Mobil
Travel Guide

Southern California

2007

ExxonMobil
Travel Publications

Acknowledgements

We gratefully acknowledge the help of our representatives for their efficient and perceptive inspections of the lodging and dining establishments listed; the establishments' proprietors for their cooperation in showing their facilities and providing information about them; and the many users of previous editions who have taken the time to share their experiences. Mobil Travel Guide is also grateful to all the talented writers who contributed entries to this book.

www.mobiltravelguide.com

Front cover photo: Santa Monica Pier, Surfer by Shutterstock, Hollywood Sign by Super Stock: age fotostock

The information contained herein is derived from a variety of third-party sources. Although every effort has been made to verify the information obtained from such sources, the publisher assumes no responsibility for inconsistencies or inaccuracies in the data or liability for any damages of any type arising from errors or omissions.

Neither the editors nor the publisher assumes responsibility for the services provided by any business listed in this guide or for any loss, damage, or disruption in your travel for any reason.

ISBN: 0-7627-4265-8 or 978-0-7627-4265-3

ISSN: 1550-1930

Manufactured in the United States of America.

10 9 8 7 6 5 4 3 2 1

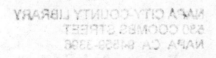

Contents

MAP SYMBOLS

TRANSPORTATION

CONTROLLED ACCESS HIGHWAYS

Freeway

Tollway

Under Construction

Interchange and Exit Number

OTHER HIGHWAYS

Primary Highway

Secondary Highway

Divided Highway

Other Paved Road

Unpaved Road
Check conditions locally

HIGHWAY MARKERS

Interstate Route

U.S. Route

State or Provincial Route

County or Other Route

Trans-Canada Highway

Canadian Provincial Autoroute

Mexican Federal Route

OTHER SYMBOLS

Distances along Major Highways
Miles in U.S.; kilometers in Canada and Mexico

Tunnel; Pass

Auto Ferry; Passenger Ferry

OTHER MAP FEATURES

Time Zone Boundary

+ Mt. Olympus   Mountain Peak; Elevation
   7,965   In Feet

Perennial; Intermittent River

RECREATION

National Park

National Forest, National Grassland

Other Large Park or Recreation Area

Small State Park
with and without Camping

Military Lands

Indian Reservation

Trail

Ski Area

Point of Interest

CITIES AND TOWNS

National Capital

State or Provincial Capital

Cities, Towns, and Populated Places
Type size indicates relative importance

Urban Area
State and province maps only

Large Incorporated Cities
City maps only

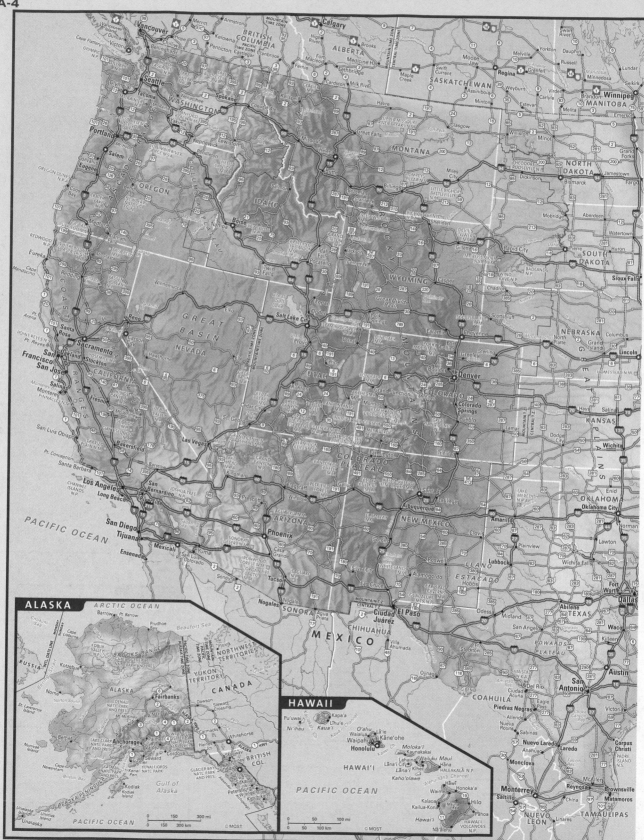

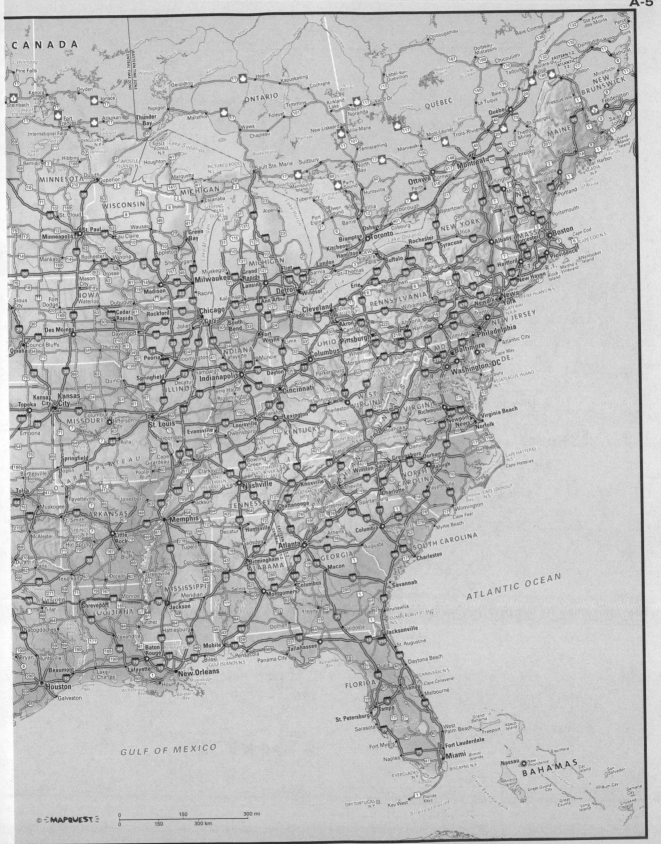

© MAPQUEST

0   150   300 mi
0   150   300 km

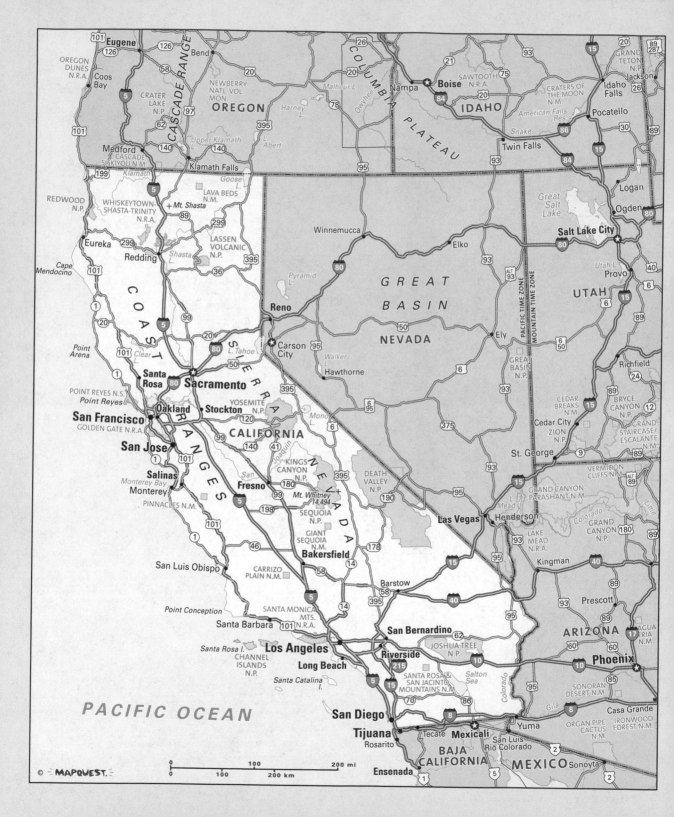

© MAPQUEST

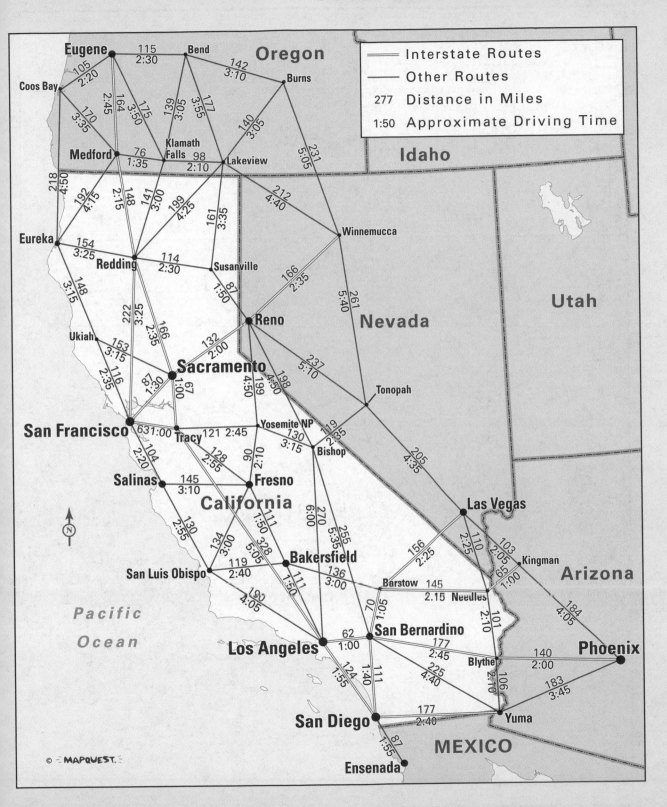

MI 30 60
KM 30 60

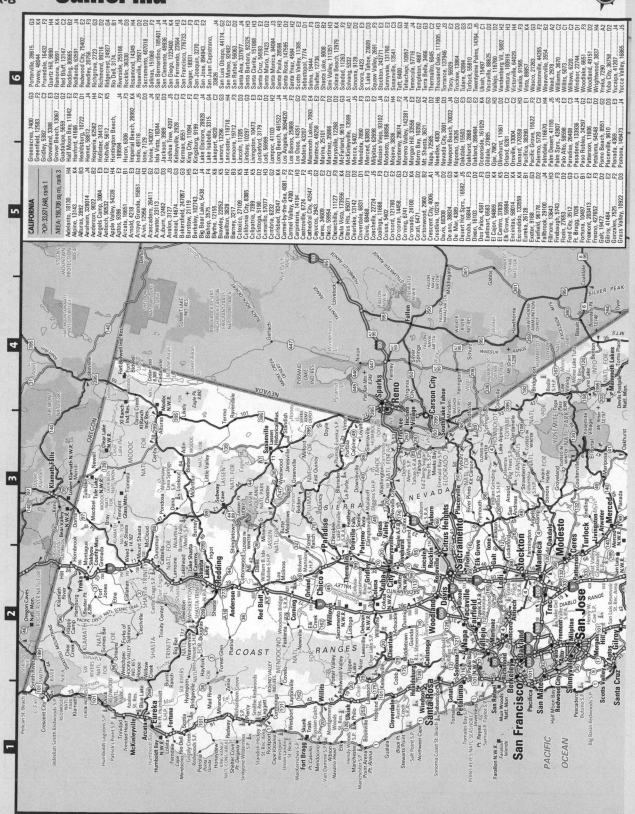

CALIFORNIA
POP: 33,871,648
AREA: 158,706 sq mi, rank 1

Place, Population	Ref.
Adelanto, 18130	H4
Alpine, 13143	J5
Alturas, 2892	B3
Anaheim, 328014	J4
Anderson, 9022	B2
Angels Camp, 3004	E3
Antioch, 90532	E2
Apple Valley, 54239	H4
Aptos, 9396	F2
Arcata, 16651	B1
Arnold, 4218	E3
Arroyo Grande, 15851	H3
Atascadero, 26411	G2
Atwater, 23113	F3
Auburn, 12462	D3
Avalon, 3127	J4
Avenal, 14674	G3
Bakersfield, 247057	H3
Barstow, 21119	H4
Berkeley, 102743	D2
Big Bear Lake, 5438	J4
Bishop, 3575	F4
Blythe, 12155	J5
Bieber, 3828	B3
Barney, 3217	K5
Calexico, 27109	K5
California City, 8385	H4
Calistoga, 5190	D2
Calipatria, 7289	K5
Camarillo, 57077	H3
Cambria, 6232	G2
Carlsbad, 78247	K4
Carmel-by-the-Sea, 4081	F2
Carmel Valley, 4700	F2
Carpinteria, 14194	H3
Castroville, 6724	F2
Cathedral City, 42547	J5
Cayucos, 2943	G2
Ceres, 34609	E3
Chico, 59954	C3
Chowchilla, 1127	F3
Chula Vista, 173556	K4
Citrus Hts., 85071	D3
Clearlake, 13142	D2
Cloverdale, 6831	D2
Clovis, 68468	G3
Coachella, 22724	J5
Coalinga, 1688	G3
Colusa, 5402	D2
Concord, 121780	E2
Corcoran, 14458	G3
Corning, 6741	C2
Coronado, 24100	K4
Corte Madera, 2960	A1
Cottonwood, 2606	B2
Crescent City, 4006	A1
Crestline, 10218	J4
Davis, 60308	D2
De Anza, 38024	H4
Del Mar, 4389	K4
Desert Hot Sprs., 16582	J5
Dinuba, 16103	G3
Dixon, 16103	D2
Dos Palos, 4581	F3
Downieville	D3
Earlimart, 6583	G3
El Cajon, 94869	K4
El Centro, 37835	K5
Elk Grove, 59984	D3
Encinitas, 58014	K4
Escondido, 133559	K4
Eureka, 26128	B1
Exeter, 9168	G3
Fairfield, 96178	D2
Fallbrook, 29100	K4
Fillmore, 13643	H3
Firebaugh, 5743	G3
Fontana, 128929	J4
Ford City, 3512	H3
Ft. Bragg, 7026	C1
Fortuna, 10497	B1
Fremont, 203413	E2
Fresno, 427652	G3
Galt, 19472	D3
Gilroy, 41464	F2
Gonzales, 7525	F2
Grass Valley, 10922	D3
Greenacres, 7400	G3
Greenfield, 12583	F2
Gridley, 5382	C3
Quartz Hill	E3
Grover Beach, 13067	G2
Guadalupe, 6059	G2
Hanford, 41686	G3
Healdsburg, 10722	D1
Hemet, 58858	J4
Hesperia, 62582	H4
Hollister, 34413	F2
Holtville, 5612	K5
Huntington Beach, 189594	J4
Huron, 6306	G3
Imperial Beach, 26992	K4
Indio, 49116	J5
Ione, 7129	D3
Isla Vista, 18344	H3
Jackson, 3989	D3
Joshua Tree, 4207	J5
Kelseyville, 2928	D2
Kerman, 8551	G3
King City, 1094	F2
Kingsburg, 9199	G3
Lake Elsinore, 28928	J4
Lake Isabella, 3315	H3
Lakeport, 4820	D2
Lamont, 13296	H3
Lake Los Angeles, 11318	H4
Lemoore, 19712	G3
Lincoln, 11205	D3
Lindsay, 10297	G3
Livingston, 10473	F3
Lodi, 56999	D3
Lockeford, 3179	D3
Lompoc, 41103	H3
Long Beach, 461522	J4
Los Angeles, 3694820	J4
Los Banos, 25869	F3
Los Gatos, 28592	E2
Madera, 43207	G3
Mammoth Lakes, 7093	E4
Manteca, 49258	E3
Marina, 25101	F2
Marysville, 12268	D3
McFarland, 9618	H3
McKinleyville, 13599	B1
Mecca, 5402	J5
Mendota, 7890	G3
Merced, 63893	F3
Mill Valley, 13600	D2
Milpitas, 62698	E2
Mission Viejo, 93102	J4
Modesto, 188856	E3
Mojave, 3836	H4
Monterey, 29674	F2
Moreno Valley, 142381	J4
Morgan Hill, 33556	F2
Morro Bay, 10350	G2
Mt. Shasta, 3621	B2
Napa, 72585	D2
Nevada City, 3001	D3
Newport Beach, 70032	J4
Nipomo, 12626	G2
Oakdale, 15503	E3
Oakhurst, 2868	F3
Oakland, 399484	D2
Oceanside, 161029	K4
Oildale, 27885	H3
Ojai, 7862	H3
Ontario, 158007	J4
Orange, 128821	J4
Orland, 6281	C2
Oroville, 13004	C3
Oxnard, 170358	H3
Pacheco, 38390	E2
Pacific Grove, 15522	F2
Pacifica, 38390	E2
Palmdale, 116670	H4
Palm Desert, 41155	J5
Palm Sprs., 42807	J5
Palo Alto, 58598	E2
Paradise, 26408	C3
Pasadena, 133936	J4
Paso Robles, 24297	G2
Patterson, 11606	E3
Petaluma, 54548	D2
Pismo Beach, 8551	G2
Placerville, 9610	D3
Planada, 4369	F3
Pomona, 149473	J4
Porterville, 39615	G3
Poway, 48044	K4
Prunedale, 16432	F2
Quartz Hill, 9890	H4
Ramona, 15691	K4
Red Bluff, 13147	C2
Redding, 80865	B2
Redlands, 63591	J4
Redwood City, 75402	E2
Reedley, 20756	G3
Richmond, 99216	D2
Rio Dell, 3174	B1
Riverside, 255166	J4
Rocklin, 36330	D3
Rosamond, 14349	H4
Roseville, 79921	D3
Salinas, 151060	F2
San Bernardino, 185401	J4
San Diego, 1223400	K4
San Fernando, 23564	J4
San Francisco, 776733	D2
Sanger, 18931	G3
San Joaquin, 3270	G3
San Jose, 894943	F2
San Juan Capistrano	J4
Santa Ana, 337977	J4
Santa Barbara, 92325	H3
Santa Clarita, 151088	H4
Santa Cruz, 54593	F2
Santa Maria, 77423	G2
Santa Monica, 84084	J4
Santa Paula, 28598	H3
Santa Rosa, 147595	D2
Santa Ynez, 4584	H3
Scotts Valley, 11385	F2
Seaside, 31696	F2
Selma, 19444	G3
Shafter, 12736	H3
Shasta Lake, 9008	B2
Simi Valley, 111351	H3
Solana Beach, 12979	K4
Soledad, 11263	F2
Solvang, 5332	H3
Sonoma, 9128	D2
Sonora, 4423	E3
S. Lake Tahoe, 23609	D3
S. San Francisco, 60552	E2
Stockton, 243771	E3
Sunnyvale, 131760	E2
Susanville, 13541	C3
Taft, 6400	H3
Tehachapi, 10957	H4
Temecula, 57716	J4
Templeton, 4687	G2
Terra Bella, 3466	G3
Thermalito, 6045	C3
Thousand Oaks, 117005	H3
Torrance, 137946	J4
Tracy, 56929	E2
Truckee, 13864	D3
Tulare, 43994	G3
Turlock, 55810	E3
Twentynine Palms, 14764	J5
Ukiah, 15497	D1
Vacaville, 88625	D2
Vallejo, 116760	D2
Vandenberg Vill., 5802	H2
Ventura, 100916	H3
Victorville, 64029	H4
Visalia, 91565	G3
Vista, 89857	K4
Wasco, 21263	H3
Watsonville, 44265	F2
Weaverville, 3554	B2
Weed, 2978	A2
Williams, 3670	C2
Willits, 5073	C1
Windsor, 27744	D1
Woodlake, 6651	G3
Woodland, 49151	D2
Wrightwood, 3837	H4
Yreka, 7290	A2
Yuba City, 36758	C3
Yucaipa, 41207	J4
Yucca Valley, 16865	J5

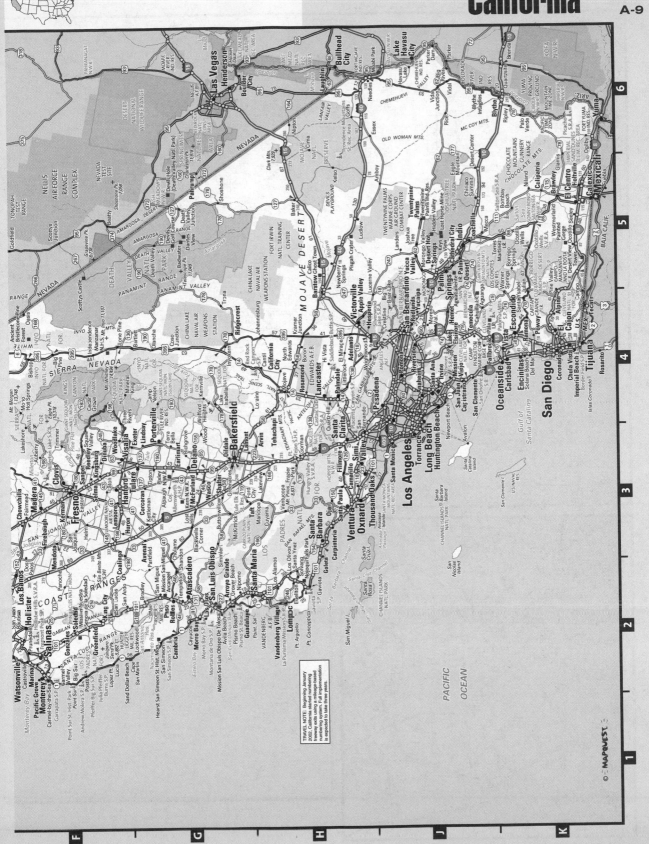

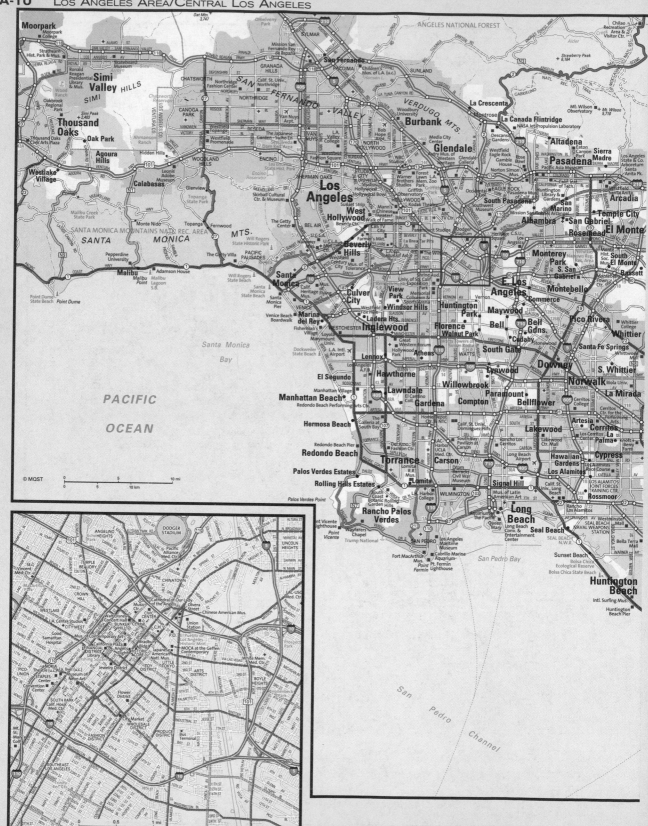

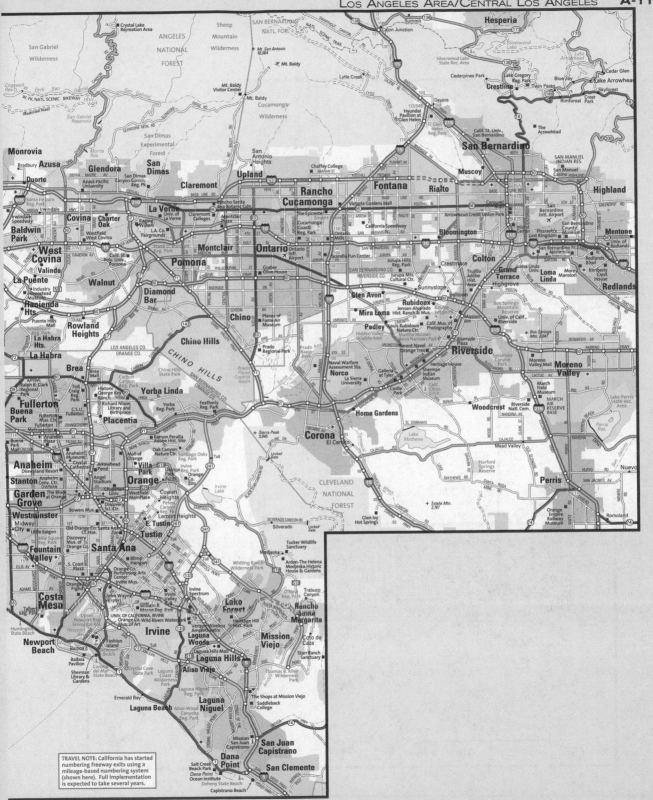

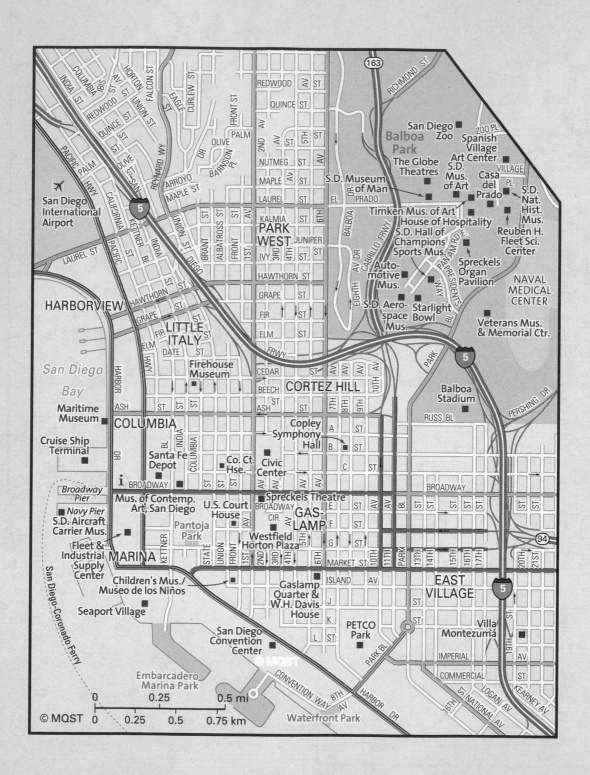

Oceanside
Vista
Carlsbad
San Marcos
Escondido
Encinitas
Solana Beach
Del Mar
Ramona
Poway
Rancho Bernardo
Rancho Penasquitos
Carmel Valley
Sorrento Valley
Mira Mesa
Scripps Ranch
Santee
Lakeside
Winter Gardens
La Jolla
Clairemont
Pacific Beach
Mission Beach
Ocean Beach
El Cajon
La Mesa
San Diego
Spring Valley
Rancho San Diego
Lemon Grove
La Presa
Jamul
Coronado
National City
Bonita
Sunnyside
Chula Vista
Imperial Beach
Tijuana
San Ysidro
Crest

PACIFIC OCEAN

Mission San Luis Rey de Francia
Antique Gas & Steam Engine Museum
Guajome Reg. Park
Deer Park Winery & Automotive Mus.
Welk Resort Center
Rancho Buena Vista Adobe
Westfield Plaza Camino Real
Carlsbad State Beach
Agua Hedionda Lagoon
McClellan Palomar Arpt.
Carlsbad Raceway
Legoland California
South Carlsbad State Beach
Batiquitos Lagoon
Lake San Marcos
Cal. St. Univ. San Marcos
La Costa
Leucadia State Beach
Quail Botanical Gardens
Moonlight State Beach
Olivenhain
Elfin Forest Ecological Reserve
Del Dios
Cal. Center for the Arts
San Diego Wild Animal Park
San Pascual Battlefield S.H.S.
Westfield North County
Lake Hodges
Cardiff-by-the-Sea
San Elijo State Beach
Cardiff State Beach
San Elijo Lagoon Co. Park
Rancho Santa Fe
San Dieguito Co. Park
Del Mar Fairgrounds
Del Mar Race Track
Blue Sky Ecological Reserve
Dos Picos Reg. Park
Torrey Pines State Beach & Res.
Los Penasquitos Canyon Preserve
Miramar Res.
BARONA RANCH INDIAN RESERVATION
Univ. of Calif. San Diego
Scripps Inst. of Oceanography / Birch Aquarium at Scripps
Museum of Contemporary Art
Westfield UTC
Miramar Marine Corps Air Station
Alliant Intl. University
Sycamore Canyon Open Space Preserve
San Vicente Reservoir
Marian Bear Mem. Nat. Pk.
Mission Trails Reg. Park
Lake Jennings Co. Park
Montgomery Field
El Monte Rd.
Westfield Mission Valley
Mission San Diego de Alcala
Cajon Speedway
Westfield Pkwy Parkway
Belmont Park
SeaWorld San Diego
Tecolote Canyon Natural Pk.
Univ. of San Diego
Lake Murray
Mission Bay Park
Qualcomm Stadium
San Diego St. Univ.
San Diego Computer Mus.
Fashion Valley
Old Town San Diego
Horton Plaza Center
San Diego Intl. Arpt.
Point Loma Nazarene Univ.
Fleet Combat Training Ctr.
U.S. NAVAL RESERVATION
Fort Rosecrans Natl. Cemetery
CABRILLO NATL. MON.
Pt. Loma Lighthouse
Pt. Loma
U.S.M.C. RECRUIT DEPOT
NORTH ISLAND N.A.S.
SAN DIEGO NAVAL STATION
SAN DIEGO NAVAL SUBMARINE BASE
Coronado Beach Hist. Mus.
Hotel del Coronado
CORONADO NAVAL AMPHIBIOUS BASE
SWEETWATER MARSH N.W.R.
Sweetwater Reservoir
Sweetwater Reg. Park
Chula Vista Nature Ctr.
Westfield Plaza Bonita
Silver Strand State Beach
NAVAL COMM. STATION
Otay Lakes
Upper Otay Res.
JAMUL MTS.
ARCO Olympic Training Center
Knott's Soak City USA
Coors Amphitheater
Lower Otay Reservoir
Naval Space Surveillance Station
Otay Mtn. 3,566
Tijuana Slough Natl. Estuarine Reserve
NAVAL AIR STATION
Border Field State Park
Abelardo L. Rodriguez Intl. Airport
SAN YSIDRO MTS.

UNITED STATES   CALIFORNIA
MEXICO   BAJA CALIFORNIA

0 1 2 3 4 mi
0 1 2 3 4 5 6 km

© MQ3T

Distances in chart are in miles. To convert miles to kilometers, multiply the distance in miles by 1.609

Example:
New York, NY to Boston, MA = 215 miles or 346 kilometers (215 x 1.609)

	ALBUQUERQUE, NM	ATLANTA, GA	BALTIMORE, MD	BILLINGS, MT	BIRMINGHAM, AL	BISMARCK, ND	BOISE, ID	BOSTON, MA	BUFFALO, NY	BURLINGTON, VT	CHARLESTON, SC	CHARLESTON, WV	CHARLOTTE, NC	CHEYENNE, WY	CHICAGO, IL	CINCINNATI, OH	CLEVELAND, OH	DALLAS, TX	DENVER, CO	DES MOINES, IA	DETROIT, MI	EL PASO, TX	HOUSTON, TX	INDIANAPOLIS, IN	JACKSON, MS	KANSAS CITY, MO	LAS VEGAS, NV	LITTLE ROCK, AR	LOS ANGELES, CA	LOUISVILLE, KY
ALBUQUERQUE, NM		1490	1902	991	1274	1333	966	2240	1808	2178	1793	1568	1649	538	1352	1409	1619	754	438	1091	1608	263	994	1298	1157	894	578	900	806	1320
ATLANTA, GA	1490		679	1889	150	1559	2218	1100	910	1158	317	503	238	1482	717	476	726	792	1403	967	735	1437	800	531	386	801	2067	528	2237	419
BALTIMORE, MD	1902	679		1959	795	1551	2401	422	370	481	583	352	441	1665	708	521	377	1399	1690	1031	532	2045	1470	600	1032	1087	2445	1072	2705	602
BILLINGS, MT	991	1889	1959		1839	413	626	2254	1796	2181	2157	1755	2012	455	1246	1552	1597	1433	554	1007	1534	1255	1673	1432	1836	1088	965	1530	1239	1547
BIRMINGHAM, AL	1274	150	795	1839		1509	2170	1215	909	1241	466	578	389	1434	667	475	725	647	1356	919	734	1292	678	481	241	753	1852	381	2092	369
BISMARCK, ND	1333	1559	1551	413	1509		1039	1846	1388	1773	1749	1347	1604	594	838	1144	1189	1342	693	675	1126	1597	1582	1024	1548	801	1378	1183	1702	1139
BOISE, ID	966	2218	2401	626	2170	1039		2697	2239	2624	2520	2182	2375	737	1708	1969	2040	1711	833	1369	1977	1206	1952	1852	2115	1376	760	1808	1033	1933
BOSTON, MA	2240	1100	422	2254	1215	1846	2697		462	214	1003	741	861	1961	1003	862	654	1819	2004	1326	741	2465	1890	940	1453	1427	2757	1493	3046	964
BUFFALO, NY	1808	910	370	1796	909	1388	2239	462		375	899	431	695	1502	545	442	197	1393	1546	868	277	2039	1513	508	1134	995	2299	1066	2572	545
BURLINGTON, VT	2178	1158	481	2181	1241	1773	2624	214	375		1061	782	919	1887	930	817	567	1763	1931	1253	652	2409	1916	878	1479	1366	2684	1437	2957	915
CHARLESTON, SC	1793	317	583	2157	466	1749	2520	1003	899	1061		468	204	1783	907	622	724	1109	1705	1204	879	1754	1110	721	703	1102	2371	900	2554	610
CHARLESTON, WV	1568	503	352	1755	578	1347	2182	741	431	782	468		265	1445	506	209	255	1072	1367	802	410	1718	1192	320	816	764	2122	745	2374	251
CHARLOTTE, NC	1649	238	441	2012	389	1604	2375	861	695	919	204	265		1637	761	476	520	1031	1559	1057	675	1677	1041	575	625	956	2225	754	2453	464
CHEYENNE, WY	538	1482	1665	455	1434	594	737	1961	1502	1887	1783	1445	1637		972	1233	1304	979	100	633	1241	801	1220	1115	1382	640	843	1076	1116	1197
CHICAGO, IL	1352	717	708	1246	667	838	1708	1003	545	930	907	506	761	972		302	346	936	1015	337	283	1543	1108	184	750	532	1768	662	2042	299
CINCINNATI, OH	1409	476	521	1552	475	1144	1969	862	442	817	622	209	476	1233	302		253	958	1200	599	261	1605	1079	116	700	597	1955	632	2215	106
CLEVELAND, OH	1619	726	377	1597	725	1189	2040	654	197	567	724	255	520	1304	346	253		1208	1347	669	171	1854	1328	319	950	806	2100	882	2374	356
DALLAS, TX	754	792	1399	1433	647	1342	1711	1819	1393	1763	1109	1072	1031	979	936	958	1208		887	752	1218	647	241	913	406	554	1331	327	1446	852
DENVER, CO	438	1403	1690	554	1356	693	833	2004	1546	1931	1705	1367	1559	100	1015	1200	1347	887		676	1284	701	1127	1088	1290	603	756	984	1029	1118
DES MOINES, IA	1091	967	1031	1007	919	675	1369	1326	868	1253	1204	802	1057	633	337	599	669	752	676		606	1283	992	481	931	194	1429	567	1703	595
DETROIT, MI	1608	735	532	1534	734	1126	1977	741	277	652	879	410	675	1241	283	261	171	1218	1284	606		1799	1338	318	960	795	2037	891	2310	366
EL PASO, TX	263	1437	2045	1255	1292	1597	1206	2465	2039	2409	1754	1718	1677	801	1543	1605	1854	647	701	1283	1799		758	1489	1051	1085	717	974	801	1499
HOUSTON, TX	994	800	1470	1673	678	1582	1952	1890	1513	1916	1110	1192	1041	1220	1108	1079	1328	241	1127	992	1338	758		1033	445	795	1474	447	1558	972
INDIANAPOLIS, IN	1298	531	600	1432	481	1024	1852	940	508	878	721	320	575	1115	184	116	319	913	1088	481	318	1489	1033		675	485	1843	587	2104	112
JACKSON, MS	1157	386	1032	1836	241	1548	2115	1453	1134	1479	703	816	625	1382	750	700	950	406	1290	931	960	1051	445	675		747	1735	269	1851	594
KANSAS CITY, MO	894	801	1087	1088	753	801	1376	1427	995	1366	1102	764	956	640	532	597	806	554	603	194	795	1085	795	485	747		1358	382	1632	516
LAS VEGAS, NV	578	2067	2445	965	1852	1378	760	2757	2299	2684	2371	2122	2225	843	1768	1955	2100	1331	756	1429	2037	717	1474	1843	1735	1358		1478	274	1874
LITTLE ROCK, AR	900	528	1072	1530	381	1183	1808	1493	1066	1437	900	745	754	1076	662	632	882	327	984	567	891	974	447	587	269	382	1478		1706	526
LOS ANGELES, CA	806	2237	2705	1239	2092	1702	1033	3046	2572	2957	2554	2374	2453	1116	2042	2215	2374	1446	1029	1703	2310	801	1558	2104	1851	1632	274	1706		2126
LOUISVILLE, KY	1320	419	602	1547	369	1139	1933	964	545	915	610	251	464	1197	299	106	356	852	1118	595	366	1499	972	112	594	516	1874	526	2126	
MEMPHIS, TN	1033	389	933	1625	241	1337	1954	1353	927	1297	760	606	614	1217	539	493	742	466	1116	720	752	1112	586	464	211	536	1611	140	1839	386
MIAMI, FL	2155	661	1109	2554	812	2224	2883	1529	1425	1587	583	994	730	2147	1382	1141	1250	1367	2069	1632	1401	1959	1201	1196	915	1466	2733	1190	2759	1084
MILWAUKEE, WI	1426	813	805	1175	763	767	1748	1100	642	1027	1003	601	857	1012	89	398	443	1010	1055	378	380	1617	1193	279	835	573	1808	747	2082	394
MINNEAPOLIS, MN	1339	1129	1121	839	1079	431	1465	1417	958	1343	1319	918	1173	881	409	714	760	999	924	246	697	1530	1240	596	1151	441	1677	814	1951	711
MONTRÉAL, QC	2172	1241	564	2093	1289	1685	2535	313	397	92	1145	822	1003	1799	841	815	588	1772	1843	1165	564	2363	1892	872	1514	1359	2596	1446	2869	920
NASHVILLE, TN	1248	242	716	1648	194	1315	1976	1136	716	1086	543	395	397	1240	474	281	531	681	1162	725	541	1328	801	287	423	559	1826	355	2054	175
NEW ORLEANS, LA	1276	473	1142	1955	351	1734	2234	1563	1254	1588	783	926	713	1502	935	820	1070	525	1409	1117	1079	1118	360	826	185	932	1854	455	1917	714
NEW YORK, NY	2015	869	192	2049	985	1641	2491	215	400	299	773	515	631	1755	797	636	466	1589	1799	1121	622	2235	1660	715	1223	1202	2552	1262	2820	739
OKLAHOMA CITY, OK	546	944	1354	1227	729	1136	1506	1694	1262	1632	1248	1022	1102	773	807	863	1073	209	681	546	1062	737	449	752	612	348	1124	355	1352	774
OMAHA, NE	973	989	1168	904	941	616	1234	1463	1005	1390	1290	952	1144	497	474	736	806	669	541	136	743	1236	910	618	935	188	1294	570	1567	704
ORLANDO, FL	1934	440	904	2333	591	2003	2662	1324	1221	1383	379	790	525	1926	1161	920	1045	1146	1847	1411	1180	1738	980	975	694	1245	2512	969	2538	863
PHILADELPHIA, PA	1954	782	104	2019	897	1611	2462	321	414	371	685	454	543	1725	768	576	437	1501	1744	1091	592	2147	1572	655	1135	1141	2500	1175	2760	678
PHOENIX, AZ	466	1868	2366	1199	1723	1662	993	2706	2274	2644	2184	2035	2107	1004	1819	1876	2085	1077	904	1558	2074	432	1188	1764	1482	1360	285	1367	369	1786
PITTSBURGH, PA	1670	676	246	1719	763	1311	2161	592	217	587	642	217	438	1425	467	292	136	1246	1460	791	292	1893	1366	370	988	857	2215	920	2476	394
PORTLAND, ME	2338	1197	520	2352	1313	1944	2795	107	560	233	1101	839	959	2059	1101	960	751	1917	2102	1424	838	2563	1988	1038	1550	1525	2855	1590	3144	1062
PORTLAND, OR	1395	2647	2830	889	2599	1301	432	3126	2667	3052	2948	2610	2802	1166	2137	2398	2469	2140	1261	1798	2405	1767	2381	2280	2544	1805	1188	2237	971	2362
RAPID CITY, SD	841	1511	1626	379	1463	320	930	1921	1463	1848	1824	1422	1678	305	913	1219	1264	1077	404	629	1201	1105	1318	1101	1458	710	1035	1093	1309	1215
RENO, NV	1020	2440	2623	960	2392	1372	430	2919	2460	2845	2741	2403	2595	959	1930	2191	2262	1933	1054	1591	2198	1315	2072	2073	2337	1598	442	2030	519	2155
RICHMOND, VA	1876	527	152	2053	678	1645	2496	572	485	630	428	322	289	1760	802	530	471	1309	1688	1126	627	1955	1330	641	914	1085	2444	983	2682	572
ST. LOUIS, MO	1051	549	841	1341	501	1053	1628	1181	749	1119	850	512	704	892	294	350	560	635	855	436	549	1242	863	239	505	252	1610	416	1856	264
SALT LAKE CITY, UT	624	1916	2100	548	1868	960	342	2395	1936	2322	2218	1880	2072	436	1406	1667	1738	1410	531	1067	1675	864	1650	1549	1813	1074	417	1507	691	1631
SAN ANTONIO, TX	818	1000	1671	1500	878	1599	1761	2092	1665	2036	1310	1344	1241	1046	1270	1231	1481	271	946	1009	1490	556	200	1186	644	812	1272	600	1356	1125
SAN DIEGO, CA	825	2166	2724	1302	2021	1765	1096	3065	2632	3020	2483	2393	2405	1179	2105	2234	2437	1375	1092	1766	2373	730	1487	2122	1780	1695	337	1703	124	2144
SAN FRANCISCO, CA	1111	2618	2840	1176	2472	1749	646	3135	2677	3062	2934	2620	2759	1176	2146	2407	2478	1827	1271	1807	2415	1181	1938	2290	2232	1814	575	2012	385	2372
SEATTLE, WA	1463	2705	2775	816	2657	1229	500	3070	2612	2997	2973	2571	2827	1234	2062	2368	2413	2208	1329	1822	2350	1944	2449	2249	2612	1872	1256	2305	1148	2364
TAMPA, FL	1949	455	960	2348	606	2018	2677	1380	1276	1438	434	845	581	1941	1176	935	1101	1161	1862	1426	1194	1753	995	990	709	1259	2526	984	2553	878
TORONTO, ON	1841	958	565	1762	958	1354	2204	570	106	419	1006	537	802	1468	510	484	303	1441	1512	834	233	2032	1561	541	1183	1028	2265	1115	2538	589
VANCOUVER, BC	1597	2838	2908	949	2791	1362	633	3204	2745	3130	3106	2705	2960	1368	2196	2501	2547	2342	1463	1956	2483	2087	2583	2383	2746	2007	1390	2439	1291	2497
WASHINGTON, DC	1896	636	38	1953	758	1545	2395	458	384	517	539	346	397	1659	701	517	370	1362	1686	1025	526	2008	1433	596	996	1083	2441	1036	2702	596
WICHITA, KS	707	989	1276	1067	838	934	1346	1616	1184	1554	1291	953	1145	613	728	785	995	367	521	390	984	898	608	674	771	192	1276	464	1513	705

	MEMPHIS, TN	MIAMI, FL	MILWAUKEE, WI	MINNEAPOLIS, MN	MONTRÉAL, QC	NASHVILLE, TN	NEW ORLEANS, LA	NEW YORK, NY	OKLAHOMA CITY, OK	OMAHA, NE	ORLANDO, FL	PHILADELPHIA, PA	PHOENIX, AZ	PITTSBURGH, PA	PORTLAND, ME	PORTLAND, OR	RAPID CITY, SD	RENO, NV	RICHMOND, VA	ST. LOUIS, MO	SALT LAKE CITY, UT	SAN ANTONIO, TX	SAN DIEGO, CA	SAN FRANCISCO, CA	SEATTLE, WA	TAMPA, FL	TORONTO, ON	VANCOUVER, BC	WASHINGTON,DC	WICHITA, KS
ALBUQUERQUE, NM	1033	2155	1426	1339	2172	1248	1276	2015	546	973	1934	1954	466	1670	2338	1395	841	1020	1876	1051	624	818	825	1111	1463	1949	1841	1597	1896	707
ATLANTA, GA	389	661	813	1129	1241	242	473	869	944	989	440	782	1868	676	1197	2647	1511	2440	527	549	1916	1000	2166	2618	2705	455	958	2838	636	989
BALTIMORE, MD	933	1109	805	1121	564	716	1142	192	1354	1168	904	104	2366	246	520	2830	1626	2623	152	841	2100	1671	2724	2840	2775	960	565	2908	38	1276
BILLINGS, MT	1625	2554	1175	839	2093	1648	1955	2049	1227	904	2333	2019	1199	1719	2352	889	379	960	2053	1341	548	1500	1302	1176	816	2348	1762	949	1953	1067
BIRMINGHAM, AL	241	812	763	1079	1289	194	351	985	729	941	591	897	1723	763	1313	2599	1463	2392	678	501	1868	878	2021	2472	2657	606	958	2791	758	838
BISMARCK, ND	1337	2224	767	431	1685	1315	1734	1641	1136	616	2003	1611	1662	1311	1944	1301	320	1372	1645	1053	960	1599	1765	1749	1229	2018	1354	1362	1545	934
BOISE, ID	1954	2883	1748	1465	2535	1976	2234	2491	1506	1234	2662	2462	993	2161	2795	432	930	430	2496	1628	342	1761	1096	646	500	2677	2204	633	2395	1346
BOSTON, MA	1353	1529	1100	1417	313	1136	1563	215	1694	1463	1324	321	2706	592	107	3126	1921	2919	572	1181	2395	2092	3065	3135	3070	1380	570	3204	458	1616
BUFFALO, NY	927	1425	642	958	397	716	1254	400	1262	1005	1221	414	2274	217	560	2667	1463	2460	485	749	1936	1665	2632	2677	2612	1276	106	2745	384	1184
BURLINGTON, VT	1297	1587	1027	1343	92	1086	1588	299	1632	1390	1383	371	2644	587	233	3052	1848	2845	630	1119	2322	2036	3020	3062	2997	1438	419	3130	517	1554
CHARLESTON, SC	760	583	1003	1319	1145	543	783	773	1248	1290	379	685	2184	642	1101	2948	1824	2741	428	850	2218	1310	2483	2934	2973	434	1006	3106	539	1291
CHARLESTON, WV	606	994	601	918	822	395	926	515	1022	952	790	454	2035	217	839	2610	1422	2403	322	512	1880	1344	2393	2620	2571	845	537	2705	346	953
CHARLOTTE, NC	614	730	857	1173	1003	397	713	631	1102	1144	525	543	2107	438	959	2802	1678	2595	289	704	2072	1241	2405	2759	2827	581	802	2960	397	1145
CHEYENNE, WY	1217	2147	1012	881	1799	1240	1502	1755	773	497	1926	1725	1004	1425	2059	1166	305	959	1760	892	436	1046	1179	1176	1234	1941	1468	1368	1659	613
CHICAGO, IL	539	1382	89	409	841	474	935	797	807	474	1161	768	1819	467	1101	2137	913	1930	802	294	1406	1270	2105	2146	2062	1176	510	2196	701	728
CINCINNATI, OH	493	1141	398	714	815	281	820	636	863	736	920	576	1876	292	960	2398	1219	2191	530	350	1667	1231	2234	2407	2368	935	484	2501	517	785
CLEVELAND, OH	742	1250	443	760	588	531	1070	466	1073	806	1045	437	2085	136	751	2469	1264	2262	471	560	1738	1481	2437	2478	2413	1101	303	2547	370	995
DALLAS, TX	466	1367	1010	999	1772	681	525	1589	209	669	1146	1501	1077	1246	1917	2140	1077	1933	1309	635	1410	271	1375	1827	2208	1161	1441	2342	1362	367
DENVER, CO	1116	2069	1055	924	1843	1162	1409	1799	681	541	1847	1744	904	1460	2102	1261	404	1054	1688	855	531	946	1092	1271	1329	1862	1512	1463	1686	521
DES MOINES, IA	720	1632	378	246	1165	725	1117	1121	546	136	1411	1091	1558	791	1424	1798	629	1591	1126	436	1067	1009	1766	1807	1822	1426	834	1956	1025	390
DETROIT, MI	752	1401	380	697	564	541	1079	622	1062	743	1180	592	2074	292	838	2405	1201	2198	627	549	1675	1490	2373	2415	2350	1194	233	2483	526	984
EL PASO, TX	1112	1959	1617	1530	2363	1328	1118	2235	737	1236	1738	2147	432	1893	2563	1767	1105	1315	1955	1242	864	556	730	1181	1944	1753	2032	2087	2008	898
HOUSTON, TX	586	1201	1193	1240	1892	801	360	1660	449	910	980	1572	1188	1366	1988	2381	1318	2072	1330	863	1650	200	1487	1938	2449	995	1561	2583	1433	608
INDIANAPOLIS, IN	464	1196	279	596	872	287	826	715	752	618	975	655	1764	370	1038	2280	1101	2073	641	239	1549	1186	2122	2290	2249	990	541	2383	596	674
JACKSON, MS	211	915	835	1151	1514	423	185	1223	612	935	694	1135	1482	988	1550	2544	1458	2337	914	505	1813	644	1780	2232	2612	709	1183	2746	996	771
KANSAS CITY, MO	536	1466	573	441	1359	559	932	1202	348	188	1245	1141	1360	857	1525	1805	710	1598	1085	252	1074	812	1695	1814	1872	1259	1028	2007	1083	192
LAS VEGAS, NV	1611	2733	1808	1677	2596	1826	1854	2552	1124	1294	2512	2500	285	2215	2855	1188	1035	442	2444	1610	417	1272	337	575	1256	2526	2265	1390	2441	1276
LITTLE ROCK, AR	140	1190	747	814	1446	355	455	1262	355	570	969	1175	1367	920	1590	2237	1093	2030	983	416	1507	600	1703	2012	2305	984	1115	2439	1036	464
LOS ANGELES, CA	1839	2759	2082	1951	2869	2054	1917	2820	1352	1567	2538	2760	369	2476	3144	971	1309	519	2682	1856	691	1356	124	385	1148	2553	2538	1291	2702	1513
LOUISVILLE, KY	386	1084	394	711	920	175	714	739	774	704	863	678	1786	394	1062	2362	1215	2155	572	264	1631	1125	2144	2372	2364	878	589	2497	596	705
MEMPHIS, TN		1051	624	940	1306	215	396	1123	487	724	830	1035	1500	780	1451	2382	1247	2175	843	294	1652	739	1841	2144	2440	845	975	2574	896	597
MIAMI, FL	1051		1478	1794	1671	907	874	1299	1609	1654	232	1211	2390	1167	1627	3312	2176	3105	954	1214	2581	1401	2688	3140	3370	274	1532	3504	1065	1655
MILWAUKEE, WI	624	1478		337	939	569	1020	894	880	514	1257	865	1892	564	1198	2063	842	1970	899	367	1446	1343	2145	2186	1991	1272	607	2124	799	769
MINNEAPOLIS, MN	940	1794	337		1255	886	1337	1211	793	383	1573	1181	1805	881	1515	1727	606	1839	1216	621	1315	1257	2014	2055	1654	1588	924	1788	1115	637
MONTRÉAL, QC	1306	1671	939	1255		1094	1632	383	1625	1300	1466	454	2637	607	282	2963	1758	2756	714	1112	2232	2043	2931	2972	2907	1522	330	3041	600	1547
NASHVILLE, TN	215	907	569	886	1094		539	906	703	747	686	818	1715	569	1234	2405	1269	2198	626	307	1675	954	2056	2360	2463	701	764	2597	679	748
NEW ORLEANS, LA	396	874	1020	1337	1632	539		1332	731	1121	653	1245	1548	1108	1660	2663	1643	2431	1002	690	1932	560	1846	2298	2731	668	1302	2865	1106	890
NEW YORK, NY	1123	1299	894	1211	383	906	1332		1469	1258	1094	91	2481	367	313	2920	1716	2713	342	956	2189	1861	2839	2929	2864	1150	507	2998	228	1391
OKLAHOMA CITY, OK	487	1609	880	793	1625	703	731	1469		463	1388	1408	1012	1124	1792	1934	871	1727	1331	505	1204	466	1370	1657	2002	1403	1295	2136	1350	161
OMAHA, NE	724	1654	514	383	1300	747	1121	1258	463		1433	1228	1440	928	1561	1662	525	1455	1263	440	932	927	1630	1672	1719	1448	971	1853	1162	307
ORLANDO, FL	830	232	1257	1573	1466	686	653	1094	1388	1433		1006	2169	963	1422	3091	1955	2884	750	993	2360	1180	2467	2918	3149	82	1327	3283	860	1434
PHILADELPHIA, PA	1035	1211	865	1181	454	818	1245	91	1408	1228	1006		2420	306	419	2890	1686	2683	254	895	2160	1774	2779	2900	2835	1062	522	2968	140	1330
PHOENIX, AZ	1500	2390	1892	1805	2637	1715	1548	2481	1012	1440	2169	2420		2136	2804	1335	1308	883	2343	1517	651	987	358	750	1513	2184	2307	1655	2362	1173
PITTSBURGH, PA	780	1167	564	881	607	569	1108	367	1124	928	963	306	2136		690	2590	1386	2383	341	611	1859	1519	2494	2599	2534	1019	321	2668	240	1046
PORTLAND, ME	1451	1627	1198	1515	282	1234	1660	313	1792	1561	1422	419	2804	690		3223	2019	3016	670	1279	2493	2189	3162	3233	3168	1478	668	3301	556	1714
PORTLAND, OR	2382	3312	2063	1727	2963	2405	2663	2920	1934	1662	3091	2890	1335	2590	3223		1268	578	2925	2057	771	2322	1093	638	170	3106	2633	313	2824	1775
RAPID CITY, SD	1247	2176	842	606	1758	1269	1643	1716	871	525	1955	1686	1308	1386	2019	1268		1151	1720	963	628	1335	1372	1368	1195	1970	1429	1328	1620	712
RENO, NV	2175	3105	1970	1839	2756	2198	2431	2713	1727	1455	2884	2683	883	2383	3016	578	1151		2718	1850	524	1870	642	217	755	2899	2426	898	2617	1568
RICHMOND, VA	843	954	899	1216	714	626	1002	342	1331	1263	750	254	2343	341	670	2925	1720	2718		834	2194	1530	2684	2934	2869	805	660	3003	108	1274
ST. LOUIS, MO	294	1214	367	621	1112	307	690	956	505	440	993	895	1517	611	1279	2057	963	1850	834		1326	968	1875	2066	2125	1008	782	2259	837	441
SALT LAKE CITY, UT	1652	2581	1446	1315	2232	1675	1932	2189	1204	932	2360	2160	651	1859	2493	771	628	524	2194	1326		1419	754	740	839	2375	1902	973	2094	1044
SAN ANTONIO, TX	739	1401	1343	1257	2043	954	560	1861	466	927	1180	1774	987	1519	2189	2322	1335	1870	1530	968	1419		1285	1737	2275	1195	1714	2410	1635	624
SAN DIEGO, CA	1841	2688	2145	2014	2931	2056	1846	2839	1370	1630	2467	2779	358	2494	3162	1093	1372	642	2684	1875	754	1285		508	1271	2481	2601	1414	2720	1531
SAN FRANCISCO, CA	2144	3140	2186	2055	2972	2360	2298	2929	1657	1672	2918	2900	750	2599	3233	638	1368	217	2934	2066	740	1737	508		816	2933	2643	958	2834	1784
SEATTLE, WA	2440	3370	1991	1654	2907	2463	2731	2864	2002	1719	3149	2835	1513	2534	3168	170	1195	755	2869	2125	839	2275	1271	816		3164	2577	140	2769	1843
TAMPA, FL	845	274	1272	1588	1522	701	668	1150	1403	1448	82	1062	2184	1019	1478	3106	1970	2899	805	1008	2375	1195	2481	2933	3164		1383	3297	916	1448
TORONTO, ON	975	1532	607	924	330	764	1302	507	1295	971	1327	522	2307	321	668	2633	1429	2426	660	782	1902	1714	2601	2643	2577	1383		2711	563	1217
VANCOUVER, BC	2574	3504	2124	1788	3041	2597	2865	2998	2136	1853	3283	2968	1655	2668	3301	313	1328	898	3003	2259	973	2410	1414	958	140	3297	2711		2902	1977
WASHINGTON, DC	896	1065	799	1115	600	679	1106	228	1350	1162	860	140	2362	240	556	2824	1620	2617	108	837	2094	1635	2720	2834	2769	916	563	2902		1272
WICHITA, KS	597	1655	769	637	1547	748	890	1391	161	307	1434	1330	1173	1046	1714	1775	712	1568	1274	441	1044	624	1531	1784	1843	1448	1217	1977	1272	

A Word to Our Readers

Travelers are on the roads in great numbers these days. They're exploring the country on day trips, weekend getaways, business trips, and extended family vacations, visiting major cities and small towns along the way. Because time is precious and the travel industry is ever-changing, having accurate, reliable travel information at your fingertips is critical. Mobil Travel Guide has been providing invaluable insight to travelers for more than 45 years, and we are committed to continuing this service well into the future.

The Mobil Corporation (known as Exxon Mobil Corporation since a 1999 merger) began producing the Mobil Travel Guide books in 1958, following the introduction of the US interstate highway system in 1956. The first edition covered only five Southwestern states. Since then, our books have become the premier travel guides in North America, covering all 50 states and Canada.

Since its founding, Mobil Travel Guide has served as an advocate for travelers seeking knowledge about hotels, restaurants, and places to visit. Based on an objective process, we make recommendations to our customers that we believe will enhance the quality and value of their travel experiences. Our trusted Mobil One- to Five-Star rating system is the oldest and most respected lodging and restaurant inspection and rating program in North America. Most hoteliers, restaurateurs, and industry observers favorably regard the rigor of our inspection program and understand the prestige and benefits that come with receiving a Mobil Star rating.

The Mobil Travel Guide process of rating each establishment includes:

- Unannounced facility inspections
- Incognito service evaluations for Mobil Four-Star and Mobil Five-Star properties
- A review of unsolicited comments from the general public
- Senior management oversight

For each property, more than 450 attributes, including cleanliness, physical facilities, and employee attitude and courtesy, are measured and evaluated to produce a mathematically derived score, which is then blended with the other elements to form an overall score. These quantifiable scores allow comparative analysis among properties and form the basis that we use to assign our Mobil One- to Five-Star ratings.

This process focuses largely on guest expectations, guest experience, and consistency of service, not just physical facilities and amenities. It is fundamentally a relative rating system that rewards those properties that continually strive for and achieve excellence each year. Indeed, the very best properties are consistently raising the bar for those that wish to compete with them. These properties proactively respond to consumers' needs even in today's uncertain times.

Only facilities that meet Mobil Travel Guide's standards earn the privilege of being listed in the guide. Deteriorating, poorly managed establishments are deleted. A Mobil Travel Guide listing constitutes a positive quality recommendation; every listing is an accolade, a recognition of achievement. Our Mobil One- to Five-Star rating system highlights its level of service. Extensive in-house research is constantly underway to determine new additions to our lists.

- The Mobil Five-Star Award indicates that a property is one of the very best in the country and consistently provides gracious and courteous service, superlative quality in its facility, and a unique ambience. The lodgings and restaurants at the Mobil Five-Star level consistently and proactively respond to consumers' needs and continue their commitment to excellence, doing so with grace and perseverance.
- Also highly regarded is the Mobil Four-Star Award, which honors properties for outstanding achievement in overall facility and for providing very strong service levels in all areas. These

award winners provide a distinctive experience for the ever-demanding and sophisticated consumer.

☉ The Mobil Three-Star Award recognizes an excellent property that provides full services and amenities. This category ranges from exceptional hotels with limited services to elegant restaurants with a less-formal atmosphere.

☉ A Mobil Two-Star property is a clean and comfortable establishment that has expanded amenities or a distinctive environment. A Mobil Two-Star property is an excellent place to stay or dine.

☉ A Mobil One-Star property is limited in its amenities and services but focuses on providing a value experience while meeting travelers' expectations. The property can be expected to be clean, comfortable, and convenient.

Allow us to emphasize that we do not charge establishments for inclusion in our guides. We have no relationship with any of the businesses and attractions we list and act only as a consumer advocate. In essence, we do the investigative legwork so that you won't have to.

Keep in mind, too, that the hospitality business is ever-changing. Restaurants and lodgings—particularly small chains and stand-alone establishments—change management or even go out of business with surprising quickness. Although we make every effort to double-check information during our annual updates, we nevertheless recommend that you call ahead to make sure the place you've selected is still open and offers all the amenities you're looking for. We've provided phone numbers; when available, we also list fax numbers and Web site addresses.

We hope that your travels are enjoyable and relaxing and that our books help you get the most out of every trip you take. If any aspect of your accommodation, dining, or sightseeing experience motivates you to comment, please drop us a line. We depend a great deal on our readers' remarks, so you can be assured that we will read your comments and assimilate them into our research. General comments about our books are also welcome. You can write to us at Mobil Travel Guide, 7373 N Cicero Ave, Lincolnwood, IL 60712, or send an e-mail to info@mobiltravelguide.com.

Take your Mobil Travel Guide books along on every trip you take. We're confident that you'll be pleased with their convenience, ease of use, and breadth of dependable coverage.

Happy travels!

How to Use This Book

The Mobil Travel Guide Regional Travel Planners are designed for ease of use. Each state has its own chapter, beginning with a general introduction that provides a geographical and historical orientation to the state and gives basic statewide tourist information, from climate to calendar highlights to seatbelt laws. The remainder of each chapter is devoted to travel destinations within the state—mainly cities and towns, but also national parks and tourist areas—which, like the states, are arranged in alphabetical order.

The following sections explain the wealth of information you'll find about those travel destinations: information about the area, things to see and do there, and where to stay and eat.

Maps and Map Coordinates

At the front of this book in the full-color section, we have provided state maps as well as maps of selected larger cities to help you find your way around once you leave the highway. You'll find a key to the map symbols on the Contents page at the beginning of the map section.

Next to most cities and towns throughout the book, you'll find a set of map coordinates, such as C-2. These coordinates reference the maps at the front of this book and help you find the location you're looking for quickly and easily.

Destination Information

Because many travel destinations are close to other cities and towns where travelers might find additional attractions, accommodations, and restaurants, we've included cross-references to those cities and towns when it makes sense to do so. We also list addresses, phone numbers, and Web sites for travel information resources—usually the local chamber of commerce or office of tourism—as well as pertinent statistics and, in many cases, a brief introduction to the area.

Information about airports, ground transportation, and suburbs is included for large cities.

Driving Tours and Walking Tours

The driving tours that we include for many states are usually day trips that make for interesting side excursions, although they can be longer. They offer you a way to get off the beaten path and visit an area that travelers often overlook. These trips frequently cover areas of natural beauty or historical significance.

Each walking tour focuses on a particularly interesting area of a city or town. Again, these tours can provide a break from everyday tourist attractions. The tours often include places to stop for meals or snacks.

What to See and Do

Mobil Travel Guide offers information about nearly 20,000 museums, art galleries, amusement parks, historic sites, national and state parks, ski areas, and many other types of attractions. A white star on a black background ★ signals that the attraction is a must-see—one of the best in the area. Because municipal parks, public tennis courts, swimming pools, and small educational institutions are common to most towns, they generally are not mentioned.

Following an attraction's description, you'll find the months, days, and, in some cases, hours of operation; the address/directions, telephone number, and Web site (if there is one); and the admission price category. The following are the ranges we use for admission fees, based on one adult:

- ✪ **FREE**
- ✪ **$** = Up to $5
- ✪ **$$** = $5.01-$10
- ✪ **$$$** = $10.01-$15
- ✪ **$$$$** = Over $15

Special Events

Special events are either annual events that last only a short time, such as festivals and fairs, or longer, seasonal events such as horse racing, theater, and summer concerts. Our Special Events listings also include infrequently occurring occasions that mark certain dates or events, such as a centennial or other commemorative celebration.

Listings

Lodgings, spas, and restaurants are usually listed under the city or town in which they're located. Make sure to check the related cities and towns that appear right beneath a city's heading for additional options, especially if you're traveling to a major metropolitan area that includes many suburbs. If a property is located in a town that doesn't have its own heading, the listing appears under the town nearest it, with the address and town given immediately after the establishment's name. In large cities, lodgings located within 5 miles of major commercial airports may be listed under a separate "Airport Area" heading that follows the city section.

LODGINGS

Travelers have different wants and needs when it comes to accommodations. To help you pinpoint properties that meet your particular needs, Mobil Travel Guide classifies each lodging by type according to the following characteristics.

Mobil Rated Lodgings

⊙ **Limited-Service Hotel.** A limited-service hotel is traditionally a Mobil One-Star or Mobil Two-Star property. At a Mobil One-Star hotel, guests can expect to find a clean, comfortable property that commonly serves a complimentary continental breakfast. A Mobil Two-Star hotel is also clean and comfortable but has expanded amenities, such as a full-service restaurant, business center, and fitness center. These services may have limited staffing and/or restricted hours of use.

⊙ **Full-Service Hotel.** A full-service hotel traditionally enjoys a Mobil Three-Star, Mobil Four-Star, or Mobil Five-Star rating. Guests can expect these hotels to offer at least one full-service restaurant in addition to amenities such as valet parking, luggage assistance, 24-hour room service, concierge service, laundry and/or dry-cleaning services, and turndown service.

⊙ **Full-Service Resort.** A resort is traditionally a full-service hotel that is geared toward recreation and represents a vacation and holiday destination. A resort's guest rooms are typically furnished to accommodate longer stays. The property may offer a full-service spa, golf, tennis, and fitness facilities or other leisure activities. Resorts are expected to offer a full-service restaurant and expanded amenities, such as luggage assistance, room service, meal plans, concierge service, and turndown service.

⊙ **Full-Service Inn.** An inn is traditionally a Mobil Three-Star, Mobil Four-Star, or Mobil Five-Star property. Inns are similar to bed-and-breakfasts (see below) but offer a wider range of services, most significantly a full-service restaurant that serves at least breakfast and dinner.

Specialty Lodgings

Mobil Travel Guide recognizes the unique and individualized nature of many different types of lodging establishments, including bed-and-breakfasts, limited-service inns, and guest ranches. For that reason, we have chosen to place our stamp of approval on the properties that fall into these two categories in lieu of applying our traditional Mobil Star ratings.

⊙ **B&B/Limited-Service Inn.** A bed-and-breakfast (B&B) or limited-service inn is traditionally an owner-occupied home or residence found in a residential area or vacation destination. It may be a structure of historic significance. Rooms are often individually decorated, but telephones, televisions, and private bathrooms may not be available in every room. A B&B typically serves only breakfast to its overnight guests, which is included in the room rate. Cocktails and refreshments may be served in the late afternoon or evening.

⊙ **Guest Ranch.** A guest ranch is traditionally a rustic, Western-themed property that specializes in stays of three or more days. Horseback riding is often a feature, with stables and trails found on the property. Facilities can range from clean, comfortable establishments to more luxurious facilities.

Mobil Star Rating Definitions for Lodgings

⊙ ★ ★ ★ ★ ★ : A Mobil Five-Star lodging provides consistently superlative service in an exceptionally distinctive luxury environment, with expanded services. Attention to detail is evident

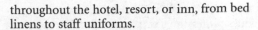

throughout the hotel, resort, or inn, from bed linens to staff uniforms.

✪ ★ ★ ★ ★ : A Mobil Four-Star lodging provides a luxury experience with expanded amenities in a distinctive environment. Services may include, but are not limited to, automatic turndown service, 24-hour room service, and valet parking.

✪ ★ ★ ★ : A Mobil Three-Star lodging is well appointed, with a full-service restaurant and expanded amenities, such as a fitness center, golf course, tennis courts, 24-hour room service, and optional turndown service.

✪ ★ ★ : A Mobil Two-Star lodging is considered a clean, comfortable, and reliable establishment that has expanded amenities, such as a full-service restaurant on the premises.

✪ ★ : A Mobil One-Star lodging is a limited-service hotel, motel, or inn that is considered a clean, comfortable, and reliable establishment.

Information Found in the Lodging Listings

Each lodging listing gives the name, address/location (when no street address is available), neighborhood and/or directions from downtown (in major cities), phone number(s), fax number, total number of guest rooms, and seasons open (if not year-round). Also included are details on business, luxury, recreational, and dining facilities at the property or nearby. A key to the symbols at the end of each listing can be found on the page following the "A Word to Our Readers" section.

For every property, we also provide pricing information. Because lodging rates change frequently, we list a pricing category rather than specific prices. The pricing categories break down as follows:

✪ **$** = Up to $150

✪ **$$** = $151-$250

✪ **$$$** = $251-$350

✪ **$$$$** = $351 and up

All prices quoted are in effect at the time of publication; however, prices cannot be guaranteed. In some locations, short-term price variations may exist because of special events, holidays, or seasonality. Certain resorts have complicated rate structures that vary with the time of year; always confirm rates when making your plans.

Because most lodgings offer the following features and services, information about them does not appear in the listings:

✪ Year-round operation

✪ Bathroom with tub and/or shower in each room

✪ Cable television in each room

✪ In-room telephones

✪ Cots and cribs available

✪ Daily maid service

✪ Elevators

✪ Major credit cards accepted

SPAS

Mobil Travel Guide is pleased to announce its newest category: hotel and resort spas. Until now, hotel and resort spas have not been formally rated or inspected by any organization. Every spa selected for inclusion in this book underwent a rigorous inspection process similar to the one Mobil Travel Guide has been applying to lodgings and restaurants for more than four decades. After spending a year and a half researching more than 300 spas and performing exhaustive incognito inspections of more than 200 properties, we narrowed our list to the 48 best spas in the United States and Canada.

Mobil Travel Guide's spa ratings are based on objective evaluations of more than 450 attributes. Approximately half of these criteria assess basic expectations, such as staff courtesy, the technical proficiency and skill of the employees, and whether the facility is maintained properly and hygienically. Several standards address issues that impact a guest's physical comfort and convenience, as well as the staff's ability to impart a sense of personalized service and anticipate clients' needs. Additional criteria measure the spa's ability to create a completely calming ambience.

The Mobil Star ratings focus on much more than the facilities available at a spa and the treatments it offers. Each Mobil Star rating is a cumulative score achieved from multiple inspections that reflects the spa management's attention to detail and commitment to consumers' needs.

Mobil Star Rating Definitions for Spas

✪ ★ ★ ★ ★ ★ : A Mobil Five-Star spa provides consistently superlative service in an exceptionally distinctive luxury environment with extensive amenities. The staff at a Mobil Five-Star spa provides extraordinary service above and beyond the traditional spa experience, allowing guests to achieve the highest level of relaxation and pampering. A Mobil Five-Star spa offers an extensive array of treatments, often incorporating international themes and products. Attention to detail is evident throughout the spa, from arrival to departure.

✪ ★ ★ ★ ★ : A Mobil Four-Star spa provides a luxurious experience with expanded amenities in an elegant and serene environment. Throughout the spa facility, guests experience personalized service. Amenities might include, but are not limited to, single-sex relaxation rooms where guests wait for their treatments, plunge pools and whirlpools in both men's and women's locker rooms, and an array of treatments, including at a minimum a selection of massages, body therapies, facials, and a variety of salon services.

✪ ★ ★ ★ : A Mobil Three-Star spa is physically well appointed and has a full complement of staff to ensure that guests' needs are met. It has some expanded amenities, such as, but not limited to, a well-equipped fitness center, separate men's and women's locker rooms, a sauna or steam room, and a designated relaxation area. It also offers a menu of services that at a minimum includes massages, facial treatments, and at least one other type of body treatment, such as scrubs or wraps.

RESTAURANTS

All Mobil Star rated dining establishments listed in this book have a full kitchen and offer seating at tables; most offer table service.

Mobil Star Rating Definitions for Restaurants

✪ ★ ★ ★ ★ ★ : A Mobil Five-Star restaurant offers one of few flawless dining experiences in the country. These establishments consistently provide their guests with exceptional food, superlative service, elegant décor, and exquisite presentations of each detail surrounding a meal.

✪ ★ ★ ★ ★ : A Mobil Four-Star restaurant provides professional service, distinctive presentations, and wonderful food.

✪ ★ ★ ★ : A Mobil Three-Star restaurant has good food, warm and skillful service, and enjoyable décor.

✪ ★ ★ : A Mobil Two-Star restaurant serves fresh food in a clean setting with efficient service. Value is considered in this category, as is family friendliness.

✪ ★ : A Mobil One-Star restaurant provides a distinctive experience through culinary specialty, local flair, or individual atmosphere.

Information Found in the Restaurant Listings

Each restaurant listing gives the cuisine type, street address (or directions if no address is available), phone and fax numbers, Web site (if available), meals served, days of operation (if not open daily year-round), and pricing category. Information about appropriate attire is provided, although it's always a good idea to call ahead and ask if you're unsure; the meaning of "casual" or "business casual" varies widely in different parts of the country. We also indicate whether the restaurant has a bar, whether a children's menu is offered, and whether outdoor seating is available. If reservations are recommended, we note that fact in the listing. When valet parking is available, it is noted in the description. In many cases, self-parking is available at the restaurant or nearby.

Because menu prices can fluctuate, we list a pricing category rather than specific prices. The pricing categories are defined as follows, per diner, and assume that you order an appetizer or dessert, an entrée, and one drink:

✪ **$** = $15 and under

✪ **$$** = $16-$35

✪ **$$$** = $36-$85

✪ **$$$$** = $86 and up

Again, all prices quoted are in effect at the time of publication, but prices cannot be guaranteed.

SPECIAL INFORMATION FOR TRAVELERS WITH DISABILITIES

The Mobil Travel Guide ⃞ symbol indicates that an establishment is not at least partially accessible to people with mobility problems. When the ⃞ symbol follows a listing, the establishment is not equipped with facilities to accommodate people using wheelchairs or crutches or otherwise needing easy access to doorways and rest rooms. Travelers with severe mobility problems or with hearing or visual impairments may or may not find the facilities they need. Always phone ahead to make sure hat an establishment can meet your needs.

Understanding the Symbols

What to See and Do

★	=	One of the top attractions in the area
$	=	Up to $5
$$	=	$5.01 to $10
$$$	=	$10.01 to $15
$$$$	=	Over $15

Lodgings

$	=	Up to $150
$$	=	$151 to $250
$$$	=	$251 to $350
$$$$	=	Over $350

Restaurants

$	=	Up to $15
$$	=	$16 to $35
$$$	=	$36 to $85
$$$$	=	Over $85

Lodging Star Definitions

★★★★★ A Mobil Five-Star lodging establishment provides consistently superlative service in an exceptionally distinctive luxury environment with expanded services. Attention to detail is evident throughout the hotel/resort/inn from the bed linens to the staff uniforms.

★★★★ A Mobil Four-Star lodging establishment is a hotel/resort/inn that provides a luxury experience with expanded amenities in a distinctive environment. Services may include, but are not limited to, automatic turndown service, 24-hour room service, and valet parking.

★★★ A Mobil Three-Star lodging establishment is a hotel/resort/inn that is well appointed, with a full-service restaurant and expanded amenities, such as, but not limited to, a fitness center, golf course, tennis courts, 24-hour room service, and optional turndown service.

★★ A Mobil Two-Star lodging establishment is a hotel/resort/inn that is considered a clean, comfortable, and reliable establishment, but also has expanded amenities, such as a full-service restaurant on the premises.

★ A Mobil One-Star lodging establishment is a limited-service hotel or inn that is considered a clean, comfortable, and reliable establishment.

Restaurant Star Definitions

★★★★★ A Mobil Five-Star restaurant is one of few flawless dining experiences in the country. These restaurants consistently provide their guests with exceptional food, superlative service, elegant décor, and exquisite presentations of each detail surrounding the meal.

★★★★ A Mobil Four-Star restaurant provides professional service, distinctive presentations, and wonderful food.

★★★ A Mobil Three-Star restaurant has good food, warm and skillful service, and enjoyable décor.

★★ A Mobil Two-Star restaurant serves fresh food in a clean setting with efficient service. Value is considered in this category, as is family friendliness.

★ A Mobil One-Star restaurant provides a distinctive experience through culinary specialty, local flair, or individual atmosphere.

Symbols at End of Listings

- Facilities for people with disabilities not available
- Pets allowed
- Ski in/ski out access
- Golf on premises
- Tennis court(s) on premises
- Indoor or outdoor pool
- Fitness room
- Major commercial airport within 5 miles
- Business center

Making the Most of Your Trip

A few hardy souls might look back with fondness on a trip during which the car broke down, leaving them stranded for three days, or a vacation that cost twice what it was supposed to. For most travelers, though, the best trips are those that are safe, smooth, and within budget. To help you make your trip the best it can be, we've assembled a few tips and resources.

Saving Money

ON LODGING

Many hotels and motels offer discounts—for senior citizens, business travelers, families, you name it. It never hurts to ask—politely, that is. Sometimes, especially in the late afternoon, desk clerks are instructed to fill beds, and you might be offered a lower rate or a nicer room to entice you to stay. Simply ask the reservation agent for the best rate available. Also, make sure to try both the toll-free number and the local number. You may be able to get a lower rate from one than from the other.

Timing your trip right can cut your lodging costs as well. Look for bargains on stays over multiple nights, in the off-season, and on weekdays or weekends, depending on the location. Many hotels in major metropolitan areas, for example, have special weekend packages that offer leisure travelers considerable savings on rooms; they may include breakfast, cocktails, and/or dinner discounts.

Another way to save money is to choose accommodations that give you more than just a standard room. Rooms with kitchen facilities enable you to cook some meals yourself, reducing your restaurant costs. A suite might save money for two couples traveling together. Even hotel luxury levels can provide good value, as many include breakfast or cocktails in the price of a room.

State and city taxes, as well as special room taxes, can increase your room rate by as much as 25 percent per day. We are unable to include information about taxes in our listings, but we strongly urge you to ask about taxes when making reservations so that you understand the total cost of your lodgings before you book them.

Watch out for telephone-usage charges that hotels frequently impose on long-distance, credit-card, and other calls. Before phoning from your room, read the information given to you at check-in, and then be sure to review your bill carefully when checking out. You won't be expected to pay for charges that the hotel didn't spell out. Consider using your cell phone if you have one; or, if public telephones are available in the hotel lobby, your cost savings may outweigh the inconvenience of using them.

Here are some additional ways to save on lodgings:

- Stay in B&B accommodations. They're generally less expensive than standard hotel rooms, and the complimentary breakfast cuts down on food costs.

- If you're traveling with children, find lodgings at which kids stay free.

- When visiting a major city, stay just outside the city limits; these rooms are usually less expensive than those in downtown locations.

- Consider visiting national parks during the low season, when prices of lodgings near the parks drop by 25 percent or more.

- When calling a hotel, ask whether it is running any special promotions or if any discounts are available; many times reservationists are told not to volunteer these deals unless they're specifically asked about them.

- Check for hotel packages; some offer nightly rates that include a rental car or discounts on major attractions.

ON DINING

There are several ways to get a less expensive meal at an expensive restaurant. Early-bird dinners are popular in many parts of the country and offer considerable savings. If you're interested in visiting a Mobil Four- or Five-Star establishment, consider going at lunchtime. Although the prices are probably still relatively high at midday, they may be half of those at dinner, and you'll experience the same ambience, service, and cuisine.

ON ENTERTAINMENT

Although many national parks, monuments, seashores, historic sites, and recreation areas may be visited free of charge, others charge an entrance fee and/or a usage fee for special services and facilities. If you plan to make several visits to national recreation areas, consider one of the following money-saving programs offered by the National Park Service:

⊙ **National Parks Pass.** This annual pass is good for entrance to any national park that charges an entrance fee. If the park charges a per-vehicle fee, the pass holder and any accompanying passengers in a private noncommercial vehicle may enter. If the park charges a per-person fee, the pass applies to the holder's spouse, children, and parents as well as the holder. It is valid for entrance fees only; it does not cover parking, camping, or other fees. You can purchase a National Parks Pass in person at any national park where an entrance fee is charged; by mail from the National Park Foundation, PO Box 34108, Washington, DC 20043-4108; by calling toll-free 888/467-2757; or at www.nationalparks .org. The cost is $50.

⊙ **Golden Eagle Sticker.** When affixed to a National Parks Pass, this hologram sticker, available to people who are between 17 and 61 years of age, extends coverage to sites managed by the US Fish and Wildlife Service, the US Forest Service, and the Bureau of Land Management. It is good until the National Parks Pass to which it is affixed expires and does not cover usage fees. You can purchase one at the National Park Service, the Fish and Wildlife Service, or the Bureau of Land Management fee stations. The cost is $15.

⊙ **Golden Age Passport.** Available to citizens and permanent US residents 62 and older, this passport is a lifetime entrance permit to fee-charging national recreation areas. The fee exemption extends to those accompanying the permit holder in a private noncommercial vehicle or, in the case of walk-in facilities, to the holder's spouse and children. The passport also entitles the holder to a 50 percent discount on federal usage fees charged in park areas, but not on con-cessions. Golden Age Passports must be obtained in person and are available at most National Park Service units that charge an entrance fee. The applicant must show proof of age, such as a driver's license or birth certificate (Medicare cards are not acceptable proof). The cost is $10.

⊙ **Golden Access Passport.** Issued to citizens and permanent US residents who are physically disabled or visually impaired, this passport is a free lifetime entrance permit to fee-charging national recreation areas. The fee exemption extends to those accompanying the permit holder in a private noncommercial vehicle or, in the case of walk-in facilities, to the holder's spouse and children. The passport also entitles the holder to a 50 percent discount on usage fees charged in park areas, but not on concessions. Golden Access Passports must be obtained in person and are available at most National Park Service units that charge an entrance fee. Proof of eligibility to receive federal benefits (under programs such as Disability Retirement, Compensation for Military Service-Connected Disability, and the Coal Mine Safety and Health Act) is required, or an affidavit must be signed attesting to eligibility.

A money-saving move in several large cities is to purchase a **CityPass.** If you plan to visit several museums and other major attractions, CityPass is a terrific option because it gets you into several sites for one substantially reduced price. Currently, CityPass is available in Boston, Chicago, Hollywood, New York, Philadelphia, San Francisco, Seattle, southern California (which includes Disneyland, SeaWorld, and the San Diego Zoo), and Toronto. For more information or to buy one, call toll-free 888/330-5008 or visit www. citypass.net. You can also buy a CityPass from any participating CityPass attraction.

Here are some additional ways to save on entertainment and shopping:

⊙ Check with your hotel's concierge for various coupons and special offers; they often have two-for-one tickets for area attractions and coupons for discounts at area stores and restaurants.

⊙ Purchase same-day concert or theater tickets for half-price through the local cheap-tickets outlet, such as TKTS in New York or Hot Tix in Chicago.

- Visit museums on their free or "by donation" days, when you can pay what you wish rather than a specific admission fee.
- Save receipts from purchases in Canada; visitors to Canada can get a rebate on federal taxes and some provincial sales taxes.

ON TRANSPORTATION

Transportation is a big part of any vacation budget. Here are some ways to reduce your costs:

- If you're renting a car, shop early over the Internet; you can book a car during the low season for less, even if you'll be using it in the high season.
- Rental car discounts are often available if you rent for one week or longer and reserve in advance.
- Get the best gas mileage out of your vehicle by making sure that it's properly tuned up and keeping your tires properly inflated.
- Travel at moderate speeds on the open road; higher speeds require more gasoline.
- Fill the tank before you return your rental car; rental companies charge to refill the tank and do so at prices of up to 50 percent more than at local gas stations.
- Make a checklist of travel essentials and purchase them before you leave; don't get stuck buying expensive sunscreen at your hotel or overpriced film at the airport.

FOR SENIOR CITIZENS

Always call ahead to ask if a discount is being offered, and be sure to carry proof of age. Additional information for mature travelers is available from the American Association of Retired Persons (AARP), 601 E St NW, Washington, DC 20049; phone 202/434-2277; www.aarp.org.

Tipping

Tips are expressions of appreciation for good service. However, you are never obligated to tip if you receive poor service.

IN HOTELS

- Door attendants usually get $1 for hailing a cab.
- Bell staff expect $2 per bag.

- Concierges are tipped according to the service they perform. Tipping is not mandatory when you've asked for suggestions on sightseeing or restaurants or for help in making dining reservations. However, a tip of $5 is appropriate when a concierge books you a table at a restaurant known to be difficult to get into. For obtaining theater or sporting event tickets, $5 to $10 is expected.
- Maids should be tipped $1 to $2 per day. Hand your tip directly to the maid, or leave it with a note saying that the money has been left expressly for the maid.

IN RESTAURANTS

Before tipping, carefully review your check for any gratuity or service charge that is already included in your bill. If you're in doubt, ask your server.

- Coffee shop and counter service waitstaff usually receive 15 percent of the bill, before sales tax.
- In full-service restaurants, tip 18 percent of the bill, before sales tax.
- In fine restaurants, where gratuities are shared among a larger staff, 18 to 20 percent is appropriate.
- In most cases, the maitre d' is tipped only if the service has been extraordinary, and only on the way out. At upscale properties in major metropolitan areas, $20 is the minimum.
- If there is a wine steward, tip $20 for exemplary service and beyond, or more if the wine was decanted or the bottle was very expensive.
- Tip $1 to $2 per coat at the coat check.

AT AIRPORTS

Curbside luggage handlers expect $1 per bag. Car-rental shuttle drivers who help with your luggage appreciate a $1 or $2 tip.

Staying Safe

The best way to deal with emergencies is to avoid them in the first place. However, unforeseen situations do happen, so you should be prepared for them.

IN YOUR CAR

Before you head out on a road trip, make sure that your car has been serviced and is in good working order. Change the oil, check the battery and belts, make sure that your windshield washer fluid is full and your tires are properly inflated (which can also improve your gas mileage). Other inspections recommended by the vehicle's manufacturer should also be made.

Next, be sure you have the tools and equipment needed to deal with a routine breakdown:

- Jack
- Spare tire
- Lug wrench
- Repair kit
- Emergency tools
- Jumper cables
- Spare fan belt
- Fuses
- Flares and/or reflectors
- Flashlight
- First-aid kit
- In winter, a windshield scraper and snow shovel

Many emergency supplies are sold in special packages that include the essentials you need to stay safe in the event of a breakdown.

Also bring all appropriate and up-to-date documentation—licenses, registration, and insurance cards—and know what your insurance covers. Bring an extra set of keys, too, just in case.

En route, always buckle up! In most states, wearing a seatbelt is required by law.

If your car does break down, do the following:

- Get out of traffic as soon as possible—pull well off the road.
- Raise the hood and turn on your emergency flashers or tie a white cloth to the roadside door handle or antenna.
- Stay in your car.
- Use flares or reflectors to keep your vehicle from being hit.

IN YOUR HOTEL

Chances are slim that you will encounter a hotel or motel fire, but you can protect yourself by doing the following:

- Once you've checked in, make sure that the smoke detector in your room is working properly.
- Find the property's fire safety instructions, usually posted on the inside of the room door.
- Locate the fire extinguishers and at least two fire exits.
- Never use an elevator in a fire.

For personal security, use the peephole in your room door and make sure that anyone claiming to be a hotel employee can show proper identification. Call the front desk if you feel threatened at any time.

PROTECTING AGAINST THEFT

To guard against theft wherever you go:

- Don't bring anything of more value than you need.
- If you do bring valuables, leave them at your hotel rather than in your car.
- If you bring something very expensive, lock it in a safe. Many hotels put one in each room; others will store your valuables in the hotel's safe.
- Don't carry more money than you need. Use traveler's checks and credit cards or visit cash machines to withdraw more cash when you run out.

For Travelers with Disabilities

To get the kind of service you need and have a right to expect, don't hesitate when making a reservation to question the management about the availability of accessible rooms, parking, entrances, restaurants, lounges, or any other facilities that are important to you, and confirm what is meant by "accessible."

The Mobil Travel Guide ⬛ symbol indicates establishments that are not at least partially accessible to people with special mobility needs (people using wheelchairs or crutches or otherwise needing easy access to buildings and rooms). Further information about these criteria can be found in the earlier section "How to Use This Book."

A thorough listing of published material for travelers with disabilities is available from the Disability Bookshop, Twin Peaks Press, Box 129, Vancouver, WA 98666; phone 360/694-2462; disabilitybookshop.virtualave.net. Another reliable organization is the Society for Accessible Travel & Hospitality (SATH), 347 Fifth Ave, Suite 610, New York, NY 10016; phone 212/447-7284; www.sath.org.

Important Toll-Free Numbers and Online Information

Hotels

Adams Mark...............................800/444-2326
www.adamsmark.com
America's Best Value Inn....................888/315-2378
www.americasbestvalueinn.com
AmericInn.................................800/634-3444
www.americinn.com
AmeriHost Inn............................800/434-5800
www.amerihostinn.com
Amerisuites..............................800/833-1516
www.amerisuites.com
Baymont Inns.............................800/621-1429
www.baymontinns.com
Best Inns & Suites.........................800/237-8466
www.bestinn.com
Best Western..............................800/780-7234
www.bestwestern.com
Budget Host Inn..........................800/283-4678
www.budgethost.com
Candlewood Suites.....................888/226-3539
www.candlewoodsuites.com
Clarion Hotels............................800/252-7466
www.choicehotels.com
Comfort Inns and Suites..................800/252-7466
www.comfortinn.com
Country Hearth Inns.......................800/848-5767
www.countryhearth.com
Country Inns & Suites.....................800/456-4000
www.countryinns.com
Courtyard by Marriott.................800/321-2211
www.courtyard.com
Crowne Plaza Hotels and Resorts...........800/227-6963
www.crowneplaza.com
Days Inn.................................800/544-8313
www.daysinn.com
Delta Hotels..............................800/268-1133
www.deltahotels.com
Destination Hotels & Resorts.................800/434-7347
www.destinationhotels.com
Doubletree Hotels.........................800/222-8733
www.doubletree.com
Drury Inn................................800/378-7946
www.druryhotels.com
Econolodge...............................800/553-2666
www.econolodge.com

Embassy Suites............................800/362-2779
www.embassysuites.com
ExelInns of America........................800/367-3935
www.exelinns.com
Extended StayAmerica......................800/398-7829
www.extendedstayhotels.com
Fairfield Inn by Marriott...............800/228-2800
www.fairfieldinn.com
Fairmont Hotels...........................800/441-1414
www.fairmont.com
Four Points by Sheraton...............888/625-5144
www.fourpoints.com
Four Seasons.............................800/819-5053
www.fourseasons.com
Hampton Inn.............................800/426-7866
www.hamptoninn.com
Hard Rock Hotels, Resorts, and Casinos.....800/473-7625
www.hardrockhotel.com
Harrah's Entertainment....................800/427-7247
www.harrahs.com
Hawthorn Suites..........................800/527-1133
www.hawthorn.com
Hilton Hotels and Resorts (US)..............800/774-1500
www.hilton.com
Holiday Inn Express.......................800/465-4329
www.hiexpress.com
Holiday Inn Hotels and Resorts.............800/465-4329
www.holiday-inn.com
Homestead Studio Suites...............888/782-9473
www.extendedstayhotels.com
Homewood Suites.........................800/225-5466
www.homewoodsuites.com
Howard Johnson..........................800/406-1411
www.hojo.com
Hyatt...................................800/633-7313
www.hyatt.com
Inns of America...........................800/826-0778
www.innsofamerica.com
InterContinental...........................888/424-6835
www.intercontinental.com
Joie de Vivre.............................800/738-7477
www.jdvhospitality.com
Kimpton Hotels........................888/546-7866
www.kimptonhotels.com
Knights Inn..............................800/843-5644
www.knightsinn.com
La Quinta................................800/531-5900
www.lq.com

Le Meridien............................... 800/543-4300
www.lemeridien.com

Leading Hotels of the World................ 800/223-6800
www.lhw.com

Loews Hotels 800/235-6397
www.loewshotels.com

MainStay Suites 800/660-6246
www.mainstaysuites.com

Mandarin Oriental 800/526-6566
www.mandarinoriental.com

Marriott Hotels, Resorts, and Suites 800/228-9290
www.marriott.com

Microtel Inns & Suites 800/771-7171
www.microtelinn.com

Millennium & Copthorne Hotels 866/866-8086
www.millenniumhotels.com

Motel 6................................... 800/466-8356
www.motel6.com

Omni Hotels 800/843-6664
www.omnihotels.com

Pan Pacific Hotels and Resorts............. 800/327-8585
www.panpacific.com

Park Inn & Park Plaza 888/201-1801
www.parkinn.com

The Peninsula Group .... Contact individual hotel
www.peninsula.com

Preferred Hotels & Resorts Worldwide....... 800/323-7500
www.preferredhotels.com

Quality Inn 800/228-5151
www.qualityinn.com

Radisson Hotels 800/333-3333
www.radisson.com

Raffles International Hotels and Resorts..... 800/637-9477
www.raffles.com

Ramada Plazas, Limiteds, and Inns 800/272-6232
www.ramada.com

Red Lion Inns............................. 800/733-5466
www.redlion.com

Red Roof Inns............................. 800/733-7663
www.redroof.com

Regent International 800/545-4000
www.regenthotels.com

Relais & Chateaux 800/735-2478
www.relaischateaux.com

Renaissance Hotels 888/236-2427
www.renaissancehotels.com

Residence Inn 800/331-3131
www.residenceinn.com

Ritz-Carlton.............................. 800/241-3333
www.ritzcarlton.com

RockResorts.......................... 888/367-7625
www.rockresorts.com

Rodeway Inn.............................. 800/228-2000
www.rodeway.com

Rosewood Hotels & Resorts 888/767-3966
www.rosewoodhotels.com

Select Inn 800/641-1000
www.selectinn.com

Sheraton 888/625-5144
www.sheraton.com

Shilo Inns 800/222-2244
www.shiloinns.com

Shoney's Inn.............................. 800/552-4667
www.shoneysinn.com

Signature/Jameson Inns.................... 800/822-5252
www.jamesoninns.com

Sleep Inn 877/424-6423
www.sleepinn.com

Small Luxury Hotels of the World........... 800/525-4800
www.slh.com

Sofitel................................... 800/763-4835
www.sofitel.com

SpringHill Suites 888/236-2427
www.springhillsuites.com

St. Regis Luxury Collection............. 888/625-5144
www.stregis.com

Staybridge Suites 800/238-8000
www.staybridge.com

Summit International 800/457-4000
www.summithotelsandresorts.com

Super 8 Motels 800/800-8000
www.super8.com

The Sutton Place Hotels............... 866/378-8866
www.suttonplace.com

Swissôtel................................. 800/637-9477
www.swissotels.com

TownePlace Suites.................... 888/236-2427
www.towneplace.com

Travelodge 800/578-7878
www.travelodge.com

Vagabond Inns............................ 800/522-1555
www.vagabondinn.com

W Hotels 888/625-5144
www.whotels.com

Wellesley Inn and Suites.................. 800/444-8888
www.wellesleyinnandsuites.com

WestCoast Hotels 800/325-4000
www.westcoasthotels.com
Westin Hotels & Resorts 800/937-8461
www.westinhotels.com
Wingate Inns 800/228-1000
www.thewingateinns.com
Woodfin Suite Hotels .800/966-3346
www.woodfinsuitehotels.com
WorldHotels 800/223-5652
www.worldhotels.com
Wyndham Hotels & Resorts 800/996-3426
www.wyndham.com

Airlines

Air Canada 888/247-2262
www.aircanada.com
AirTran 800/247-8726
www.airtran.com
Alaska Airlines 800/252-7522
www.alaskaair.com
American Airlines 800/433-7300
www.aa.com
ATA 800/435-9282
www.ata.com
Continental Airlines 800/523-3273
www.continental.com
Delta Air Lines 800/221-1212
www.delta.com
Frontier Airlines 800/432-1359
www.frontierairlines.com
Hawaiian Airlines 800/367-5320
www.hawaiianairlines.com
Jet Blue Airlines 800/538-2583
www.jetblue.com

Midwest Airlines 800/452-2022
www.midwestairlines.com
Northwest Airlines 800/225-2525
www.nwa.com
Southwest Airlines 800/435-9792
www.southwest.com
Spirit Airlines 800/772-7117
www.spiritair.com
United Airlines 800/241-6522
www.united.com
US Airways 800/428-4322
www.usairways.com

Car Rentals

Advantage 800/777-5500
www.arac.com
Alamo 800/327-9633
www.alamo.com
Avis 800/831-2847
www.avis.com
Budget 800/527-0700
www.budget.com
Dollar 800/800-4000
www.dollar.com
Enterprise 800/325-8007
www.enterprise.com
Hertz 800/654-3131
www.hertz.com
National 800/227-7368
www.nationalcar.com
Payless 800/729-5377
www.paylesscarrental.com
Rent-A-Wreck.com 800/535-1391
www.rentawreck.com
Thrifty 800/847-4389
www.thrifty.com

Meet The Stars

Mobil Travel Guide 2007 *Five-Star* Award Winners

CALIFORNIA
Lodgings
The Beverly Hills Hotel, *Beverly Hills*
Chateau du Sureau, *Oakhurst*
Four Seasons Hotel San Francisco,
  San Francisco
Hotel Bel-Air, *Los Angeles*
The Peninsula Beverly Hills, *Beverly Hills*
Raffles L'Ermitage Beverly Hills, *Beverly Hills*
St. Regis Monarch Beach Resort & Spa, *Dana Point*
St. Regis San Francisco, *San Francisco*
The Ritz-Carlton, San Francisco, *San Francisco*

Restaurants
The Dining Room, *San Francisco*
The French Laundry, *Yountville*

COLORADO
Lodgings
The Broadmoor, *Colorado Springs*
The Little Nell, *Aspen*

CONNECTICUT
Lodging
The Mayflower Inn, *Washington*

DISTRICT OF COLUMBIA
Lodging
Four Seasons Hotel Washington, DC
  Washington

FLORIDA
Lodgings
Four Seasons Resort Palm Beach, *Palm Beach*
The Ritz-Carlton Naples, *Naples*
The Ritz-Carlton, Palm Beach, *Manalapan*

GEORGIA
Lodgings
Four Seasons Hotel Atlanta, *Atlanta*

The Lodge at Sea Island Golf Club,
  St. Simons Island

Restaurants
The Dining Room, *Atlanta*
Seeger's, *Atlanta*

HAWAII
Lodging
Four Seasons Resort Maui, *Wailea, Maui*

ILLINOIS
Lodgings
Four Seasons Hotel Chicago, *Chicago*
The Peninsula Chicago, *Chicago*
The Ritz-Carlton, A Four Seasons Hotel, *Chicago*

Restaurants
Alinea, *Chicago*
Charlie Trotter's, *Chicago*

MAINE
Restaurant
The White Barn Inn, *Kennebunkport*

MASSACHUSETTS
Lodgings
Blantyre, *Lenox*
Four Seasons Hotel Boston, *Boston*

NEVADA
Lodging
Tower Suites at Wynn, *Las Vegas*

Restaurants
Alex, *Las Vegas*
Joel Robuchon at the Mansion, *Las Vegas*

NEW YORK
Lodgings
Four Seasons, Hotel New York, *New York*
Mandarin Oriental, *New York*
The Point, *Saranac Lake*

The Ritz-Carlton New York, Central Park,
  New York
The St. Regis, *New York*

Restaurants
Alain Ducasse, *New York*
Jean Georges, *New York*
Masa, *New York*
per se, *New York*

NORTH CAROLINA
Lodging
The Fearrington House Country Inn, *Pittsboro*

PENNSYLVANIA
Restaurant
Le Bec-Fin, *Philadelphia*

SOUTH CAROLINA
Lodging
Woodlands Resort & Inn, *Summerville*

Restaurant
Dining Room at the Woodlands, *Summerville*

TENNESSEE
Lodging
The Hermitage, *Nashville*

TEXAS
Lodging
The Mansion on Turtle Creek, *Dallas*

VERMONT
Lodging
Twin Farms, *Barnard*

VIRGINIA
Lodgings
The Inn at Little Washington, *Washington*
The Jefferson Hotel, *Richmond*

Restaurant
The Inn at Little Washington, *Washington*

Mobil Travel Guide has been rating establishments with its Mobil One- to Five-Star system since 1958. Each establishment awarded the Mobil Five-Star rating is one of the best in the country. Detailed information on each award winner can be found in the corresponding regional edition listed on the back cover of this book.

Four- and Five-Star Establishments in Southern California

★ ★ ★ ★ ★ Lodgings

The Beverly Hills Hotel, *Beverly Hills*

Hotel Bel-Air, *Bel-Air*

The Peninsula Beverly Hills, *Beverly Hills*

Raffles L'Ermitage Beverly Hills, *Beverly Hills*

The St. Regis Monarch Beach Resort & Spa, *Dana Point*

★ ★ ★ ★ ★ Spa

Spa Montage at Montage Resort, *Laguna Beach*

★ ★ ★ ★ Lodgings

Bacara Resort & Spa, *Santa Barbara*

Casa Palmero at Pebble Beach, *Pebble Beach*

Four Seasons Hotel Los Angeles at Beverly Hills, *Beverly Hills*

Four Seasons Resort Aviara, North San Diego, *Carlsbad*

Four Seasons Resort Santa Barbara, *Santa Barbara*

The Inn at Spanish Bay, *Pebble Beach*

The Inn on Mount Ada, *Avalon*

The Island Hotel Newport Beach, *Newport Beach*

Lodge at Pebble Beach, *Pebble Beach*

Lodge at Torrey Pines, *La Jolla*

Montage Resort & Spa, *Laguna Beach*

Rancho Valencia Resort, *Rancho Santa Fe*

The Regent Beverly Wilshire, *Beverly Hills*

The Ritz-Carlton, Huntington Hotel & Spa, *Pasadena*

The Ritz-Carlton, Laguna Niguel, *Dana Point*

★ ★ ★ ★ Spas

The Beverly Hills Hotel Spa by La Prairie, *Beverly Hills*

The Four Seasons Spa, Los Angeles at Beverly Hills, *Los Angeles*

Spa at Four Seasons Resort Aviara, North San Diego, *Carlsbad*

Spa at Four Seasons Resort Santa Barbara, *Santa Barbara*

Spa Gaucin, *Dana Point*

Spa Ojai, *Ojai*

The Spa at Pebble Beach, *Pebble Beach*

The Spa at The Peninsula Beverly Hills, *Beverly Hills*

The Spa at Torrey Pines, *La Jolla*

★ ★ ★ ★ Restaurants

The Belvedere, *Beverly Hills*

Diaghilev, *West Hollywood*

Laurel, *San Diego*

L'Orangerie, *West Hollywood*

Melisse, *Santa Monica*

Ortolan, *Los Angeles*

Patina, *Los Angeles*

The Restaurant at Hotel Bel-Air, *Bel-Air*

Sona, *West Hollywood*

Stonehill Tavern, *Dana Point*

Southern California

California has the largest
population of any state in the
United States. Within it, only
80 miles apart, are the lowest and highest points in the contiguous United
States—Death Valley and Mount
Whitney. California has ski areas and
blistering deserts, mountains and
beaches, giant redwoods and giant missiles, Spanish missions and skyscrapers. The oldest living things on earth
grow here—a stand of bristlecone pine
said to be 4,600 years old. Los Angeles,
in Southern California, is bright and
brazen, growing, and modern. California, with 1,264 miles of coastline and
a width of up to 350 miles, does things
in a big way.

Almost every crop of the United States
grows here. Prunes, oranges, bales of
cotton, and tons of vegetables roll out
from the factory farms in the fertile
valleys. California leads the nation in
the production of 75 crop and livestock
commodities, including grapes, peaches,
apricots, olives, figs, lemons, avocados, walnuts,
almonds, rice, plums, prunes, dates, and nectarines.
It also leads in the production of dried, canned, and
frozen fruits and vegetables, wine, eggs, turkeys, saf-
flower, beeswax, and honey. Homegrown industries
include Hollywood movies, television, electronics,
aircraft, and missiles.

Spaniards, Mexicans, English, Russians, and others helped write the history of the state. The first
explorer to venture into the waters of California was
Portuguese—Juan Rodriguez Cabrillo, in 1542. In
1579, Sir Francis Drake explored the coastal waters
and is believed to have landed just northwest of what
is now San Francisco. Beginning in 1769, Spanish

Population: 33,871,648

Area: 158,693 square miles

Elevation: 282 feet below sea level–14,494 feet

Peak: Mount Whitney (between Inyo and Tulare coun-
ties)

Entered Union: September 9, 1850 (31st state)

Capital: Sacramento

Motto: Eureka (I Have Found It)

Nickname: The Golden State

Flower: Golden Poppy

Bird: California Valley Quail

Tree: California Redwood

Fair: Late August in Sacramento

Time Zone: Pacific

Web Site: www.gocalif.ca.gov

Fun Facts:

- More than 300,000 tons of grapes are grown in
California annually.
- More turkeys are raised in California than in any other
state in the US.
- The first motion picture theater opened in Los
Angeles on April 2, 1902.

colonial policy sprinkled a trail of missions around
which the first towns developed. The Mexican flag
flew over California after Mexico won independence
from Spain in 1821. American settlers later wrenched
the colony from Mexico and organized the short-
lived Bear Flag Republic. On July 7, 1846, Commo-
dore John D. Sloat raised the United States flag at
Monterey. Under the Treaty of Guadalupe Hidalgo,
California became part of what was to be the coastal
boundary of the United States in 1848.

Perhaps the most important event in California's
history was the discovery of gold in January of
1848, which set off a sudden mass migration that
transformed the drowsy, placid countryside and
accelerated the opening of the Far West by sev-

Calendar Highlights

JANUARY

Bob Hope Chrysler Classic *(Palm Desert). Phone 760/346-8184.* Golf pros and celebrities play at four country clubs at Bermuda Dunes, La Quinta, Palm Desert, and Indian Wells.

Tournament of Roses Parade *(Pasadena). Phone 626/449-4100.* This spectacular floral parade on Colorado Boulevard attracts more than a million people each year. It culminates with the Rose Bowl football game in the afternoon.

APRIL

Toyota Grand Prix *(Long Beach). Phone 562/981-2600.* An international race held on downtown streets.

MAY

Cinco de Mayo *(Los Angeles). El Pueblo de Los Angeles Historic Monument. Phone 213/689-8822.* Arts and crafts, music, and dancing. Contact Hollywood Visitors Information Center.

JULY

Mozart Festival *(San Luis Obispo). Phone 805/781-3008.* www.mozartfestival.*com.* Recitals, chamber music, orchestra concerts, and choral music. Held at various locations throughout the county, including Mission San Luis Obispo de Tolosa and Cal Poly State University campus.

SEPTEMBER

Los Angeles County Fair *(Pomona). Fairplex. Phone 909/623-3111. www.lacountyfair.com.* Thoroughbred racing, carnival, exhibits, free stage shows, food booths, and a monorail.

NOVEMBER

Hollywood Christmas Parade *(Hollywood). Phone 323/469-2337.* The largest celebrity parade in the world, televised worldwide, features floats and marching bands; more than 50 of Hollywood's famous stars. For information, contact the Hollywood Chamber of Commerce.

DECEMBER

Christmas-Light Boat Parade *(San Diego). San Diego Harbor, Shelter Island Yacht Basin. www.sdparadeoflights.org.*

eral decades. The 49ers who came for gold found greater riches in the fertile soil of the valleys and the markets of the young cities.

During and after World War II, California grew at an astounding pace in both industry and population. Jet travel across the Pacific makes the state a gateway to the Orient.

When to Go/Climate

We recommend visiting California in the mid- to late spring or early to mid-fall, when the fog generally lifts and the heavy tourist traffic is over. Winters are rainy; summers are dry and hot in much of the state.

AVERAGE HIGH/LOW TEMPERATURES (°F)

Los Angeles

Jan 68/49	May 74/58	Sept 83/65
Feb 69/51	Jun 78/61	Oct 79/60
Mar 70/52	July 84/65	Nov 72/54
Apr 72/54	Aug 85/66	Dec 68/49

Parks and Recreation

Water-related activities, hiking, riding, various other sports, picnicking, nature trails, and visitor centers, as well as camping, are available in many of California's parks. Some parks limit camping to a maximum consecutive period of 7-30 days, depending on the season and the popularity of the area. Campsite charges are $10-$29 per night per vehicle; trailer hook-ups are $9-$25. For campsite reservations, phone toll-free 800/444-7275 from anywhere in the continental United States; outside the country, phone customer service at toll-free 800/695-2269. Day-use fee is $2-$6 per vehicle; vehicle with sailboat over 8 feet and all motor vessels, $3-$5 additional; all other boats, $1 additional; annual pass for $75 includes unlimited day use, $125 with boat; boat launching $3-$5. Fees may vary in some areas. There are also small fees for some activities at some areas. Pets on a leash permitted in campground and day-use areas only, $1 per night (camping), $1 (day-use). Reservations for Hearst-San Simeon State Historical Monument (Hearst Castle) (see) can be made by calling toll-free 800/444-4445. For a map folder listing and describing state parks ($2), contact the California State Parks Store, PO Box 942896, Sacramento 94296-0001; phone 916/653-4000; www.parks.ca.gov. For general park information, phone 916/653-6995.

FISHING AND HUNTING

Streams, rivers, canals, and lakes provide a great variety of freshwater fish. Salmon and steelhead trout run in great numbers in major coastal rivers north of San Francisco. Everything from barracuda to smelt may be found along or off the shore.

Hunting for deer, bear, and other big game is available in most national forests, other public lands, and some private lands (by permission), except in national and state parks, where firearms are prohibited. Waterfowl, quail, and dove shooting can be arranged at public management areas and in private shooting preserves. Tidepool collecting is illegal without a special permit.

A fishing license is required for all persons 16 and older to fish in either inland or ocean waters. Some public piers in ocean waters allow fishing without a license (a list is available on request). A hunting license is required to hunt any animal. For information, contact the California Department of Fish and Game, 3211 S St, Sacramento 95816. For general information, phone 916/653-7664; for license information, phone 916/227-2282.

Driving Information

Safety belts are mandatory for all persons anywhere in a vehicle. Children under 4 years and weighing under 40 pounds must be in approved safety seats anywhere in vehicle.

INTERSTATE HIGHWAY SYSTEM

Use the following list as a guide to access interstate highways in California. Consult a map to confirm driving routes.

Highway Number	Cities/Towns within 10 Miles
Interstate 5	Anaheim, Buena Park, Carlsbad, Costa Mesa, Del Mar, Dunsmuir, Fullerton, Garden Grove, Irvine, Lodi, Mount Shasta, Oceanside, Orange, Rancho Santa Fe, Red Bluff, Redding, Sacramento, San Clemente, San Diego, San Juan Capistrano, Santa Ana, Stockton, Valencia, Willows, Yreka.
Interstate 8	Calexico, El Cajon, El Centro, San Diego.
Interstate 10	Beaumont, Blythe, Claremont, Desert Hot Springs, Indio, Ontario, Palm Desert, Palm Springs, Pomona, Redlands, San Bernardino, Santa Monica, West Covina.
Interstate 15	Barstow, Corona, Escondido, Redlands, Riverside, San Bernardino, San Diego, Temecula, Victorville.
Interstate 40	Barstow, Needles.
Interstate 80	Auburn, Berkeley, Davis, Fairfield, Oakland, Sacramento, San Francisco, Truckee, Vacaville, Vallejo.
Interstate 110	Arcadia, Beverly Hills, Burbank, Culver City, Glendale, Long Beach, Los Angeles, Los Angeles International Airport Area, Marina del Rey, Pasadena, Redondo Beach, San Gabriel, San Marino, San Pedro, Torrance, Westwood, and Westwood Village.

Additional Visitor Information

For material on Southern California, contact the Los Angeles Convention and Visitors Bureau, 633 W 5th St, Suite 6000, Los Angeles 90007, phone 213/624-7300, www.lacvb.com; the San Diego Visitor Information Center, 2688 E Mission Bay Dr, San Diego 92109, phone 619/276-8200, www.infosandiego.com, is also

JOSHUA TREE NATIONAL PARK

Joshua Tree makes an easy day trip from the desert resort of Palm Springs and offers views of some of California's most dramatic high-desert landscapes where the Mojave Desert meets the Colorado River. From Palm Springs, a short drive on Interstate 10 west and Highway 62 north leads to the western entrance of Joshua Tree in about an hour. The dramatic 30-mile-long Northern Loop passes thousands of Joshua trees, known for their distinctive-looking arms, as well as clusters of massive boulders and hiking trails that lead up mountains and through old rustlers' hideouts. A number of campgrounds lie along the route (bring water). Those with just a few hours can loop back to Highway 62 on the Northern Loop and head back west and south to Palm Springs. Those with more time can leave the Northern Loop at the Pinto Wye Junction and follow the signs toward Cottonwood Springs. The road leads southeast through the park, spanning two deserts and passing cholla and ocatillo cactus gardens and rugged hiking trails. The road reaches Interstate 10 after 40 miles, just past Cottonwood Springs oasis; Interstate 10 then leads west back to Palm Springs. **(Approximately 150 miles; add approximately 200 miles if starting in Los Angeles)**

RIM OF THE WORLD HIGHWAY

Rugged lake and mountain scenery and bracing mountain air lie just a few hours east of Los Angeles. If you get an early start (to beat traffic), you can make this round-trip in a long day, but staying overnight in Big Bear makes for a more relaxed tour. From Los Angeles, Interstate 10 leads east to Redlands; from there, head northeast (Routes 30 and 300) toward Running Springs. The roads rise steadily into the mountains and then wind along Highway 18, the Rim of the World Highway, which offers sweeping views south to forests and deserts on a clear day. Big Bear Lake lies about 15 miles east of Running Springs and is a popular public resort area lined with motels, lodges, restaurants, and, in summer, places to go fishing and boating. In winter, Big Bear has Southern California's largest concentration of ski resorts. Weather and road conditions permitting, its worthwhile to drive all the way around the lake, along both the more developed south shore and the rustic north shore. The road loops back onto the Rim of the World Highway going west, then drops steeply down to the flatlands and back to Los Angeles via Interstate 10. **(Approximately 275 miles)**

SANTA BARBARA TO SAN SIMEON

This route combines exceptional coastal and mountain scenery; several interesting towns, wineries, and vineyards; and historic sites including old missions and Hearst Castle. Two days are necessary to complete the entire route with sightseeing stops. From the popular coastal resort town of Santa Barbara, head north into the Santa Ynez Mountains via Route 154; the road passes Native American painted caves and a recreational lake. Follow Route 246 west through the Santa Ynez wine country to the Danish-influenced town of Solvang, where shops abound. Continue on 246 to Highway 1; near that junction is La Purisima, one of the most interesting of the state's old Franciscan missions. Highway 1 then goes north to dune-swept Pismo Beach, where there are plenty of restaurants to stop at for lunch. Highway 1 (joining Highway 101) then veers back inland to the town of San Luis Obispo, site of another historic mission. If you have only one day, this is a good turnaround point, making for a 200-mile round-trip (return to Santa Barbara via Highway 101). If continuing, follow Highway 1 (not 101) north back to the coast at Morro Bay, which is a nice place to spend the night. The seafront is lined with restaurants, many with views of Morro Rock, a bird sanctuary known as the Gibraltar of the Pacific. The area has a number of good beaches; Montana de Oro State Park, a few miles south of Morro Bay, is one of the great undiscovered Central Coast gems. From Morro Bay, Highway 1 leads north to Hearst Castle; tour reservations should be made in advance, and tours require about two hours. To return, take Highway 46 east off Highway 1 and then head to Highway 101; follow that south back to Santa Barbara. **(Approximately 300 miles)**

THE ROAD TO JULIAN

This route travels from San Diego to the mountain town of Julian and offers chances to hike in rugged state parks along the way. About 100 miles total, it involves some mountain driving and winding roads, so allow ample time. From San Diego, take I-8 (east) to Route 67 (north) to Highway 78 (east) to the picturesque hill town of Julian, a popular site for prowling through antique stores. Wineries and old mines are also nearby. Huge Anza-Borrego Desert State Park lies to the east (don't try to drive there unless you have two days for this tour). With restaurants and bed-and-breakfasts available, Julian is the best place to spend the night for those with more than one day. Highway 79 then heads south from Julian, passing Cuyamaca Reservoir and rugged Cuyamaca Rancho State Park, San Diego's nearest forest recreation and home to 6,500-foot Cuyamaca Peak. Highway 79 then continues south to I-8, which leads west back to San Diego. **(Approximately 100 miles)**

YOSEMITE VALLEY

This tour takes the most picturesque route into Yosemite Valley and includes the valley's most dramatic scenic points, as well as other beautiful stretches of the park. From Fresno, Highway 41 leads north toward the park. The route starts off flat but gets quite hilly and winding by the town of Oakhurst, the southernmost point on Highway 49. Follow Highway 49 northwest to the old mining town of Mariposa, where Highway 140 heads north and then east toward Yosemite. On the way into the park, Highway 140 runs along a very pretty stretch of the Merced River, popular with rafters in summer. From the park's western entrance, follow the signs leading to Yosemite Valley. Expect heavy traffic on a weekend in the height of summer or over a holiday (cars are occasionally banned from the valley on peak summer holidays); the best times to visit are fall and spring. Snowy winters can be beautiful, but the roads may be slick and require four-wheel drive or tire chains; some high-elevation roads typically close. Southside and northside drives make a loop around the valley, passing spectacular waterfalls (best in spring) and granite monoliths such as Half Dome and El Capitn. There are plenty of pullouts where tourists can stop to take pictures or embark on a short hike. If you want to stay overnight in the valley, make reservations in advance; otherwise, your chances of finding lodging here are slim. When leaving the valley, take Highway 41 south. If the access road to Glacier Point is open (it closes in winter) and you have an extra hour or two, follow the signs to Glacier Point for panoramic views of the valley, Yosemite Falls, and Half Dome. Continue south on Highway 41 through the parks Wawona section, where the Mariposa Grove of Big Trees awaits; a short hike leads to several ancient giant sequoias. Highway 41 then leads south out of the park and back to Fresno. **(Approximately 200 miles)**

helpful. Serious hikers should consult *Sierra North* or *Sierra South*, available from Wilderness Press, 1200 5th St, Berkeley 94710, phone toll-free 800/443-7227, www.wildernesspress.com. For general information, contact the California Division of Tourism, 801 K St, Suite 1600, Sacramento 95814, phone 916/322-2881 or toll-free 800/862-2543, gocalif.ca.gov. The monthly magazine *Sunset* gives special attention to West Coast travel and life. Contact Sunset Publishing Corporation, 80 Willow Rd, Menlo Park 94025-3691, phone toll-free 800/227-7346 outside California and toll-free 800/321-0372 in California, www.sunset.com.

Alpine (K-4)

Population 13,143
Area Code 619
Information Chamber of Commerce, 2157 Alpine Blvd, 91903; phone 619/445-2722
Web Site www.alpinechamber.com

What to See and Do

Holidays on Horseback. *24928 Viejas Blvd, Descanso (91916). Phone 619/445-3997.* Based in Descanso, at the foot of the oak- and pine-crowned Cuyamaca

Mountains, this company offers rejuvenating horseback rides along scenic wilderness trails. Riders climb from the rocky terrain at the trailhead through the chaparral country and on into the mountains, where seedlings sprout through the ruins of a forest fire and a private lake beckons. Southern California's climate keeps the air clean, and the experienced horses will keep even amateur riders in the saddle. Rides can last for an hour, a day, or overnight; there are even packages with ranches that will put you up in a room with a fireplace or spa. **$$$$**

Viejas Casino. *5000 Willows Rd, Alpine (91901). Phone 619/445-5400; toll-free 800/847-6537. www.viejas.com.* Drawing an inside straight is good. Being able to head straight to Black & Decker, the Gap, or the Nike store afterwards is better. The Viejas has hit on a great idea: offer gamblers a wide array of slots, tables, and other games and then put an outlet mall next door for them to spend their winnings. Unlike some of the other area casinos, Viejas is also big on entertainment. There's a live band playing in the lounge on most nights and big band music on Sunday. For those with a taste for the exotic, or perhaps a longing for home, a number of ethnically oriented concerts in the showroom (including Latino Night, Filipino Night, and Vietnamese Night) are scheduled throughout the year. (Daily, 24 hours) **FREE**

Anaheim (J-4)

See also Buena Park, Corona, Disneyland, Fullerton, Garden Grove, Long Beach, Los Angeles, Orange, San Bernardino, San Clemente, San Juan Capistrano, Santa Ana, Whittier

Founded 1857
Population 328,014
Elevation 160 ft
Area Code 714
Information Anaheim/Orange County Visitor & Convention Bureau, 800 W Katella Ave, 92803; phone 714/765-8888
Web Site www.anaheimoc.org

Once part of a Spanish land grant, Anaheim was bought and settled by German colonists who came to this land to grow grapes and produce wine. The town takes its name from the Santa Ana River and the German word for "home." Today, Anaheim is known as the home of Disneyland.

What to See and Do

Anaheim Angels (MLB). *Edison Field, 2000 Gene Autry Way, Anaheim (92806). Phone 714/940-2000. angels. mlb.com.* Professional baseball team.

⭐ **Disneyland.** *1313 S Harbor Blvd, Anaheim (92802). Off Santa Ana Frwy. Phone 714/781-4565. www.disneyland.com.* (See information under the city heading of Disneyland)

Disney's California Adventure. *1313 S Harbor Blvd, Anaheim (92802). Phone 714/781-4565. www.disneyland.com.* This Disney theme park celebrates the history, culture, landscape, and industry of California. Located adjacent to Disneyland, Disney's California Adventure features four main areas, each with a different California-related theme. **Sunshine Plaza,** the gateway to all areas of the park, includes a 50-foot-tall sun atop a perpetual wave fountain. Events that draw crowds include a parade and a light show (daily). The **Golden State** area focuses on the diversity of California's people and landscape. Six areas explore the state's history, agriculture, and industry: Condor Flats, Bountiful Valley Farm, Pacific Wharf, Bay Area, Grizzly Peak Recreation Area, and Golden Vine Winery. This area also features opportunities for hiking and climbing, as well as art and music shows and wine tastings. **Paradise Pier** is a surfside boardwalk that features classic amusement park rides, diners, and shops. Rides include California Screamin' roller coaster, Sun Wheel Ferris wheel, Maliboomer 180-foot launch tower, Mulholland Madness, Golden Zephyr spinning spaceships, Orange Stinger, King Triton's Carousel, Games of the Boardwalk, and two floating interactive exhibits: Jumpin' Jellyfish and SS *rustworthy.* **Hollywood Pictures Backlot** lets visitors explore Hollywood Boulevard during the "Golden Age" of filmmaking. It includes Jim Henson's Muppet Vision 3-D, Disney Animation, Hyperion Theater, and Superstar Limo, as well as a musical theater, rides, and films. (Under 3 years free) (Daily) **$$$$**

Gray Line Anaheim. *2001 S Manchester Ave, Orange (92868). Phone 714/978-8855; toll-free 800/828-6699. www.socaltours.com.* This Coach USA company offers sightseeing and package tours, including Universal Studios Hollywood; SeaWorld San Diego; and Tijuana, Mexico. **$$$$**

Mighty Ducks of Anaheim (NHL). *Arrowhead Pond, 2695 Katella Ave, Anaheim (92806). Phone 714/704-2500. www.mightyducks.com.* Professional hockey team.

Special Event

Obon Festival. *909 S Dale Ave, Anaheim (92804). Phone 714/827-9590. www.bca-ocbc.org.* Japanese-American outdoor celebration with hundreds of costumed dancers and Taiko drummers; games, food, crafts. Mid-July. **FREE**

Limited-Service Hotels

★ **AYRES HOTEL.** *2550 E Katella Ave, Anaheim (92806). Phone 714/634-2106; toll-free 800/448-7162; fax 714/634-2108. www.ayresanaheim.com.* The biggest thing the Ayres Hotel has going for it is its location. Just 2 miles from Disneyland, it is a nice alternative to staying on-site at the theme park, making it ideal for those who want a more diverse sight-seeing experience in Southern California. As a suite hotel, it offers a little more in the way of travelers' amenities, such as a washer and dryer on-site and in-room refrigerators and microwaves. The hotel has a small outdoor pool and hot tub, and the interior is decorated in what is billed as something reminiscent of a French country inn. 133 rooms, all suites. Complimentary full breakfast. Check-in 3 pm, check-out noon. Outdoor pool, whirlpool. **$**

★ **AYRES-COUNTRY SUITES YORBA LINDA.** *22677 Oakcrest Cir, Yorba Linda (92887). Phone 714/921-8688; toll-free 800/706-4891; fax 714/283-3927. www.ayreshotels.com.* This suite hotel, with its antique décor, offers all the amenities you'd expect, plus a location that's convenient to many of Southern California's major tourist attractions, including Disneyland, Disney's California Adventure, and Angel Stadium, home of the California Angels baseball team. If you want a break from all things Mickey, head over to the Richard M. Nixon Presidential Library in nearby Whittier for a lesson in history. Forty miles from both Los Angeles and Long Beach, the hotel makes a great resting point for business and leisure travelers, including families. 112 rooms, 4 story, all suites. Complimentary full breakfast. Check-in 3 pm, check-out noon. Fitness room. Outdoor pool, whirlpool. **$**

★ ★ **DISNEY'S PARADISE PIER HOTEL.** *1717 S Disneyland Dr, Anaheim (92802). Phone 714/999-0990; fax 714/776-5763. www.disneylandresort.com.* This family-friendly Disney hotel gets its name from Paradise Pier in Disney's California Adventure park, which is just across the street. When you stay here, you get exclusive park access. In addition to convenient access to all that Disneyland has to offer, the hotel has a rooftop pool and spa, a workout room for adults, a game room, and Paradise Theater, where kids come to be transfixed by Disney movies. At Disney's PCH Grill, you can have breakfast with Lilo and Stitch, and in the afternoons and evenings, kids enjoy designing their own pizzas or noshing on burgers and fries. 489 rooms, 15 story. Check-in 3 pm, check-out 11 am. Two restaurants, bar. Children's activity center. Fitness room. Outdoor pool, whirlpool. Business center. **$$**

★ **FAIRFIELD INN.** *1460 S Harbor Blvd, Anaheim (92802). Phone 714/772-6777; toll-free 800/403-3818; fax 714/999-1727. www.marriott.com.* This hotel is a perfect base from which to explore the park. Kid-friendly features include an impressive children's arcade and pull-out sofa beds in the guest rooms. 467 rooms, 9 story. Check-in 4 pm, check-out noon. Outdoor pool, whirlpool. **$$**

★ **RAMADA.** *1650 S Harbor Blvd, Anaheim (92802). Phone 714/772-0440; fax 714/991-8219. www.ramada.com.* Perfect for families and visitors to Disneyland, this comfortable hotel is close to the freeway, not to mention right across the street from the famous amusement park. 185 rooms, 4 story. Complimentary continental breakfast. Check-in 3 pm, check-out noon. Outdoor pool, whirlpool. **$**

★ ★ ★ **SHERATON ANAHEIM HOTEL.** *900 S Disneyland Dr, Anaheim (92802). Phone 714/778-1700; toll-free 800/331-7251; fax 714/535-3889. www.starwoodhotels.com.* This Disneyland-adjacent, English manor-style lodge—replete with a grand rotunda, massive stone fireplace, fine European antiques, and romantic courtyards—might seem a tad misplaced in the midst of Ocean County. But with Fantasyland next door, its stately-yet-casual atmosphere is right at home. And its family-friendly amenities, including an outdoor heated pool, well-stocked game and billiards rooms, and the indoor/outdoor Garden Court Bistro, are of a quality that discerning Disney visitors have come to expect. A koi pond that meanders through the lobby outside to a rose garden and fountain offers the perfect post-theme park refuge. 489 rooms, 4 story. Pets accepted; fee. Check-in 3 pm, check-out noon. High-speed Internet access, wireless Internet access. Two restaurants, bar. Fitness room. Outdoor pool, whirlpool. Business center. **$**

Full-Service Hotels

★ ★ ★ DISNEY'S GRAND CALIFORNIAN.
1600 S Disneyland Dr, Anaheim (92802). Phone 714/778-6600; toll-free 800/207-6900; fax 714/956-6597. www.disneyland.com. This Disneyland resort truly earns the "grand" of its moniker. Set amid towering evergreens, this beautiful full-service luxury hotel—conveniently situated between Disney's California Adventure theme park and the vibrant Downtown Disney entertainment complex—is a giant alpine lodge designed in its home state's romantic, early 20th–century Arts & Crafts style. From the vaulted lobby to the homey guest rooms, the style resonates in handsome, custom-made appointments, and artwork. Complete concierge service and a surprising array of amenities, including The Napa Rose, a gourmet restaurant featuring the consummate California wine list, offer enough sensory pleasure to compete with the nearby rides and shows. 751 rooms, 6 story. Check-in 3 pm, check-out 11 am. High-speed Internet access. Two restaurants, two bars. Fitness room. Outdoor pool, children's pool, whirlpool. Business center. **$$**

★ ★ DISNEYLAND HOTEL.
1150 W Magic Way, Anaheim (92802). Phone 714/778-6600; fax 714/956-6597. www.disneyland.com. A Disneyland tradition since 1955, this family lodge remains as bright and fresh as the classic Disney-costumed characters who welcome guests in the lobby. Many rooms offer spectacular views of the Magic Kingdom, the Downtown Disney shopping district, and Disney's California Adventure park, and direct Interstate 5 access makes it easy to reach. The lagoon-style pool area and no-charge policy for parent-accompanied guests 18 and under warrant Mouseketeer cheers. 990 rooms, 14 story. Check-in 3 pm, check-out 11 am. Three restaurants, bar. Children's activity center. Fitness room. Two outdoor pools, whirlpool. Business center. **$$**

★ ★ ★ HYATT REGENCY ORANGE COUNTY.
11999 Harbor Blvd, Garden Grove (92840). Phone 714/750-1234; toll-free 800/233-1234; fax 714/740-0465. www.hyatt.com. Just a short, complimentary shuttle hop to the Anaheim Convention Center and the Disneyland Resort, this gleaming hotel caters to a mix of business and leisure clientele—bringing sophistication and calm to a bustling tourist area. Practice your golf swing on the adjacent driving range, slip into the rooftop pool, or sip drinks beneath the soaring 17-story atrium. Four eateries, a complete fitness center, and family-ready one- and two-bedroom suites offer self-contained convenience and comfort. Knott's Berry Farm, Crystal Cathedral, and the Discovery Science Center are among top attractions within a 10-mile radius; popular Southern California beaches are a short drive away. 654 rooms, 17 story. Check-in 3 pm, check-out noon. High-speed Internet access. Two restaurants, bar. Fitness room. Two outdoor pools, whirlpool. Tennis. Airport transportation available. Business center. **$**

Restaurants

★ ★ ★ ANAHEIM WHITE HOUSE.
887 S Anaheim Blvd, Anaheim (92805). Phone 714/772-1381; fax 714/772-7062. www.anaheimwhitehouse.com. Many celebrities have visited this converted Victorian-style mansion built in 1909 and modeled after that famous residence in Washington, DC. Eight intimate and old-fashioned dining rooms, each named after a US president, are romantic havens of candlelight, with fabric-draped ceilings in tones of cream and gold. A roaring fireplace warms the Reagan Room, while those who prefer a porch setting can reserve a table in the Nixon Room. The contemporary Italian menu includes many fresh seafood entrées, and the wine list includes more than 200 selections. Free shuttle service is offered to and from area hotels. French, Italian menu. Lunch, dinner. Closed holidays. Bar. Business casual attire. Reservations recommended. Outdoor seating. **$$$**

★ ★ FOXFIRE.
5717 E Santa Ana Canyon Rd, Anaheim Hills (92807). Phone 714/974-5400; fax 714/974-3302. www.foxfirerestaurant.com. Billing itself as "an American chophouse," Foxfire offers an à la carte menu featuring hearty portions of aged prime Angus beef, as well as veal, lamb, and seafood selections. Dancing and karaoke liven things up in the evenings, with live music in the nicely landscaped outdoor patio area and on the stage inside. American menu. Lunch, dinner, Sun brunch. Closed holidays. Bar. Children's menu. Business casual attire. Reservations recommended. Outdoor seating. **$$**

★ ★ MR. STOX.
1105 E Katella Ave, Anaheim (92805). Phone 714/634-2994; fax 714/634-0561. www.mrstox.com. The fresh-baked gourmet breads are not to be missed at this family-run restaurant that specializes in fresh seafood, top-quality meats, and pasta dishes. Many of the herbs used in the kitchen, which turns out contemporary California fare, are grown on the premises. The wine list offers more than 25,000 bottles from 12 countries and ten US states. American

menu. Lunch, dinner. Closed holidays. Bar. Business casual attire. Reservations recommended. Valet parking. Outdoor seating. **$$$**

★ ★ **YAMABUKI.** *1717 S Disneyland Dr, Anaheim (92802). Phone 714/956-6755. www.disneyland.com.* Sushi and Disney may not seem to go hand in hand, but they pair nicely at this restaurant in Disney's Paradise Pier Hotel (see), an appealing option for parents who are tired of kid food but still need to find a family-friendly place to eat. The restaurant features a full sushi bar, teriyaki and tempura entrées, and Japanese beers and sake. Japanese menu. Lunch, dinner. Bar. Children's menu. Casual attire. Reservations recommended. Valet parking. **$$**

Anza-Borrego Desert State Park (K-5)

See also Borrego Springs

Web Site www.anzaborrego.statepark.org

Approximately 600,000 acres of desert wilderness are preserved here, relieved by an occasional spring-fed oasis and colorful canyons. Highway 78 bisects the park, with Borrego Springs (see), the park headquarters, and the visitor center to the north. Other improved roads are County S-2, S-3, and S-22. Anyone who wants to explore seriously must use a four-wheel-drive vehicle; road condition information is available at the visitor center. Driving across sand can be rough on vehicles and passengers. The best time to visit is November through mid-May. Six hundred species of flowering plants in the park soften the somewhat austere landscape during the spring months. Elephant trees reach the northernmost limits of their range in Anza-Borrego Park; rare smoke trees and fan palms grow here around natural seeps and springs. The park provides a refuge for wildlife, including roadrunners, rare bighorn sheep, and kit foxes. There are nature, hiking, and bridle trails and picnic grounds. Improved campsites (trailer hook-ups in Borrego Springs) are scattered in the park; primitive camping (fee) is allowed throughout the park, and there is a horse campground. Naturalist programs, tours, and campfire programs are offered on weekends (Nov-May). Self-guided auto tour brochures are available at the visitor center (Oct-May, daily; rest of year, weekends and holidays), west of Borrego Springs. For more information, phone 760/767-5311 or 760/767-4205 (visitor center).

Arcadia (J-4)

See also Los Angeles, Pasadena, Port Charlotte, San Marino

Population 53,054
Elevation 485 ft
Area Code 626
Information Chamber of Commerce, 388 W Huntington Dr, 91007; phone 626/447-2159 or 626/445-1400
Web Site www.arcadiachamber.com

Arcadia is known as the home of Santa Anita Park racetrack, a world-class thoroughbred racing facility.

What to See and Do

Irwindale Speedway. *500 Speedway Dr, Irwindale (91706). Phone 626/358-1100. www.irwindalespeedway. com.* Located in California's San Gabriel Valley, less than 25 minutes from downtown Los Angeles and about 35 miles from California Speedway, Irwindale's banked 1/2-mile oval hosts NASCAR events mid-March through November. The award-winning NASCAR Toyota All-Star Showdown, which the track ran starting in 2003, brings together the top regional touring drivers from across the country in a one-of-a-kind, head-to-head event. The stands seat more than 6,000. Ticket prices vary.

✪ **Los Angeles County Arboretum & Botanic Garden.** *301 N Baldwin Ave, Arcadia (91007). 6 miles N of San Bernardino Frwy and just S of Foothill Frwy. Phone 626/821-3222. www.arboretum.org.* This 127-acre public garden has been a Los Angeles area oasis since 1948. Enjoy beautiful plants from around the world and wildlife such as fish, turtles, and migrating birds, which roam the arboretum's lakes and grounds. Classes, lectures, workshops, and resources abound. Take advantage of everything from the Botanical Watercolor Workshop to the Plant Science Library, a reference collection for the general public that contains information on everything from garden design and flower gardening to vegetable and fruit growing. (Daily 9 am-4:30 pm; extended summer hours; closed Dec 25) **$$**

Santa Anita Park. *285 W Huntington Dr, Arcadia (91007). Phone 626/574-7223. www.santaanita.com.* Located on 320 acres at the base of the San Gabriel Mountains, Santa Anita has been a favorite of Southern California horseracing fans since it opened in 1934. In 1940, the ever-popular Seabiscuit won the 1940 Santa Anita Handicap in his last race ever. Today, the track is popular with Hollywood celebrities, including Jack Nicholson and Michelle Pfeiffer. (Wed-Sun, some Mon; closed late Apr-late Dec) **$**

Limited-Service Hotels

★ ★ **EMBASSY SUITES.** *211 E Huntington Dr, Arcadia (91006). Phone 626/445-8525; fax 626/445-8548. www.embassy-suites.com.* 192 rooms, 7 story, all suites. Complimentary full breakfast. Check-in 3 pm, check-out 1 pm. Restaurant, bar. Indoor pool, whirlpool. Airport transportation available. **$**

★ **HAMPTON INN.** *311 E Huntington Dr, Arcadia (91006). Phone 626/574-5600; toll-free 800/426-7866; fax 626/446-2748. www.hampton-inn.com.* 131 rooms, 4 story. Complimentary continental breakfast. Check-in 3 pm, check-out noon. Outdoor pool. **$**

★ ★ **HOLIDAY INN.** *924 W Huntington Dr, Monrovia (91016). Phone 626/357-1900; fax 626/359-1386. www.holiday-inn.com.* 174 rooms, 10 story. Complimentary continental breakfast. Check-in 3 pm, check-out noon. Restaurant, bar. Outdoor pool, whirlpool. **$**

Restaurants

★ ★ **THE DERBY.** *233 E Huntington Dr, Arcadia (91006). Phone 626/447-8174; fax 626/447-2430. www.thederbyarcadia.com.* Portraits of famous thoroughbreds and jockeys. Seafood, steak menu. Dinner. Closed Dec 25. Valet parking. **$$$**

★ ★ ★ **LA PARISIENNE.** *1101 E Huntington Dr, Monrovia (91016). Phone 626/357-3359; fax 626/357-9649. www.laparisiennerestaurant.net.* This attractive country inn, in a quiet, romantic setting, is located in the heart of the San Gabriel Valley. French menu. Lunch, dinner. Closed Dec 25. Bar. **$$**

Atascadero (G-2)

See also Morro Bay, Paso Robles, Pebble Beach, San Luis Obispo

Founded 1913
Population 26,411
Elevation 855 ft

Area Code 805
Zip 93422
Information Chamber of Commerce, 6550 El Camino Real; phone 805/466-2044

In the foothills of the Santa Lucia Mountains, Atascadero was founded by St. Louis publisher E. G. Lewis, who also founded University City, Missouri. Lewis developed the town to be a self-sustaining community or colony.

What to See and Do

Atascadero Lake Park. *2 miles W of Hwy 101 on Hwy 41. Phone 805/461-5000.* Fishing. Picnicking, playground. On the premises is

> **Charles Paddock Zoo.** *9305 Pismo Ave, Atascadero (93422). Phone 805/461-5080.* Assortment of domestic, native, and exotic animals. (Apr-late Oct: daily 10 am-5 pm; Nov-late Mar: daily 10 am-4 pm; closed Thanksgiving, Dec 25) **$**

Special Event

Colony Days. *www.atascaderochamber.org.* Parade, activities, arts and crafts, displays, food booths. Third Sat in Oct.

Avalon (Catalina Island) (J-3)

See also Laguna Beach, Long Beach, Newport Beach, San Pedro

Population 3,127
Elevation 20 ft
Area Code 310
Zip 90704
Information Catalina Island Visitors Bureau and Chamber of Commerce, PO Box 217; phone 310/510-1520
Web Site www.catalinachamber.com

Avalon is the sport fishing and resort capital of 21-mile-long, 8-mile-wide Santa Catalina Island. The peaks of the island rise from the Pacific 21 miles southwest of Los Angeles harbor. Scuba diving, kayaking, golf, tennis, horseback riding, swimming, and hiking are popular.

Discovered in 1542 by Juan Rodriguez Cabrillo, the Portuguese navigator, it was named by the Spanish explorer Sebastian Viscaino in 1602. Later, Russians and Aleuts used the island as a base to hunt sea otter. The town experienced a brief miniature gold rush in 1863. In 1919, William Wrigley Jr., chewing gum magnate and owner of the Chicago Cubs major league baseball team, bought controlling interest in the Santa Catalina Island Company from the Banning brothers, who had incorporated the island. Wrigley established a program of conservation that still applies; today, 86 percent of Catalina Island is protected by the Santa Catalina Island Conservancy. Tourism is the island's only industry and source of revenue today.

Daily air or boat service to the island is available all year from Long Beach (see) and San Pedro; boat service only from Newport Beach.

What to See and Do

Catalina Island Museum. *Casino Building, 1 Casino Way, Avalon (Catalina Island). Phone 310/510-2414. www.catalinamuseum.org.* Permanent exhibits on the history of the island; natural history and archaeology displays. (Daily 10 am-4 pm; Jan-Mar, closed Thurs; also closed Dec 25) **$**

Catalina tours and trips. *150 Metropole Ave, Avalon (Catalina Island). Phone 310/510-2500.* Santa Catalina Island Company Discovery Tours (www.scico.com) and Catalina Adventure Tours (www.catalinaadventuretours.com) offers boat and bus tours to several points of interest.

Wrigley Memorial and Botanical Garden. *1400 Avalon Canyon Rd, Avalon (Catalina Island). Phone 310/510-2897.* Native trees, cactus, succulent plants, and flowering shrubs on 38 acres surround the memorial to a man who contributed much to Catalina Island. (Daily) Tram may run here from Island Plaza (summer only; fee). **$$**

Limited-Service Hotels

★ **HOTEL ST. LAUREN.** *231 Beacon St, Avalon (90704). Phone 310/510-2299; fax 310/510-1369. www.stlauren.com.* This Victorian-style hotel is one block from the beach/ocean. The sixth-floor patio has splendid views of the city, bay, and ocean. 42 rooms, 6 story. Complimentary continental breakfast. Check-in 3 pm, check-out 11 am. **$**

★ ★ **HOTEL VILLA PORTOFINO.** *111 Crescent Ave, Avalon (90704). Phone 310/510-0555; toll-free 888/510-0555; fax 310/510-0839. www.hotelvillaportofino.com.* 44 rooms, 3 story. Complimentary continental breakfast. Check-in 2 pm, check-out 11 am. Restaurant, bar. **$$**

★ **HOTEL VISTA DEL MAR.** *417 Crescent Ave, Avalon (90704). Phone 310/510-1452; toll-free 800/601-3836; fax 310/510-2917. www.hotel-vistadelmar.com.* This bayfront hotel features Spanish-style archways and a tiled roof and is just steps from the beach. Some rooms adjoin a quiet atrium courtyard, while others boast private ocean-view balconies. All guests receive fresh-baked cookies and milk each evening. 15 rooms. Complimentary continental breakfast. Check-in 2 pm, check-out 11 am. Beach. **$**

Full-Service Hotel

★ ★ ★ **HOTEL METROPOLE.** *205 Crescent Ave, Avalon (90704). Phone 310/510-1884; toll-free 800/300-8528; fax 310/510-2534. www.hotel-metropole.com.* The guest rooms and suites, finished with blue tones and quilted bedspreads, have ocean, mountain, or courtyard views. You are only steps from the beach at this charming hotel. 48 rooms, 3 story. Complimentary continental breakfast. Check-in 3 pm, check-out 11 am. **$**

Full-Service Inn

★ ★ ★ ★ **THE INN ON MOUNT ADA.** *398 Wrigley Rd, Avalon (90704). Phone 310/510-2030; toll-free 800/608-7669; fax 310/510-2237. www.catalina.com/mtada.* Visitors arrive on Catalina Island by boat or helicopter to rediscover a bygone era at the Inn on Mount Ada. Resting 22 miles off the coast of Los Angeles, this unique island getaway is imbued with history. Once the private stomping grounds of chewing gum magnate William Wrigley Jr., the island is now home to a variety of wildlife, including sea otters, seals, and bald eagles. Completed in the early 1920s, Wrigley's white palace, with its recognizable red conical roof, now hosts lucky visitors who book one of the six special rooms. Appointed with a sophisticated country style, the inn affords fantastic views of the harbor and town from its hilltop location. But be sure to get out and about: guests can tool around town in their inn-provided golf carts (after a proper driving lesson from the staff, of course!). From the palatial yet comfortable style to the deliciously prepared meals and snacks, guests feel very much at home here. 6 rooms, 2 story. Children over 14 years only. Check-in 2 pm, check-out 11 am. **$$$$**

Restaurants

★ **ANTONIO'S PIZZERIA & CABARET.** *230 Crescent Ave, Avalon (90704). Phone 310/510-0008; fax 310/510-2949.* There is a 1955 Seeberg jukebox at each table. Italian, American menu. Breakfast, lunch, dinner. Bar. Outdoor seating. **$$**

★ ★ **ARMSTRONG'S FISH MARKET AND SEAFOOD.** *306 Crescent Ave, Avalon (90704). Phone 310/510-0113; fax 310/510-0266. www.armstrongsea food.com.* Seafood menu. Lunch, dinner. Closed the first three weeks in Dec. Bar. Outdoor seating. **$$**

★ ★ **BLUE PARROT.** *205 Crescent Ave, Avalon (90704). Phone 310/510-2465; fax 310/510-2039. www.blueparrotcatalina.com.* American, seafood menu. Lunch, dinner. Closed Jan. Bar. Children's menu. **$$$**

★ ★ **CHANNEL HOUSE.** *205 Crescent Ave, Avalon (90704). Phone 310/510-1617.* International menu. Lunch, dinner. Bar. Children's menu. Outdoor seating. **$$**

Bakersfield (G-3)

See also Tehachapi

Founded 1869
Population 174,820
Elevation 408 ft
Area Code 661
Information Chamber of Commerce, 1725 Eye St, 93301; phone 661/327-4421
Web Site www.bakersfield.org/chamber

Surrounded by oil wells and fields of cotton and grain, Bakersfield is an important trading center–the hub of a network of highways that carries its produce and products to major cities. Founded by Colonel Thomas Baker, the town awakened in 1885 when gold was discovered in the Kern River Canyon. Overnight it changed from a placid farm town to a wild mining community, complete with gunfights and gambling halls. A fire in 1889 destroyed most of the old town and resulted in considerable modernization. The discovery of oil in 1899 rekindled the gold rush hysterics.

Unlike gold, oil has remained an important part of the city's economy. Bakersfield is the seat of Kern County (8,064 square miles; third-largest county in the state). Nearby vineyards produce 25 percent of California's wine, and surrounding fields provide a colorful flower display in spring. A Ranger District office of the Sequoia National Forest is located here.

What to See and Do

California Living Museum. *10500 Alfred Harrell Hwy, Bakersfield. 12 miles NE via Hwy 178. Phone 661/872-2256. www.calmzoo.org.* Botanical garden and zoo house plants and animals native to California; natural history museum; interpretive tours. (Daily 9 am-5 pm; closed Thanksgiving, Dec 25) **$$**

Colonel Allensworth State Historic Park. *4129 Palmer Ave, Allensworth. Phone 661/849-3433. www.parks. ca.gov.* This park honors the only California town founded, settled, and financed entirely by African Americans; it's now a ghost town with restored buildings. Camping. (Daily) **$$**

Kern County Museum. *3801 Chester Ave, Bakersfield (93301). Phone 661/852-5000. www.kcmuseum.org.* Complete 16-acre outdoor museum of 60 restored or representational buildings including a Queen Anne-style mansion (1891), log cabin, wooden jail, hotel, drugstore; 1898 locomotive, oil-drilling rig, and horse-drawn vehicles. Main museum building contains changing exhibits on natural and cultural history of the area. (Mon-Sat 10 am-5 pm, Sun from noon; closed holidays) **$$**

Scenic drive. *Go E on Hwy 178 and follow the Kern River through a rock-dotted canyon.* Many fine places for picnicking, camping, and fishing along the road.

Tule Elk State Reserve. *8653 Station Rd, Bakersfield. 20 miles W via Stockdale Hwy, then S on Morris Rd to Station Rd, then 1/4 mile W. Phone 661/764-6881.* This 969-acre reserve is home for a small herd of elk native only to California. Picnic shelters. (Daily) **$**

Special Event

Great Kern County Fair. *1142 South P St, Bakersfield (93307). Phone 661/833-4900. www.kerncountyfair. com.* The annual fair provides a stage for country music stars such as Gretchen Wilson and Gary Allan and for local talents in events like colorguard and cheering competitions. Late Sept-early Oct. **$$**

Limited-Service Hotels

★ ★ **BEST WESTERN HILL HOUSE.** *700 Truxton Ave, Bakersfield (93301). Phone 661/327-4064; fax 661/327-1247. www.bestwestern.com.* 97 rooms, 2 story. Pets accepted; restrictions; fee. Complimentary continental breakfast. Check-in 3 pm, check-out noon. Restaurant, bar. Fitness room. Outdoor pool. **$**

★ ★ **FOUR POINTS BY SHERATON.** *5101 California Ave, Bakersfield (93309). Phone 661/325-9700; toll-free 800/500-5399; fax 661/323-3508. www.fourpoints. com/bakersfield.* 198 rooms, 2 story. Complimentary continental breakfast. Check-in 3 pm, check-out noon. Restaurant, bar. Fitness room. Indoor pool, outdoor pool, whirlpool. Airport transportation available. **$**

★ **HOLIDAY INN EXPRESS.** *4400 Hughes Ln, Bakersfield (93309). Phone 661/833-3000; toll-free 800/465-4329; fax 661/833-3736. www.hiexpress. com.* 108 rooms, 4 story. Complimentary continental breakfast. Check-in 2 pm, check-out 11 am. Indoor pool, whirlpool. Business center. **$**

★ **QUALITY INN.** *1011 Oak St, Bakersfield (93304). Phone 661/325-0772; toll-free 800/228-5050; fax 661/325-4646. www.qualityinn.com.* 89 rooms, 2 story. Pets accepted, some restrictions; fee. Complimentary full breakfast. Check-in 10 am, check-out noon. Indoor pool, whirlpool. **$**

Specialty Lodging

RANKIN RANCH. *23500 Walkers Basin Rd, Caliente (93518). Phone 661/867-2511; fax 661/867-0105. www. rankinranch.com.* Cattle ranch (31,000 acres) founded in 1863, in the Tehachapi Mountains. 21 rooms. Closed the first week in Sept through the week before Easter. Check-in 3 pm, check-out 1 pm. Restaurant. Children's activity center. Outdoor pool, whirlpool. Tennis. **$$**

Restaurants

★ ★ **MAMA TOSCA'S.** *9000 Ming Ave, Bakersfield (93311). Phone 661/831-1242.* Italian menu. Lunch, dinner. Closed Sun; holidays. Bar. Children's menu. Casual attire. Reservations recommended. Outdoor seating. **$$$**

★ **ROSA'S.** *2400 Columbus, Bakersfield (93306). Phone 661/872-1606.* Italian menu. Lunch, dinner. Closed holidays. Children's menu. Casual attire. Outdoor seating. **$$**

★ ★ **WOOL GROWERS.** *620 E 19th St, Bakersfield (93305). Phone 661/327-9584.* French menu. Lunch, dinner. Closed Sun; Thanksgiving, Dec 25. Bar. Children's menu. Casual attire. **$$**

Barstow (H-5)

See also Victorville

Founded 1880
Population 21,119
Elevation 2,106 ft
Area Code 760
Zip 92311
Information Barstow Area Chamber of Commerce, 401 E Fredricks St; phone 760/256-8617
Web Site www.barstowchamber.com

In the heart of the beautiful high-desert country, Barstow is a former frontier town that has become one of the fastest growing cities in San Bernardino County. Once a desert junction for overland wagon trains and an outfitting station for Death Valley expeditions, Barstow thrives on nearby military installations and a $15 million tourist trade. It is the hub of three major highways that carry tourists into the Mojave Desert.

What to See and Do

Afton Canyon. *40 miles E on I-15. www.recreation.gov.* Created in prehistoric times when Lake Manix broke through, chiseling a gorge through layers of multicolored rock. Primitive camping (fee).

Calico Early Man Site. *831 Barstow Rd, Barstow. 18 miles E via I-15, Minneola Rd exit, then 2 3/4 miles on graded dirt road.* Archaeological digs; stone tool artifacts fashioned by man approximately 200,000 years ago are still visible in the walls of the excavations. Oldest evidence of human activity in the Western Hemisphere. Only New World site that Louis S. B. Leakey ever worked on; he served as project director until his death. Two master pits open for viewing; small museum. Guided tours. (Wed 12:30-4:30 pm, Thurs-Sun 9 am-4:30 pm) **$**

Calico Ghost Town Regional Park. *36600 Ghost Town Rd, Barstow. 10 miles E via I-15, then 4 miles N on Ghost Town Rd. Phone 760/254-2122. www.calicotown.com.* Restored

1880s mining town. For six decades, a dust-shrouded ghost town; privately restored in 1954. General store; old schoolhouse; the Maggie Mine; collection of paintings in "Lil's Saloon"; print, pottery, basket, and leather shops; tramway, railroad, mine tours. (See SPECIAL EVENTS) Nearby are the Calico Mountains, which yielded $86 million in silver in 15 years. Camping (some hook-ups; fee). (Daily; closed Dec 25) **$$** East of Calico is

Odessa Canyon. Rock-studded landscape created by volcanic action. Erosion has etched striking rock formations. No cars.

Factory Merchants Outlet Mall. *2552 Mercantile Way, Barstow (92311). Phone 760/253-7342. www.factory-merchantsbarstow.com.* More than 90 outlet stores. (Daily 10 am-8 pm)

Mojave River Valley Museum. *270 Virginia Way, Barstow (92311). Phone 760/256-5452. www.mojaverivervalleymuseum.org.* Rock and mineral displays, photographs, archaeology and railroad displays, Native American exhibits. (Daily 11 am-4 pm) **FREE**

Mule Canyon and Fiery Gulch. *14 miles NE.* Cathedral-like rocks, S-shaped formations, crimson walls, natural arches. No cars.

Rainbow Basin. *Frwys 91 and 15, Barstow. 10 miles N on Old Irwin Rd.* Colorful geologic display of a syncline and hogbacks on the 4-mile, one-way drive. No motor homes.

Special Events

Calico Days. *Calico Ghost Town, 36600 Ghost Town Rd, Barstow (92398). Phone 760/254-2122. www.calicotown.com/calicodays.* Country music, Wild West parade, national gunfight stunt championship, burro race, 1880s games. Columbus Day weekend.

Calico Spring Festival. *Calico Ghost Town, 36600 Ghost Town Rd, Barstow (92398). Phone 760/254-2122. www.calicotown.com/springfestival.* Fiddle and banjo contests, bluegrass music, gunfights, 1880s games, clogging hoedown. Mother's Day weekend. **$$**

Limited-Service Hotel

★ ★ **BEST WESTERN DESERT VILLA INN.** *1984 E Main St, Barstow (92311). Phone 760/256-1781; fax 760/256-9265. www.bestwestern.com.* 95 rooms, 2 story. Fee. Complimentary continental breakfast. Check-in 2 pm, check-out 11 am. Bar. Outdoor pool, whirlpool. **$**

Restaurant

★ ★ **IDLE SPURS STEAK HOUSE.** *690 Old Hwy 58, Barstow (92311). Phone 760/256-8888; fax 760/256-0548. www.idlespurssteakhouse.com.* Steak menu. Lunch, dinner. Closed holidays. Bar. Outdoor seating. **$$**

Beaumont (J-4)

See also Hemet, Palm Springs, Redlands, Riverside, San Bernardino

Population 11,384
Elevation 2,573 ft
Area Code 951
Zip 92223
Information Chamber of Commerce, PO Box 637; phone 951/845-9541
Web Site www.beaumontcachamber.com

What to See and Do

Edward-Dean Museum of Decorative Arts. *9401 Oak Glen Rd, Cherry Valley (92223). Phone 951/845-2626. www.edward-deanmuseum.org.* European and Asian furniture, bronzes, porcelains, rugs, paintings from 17th and 19th centuries. (Fri-Sun 10 am-5 pm; closed holidays) **$**

Special Event

Cherry Festival. *Stewart Park, 9th St and Orange Ave, Beaumont (92223). Phone 951/845-9541. www.ci.beaumont.ca.us/cherryfestival.htm.* This annual festival celebrates the area's cherry harvest, selling cherries and other cherry treats throughout the park. Festivities include a parade, entertainment, and carnival rides. Early June.

Limited-Service Hotel

★ ★ **BEST WESTERN EL RANCHO MOTOR INN.** *550 E 5th St, Beaumont (92223). Phone 951/845-2176; fax 951/845-7559. www.bestwestern.com.* 52 rooms, 2 story. Pets accepted, some restrictions; fee. Complimentary continental breakfast. Check-in noon, check-out 11 am. Restaurant, bar. Fitness room. Outdoor pool. **$**

Bel-Air (J-4)

The cloistered neighborhood of Bel-Air is perhaps the most elite, quiet, and wealthy neighborhood in Los Angeles. This residential enclave is tucked away in the hills above Westwood and Beverly Hills, and entered into through massive gated porticos that lend the exclusive neighborhood a secretive aura. The sprawling, curvy streets are graced with mature tall trees, and sprawling lawns frame the castlelike mansions of the extremely privileged. This ultra-reserved hideaway is a favorite spot for camera-shy movie stars, powerful CEOs, and international VIPs who crave privacy.

There are few public destinations within Bel-Air, with the exception of the fairy-tale Hotel Bel-Air (see). This grand old-California hotel is a favorite for upscale weddings and special occasion dining and often hosts A-list stars.

Full-Service Hotel

★ ★ ★ ★ ★ **HOTEL BEL-AIR.** *701 Stone Canyon Rd, Los Angeles (90077). Phone 310/472-1211; toll-free 800/648-4097; fax 310/476-5890. www.hotelbelair.com.* Special memories are made at the Hotel Bel-Air. Close to the action of Los Angeles, this magical hotel transports visitors to a romantic, unhurried world. It enjoys a parklike setting on 12 acres of gardens dotted with intimate courtyards, trickling fountains, winding creeks, and intoxicating aromas. The centerpiece of the garden is the signature Swan Lake, where visitors marvel at the graceful movements of these elegant creatures. A favorite of guests seeking anonymity, the guest rooms are spread throughout the grounds, lending a special privacy to each accommodation. Reflecting a timeless décor, the rooms are luxurious. Amenities are plentiful, including Kiehl's products in the guest rooms and a well-equipped fitness center. The pool offers a wonderful way to spend the afternoon. Guests are romanced and charmed in the restaurants as well, whether dining in the distinguished Restaurant (see) the beautiful garden setting of the Terrace, or the unique in-kitchen Table One. 91 rooms. Pets accepted, some restrictions; fee. Check-in 3 pm, check-out noon. High-speed Internet access. Restaurant, bar. Fitness room. Outdoor pool. Business center. **$$$$**

🐾 🏋 🏊 🏃

Restaurants

★ ★ **FOUR OAKS.** *2181 N Beverly Glen, Los Angeles (90077). Phone 310/470-2265; fax 310/475-5492. www.fouroaksrestaurant.com.* A favorite for special occasions, this gorgeous gem tucked high in the canyon has a longstanding tradition of romance and celebration. Appointed like a luxury cabin with sprawling gardens and windows offering panoramic views, the dining room matches the elegance of the ever-changing menu, which includes impeccable preparations of the season's finest ingredients. Despite its lushness, Four Oaks has become an institution because of its fine yet unpretentious attention to detail. French, California menu. Lunch, dinner, Sun brunch. Closed Mon; holidays. Bar. Casual attire. Reservations recommended. Valet parking. Outdoor seating. **$$$**

★ ★ ★ ★ **THE RESTAURANT AT HOTEL BEL-AIR.** *701 Stone Canyon Rd, Los Angeles (90077). Phone 310/472-5234; fax 310/440-5865. www.hotelbelair.com.* The resident eatery of the haute Hotel Bel-Air (see) suitably cossets diners in elegant surroundings. Indoors, the restaurant is formal and flower-filled; outdoors, lush landscaping and a swan pond surround the terrace. No wonder it's the scene of many a romantic affair. The California-French cuisine distinguishes itself with entrées such as seared foie gras, sea bass with squid ink, and rack of lamb with goat cheese. After dessert, retire to the cozy fire-lit bar for a glass of port. California; French menu. Breakfast, lunch, dinner, Sun brunch. Bar. Children's menu. Casual attire. Reservations recommended. Valet parking. Outdoor seating. **$$$**

Bell Gardens (J-4)

See also Hemet, Palm Springs, Redlands, Riverside, San Bernardino

Web Site www.ci.bell-gardens.ca.us

What to See and Do

The Bicycle Casino. *7301 Eastern Ave, Bell Gardens (90201). Phone 562/806-4646. www.thebike.com.* Opened in 1984, the Bicycle Casino is one of the biggest card casinos in the world, with more than 130 tables and 81,000 square feet of room to roam. If you want to relax (and get your mind off how much money you've lost), you can have a massage while you play. Though hotel accommodations are not connected with the casino, many options are available nearby, and the casino will help you find a place to rest. (Daily, 24 hours) **FREE**

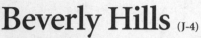

Beverly Hills (J-4)

See also Hollywood, Los Angeles, Santa Monica, West Hollywood

Population 33,784
Elevation 225 ft
Area Code 310
Information Visitors Bureau, 239 S Beverly Dr, 90212; phone 310/248-1015 or toll-free 800/345-2210
Web Site www.lovebeverlyhills.org

The 5.7 square miles of Beverly Hills enclose a domain reminiscent of the fabled small principalities of Europe. Wedged between the tiny West Side Los Angeles communities of Bel-Air, Brentwood, Century City, and Westwood, Beverly Hills is, in many ways, a world of its own. You could easily spend $10,000 a day here without being noticed. Many come to Beverly Hills to shop the stores of Rodeo Drive and Wilshire Boulevard, not so much for the bargains as for the experience.

Among the locals is a favored saying: "There's so much going on in Beverly Hills at any one time that it needs two Santa Monica Boulevards." Indeed, Big Santa Monica Boulevard and Little Santa Monica Boulevard are two perfect starting points to get the feel of the place. The former is a main artery, giving you access to the residential and traffic sense of the city; the latter is a cook's tour of smart shops, quirky restaurants, and hip clothing outlets.

Just as the English can nail your social point of origin by the way you speak, locals identify you by where you live in relation to Sunset Boulevard (north or south of it). North means one of the more spacious mansions, while south means a comfy older house, a posh condo, or a roomy apartment. As you drive through the residential streets on either side of the east/west-running Sunset Boulevard, you're bound to intersect one of the three great canyons that add to Beverly Hills' character—Coldwater, Benedict, and Franklin. These canyons bring the moisture and year-round variety of ground covering that typify the Southern California flora. The canyons also point to a physical heart of the city where Sunset and Beverly boulevards converge. Follow Coldwater north to get a timeless sense of why so many people are drawn to make their homes in the steep, sometimes slippery, rock-and-sandstone foothills.

Beverly Hills High School on Moreno Drive has its own oil well; the splendidly stocked Beverly Hills Library on North Rexford Drive is a great spot for frequent literary events and for spotting movie and television stars.

What to See and Do

Beverly Hills Public Art Walking Tour. *450 N Crescent Dr, Beverly Hills (90210). Phone 310/550-4796. www. beverlyhills.org.* If you're interested in seeing more in Beverly Hills than the latest designer labels, the Beverly Hills Public Art Walking Tour is a good bet. Free of charge, the hour-long guided tour takes you past outdoor artworks in the vicinity of the Civic Center. You'll see works by artists such as Auguste Rodin and Henry Moore. (First Sat of the month, May-Aug 1 pm) **FREE**

Golden Triangle. *Rodeo Dr and Wilshire Blvd, Beverly Hills. Phone toll-free 800/345-2210.* High-end shopping lures celebrities and their platinum cards to this exclusive area, the heart of Beverly Hills' business district and home to one of the world's most famous streets, Rodeo Drive. Big spenders with fabulous fashion sense will feel right at home in the many pricey designer boutiques that line this chichi shopping avenue. And just a short walk away, on Wilshire Boulevard, three tony department stores—Barney's New York, Neiman Marcus, and Saks Fifth Avenue—sell only the best as well. If you don't bring home million-dollar paychecks like the stars who shop here do, and your budget demands that you spend more modestly, Beverly Drive is home to more affordable retailers such as Banana Republic, Club Monaco, Gap, and Williams-Sonoma. The area also offers some of LA's hottest restaurants (Crustacean and Spago, in particular) and poshest hotels (think the Regent Beverly Wilshire and the Luxe).

Museum of Television and Radio. *465 N Beverly Dr, Beverly Hills (90210). Phone 310/786-1000. www.mtr. org.* Founded in New York in 1975 by William Paley, the former head of CBS, the Los Angeles branch of this museum opened in 1996. With an archive of more than 100,000 television and radio programs to choose from, you can watch scheduled screenings or sit back in a private console in the library and view that lost episode of your favorite show that you've been dying to see. From the comedy of Burns and Allen to the Beatles in America, from a teary-eyed Walter Cronkite reporting JFK's assassination to a tireless Peter Jennings persevering through an endless 9/11, it's all there for the asking. (Wed-Sun noon-5 pm; closed holidays) **FREE**

Rodeo Drive. *Between Santa Monica and Wilshire blvds, Beverly Hills (90210). Phone 310/248-1000. www. rodeodrive.com.* Julia Roberts's roommate in *Pretty Woman* had it right when she was asked where to go for the best clothes in Los Angeles and replied: "Rodeo Drive, baby!" From Prada and Gucci to Louis Vuitton and Giorgio Armani, you can find the finest designer fashions on this three-block stretch. Whether you have the money to drop or you just want to walk among those who do, you'll get a kick out of seeing the most famous shopping street in the world. At the southeast end of Rodeo Drive, you'll find 2 Rodeo, a pedestrian street created in 1990, resembling something out of a European village (or a Hollywood movie set made to resemble one).

Limited-Service Hotel

★ ★ ★ **LUXE HOTEL RODEO DRIVE.** *360 N Rodeo Dr, Beverly Hills (90210). Phone 310/273-0300; toll-free 866/589-3411; fax 310/859-8730. www. luxehotels.com.* Well-heeled shoppers and discriminating travelers who would rather spot celebrities than loll by a pool should find this richly styled boutique hotel—the only hotel situated in the middle of world-famous Rodeo Drive—an ideal fit. Having recently completed a $15 million renovation highlighted by gorgeous artwork, brushed metal, mahogany accents, and mirrored surfaces, the Luxe is big on personal amenities, which include complimentary fruit baskets, Frette linens, signature bathrobes, private sundecks, and Swiss truffles at turndown. Café Rodeo features inspired California cuisine, and its Bar 360 serves martinis made to impress. Concierge, business, and babysitting services are available. 88 rooms, 5 story. Pets accepted, some restrictions; fee. Check-in 3 pm, check-out noon. High-speed Internet access, wireless Internet access. Restaurant, bar. Fitness room. Business center. **$$**

Full-Service Hotels

★ ★ ★ **AVALON HOTEL BEVERLY HILLS.** *9400 W Olympic Blvd, Beverly Hills (90212). Phone 310/277-5221; toll-free 800/535-4715; fax 310/277-4928. www. avalonbeverlyhills.com.* Channeling the mid-century modernist spirit of Marilyn Monroe's age (she once bunked here), the Avalon has become one of the coolest scenes in Beverly Hills. The boutique hotel's sleek lobby serves as a meeting spot overlooking the hourglass-shaped swimming pool and funneling patrons into Blue on Blue restaurant and bar. Each of its guest

rooms is different; options range from see-and-be-seen poolside quarters to cityscape tower rooms and junior suites with kitchenettes. Aura Spa provides in-room massages. 82 rooms, 5 story. Pets accepted; fee. Complimentary continental breakfast. Check-in 3 pm, check-out noon. High-speed Internet access. Restaurant, bar. Fitness room. Outdoor pool. **$$**

★ ★ ★ ★ ★ **THE BEVERLY HILLS HOTEL.** *9641 Sunset Blvd, Beverly Hills (90210). Phone 310/276-2251; toll-free 800/283-8885; fax 310/887-2887. www.beverlyhillshotel.com.* Hovering above Sunset Boulevard in a magnificent setting of lush gardens, The Beverly Hills Hotel epitomizes the glamour of Hollywood. Affectionately known as the "pink palace," this legendary hotel has long been the favorite hideaway of the silver screens biggest stars. Taking a cue from its most famous guests, the hotel evokes the allure of 1940s Hollywood in its public and private rooms. The guest rooms and suites are an ideal refuge with soothing pastel color schemes and luxurious furnishings. Fireplaces add a romantic touch, and terraces and balconies focus attention on the lush gardens below. Guests seeking a true getaway opt for the bungalows privately tucked away along paths of fragrant tropical plants, where pets are allowed. A variety of dining venues attract producers and stars, but visitors in the know head for the pool, where the scene is best viewed from a fantastic private cabana. 204 rooms, 4 story. Pets accepted; restrictions; fee. Check-in 3 pm, check-out noon. High-speed Internet access, wireless Internet access. Three restaurants, bar. Fitness room, spa. Outdoor pool, whirlpool. Tennis. **$$$$**

★ ★ ★ **THE BEVERLY HILTON.** *9876 Wilshire Blvd, Beverly Hills (90210). Phone 310/274-7777; toll-free 800/774-1500; fax 310/285-1313. www.beverlyhilton.com.* The late and former TV talk show host Merv Griffin owned it and Trader Vic's resides in it, giving the historic Beverly Hilton its share of Tinseltown caché. Filled with pictures of Golden Globe and Oscar parties, the Old Hollywood standby resides walking distance from the shops of Rodeo Drive. In-house leisure seekers will appreciate the Olympic-sized swimming pool adjacent to a well-equipped fitness center. After hours, sip from an umbrella-garnished coconut at Trader Vic's Polynesian-themed cocktail bar, an authentic retro spot turned hot bote. With its many rooms, you can bet they come in different configurations, from tropical, poolside cabana rooms to balconied suites. 570 rooms, 8 story. Pets accepted, some restrictions; fee. Check-in 3 pm, check-out noon. Wireless Internet access. Two restaurants, two bars. Fitness room. Outdoor pool. Business center. **$$$**

★ ★ ★ **THE CRESCENT HOTEL.** *403 N Crescent Dr, Beverly Hills (90210). Phone 310/247-0505; toll-free 800/451-1566; fax 310/247-9053. www.crescentbh. com.* Just three blocks off Rodeo Drive, in the heart of Beverly Hills, this hotel is the epitome of hip. All the rooms—ultramodern and minimalist, with crisp white sheets and down comforters and pillows, offset by dark wood furniture and fresh flowers—have wireless Internet access, flat-screen TVs, DVD/CD players, cordless phones, fax machines, and printers. When you step outside your room—if you ever want to leave it, that is—you'll find the lobby's lounge and bar, which is the only indoor-outdoor hotel lounge in Beverly Hills with a fireplace. The hotel restaurant, Boe, is open for breakfast, lunch, and dinner, and offers high-end cuisine. 35 rooms. Pets accepted; some restrictions. Check-in 3 pm, check-out noon. Wireless Internet access. Restaurant, bar. **$$**

★ ★ ★ ★ **FOUR SEASONS HOTEL LOS ANGELES AT BEVERLY HILLS.** *300 S Doheny Dr, Beverly Hills (90048). Phone 310/273-2222; toll-free 800/819-5053; fax 310/859-3824. www.fourseasons. com.* A bastion of chic, the hotel is only 1 mile from the exclusive boutiques of Rodeo Drive. Refreshing and elegant, the guest rooms are luxuriously appointed with European élan and Californian comfort. The hotel is honed to perfection, down to the smallest details. Enlivened by rich colors and abundant floral displays, the Florentine-style Gardens restaurant (see) is a showpiece for California-Pacific cuisine, and the Café is a sun-filled Mediterranean-style bistro. Bathed by the glorious Southern Californian sun, the heated outdoor pool is a popular gathering spot, and the Poolside Café satisfies hungry sun worshipers with spa cuisine and traditional favorites. The spa is a standout, from tequila massages to European body kurs. The marvelous California sunset massage, conducted in a private candlelit cabana, is a massage that's not to be missed. 285 rooms, 16 story. Pets accepted, some restrictions. Check-in 3 pm, check-out noon. High-speed Internet access. Three restaurants, bar. Fitness room, spa. Outdoor pool, whirlpool. Business center. **$$$$**

★ ★ ★ **MAISON 140.** *140 S Lasky Dr, Beverly Hills (90212). Phone 310/281-4000; toll-free 800/670-6182; fax 310/281-4001. www.maison140.com.* Maison 140 is located almost exactly halfway between the ultra-high-end shopping of Rodeo Drive and the popular outdoor Westfield Shoppingtown Century City. When you step inside this boutique hotel, its European and Asian style, with deep color palettes and bold patterns, transports you to another place. But the guest rooms—equipped with amenities such as high-speed Internet access, Egyptian cotton bedding, Philosophy toiletries, flat-screen TVs with DVD and CD players, and in-room spa treatments, not to mention original abstract artworkare all LA. The hotel's bar, Bar Noir, decorated in black, white, and red, is just right for before- or after-dinner cocktails. Though the hotel doesn't have an on-site pool, as a hotel guest you can use the pool at the Avalon Hotel (see), a half-mile's drive away. 43 rooms. Check-in 3 pm, check-out noon. High-speed Internet access. Restaurant, bar. Fitness room. **$$**

★ ★ ★ ★ ★ **THE PENINSULA BEVERLY HILLS.** *9882 S Santa Monica Blvd, Beverly Hills (90212). Phone 310/551-2888; toll-free 800/462-7899; fax 310/788-2319. www.peninsula.com.* The Peninsula embodies the grace and elegance synonymous with Beverly Hills. This French Renaissance-style hotel remains close to the enticing boutiques of Rodeo Drive and Century City, yet feels very private and secluded. Meticulously maintained, the luscious gardens are a kaleidoscope of colors and fragrances, from rare and exotic plantings to familiar favorites. The sun-filled lobby mimics the bounty of the gardens in its sophisticated, tropical-inspired décor. A particularly convenient feature is the flexibile check-in/check-out policy: whenever you check in, you have 24 hours before you must check out. The guest rooms and suites, fitted with the Peninsula's renowned amenities, are the last word in luxury. Swimmers drink in a view of the city from the rooftop lap pool, while spa-goers retreat to the Zen-like spa, complete with fitness center. Dining is exceptional, from the delicious West Coast cuisine of The Belvedere (see) and the wonderful afternoon tea of the Living Room to the health-conscious spa menu at the Rooftop Garden. Even pets are pampered here, with doggie beds (including turndown!) and a pet-friendly room service menu. 196 rooms, 5 story. Pets accepted, some restrictions; fee. Check-in 24 hours, check-out 24 hours. Wireless Internet access. Two restaurants, bar. Fitness room, spa. Outdoor pool, whirlpool. Business center. **$$$$**

★ ★ ★ ★ ★ **RAFFLES L'ERMITAGE BEVERLY HILLS.** *9291 Burton Way, Beverly Hills (90210). Phone 310/278-3344; toll-free 800/800-2113; fax 310/278-8247. www.raffles-lermitagehotel.com.* Satisfying the cool quotient in Beverly Hills with its stylish and serene Asian-inspired contemporary décor, Raffles L'Ermitage is the haven of choice for the jet set. Conveniently located, this hotel maintains a sanctuary-like ambience in the heart of Beverly Hills. The guest rooms and suites are a harmony of European and Asian influences with light woods, simple furnishings, and shoji-style screens. All accommodations are outfitted with high-tech accoutrements, including 40-inch televisions, Bose speakers, and ten jacks for audiovisual needs and DSL lines. A flexible check-in/check-out policy allowing guests to stay for a full 24 hours is the ultimate in convenience. Hipsters flock to JAAN's sensuous setting for delicious French dishes infused with Indochine flavors. The Living Room and Writers Bar encourage visitors to sink into their inviting surroundings and enjoy cocktails or light meals. The rooftop pool provides guests with a bird's-eye view of the prestigious neighborhood, while the Amrita spa takes guests to a higher level of relaxation with its Ayurvedic techniques. Pets are welcome here and get their own beds, snacks, and toys; a gourmet room service menu is available, as are private dog walkers and an on-site veterinarian. 119 rooms, 8 story. Pets accepted, some restrictions; fee. Complimentary continental breakfast. Check-in 3 pm; flexible, check-out noon; flexible. Wireless Internet access. Restaurant, bar. Fitness room, spa. Outdoor pool. **$$$$**

★ ★ ★ ★ **THE REGENT BEVERLY WILSHIRE.** *9500 Wilshire Blvd, Beverly Hills (90212). Phone 310/275-5200; toll-free 800/545-4000; fax 310/275-5986. www.fourseasons.com.* For a taste of the good life, savvy travelers check in at the Regent Beverly Wilshire, a Four Seasons hotel. It doesn't get any better than this prestigious address in the heart of world-famous Beverly Hills, at the intersection of Rodeo Drive and Wilshire Boulevard. Bridging old and new, this Italian Renaissance-style hotel is a happy marriage of two distinctive sensibilities. The guest rooms of the Beverly Wing are a triumph of contemporary décor, while the Wilshire Wing's rooms appeal to classic-minded guests. The service is exemplary, as guests have come to expect from the Four Seasons, from the attentive room service to the

helpful staff in the business and fitness centers. A very British afternoon tea is served at the Lobby Lounge, and the convivial bar is a perfect place to sit back and watch the glamorous parade of this star-studded city. 399 rooms, 12 story. Pets accepted, some restrictions. Complimentary continental breakfast. Check-in 3 pm, check-out noon. High-speed Internet access. Two restaurants, two bars. Fitness room, spa. Outdoor pool, whirlpool. Business center. **$$$**

Spas

★ ★ ★ ★ **THE BEVERLY HILLS HOTEL SPA BY LA PRAIRIE.** *9641 Sunset Blvd, Beverly Hills (90210). Phone 310/887-2505. www.beverlyhills. com.* The La Prairie Spa at the Beverly Hills Hotel is a perfect marriage of Swiss innovation and American elegance. The Clinic La Prairie in Montreux, Switzerland, is among the world's leading spa innovators, and its anti-aging treatments are considered revolutionary. Exclusive and intimate, this spa truly makes every guest feel like a star with its individualized attention, white glove service, plush surroundings, and advanced therapies. La Prairie's commitment to anti-aging is perhaps best experienced through one of the spa's many decadent facials. From stress relief and re-hydration to deep cleansing, the facial menu has something to soothe, treat, and heal your skin. The caviar firming facial is a particularly extravagant treat, using the concentration of caviar extracts to lift and polish skin. Wrinkle fighters take refuge in the intensive de-aging facial, which uses a cellular complex and glycolic acid blend to reduce the appearance of fine lines, and the refining microdermabrasion facial, which takes wrinkle reduction one step further with a blend of technology and coveted La Prairie formulations. Wind down with one of the spas many massage therapies, including Swedish, deep tissue, Shiatsu, or hot stone. Massages and nail services are available at the spa, in a poolside cabana, or in the privacy of a guest room. The spa also features a bath menu with varieties targeting muscle relief, stress reduction, sleep enhancement, and body balancing.

★ ★ ★ ★ **THE FOUR SEASONS SPA, LOS ANGELES AT BEVERLY HILLS.** *300 S Doheny Dr, Los Angeles (90048). Phone 310/786-2229; toll-free 800/819-5053. www.fourseasons.com.* Intimate and deluxe, The Four Seasons Spa, Los Angeles at Beverly Hills is a true urban retreat. This facility perfects the experience down to every last detail. Like all Four Seasons hotels, excellent service is a hallmark, and the spa is no exception. Treat yourself to a massage; Swedish, shiatsu, deep tissue, reflexology, aromatherapy, and pregnancy therapies are available. For an even more memorable experience, book the spa's private poolside cabana for a signature California sunset massage. The punta mita massage is another signature treatment, combining tequila and sage for a wonderfully intoxicating feeling—without the alcohol! Body scrubs use an array of products, including chamomile and Turkish salt, to exfoliate and polish skin. The margarita scrub blends the essential oils of limes, oranges, apples, and tangerines with tequila, sunflower oil, and salt to rub your body to baby-soft perfection. Revel in the restorative properties of the thermal mineral kur. This exhilarating treatment begins with a moor mud wrap, followed by a bath filled with mineral crystals from Hungary's renowned Sarvar Springs, and ends with a soothing massage. Ocean lovers enjoy the nourishing and relaxing benefits of the from the sea treatment, which combines a wrap in warm algae, a bath with sea salts and algae, and a massage with lavender and mineral cream. The spa's divine facials cleanse, refresh, and revive with a variety of options, including European deep-cleansing, aromatherapy stone, and oxyliance cellular. The deep skin ionization facial is a Four Seasons signature.

★ ★ ★ ★ **THE SPA AT THE PENINSULA BEVERLY HILLS.** *9882 S Santa Monica Blvd, Beverly Hills (90212). Phone 310/551-2888; toll-free 800/462-7899. www.beverlyhills.peninsula.com.* From the golden sunshine streaming into the lobby to the lush gardens surrounding the property, The Peninsula knows how to help guests relax, and the spa is no exception. The facility includes a well-equipped fitness center, a relaxation space overlooking the Hollywood Hills, and a 60-foot rooftop lap pool lined with private cabanas. Tucked away yet conveniently located, this spa is an urban retreat. After a rigorous workout or a day at the spa, head for the Roof Garden, where sensational cuisine will satisfy your appetite. From the geranium, mandarin orange, and papaya-pineapple enzyme body scrubs to sea kelp manicures and pedicures, natures gifts inspire many of the therapies at The Peninsula Spa. Enjoy the gentle pulses of the Rosemary Rhapsody body treatment, or sink into the pleasures of an aroma-infused, athletic, or classic Californian massage. Indulge in treatments that draw upon the healing powers of rubies, emeralds, sapphires, and diamonds with one of The Spa's exclusive Shiffa Precious Gem Treatments, where precious gem oils provide a luxurious way to achieve tranquility, strength, vitality, and harmony. Revel in the healthy glow you achieve with a sunless tanning treatment, or battle cellulite with a targeted body treatment. Facials also are a specialty here, whether you hydrate your skin with oxygen therapy, nourish with antioxidants, or indulge with a crystalline gemstone mask in The Walk of Fame Facial. Fresh-faced visitors owe their supple looks to advanced treatments, such as machine-free microdermabrasion, that utilize the latest antiaging techniques. In addition to more traditional facials, body scrubs, and massages, The Peninsula Spa offers Eastern-influenced therapies—including Ayurvedic treatments such as shirodhara, shakti karma, and ama mokshah—to relax you, increase your energy, and rid your body of toxins. Men find ways to pamper themselves, too, with facials, sports therapies, and body, hand, and foot experiences designed especially for them, while couples can enjoy massages and body treatments together in the couples treatment room.

Restaurants

★ **BARNEY GREENGRASS.** *9570 Wilshire Blvd, Beverly Hills (90212). Phone 310/777-5877; fax 310/777-5760.* On the upper floor of famed shopping mecca Barney's, this power lunch institution is the ultimate spot to grab a quick bite for talent agents, Beverly Hills matrons, Manolo Blanik fanatics, and New Yorkers who miss the taste of home. The menu is poised as a deli's but is strictly upscale, with its famed smoked fish (especially the sturgeon), luscious matzo brei, and refined salads and sandwiches. The dining room is cool and civilized in various shades of taupe, and outdoor patio tables with city views are always in demand. American menu. Breakfast, lunch. Bar. Casual attire. Valet parking. Outdoor seating. **$$**

★ ★ ★ ★ **THE BELVEDERE.** *9882 S Santa Monica Blvd, Beverly Hills (90212). Phone 310/788-2736; fax 310/975-2736.* Packed with financial VIPs by day and doe-eyed, hand-holding romance seekers by night, The Belvedere is one of the hottest tickets in hotel dining in Los Angeles. The intimate but spacious dining room is dressed in cream tones, with elegant tables topped with Villeroy & Boch china and pewter vases filled with fresh seasonal flowers. The cuisine is eclectic "left coast"—a lively combination of heartland staples and edgy, global-accented fare. Diners are encouraged to invent their own menus by mixing and matching appetizer-sized plates with tapas-style mouthfuls and larger entrée dishes. The waitstaff is skilled at helping with menu planning and attending to any other details. The management has a terrific sense of humor; the bottom of the menu reads, "The use of mobile phones interferes with the chef's orange reduction on his potato-crusted sea bass." The food may be seriously good, but at The Belvedere, it's still taken with a grain of salt. American menu. Breakfast, lunch, dinner. Bar. Children's menu. Business casual attire. Reservations recommended. Valet parking. Outdoor seating. **$$$$**

★ ★ **CHIN CHIN.** *206 S Beverly Dr, Beverly Hills (90212). Phone 310/248-5252. www.chinchin.com.* This sunny Chinese bistro is always abuzz with young executives taking quick business lunches, post-yoga beauties munching on salads, and shoppers refueling for the next boutique. The interior is pure SoCal, with lots of peach and green appointments surrounding the blonde wood tables and the model-like waitstaff. From mu shu pork to fried rice, hot-and-sour soup to chow fun, classic Chinese fare gets a healthy twist with light preparations and fresh ingredients. Chinese menu. Lunch, dinner. Casual attire. Outdoor seating. **$$**

★ ★ **COBRA LILY.** *8442 Wilshire Blvd, Beverly Hills (90211). Phone 323/651-5051.* This sultry little tapas bar tucked into a corner on the Miracle Mile has a sexy European feel, with candlelit tables, polished wood, and cigar box covers hammered into the wall. Along the entrance, a polished bar turns out pitchers of sangria and cool mojitos to a crowd of young Hollywood executives and patrons of the adjacent theater. Small dining tables dot the room where modelesque waiters serve small plates of artisanal Spanish cheeses, grilled shrimp, and skirt steak. Cobra Lily is the perfect launching point for a spirited evening or a swinging post-work happy hour. Spanish, tapas menu. Lunch, dinner. Closed Sun. Casual attire. Reservations recommended. Valet parking. **$$**

★ ★ ★ **CRUSTACEAN.** *9646 Little Santa Monica Blvd, Beverly Hills (90210). Phone 310/205-8990; fax 310/271-0737. www.anfamily.com.* The buzz surrounding this white-hot restaurant tends to center on the Mason-like secrecy surrounding the kitchen, where nonfamily members are prohibited. In the end, however, you won't care who's in there as long as they continue to churn out the satays, rolls, and entrées LA has grown to love. The atmosphere is reminiscent of a French colonial estate, and the dining room overlooks bamboo garden verandas. Vietnamese menu. Lunch, dinner. Closed Sun; holidays. Bar. Business casual attire. Reservations recommended. Valet parking. **$$$**

★ ★ **DA PASQUALE.** *9749 Little Santa Monica Blvd, Beverly Hills (90210). Phone 310/859-3884; fax 310/859-2911.* In a neighborhood known for exorbitant prices and snooty service, this Tuscan-style Italian restaurant breaks all the rules. A charming family-owned trattoria on a stretch of busy street, Da Pasquale is always aroar with activity. Energetic parties of friends and families congregate here for the affordable and tasty cuisine, including bruschetta al pomodoro, crisp pizzas, and daily pasta specials. Another perk: delivery is free to immediate neighboring areas. Italian menu. Lunch, dinner. Closed Sun; holidays. Casual attire. Reservations recommended. Outdoor seating. **$$$**

★ ★ **DELMONICO'S SEAFOOD GRILLE.** *9320 W Pico Blvd, Los Angeles (90035). Phone 310/550-7737; fax 310/550-0929. www.delmonicos.com.* This cavernous brasserie can get loud and raucous, so opt for one of the large enclosed booths for a cozy dinner away from the fracas. With lots of space and an old-school aura, this is a perfect and unpretentious family spot. The kitchen offers up almost every fish in the sea, either simply grilled or prepared crusted, seared, sautéed, or any other way imaginable. Carnivores will be pleased to find steaks and chops on the menu as well, and even the generously sized salads can be meals in themselves. American, seafood menu. Lunch, dinner. Closed Jan 1. Bar. Casual attire. Valet parking. **$$$**

★ ★ ★ **FRIDA RESTAURANT.** *236 S Beverly Dr, Beverly Hills (90212). Phone 310/278-7666; fax 310/278-9699. www.fridarestaurant.com.* On Beverly's restaurant row, Frida is consistently the most festive place to dine. Customers spill out onto the sidewalk patio, sipping world-class margaritas and munching on generous portions of appetizers. The interior is adorned with a bizarre collection of religious antiquities and folk art, but the upscale diners are focused on the creative Latin fare. Standards like chicken mole are great, and innovative dishes like chicken in pumpkin seed sauce and steak cloaked in huitlacoche (corn fungus) are scrumptious. Mexican menu. Lunch, dinner. Closed holidays. Bar. Casual attire. Reservations recommended. Valet parking. Outdoor seating. **$$**

★ ★ ★ **GARDENS.** *300 S Doheny Dr, Beverly Hills (90048). Phone 310/273-2222; fax 310/859-3824. www.fourseasons.com.* The elegant dining room of the Four Seasons Los Angeles (see), Gardens goes haute-theatrical with patterned carpet, gold-framed oils, upholstered dining chairs, and abundant flower arrangements. The food favors contemporary regional and seasonal preparations with Asian accents. In addition to salads and pastas, dishes might include Pacific halibut with butternut squash risotto and grilled ahi tuna with saffron aioli. For all its formality, Gardens also welcomes kids with a special children's menu, and the more relaxed terrace takes in the lavish landscaping. Mediterranean menu. Breakfast, lunch, dinner, Sun brunch. Bar. Children's menu. Business casual attire. Reservations recommended. Valet parking. Outdoor seating. **$$$**

★ ★ **GRILL ON THE ALLEY.** *9560 Dayton Way, Beverly Hills (90210). Phone 310/276-0615; fax 310/276-0284. www.thegrill.com.* Entertainment industry bigwigs huddle over steaks and business deals at Beverly Hills Grill on the Alley. Famed for its power lunches (do make a reservation), this men's-clubbish grill makes for great people-watching, while its kitchen makes great grill classics. Steaks and chops are supplemented by upscale comfort foods (like chicken pot pie and meatloaf), pastas, and fish. Although the Grill is located in an alley near Wilshire Boulevard, you can simply follow the streams of devotees to find it. American menu. Lunch, dinner. Closed holidays. Bar. Business casual attire. Reservations recommended. Valet parking. **$$$**

★ ★ ★ **IL CIELO.** *9018 Burton Way, Beverly Hills (90211). Phone 310/276-9990; fax 310/276-5431. www.ilcielo.com.* A cozy cottage spilling into a lush, Tuscan-style garden, Il Cielo has earned its reputation for romance. Dine indoors under hand-painted ceilings or outdoors amid the twinkling lights of the patio. From owner Pasquale Vericella on down, the entire staff is Italian, lending old-world authenticity to the restaurant. The bilingual menu rests heavily on seafood pastas, though the Florentine steak will please heartier appetites. To avoid heartbreak—this is a popular place for parties and wedding receptions—do phone ahead for a reservation. Italian menu. Lunch, dinner. Closed Sun; holidays. Bar. Business casual attire. Reservations recommended. Valet parking. Outdoor seating. **$$$**

★ ★ **IL FORNAIO.** *301 N Beverly Dr, Los Angeles (90210). Phone 310/550-8330. www.ilfornaio.com.* This popular Italian chain is a massive, always-packed place serving upscale fare at reasonable prices. Booths and tables are large and perfect for families; the servers are courteous and prompt; and the dependable menu features classics like butternut squash ravioli and veal scaloppini. Each month, a different region of Italy is featured in a special dinner menu—a nice way to sample specialties of Umbria or Tuscany without the cost of airfare. Italian menu. Lunch, dinner, late-night. Bar. Casual attire. Outdoor seating. **$$**

★ ★ **IL PASTAIO.** *400 N Canon Dr, Beverly Hills (90210). Phone 310/205-5444; fax 310/205-5445.* From the famed Drago family comes this upbeat trattoria, which is constantly packed with enthusiastic locals who gladly wait for a table and cool their heels at the sparkling and enchanting bar. The egalitarian atmosphere is evident with the no-reservation policy, exuberant service, and affordable Italian cuisine. Start with the beef carpaccio or the goat cheese-stuffed eggplant and a glass of the house Chianti. Creative pastas and pizzas dazzle, as do the half-dozen nightly risotto offerings. Italian menu. Lunch, dinner. Closed holidays. Bar. Casual attire. Reservations recommended. Valet parking. Outdoor seating. **$$**

★ ★ **KATE MANTILINI.** *9101 Wilshire Blvd, Beverly Hills (90210). Phone 310/278-3699.* Full of soaring metal sculptures and high-walled booths, this cavernous diner is large enough to shoot a cannon through. That's the way the food is, too big. The menu is extensive, with deli classics, gourmet diet fare, mountainous salads, and refined entrées like pork chops and frog legs. Always open from early morning to late at night, and always packed with celebrities, wheeling-and-dealing producers, post-theater diners, and retirees, this upscale yet casual joint has something for everyone who has too much cash and flash to be seen in a Denny's. American menu. Breakfast, lunch, dinner, late-night. Closed Thanksgiving, Dec 25. Casual attire. **$$$**

★ ★ **MAKO.** *225 S Beverly Dr, Beverly Hills (90212). Phone 310/288-8338. www.makorestaurant.com.* Blond wood walls, panels of mirrors, a sleek marble bar, and artful orchid arrangements create a clean and simple backdrop to showcase Maketo Tanaka's imaginative Asian dishes, which have a distinctly Mediterranean flair. Specialties like lobster in a coconut-saffron sauce over angel hair pasta and foie gras with lychee fruit make for elegant dinners, and Beverly Hills shoppers flock here for exquisite sushi and salads in the afternoon. Diners swear by the yuzu meringue tart. Asian menu. Dinner. Closed Sun; holidays. Bar. Casual attire. **$$**

★ ★ ★ **MASTRO'S STEAKHOUSE.** *246 N Canon Dr, Beverly Hills (90210). Phone 310/888-8782; fax 310/858-7036. www.mastrossteakhouse.com.* Everything is gargantuan at this swanky steakhouse—the massive cutlery, the towering seafood appetizers chilling on dry ice, and the huge slabs of world-class aged beef. The Beverly Hills' elite dine here while doing business, impressing their dates, and scanning for stars in the celebrity-heavy dining room. Upstairs, a miraculous one-man band plays standards to a sophisticated older crowd that sips champagne in sleek and modern surroundings. VIPs, like former president Bill Clinton, often dine in the private back room, away from mere mortals. Steak menu. Dinner. Bar. Business casual attire. Reservations recommended. Valet parking. **$$$$**

★ ★ ★ **MATSUHISA.** *129 N La Cienega Blvd, Beverly Hills (90211). Phone 310/659-9639; fax 310/659-0492. www.nobumatsuhisa.com.* Acclaimed chef Nobu Matsuhisas flagship serves signature fusion fare to fans both celebrated and unknown. Established in 1987, this sushi bar broke culinary ground serving the likes of lobster ceviche and sashimi sparked by cilantro or garlic, influences Matsuhisa picked up cooking in Peru. Given a vast menu, aficionados recommend putting yourself in the chef's hands with the "omakase" tasting menu. Although Matsuhisa later opened the more self-consciously stylish Nobu chain with partners that include actor Robert De Niro, the original restaurant is determinedly casual with bright lighting and wall posters. Japanese menu. Lunch, dinner. Closed holidays. Bar. Business casual attire. Reservations recommended. Valet parking. **$$$**

★ ★ **MR. CHOW.** *344 N Camden Dr, Beverly Hills (90210). Phone 310/278-9911. www.mrchow.com.* Everybody who's anybody has dined at this Asian institution, with high white walls, mobile kite sculptures hanging from the ceiling, and a crowd that's a veritable who's who of Hollywood. Regulars don't even ask for a menu, ordering up shocking orange chicken skewers, hand-pulled dragon noodles, electric green prawns, and heavenly drunken fish. Most of the time, knowledgeable waiters will choose dishes for you, leaving you time to stargaze over lychee martinis. Watch out for the paparazzi outside. Chinese menu. Lunch, dinner. **$$$**

★ **NATE 'N AL'S DELICATESSEN.** *414 N Beverly Dr, Beverly Hills (90210). Phone 310/274-0101; fax 310/274-0485. www.natenal.com.* The world's most elite shops, expensive salons, and outrageous antique dealers are neighbors of this timeless Jewish deli that has been serving comfort food to affluent customers since 1945. The room is a tacky study in orange and brown synthetics, the waitstaff short-tempered, and the menu old-fashioned, but that's why this institution is so beloved by the 90210 old guard, NYC transplants, and shoppers who crave the comfort of matzo ball soup and pastrami sandwiches. The take-out deli is a smorgasbord of salads, cured meats, and other Jewish delicacies. Deli menu. Breakfast, lunch, dinner. Children's menu. Casual attire. **$$**

★ ★ **NYALA.** *1076 S Fairfax Ave, Los Angeles (90019). Phone 323/936-5918; fax 323/936-1261. www.nyala-la.com.* In Fairfaxs Little Ethiopia district, you'll find an array of restaurants, but Nyala is the crown jewel of them all. The dining room is modest, yet rich in rust and earth tones, and tables can be chummy and communal. Authentic stews studded with lamb or chicken are complex in flavor and intricately spiced. You use a sour crepe as fork, knife, and wrapper, so unless you're a pro, prepare to get delightfully messy. Middle Eastern menu. Lunch, dinner. Bar. Casual attire. **$$**

★ ★ ★ **POLO LOUNGE.** *9641 Sunset Blvd, Beverly Hills (90210). Phone 310/281-2907; fax 310/281-2988. www.beverlyhillshotel.com.* Dimly lit despite—or perhaps because of—its A-list clientele, the Polo Lounge remains the place to see and be seen in LA. Hollywood stars from Marlene Dietrich to Gwyneth Paltrow have powwowed with dealmakers in the generous velvet booths of the Beverly Hills Hotel landmark, a regular in the gossip columns. The food keeps pace with classic but well-executed California-meets-the-continent fare. But, beware: if you don't have a production deal, you might balk at the prices. California menu. Breakfast, lunch, dinner. Bar. Children's menu. Business casual attire. Reservations recommended. Valet parking. Outdoor seating. **$$$**

★ ★ ★ **RUTH'S CHRIS STEAK HOUSE.** *224 S Beverly Dr, Beverly Hills (90212). Phone 310/859-8744; fax 310/859-2576. www.ruthschris.com.* Born from a single New Orleans restaurant that Ruth Fertel bought in 1965 for $22,000, the Ruth's Chris Steak House chain has made it to the top of every steak lover's list. Aged prime Midwestern beef is broiled to your liking at 1,800 degrees and served on a heated plate, sizzling in butter, a staple ingredient used generously in most entrées; even "healthier" alternatives like chicken arrive at your table drenched in the savory substance. Sides like creamed spinach and fresh asparagus with hollandaise are not to be missed. And who can forget the potatoes? Choose from seven different preparations, from a 1 pound baked potato with "everything" to au gratin potatoes with cream sauce and topped with cheese. Steak menu. Dinner. Bar. Business casual attire. Reservations recommended. Valet parking. **$$$**

★ ★ ★ **SPAGO BEVERLY HILLS.** *176 N Canon Dr, Beverly Hills (90210). Phone 310/385-0880; fax 310/385-9690. www.wolfgangpuck.com.* The first restaurant from the Wolfgang Puck-Barbara Lazar culinary dynasty (they also own Postrio and Chinois, among others), Spago remains white-hot and is often bursting at the seams with celebrities, VIPs, studio executives, models, media moguls, and other generally fabulous folks. Set in the posh Golden Triangle of Beverly Hills, the restaurant is as famous for its late-night Oscar bashes as it is for its innovative, sophisticated American cuisine prepared with European and Asian influences. The stylish, upscale room is awash in rich wood and accented with tones of amethyst, jade, and amber. The open-air garden with a sculpted fountain and a pair of 100-year-old olive trees adds a dose of serenity to the restaurant's high-energy atmosphere. Delicately devouring the restaurant's signature gourmet pizza while bathing in the dining room's soft, flattering golden light, you'll feel like a star and look like one, too. American menu. Lunch, dinner. Bar. Business casual attire. Reservations recommended. Valet parking. **$$$$**

★ ★ **XI'AN.** *362 N Canon Dr, Beverly Hills (90210). Phone 310/275-3345. www.xian90210.com.* This trendy Chinese restaurant is informal and mod, with green tile floors, blond wood walls, a curvaceous bar, and scattered bistro tables. Lunching professionals, shopping families, and casual couples flock here for the "healthy" Chinese menu, sharing plates of guilt-free potstickers, chicken teriyaki, and ubiquitous lettuce cups. Unlike some of the snooty surrounding boutiques and restaurants, this joint is always a friendly and low-key spot to grab a bite. Chinese menu. Lunch, dinner. Bar. Casual attire. Reservations recommended. Valet parking. Outdoor seating. **$$**

Big Bear Lake (J-4)

See also Lake Arrowhead, Redlands, Riverside, San Bernardino, Victorville

Population 5,438
Elevation 6,754 ft
Area Code 909
Zip 92315
Information Big Bear Lake Resort Association, 630 Bartlett Rd; phone 909/866-6190, 909/866-7000, or toll-free 800/424-4232
Web Site www.bigbearinfo.com

This is a growing, year-round recreation area in the San Bernardino National Forest (see SAN BERNARDINO). Fishing, canoeing, parasailing, windsurfing, riding, golfing, bicycling, picnicking, hiking, and camping are available in summer; skiing and other winter sports are also popular in season.

What to See and Do

Alpine Slide at Magic Mountain. *660 Cherry Ln, Big Bear Lake. Approximately 1/4 mile W on Hwy 18. Phone 909/866-4626. www.alpineslideatmagicmountain.com.* Includes Alpine bobsled-type ride (all year), water slide (summer), and inner tubing (winter). Miniature golf (all year). Video games; snack bar. (Daily) **$$$**

Big Bear Mountain Resort. *N on I-215 (Hwy 395), exit E on Frwy 10, exit Orange Ave in Redlands, left at Hwy 38 (Lagonia Ave), left on Big Bear Blvd, left on Moonridge Rd. Phone 909/585-2519. www.bearmtn.com.* Skiing, seasonal passes; also golf course and driving range; resort.

Big Bear Mountain Ski Resort. *2 miles S off Hwy 18. Phone 909/585-2519; toll-free 800/232-7686. www.bigbearmountainresorts.com.* Quad, two high-speed quads, three triple, four double chairlifts, two Poma-lifts; patrol, school, rentals; snowmaking; cafe, two restaurants, two bars. Longest run 2 1/2 miles; vertical drop 1,665 feet. (Mid-Nov-Apr, Mon-Fri 8:30 am-4 pm, Sat-Sun from 8:30 am) Hiking; nine-hole golf course (May-mid-Oct, daily). **$$$$**

Big Bear Queen **Tour Boat.** *Big Bear Marina, 500 Paine Rd, Big Bear Lake (92315). Paine Rd at Lakeview Dr. Phone 909/866-3218. www.bigbearmarina.com/queen.html.* Paddlewheeler provides 90-minute narrated tour of Big Bear Lake. Dinner and champagne cruises also available. (Apr-Oct, daily at noon, 2 pm, and 4 pm) **$$$**

Snow Summit. *880 Summit Blvd, Big Bear Lake. 1/2 mile S off Hwy 18. Phone 909/866-5766. www.snowsummit.com.* Two high-speed quads, two quads, two triples, five double chairlifts; patrol, school, rentals; snowmaking; five restaurants, two bars. Longest run 1 1/4 miles; vertical drop 1,200 feet. (Mid-Nov-Apr, daily) Night skiing, snowboarding. Chairlift also operates in summer (May-early Sept). **$$$$**

Special Event

Old Miners' Days. *Phone 909/866-4607. www.oldminers.org.* Festival celebrating 19th-century frontier heritage with cowboy music, parades, quick-draw contest, children's activities. Three weekends in July.

Limited-Service Hotels

★ ★ **BEST WESTERN BIG BEAR CHATEAU.** *42200 Moonridge Rd, Big Bear Lake (92315). Phone 909/866-6666; toll-free 800/232-7466; fax 909/866-8988. www.bestwestern.com.* European chteau-style décor. 80 rooms, 3 story. Pets accepted, some restrictions; fee. Check-in, check-out noon. Restaurant, bar. Outdoor pool, whirlpool. **$**

★ **ROBIN HOOD RESORT.** *40797 Lakeview Dr, Big Bear Lake (92315). Phone 909/866-4643; toll-free 800/990-9956; fax 909/866-4645. www.robinhoodresort.info.* 54 rooms, 2 story. Check-in 3 pm, check-out 11 am. **$**

Full-Service Resort

★ ★ ★ **NORTHWOODS RESORT AND CONFERENCE CENTER.** *40650 Village Dr, Big Bear Lake (92831). Phone 909/866-3121; toll-free 800/866-3121; fax 909/878-2122. www.northwoodsresort.com.* This rustic Southern California mountain resort and conference center offers rooms and suites filled with handcrafted wood furniture. 147 rooms, 4 story. Check-in 4 pm, check-out noon. Restaurant, bar. Fitness room. Outdoor pool, whirlpool. **$**

Specialty Lodgings

EAGLES NEST BED AND BREAKFAST. *41675 Big Bear Blvd, Big Bear Lake (92315). Phone 909/866-6465; toll-free 888/866-6465; fax 909/866-6025. www.eaglesnestlodgebigbear.com.* High in the Bernardino Mountains and in the heart of Bear Valley, this bed-and-breakfast is conveniently located close to Snow Summit and Big Bear Mountain ski resorts. 5 rooms, 2 story. Pets accepted, some restrictions. Complimentary full breakfast. Check-in 3-10 pm, check-out 11 am. **$**

SWITZERLAND HAUS BED AND BREAKFAST. *41829 Switzerland Dr, Big Bear Lake (92315). Phone 909/866-3729; toll-free 800/335-3729; fax 909/866-4073. www.switzerlandhaus.com.* This Swiss chalet, at the base of Snow Summit, is close to the lake and village. Recharge with a full breakfast and afternoon snacks in front of the fireplace or on the deck with a great view of the slopes. 5 rooms, 2 story. Complimentary full breakfast. Check-in 2 pm, check-out noon. **$$**

Blythe (K-6)

See also Parker

Settled 1910

Population 12,155
Elevation 270 ft
Area Code 760
Zip 92225
Information Chamber of Commerce, 201 S Broadway; phone 760/922-8166 or toll-free 800/443-5513
Web Site www.blytheareachamberofcommerce.com

Thomas Blythe, an Englishman, came here with an idea of turning this portion of the Colorado River valley into another Nile River valley. The techniques of modern irrigation have allowed that dream to come true, as a series of dams has converted the desert into rich farmland and a vast recreational area. There is still some mining in the Palo Verde valley, and rockhounding is good in some nearby areas.

What to See and Do

Canoe trips. *12400 W 14th Ave, Blythe. Phone 760/922-8753.* One- to five-day self-guided trips on the lower Colorado River. Fishing, boating, water-skiing, camping. Canoe rentals; delivery and pickup. For schedule and fee information, contact Desert Canoe Rentals.

Cibola National Wildlife Refuge. *17 miles S of I-10, on Colorado River near Cibola, AZ. Phone 928/857-3253. southwest.fws.gov.* Large flocks of Canada geese, ducks, sandhill cranes, and wintering passerine birds. Swimming, fishing, boating; hunting; picnicking, visitor center (Mon-Fri; closed holidays).

Palo Verde Lagoon. *20 miles S on Hwy 78.* A natural lake with fishing, picnicking, and camping facilities.

Riverfront camping. There are 30 camps for sports enthusiasts along the banks of the Colorado River, Mayflower Park among them. Approximately 30,000-50,000 people visit here each winter to hunt deer, duck, pheasant, quail, doves, and geese and to fish for bass, crappie, bluegill, and catfish.

Special Events

Blythe Bluegrass Festival. *Colorado River Fairgrounds, 11995 Olive Lake Blvd, Blythe (92225). Phone 760/922-8166. www.blytheareachamberofcommerce.com/bluegrass.* Blythe's first festival of the year features two stages with live Bluegrass music as well as the Husband Calling Contest, a quilt show, and food vendors. Third weekend in Jan.

Colorado River Country Fair. *11995 Olive Lake Blvd, Blythe (92225). Phone 760/922-3247. www.colorador-*

iverfair.com. Stock car races, carnival rides, comedy shows...this fair provides all sorts of entertainment in addition to traditional country fair exhibits like agriculture and 4-H livestock projects. Late Mar-early Apr.

Limited-Service Hotel

★ **HAMPTON INN.** *900 W Hobson Way, Blythe (92225). Phone 760/922-9000; toll-free 800/426-7866; fax 760/922-9011. www.hamptoninn.com.* 59 rooms, 2 story. Check-in 1 pm, check-out 11 am. Wireless Internet access. Fitness room. Outdoor pool, whirlpool. **$**

Borrego Springs (K-5)

See also Anza-Borrego Desert State Park

Population 2,535
Elevation 700 ft
Area Code 760
Zip 92004
Information Chamber of Commerce, 786 Palm Canyon Dr, PO Box 420; phone 760/767-5555 or toll-free 800/559-5524
Web Site www.borregospringschamber.com

Artifacts from the area show that nomadic tribes lived here at least 5,000 years ago. Although prospectors and cattle ranchers had driven through the desert in the late 19th century, it wasn't until 1906 that the first permanent white settler arrived.

In the winter and spring, wildflowers transform the desert's valleys, canyons, and washes into a rainbow of colors, creating an oasis of this charming resort village in the midst of the desert.

What to See and Do

Anza-Borrego Desert State Park. *200 Palm Canyon Dr, Borrego Springs (92004). Phone 760/767-5311. www. anzaborrego.statepark.org.* Approximately 600,000 acres of desert wilderness are preserved here, relieved by an occasional spring-fed oasis and colorful canyons. Highway 78 bisects the park, with Borrego Springs (see), the park headquarters, and the visitor center to the north. Other improved roads are County S-2, S-3, and S-22. Anyone who wants to explore seriously must use a four-wheel-drive vehicle; road condition information is available at the visitor center. Driving across sand can be rough on vehicles and passengers. The best time to visit is November through mid-May. Six hundred species of flowering plants in the park soften the somewhat austere landscape during the spring months. Elephant trees reach the northernmost limits of their range in Anza-Borrego Park; rare smoke trees and fan palms grow here around natural seeps and springs. The park provides a refuge for wildlife, including roadrunners, rare bighorn sheep, and kit foxes. There are nature, hiking, and bridle trails and picnic grounds. Improved campsites (trailer hook-ups in Borrego Springs) are scattered in the park; primitive camping (fee) is allowed throughout the park, and there is a horse campground. Naturalist programs, tours, and campfire programs are offered on weekends (Nov-May). Self-guided auto tour brochures are available at the visitor center (Oct-May, daily; rest of year, weekends and holidays), west of Borrego Springs. For more information, phone 760/767-5311 or 760/767-4205 (visitor center). **$**

Limited-Service Hotel

★ ★ **BORREGO SPRINGS RESORT.** *1112 Tilting T Dr, Borrego Springs (92004). Phone 760/767-5700; toll-free 888/826-7734; fax 760/767-5710. www. borregospringsresort.com.* 100 rooms, 2 story. Pets accepted; restrictions; fee. Complimentary continental breakfast. Check-in 4 pm, check-out noon. Restaurant. Fitness room. Outdoor pool, whirlpool. Golf. Tennis. Airport transportation available. **$$**

Full-Service Resort

★ ★ ★ **LA CASA DEL ZORRO.** *3845 Yaqui Pass Rd, Borrego Springs (92004). Phone 760/767-5323; fax 760/767-5963. www.lacasadelzorro.com.* Peaceful and scenic, La Casa del Zorro is the type of place travelers visit to relax and recharge. This historic resort dating to 1937 is situated in the heart of San Diego County's striking Anza Borrego Desert. The region's Spanish history inspires the décor in the spacious and inviting rooms, suites, and casitas. Groups or those planning longer visits often opt for the one- to four-bedroom casitas, most of which have private pools or Jacuzzis. This desert paradise's laid-back attitude appeals to overworked individuals who need a break from the hectic pace, while its sophistication draws city slickers who can't quite leave inspired American cuisine, salon services, and fitness facilities behind. 79 rooms. Check-in 4 pm, check-out noon. Restaurant, bar. Children's activity center. Fitness room, spa. Outdoor pool, whirlpool. Tennis. Business center. **$$$**

Full-Service Inn

★ ★ ★ **THE PALMS AT INDIAN HEAD.** *2220 Hoberg Rd, Borrego Springs (92004). Phone 760/767-7788; toll-free 800/519-2624; fax 760/767-9717. www. thepalmsatindianhead.com.* 12 rooms, 2 story. Complimentary continental breakfast. Check-in 3 pm. Check-out noon. Restaurant. Outdoor pool, whirlpool. **$**

Specialty Lodging

BORREGO VALLEY INN. *405 Palm Canyon Dr, Borrego Springs (92004). Phone 760/767-0311; toll-free 800/333-5810; fax 760/767-0900. www.borregovalley-inn.com.* 15 rooms. Closed June-Sept (weekdays). Pets accepted; fee. Children over 14 yers only. Complimentary continental breakfast. Check-in 4 pm, check-out 11 am. Outdoor pool, whirlpool. Airport transportation available. **$$**

Restaurants

★ **BERNARD'S.** *575 Palm Canyon Dr, Borrego Springs (92004). Phone 760/767-5666.* American menu. Lunch, dinner. Closed Sun. Bar. Casual attire. **$**

★ ★ **BUTTERFIELD ROOM.** *3845 Yaqui Pass Rd, Borrego Springs (92004). Phone 760/767-5323; fax 760/767-5963. www.lacasadelzorro.com.* Beautiful oil paintings of the Old West Butterfield Stageline adorn the thick white-washed adobe walls of this sophisticated restaurant. Candlelight and sparkling table settings create a romantic atmosphere in which to enjoy chef Peter Brinckerhoff's creative California cuisine. The menu changes throughout the year, taking advantage of the freshest seasonal ingredients. American menu. Breakfast, lunch, dinner. Bar. Jacket required. Reservations recommended. Outdoor seating. **$$$**

Brentwood (J-4)

Brentwood is an upscale community, with trendy boutiques, gourmet grocery stores, and posh restaurants, which center around San Vicente Boulevard.

What makes San Vicente different from Rodeo Drive is the community that surrounds it. Large luxury apartment complexes house wealthy divorces, young urban professionals, and children of the rich and famous. Further up the hill, mostly families inhabit large houses—so Brentwood has a young and whole-some air about it.

The local Starbucks is filled with yoga-mat-toting ladies, the boutiques crammed with young mothers buying hip gear for their trendy tots, and watering holes are more about a quiet cocktail than a randy pickup scene. The geographic intersection between the West Side and the beach, Brentwood has a fervent urban energy infused with a breezy beach vibe.

Restaurants

★ ★ **CHIN CHIN.** *11740 San Vincente Blvd, Brentwood (90049). Phone 310/826-2525. www.chinchin. com.* Chinese menu. Lunch, dinner. Casual attire. **$$**

★ ★ **TAKAO.** *11656 San Vicente Blvd, Los Angeles (90049). Phone 310/207-8636.* Gracing Brentwood's Restaurant Row with raw-fish delicacies that many foodies and sushi-savvy Hollywood players place among the city's best, Takao dispenses with ambitious ambience to concentrate on its customers palates. The small, basic, pseudo-diner-style space serves as a neutral canvas for colorful specialties (some flown in fresh from Japan) like bonito and kampachi yellowtail. While extolling the restaurants delightfully spicy rolls, the smart, very helpful waitstaff also highlights the non-fish and more budget-friendly offerings, which include tempura, teriyaki, and a satisfying bento box lunch special. Japanese menu. Lunch, dinner. Casual attire. Reservations recommended. Valet parking. **$$**

★ ★ **TOSCANA.** *11633 San Vicente Blvd, Los Angeles (90049). Phone 310/820-2448.* This clubby Italian restaurant oozes subdued style with its glossy wooden shades, dazzling copper pizza oven, and golden hues that bathe the dining room in soothing light. Powerful men in suits do business over grilled steaks, while couples on romatic dates share pizza and wine. Effusive waiters with thick accents will steer you through the superb menu, which includes fresh pastas, creamy risottos, and manly cuts of meat. Although you will likely be seated next to a studio head, everyone here is treated like a VIP. Italian menu. Lunch, dinner. Casual attire. Reservations recommended. **$$$**

★ ★ **VINCENTI.** *11930 San Vicente Blvd, Los Angeles (90049). Phone 310/207-0127. www.vincentiristorante. com.* A West Side favorite for fine Italian fare, Vincenti draws high-powered business types, village-dwelling celebrities, and inveterate people watchers who can afford to dress the part. The restaurants discreetly-lit contemporary décor—lush shades of red with highlights of blonde wood and marble surround plush banquettes

and impeccably set tables—is warmed considerably by the open kitchen, from which signature entrées like roasted quail and filet of Mediterranean sea bass emerge. The menu and atmosphere are rich enough to make the excellent handmade pastas, extensive wine list, and superior service feel like pleasant afterthoughts. Italian menu. Dinner. Closed Sun. Bar. Casual attire. Reservations recommended. Valet parking. **$$$**
🅳

Buena Park (J-4)

See also Anaheim, Disneyland, Fullerton, La Habra, Long Beach, Santa Monica, Whittier

Population 78,282
Elevation 74 ft
Area Code 714
Information Convention & Visitors Office, 6601 Beach Blvd, 90621; phone 714/521-0261
Web Site www.buenapark.com

What to See and Do

Knott's Berry Farm. *8039 Beach Blvd, Buena Park (90620). 2 miles S of Santa Ana Frwy (Hwy 101, I-5) on Hwy 39. Phone 714/220-5200. www.knotts.com.* At this thrill-a-minute amusement park, the official home of Snoopy and the other beloved Peanuts characters, be sure to test your moxie on GhostRider—at 4,533 feet, it's the longest wooden roller coaster in the Western United States. The hair-rising ride starts with a 108-foot swooping drop, then continues with 13 additional hills and banked turns, sometimes reaching speeds that exceed 60 mph. But it's just one of the more than 165 rides, shows, attractions, restaurants, and shops that make this 160-acre park a favorite with families. The youngest of the bunch especially go gaga over Camp Snoopy, a 6-acre playland packed with fun for the little ones, such as Snoopy's Red Baron airplanes and Charlie Brown Speedway. (Opens at 10 am daily; closing times vary by season; closed Dec 25) **$$$$**

Ripley's Believe It or Not Museum. *7850 Beach Blvd, Buena Park (90620). Opposite Movieland Wax Museum. Phone 714/522-7045. www.ripleysbuenapark.com.* Houses a collection of oddities and anthropological artifacts that allow visitors to experience firsthand that truth is indeed stranger than fiction. (Mon-Fri 11 am-5 pm, Sat-Sun 10 am-6 pm) **$$**

Limited-Service Hotels

★ **BEST WESTERN INNSUITES HOTEL & SUITES.** *7555 Beach Blvd, Buena Park (90620). Phone 714/522-7360; toll-free 888/522-5885; fax 714/523-2883. www.bestwestern.com.* 172 rooms, 2 story, all suites. Complimentary continental breakfast. Check-in 3 pm, check-out noon. Outdoor pool, whirlpool. **$**
🏊

★★ **COURTYARD BY MARRIOTT.** *7621 Beach Blvd, Buena Park (90620). Phone 714/670-6600; toll-free 800/321-2211; fax 714/670-0360. www.buenapark-courtyard.com.* 145 rooms, 2 story. Check-in 3 pm, check-out 1 pm. High-speed Internet access. Restaurant, bar. Fitness room. Outdoor pool, whirlpool. Business center. **$**
🏋 🏊 🏃

★ **GOOD NITE INN.** *7032 Orangethorpe Ave, Buena Park (90621). Phone 714/523-1488; fax 714/523-8474. www.hotels.com.* 134 rooms, 3 story. Complimentary continental breakfast. Check-in 3 pm, check-out noon. Outdoor pool. **$**
🏊

★★ **HOLIDAY INN.** *7000 Beach Blvd, Buena Park (90620). Phone 714/522-7000; fax 714/522-3230. www.hibuenapark.com.* 248 rooms, 5 story. Check-in 3 pm, check-out noon. High-speed Internet access. Restaurant, bar. Fitness room. Outdoor pool, whirlpool. Business center. **$**
🏋 🏊 🏃

Full-Service Hotels

★★ **EMBASSY SUITES.** *7762 Beach Blvd, Buena Park (90620). Phone 714/739-5600; toll-free 800/362-2779; fax 714/521-9650. www.embassy-suites.com.* This branch of the Hilton chain is conveniently located near Disneyland, Knott's Berry Farm (one block), and the Anaheim Convention Center. Enjoy complimentary breakfast each morning and two hours of beverages and cocktails in the evening. 201 rooms, 4 story, all suites. Complimentary full breakfast. Check-in 3 pm, check-out noon. Restaurant, bar. Fitness room. Outdoor pool, children's pool, whirlpool. Business center. **$$**
🅳 🏋 🏊 🏃

★★★ **MARRIOTT NORWALK.** *13111 Sycamore Dr, Norwalk (90650). Phone 562/863-5555; toll-free 800/228-9290; fax 562/868-4486. www.marriotthotels.*

com/laxnk. 173 rooms, 8 story. Check-in 3 pm, check-out noon. Restaurant, bar. Fitness room. Outdoor pool, whirlpool. **$**

🏃 🛏️

★ ★ ★ **SHERATON CERRITOS HOTEL AT TOWNE CENTER.** *12725 Center Court Dr, Cerritos (90703). Phone 562/809-1500; toll-free 800/598-1753; fax 562/403-2080. www.sheraton.com.* 203 rooms, 8 story. Check-in 3 pm, check-out noon. Restaurant, bar. Fitness room. Outdoor pool, whirlpool. Business center. **$**

🏃 🛏️ 🚶

Burbank (J-4)

Population 100,316
Elevation 598 ft
Web Site www.ci.burbank.ca.us

One of the many satellite-bedroom communities ringing central Los Angeles, Burbank has a mind, ambience, and mythology of its own. For instance, not only was it not founded by noted botanist Luther Burbank, it was in fact the creation of a dentist who wanted to branch out into real-estate speculation. The subject of frequent humor on the classic TV comedy series *Laugh-In,* beautiful downtown Burbank is thriving with television (NBC Studios) and independent motion-picture activities as well as first-rate lodging, dining, and shopping outlets.

Long a favorite with LA Basin locals, the Burbank airport has direct and convenient connecting flights to major California and US cities. By taking the venerable Cahuenga Pass heading east off the 101 in Hollywood, you could be in beautiful downtown Burbank in minutes, to see mountainous corridors to the north and west, a variety of local parks, and several neighborhoods off Burbank Boulevard with excellent samples of classic California/Spanish/Mediterranean architecture. It is convenient to Glendale and downtown LA to the southeast, the Simi Valley and Thousand Oaks to the west. Major arteries (the 5, 110, and 210) lead directly to or nearby Burbank.

What to See and Do

NBC Studios Tour. *3000 W Alameda Ave, Burbank (91523). Phone 818/840-4444. www.nbc.com.* This hour-long walking tour of the interior of the NBC television studio is your chance to see a studio devoted to television production, as opposed to the movie studios you'll find in the area. You'll see where *The Tonight Show* is filmed, and you'll catch a peek at wardrobe, makeup, and set design departments. The tour is limited, however, which is reflected in the relatively low admission price. If you're interested in a more extensive behind-the-scenes tour, try the Warner Brothers Studios VIP Tour or the tour at Universal Studios. (Mon-Fri 9 am-3 pm; closed holidays) **$$**

Warner Brothers Studios VIP Tour. *3400 Warner Blvd, Burbank (91522). Phone 818/846-1403. www.studio-tour.com.* This tour, lasting 2 hours and 15 minutes, is one of the best tours of a Hollywood studio you'll find. Here, you'll hop aboard a tour cart that's similar to a golf cart, but about twice the size, and you're not restricted to staying on the cart at all times—you'll have opportunities to get out and walk around, seeing some of the sets up close. Every tour is different, because this is a working studio, but you may be able to see New York Street, which has been used in the filming of the hit NBC show *ER;* French Street, where the Paris scenes from *Casablanca* were filmed; or even the sets of shows like *Gilmore Girls, Two and a Half Men,* and *Joey.* A highlight of the tour is the possibility of seeing a real-live celebrity walking around the lots. *Note:* no children under 8 years old allowed. (Oct-Apr: Mon-Fri 9 am-3 pm; May-Sept: Mon-Fri 9 am-4 pm; closed Sat-Sun, Jan 1, Thanksgiving, Dec 25) **$$$$**

Full-Service Hotel

★ ★ ★ **GRACIELA.** *322 N Pass Ave, Burbank (91505). Phone 818/842-8887; fax 818/260-8999. www.thegraciela.com.* Located in the heart of Burbank, the Graciela is a modern, luxurious place from which to access the areas many draws, including the entertainment-industry hot spots of Universal Studios and NBC Studios, not to mention Disneyland and the many museums, theaters, and sporting events of Los Angeles. Though you won't find a restaurant in the hotel itself, the area has hundreds of possibilities—at least 37 of which are in the nearby Universal City Walk. The guest rooms are modern with simple, clean lines, decorated with white bed linens and light wood furniture. Though the hotel doesn't have a pool, you can soak in the Jacuzzi or lounge in the sun on the rooftop deck to get that tan that proves you've spent some time in Southern California. 101 rooms. Pets accepted; fee. Check-in 3 pm, check-out noon. High-speed Internet access. Restaurant, bar. Fitness room. Whirlpool. Airport transportation available. Business center. **$$**

🐾 🏃 🚶

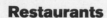

Restaurants

★ **BOB'S BIG BOY.** *4211 Riverside Dr, Burbank (91505). Phone 818/843-9334. www.bobs.net.* Built in 1949, this 24-hour diner is a blast from the past, with neon signage, tacky orange awnings, plastic booths, and the ubiquitous sculpture of Big Boy himself. High school kids, families, night-clubbers, and senior citizens alike opt for the historic Big Boy burger, reportedly the first triple-level burger in existence. A classic car show is held in the parking lot every Friday night, and on Saturday and Sunday nights, there's actual carhop service. American menu. Breakfast, lunch, dinner, late-night. Children's menu. Casual attire. Outdoor seating. **$**

★ **ZEKE'S SMOKEHOUSE.** *2209 Honolulu Ave, Montrose (91020). Phone 818/957-7045; toll-free 888/900-1434; fax 818/957-2545. www.zekessmokehouse.com.* LA's brimming culinary melting pot has chased some of the city's best American barbecue to the suburbs. About 20 miles north of downtown in the foothill hamlet of Montrose, Zeke's Smokehouse is the real deal: a neighborhood fire pit tucked behind a tidy storefront and busy counter—where customers can place their orders or request a checker-clothed table for service. Baby back ribs, spareribs, pulled pork, chicken and sausage—all slow-cooked over wood chips and glazed with pungent sauces—make for hearty eating. The Zeke's Feast menu option incorporates three of the featured meats. Barbecue menu. Lunch, dinner. Bar. Children's menu. Casual attire. Outdoor seating. **$$**

Calabasas

See also Anaheim, Fullerton, La Habra, Long Beach, Santa Monica, Whittier, Disneyland

The 101 southbound from Ventura directs you to the bedroom community of Calabasas, which is less than a mile south of the freeway, on Calabasas Road, and a few miles short of fabled Mulholland Drive, which runs north and south and serves as the gateway to the Los Angeles complex of cities. Look for Park Moderne, a nature lover's dream masquerading at a housing tract. Located just behind the sprawling campus of Calabasas High School, Park Moderne features what the locals call "the Bird Streets." Turn east off Old Topanga Road onto Blue Bird Drive. Park, and then walk to the footpath running between Meadowlark Drive and Black Bird Way for a memorable stroll

through rich varieties of trees, shrubs, gentle hills, patches of volunteer flowers, and a seemingly endless variety of birds and ground squirrels. Check out Old Town (on Calabasas Road) for restaurants, boutiques, and specialty shops that not only reflect Calabasas's early Spanish ranch days ("Calabasas" means "gourds" in Spanish) but the contemporary denizens' eclectic tastes in food, art, and antiques. Grape Arbor Park at the Corner of Canwood and Parkville is an excellent site for an impromptu picnic, a rest from the road, and a chance to see more of the chaparral and flowers that flood the area year-round with bright colors.

Restaurant

★ ★ ★ **SADDLE PEAK LODGE.** *419 Cold Canyon Rd, Calabasas (91302). Phone 818/222-3888; fax 818/222-1054. www.saddlepeaklodge.com.* A destination-worthy refuge from LA, Saddle Peak rewards trek-making diners with both atmosphere and cuisine. Set in a former hunting lodge in the hills above Malibu, the 100-plus-year-old landmark is filled with the trappings of the Old West, including badger and buffalo heads, old fishing tackle, and antique landscapes busily decorating the walls. Chef Warren Schwartz seizes the rustic moment to present his specialty: game. The menu proffers elk, buffalo, deer, boar, quail, and partridge. Like wedding parties and birthday celebrants, go for a memorable special event. Wild game menu. Dinner, Sun brunch. Closed Mon-Tues. Jacket required. Reservations recommended. **$$$**

Calexico (K-5)

See also El Centro

Founded 1908
Population 27,109
Elevation 2 ft
Area Code 760
Information Chamber of Commerce, 1100 Imperial Ave, PO Box 948, 92232; phone 760/357-1166
Web Site www.calexicochamber.ca.gov

Once a tent town of the Imperial Land Company, this community at the south end of the Imperial Valley is separated from its much larger sister city, Mexicali, Mexico, by only a fence. The town represents the marriage of two diverse cultures. It serves as a port of entry to the United States. (For Border Crossing Regulations see MAKING THE MOST OF YOUR TRIP.)

Limited-Service Hotel

★ ★ **GUESTHOUSE INTERNATIONAL HOTEL & SUITES.** *801 Imperial Ave, Calexico (92231). Phone 760/357-3271; fax 760/357-7975.* 57 rooms, 2 story. Check-in 1 pm, check-out noon. Restaurant. Outdoor pool. **$**

Camarillo

See also Oxnard, Thousand Oaks, Ventura

Population 57,077
Elevation 160 ft
Area Code 805
Zip 93010
Information Chamber of Commerce, 2400 E Ventura Blvd; phone 805/484-4383
Web Site www.camarillochamber.org

What to See and Do

Camarillo Factory Stores. *740 Ventura Blvd, Camarillo (93010).* Hwy 101, Las Posas Rd exit. *Phone 805/445-8520.* www.premiumoutlets.com. Over 100 outlet stores.

Channel Islands Aviation. *305 Durley Ave, Camarillo (93010). Phone 805/987-1301.* www.flycia.com. This company, the official provider of flights for Channel Islands National Park, offers day trips to Santa Rosa Island. The flight takes just 25 minutes. Surf fishing safaris and camping trips are available as well. (Daily; closed Jan 1, Dec 25) **$$$$**

Limited-Service Hotels

★ **BEST WESTERN CAMARILLO INN.** *295 Daily Dr, Camarillo (93010). Phone 805/987-4991; fax 805/388-3679.* www.bestwestern.com. 58 rooms, 2 story. Complimentary continental breakfast. Check-in noon, check-out 11 am. Outdoor pool, whirlpool. **$**

★ **COUNTRY INN & SUITES BY CARLSON.** *1405 Del Norte Rd, Camarillo (93010). Phone 805/983-7171; toll-free 800/456-4000; fax 805/983-1838.* www.countryinns.com. This branch of the Carlson chain has rooms with country décor. Located on scenic Highway 101, you'll be near Magic Mountain and various shops. 100 rooms, 3 story. Complimentary full breakfast. Check-in 3 pm, check-out noon. Outdoor pool, whirlpool. **$**

★ **HOLIDAY INN EXPRESS.** *4444 Central Ave, Camarillo (93010). Phone 805/485-3999; fax 805/485-1820.* www.holiday-inn.com. 110 rooms, 3 story. Complimentary continental breakfast. Check-in 3 pm, check-out noon. Outdoor pool, whirlpool. **$**

Restaurants

★ ★ **MONEY PANCHO.** *3661 Las Posas Rd, Camarillo (93010). Phone 805/484-0591; fax 805/484-0593.* Mexican menu. Breakfast, lunch, dinner. Children's menu. **$$**

★ ★ **OTTAVIO'S.** *1620 Ventura Blvd, Camarillo (93010). Phone 805/482-3810; fax 805/987-3714.* www.ottavio.com. Italian menu. Lunch, dinner. Closed holidays. Bar. **$$**

Cambria (G-2)

See also Morro Bay, San Simeon

Population 6,232
Elevation 65 ft
Area Code 805
Zip 93428
Information Chamber of Commerce, 767 Main St; phone 805/927-3624
Web Site www.cambriachamber.org

Cambria's early commerce centered on lumbering, ranching, mining, and shipping. However, the town's shipping and whaling volume declined as trade relied on the railroad extending to San Luis Obispo. Today, Cambria is known as an artists' colony on California's central coast; there are many art galleries and gift and antique shops throughout town.

What to See and Do

Beach recreation. Rock and surf fishing at Moonstone Beach. Whale-watching late Dec-early Feb. The large rocks at Piedras Blancas are a prime refuge for sea lions and sea otters.

Limited-Service Hotel

★ **BEST WESTERN FIRESIDE INN ON MOONSTONE BEACH.** *6700 Moonstone Beach Dr, Cambria (93428). Phone 805/927-8661; toll-free 888/910-7100; fax 805/927-8584.* www.bestwestern-firesideinn.com. 46 rooms. Complimentary continental breakfast. Check-in 3 pm, check-out 11 am. Outdoor pool, whirlpool. **$**

Specialty Lodgings

BURTON DRIVE INN. *4022 Burton Dr, Cambria (93428). Phone 805/927-5125; toll-free 800/572-7442; fax 805/927-9637. www.burtoninn.com.* A bright blue entrance welcomes you to this property located in the center of town. All units are spacious at 600 square feet each. Drive to historic Hearst Castle (see) and area wineries or walk to local restaurants and shops. 10 rooms, 2 story. Complimentary continental breakfast. Check-in 3 pm. Check-out 11 am. **$**

J. PATRICK HOUSE BED AND BREAKFAST. *2990 Burton Dr, Cambria (93428). Phone 805/927-3812; toll-free 800/341-5258; fax 805/927-6759. www.jpatrickhouse.com.* A refreshing, wooded setting minutes from the ocean is home to a main log cabin and a charming seven-room Carriage House. A full breakfast is served each morning in the cozy living room before you head out to antiquing and wine tasting. 8 rooms, 2 story. Complimentary full breakfast. Check-in 3-7 pm, check-out 11 am. **$$**

SQUIBB HOUSE. *4063 Burton Dr, Cambria (93428). Phone 805/927-9600; toll-free 866/927-9600; fax 805/927-9606. www.squibbhouse.net.* The current owner painstakingly restored this yellow Italianate structure to its original 1877 splendor. You'll find the same handcrafted pine furniture that's in your room in the 100-year-old Shop Next Door. A nice find in the heart of the village. 5 rooms, 2 story. Complimentary continental breakfast. Check-in 3-6 pm, check-out 11 am. **$$**

Restaurants

★ ★ **THE BRAMBLES DINNER HOUSE.** *4005 Burton Dr, Cambria (93428). Phone 805/927-4716; fax 805/927-3761. www.bramblesdinnerhouse.com.* Victorian décor; antiques. American menu. Dinner, Sun brunch. Bar. Children's menu. Outdoor seating. **$$**

★ ★ **ROBIN'S.** *4095 Burton Dr, Cambria (93428). Phone 805/927-5007; fax 805/927-1320. www.robinsrestaurant.com.* Asian, vegetarian menu. Lunch, dinner. Closed Thanksgiving, Dec 25. Outdoor seating. **$$**

Campo
See also Morro Bay, San Simeon

What to See and Do

Golden Acorn Casino. *1800 Golden Acorn Way, Campo (91906). From San Diego, take I-8 east to the Crestwood exit. Phone toll-free 866/794-6244. www.goldenacorn-casino.com.* This combination casino-truck stop, operated by the Campo Band of the Kumeyaay Nation, is just off the interstate. Gamblers can choose from 750 slots or a variety of card games. There's a trucker's lounge for those making hauls of another kind. Attached to the casino is the Golden Grill, a 24-hour restaurant serving night owls and anyone needing a break from the dark desert highway. (Daily) **FREE**

Carlsbad (K-4)
See also Del Mar, Escondido, La Jolla, Oceanside, San Diego, San Juan Capistrano

Population 78,247
Elevation 39 ft
Area Code 760
Information Convention & Visitors Bureau, 400 Carlsbad Village Dr, PO Box 1246, 92018; phone 760/434-6093 or toll-free 800/227-5722
Web Site www.visitcarlsbad.com

Named for Karlsbad, Bohemia (now in the Czech Republic), a famous European spa, this beach-oriented community is a playground for golfers, tennis players, water-skiers, and fishing enthusiasts.

What to See and Do

Legoland. *1 Legoland Dr, Carlsbad (92008). Phone 760/918-5346. www.legoland.com.* A bright red dinosaur—9 feet tall, 34 feet from head to tail, and made entirely from Lego bricks—is the first thing guests see upon entering Legoland. Everything here is made of Legos, from the fairy-tale characters along Fairy Tale Brook to the horses that kids ride through an enchanted forest. Designed for children ages 2-12, the 128-acre park has 60 family rides, hands-on attractions, and shows, plus a special area designed to interest toddlers. The park's centerpiece is Miniland, which replicates areas of New York, Washington, DC, the California coastline, New Orleans, and an interactive New England harbor scene in 1:20 scale, using 20 million Lego bricks. (Daily, opens at 10 am) **$$$$**

Leo Carrillo Ranch Historic Park. *6200 Flying LC Ln, Carlsbad (92009). E of I-5 and S of Palomar Airport Rd; turn on Carrillo Way from Melrose Dr. Phone 760/476-1042. www.carrillo-ranch.org.* This 27-acre park, once part of a working ranch, was made possible by actor Leo Carrillo, best known for his role as Pancho on the television show *The Cisco Kid.* Carrillo participated in a number of conservation efforts in Southern California and conceived of this ranch in the 1930s as a tribute to his Mexican ancestors who helped settle the area. (Carrillo's great-grandfather was the first provisional governor of California.) A number of buildings have been restored, including the main hacienda, cantina, barn, wash house, and foundry. Guided tours are given Saturday and Sunday. (Summer: Tues-Sat 9 am-6 pm, Sun 11 am-6 pm; fall, winter, and spring: Tues-Sat 9 am-5 pm, Sun 11 am-5 pm) **FREE**

Museum of Making Music. *5790 Armada Dr, Carlsbad (92008). Phone 760/438-5996. www.museumofmaking-music.org.* Take the whole family on a journey through 100 years of music as you explore all genres from the Victorian era up through the MTV generation. This relatively new museum tells musics stories through more than 450 vintage instruments, multimedia presentations, and interactive listening stations where visitors can tune into some of culture's most influential music. One hundred years of music is put into an historical perspective and made fun for every age level; while the kids are making their own music with guitars, drums, and pianos, you can try your hand at a *theremin*—a wooden box with two antennas that works when you interrupt sound waves with your hand—and learn how the Beach Boys made those high-pitched sounds at the beginning of "Good Vibrations." (Tues-Sun 10 am-5 pm; closed holidays) **$**

South Carlsbad State Beach. *3 miles S on Carlsbad Blvd. Phone 760/438-3143; toll-free 800/444-7275.* Swimming, surfing, fishing; improved camping (dump station).

Special Events

Carlsbad Village Street Faire. *414 Carlsbad Village Dr, Carlsbad (92008).* More than 850 art, craft, and antique vendors; food, entertainment. First Sun in May and first Sun in Nov.

Flower Fields at Carlsbad Ranch. *5704 Paseo Del Norte, Carlsbad (92008). Phone 760/431-0352. www.*

theflowerfields.com. From its roots as a family-owned flower operation, the annual Flower Fields at Carlsbad Ranch has bloomed into a local phenomenon—all thanks to the beautiful Tecolote Giant Ranunculus. Brought to California by a British immigrant and horticulturist, this Asian relative of the buttercup first decorated his garden. Now it grows on 50 rainbow-splashed acres. Locals consider the March flowering to be a harbinger of spring, and more than 150,000 visitors per year agree. To avoid the crowds, your best bet is to visit on a weekday before noon, although this means sacrificing the fairs and festivals scheduled for weekends in March and April. Either way, and whatever the color of your thumb, the experience is rejuvenating. Mar-May, daily. **$$**

Limited-Service Hotels

★ **BEACH TERRACE INN.** *2775 Ocean St, Carlsbad (92008). Phone 760/729-5951; fax 760/729-1078. www.beachterraceinn.com.* This Best Western, located right on the beach, is a step up from many others in the chain. The outdoor pool is small, but it has a generous pool deck overlooking the beach. Plenty of lounge chairs are available, as well as tables with umbrellas. The rooms are serviceable; many have a fireplace and ocean view. The hotel is just a short walk from shops and restaurants, and only a few miles from Legoland (see) and other recreational activities. 49 rooms, all suites. Check-in 3 pm, check-out 11 am. Beach. Outdoor pool. **$**
🏖

★ **CARLSBAD INN BEACH RESORT.** *3075 Carlsbad Blvd, Carlsbad (92008). Phone 760/434-7020; toll-free 800/235-3939; fax 760/729-4853. www. carlsbadinn.com.* 56 rooms, 3 story. Check-in 4 pm, check-out 11 am. Children's activity center. Fitness room. Near the beach. **$$**
🧍

★ ★ **HILTON GARDEN INN CARLSBAD BEACH.** *6450 Carlsbad Blvd, Carlsbad (92011). Phone 760/476-0800; toll-free 800/774-1500; fax 760/476-0801. www.hiltongardeninn.com.* This hotel is particularly well suited to the business traveler, but families will find much to enjoy here as well. The rooms are traditionally decorated in mauves, greens, and blues, with floral bedspreads. You'll also find a large desk, high-speed Internet access, and a refrigerator and microwave. The outdoor pool has a an attractive deck area where you can work on your tan, and you're located a stone's throw from the beach. Within 2 miles of the hotel is Legoland (see). Thirty miles away are the San Diego Zoo, SeaWorld, and the Wild Animal Park. 161 rooms. Check-in 3 pm, check-out noon. High-speed Internet access. Restaurant, bar. Fitness room. Beach. Outdoor pool, whirlpool. Airport transportation available. Business center. **$$**

Full-Service Resorts

★ ★ ★ ★ **FOUR SEASONS RESORT AVI-ARA, NORTH SAN DIEGO.** *7100 Four Seasons Point, Carlsbad (92009). Phone 760/603-6800; toll-free 800/819-5053; fax 760/603-6801. www.fourseasons.com/aviara.* The Four Seasons Resort Aviara is a world away from everyday distractions, yet it is only 30 minutes from San Diego. This splendid resort is nestled on 200 lush acres overlooking the Batiquitos Lagoon, the Pacific Ocean, and a nature preserve that's home to a wide variety of wildlife. The architecture pays homage to the region's history in its Spanish colonial design. An unpretentious elegance is felt throughout the property, especially in the guest rooms. Recognized for its 18-hole course designed by Arnold Palmer, the resort is a favorite of golfers. Carefully preserving the natural landscape, the course is a visual and athletic delight. Relaxation is guaranteed at this resort, whether poolside or at the spa. From the Pool Bar & Grill, California Bistro, and Argyle, with views over the verdant links, to Vivace (see), with floor-to-ceiling windows framing the Pacific Ocean, dining is always with a view. 349 rooms, 5 story. Pets accepted, some restrictions. Check-in 3 pm, check-out noon. Two restaurants, bar. Children's activity center. Fitness room, spa. Outdoor pool, whirlpool. Golf, 18 holes. Tennis. Business center. **$$$$**

★ ★ ★ **LA COSTA RESORT AND SPA.** *2100 Costa Del Mar Rd, Carlsbad (92009). Phone 760/438-9111; toll-free 800/854-5000; fax 760/930-7070. www.lacosta.com.* Guests come to La Costa Resort and Spa to hit the links, bliss out in the spa, feast on mouthwatering meals, and dip their toes in the pool. Blessed with sunny skies and temperate weather, this San Diego-area resort has cornered the market on relaxation. Designed to resemble a Spanish Colonial village, La Costa has a warm, inviting spirit. Two PGA 18-hole golf courses and the US Golf Fitness Association win praise from loyal golfers, while the 21-court tennis center is a big hit with players. The dazzling spa with a Roman waterfall is a light-filled oasis of well-being, and the resort is also home to the renowned Chopra Center, which focuses on helping guests achieve total harmony through ancient Indian Ayurvedic principles. 480 rooms, 3 story. Check-in 4 pm, check-out noon. Restaurant, bar. Children's activity center. Fitness room. Outdoor pool, children's pool, whirlpool. Golf, 36 holes. Tennis. Airport transportation available. Business center. **$$$**

Spa

★ ★ ★ ★ **SPA AT FOUR SEASONS RESORT AVIARA, NORTH SAN DIEGO.** *7100 Four Seasons Point, Carlsbad (92009). Phone 760/603-6800; toll-free 800/819-5053. www.fourseasons.com/aviara.* This resort's love affair with the outdoors comes alive at the spa, where a light-filled, solarium-style lounge brings the outside in. Expansive windows and white wicker furnishings create an airy atmosphere, mimicking the resorts relaxed elegance. Ample seating and plentiful refreshments create a welcoming environment in which to begin or end your spa experience. Both indoor and outdoor treatment rooms are available, and a couples suite is provided for spa sampling à deux. Stress is a four-letter word at this spa, where the treatments focus on relaxing and re-energizing body and spirit. Skin is pampered and perfected here, from the exfoliating and hydrating benefits of a clay sage body treatment and an avocado body wrap to the customized facials. Sugar scrubs buff and polish skin with an intoxicating choice of citrus blend or spicy ginger sugar. Watsu treatments invite you to take a dip in a heated pool, and then let your tensions ease as you are stretched and massaged into delirium. The Four Seasons In One treatment is highly creative and invokes the spirit of the four different seasons. From winter's cooling scrub and spring's floral body wrap to summer's different massages and fall's herbal scalp treatment, this is one memorable way to pass time. Exceeding expectations is all in a day's work here, and thoughtful touches create lasting memories. After your aromatherapy massage ends, you are presented with a sweet-smelling reminder of your visit—a velvet pouch containing the fragrant blend created especially for you.

Restaurants

★ ★ **TUSCANY.** *6981 El Camino Real, Carlsbad (92009). Phone 760/929-8111; fax 760/929-0421. www.tomasos.com/CarlsbadHome.htm.* Italian menu. Lunch, dinner. Closed Thanksgiving. Bar. **$$**

★ **VIGILUCCI'S TRATTORIA ITALIANA.** *505 S Coast Hwy 101, Encinitas (92024). Phone 760/942-7332. www.vigiluccis.com.* Italian menu. Lunch, dinner. Closed Thanksgiving, Dec 25. Bar. Children's menu. Outdoor seating. **$$**

★ ★ ★ **VIVACE.** *7100 Four Seasons Point, Carlsbad (92009). Phone 760/603-3773; fax 760/603-3776. www.fourseasons.com/aviara.* An eclectic mixture of Four Seasons elegance and modern design, Vivace offers rustic yet refined cuisine. The attentive and professional staff takes good care of diners who sup here. Italian menu. Dinner. Children's menu. Valet parking. Outdoor seating. **$$$**

Channel Islands National Park (J-2)

Web Site www.nps.gov/chis

Off the coast of Southern California.

Eight islands extending over a range of 150 miles in the Pacific Ocean make up this chain, of which five islands have been set aside by the government as Channel Islands National Park. Visitors can reach the park by commercial boat (see SANTA BARBARA and VENTURA). Anacapa Island, 14 miles south of Ventura, is actually a slender chain of three islands, 5 miles long with an average width of 1/2 mile; Santa Barbara Island, 38 miles west of San Pedro, is roughly triangular, its greatest dimension being 1 1/4 miles. Santa Cruz Island (30 miles offshore), Santa Rosa Island (40 miles offshore), and San Miguel Island (45 miles offshore) are also part of the park. Santa Rosa can be reached by commercial flights (see CAMARILLO). Camping is permitted on Anacapa, Santa Barbara, Santa Rosa, Santa Cruz, and San Miguel Islands. Permits are issued in advance and may be obtained by calling toll-free 800/365-2267. No pets are permitted on the islands.

On **Anacapa Island** in early spring, there is a spectacular display of wildflowers; a yellow table of the giant coreopsis, with its large flowers, is visible from a great distance. Sea mammals, including the California sea lion and harbor seal, are observed around the island's rocky shores. From January through March, the annual migration of gray whales passes close to Anacapa. The island also has a self-guided nature trail and a museum. Ranger-guided tours are available all year. Scuba and skin diving are popular sports, as the islands are noted for their variety of marine life.

Santa Barbara Island is a marine terrace with steep cliffs, some rising to more than 500 feet. Numerous caves, coves, offshore pillars, and blowholes are also found. Because Santa Barbara is so isolated, sea mammals, including the huge elephant seal, are occasional visitors. Bird-watching is excellent on this island, and numerous species may be observed, including Xantus' murrelet, American kestrel, brown pelican, black oystercatcher, and orange-crowned warbler. Self-guided trails and ranger-conducted walking tours are available.

San Miguel Island (14 square miles) contains an outstanding number of natural features, including caliche, or "fossil forests," which give the island landscape an eerie, almost alien appearance. It is the only island where six pinniped (seals and sea lions) species are found, more than are found in any other single location in the world. To land on the island, you must acquire a permit from the park headquarters prior to your visit.

Santa Rosa Island (53 square miles) is now owned by Channel Islands National Park. Visitors to the island must be accompanied by a park ranger. For camping, a permit is required (phone 805/658-5711). A landing permit is required for ranger-led walks and hikes (arranged by appointment).

Santa Cruz Island (96 square miles) is divided between the National Park Service, which owns and manages the eastern 10 percent, and the Nature Conservancy, which owns and manages the remainder. Information about public access to this island can be obtained from the Santa Cruz Nature Conservancy, 213 Stearns Wharf, Santa Barbara 93101; phone 805/962-9111. A visitor center (open all year) at 1901 Spinnaker Drive in Ventura offers information, exhibits, and audiovisual programs; phone 805/658-5730. For further information, contact the Park Superintendent, 1901 Spinnaker Dr, Ventura 93001; phone 805/658-5700 or 805/658-5730. Camping **$$$**. **FREE**

Chula Vista (K-4)

Population 173,556
Elevation 75 ft
Area Code 619
Web Site www.ci.chula-vista.ca.us

The name Chula Vista is Spanish for "beautiful view." Set between the mountains and the sea, the city lives up to its name.

What to See and Do

Olympic Training Center. *1750 Wueste Rd, Chula Vista (91915). Phone 619/656-1500.* The nation's first year-round, warm-weather, multisport Olympic training facility. Narrated 1 1/2-mile tours (hourly) show Olympic-hopeful athletes training for track and field, tennis, archery, kayaking, rowing, cycling, and soccer. (Daily) **FREE**

Limited-Service Hotel

★ **RAMADA INN SOUTH.** *91 Bonita Rd, Chula Vista (91910). Phone 619/425-9999; toll-free 800/272-6232; fax 619/425-8934. www.ramada.com.* 198 rooms, 4 story. Complimentary continental breakfast. Check-in 4 pm, check-out noon. Outdoor pool, whirlpool. **$** 🏊

Restaurants

★ ★ **BUON GIORNO.** *4110 Bonita Rd, Bonita (91902). Phone 619/475-2660; fax 619/475-5929.* Old-world Italian setting; prints of opera stars adorn walls. Italian menu. Lunch, dinner. Closed Jan 1, Thanksgiving, Dec 25. Bar. Children's menu. Casual attire. **$$**

★ **BUTCHER SHOP.** *556 Broadway, Chula Vista (91910). Phone 619/420-9440.* American, steak menu. Lunch, dinner. Closed Thanksgiving, Dec 25. Bar. Casual attire. **$$$**

Claremont (J-4)

See also Ontario, Pasadena, Pomona, Rancho Cucamonga, Riverside

Population 33,998
Elevation 1,169 ft
Area Code 909
Zip 91711
Information Chamber of Commerce, 205 Yale Ave; phone 909/624-1681
Web Site www.claremontchamber.org

What to See and Do

The Claremont Colleges. *747 N Dartmouth Ave, Claremont. College Ave between 1st St and Foothill Blvd*

(Hwy 66). Phone 909/621-8000. www.claremont.edu. A distinguished group of institutions comprised of Pomona College (1887) (1,500 students), Claremont Graduate School (1925) (1,800 students), Scripps College (1926) (550 students), Claremont McKenna College (1946) (900 students), Harvey Mudd College (1955) (650 students), and Pitzer College (1963) (700 students). On campus are

> **Graduate School Art Building.** *251 E 10th St, Claremont (91711). 10th St and Columbia Ave. Phone 909/621-8071.* Exhibits. (Daily, weekends by appointment)

> **Montgomery Art Gallery.** *330 N College Ave, Claremont. Phone 909/621-8283.* Exhibits. (Tues-Sun afternoons; closed school holidays, also June-Aug)

> **Rancho Santa Ana Botanic Garden.** *1500 N College Ave, Claremont (91711). N of Foothill Blvd. Phone 909/625-8767.* More than 6,000 kinds of native plants. 86 acres laid out in three areas: Indian Hill Mesa, East Alluvial Gardens, and Plant Communities. (Daily; closed holidays) **DONATION**

Limited-Service Hotel

★ **CLAREMONT HOTEL.** *840 S Indian Hill Blvd, Claremont (91711). Phone 909/621-4831; fax 909/621-0411. www.hotelclaremontca.com.* 122 rooms, 2 story. Pets accepted, some restrictions; fee. Complimentary continental breakfast. Check-in 3 pm, check-out noon. Outdoor pool, children's pool, whirlpool. Tennis. **$** 🐾🏊🎾

Restaurant

★ ★ **YIANNIS.** *238 Yale Ave, Claremont (91711). Phone 909/621-2413.* Greek menu. Lunch, dinner, Sun brunch. Bar. Outdoor seating. **$**

Cleveland National Forest (K-4)

What to See and Do

Cleveland National Forest. *3348 Alpine Blvd, Alpine (91901). Phone 858/673-6180. www.fs.fed.us/r5/cleveland.* Nearly 420,000 acres; a dense chaparral environment with conifers at higher levels, treelike manzanitas, and the Palomar Observatory (see ESCONDIDO). Fishing;

hiking, riding, nature trails, guided walks; picnicking; camping. Includes Laguna Mountain Recreation Area, 10 miles NE of I-8 on County S1. Fees at developed recreation sites. Contact Forest Supervisor, 10845 Rancho Bernardo Dr, Suite 200, San Diego 92127-2107.

Corona (J-4)

See also Anaheim, Ontario, Riverside

Population 124,966
Elevation 678 ft
Area Code 951
Zip 91719
Information Chamber of Commerce, 904 E 6th St; phone 951/737-3350
Web Site www.coronachamber.org

A Ranger District office of the Cleveland National Forest (see PINE VALLEY) is located in Corona.

What to See and Do

Glen Ivy Hot Springs. *25000 Glen Ivy Rd, Corona (92883). 8 miles S via I-15 at Temescal Canyon Rd exit. Phone 951/277-3529. www.glenivy.com.* Natural hot mineral spa. Swimming, 15 outdoor mineral baths, massage, sauna, clay bath, outdoor poolside dining. Admission limited to guests over 16. (Daily 9:30 am-6 pm; to 5 pm in the cooler season; closed Jan 1, Thanksgiving, Dec 25) **$$$$**

Limited-Service Hotels

★ **AYRES INN CORONA EAST.** *2260 Griffin Way, Corona (92879). Phone 951/734-2140; toll-free 800/451-7463; fax 951/734-4056. www.ayreshotels. com.* 101 rooms, 2 story. Complimentary full breakfast. Check-in 3 pm, check-out noon. Outdoor pool, whirlpool. **$**

★ **DYNASTY SUITES.** *1805 W 6th St, Corona (92882). Phone 951/371-7185; toll-free 800/842-7899; fax 951/371-0401. www.dynastysuites.com.* 56 rooms, 2 story. Pets accepted, some restrictions; fee. Complimentary continental breakfast. Check-out noon. Outdoor pool, whirlpool. **$**

Corona del Mar

See also Newport Beach

Elevation 75 ft
Area Code 949
Zip 92625

This community is part of Newport Beach (see).

Restaurants

★ ★ **THE BUNGALOW.** *2441 E Coast Hwy, Corona del Mar (92625). Phone 949/673-6585; fax 949/673-9583. www.thebungalowrestaurant.com.* Seafood, steak menu. Dinner. Bar. Casual attire. Reservations recommended. Valet parking. Outdoor seating. **$$$**

★ ★ **THE QUIET WOMAN.** *3224 E Pacific Coast Hwy, Corona del Mar (92625). Phone 949/640-7440; fax 949/640-5869. www.quietwoman.com.* American menu. Lunch, dinner, late-night. Closed holidays. Bar. Children's menu. Casual attire. **$$**

Coronado (K-4)

See also San Diego

Population 24,100
Elevation 25 ft
Area Code 619
Zip 92118
Information Coronado Chamber of Commerce, 875 Orange Ave, Suite 107; phone 619/435-9260
Web Site www.coronadochamber.com

Known as the Crown City, Coronado lies across the bay from San Diego and is connected to the mainland by a long, narrow sandbar called the Silver Strand and by the beautiful Coronado Bridge. It is the site of the famous Hotel del Coronado (1888).

What to See and Do

Art in the Park. *1142 Orange Ave, Coronado (92118). www.coronadoartassn.com.* On the first and third Sunday of every month, more than 50 top artists from throughout San Diego County set up their treasures in the center of Coronado Village. They work in every genre, from watercolor to ceramic, metal to oil. This is a juried show, and one of the conditions is that the artists must be there to show their work, so the conversation is guaranteed to be as interesting as the art. (Jan-Dec, first and third Sun)

⭐ **Coronado Walking Tour.** *www.coronadovisitors.com.* Coronado is a place for walkers. Once you drive over the bridge—note that its *the* bridge, so beware of traveling during opportunities for traffic—park your car and start the stroll. The area is beautiful, lush with greenery; the homes have gardens of flowers native only to this part of the country; and the sky is almost always blue. And if shopping is what you want, here it is. Take a walk down Orange Street, where quaint becomes common-place. Everything from San Diegos largest independent bookstore (Bay Books) to clothes that glitter (Kippy's) to gifts that celebrate animals (Art for Wildlife) is here. And when you're tired of walking, hop the ferry to Ferry Landing Marketplace, a center of fine dining, specialty shops, art galleries, and bike rentals. There's also a waterfront park, fishing pier, beach, bike path, and a family amusement center. If that's not enough, don't forget the Farmers' Market every Tuesday from 2:30 to 6 pm.

Limited-Service Hotels

★ **BEST WESTERN SUITES HOTEL CORONADO ISLAND.** *275 Orange Ave, Coronado (92118). Phone 619/437-1666; fax 619/437-0188. www.best-western.com.* If your goal is stay on Coronado Island, but you don't want to spend a fortune, this hotel may be what you're looking for. The hotel itself is nothing out of the ordinary. It offers a very small outdoor pool, with an equally small pool deck for sunbathing. The rooms are serviceable but not fancy. A mile or less from the beach, shopping, golfing, and a movie theater, plus a short drive from San Diego's many attractions, this hotel's location is a major selling point. 63 rooms. Complimentary continental breakfast. Check-in 3 pm, check-out noon. Outdoor pool. **$**
🏊

★ ★ **CROWN CITY INN.** *520 Orange Ave, Coronado Island (92118). Phone 619/435-3116; toll-free 800/422-1173; fax 619/435-6750. www.crowncityinn. com.* 33 rooms, 2 story. Pets accepted, some restrictions; fee. Check-in 3 pm. Check-out 11 am. Restaurant. Outdoor pool. **$**
🐾 🏊

★ ★ **EL CORDOVA HOTEL.** *1351 Orange Ave, Coronado (92118). Phone 619/435-4131; toll-free 800/229-2032; fax 619/435-0632. www.elcordovahotel. com.* Historic mansion (1902). 9 rooms, 2 story. Check-in 3 pm, check-out noon. Restaurant. Outdoor pool. **$**
🐾 🏊

Full-Service Resorts

★ ★ ★ **HOTEL DEL CORONADO.** *1500 Orange Ave, Coronado (92118). Phone 619/435-6611; toll-free 800/468-3533; fax 619/522-8238. www.hoteldel.com.* Few hotels have earned a place in American history like the Hotel del Coronado. Charles Lindbergh was honored here after his first transatlantic flight, and it was at the Del that Marilyn Monroe romped on the beach in *Some Like It Hot.* It is even rumored that the Duke of Windsor met his future wife, Wallis Simpson, here. Set on 31 acres on the charming island of Coronado just off San Diego, this beachfront, Victorian-style paradise is the ultimate sand and surf getaway. A full-service spa lures world-weary travelers, while others indulge in a little retail therapy at the resorts 20 upscale boutiques. Three restaurants are committed to providing exceptional dining in romantic, sophisticated, and casually elegant settings. 688 rooms. Check-in 4 pm, check-out noon. Three restaurants, bar. Children's activity center. Fitness room, spa. Beach. Outdoor pool, whirlpool. Tennis. Business center. **$$$**
🧍 🏊 🏋 🧍

★ ★ ★ **LOEWS CORONADO BAY RESORT.** *4000 Coronado Bay Rd, Coronado (92118). Phone 619/424-4000; toll-free 800/235-6397; fax 619/424-4400. www.loewshotels.com.* Scenically situated on a 15-acre peninsula overlooking San Diego Bay, this romantic yet family-friendly resort has an exclusive air fanned by lush tropical landscaping and the ocean breezes that sweep through its private marina. Casual, Mediterranean-style elegance and expansive water views define the décor from the sunny lobby to the luxe accommodations, which feature spacious balconies and oversized tubs. Stunning sunsets are a frequent highlight at the Azzura Point restaurant (see). Year-round activities include gondola rides, complimentary sailing lessons, and dive-in movies—which unspool poolside on a large screen. San Diego's airport and top attractions are within a 15-mile drive. 450 rooms. Pets accepted. Check-in 4 pm, check-out noon. Restaurant. Children's activity center. Fitness room, spa. Beach. Outdoor pool, children's pool. Tennis. Business center. **$$**
🐾 🧍 🏊 🏋 🧍

★ ★ ★ **THE MANSION AT GLORIETTA BAY.** *1630 Glorietta Blvd, Coronado (92118). Phone 619/435-3101; toll-free 888/267-6236; fax 619/435-6182. www.gloriettabayinn.com.* The Mansion at Glorietta Bay Inn sits on beautiful Coronado Island, just a mile from San Diego's numerous attractions, including the famed San Diego Zoo. Built in 1908 by John Spreckels, one of San Diego's earliest developers, the mansion was converted to a hotel in the mid-1970s. You can choose between staying in the mansion itself, which offers more-luxurious rooms that bespeak the mansion's history, or in the surrounding inn buildings, which are a more modern alternative, perfect for families or business travelers. A complimentary continental breakfast is served daily, but otherwise, you'll need to leave the hotel grounds for dining. Not to worry—many options are within a short walk, and the hotel will make reservations for you upon request. 183 rooms, 2 story. Complimentary continental breakfast. Check-in 3 pm, check-out 11 am. Outdoor pool, whirlpool. Business center. **$$**

★ ★ ★ **MARRIOTT CORONADO ISLAND RESORT.** *2000 Second St, Coronado (92118). Phone 619/435-3000; fax 619/435-4183. www.marriott. com.* At this bayfront resort 5 miles from San Diego's Gaslamp Quarter, a crisp white entrance is a minimalist beginning to 16 tropical acres that are home to waterfalls, koi ponds, strolling flamingos, and two Mediterranean restaurants. For a special getaway, reserve a villa with a private entrance and pool. 300 rooms, 3 story. Pets accepted. Check-in 4 pm, check-out noon. High-speed Internet access. Two restaurants. Fitness room, spa. Three outdoor pools, whirlpool. Tennis. Business center. **$$**

Restaurants

★ ★ ★ **AZZURA POINT.** *4000 Coronado Bay Rd, Coronado (92118). Phone 619/424-4000. www.loewshotels.com.* This space of huge curving windows dresses in some funky but tasteful leopard print. The glorious views of the bay and Pacific will romance you, while you enjoy the imaginative cuisine. California menu. Dinner. Closed Mon. Bar. Children's menu. Valet parking. **$$$**

★ ★ **BRIGANTINE.** *1333 Orange Ave, Coronado (92118). Phone 619/435-4166; fax 619/435-2499. www. brigantine.com.* California menu. Lunch, dinner. Closed holidays. Bar. Children's menu. Casual attire. **$$**

★ ★ **CHEZ LOMA.** *1132 Loma Ave, Coronado (92118). Phone 619/435-0661; fax 619/435-3770. www.chezloma.com.* Historic landmark house (1889). French menu. Dinner. Closed holidays. Bar. Casual attire. Reservations recommended. **$$$**

★ ★ **PEOHE'S.** *1201 1st St, Coronado (92118). Phone 619/437-4474; fax 619/437-8471. www.peohes.com.* American, seafood. Lunch, dinner, Sun brunch. Bar. Children's menu. Casual attire. Outdoor seating. **$$$**

★ ★ **PRIMAVERA.** *932 Orange Ave, Coronado (92118). Phone 619/435-0454; fax 619/435-5381. www.primavera1st.com.* Italian menu. Dinner. Closed Thanksgiving. Bar. **$$$**

★ ★ ★ **PRINCE OF WALES.** *1500 Orange Ave, Coronado (92118). Phone 619/522-8490; fax 619/522-8202. www.hoteldel.com.* Whether inside or alfresco, by candlelight or sunset, this restaurant in the grand Hotel del Coronado (see) is an amazingly romantic dinner spot. The magnificent view of the Pacific and live piano jazz complement the delectable food. California, French menu. Dinner. Closed Mon. Bar. Casual attire. Reservations recommended. Valet parking. Outdoor seating. **$$$**

Costa Mesa (J-4)

See also Huntington Beach, Irvine, Laguna Beach, Newport Beach, Santa Ana

Population 108,724
Elevation 101 ft
Area Code 714 and 949
Information Chamber of Commerce, 1700 Adams Ave, Suite 101, 92626; phone 714/885-9090
Web Site www.costamesa-ca.com/

What to See and Do

Noguchi Garden. *South Coast Plaza Town Center, Costa Mesa. San Diego Frwy at Bristol St. Phone 714/384-5500.* This 1 1/2-acre sculpture garden is world-renowned sculptor Isamu Noguchi's tribute to California's environment. Flanked by two reflective glass buildings and two 40-foot-high concrete walls, the garden features tranquil walks, fountains, flowers, and native grasses and trees. Noguchi's *The Spirit of the Lima Bean* is the centerpiece. (Daily) **FREE**

Special Events

Highland Gathering and Games. *Fairplex, 1101 W McKinley Ave, Pomona (91768). Phone 909/623-3111. www.unitedscottishsociety.com.* Scottish games; dancing; soccer, rugby; piping, drumming competition. Memorial Day weekend.

Orange County Fair. *Orange County Fairgrounds, 88 Fair Dr, Costa Mesa. Phone 714/708-3247. www.ocfair. com.* Rodeo, livestock, exhibits, home arts, contests, photography, nightly entertainment, floriculture display, wine show, carnival, motorcycle races. July. **$$**

Limited-Service Hotels

★ ★ ★ **AYRES HOTEL & SUITES COSTA MESA-NEWPORT BEACH.** *325 Bristol St, Costa Mesa (92626). Phone 714/549-0300; toll-free 800/454-1692; fax 714/662-0717. www.countrysuites.com.* Hand-painted frescoes in the lobby, mahogany furniture in the rooms, and cobblestones and lush flowers in the courtyard welcome, relax, and charm guests of this inn. 171 rooms, 4 story. Complimentary full breakfast. Check-in 3 pm, check-out noon. Restaurant, bar. Fitness room. Two outdoor pools, whirlpools. Airport transportation available. Business center. **$$**

★ **BEST WESTERN NEWPORT MESA INN.** *2642 Newport Blvd, Costa Mesa (92627). Phone 949/650-3020; toll-free 800/554-2378; fax 949/642-1220. www.bestwestern.com.* 97 rooms, 3 story. Complimentary continental breakfast. Check-in noon, check-out noon. Outdoor pool, whirlpool. **$**

★ **COZY INN.** *325 W Bay St, Costa Mesa (92627). Phone 949/650-2055; fax 949/650-6281. www.cozyinn. com.* Near Orange County Airport and Newport Beach and just off Interstate 55, this small, friendly, tidy establishment is perfect for families on a budget. 28 rooms, 2 story. Check-in 2-6 pm, check-out 11 am. Outdoor pool. **$**

★ ★ ★ **HILTON COSTA MESA.** *3050 Bristol St, Costa Mesa (92626). Phone 714/540-7000; toll-free 800/774-1500; fax 714/540-9176. www.hilton.com.* 484 rooms, 7 story. Pets accepted, some restrictions; fee. Check-in 3 pm, check-out noon. Restaurant, bar. Fitness room. Outdoor pool, whirlpool. Airport transportation available. Business center. **$**

★ ★ **HOLIDAY INN.** *3131 S Bristol St, Costa Mesa (92626). Phone 714/557-3000; toll-free 800/221-7220; fax 714/957-8185. www.holiday-inn.com.* 230 rooms, 5 story. Pets accepted. Check-in 3 pm, check-out noon. Restaurant, bar. Fitness room. Outdoor pool, children's pool. Airport transportation available. **$**

★ **RAMADA.** *1680 Superior Ave, Costa Mesa (92627). Phone 949/645-2221; toll-free 800/272-6232; fax 949/650-9125. www.ramada.com.* 140 rooms, 3 story. Pets accepted, some restrictions. Complimentary continental breakfast. Check-in 3 pm, check-out noon. Fitness room. Outdoor pool, whirlpool. Airport transportation available. **$**

★ **VAGABOND INN.** *3205 Harbor Blvd, Costa Mesa (92626). Phone 714/557-8360; toll-free 800/522-1555; fax 714/662-7596. www.vagabondinn.com.* Mission-style building. 133 rooms, 2 story. Pets accepted, some restrictions; fee. Complimentary continental breakfast. Check-in 3 pm, check-out noon. Fitness room. Outdoor pool. **$**

★ ★ **WYNDHAM ORANGE COUNTY AIRPORT.** *3350 Ave of the Arts, Costa Mesa (92626). Phone 714/751-5100; fax 714/751-0129. www.wyndham.com.* Set on nicely landscaped grounds with a lake in back, this business park hotel appeals mainly to business travelers. Terra Nova Cal-Ital Bar & Grille, the on-site restaurant, serves California-Italian fare. 238 rooms, 6 story. Pets accepted; fee. Check-in 3 pm, check-out noon. High-speed Internet access. Restaurant, bar. Fitness room. Outdoor pool, whirlpool. Airport transportation available. **$**

Full-Service Hotels

★ ★ ★ **MARRIOTT SUITES COSTA MESA.** *500 Anton Blvd, Costa Mesa (92626). Phone 714/957-1100; fax 714/966-8495. www.marriott.com.* Offering suites with separate living and sleeping areas, this hotel is located in the heart of the business district. It is minutes from the John Wayne Airport (Orange County), golf, beaches, and more. 253 rooms, 11 story, all suites. Pets accepted; fee. Check-in 4 pm, check-out noon. Restaurant, bar. Fitness room. Outdoor pool, whirlpool. Airport transportation available. Business center. **$$**

★ ★ ★ **WESTIN SOUTH COAST PLAZA.** *686 Anton Blvd, Costa Mesa (92626). Phone 714/540-2500; fax 714/662-6695. www.westin.com.* This hotel is connected to the South Plaza Mall and is near the Anaheim Convention Center, Disneyland, and John Wayne Airport, as well as the South Coast Plaza Retail Center and the Orange County Performing Arts Center. 400 rooms, 16 story. Pets accepted. Check-in 3 pm, check-out 1 pm. Restaurant, bar. Fitness room.

Outdoor pool. Tennis. Airport transportation available. Business center. **$$**

Restaurants

★ ★ ★ **GOLDEN TRUFFLE.** *1767 Newport Blvd, Costa Mesa (92627). Phone 949/645-9858; fax 949/645-7831.* This truffle is a special find! This menu is innovative yet unpretentious. Alan Greeley's trendy restaurant features unforgettable food. Caribbean, French menu. Lunch Tues-Fri, dinner. Closed Sun-Mon; holidays. Outdoor seating. **$$$**

★ ★ **HABANA.** *2930 Bristol St, Costa Mesa (92626). Phone 714/556-0176; fax 714/556-5862. www.restauranthabana.com.* Latin American menu. Lunch, dinner. Closed holidays. Bar. Casual attire. Outdoor seating. **$$**

★ **MEMPHIS CAFE.** *2920 S. Bristol St, Costa Mesa (92626). Phone 714/432-7685; fax 714/708-3785. www.memphiscafe.com.* Roadhouse cafe. American, Cajun/Creole menu. Lunch, dinner, brunch. Closed holidays. Bar. Casual attire. Outdoor seating. **$$**

★ **NELLO CUCINA.** *3333 S Bear St, Costa Mesa (92704). Phone 714/540-3365; fax 714/540-2285. www.nellocucina.com.* Trattoria-style dining in inner courtyard of mall. Italian menu. Lunch, dinner. Closed Jan 1, Easter, Dec 25. Bar. Outdoor seating. **$$**

★ ★ **PINOT PROVENCE.** *686 Anton Blvd, Costa Mesa (92626). Phone 714/444-5900; fax 714/444-5906. www.patinagroup.com.* Housed in the Westin South Coast Plaza, this rustically upscale bistro serves hearty, full-flavored French foods that take advantage of local fresh seafood, top-quality meats, and beautiful produce. Chef Florent Marneau's sauces and accompaniments artfully enhance and complement natural flavors. French menu. Breakfast, lunch, dinner, brunch. Casual attire. **$$$**

★ ★ **SCOTT'S SEAFOOD GRILL & BAR.** *3300 Bristol St, Costa Mesa (92626). Phone 714/979-2400; fax 714/432-8640. www.scottsseafood.com.* Seafood menu. Lunch, dinner, brunch. Closed holidays. Bar. Valet parking. Outdoor seating. **$$$**

★ **TEA AND SYMPATHY.** *369 E 17th St, Costa Mesa (92627). Phone 949/645-4860; fax 949/850-0188. www.englishtearooms.com.* Traditional English tea room. Continental menu. Lunch and afternoon tea. Closed Sun-Mon; Dec 25; July 4. **$**

Crestline (J-4)

See also Lake Arrowhead

Population 10,218
Elevation 5,000 ft
Area Code 909
Zip 92325
Information Chamber of Commerce, 24385 Lake Dr; phone 909/338-2706
Web Site www.crestlinechamber.net

What to See and Do

Lake Gregory Regional Park. *24171 Lake Dr, Crestline. Lake Dr at Gregory Rd, E of town. Phone 909/338-2233.* Swimming beach (late June-Labor Day weekend), waterslide (fee), fishing, rowboats (rentals); picnicking, snack bars, park. **$$**

Silverwood Lake State Recreation Area. *14651 Cedar Cir, Hesperia (92345). 12 miles E off I-15 on Hwy 138. Phone 760/389-2303. www.parks.ca.gov.* Swimming, fishing, boating (rentals); nature and bicycle trails, picnicking, concession, camping (dump station). Visitor center.

Dana Point (J-3)

See also Laguna Beach, Laguna Niguel

This quiet, unhurried town is about halfway between Los Angeles and San Diego. It has nearly 7 miles of prominent ocean-facing bluffs and an exquisite man-made marina, was once named Capistrano Bay. But in honor of the noted author Richard Henry Dana (of Two Years Before the Mast fame), it was renamed. The harbor, with its commodious accommodations for mooring, has more than 50 specialty shops and restaurants; it is a magnet for seagoing Californians and tourists from the world over. It is also the main funnel to the 62-acre Doheny State Park, a popular beach facility for surfing, snorkeling, tidepool examination, and camping.

Full-Service Hotel

★ ★ ★ **MARRIOTT LAGUNA CLIFFS RESORT.** *25135 Park Lantern, Dana Point (92629). Phone 949/661-5000; toll-free 800/533-9748; fax 949/661-5358. www.lagunacliffs.com.* This hotel has great views of the Pacific Ocean; it is located on the cliffs above the bay with 42 acres of lawn and parkland. 376 rooms, 4 story. Pets accepted, some restrictions; fee. Check-in 4 pm, check-out noon. High-speed Internet access. Restaurant, bar. Fitness room, fitness classes available, spa. Two outdoor pools, three whirlpools. Tennis. Business center. **$$$**

Full-Service Resorts

★ ★ ★ ★ THE RITZ-CARLTON, LAGUNA NIGUEL. *1 Ritz-Carlton Dr, Dana Point (92629). Phone 949/240-2000; toll-free 800/241-3333; fax 949/240-1061. www.ritzcarlton.com.* Reminiscent of a Mediterranean villa, The Ritz-Carlton, Laguna Niguel, embodies the best in luxury resort living. Perched atop a 150-foot bluff overlooking the ocean, this resort is a Pacific paradise halfway between Los Angeles and San Diego. Two miles of golden beaches beckon guests, while eight spectacular courses surrounding the property attract avid golfers. Restful sleep is assured in the guest rooms, where California cool meets traditional Europe. Both private and public spaces show off expansive views of the sparkling ocean. Dining venues are plentiful and suit all tastes. 393 rooms, 4 story. Pets accepted, some restrictions; fee. Check-in 4 pm, check-out noon. High-speed Internet access, wireless Internet access. Two restaurants, bar. Fitness room, spa. Beach. Outdoor pool, whirlpool. Tennis. Business center. **$$$$**

★ ★ ★ ★ ★ THE ST. REGIS MONARCH BEACH RESORT & SPA. *One Monarch Beach Resort, Dana Point (92629). Phone 949/234-3200; toll-free 800/722-1543; fax 949/234-3201. www.stregismb. com.* Tucked away on 200 acres high above the Pacific Ocean, The St. Regis Monarch Beach Resort & Spa is a place for exceptional holidays. Well-heeled travelers swoon over the luscious, secluded setting and the playful yet sophisticated Mediterranean design. Elegant marble floors, plush carpets, and massive sofas and chairs grace the public areas. The guest rooms are ravishing, from the swirled rugs and sensual furnishings to the glimmering silk fabrics and decorative accents. Private balconies flaunt ocean or golf course views, and all rooms are fitted with the finest amenities. This full-service resort entices guests to partake in a round of golf, a game of tennis, or a treatment at the Spa Gaucin, while three heated pools complete the beautifully landscaped pool deck. Nature trails encourage others to take the less-traveled path to private beaches, where surfing lessons are available. The joie de vivre of this resort extends to the restaurants,

where chic settings focus attention on the gorgeous views. Pets receive a welcome letter and their own food and water bowls. 400 rooms, 7 story. Pets accepted, some restrictions; fee. Check-in 3 pm, check-out noon. High-speed Internet access. Six restaurants, three bars. Fitness room, fitness classes available, spa. Beach. Three outdoor pools, whirlpool. Golf, 18 holes. Tennis. Business center. **$$$$**

Specialty Lodging

BLUE LANTERN INN. *34343 St of the Blue Lantern, Dana Point (92629). Phone 949/661-1304; toll-free 800/950-1236; fax 949/496-1483. www.bluelanterninn. com.* This inn is located on a bluff overlooking yacht harbor; some rooms have view of the coast. 29 rooms, 3 story. Complimentary full breakfast. Check-in 3 pm, check-out noon. High-speed Internet access. Fitness room. **$$**

Spa

★ ★ ★ ★ SPA GAUCIN. *One Monarch Beach Resort, Dana Point (92629). Phone 949/234-3200; toll-free 800/722-1543. www.stregismonarchbeach.com.* The Spa Gaucin at the St. Regis is the picture of Mediterranean elegance. This facility calms the body and mind with dark woods, Asian-style accents, and mesmerizing features, including three-story water walls and waterfalls. The serenity is palpable and symbolic, as each treatment begins with a guest tossing a coin (and their cares) into the spa's well of desires. European expertise and glorious indulgence influence the treatment menu at the Spa Gaucin. The facials refresh and revitalize with tantalizing treatments. Vitamin C heals dehydrated skin and smooth fine lines, while European deep-cleansing treatments nourish and protect. The four hands healing facial or the Ultralift Facial are the last word in indulgence. The body treatment menu is good enough to eat, with treatments such as the Barely Pear Polish and Orange Silk Body Wrap. The signature Swedish massage is a good bet for total body relaxation, and aromatherapy, sports, shiatsu, and reflexology are also featured. This spa is a terrific spot for couples, where massages, baths, and body treatments may be enjoyed together in the privacy of one of the specially designed couples suites, complete with fireplaces. From teeth whitening and microdermabrasion to sunless tanning, this spa also offers a complete beautifying menu in addition to regular salon services. Fitness regimes are reworked with personal training sessions or time spent

at the fitness center, and this spa also helps get your chi back on track with reiki energy balancing, meditation sessions, and life coaching consultations.

Restaurant

★ ★ ★ ★ **STONEHILL TAVERN.** *One Monarch Beach Resort, Dana Point (92629). Phone 949/234-3318. www.michaelmina.com.* Famed San Francisco chef-turned-restaurateur Michael Mina returns to the site of his first restaurant concept at the St. Regis Monarch Beach Resort & Spa (see) with Stonehill Tavern, an urban bistro offering twists on classic American tavern fare. The space that formerly housed Mina's seafood-only restaurant, Aqua, has been transformed into a sleek, intimate spot by acclaimed New York-based interior designer Tony Chi. The strikingly sophisticated surroundings, with neutral tones, comfortable couches, glass-enclosed booths, and a 500-square-foot terrace offering glorious views of the Pacific Ocean, are the perfect accompaniment to the innovative Modern American cuisine. Highlighting seasonal products from some of California's best farms, the menu includes Mina's signature appetizer "trios"—three different preparations of one ingredient, such as tuna, lobster, or duck. Main courses include an American Kobe burger with truffle cheese, pickled onions, and watercress; and prime short rib with glazed mirepoix, potato puree, and Worcestershire. An impressive wine program focuses on boutique California producers but also includes a diverse selection from Austria, Burgundy, and Champagne and offers many eclectic by-the-glass options. For the finale, top off your meal of comfort food with desserts that are just as…well, comforting. With choices like a root beer float with warm chocolate chip cookies and a peanut butter cake, there aren't any worries Stonehill Tavern can't make disappear. American menu. Dinner. Bar. Business casual attire. Reservations recommended. Outdoor seating. **$$$**

Death Valley National Park (G-5)

See also Huntington Beach, Irvine, Laguna Beach, Newport Beach, Santa Ana

Information PO Box 579, Death Valley, CA 92328; phone 760/786-3200
Web Site www.nps.gov/deva/

Here, approximately 300 miles northeast of Los Angeles, are more than 5,200 square miles of rugged desert, peaks, and depressions—an unusual and colorful geography. The park is one vast geological museum, revealing secrets of ages gone by. Millions of years ago, this was part of the Pacific Ocean; then violent uplifts of the earth occurred, creating mountain ranges and draining water to the west. Today, 200 square miles of the valley are at or below sea level. The lowest point on the continent (282 feet below sea level) is here; Telescope Peak, at 11,049 feet, towers directly above it. The valley itself is about 140 miles long and 4-16 miles wide. The average rainfall is less than two inches a year. From October to May, the climate is very pleasant. In summer, it's extremely hot; a maximum temperature of 134° F in the shade has been recorded. If considered all together, this is the lowest, hottest, and driest area in North America.

Death Valley was named in 1849 when a party of gold hunters took a shortcut here and were stranded for several weeks awaiting help. The discovery and subsequent mining of borax, hauled out by the famous 20-mule teams, led to development of the valley as a tourist attraction.

The visitor center at Furnace Creek is open daily, and offers guided walks, evening programs, and talks (Nov-Apr). Golden Age, Golden Eagle, Golden Access passports (see MAKING THE MOST OF YOUR TRIP) are accepted. Per vehicle **$$**.

Note: Venturing off paved roads in this area in the summer months can be very dangerous. Carefully obey all National Park Service signs and regulations. Make sure that your vehicle has plenty of gas and oil. Carry water when you explore this park, especially in hot weather.

What to See and Do

20-Mule-Team Canyon. *Lone Pine. Phone 760/786-2331.* Viewed from a twisting road on which RVs and trailers are not allowed. (This is an unpaved, one-way road; watch carefully for the entrance sign.)

Artist's Palette. A particularly scenic auto drive (9 miles one way), with spectacular colors. Because of difficult roads, RVs and trailers are advised not to drive here.

Badwater. *Lone Pine. Phone 760/786-2331.*At 279 feet below sea level, near the lowest spot on the North American continent; look for the sea level sign.

Camping. *Phone 760/786-2331.* Developed and primitive camping in the area; limited hook-ups. It is suggested that campers check with the visitor center for important information on camping facilities and road conditions. (Daily) **FREE**

Charcoal kilns. *Phone 760/786-2331.* Beehive-shaped stone structures, formerly used to make charcoal for nearby mines. *Note:* The last mile of the access road is unpaved.

Dante's View. *Phone 760/786-2331.* (5,475 feet) View of Death Valley with a steep drop to 279 feet below sea level at Badwater.

Devil's Golf Course. *Phone 760/786-2331.* Vast beds of rugged salt crystals.

Golden Canyon. *Phone 760/786-2331.* Offers a display of color ranging from deep red to rich gold. A 1-mile trail provides access.

Natural Bridge. *Phone 760/786-2331.* A bridge spanning a rugged canyon in the Black Mountains; 1-mile walking trail.

Rhyolite Ghost Town. *Phone 760/786-2331. www.nps. gov/deva/rhyolite.htm.* This was the largest town in the mining history of Death Valley in the early 1900s; 5,000-10,000 people lived here then. The town bloomed from 1905 to 1910; by 1911, it was a ghost town. One structure still left standing from that era is the "bottle house," constructed of 12,000-50,000 beer and liquor bottles (depending on who does the estimating).

Sand dunes. *Phone 760/786-2331.* Sand blown by the wind into dunes 5 to 100 feet high.

Scotty's Castle. *Phone 760/786-2392.* A desert mansion (circa 1922-1931), designed and built to be viewed as a work of art, as well as a house. The furnishings are typical of the period; many were especially designed and handcrafted for this house. Living history tours are led by costumed interpreters. (Daily 8 am-5 pm) **FREE**

Telescope Peak. *Phone 760/786-2331.* Highest point in the Panamint Range (11,049 feet). Although there is a 14-mile round-trip hiking trail, it is inaccessible in the winter months.

Ubehebe Crater. *Phone 760/786-2331.* Colorful crater left by a volcanic steam explosion.

Visitor center. *Hwy 190, Death Valley (92328). At Furnace Creek. Phone 760/786-3200.* Before continuing on, we recommend that visitors stop here for an orientation film, day-trip suggestions, help in organizing sightseeing routes, and important information on camping areas and road conditions. (Daily 8 am-5 pm)

Zabriskie Point. *Phone 760/786-2331.* View of Death Valley and the Panamint Range from the rugged badlands of the Black Mountains.

Limited-Service Hotels

★ ★ **CARRIAGE INN.** *901 N China Lake Blvd, Ridgecrest (93555). Phone 760/446-7910; toll-free 800/772-8527; fax 760/446-6408. www.carriageinn.biz.* This family-run hotel offers a mix of luxury suites and poolside cabanas. 160 rooms, 1 story. Outdoor pool. **$$**

★ ★ **HERITAGE INN AND SUITES.** *1050 N Norma St, Ridgecrest (93555). Phone 760/446-6543; toll-free 800/843-0693; fax 760/446-3139. www. heritageinnsuites.com.* 169 rooms, 2 story, all suites. Restaurant. **$**

★ ★ **STOVEPIPE WELLS VILLAGE.** *Hwy 190, Death Valley (92328). Phone 760/786-2387; fax 760/786-2389. www.stovepipewells.com.* Landing strip. Panoramic view of the mountains, desert, and dunes. 83 rooms. Pets accepted; fee. Check-in 2 pm, check-out noon. High-speed Internet access. Restaurant, bar. Outdoor pool. **$**

Restaurants

★ **THE 19TH HOLE.** *Hwy 190, Furnace Creek (92328). Phone 760/786-2345. www.furnacecreekresort. com.* Located on a site overlooking the world's lowest golf course (214 feet below sea level), this establishment also offers drive-through service for golf carts. American menu. Breakfast, lunch. Closed June-Sept. **$**

★ **CHARLIE'S PUB & GRILL.** *901 N China Lake Blvd, Ridgecrest (93555). Phone 760/446-7910. www. carriageinn.biz.*Serves family-style food in a unique environment of aircrew memorabilia donated from squadrons around the world. American menu. Dinner. **$**

★ **FARRIS RESTAURANT.** *1050 N Norma St, Ridgecrest (93555). Phone toll-free 800/843-0693.* A favorite dining spot for locals, the Farris Restaurant offers regional American cuisine in a comfortable atmosphere. American menu. Lunch, dinner. **$**

★ ★ ★ **FURNACE CREEK INN DINING ROOM.** *Hwy 190, Death Valley (92328). Phone 760/786-2345; fax 760/786-2423. www.furnacecreekresort.com.* When you are in Death Valley, visit this inn for delicious food. Try their steak while enjoying the 1930s décor under beamed ceilings. American menu. Breakfast, lunch, dinner, brunch. Closed mid-May-mid-Oct. Bar. Children's menu. Business casual attire. Reservations recommended. Valet parking. **$$**

Del Mar (K-4)

See also Carlsbad, La Jolla, Rancho Santa Fe, San Diego

Population 4,389
Elevation 100 ft
Area Code 858
Zip 92014
Information Greater Del Mar Chamber of Commerce, 1104 Camino Del Mar; phone 858/793-5292
Web Site www.delmar.ca.us

This village-by-the sea community offers beautiful white beaches and brilliant sunsets. It is also an attractive area for year-round ballooning.

Special Event

Del Mar Thoroughbred Club. *County Fairgrounds, 2260 Jimmy Durante Blvd, Del Mar. Phone 858/792-4242. www.dmtc.com.* Thoroughbred horse racing. Late July-mid-Sept.

Limited-Service Hotels

★ **BEST WESTERN STRATFORD INN.** *710 Camino del Mar, Del Mar Heights (92014). Phone 858/755-1501; toll-free 800/780-7234; fax 858/794-4055. www.bestwestern.com.* 94 rooms, 2 story. Complimentary continental breakfast. Check-in 4 pm, check-out noon. Two outdoor pools, whirlpool. **$$**

★ **CLARION HOTEL.** *720 Camino Del Mar, Del Mar (92014). Phone 858/755-9765; toll-free 800/451-4515; fax 858/792-8196. www.delmarinn.com.* 81 rooms, 3 story. Pets accepted, some restrictions. Complimentary continental breakfast. Check-in 4 pm, check-out 11 am. Outdoor pool, whirlpool. **$**

Full-Service Hotel

★ ★ ★ **HILTON SAN DIEGO/DEL MAR.** *15575 Jimmy Durante Blvd, Del Mar (92014). Phone 619/792-5200; toll-free 800/833-7904; fax 619/792-9538. www.hilton.com.* This comfortable hotel is located next door to the Del Mar Thoroughbred Club (race track). 256 rooms, 3 story. Pets accepted. Check-in 4 pm, check-out noon. Restaurant, bar. Fitness room. Outdoor pool, whirlpool. Business center. **$$**

Full-Service Resort

★ ★ ★ **L'AUBERGE DEL MAR RESORT AND SPA.** *1540 Camino del Mar, Del Mar (92014). Phone 858/259-1515; toll-free 800/901-9514; fax 858/755-4940. www.laubergedelmar.com.* The natural beauty of Southern California comes alive at L'Auberge Del Mar. Located in the wonderful coastal village of Del Mar near San Diego, the resort occupies more than 5 lush acres on the Pacific Ocean. Feeling every bit the tropical paradise, it is a wondrous hideaway for guests seeking relaxation and rejuvenation. Soft yellow walls and striped fabrics reinforce the sophisticated beach-cottage style of the guest rooms, and fireplaces, terraces, or patios further raise the comfort level. Guests rejoice in the great outdoors here, whether playing a round of golf on the celebrated Tom Fazio-designed course, gazing at the views from a hot air balloon, or enjoying a sunrise hike. The spa is a destination in its own right, luring weary travelers with its tempting array of pampering treatments. J. Taylor's of Del Mar (see) echoes the resort's fresh, energetic vibe with its airy setting and sensational menu. 120 rooms, 3 story. Check-in 4 pm, check-out noon. Restaurant, bar. Fitness room, spa. Outdoor pool, whirlpool. Tennis. **$$$$**

Restaurants

★ ★ ★ **CUVEE.** *2334 Carmel Valley Rd, Del Mar (92014). Phone 858/259-5878; fax 858/259-6968. www.cuveerestaurant.com.* Chef/owner Chuck Samuelson has designed the menu so his guests can order small, medium, or large dishes depending on their appetite. Located less than a mile from the ocean, the dining room has unobstructed views of the lagoon. California menu. Lunch, dinner, Sun brunch. Closed holidays. Children's menu. Outdoor seating. **$$**

★ ★ **EPAZOTE.** *1555 Camino del Mar, Del Mar (92014). Phone 858/259-9966; fax 858/259-0611. www.*

epazote.signonsandiego.com. Southwestern menu. Lunch, dinner, Sun brunch. Closed Dec 25. Bar. Casual attire. Valet parking. Outdoor seating. **$$**

★ **FISH MARKET.** *640 Via De La Valle, Solana Beach (92075). Phone 858/755-2277; fax 858/755-3912. www.thefishmarket.com.* Seafood menu. Lunch, dinner. Closed holidays. Children's menu. Casual attire. **$$**

★ ★ **IL FORNAIO.** *1555 Camino del Mar, Del Mar (92014). Phone 858/755-8876; fax 858/755-8906. www.ilfornaio.com.* Italian menu. Lunch, dinner, Sun brunch. Closed Thanksgiving, Dec 25. Bar. Children's menu. Casual attire. Outdoor seating. **$$**

★ ★ **J. TAYLOR'S OF DEL MAR.** *1540 Camino del Mar, Del Mar (92014). Phone 858/793-6460; fax 858/793-6482. www.jtaylors.com.* Located in the L'Auberge Del Mar Resort and Spa (see), a European cottage-style hotel, guests in this dining room will enjoy the lovely setting. California menu. Breakfast, lunch, dinner. Bar. Valet parking. Outdoor seating. **$$$**

★ ★ **JAKE'S DEL MAR.** *1660 Coast Blvd, Del Mar (92014). Phone 858/755-2002; fax 858/755-3240. www.jakesdelmar.com.* Seafood, steak menu. Lunch, dinner, Sun brunch. Closed Dec 25. Bar. Valet parking. Outdoor seating. **$$$**

★ **PACIFICA DEL MAR.** *1555 Camino del Mar, Del Mar (92014). Phone 858/792-0476; fax 858/792-0848. www.pacificadelmar.com.* Seafood menu. Lunch, dinner. Children's menu. **$$$**

Desert Hot Springs (J-5)

See also Idyllwild, Indio, Joshua Tree National Park, Palm Desert, Palm Springs

Population 16,582
Elevation 1,070 ft
Area Code 760
Zip 92240
Information Chamber of Commerce, 11-711 West Dr; phone 760/329-6403 or toll-free 800/346-3347
Web Site www.deserthotsprings.com

Full-Service Resort

★ ★ ★ **TWO BUNCH PALMS RESORT AND SPA.** *67-425 Two Bunch Palms Trail, Desert Hot Springs (92240). Phone 760/329-8791; toll-free 800/472-4334; fax 760/329-1317. www.twobunchpalms. com.* This tranquil oasis on 256 acres of rolling, wooded terrain sets out to give you the ultimate relaxation experience. Swim in the grotto pool sourced by a hot spring or indulge in one of the many spa treatments such as a sea algae body wrap. 45 rooms. No children allowed. Complimentary continental breakfast. Check-in 3 pm, check-out noon. Restaurant, bar. Spa. Two outdoor pools, whirlpool. Tennis. **$$**

Disneyland (J-4)

See also Anaheim, Buena Park, Los Angeles, Orange

Web Site www.disneyland.com

Since 1955, Disneyland has been the "happiest place on Earth," though it has certainly changed during those five decades. It opened in 1955 with 18 major attractions, but now has 60 of them on 85 acres. One attraction—The Many Adventures of Winnie the Pooh—features the popular story's characters in a magical journey that incorporates music, special effects, scenic design, and dark-ride technology. The park is divided into eight themed lands, each packed with exciting rides and upbeat entertainment. For example, in Frontierland, board the Big Thunder Mountain Railroad, then take in a rousin' show at the Golden Horseshoe Stage. In Fantasyland, fly off to Never Land or attend a mad tea party. Everyone leaves this happy place feelin' darn good—and a little pooped.

Disneyland attractions are open daily, with extended hours during holidays. Passports to Disneyland are good for unlimited use of rides and attractions (except arcades). Guided tours are available. Facilities for the disabled include wheelchair rentals, ramps, and audiocassettes for the visually impaired.

What to See and Do

Adventureland. *1313 S Harbor Blvd, Disneyland (92802).* "Jungle Cruise" through tropical rivers of the world, with lifelike alligators, hippos, gorillas, monkeys, water buffalo, and Indian elephants; Swiss Family Tree House. Enchanted Tiki Room shows musical fantasy with Audio-Animatronics: birds, flowers, talking and singing Tiki gods. The Indiana Jones Adventure thrill ride is also here.

Critter Country. *1313 S Harbor Blvd, Disneyland (92802).* Home of Splash Mountain log flume ride;

Country Bear Playhouse, a 15-minute country and western revue featuring musical Audio-Animatronic bears; and Davy Crockett Explorer Canoes.

Fantasyland. *1313 S Harbor Blvd, Disneyland (92802).* Favorite Disney classics come to life in exciting adventures. Major attractions include It's a Small World, Pinocchio, Snow White, Dumbo, Peter Pan, and Alice in Wonderland.

Frontierland. *1313 S Harbor Blvd, Disneyland (92802).* Relive the Old West and capture the pioneer spirit with the *Mark Twain* sternwheel riverboat, keel boats, the Golden Horseshoe Stage, and Big Thunder Mountain Railroad. FANTASMIC! is a special effects and character presentation (nightly anytime Disneyland is open after dark) on the Rivers of America, which flow between Frontierland and Tom Sawyer Island.

Main Street, U.S.A. *1313 S Harbor Blvd, Disneyland (92802).* Revives turn-of-the-century nostalgia with steam-powered Disneyland railroad, old-time cinema, Market House, 1900 emporium; an inspiring Audio-Animatronics presentation, "The Walt Disney Story," featuring "Great Moments with Mr. Lincoln."

Mickey's Toontown. *1313 S Harbor Blvd, Disneyland (92802).* A 3-D cartoon environment where guests can visit the homes of Mickey Mouse and his friends, including Goofy's Bounce House and Chip 'n Dale's Tree Slide and Acorn Crawl. Other attractions include The Jolly Trolley, Gadget's Go Coaster, and Roger Rabbit's Car Toon Spin.

New Orleans Square. *1313 S Harbor Blvd, Disneyland (92802).* Shops, cafés, nostalgic courtyards, the "Pirates of the Caribbean" cruise, and the Haunted Mansion.

Tomorrowland. *1313 S Harbor Blvd, Disneyland (92802).* This land of the future explores inner and outer space; features include Space Mountain roller coaster, Autopia, Submarine Voyage, a 2 1/2-mile monorail, rocket ride; Star Tours is an exciting out-of-this-world trip through the galaxy.

El Cajon (K-4)

See also Calexico

Population 94,869
Elevation 435 ft
Area Code 619
Web Site www.ci.el-cajon.ca.us

What to See and Do

Sycuan Casino. *5469 Casino Way (Dehesa Rd), El Cajon (92019).* Phone 619/445-6002; toll-free 800/279-2826. www.sycuancasino.com. Owned by the Sycuan Band of the Kumeyaay Nation, this casino, painted in pastels and located 10 miles east of San Diego, offers a variety of gaming options, plus off-track wagering and a 1,200-seat bingo parlor. Nonsmokers tired of cloudy pits at last have their own smoke-free area in which to play the slots. Six eateries, offering everything from deli fare to Asian cuisine, are available for celebratory dinners—or comfort food. (Daily) **FREE**

Special Event

Mother Goose Parade. *Chambers and Main, El Cajon (92020).* Phone 619/444-8712. www.mothergooseparade.com. From Clydesdales to Claus (Santa, that is) with a lot of kid-friendly characters in between, the 2.2-mile Mother Goose Parade is the largest single-day event in San Diego County. It's also one of the biggest parades in the country, with more than 200 colorful floats, clowns, marching bands, and celebrities entertaining crowds of several hundred thousand spectators. The parade is in El Cajon, approximately 14 miles from San Diego. Sun before Thanksgiving. **FREE**

Limited-Service Hotels

★ **BEST WESTERN CONTINENTAL INN.** *650 N Mollison Ave, El Cajon (92021).* Phone 619/442-0601; toll-free 800/780-7234; fax 619/442-0152. www.bestwestern.com/continentalinnelcajon. 97 rooms, 3 story. Complimentary full breakfast. Check-in 1 pm, check-out 11 am. Outdoor pool, whirlpool. **$**

★ **DAYS INN EL CAJON.** *683 N Mollison Ave, El Cajon (92021).* Phone 619/442-0973; toll-free 800/329-7466; fax 619/593-0772. www.daysinn.com. 60 rooms, 2 story. Check-in 2 pm, check-out 11 am. Outdoor pool, whirlpool. **$**

★ **ROADWAY INN.** *471 N Magnolia Ave, El Cajon (92020).* Phone 619/447-3999; toll-free 800/578-7878; fax 619/447-8403. www.travelodge.com. 49 rooms, 3 story. Complimentary continental breakfast. Check-in 3 pm, check-out 11 am. Outdoor pool. **$**

Full-Service Resort

★ ★ ★ **SINGING HILLS COUNTRY CLUB AT SYCUAN.** *3007 Dehesa Rd, El Cajon (92019). Phone 619/442-3425; toll-free 800/457-5568; fax 619/442-9574. www.singinghills.com.* This 425-acre golf resort, laying in the tranquil Dehesa Valley, is just 30 minutes east of the San Diego airport. 103 rooms, 2 story. Check-in 4 pm, check-out 1 pm. Restaurant, bar. Fitness room. Outdoor pool, whirlpool. Golf. Tennis. Airport transportation available. **$**

El Centro (K-5)

See also Calexico

Settled 1901
Population 37,835
Elevation 40 ft below sea level
Area Code 760
Zip 92243
Information Chamber of Commerce, 1095 S 4th St; phone 760/352-3681
Web Site www.elcentrochamber.com

This busy marketplace in the center of the Imperial Valley, which was once part of the Gulf of California, is the largest town in the United States entirely below sea level. Water from the All-American Canal and Hoover Dam has turned arid desert into lush farmland, which produces great crops of sugar beets, melons, and lettuce. Mountains east of El Centro are ringed with coral reefs. Other points of geological interest are Fossil Canyon, north of town, and Painted Gorge, northwest off Interstate 8.

Limited-Service Hotels

★ ★ **RAMADA.** *1455 Ocotillo Dr, El Centro (92243). Phone 760/352-5152; toll-free 800/805-4000; fax 760/337-1567. www.ramada.com.* 147 rooms, 2 story. Pets accepted, fee. Check-in 3 pm, check-out noon. Restaurant, bar. Fitness room. Outdoor pool, children's pool, whirlpool. Airport transportation available. **$**

★ ★ **VACATION INN.** *2015 Cottonwood Cr, El Centro (92243). Phone 760/352-9523; toll-free 800/328-6289; fax 760/353-7620.* 170 rooms, 2 story. Pets accepted; fee. Complimentary continental breakfast. Check-in 3 pm. Check-out noon. Restaurant, bar. Fitness room. Outdoor pool, whirlpool. **$**

Full-Service Resort

★ ★ **BARBARA WORTH GOLF RESORT AND CONVENTION CENTER.** *2050 Country Club Dr, Holtville (92250). Phone 760/356-2806; fax 760/356-4653. www.bwresort.com.* 104 rooms, 2 story. Pets accepted. Check-in 3 pm, check-out noon. Restaurant, bar. Fitness room. Two outdoor pools, children's pool, whirlpool. Golf. Business center. **$**

Restaurant

★ **SCRIBBLES.** *2015 Cottonwood Cir, El Centro (92243). Phone 760/352-9523.* American menu. Breakfast, lunch, dinner. Closed Sun; Dec 25. Bar. Children's menu. Casual attire. **$$**

Escondido (K-4)

See also Carlsbad, La Jolla, Oceanside, San Diego

Population 133,559
Elevation 684 ft
Area Code 760
Information San Diego North Convention and Visitors Bureau, 360 N Escondido Blvd, 92025; phone 760/745-4741 or toll-free 800/848-3336
Web Site www.sandiegonorth.com

A Ranger District office of the Cleveland National Forest is located here.

What to See and Do

California Center for the Performing Arts. *340 N Escondido Blvd, Escondido (92025). Phone 760/839-4100. www.artcenter.org.* The California Center for the Performing Arts is building a world by building a neighborhood. Designed by renowned architect Charles Moore, this 12-acre campus of postmodern buildings includes two theaters, an art museum, a conference center, and a café. Its simple mission is to "promote the arts and their power for community building and enhancement." The centers museum presents work of upcoming and established Mexican and American artists, particularly those who live in and around Southern California. Other facilities include the Concert Hall, a 1,535-seat venue with superb acoustics and no seat farther than 100 feet from the stage, and the intimate 408-seat Center Theater, which host local and internationally known performers of opera, country, ballet, tap, folk, and just about everything in between. (Tues-Sat) **$**

Escondido Heritage Walk. *321 N Broadway, Escondido. Phone 760/743-8207.* Escondido Historical Society history museum. Artifacts, books, preservation displays. Victorian ranch house; working blacksmith shop, early 1900s barn and windmill, 1888 Santa Fe train depot, railroad car with model train replica of the Oceanside to Escondido run (circa 1920). (Tues-Sat; closed holidays except July 4) **DONATION**

Ferrara. *1120 W 15th Ave, Escondido. Phone 760/745-7632.* Producers of wine and grape juice. Self-guided tours, wine tasting. (Daily 10 am-5 pm; closed holidays) **FREE**

Orfila. *13455 San Pasqual Rd, Escondido (92025). Phone 760/738-6500; toll-free 800/868-9463. www. orfila.com.* Guided and self-guided tours, wine tasting room; picnic area beneath grape arbor overlooks the vineyards and San Pasqual Valley. (Daily 10 am-6 pm; closed holidays) **FREE**

Palomar Observatory. *35899 Canfield Rd, Escondido. 35 miles NE on County S6. Phone 760/742-2119. www. astro.caltech.edu/observatories/palomar.* Here are a 200-inch Hale telescope (second-largest in the United States) and 48-inch and 60-inch telescopes. There is a visitors' gallery in the dome of the Hale telescope; Greenway Museum has photography from telescopes, exhibits explaining equipment. Self-guided tours. Gift shop. (Daily; closed Dec 24-25) **FREE**

San Pasqual Battlefield State Historic Park and Museum. *15808 San Pasqual Valley Rd, Escondido (92025). 8 miles E on Hwy 78. Phone 760/737-2201. www.parks. ca.gov.* One of the deadliest battles of the Mexican-American War took place here on December 6, 1846. Twenty-one Americans died, 16 more were wounded during the brutal fighting, and the Americans were forced to retreat. A short video at the visitor center places the battle in the context of the war. The park features hiking trails and hosts living history programs the first Sunday of each month, as well as a reenactment of the battle every December to mark its anniversary. (Fri-Mon 10 am-5 pm; closed Jan 1, Thanksgiving, Dec 25) **FREE**

Welk Resort Center Theatre-Museum. *8860 Lawrence Welk Dr, Escondido (92026). At the Welk Resort (see). Phone 760/749-3448.* Music center houses memorabilia marking the milestones of Lawrence Welk's career. (Daily) Theater and dance performances (fee). **FREE**

Limited-Service Hotels

★ ★ **CASTLE CREEK INN & SPA.** *29850 Circle R Way, Escondido (92026). Phone 760/751-8800; toll-free 800/253-5341; fax 760/751-8787. www.castlecreekinn. com.* 30 rooms, 2 story. Pets accepted; fee. Check-in 3 pm, check-out noon. Restaurant. Fitness room. Outdoor pool. Tennis. **$**

★ **COMFORT INN.** *1290 W Valley Pkwy, Escondido (92029). Phone 760/489-1010; toll-free 800/541-6012; fax 760/489-7847. www.choicehotels.com.* 93 rooms, 3 story. Complimentary continental breakfast. Check-in 2 pm, check-out noon. Fitness room. Outdoor pool, whirlpool. **$**

Full-Service Resorts

★ ★ **LAKE SAN MARCOS RESORT.** *1025 La Bonita Dr, San Marcos (92078). Phone 760/744-0120; toll-free 800/447-6556; fax 760/744-0748. www.lakesan-marcosresort.com.* The price is right at this clean, quiet getaway on Lake San Marcos. Guests can choose from lake- or pool-view rooms. 140 rooms, 2 story. Pets accepted, some restrictions; fee. Check-in 3 pm, check-out noon. Fitness room. Two outdoor pools, whirlpool. **$**

★ ★ ★ **WELK RESORT SAN DIEGO.** *8860 Lawrence Welk Dr, Escondido (92026). Phone 760/749-3000; toll-free 800/932-9355; fax 760/749-9537. www. welkresort.com.* 100 rooms, 2 story. Check-in 4 pm, check-out noon. Restaurant, bar. Children's activity center. Fitness room. Two outdoor pools, whirlpool. Tennis. Dinner theater. **$$**

Specialty Lodging

ZOSA GARDENS BED AND BREAKFAST. *9381 W Lilac Rd, Escondido (92026). Phone 760/723-9093; toll-free 800/711-8361; fax 760/723-3460. www. zosagardens.com.* Awake to birds chirping, take in the mountain view, or explore 22 picturesque acres. You can do it all at this quiet retreat north of the city. In case that's not enough, the omnipresent owner will honor special requests. 10 rooms. Complimentary full breakfast. Check-in 3 pm. Check-out 11 am. Whirlpool. Tennis. **$**

Restaurants

★ ★ ★ **150 GRAND CAFE.** *150 W Grand Ave, Escondido (92025). Phone 760/738-6868; fax 760/738-8072. www.150grandcafe.com.* This comfortably elegant restaurant featuring a patio full of fresh flowers is lovely for seasonal dining. In the winter months the dining room, with a crackling fire in the fireplace, is cozy and romantic. American menu. Lunch, dinner. Closed Sun; holidays. Bar. Outdoor seating. **$$**

★ ★ **SANDCRAB CAFE.** *2229 Micro Pl, Escondido (92029). Phone 760/480-2722. www.sandcrabcafe.com.* Seafood menu. Lunch, dinner. Closed Dec 25. Bar. Children's menu. Casual attire. **$$**

★ ★ ★ **VINCENT'S SIRINO'S.** *113 W Grand Ave, Escondido (92025). Phone 760/745-3835; fax 760/745-8401. www.vincentssirinos.com.* Café-style dining. California, French menu. Lunch, dinner. Closed Mon; holidays. Bar. Children's menu. Reservations recommended. Outdoor seating. **$$$**

Fallbrook (J-4)

See also Temecula

Settled 1880s
Population 29,100
Elevation 685 ft
Area Code 760
Zip 92028
Web Site www.fallbrookca.org

Special Event

Fallbrook Avocado Festival. *233 E Mission Rd, Fallbrook (92028). Phone 760/728-5845. www.fallbrookca. org/avofest.htm.* If you're an avocado lover, welcome to Nirvana. Fallbrook is the self-proclaimed avocado capital of the world, and one can see why: 28 square miles are devoted to growing and packing the rich, delicate-flavored fruit. One day in mid-April (call for the exact date) is set aside to celebrate the joys of the avocado with a festival that includes crafts, games, contests, entertainment, and a packing house tour of the Del Rey Avocado Company. But the real reason for coming is to taste the world-class guacamole, avocado sandwiches, grilled avocado halves with lemon, and other samples. Mid-Apr. **FREE**

Limited-Service Hotel

★ **BEST WESTERN FRANCISCAN INN.** *1635 S Mission Rd, Fallbrook (92028). Phone 760/728-6174; toll-free 800/780-7234; fax 760/731-6404. www. bestwestern.com/franciscaninn.* 51 rooms, 1 story. Pets accepted; some restrictions, fee. Complimentary con-

tinental breakfast. Check-in 3 pm, check-out 11 am. Outdoor pool, whirlpool. **$**
🅿 🐾 🏊

Full-Service Resort

★ ★ ★ **PALA MESA RESORT.** *2001 Old Hwy 395, Fallbrook (92028). Phone 760/728-5881; toll-free 800/722-4700; fax 760/723-8292. www.palamesa. com.* As one of California's most unique golf settings, guests can enjoy a round of golf, as well as winery and antique tours. 133 rooms, 2 story. Pets accepted, fee. Check-in 4 pm, check-out noon. Restaurant, bar. Outdoor pool, whirlpool. Golf, 18 holes. Tennis. **$$**
🐾 🏊 🏌 🎿

Fresno (F-3)

Founded 1874
Population 427,652
Elevation 296 ft
Area Code 559
Information Convention & Visitors Bureau, 848 M St, 3rd floor, 93721; phone 559/445-8300 or toll-free 800/788-0836
Web Site www.fresnocvb.org

Fresno was founded when the population of Millerton moved from that town to the railroad line. In the geographic center of the state and the heart of the San Joaquin Valley—the great central California "Garden of the Sun"—Fresno and Fresno County are enjoying tremendous growth. The county claims the greatest agricultural production of any in the United States, handling more than $3 billion annually. The world's largest dried fruit packing plant, Sun-Maid, is here.

What to See and Do

California State University, Fresno. *5241 N Maple Ave, Fresno (93740). Phone 559/278-4240. www.csufresno. edu.* (1911) (20,000 students) Includes a farm, arboretum, and California wildlife habitat exhibits. Tours available.

Discovery Center. *1937 N Winery Ave, Fresno (93703). Phone 559/251-5533. www.thediscoverycenter.net.* Participatory natural and physical science exhibits for families; outdoor exhibits, cactus garden; picnicking; Native American room. $3 donation suggested. (Tues-Fri 9 am-4 pm) **DONATION**

Forestiere Underground Gardens. *5021 W Shaw, Fresno (93722). Phone 559/271-0734. www.undergroundgardens.com.* This former home of Italian immigrant Baldasare Forestiere has 10 acres of underground tunnels filled with citrus plants, grape vines, rose bushes, and other flora. (Apr-Sept, Wed-Sun) **$$**

Fresno Art Museum. *2233 N First St, Fresno (93703). Phone 559/441-4221. www.fresnoartmuseum.org.* The only modern art museum between Los Angeles and San Francisco, the Fresno Art Museum has been the centerpiece of Radio Park since it opened in the 1950s. The museum's exhibits display works from an international group of contemporary artists, as well as an impressive collection of Mexican art, dating from the pre-Columbian era to present day. The museum also plays host to a series of performances, lectures, and films. (Tues-Wed, Fri-Sun 11 am-5 pm; Thurs to 8 pm; closed Jan 1, Thanksgiving, Dec 25) **$**

Fresno Metropolitan Museum. *1555 Van Ness Ave, Fresno (93721). Phone 559/441-1444. www.fresnomet.org.* Displays on the heritage and culture of the San Joaquin Valley; hands-on science exhibits; touring exhibits. (Tues-Wed, Fri-Sun 11 am-5 pm, Thurs to 8 pm; closed holidays) **$$**

Kearney Mansion Museum. *7160 W Kearney Blvd, Fresno (93706). Phone 559/441-0862. www.valleyhistory.org.* (1900-1903) Historic mansion has been restored; contains many original furnishings, including European wallpapers and Art Nouveau light fixtures. Adjacent servants' quarters house ranch kitchen and museum gift shop. Narrated 45-minute tour of mansion. (Fri-Sun 1 pm, 2 pm, and 3 pm; closed Jan 1, Easter, Dec 25) **$**

Kingsburg. *Chamber of Commerce, 1475 Draper St, Fresno. 18 miles S via Hwy 99. Phone 559/897-1111.* Settled by Swedes, their colorful influence remains in this town. Swedish architectural design on buildings; dala horses and flags decorate streets. **Historical Society Museum** is at 2321 Sierra Street.

Millerton Lake State Recreation Area. *5290 Millerton Rd, Fresno. 21 miles NE via Hwy 41, Friant Rd. Phone 559/822-2332. www.parks.ca.gov.* 14,107 acres. Swimming, water-skiing (lifeguards), fishing, boat launching; hiking and riding trails; picnicking, concession, store nearby; camping (dump station). **$$$**

Roeding Park. *890 W Belmont Ave, Fresno (93728). Phone 559/621-2900. www.fresno.gov/parks-rec/roeding.* Variety of trees and shrubs, ranging from high mountain to tropical species, on 157 acres. Boating (rentals). Tennis. Camellia garden, picnic areas; children's storyland (fee), playland (fee/ride), amphitheater. (Daily) In the park is

Chaffee Zoological Gardens. *894 W Belmont, Fresno (93728). At the S end of the park, near Olive Ave. Phone 559/498-2671.* This 18-acre zoo has more than 650 animals representing 200 species. Includes a reptile house, elephant exhibit, sunda forest; also tropical rain forest exhibit containing plants and animals found primarily in South American regions. (Feb-Oct: daily 9 am-4 pm; Nov-Jan: daily 10 am-3 pm) **$$**

⭐ **Sierra National Forest.** *1600 Tollhouse Rd, Clovis (93611). Sections NE and E reached via Hwys 41, 99, 168. Phone 559/297-0706; toll-free 877/444-6777. www.fs.fed.us/r5/sierra.* Nearly 1.3 million acres ranging from rolling foothills to rugged, snow-capped mountains; two groves of giant sequoias, hundreds of natural lakes, 11 major reservoirs, and unique geological formations. The topography can be rough and precipitous in higher elevations, with deep canyons and many beautiful meadows along streams and lakes; five wilderness areas. Rafting, boating, sailing, fishing; hunting, downhill and cross-country skiing, picnicking, camping.

Sierra Summit Ski Area. *59265 Hwy 168, Huntington Lake. 65 miles NE on Hwy 168, in Sierra National Forest. Phone 559/233-2500. www.sierrasummit.com.* Three triple, two double chairlifts, four surface lifts; patrol, school, rentals; snowmaking; snack bar, cafeteria, restaurant, bar; lodge. Twenty-five runs; longest run 2 1/4 miles; vertical drop 1,600 feet. Half-day rates (weekends and holidays). (Mid-Nov-mid-Apr, daily) **$$$$**

Wild Water Adventures. *11413 E Shaw Ave, Clovis (93611). Phone 559/299-9453; toll-free 800/564-9453. www.wildwater1.com.* This water park with rides, slides, and picnicking has one of the West's largest wave pools, plus water slides for teens and a water play area for children. (June-mid-Aug: daily) **$$$$**

Woodward Park. *7775 N Friant Rd, Fresno (93720). Phone 559/621-2900. www.fresno.gov/parks-rec/woodward.* Approximately 300 acres. Authentic Japanese garden (weekends only; summer weekday evenings, fee); fishing ponds for children under 16; jogging course; picnic area; bird sanctuary. (Daily)

Special Events

Big Fresno Fair. *1121 S Chance Ave, Fresno (93702). Phone 559/650-3247. www.fresnofair.com.* Carnival, horse racing, livestock exhibits, and arts and crafts. Oct. **$$**

Clovis Rodeo. *Clovis Arena. Phone 559/299-5203. www. clovisrodeo.com.* First a venue for local cowboys to compete, the Clovis Rodeo has evolved into a four-day festival featuring a parade, kids rodeo, and competition categories that include bull riding, team roping, barrel racing, bareback riding, and saddle broncriding. Late Apr. **$$$**

Fresno County Blossom Trail. *2629 S Clovis Ave, Fresno (92725). Phone 559/495-4800. www.co.fresno. ca.us/4510/tourism/agtrails.aspx.* This 62-mile self-guided driving tour features the beauty of California agriculture during peak season (weather permitting). Highlights of the trail are fruit orchards, citrus groves, vineyards, and historical points of interest. The visitors bureau has maps and information. Peak season is late Feb-mid-Mar.

Highland Gathering and Games. *Coombs Ranch. Phone 559/265-6507.* Scottish athletics, dancing contests, bagpipe competition. Mid-Sept.

Swedish Festival. *1475 Draper St, Kingsburg (93631). Phone 559/897-1111.* Celebrate everything Swedish at this three-day festival. After a traditional Svenska pancake breakfast, stick around for a parade, entertainment, arts and crafts, carnival, Maypole, folk dancing, and more Swedish food. Third weekend in May.

Limited-Service Hotels

★ ★ **FOUR POINTS BY SHERATON.** *3737 N Blackstone Ave, Fresno (93726). Phone 559/226-2200; toll-free 800/742-1911; fax 559/222-7147. www.four-points.com.* 204 rooms, 2 story. Check-in 3 pm, check-out noon. High-speed Internet access. Restaurant, bar. Fitness room. Outdoor pool, whirlpool. Airport transportation available. Business center. **$$**

★ **PICCADILLY INN-UNIVERSITY.** *4961 N Cedar Ave, Fresno (93726). Phone 559/224-4200; toll-free 800/468-3587; fax 559/227-2382. www.piccadillyinn.com.* In the center of the financial district, this inn is conveniently located near Fresno State University. 90 rooms, 3 story. Complimentary continental breakfast. Check-in 3 pm, check-out noon. Fitness room. Outdoor pool, whirlpool. Airport transportation available. **$$**

★ ★ **RADISSON HOTEL & CONFERENCE CENTER FRESNO.** *2233 Ventura St, Fresno (93721). Phone 559/268-1000; toll-free 800/333-3333; fax 559/441-2954. www.radisson.com.* This hotel is situated adjacent to the Fresno Convention Center.

Yosemite National Park and Sequoia and Kings Canyon National Parks are within driving distance. 321 rooms, 8 story. Check-in 3:30 pm, check-out noon. Restaurant, bar. Fitness room. Indoor pool, outdoor pool, whirlpool. Airport transportation available. Business center. **$**

Restaurant

★ ★ **RIPE TOMATO.** *5064 N Palm Ave, Fresno (93704). Phone 559/225-1850.* French menu. Lunch, dinner. Closed Sun-Mon. Business casual attire. Reservations recommended. Outdoor seating. **$$$**

Fullerton (J-4)

See also Anaheim, Buena Park, Santa Monica

Population 126,003
Elevation 155 ft
Area Code 714 or 657
Web Site www.ci.fullerton.ca.us

Limited-Service Hotels

★ ★ **FOUR POINTS BY SHERATON.** *1500 S Raymond Ave, Fullerton (92831). Phone 714/635-9000; toll-free 888/635-9000; fax 714/520-5831. www.four-points.com.* 256 rooms, 6 story. Check-in 3 pm, check-out noon. Restaurant, bar. Fitness room. Outdoor pool. Business center. **$**

★ ★ **WYNDHAM ANAHEIM PARK.** *222 W Houston Ave, Fullerton (92832). Phone 714/992-1700; fax 714/992-4843.* This hotel is located 3 miles from Disneyland. 287 rooms, 7 story. Check-in 3 pm, check-out noon. Restaurant, bar. Fitness room. Outdoor pool. **$$**

Full-Service Hotel

★ ★ ★ **FULLERTON MARRIOTT AT CALIFORNIA STATE UNIVERSITY.** *2701 E Nutwood Ave, Fullerton (92831). Phone 714/738-7800; toll-free 800/228-9290; fax 714/738-0288. www.marriott. com.* Adjacent to California State University. 224 rooms, 6 story. Pets accepted, some restrictions; fee. Check-in 4 pm, check-out noon. Restaurant, bar. Fitness room. Outdoor pool, whirlpool. Business center. **$**

Restaurants

★ ★ ★ **THE CELLAR.** *305 N Harbor Blvd, Fullerton (92832). Phone 714/525-5682; fax 714/525-3853.* Located underneath the beautiful Villa del Sol (the old California Hotel), the dining rooms of this restaurant can be reached by venturing down a flight of stairs into the cellar. The cavelike walls are decorated with wine casks and lanterns; guests feel as though they've stepped into their own winery! French menu. Dinner. Closed Sun-Mon; holidays. Bar. Valet parking. **$$$**

★ ★ ★ **LA VIE EN ROSE.** *240 S State College Blvd, Brea (92821). Phone 714/529-8333; fax 714/529-2751. www.lavnrose.com.* "Life is rosy" at this reproduction of a Normandy farmhouse serving recipes native to the Gascony and Province regions of France. Tapestry-covered booths create an intimate place for conversation. Choose one of the several picturesque dining rooms for a truly enjoyable meal. French menu. Lunch, dinner. Closed Sun; holidays. Bar. **$$$**

★ **MULBERRY STREET.** *114 W Wilshire Ave, Fullerton (92832). Phone 714/525-1056; fax 714/447-0542. www.mulberry-st.com.* Italian menu. Lunch, dinner. Closed holidays. Bar. Casual attire. **$$**

★ ★ ★ **SUMMIT HOUSE.** *2000 E Bastanchury Rd, Fullerton (92835). Phone 714/671-4111; fax 714/671-3087. www.summithouse.net.* Situated high atop the hilltop of Vista Park, this restaurant offers one of the finest views available in Orange County. Take some time to walk around the property and enjoy sights. American menu. Lunch, dinner. Closed holidays. Bar. Valet parking. Outdoor seating. **$$$**

Garden Grove (J-4)

See also Anaheim, Orange, Santa Ana

Population 165,196
Elevation 90 ft
Area Code 714
Web Site www.ci.garden-grove.ca.us

What to See and Do

Crystal Cathedral. *12141 Lewis St, Garden Grove (92840). Phone 714/971-4000. www.crystalcathedral.org.* The all-glass church resembles a four-pointed crystal star. Designed by Philip Johnson; set on 36 acres of landscaped grounds. Guided tours. (Mon-Sat 9 am-3:30 pm; closed holidays) **DONATION**

Limited-Service Hotel

★ **GUESTHOUSE INTERNATIONAL INN.** *7912 Garden Grove Blvd, Garden Grove (92841). Phone 714/894-7568; fax 714/894-6308.* 100 rooms, 2 story. Check-in 11 am, check-out 11 am. Outdoor pool. **$**

Glendale (J-4)

See also Pasadena

Population 194,973
Elevation 571 ft
Web Site www.ci.glendale.ca.us

Set at the foot of the Verdugo Mountains and bordered on the west by Burbank and on the east by Pasadena, Glendale is the third-largest city in Los Angeles County. With more than half of its population being foreign-born, this city of more than 200,000 residents is richly diverse.

What to See and Do

Glendale Galleria. *2148 Glendale Galleria, Glendale (91210). Phone 818/240-9481. www.glendalegalleria.com.* In its promotional material, this megamall uses the slogan "Find It All Here"—and, with more than 250 retailers, this shoppers' paradise more than lives up to that promise. Not one, not two, but five large department stores serve as the anchors: JCPenney, Macy's, Mervyn's, Nordstrom, and Robinsons May. These big draws are surrounded by other familiar chains, such as Aveda, Bath & Body Works, Brookstone, Coach, the Discovery Channel Store, Eddie Bauer, the Gap, Mont Blanc, the Wherehouse, and Williams-Sonoma. A savory food court, attractive foliage, and handsome marble floors give the mall added appeal. (Mon-Fri 10 am-9 pm, Sat to 8 pm, Sun 11 am-7 pm)

Limited-Service Hotels

★ **BEST WESTERN EAGLE ROCK INN.** *2911 Colorado Blvd, Los Angeles (90041). Phone 323/256-7711; toll-free 888/255-7970; fax 323/255-6750. www.bestwestern.com.* 49 rooms, 3 story. Complimentary continental breakfast. Check-in 2 pm, check-out noon. High-speed Internet access. Outdoor pool, whirlpool. **$**

★ **BEST WESTERN GOLDEN KEY MOTOR HOTEL.** *123 W Colorado St, Glendale (91204). Phone 818/247-0111; toll-free 800/651-1155; fax 818/545-9393. www.bestwestern.com/goldenkeyglendale.* 55 rooms, 3 story. Complimentary continental breakfast. Check-in 3 pm, check-out noon. Outdoor pool, whirlpool. **$**

Restaurant

★ ★ **FAR NIENTE.** *204 1/2 N Brand Blvd, Glendale (91203). Phone 818/242-3835; fax 818/242-4804. www. farnienteristorante.net.* Family-style Italian comfort cuisine dished up generously with good cheer (and with lots of fabulous focaccia bread) is the rule here. Pasta lovers may find the ricotta-and-spinach ravioli with sage cream sauce a real dream; the grilled veal chop with a sauce of balsamic vinegar and sweet onion has long been a favorite among non-pasta entrées. As dusk falls, a multitude of candles are lit, transforming Far Niente's pair of spacious dining areas—where pretty replicas of classic statuary are framed by walls of ocher—into romantic refuges. Italian menu. Lunch, dinner. Closed holidays. Bar. Casual attire. Reservations recommended. Valet parking. Outdoor seating. **$$**

Hearst-San Simeon State Historical Monument (Hearst Castle) (G-2)

See also San Simeon

750 Hearst Castle Rd, San Simeon (93452). Phone 805/927-2020. www.hearstcastle.com.

Crowning La Cuesta Encantada—the Enchanted Hill—is a princely domain of castle, guest houses, theater, pools, and tennis courts created by William Randolph Hearst as his home and retreat. After his death in 1951, the estate was given to the state as a memorial to the late publisher's mother, Phoebe Adderson Hearst. For years, Hearst Castle could be glimpsed by the public only through a telescope at the nearby village of San Simeon, but today it is open to the public. A "carefully planned, deliberate attempt to create a shrine of beauty," it was begun in 1919 under the direction of

noted architect Julia Morgan. An army of workers built the castle with its twin towers and surrounded it with formal Mediterranean gardens; construction continued for 28 years. And, though three guest houses and 115 rooms of the main house were completed, there was still much more Hearst had hoped to build.

Items collected by Hearst can be viewed in the castle and on the grounds. Features of the castle itself are the Refectory, an unbelievable "long, high, noble room" with a hand-carved ceiling and life-size statues of saints, silk banners from Siena, and 15th-century choir stalls from a Spanish cathedral; the Assembly Room, with priceless tapestries; and the lavish theater where the latest motion pictures were shown.

The estate includes three luxurious "guest houses"; the Neptune Pool, with a colonnade leading to an ancient Roman temple facade and an array of marble statuary; an indoor pool; magnificent gardens; fountains; walkways; and, of course, the main house of 115 rooms.

Visitors may explore an exhibit on the life and times of William Randolph Hearst inside the visitor center at the bottom of the hill. Also here is an iWERKS giant-screen theater showing "Hearst Castle: Building the Dream," a 40-minute film detailing the rich history and architectural precedents of Hearst and his estate (phone 805/927-6811). Food and gift concessions are also located here. There is an area to observe artifact restoration in progress; entrance to the exhibit is free.

Parking is available in a lot near Highway 1, where buses transport visitors to the castle. Access to the castle and grounds is by guided tour only. Tour One takes in the grounds, a guest house, the pools, and the lower level of the main house; Tour Two visits the upper levels of the main house, which include Hearst's private suite; Tour Three covers the north wing and a guest house and includes a video about the construction of the castle; Tour Four (available April-October) is spent mostly outside in the gardens and around the pools, but also includes behind-the-scenes areas such as the wine cellar and two floors of the largest guest house. Tours are available for selected evenings in the spring and fall; these tours take in the highlights of the estate and include a living history program developed to give visitors a glimpse of life at the castle in the early 1930s. All tours include the outdoor and indoor pools.

Day tours take approximately one hour and 45 minutes; evening tours take approximately two hours and 15 minutes. No pets. Reservations are recommended and are available up to eight weeks in advance by phoning toll-free 800/444-4445. Tickets are also available at the ticket office in the visitor center. Tours entail much walking and stair climbing; wheelchairs can be accommodated under certain conditions and with ten days advance notice by phoning 805/927-2020; strollers cannot be accommodated. (Daily; closed Jan 1, Thanksgiving, Dec 25) **$$$**

Hemet

See also Beaumont, Palm Springs, Riverside

Founded 1890
Population 63,779
Elevation 1,596 ft
Area Code 951
Web Site www.ci.hemet.ca.us

Located in the beautiful San Jacinto Valley, Hemet was once the largest producer of alfalfa and herbs in the country. Today, it is near the hub of an area that includes ocean, desert, mountains, lakes, health resorts, and springs, along with neighboring historic Native American reservations and large cattle ranches, all within an hour's drive.

What to See and Do

San Jacinto Valley Museum. *150 N Dillon Ave, San Jacinto (92583). Phone 951/654-4952.* Permanent and temporary exhibits of genealogy, Native American archaeology, and a variety of historical items of San Jacinto Valley. (Daily, mornings; closed Jan 1, Thanksgiving, Dec 25) **FREE**

Special Events

Ramona Pageant. *27400 Ramona Bowl Rd, Hemet. Phone 951/658-3111; toll-free 800/645-4465. www.ramonapageant.com.* Ramona Bowl is a 5,959-seat outdoor amphitheater built into the side of a mountain. Beautiful setting among the rolling hills, where most of the action of Helen Hunt Jackson's story takes place. More than 350 persons participate in this romance of early California, presented annually since 1923. Three weekends in late Apr-early May.

Southern California Fair. *Lake Perris Fairgrounds, 18700 Lake Perris Dr, Perris (92571). 10 miles W on Hwy 74. Phone 951/657-4221. www.socalfair.com.* Competitions and exhibits, food, activities, entertainment. Mid-Oct. **$$**

Limited-Service Hotel

★ **BEST WESTERN INN OF HEMET.** *2625 W Florida Ave, Hemet (92545). Phone 951/925-6605; toll-free 800/605-0001; fax 951/925-7095. www.bestwestern.com.* 70 rooms, 2 story. Pets accepted, some restrictions; fee. Complimentary full breakfast. Check-in 2 pm, check-out 11 am. Outdoor pool, whirlpool. **$**

Restaurant

★ ★ **DATTILO.** *2288 E Florida Ave, Hemet (92544). Phone 951/658-4248; fax 951/658-9989.* Italian menu. Lunch, dinner. Closed holidays. Bar. **$$$**

Hermosa Beach (J-4)

Limited-Service Hotels

★ ★ **BEACH HOUSE.** *1300 The Strand, Hermosa Beach (90254). Phone 310/374-3001; fax 310/372-2115.* When you think of Southern California, chances are you picture wide beaches, eternal sunshine, and a slower pace. If that's the case, the Beach House is the perfect Southern California hotel. Located right on the beach, on the 26-mile bike and jogging path that stretches up the coast toward Malibu, each suite has separate bedroom and living room areas, with a private balcony, Frette linens, a wet bar and full sink with a refrigerator, a wood-burning fireplace, two TVs, and a CD stereo. If you can muster the discipline to get some work done during your stay, you'll have high-speed Internet access, with teleconferencing equipment available. The location can't be beat—the beach is just outside the hotel's door, as are shops and restaurants, beach volleyball and inline skating, surfing, and swimming. Within a 30-minute drive are Hollywood, the Getty Center, Rodeo Drive, Venice Beach, and Santa Monica's Third Street Promenade. Or stay in and take advantage of the hotel's spa services. 96 rooms, 3 story. Complimentary continental breakfast. Check-in 3 pm, check-out noon. High-speed Internet access. Fitness room. Beach. Whirlpool. **$$$**

★ **HAMPTON INN & SUITES.** *1530 Pacific Coast Hwy, Hermosa Beach (90254). Phone 310/318-7800; toll-free 800/426-7866; fax 310/318-7801. www.hermosabeach.hamptoninn.com.* Geared toward business travelers, there is a lot to like in this hotel. The rooms are clean and serviceable, with an emphasis on getting work done. You'll find a refrigerator, microwave, and coffeemaker in every room. All the rooms have free high-speed Internet access, as does the meeting room. Decorated with aqua-colored carpeting and shades of mauve and gold, the rooms are clean, but cookie-cutter in their design. Conveniently located only 6 miles from the Los Angeles International Airport (LAX), the hotel is also near many area businesses, including Toyota, Nissan, Xerox, and TRW. For recreation, you can walk or jog to the Hermosa Pier or even the Manhattan or Redondo piers (each 1 1/2 miles away). The hotel's sun deck has a view of the ocean (as do more than over half of the hotel rooms), so if you can only steal a few minutes to work on your tan, you don't have to make your way to the beach to do so. 70 rooms. Complimentary continental breakfast. Check-in 3 pm, check-out 11 am. High-speed Internet access. Fitness room. **$$**

🏃

Hollywood (J-4)

See also Beverly Hills, Los Angeles, West Hollywood

Elevation 385 ft
Area Code 213,323
Information Chamber of Commerce, 7018 Hollywood Blvd, 90028; phone 323/469-8311; or Hollywood Convention & Visitors Information Center, 685 S Figueroa St; phone 213/689-8822
Web Site www.seemyla.com

To most tourists, Hollywood is synonymous with Los Angeles—it symbolizes the glitz and glamour of the movie industry, the celebrity mill, and the endless tabloid parade. In fact, Hollywood is more than a state of mind—it is a real place, a diverse neighborhood that is a social cross-section of LA itself.

Movies actually have to be made, and the process is not all about exotic location shoots. On the side streets of Hollywood, thousands of workers in production houses edit miles of footage, mix and edit sound, color-correct, and physically compose the movies themselves. These neighborhoods appear more industrial than swanky, but this is the true buzzing underbelly of movie making, the important cogs of the machine.

Several major motion picture studios call Hollywood home—and they are microcosmic cities within themselves. Studios have a campus-like feel, with their own

transit, restaurants, shops, barbers, and stores. These gated oases are surrounded by a smattering of trendy dining spots for power lunches, and not much else.

Famed Hollywood Boulevard is an ultimate tourist destination. Tour groups from around the globe gather here to snap photos of the stars embedded in the sidewalk, gawk at the outlandish Grauman's Chinese Theatre, and get photo ops with celebrity impersonators. They also do some shopping at the Hollywood and Highland shopping mall, which houses upscale chain stores and restaurants, as well as the Kodak Theatre, the home of the Oscars.

From the rotunda of the mall, one can spot the famed Hollywood sign in the Hollywood Hills. In the hills, the Hollywood Bowl is the iconic alfresco concert venue, with its white shell-shaped stage; this is the summer home to the LA Philharmonic. The hills are also home to the very privileged of society—the estates of movie stars, powerful producers, and other heavy hitters are nestled among the windy streets and hidden canyons.

Outdoor enthusiasts love the hills for the countless secluded hiking trails—and dog lovers congregate at Runyon Canyon and Laurel Canyon for off-leash adventures. Even a drive on the ridge of the hill on historic Mulholland Drive feels like a nature excursion, with plenty of vistas, scenery, and fresh air above the bustling city below.

What to See and Do

⭐ **Barnsdall Art Park.** *4800 Hollywood Blvd, Hollywood (90027). www.barnsdallartpark.com.* Named after socialite Aline Barnsdall, who commisioned Frank Lloyd Wright to build her home and later gave the property to the city of Los Angeles. (Daily) **FREE** Within the park is

> **Municipal Art Gallery.** *4800 Hollywood Blvd, Hollywood (90027). Phone 323/644-6269.* Features works by regional and local artists. (Thurs-Sun noon-5 pm) **$**

CBS Television City. *7800 Beverly Blvd, Hollywood (90036). At Fairfax Ave. Phone 323/575-2458.* This is the location of the West Coast studios of CBS Television and the source of many of its network telecasts. Write for free tickets well in advance (specify dates and shows preferred) and enclose a stamped, self-addressed envelope. Tickets may also be picked up at the information window (daily) on a first-come, first-

Hollywood Boulevard

In the first half of the 20th century, Hollywood Boulevard was a legendary place replete with glamorous stars and nightclubs; in the latter part of the century, as film studios deserted Hollywood for other parts of greater LA, it fell into decline. But now the once-glittering boulevard is making a comeback. Walking is the best way to see its sights, which include renowned theaters, old-time restaurants and hotels, and much of the Hollywood Walk of Fame. Start at the celebrated corner of Hollywood and Vine. The Walk of Fame heads north on Vine Street up to Sunset Boulevard. You can also view the famous circular Capitol Records Building (1750 N Vine St), designed to resemble a stack of records. Needless to say, this building predated the CD era. Return to Hollywood Boulevard and walk west, continuing to follow the Walk of Fame; keep your eyes open for the stars of Marilyn Monroe, Charlie Chaplin, Clark Gable, Jack Nicholson, Elvis Presley, and Mickey Mouse. But don't forget to look up either—in the hills to the north, you should be able to spot the 50-foot-high letters of the Hollywood sign. Meanwhile, at eye level, you'll pass several vintage theaters, each more ornate (and gaudy) than the last, including the Pantages (6233 Hollywood Blvd), the Egyptian (6712), and El Capitan (6838). Most legendary of all is Mann's Chinese (6925), where stars ranging from Shirley Temple to Harrison Ford have left their handprints and footprints (and, in Lassie's case, pawprints) in the cement in the theater's courtyard. Next to Mann's is the Academy of Motion Pictures Arts and Sciences Complex, which is helping to put the Hollywood back into Hollywood. And just across the street is the venerable Hollywood Roosevelt Hotel (7000 Hollywood Blvd), where Hollywood's golden years are chronicled in a photo exhibit on the Mezzanine level. At the end of your stroll, head to Musso & Frank Grill (6667 Hollywood Blvd), an oldtime Hollywood hangout that retains its vintage flavor; its a good place to eat or have a drink at the splendid bar.

served basis. Age limits for admittance vary and are specified on tickets; children under 16 not admitted to any broadcast. (Mon-Fri) **FREE**

Farmers' Market. *6333 W 3rd St, Hollywood (90036). Corner of 3rd St and Fairfax Ave. Phone 323/933-9211. www.farmersmarketla.com.* This historic landmark features outdoor food stalls, restaurants, and shops. (Mon-Fri 9 am-9 pm, Sat 9 am-8 pm, Sun 10 am-7 pm)

⭐ **Grauman's Chinese Theatre.** *6925 Hollywood Blvd, Hollywood (90028). Between Highland and LaBrea aves. Phone 323/464-8111. www.manntheatres.com/chinese.* Grauman's Chinese Theatre opened in 1927 and has been an operating movie theater ($$) ever since. But what makes this pagoda-shaped façade famous is the forecourt, which is the home to footprints and handprints of more than 100 movie stars, including Marilyn Monroe, John Wayne, Clark Gable, Cary Grant, Jack Nicholson, Harrison Ford, Al Pacino, and Meryl Streep. For more than 50 years, tourists have flocked to Grauman's Chinese—though Lucy Ricardo and Ethel Mertz may be the only ones who succeeded in removing one of the giant cement blocks as a souvenir. You'll face dozens of overpriced souvenir stands and hordes of other camera-toting travelers, but this landmark is worth the trip. Compare your foot size to those of your favorite stars, and know for a second or two what it feels like to stand, if not in their shoes, then at least in the exact place where they once stood. Daily guided tours of the theater are available; phone 323/463-9576. (Forecourt open daily, 24 hours) **$**

⭐ **Griffith Park.** *4730 Crystal Springs Dr, Los Angeles (90027). N end of Vermont Ave, bordered by Ventura Frwy on N, Golden State Frwy on E, Los Feliz Blvd entrances on S. Phone 323/913-4688. www.laparks.org/dos/parks/griffithPK/griffith.htm.* If you want to escape city life without ever leaving town, head to this wonderfully wild retreat only about 8 miles from downtown Los Angeles. With more than 4,100 acres, it's one of the country's largest municipal park and urban wilderness. The recreational opportunities are many, including camping, golf, hiking, horseback riding, jogging, swimming, soccer, and tennis. There is a fee for some activities. The park is also home to numerous top-rate attractions, such as the Museum of the American West, the Griffith Observatory (currently closed for renovation), and the Los Angeles Zoo. (Daily 6 am-10 pm; bridle trails, hiking paths, and mountain roads close at sunset) **FREE** Also in the park are

Greek Theatre. *2700 N Vermont Ave, Los Angeles (90027). Phone 323/665-5857.* The Greek Theatre in Los Angeles's Griffith Park is a concert-goer's paradise. An outdoor theater set in a tree-enveloped canyon, the Greek Theatre has been host to some of the music world's biggest stars, including James Taylor, Elton John, Tina Turner, Santana, and Pearl Jam, to name just a few. You can even have a world-famous Pink's hot dog, available at the concession stand, while you watch the show.

Griffith Park Golf Course. *4730 Crystal Springs Dr, Los Angeles (90027). Phone 323/664-2255.* Nestled into downtown Los Angeles is Griffith Park, which houses four golf courses (two 18-hole and two 9-hole): the Woodrow Wilson, the Warren Harding, the Franklin Roosevelt, and the Los Feliz. The park hosts the city's junior golf championship every year and has been in operation since the 1930s, when it hosted the PGA's Los Angeles Open three years straight. The Barber Shop is one of the best golf shops in the country and is located in the clubhouse at Griffith Park. It offers club fitting, junior instruction, and even demo days to try out new equipment. **$$$$**

Hollywood Sign. *Mount Lee, Los Angeles (90027). In Griffith Park.* Originally constructed in 1923 to advertise the Hollywoodland housing development, the letters spelling LAND on this larger-than-life sign somehow disappeared, and the world-famous landmark that we know today was born. Although you can see the Hollywood sign from all over Los Angeles, head to Beachwood Drive off of Franklin Avenue in Hollywood near the 101 Freeway for a great snapshot. You can follow Beachwood all the way to its ending point, park your car, and hike up the Hollyridge Trail to the sign itself. Although a fence surrounds the sign, you'll be rewarded with a great view from above and behind its nine famous letters, with breathtaking views of Los Angeles and (on a clear day) the Pacific Ocean.

Los Angeles Zoo. *5333 Zoo Dr, Los Angeles (90027). In the center of Griffith Park. Phone 323/644-4200.* Crested capuchin monkeys, uakaries, ploughshare tortoises, Komodo dragons, and snow leopards—these are just some of the unique creatures that keep bug-eyed visitors at this 80-acre animal kingdom oohing and ahhing at every turn. In all, the zoo displays more than 1,200 amphibians, birds, mammals, and reptiles representing more than 370 different species. Two especially notable exhibits feature crowd-pleasing critters in replicas of their natural habitats: the Red Ape Rain Forest, home to those lovable orangutans, and the Chimpanzees of Mahale Mountain in Tanzania. (Sept-June: daily 10 am-5 pm, July-early Sept: daily 10 am-6 pm; closed Dec 25) **$$**

Museum of the American West. *4700 Western Heritage Way, Los Angeles (90027). Phone 323/667-2000.* Located in beautiful Griffith Park, the Museum of the American West is your ticket to the Wild West. Founded in 1988 by the "singing cowboy" himself, Gene Autry, the museum is a treasure trove of more than 70,000 objects relating to the American West, including everything from paintings by Bierstadt, Moran, and Remington to Western furniture and clothing. You'll also see an excellent collection of radio, TV, and film memorabilia, such as Gene Autrys guitar; Hopalong Cassidy's hat and his horse, Topper's, saddle; and artifacts from legendary filmmaker Cecil B. DeMille. (Tues-Wed, Fri-Sun 10 am-5 pm, Thurs to 8 pm; closed Thanksgiving, Dec 25) Free admission on Thurs after 4 pm. **$$**

Travel Town. *5200 W Zoo Dr, Los Angeles. Phone 323/662-5874.* Travel Town is an outdoor transportation museum in Los Angeles's Griffith Park, where you can see trains and motorcars up close. With 15 locomotives (the oldest dating to 1864), 11 freight cars and cabooses, 9 passenger cars, and 4 interurbans and motorcars, the museum offers plenty to see. You can also take a ride on the miniature train that runs around the park's perimeter. (Mon-Fri 10 am-5 pm, Sat-Sun 10 am-6 pm; closed Dec 25) **FREE**

Hollywood Boulevard. *Hollywood Blvd, Hollywood.* There is no greater testament to Hollywood than Hollywood Boulevard. From the storefront murals to the world-renowned Walk of Fame, the legends of Hollywood are immortalized here. Take the Walk to Hollywood and Highland, the must-see hotel-retail complex that houses the Kodak Theatre, permanent home to the Academy Awards, and continue past Grauman's Chinese Theatre, the Guinness World of Records Museum, and famous restaurants and clubs, such as the Pig N' Whistle.

Hollywood Bowl. *2301 N Highland Ave, Hollywood (90078). Just SW of the Hollywood Frwy. Phone 323/850-2000. www.hollywoodbowl.org.* This huge outdoor amphitheater has been a Los Angeles landmark for more than 80 years, with performances ranging from symphony orchestras to rock 'n' roll. Over the years, performers including Sinatra, Streisand, and

Pavarotti have graced the stage; bands have included the Beatles and The Who. Even if you're not able to attend a performance while you're in town, stop by the Hollywood Bowl Museum, open daily throughout the year and two hours before every performance, to find out more about this landmark venue.

Hollywood Entertainment Museum. *7021 Hollywood Blvd, Hollywood (90028). Phone 323/465-7900. www. hollywoodmuseum.com.* Who needs Captain Picard? At this fun-packed, interactive museum you can assume command of the *Starship Enterprise* from the *Star Trek* series. When you return to planet Earth, take at seat in Norm's chair from *Cheers,* or tour one of the actual sets from *The X-Files.* These exhibits and the many others in this 33,000-square-foot salute to Hollywood celebrate the entertainment industry and offer an exciting behind-the-scenes look at Tinseltown's magic. (Memorial Day-Labor Day: daily 10 am-6 pm; rest of year: Thurs-Tues 11 am-6 pm; closed Thanksgiving, Dec 25 and Jan 1) **$$$**

Hollywood Heritage Museum. *2100 N Highland Ave, Hollywood (90068). Phone 323/874-2276. www.hollywood-heritage.org.* Right across the street from the Hollywood Bowl, in a restored barn, you'll find this treasure trove packed with the largest public display of mesmerizing memorabilia from Hollywood's heyday: rare photos of silent film sets and casts; original props and weapons from director Cecil B. DeMille's films, including *Cleopatra* and *Samson and Delilah*, and historic photos and postcards of Hollywood streets and buildings. As the song goes, "there's no business like show business," and you just might leave this small jewel of a museum singing that catchy tune. Way back in 1913, it was the site of Hollywood's first feature-length Western, *The Squaw Man.* (Sat-Sun 11 am-4 pm; closed holidays) **$**

⭐ **Hollywood Walk of Fame.** *Hollywood Blvd and La Brea Ave, Hollywood (90028). Hollywood Blvd from Gower St to La Brea Ave, Vine St from Yucca St to Sunset Blvd. Phone 323/469-8311. www.hollywoodchamber. net.* Begun in 1960, the Walk of Fame is one of Hollywood's most recognized landmarks. Honoring celebrities from film, television, theater, and music, there are well over 2,000 stars on the Walk, with roughly one or two new stars added every month. If you want to try to catch a glimpse of a celebrity getting his or her star on the Walk of Fame, check out the Web site for information about upcoming ceremonies.

Hollywood Wax Museum. *6767 Hollywood Blvd, Hollywood (90028). Phone 323/462-8860. www.holly-woodwax.com.* This is not your typical wax museum.

Located in the heart of famous Hollywood Boulevard, the Hollywood Wax Museum steers clear of obscure political figures and instead immortalizes more than 350 of Hollywood's legends with lifelike wax sculptures. Expertly designed and created by the Masters FX studio and curator Ken Horn, sculptures of film and TV stars such as Clark Gable, Elvis Presley, Tom Cruise, and even Super Mario are part of elaborate movie sets designed to entertain and inform visitors about films and their actors. (Daily 10 am-midnight) **$$$**

Melrose Avenue. *Melrose and Highland aves, Los Angeles. E of Beverly Hills, between Doheny Dr and Highland Ave. Phone 323/469-8311.* On this street synonymous with bohemian shopping, funky fashions definitely have the right of way. Some shops offer great buys on vintage clothing, while others offer great-looking cutting-edge designs at prices to match. If you're a trendsetting style maven not deterred by cost, check the racks at chic boutiques such as Betsey Johnson, Liza Bruce, and Miu Miu for what's new and hip. Galleries and restaurants also do business along this main thoroughfare east of Beverly Hills.

Mulholland Drive. *Mulholland Dr, Hollywood. Reached by Laurel Canyon Blvd, Hollywood Blvd, Coldwater Canyon Dr, Beverly Glen Blvd, and other roads.* The best way to take advantage of Los Angeles's beautiful Santa Monica Mountains is to take a ride on Mulholland Drive. This 21-mile road takes you along the top of the range from Hollywood to Ventura, dipping through the peaks and canyons of the Hollywood Hills. The views of the San Fernando Valley and the LA Basin are breathtaking, as are the celebrity homes you'll spot along the way.

Pantages Theater. *6233 Hollywood Bvd, Hollywood (90028). Phone 213/480-3232.* Take a seat in this ornate theater, and you take a walk down Hollywood's Memory Lane. Since its opening in 1930, the Pantages has hosted A-list movie premieres, the Academy Awards, performances by some of the world's greatest musicians, and, more recently, national touring productions of Broadway's biggest hits. Just seeing the 2,691-seat theater itself, however, is worth the price of any show ticket ($$$$). Art Deco statues. Gilded columns. Hand-painted murals. They just don't make 'em like this anymore.

Sunset Ranch/Hollyridge Trail. *3400 Beachwood Dr, Hollywood (90068). Head N on Beachwood Dr off of Franklin Ave in Hollywood and follow Beachwood until it dead-ends at the Sunset Ranch. Either park on the residential street outside the ranch or enter the ranchs driveway and park at the small dirt lot on your right. Phone 323/464-9612. www.*

sunsetranchhollywood.com. Located in the Hollywood Hills, on the edge of Griffith Park (the largest municipal park in the United States), is the Sunset Ranch. When you walk onto the grounds, you'll swear that you've stepped back in time (or, at the very least, onto a Hollywood movie set). Rent a horse, and the ranch will provide a guide to take you up into the trails that weave through the hills of Griffith Park. Or, if you prefer to hoof it without horsepower, walk partway up the driveway until you come to the trailhead of the Hollyridge Trail. A relatively easy hike on a wide dirt fire road, you'll circle around the east side of Mount Lee, where you can see the San Fernando Valley from the one vantage point where it'll make you ooh and aah. Continue around the mountain and you'll come to the Hollywood sign, where you'll be rewarded with breathtaking views of Los Angeles. (Daily 9 am-5 pm) **$$$$**

Special Events

Easter Sunrise Services. *Hollywood Bowl, 2301 N Highland Ave, Hollywood (90078). Phone 323/850-2000.* An interdenominational service with music of select choral groups.

Hollywood Christmas Parade. *6925 Hollywood Blvd, Los Angeles (90028).* Features floats, marching bands, and more than 50 of Hollywood's famous stars. Televised worldwide. Sun after Thanksgiving.

Full-Service Hotel

★ ★ ★ **RENAISSANCE HOLLYWOOD HOTEL.** *1755 N Highland Ave, Los Angeles (90028). Phone 323/856-1200; toll-free 800/468-3571; fax 323/856-1205. www.renaissancehollywood.com.* Anchoring the dynamic Hollywood and Highland retail/entertainment complex, home of the Kodak Theatre and the Academy Awards, this luxury hotel in the heart of the movie-making capital boasts a sophisticated, mid-century design, a rooftop pool, and spectacular city views. Deluxe accommodations featuring chic furnishings, work desks, and complimentary weekday newspapers should please any business or leisure traveler, and the house restaurant, Twist, offers eclectic eats. The Hollywood Walk of Fame and numerous restaurants and shops are within the complex; the Hollywood Bowl, Universal Studios, and other attractions are within a short drive. Concierge, secretarial, and childcare services are available. 637 rooms. Check-in 4 pm, check-out noon. High-speed Internet access. Restaurant, bar. Fitness room. Outdoor pool. Business center. **$$$**

Restaurants

★ ★ ★ **BRASSERIE VERT.** *6801 Hollywood Blvd, Suite 411, Hollywood (90028). Phone 323/491-1300; fax 323/491-1293. www.wolfgangpuck.com.* Within the vortex of the Hollywood and Highlands mall, Wolfgang Puck's chic brasserie is a welcome respite for weary shoppers, hungry tourists, and dressed-up locals on their way to the Bowl or the theater. The room is large and cheerful, with green walls, blue booths, funky lighting, and an open kitchen. The bistro-style menu is chock full of European classics like steamed mussels, fritto misto, pork chops, and of course, gourmet pizzas. Puck has proven that mall dining need not involve a hot dog on a stick. French menu. Lunch, dinner. Bar. Children's menu. Casual attire. Reservations recommended. Valet parking. **$$$**

★ ★ ★ **CAFE DES ARTISTES.** *1534 N McCadden Pl, Hollywood (90028). Phone 323/469-7300; fax 323/469-7375. www.cafedesartistes.info.* This intimate French restaurant, located in a converted house on a Sunset Boulevard side street, transports you from Hollywood to France, despite the evident movie industry types who hew to the place. The firelit, parquet-floored room is dimly lit, making the beautiful people ever more beautiful, and the outdoor patio is tented to romantic effect. There's plenty of food on the menu to please a Francophile, including escargot and duck leg confit. But the restaurant's mac 'n' cheese, a comfort food staple, has made it famous with foodies. French menu. Lunch, dinner. Bar. Casual attire. Reservations recommended. Outdoor seating. **$$$**

★ ★ ★ **FALCON.** *7213 Sunset Blvd, Hollywood (90046). Phone 323/850-5350; fax 323/850-5319. www.falconslair.com.* This sleek spot with a sexy 1970s aura is evocative of a case-study house, with clean lines and layout, where the indoor dining room seems to pour into a fire-lit back patio. Shag carpets and leather blocks are strewn about in the uber-chic cocktail lounge, and geometric booths line the walls. The terminally hip clientele nibble on organic salads and crisp pizzas made with farmers' market-fresh ingredients. Later in the evening, the crowd spills into the patio to carouse, and a DJ turns the dining room into a nightclub. American menu. Dinner, late-night. Closed Sun. Bar. Casual attire. Outdoor seating. **$$**

★ **LA SERENATA DE GARIBALDI.** *1842 E 1st St, Los Angeles (90039). Phone 323/265-2887; fax 323/265-9732. www.laserenataonline.com.* This traditional Mexican restaurant full of authentic folk art is the dining destination for authentic south-of-the-border cuisine. Its West Side sister dining room (1416 Fourth St, Santa Monica; phone 310/656-7017) is awash in pastel hues and frequented by upscale beach-goers who appreciate the simple and powerful food. The casual atmosphere seems appropriate for this seafood nirvana, where offerings of super-fresh fish are paired with complex house-made sauces like smoky chipotle and mojo de ajo. Mexican menu. Lunch, dinner. **$$**

★ **MUSSO & FRANK GRILL.** *6667 Hollywood Blvd, Los Angeles (90028). Phone 323/467-5123; fax 323/467-7788.* Not much has changed since this historic institution opened in 1919, and that's just the way the loyal customers like it. You can still order Welsh rarebit from a grumpy old waiter and enjoy what many swear is the most perfect martini on the planet. The dining room is as frozen in time as the menu, with lots of dark wood, lumpy booths, and archival photos. Hollywood old-timers and up-and-comers meet here to do deals over meat and potatoes. The famed "Round Table" of Saroyan, Thurber, Faulkner, and Fitzgerald met here. American menu. Lunch, dinner. Closed Sun-Mon; holidays. Bar. **$$$**

★ ★ **UZBEKISTAN.** *7077 Sunset Blvd, Hollywood (90028). Phone 323/464-3663.* Los Angeles is punctuated with ethnic neighborhoods, and Little Russia lands smack dab in the middle of the city. So it's no surprise to see a fine Russian restaurant tucked into a mini mall next to a fast-food joint. The charming and kitschy dining room is colorful and vibrant, with somewhat authentic live music. Meat dumplings, skewered lamb, and other Eurasian specials grace the tables of Russian expats and Hollywood hipsters alike. Eastern European menu. Lunch, dinner. Bar. Casual attire. Reservations recommended. **$$**

★ ★ **WHITE LOTUS.** *1743 Cahuenga Blvd, Los Angeles (90028). Phone 323/463-0060. www.whitelotushollywood.com.* More renowned for its celebrity sightings than its cuisine, White Lotus is a white-hot spot to beif you can get by the bouncer and his velvet rope. Or you can do the civilized thing and make reservations to dine on the massive tent-covered patio, complete with palms, fountains, and a giant Buddha. Sushi is available, but the prepared entrées are the real stars of the menu. After dinner, toss back a few cocktails in the adjacent nightclub and try to catch a glimpse of Ashton or Demi. Pan-Asian menu. Dinner. Bar. Casual attire. Reservations recommended. Valet parking. Outdoor seating. **$$$**

Huntington Beach (J-4)

See also Costa Mesa, Newport Beach

Population 189,594
Elevation 28 ft
Area Code 714
Web Site www.hbvisit.com

This quirky city with a nearly unbelievable history features more than 8 miles of beaches, all of them favorable to swimmers, many favorable to surfers, and some even hospitable to dogs. Pacific Coast Highway at Sea Point Avenue is officially known as Huntington Cliffs, but the locals call it Dog Beach because, well, dogs are welcomed along with their owners. You'll find Dog Beach if you investigate the fabled and most recent incarnation of the Huntington Pier, a structure that has had its ups and downs thanks to heavy surf, earthquake, fire, and dramatic disasters. This version, the locals say, is built to last. They'll also tell you to take a hike out to the very end and have a meal at Ruby's Restaurant.

Named after Henry E. Huntington, a fabled entréepreneur from California's freewheeling past, Huntington Beach was a vital rail terminus, an oil boom town, and a posh resort. The Newland House (Beach Blvd at Adams) evokes the feel and architecture of the first decade of the 20th century in California. The City Gym and Pool on Palm Avenue dates to the early 1930s, surviving numerous earthquakes.

Huntington Beach is one of the few Orange County beaches that allows fire pits.

Limited-Service Hotels

★ **COMFORT INN.** *16301 S. Beach Blvd, Huntington Beach (92647). Phone 714/841-1812; fax 714/841-0214. www.comfortsuites.com.* 102 rooms, 3 story. Complimentary continental breakfast. Check-in 3 pm. Check-out 11 am. Fitness room. Outdoor pool, whirlpool. **$** 🏋 🏊

★ ★ **HOTEL HUNTINGTON BEACH.** *7667 Center Ave, Huntington Beach (92647). Phone 714/891-0123; toll-free 877/891-0123; fax 714/895-4591. www.hotelhb.com.* 224 rooms, 8 story. Complimentary continental breakfast. Check-in 2 pm, check-out noon. Restaurant, bar. Fitness room. Indoor pool, children's pool, whirlpool. Airport transportation available. Business center. **$** 🏋 🏊 🧍

★ **RAMADA LIMITED OCEAN FRONT.** *17205 Pacific Coast Hwy, Sunset Beach (90742). Phone 714/840-2431; fax 562/592-4093. www.ramada.com.* 50 rooms, 2 story. Complimentary continental breakfast. Check-in 3 pm, check-out 11 am. **$$**

Full-Service Resort

★ ★ ★ **HILTON WATERFRONT BEACH RESORT.** *21100 Pacific Coast Hwy, Huntington Beach (92648). Phone 714/845-8000; toll-free 800/822-7873; fax 714/845-8425. www.waterfrontbeachresort.hilton. com.* Waterfalls, fountains, and the view of the Pacific Ocean are only part of the charm of this resort. 290 rooms, 12 story. Pets accepted. Check-in 4 pm, check-out noon. Restaurant, bar. Fitness room. Outdoor pool, whirlpool. Tennis. Airport transportation available. Business center. **$$**

Restaurants

★ ★ ★ **RED PEARL KITCHEN.** *412 Walnut Ave, Huntington Beach (92648). Phone 714/969-0224. www. redpearlkitchen.com.* Its smallish interior sports a pop Asian/industrial aesthetic—a big video screen shows old Godzilla and kung fu clips; utility conduits have been left exposed—that may be a bit self-consciously hip even for this freewheeling shore town. But the largely preppy, post-bohemian patronage doesn't mind that or the forced neighborliness of the banquet-style table-and-stool seating, because Red Pearl Kitchen's Asian-based mains are "hot" in every sense. Along with taste sensations, an entrée of coriander-seasoned shrimp satay, for example, might induce a waiter-summoning shout of "Sake to me!" And, fortunately, Red Pearl Kitchen stocks plenty of the chilled adult beverage to douse flavorful fires. Pan-Asian menu. Dinner. Closed. Bar. Casual attire. Reservations recommended. **$$**

★ ★ ★ **TROQUET.** *3333 Bristol St, Costa Mesa (92626). Phone 714/708-6865; fax 714/708-6869. www. troquetrestaurant.com.* Mall dining doesn't get any better than Troquet, which effectively diverts attention from its location with an open kitchen, lots of artfully arranged flowers, and an elegant dark cherry wood bar. Another welcome distraction: the starters, which are so varied and substantial—the foie gras terrine and steak tartare with black olive tapanade among them—that they end up being "finishers" for some patrons. Main dishes, including the Niman Ranch pork chop with lavender-scented shell beans and the crispy veal sweet-

breads, are innovative and exceptionally aromatic. A la carte and chef's tasting menus are available daily, and the wine list offers ideal pairings for all parts of the repast. French menu. Lunch, dinner. Bar. Children's menu. Valet parking. Outdoor seating. **$$$**

Idyllwild (J-5)

See also Desert Hot Springs, Indio, Palm Desert, Palm Springs

Population 3,504
Elevation 5,500 ft
Area Code 951
Zip 92549
Information Chamber of Commerce, 54295 Village Center Dr; phone 951/659-3259 or toll-free 888/659-3259
Web Site www.idyllwild.com

Idyllwild, located in the San Jacinto Mountains amid pine and cedar forests with towering mountains providing the backdrop, is a small alpine village at the gateway to thousands of acres of national forest and state and county parks. This popular resort and vacation area provides fishing in backcountry streams and lakes, hiking, rock climbing, and riding. A Ranger District office of the San Bernardino National Forest (see SAN BERNARDINO) is located here.

What to See and Do

Mount San Jacinto State Park. *On Hwy 243. Phone 951/659-2607. www.sanjac.statepark.org.* On 14,000 acres. Nature and hiking trails; picnicking; camping (reservations required). Interpretive programs.

Riverside County parks. *5400 County Playground Rd, Idyllwild (92549). Phone toll-free 800/234-7275.*

　Hurkey Creek. *56375 Hwy 74, Mountain Center (92561). 4 miles SE via Hwys 243, 74, near Lake Hemet. Phone 951/659-2050.* Camping (fee), picnicking (fee), play area, hiking. Pets on leash.

　Idyllwild. *54000 County Park Rd, Idyllwild. 1 mile W at end of County Park Rd. Phone 951/659-3850.* Camping (fee; reservations phone 951/659-2656), picnicking (fee), play area, hiking. Pets on leash only. Visitor center with museum. **$**

Full-Service Inn

★ ★ ★ **STRAWBERRY CREEK INN.** *26370*

Scenic Hwy 243, Idyllwild (92549). Phone 951/659-3202; toll-free 800/262-8969. www.strawberrycreekinn.com. If your idea of relaxing is reading in the library, basking in the summer sun, or walking along Strawberry Creek, then this inn is for you. For the more adventurous person, there are hundreds of miles of hiking trails, or you can just dream the day away in a hammock. 9 rooms. Complimentary full breakfast. Check-in 2-6 pm. Check-out 11 am. **$**

Restaurant

★ ★ **GASTROGNOME.** 54381 Ridgeview, Idyllwild (92549). Phone 951/659-5055; fax 951/659-5719. www.thegnome.com. Seafood menu. Lunch, dinner. Closed Mon. Bar. Outdoor seating. **$$$**

Indian Wells (J-5)

See also Palm Desert, Palm Springs

Web Site www.indianwells.org

Full-Service Resorts

★ ★ ★ **HYATT GRAND CHAMPIONS.** 44600 Indian Wells Ln, Indian Wells (92210). Phone 760/341-1000; toll-free 800/554-9288; fax 760/568-2236. www.grandchampions.hyatt.com. Located 120 miles east of Los Angeles and 135 miles north of San Diego, Palm Springs has long been the vacation getaway for Southern California's elite. It's a desert oasis complete with swimming pools, golf courses, and fine dining. In January 2003, the Hyatt Grand Champions wrapped up a $65 million renovation, and when you stay here, you'll reap the rewards. Every room, elegantly decorated in cream and beige tones, comes with all the modern amenities you'd expect, plus the less-modern pull-out sofa, which makes staying here with kids more feasible. The hotel has a 30,000-square-foot spa plus the adults-only Oasis Pool. But don't worry—there are five other heated pools, plus a water slide, all of which allow children. If golf is your passion, hit the links at the 36 holes of the Golf Resort at Indian Wells, which surrounds the hotel. For food and drinks, the resort has five options, including an espresso bar, a cocktail lounge, an outdoor grill, and a café offering light fare. 479 rooms, 5 story. Pets accepted, fee. Check-in 4 pm, check-out noon. Restaurant, bar. Children's activity center. Spa. Outdoor pool, children's pool, whirlpool. Golf, 36 holes. Tennis. Business center. **$$$**

★ ★ ★ **INDIAN WELLS RESORT HOTEL.** 76-661 Hwy 111, Indian Wells (92210). Phone 760/345-6466; toll-free 800/248-3220; fax 760/772-5083. www.indianwellsresort.com. A beautifully landscaped desert oasis, this intimate property appeals to the escapist tendencies of leisure and business travelers with its serene mountain vistas and proximity to top shopping and recreation. European boutique-hotel styling informs the personalized service and spacious, casually elegant accommodations. The unique array of stores and galleries along El Paseo is within an easy drive. 155 rooms, 3 story. Complimentary continental breakfast. Check-in 3 pm, check-out noon. Restaurant, two bars. Fitness room. Outdoor pool, whirlpool. Tennis. Airport transportation available. **$$**

★ ★ ★ **RENAISSANCE ESMERALDA RESORT.** 44-400 Indian Wells Ln, Indian Wells (92210). Phone 760/773-4444; fax 760/346-9308. www.renaissanceesmeralda.com. The resorts of Palm Springs are oases in the desert, and the Renaissance Esmeralda is no exception. On-site you'll find a full-service spa, lighted tennis courts, and the Golf Resort at Indian Wells, which offers two championship courses. Kids aren't left out of the fun, either—a special Kids Camp offers arts-and-crafts activities, swimming, and poolside play at the hotel's sandy "beach." Each room has a private balcony, with a stunning view of the surrounding mountains, golf courses, and desert. Two restaurants are on-site—the Sirocco, offering Italian cuisine, and the more casual Charisma, where you can dine indoors or out. Whether you're traveling for business or pleasure, alone or with children, the Renaissance Esmeralda is sure to please. 560 rooms, 7 story. Check-in 4 pm, check-out noon. Restaurant, bar. Children's activity center. Fitness room, spa. Beach. Outdoor pool, children's pool, whirlpool. Golf. Tennis. Airport transportation available. Business center. **$$**

Spa

★ ★ ★ **THE WELL SPA AT MIRAMONTE RESORT & SPA.** 45000 Indian Wells Ln, Indian Wells (92210). Phone 760/341-2200; toll-free 800/237-2926; fax 760/568-0541. www.miramonteresort.com. Pampering, relaxation, and rejuvenation lure guests to the intimate and luxurious Well Spa at the Miramonte Resort. This Tuscan-inspired jewel will awaken your senses in a setting that is distinctive and tranquil. Outdoor and indoor treatment rooms are available to ensure the ultimate spa experience. Guests can indulge themselves in the Tuscan living-inspired spa services and treatments that incorporate therapeutic muds, wine extracts, pure essential oils, and refreshing waters. Signature services at The Well Spa are very unique and include wine baths and Vichy showers provided on tables built from 100-year-old Acacia cedar. Relax in a shallow stream of water on one of the spa's unique river benches sculpted from stone. The Well Spa features a complete fitness center with an array of classes and activities, a full service salon, a spa boutique, and a beverage bar serving healthy fare. Other options available include wellness and cooking classes, plus fitness and spa events.

Restaurant

★ ★ ★ LE SAINT GERMAIN. *74985 Hwy 111, Indian Wells (92210). Phone 760/773-6511; fax 760/773-6510. www.lestgermain.com.* French, Mediterranean menu. Dinner. Closed Sun in summer. Bar. Casual attire. Valet parking. Outdoor seating. **$$$**

Indio (J-5)

See also Desert Hot Springs, Idyllwild, Joshua Tree National Park, Palm Desert, Palm Springs

Founded 1876
Population 49,116
Elevation 14 ft below sea level
Area Code 760
Information Chamber of Commerce, 82-503 Hwy 111, 92201; phone 760/347-0676 or toll-free 800/444-6346
Web Site www.indiochamber.org

Founded as a railroad construction camp, the town took its name from the large number of Native Americans nearby. Few settlers came until the All-American Canal and its 500 miles of pipeline turned the Coachella Valley into an area so fertile that it now produces 59 types of crops, including 95 percent of all American dates. The groves in the valley are the thickest in the Western Hemisphere. Today, Indio is a marketing and transportation hub for this agricultural outpouring. It is also known for its variety of festivals (see SPECIAL EVENTS).

What to See and Do

All-American Canal. *N, E, and W of the city.* Brings water 125 miles from Colorado River.

Fantasy Springs Casino. *84-245 Indio Springs Pkwy, Indio (92203). Phone 760/342-5000. www.fantasyspringsresort.com.* Gaming and entertainment center offers

off-track betting, video gaming machines, 1,200-seat bingo room, and more than 35 card tables. Also entertainment shows and dining. (Daily, open 24 hours)

General George S. Patton Memorial Museum. *2 Chiriaco Rd, Indio (92201). 30 miles E on Hwy 60, I-10, at Chiriaco Summit. Phone 760/227-3483. www.generalpattonmuseum.com.* Once the desert training headquarters on approximately 18,000 square miles in the California, Arizona, and Nevada deserts. General Patton selected this site to prepare his soldiers for combat in North Africa. Patton memorabilia, artifacts; animal exhibits; natural science exhibits. (Daily 9:30 am-4:30 pm; closed Thanksgiving, Dec 25) **$**

Salton Sea State Recreation Area. *100-225 State Rd, North Shore (92254). N shore of Salton Sea, Hwy 111 at State Park Rd. Phone 760/393-3052. www.saltonsea.statepark.org.* The Salton Sea, located in the Colorado Desert, is a popular inland boating and fishing area. In 1905, the Colorado River flooded through a broken canal gate into the Salton Basin, creating a vast new lake. Anglers catch corvina, croakers, sargo, and tilapia year-round. A launch ramp is available and can accommodate any trailer boat. The recreation area covers 17,913 acres and has areas for swimming and water-skiing. There are nature trails for birdwatching, interpretive programs (Nov-May), picnic grounds, and 148 developed campsites (dump station, hookups), plus 2 miles of primitive camping at Corvina Beach, Salt Creek, and Bombay Beach campgrounds. (Daily).

Special Events

Indio Desert Circuit Horse Show. *81500 Ave 52, Indio (92201).* The largest hunter/jumper horse show west of the Mississippi River. Six weeks from Jan-Mar.

Indio International Tamale Festival. *100 Civic Center Mall, Indio (92201). Phone 760/342-6532. www.tamalefestival.org.* Celebration of traditional Latin American fare. Tamales prepared in various ways; traditional dance, music, entertainment. Carnival, petting zoo, arts and crafts, holiday parade. First weekend in Dec. **FREE**

Riverside County Fair and National Date Festival. *Riverside County Fairgrounds, 40350 Arabia St, Indio (92202). Hwy 111 between Oasis and Arabia sts. Phone 760/863-8247. www.datefest.org.* Fair and pageant done in Arabian Nights style. Mid-late Feb. **$$**

Limited-Service Hotels

★ BEST WESTERN DATE TREE HOTEL. *81909*

Indio Blvd, Indio (92201). Phone 760/347-3421; toll-free 800/720-7234; fax 760/863-1338. www.datetree. com. 119 rooms, 2 story. Pets accepted; fee. Complimentary continental breakfast. Check-in 4 pm, check-out noon. Fitness room. Outdoor pool, whirlpool. **$**

★ **QUALITY INN.** *43505 Monroe St, Indio (92201). Phone 760/347-4044; toll-free 877/424-6423; fax 760/347-1287. www.qualityinnindio.com.* 62 rooms, 2 story. Pets accepted, restrictions. Complimentary continental breakfast. Check-in 1 pm, check-out 11 am. Outdoor pool, whirlpool. **$**

Inglewood

See also Desert Hot Springs, Idyllwild, Palm Desert, Palm Springs, Joshua Tree National Park

What to See and Do

Hollywood Park. *1050 S Prairie Ave, Inglewood (90301). Phone 310/419-1500. www.hollywoodpark. com.* Founded in 1938 by Jack Warner (of Warner Brothers Studios fame), Hollywood Park is a major draw for horseracing fans, with a typical schedule of eight races on weekdays, nine on Saturdays, and ten on Sundays and holidays. If it's thoroughbreds you're after, it's thoroughbreds you'll get. Bring the whole family—kids will enjoy the playground on the north side of the grandstand. (Wed-Sun) **$$**

Irvine (J-4)

See also Costa Mesa, Laguna Beach, Newport Beach, Santa Ana

Population 143,072
Elevation 195 ft
Area Code 949
Information Chamber of Commerce, 2485 McCabe Way, Suite 150; phone 949/660-9112
Web Site www.irvinechamber.com

The land on which the community of Irvine lies was once the property of the Irvine Ranch. In the heart of Orange County, Irvine is a totally planned community.

What to See and Do

University of California, Irvine. *Campus and University drs, Irvine (92697). 2 miles W of I-405, closest off-ramp Jamboree. Phone 949/824-5011. www.uci.edu.* (1965) (17,000 students) Undergraduate, graduate, and medical schools on 1,489-acre campus. Taped and guided tours of campus (daily). **FREE**

Wild Rivers Waterpark. *8770 Irvine Center Dr, Irvine. Phone 949/768-9453. www.wildrivers.com.* One of Southern California's biggest water parks (20 acres), with rides designed for children, teens, and adults. (Mid-May-late Sept: days and times vary; call or visit Web site for information) **$$$$**

Limited-Service Hotel

★ ★ **ATRIUM HOTEL AT ORANGE COUNTY AIRPORT.** *18700 MacArthur Blvd, Irvine (92612). Phone 949/833-2770; toll-free 800/854-3012; fax 949/757-1670. www.atriumhotel.com.* 215 rooms, 3 story. Check-in 3 pm, check-out noon. Restaurant, bar. Fitness room. Outdoor pool. Airport transportation available. Business center. **$**

Full-Service Hotels

★ ★ ★ **CROWNE PLAZA.** *17941 Von Karman Ave, Irvine (92614). Phone 949/863-1999; fax 949/474-7236. www.crowneplaza.com.* This hotel is located in Orange County's prestigious Irvine Concourse Corporate Center. 335 rooms, 14 story. Complimentary continental breakfast. Check-in 3 pm, check-out noon. Restaurant, bar. Fitness room. Indoor pool, whirlpool. Tennis. Airport transportation available. Business center. **$$**

★ ★ ★ **HYATT REGENCY.** *17900 Jamboree Rd, Irvine (92614). Phone 949/975-1234; toll-free 800/233-1234; fax 949/852-1574. www.irvine.hyatt.com.* Visitors will find this hotel central to the business districts of Irvine and Newport. 536 rooms, 14 story. Check-in 3 pm, check-out noon. Restaurant, bar. Fitness room, spa. Outdoor pool, whirlpool. Tennis. Airport transportation available. Business center. **$$**

Restaurants

★ ★ ★ **CHANTECLAIR.** *18912 MacArthur Blvd, Irvine (92612). Phone 949/752-8001; fax 949/955-1394. www.chanteclairirvine.com.* Filled with rich dark woods, comfortably worn colonial furnishings, soaring open-beamed ceilings, and intimate, fireplace-centered rooms, this Orange County institution feels more like a country manor than an award-winning French restaurant. Executive chef Yves Fournier matches the considerable atmospheric charm with a menu anchored by exquisite entrées of steak (including a super-juicy, melts-in-your-mouth filet mignon) and seafood (witness the mahi mahi crusted with sun-dried tomatoes and shiitake mushrooms bathed in a citrus-tinged barnaise). The on-point waitstaff upholds Chanteclair's long tradition of impeccable service. That said, the owner has expanded the bar and commenced an after-hours party nightly at 10 pm—attracting a younger, club-type crowd that tends to hasten the departure of the older, more moneyed dinner clientele. French menu. Lunch, dinner. Closed Sun. Bar. Jacket required. Reservations recommended. Outdoor seating. **$$$$**

★ ★ ★ **RUTH'S CHRIS STEAK HOUSE.** *2961 Michelson Dr, Irvine (92612). Phone 949/252-8848; fax 949/252-0104. www.ruthschris.com.* Born from a single New Orleans restaurant that Ruth Fertel bought in 1965 for $22,000, the Ruth's Chris Steak House chain has made it to the top of every steak lover's list. Aged prime Midwestern beef is broiled to your liking and served on a heated plate, sizzling in butter, a staple ingredient used generously in most entrées; even healthier alternatives like chicken arrive at your table drenched in the savory substance. Sides like creamed spinach and fresh asparagus with hollandaise are not to be missed, and are the perfect companion to any entrée. And who can forget the potatoes? Choose from seven different preparations, from a 1-pound baked potato with "everything" to au gratin potatoes with cream sauce and topped with cheese. Steak menu. Dinner. Bar. Children's menu. Casual attire. **$$$**

Joshua Tree National Park (J-5)

See also Desert Hot Springs, Indio, Palm Desert

Web Site www.nps.gov/jotr/

Covering more than 1,236 square miles, this park preserves a section of two deserts: the Mojave and the Colorado. Particularly notable are the variety and richness of desert vegetation. The park shelters many species of desert plants. The Joshua tree, which gives the park its name, was christened thus by the Mormons because of its upstretched "arms." A member of the Lily family, this giant yucca attains heights

of more than 40 feet. The area consists of a series of block mountains ranging in altitude from 1,000 to 5,800 feet and separated by desert flats. The summer gets very hot, and the temperature drops below freezing in the winter. Water is available only at the Black Rock Canyon Visitor Center/Campground, Cottonwood Campground, the Indian Cove Ranger Station, and the Twentynine Palms Visitor Center. Pets are permitted on leash only; pets are not allowed on trails. Guided tours and campfire programs (Feb-May and Oct-Dec). Picnicking is permitted in designated areas and campgrounds, but no fires may be built outside the campgrounds. For additional information, contact 74485 National Park Dr, Twentynine Palms 92277; phone 760/367-5500.

What to See and Do

Camping. *74485 National Monument Dr, Joshua Tree National Park. Phone toll-free 800/365-2267.* Restricted to nine campgrounds with limited facilities; bring your own firewood and water. Thirty-day limit, July-Sept; 14-day limit the rest of the year. Cottonwood, Black Rock Canyon, and Indian Cove campgrounds (fee); other campgrounds free. Group camping at Cottonwood, Indian Cove, and Sheep Pass. Campgrounds are operated on a first-come, first-served basis, except for Indian Cove, Sheep Pass, and Black Rock Canyon.

Hidden Valley Nature Trail. *74485 National Park Dr, Joshua Tree National Park (92277). Phone 760/367-5500.* One-mile loop; access from picnic area across Hidden Valley Campground. Valley enclosed by wall of rocks.

Keys View. *74485 National Park Dr, Joshua Tree National Park (92277). Phone 760/367-5500.* (5,185 feet) Sweeping view of Coachella valley, desert, and mountain. A paved path leads off the main road.

Lost Palms Canyon. *74485 National Park Dr, Joshua Tree National Park (92277). Phone 760/367-5500.* Eight-mile round-trip hike. Reached by 4-mile trail from Cottonwood Spring. Shelters the largest group of palms (120) in the park. Day use only.

✪ **Oasis Visitor Center.** *74485 National Park Dr, Joshua Tree National Park (92277). Park headquarters, just N of park at Twentynine Palms entrance. Phone 760/367-5500.* Exhibits; self-guided nature trail through the Oasis of Mara, discovered by a government survey party in 1855. (Daily)

Stands of Joshua trees. *74485 National Park Dr, Joshua Tree National Park (92277). Phone 760/367-5500.* In Queen and Lost Horse valleys.

Special Event

Pioneer Days. *Twentynine Palms. Phone 760/367-3445.* Pioneer Days provides fun for the entire family with a children's carnival, parade, rodeo, concerts, outhouse races, and much more. Third weekend in Oct.

Limited-Service Hotels

★ **BEST WESTERN GARDEN INN & SUITES.** *71487 Twentynine Palms Hwy, Twentynine Palms (92277). Phone 760/367-9141; toll-free 800/780-7234; fax 760/367-2584. www.bestwestern.com.* 84 rooms, 2 story. Pets accepted; fee. Complimentary continental breakfast. Check-in 3 pm, check-out 11 am. Fitness room. Outdoor pool. **$**

★ **HOLIDAY INN EXPRESS TWENTYNINE PALMS.** *71809 Twentynine Palms W, Twentynine Palms (92277). Phone 760/361-4009; fax 760/361-3350. www.hiexpress.com.* 53 rooms. Complimentary continental breakfast. Check-in 3 pm, check-out 11 am. High-speed Internet access. Fitness room. Outdoor pool. **$**

★ **OASIS OF EDEN INN & SUITES.** *56377 Twentynine Palms Hwy, Yucca Valley (92284). Phone 760/365-6321; toll-free 800/606-6686; fax 760/365-9592. www.oasisofeden.com.* 39 rooms, 2 story. Pets accepted, some restrictions; fee. Complimentary continental breakfast. Check-in 3 pm, check-out 11 am. Outdoor pool, whirlpool. **$**

Specialty Lodging

JOSHUA TREE INN. *61259 Twentynine Palms Hwy, Joshua Tree (92252). Phone 760/366-1188; fax 760/366-3805. www.jtinn.com.* 10 rooms. Complimentary continental breakfast. Check-in 3-8 pm. Check-out 11 am. Outdoor pool. **$**

Julian

See also San Diego

Web Site www.julianca.com

What to See and Do

⭐ **Eagle and High Peak Mines.** *At the end of C St. Phone 760/765-0036.* A century ago, miners worked by candlelight, with wet bandanas over their faces to keep out dust. This image from the past becomes real when you tour these former gold mine tunnels and learn about Julian's early families and the one-time economic mainstay of this historic little town. Tours, which last about one hour, take you into a 1,000-foot hard-rock tunnel, where you can see the gold mining and milling processes. On display are the hand tools used to dig out all the ore, wooden trusses that braced the tunnels, chutes that carried ore to the ore carts, hoist room machinery that carried miners from the lower levels, and huge stamp machines that crushed the ore to extract the gold. **$$**

Julian Pioneer Museum. *2811 Washington St, Julian. Phone 760/765-0227.* This interesting little museum, one hour east of San Diego in the Cuyamaca Mountains, was originally a blacksmith shop and later a brewery for Peter Meyerhof. It now displays more than 2,120 square feet of historical exhibits of this mid-19th-century gold rush town. It is also said to have the finest lace collection in California. There is a shaded picnic area with restrooms, and many nearby restaurants and shops sell the famous Julian apple pie. (Apr-Nov Fri-Sun 10 am-4 pm; Dec-Mar Sat-Sun 10 am-4 pm; closed Jan 1, Thanksgiving, Dec 25) **DONATION**

Specialty Lodgings

JULIAN GOLD RUSH HOTEL. *2032 Main St, Julian (92036). Phone 760/765-0201; toll-free 800/734-5854; fax 760/765-0327. www.julianhotel.com.* Built in 1897 and lovingly restored, this tree-shaded landmark—the oldest continuously operating hotel in Southern California—affords leisure seekers a look back in time by maintaining the Victorian-era flavor of the old mining town it anchors. All rooms feature private baths and are decorated with antiques and authentic period furniture; the adjoining patio cottage and honeymoon house offer additional privacy along with romantic amenities like fireplaces, verandas and claw-footed tubs. Situated in the heart of Julian's Historic District, the hotel is within a short walk of antique stores, gift shops, a museum and the fabled local gold mines. 16 rooms, 2 story. Complimentary full breakfast. Check-in 3 pm, check-out noon. **$**

ORCHARD HILL COUNTRY INN. *2502 Washington St, Julian (92036). Phone 760/765-1700; toll-free 800/716-7242; fax 760/765-0290. www.orchardhill.com.* Opened in 1994, the Orchard Hill Country Inn has the feel of a rustic mountain lodge, in keeping with its location in Julian, a historic gold-mining town. Larger than you might expect, the inn accommodates both business travelers and vacationers. Each of the rooms is individually decorated, and they range in price—from the spa suite, which has a jetted over-sized bathtub, to the lodge rooms, which are simple but nicely decorated bedrooms, each one unique. (Photographs of the rooms are available on the hotel's Web site, which may help you decide which one is right for you.) Breakfast is included in your hotel stay, as are evening hors doeuvres. A gourmet dinner is served four nights a week. For recreation, you can hike or walk the trails surrounding the inn, take a nap in a hammock, or relax in the game room, where you can watch movies or play games. You can tour the historic goldmines of Julian, shop for antiques, or visit some of the local vineyards (about an hour away). Horseback riding, golfing, and tour of the desert (via air-conditioned jeep) are also popular activities. 22 rooms. Closed Dec 24-25. Complimentary full breakfast. Check-in 3 pm, check-out noon. **$$**

Kernville

Population 1,736
Elevation 2,650 ft
Area Code 760
Zip 93238
Information Chamber of Commerce, 11447 Kernville Rd, PO Box 397; phone 760/376-2629
Web Site www.kernvillechamber.org

A Ranger District office of the Sequoia National Forest (see PORTERVILLE) is located in Kernville. Trout fishing is enjoyed in nearby Kern River.

What to See and Do

Greenhorn Mountain Park. *12 miles W via Hwy 155 in Sequoia National Forest.* Phone 559/565-3341. Park has 90 campsites with barbecue pits, 115 picnic tables, camping supplies. Camping limited to 14 days, no reservations; pets on leash only. **$$$**

Isabella Lake. *4875 Ponderosa Dr, Kernville. S of town.* Phone 760/379-5646. Swimming, water-skiing, fishing, boating (marinas); more than 700 improved camp-sites with showers, restrooms (site/night); auxiliary (primitive) camp area (fee). Contact Sequoia National Forest, Lake Isabella Visitors Center, PO Box 3810, Lake Isabella, 93240.

Kern River Tours. *2712 Mayfair Rd, Lake Isabella (93240).* Phone 760/379-4616. www.kernrivertours.com. Rafting trips down the upper and lower Kern River, a Class II-V river. (Apr-Sept) **$$$$**

Special Events

Kernville Rod Run. Features more than 350 vintage hot rods and classic cars on display. Oct.

Whiskey Flat Days. *Hwy 178, Kernville (93238). 50 miles E of Bakersfield on Hwy 178.* Phone 760/376-2629. Celebrate the gold rush days, when Kernville was known as "Whiskey Flat." There's a ton of fun to be had, with carnival rides, activities for kids, games, a pet parade, and costume contests. Early Jan.

Specialty Lodgings

KERN RIVER INN BED AND BREAKFAST. *119 Kern River Dr, Kernville (93238). Phone 760/376-6750; toll-free 800/986-4382; fax 760/376-6643. www.kern-riverinn.com.* 5 rooms, 2 story. Complimentary full breakfast. Check-in 3-5 pm, check-out 11 am. **$**

WHISPERING PINES LODGE. *13745 Sierra Way, Kernville (93238). Phone 760/376-3733; toll-free 877/241-4100; fax 760/376-6513. www.kernvalley.com/whispering-pines.* 17 rooms. Complimentary full breakfast. Check-in 3 pm, check-out 11 am. Outdoor pool. **$**

Restaurant

★ **JOHNNY MCNALLY'S FAIRVIEW LODGE.** *Star Rte 1, Box 95, Kernville (93238). Phone 760/376-2430. Seafood, steak menu. Dinner. Closed Dec-Feb. Bar. Children's menu.* **$$**

King City (F-2)

See also Pinnacles National Monument

Population 11,094
Elevation 330 ft
Area Code 831
Zip 93930
Information Chamber of Commerce, 200 Broadway St; phone 831/385-3814
Web Site www.kingcity.com

What to See and Do

Los Padres National Forest. *406 S Mildred, King City.*

The forest's northernmost section is W of town. Phone 831/385-5434. www.fs.fed.us/r5/lospadres. Contains the Santa Lucia Mountains, which feature the southernmost groves of coastal redwoods and the only natural stands of bristlecone fir. The 164,575-acre Ventana Wilderness was almost completely burned in a 1977 fire, but vegetation in the fire area reestablished itself and provides an excellent opportunity to witness the changing conditions. Fishing; hiking, camping. (Daily) **$$**

Mission San Antonio de Padua. *Jolon Rd, Jolon. I-101 S, exit King City, then 19 miles S on County G14. Or I-101 N, exit past Bradley at other end of Jolon Rd. Phone 831/385-4478. www.sanantoniomission.org.* Founded in 1771 as the third in the chain of missions. Restoration includes gristmill, waterwheel, wine vat; tannery; museum; Padres Garden. (June-Sept: daily 8 am-6 pm; rest of year: daily 8 am-5 pm; closed Dec 25) **DONATION**

Pinnacles National Monument. *www.nps.gov/pinn.* (See).

Special Event

Mission San Antonio de Padua Fiesta. *End of Mission Rd, King City (93930). Phone 831/385-4478.* This celebration commemorates the founding of the mission in 1771 by Father Junipera Serra and is held in conjunction for the Feast of St. Anthony. Along with a special mass, there is a barbecue as well as music and dancing. Second Sun in June.

Limited-Service Hotel

★ **BEST WESTERN KING CITY INN.** *1190 Broadway, King City (93930). Phone 831/385-6733; fax 831/385-0714. www.bestwestern.com.* King City makes a nice resting point for trips between San Francisco and Los Angeles—sits situated halfway between the two—and the Best Western makes for an inexpensive stopover. Don't expect anything fancy or unique here. The hotel has a small outdoor pool with plastic poolside furniture; rooms come with refrigerators and microwaves. Your dining options include an array of fast-food restaurants all within a mile. 47 rooms. Check-in 2 pm, check-out 11 am. Outdoor pool. **$**

La Habra (J-4)

See also Buena Park, Whittier

Population 58,974
Elevation 298 ft

Area Code 562
Zip 90631
Web Site www.ci.la-habra.ca.us

Restaurant

★ ★ ★ **CAT AND THE CUSTARD CUP.** *800 E Whittier Blvd, La Habra (90631). Phone 562/694-3812; fax 562/694-6753. www.catandcustardcup.com.* Chef/Owner Creed Salisbury welcomes guests to this charming property that has the feel of a contemporary European inn. The fireplace crackles year-round. California menu. Dinner. Closed July 4, Dec 25. Bar. Outdoor seating. **$$$**

La Jolla (K-4)

See also Carlsbad, Del Mar, Escondido, San Diego

Area Code 858
Zip 92037
Information La Jolla Town Council, PO Box 1101; phone 858/454-1444
Web Site www.lajolla.com

This resort community is known as the "Jewel of San Diego." Sandstone bluffs laced with white sand and sparkling ocean suggest the look of the French Riviera. La Jolla is also a recognized center for scientific research.

What to See and Do

Birch Aquarium at Scripps. *2300 Expedition Way, La Jolla (92037). Entrance at N Torrey Pines. Phone 858/534-3474. aquarium.ucsd.edu.* At Scripps Institution of Oceanography, University of California, San Diego; situated on a hilltop, with a spectacular view of the ocean. Visitors can explore the "blue planet," from the depths of the ocean to the far reaches of outer space, at this impressive interpretive center. This facility presents undersea creatures in realistic habitats and allows visitors to experience the frontiers of marine science through interactive museum exhibits. Tidepool exhibit. Bookshop. Beach and picnic areas nearby. (Daily 9 am-5 pm; closed Jan 1, Thanksgiving, Dec 25) **$$**

The Comedy Store. *916 Pearl St, La Jolla (92037). Phone 858/454-9176. www.thecomedystore.com.* We could give you the top ten reasons to check out the talent at the La Jolla branch of LA's famous Comedy Store, but here's just one: it's where David Letterman broke out of the pack. It also can be a hilariously risky evening out, since you're never sure exactly who—or what—you might see. LA talent comes south to headline the Friday and Saturday shows, and lesser-known professional comics perform live Tuesday through Thursday. Sunday is open-mike night, when your two-drink minimum will seem either like enjoyable refreshment or like its not nearly enough. (Wed-Thurs, Sun 8 pm; Fri-Sat 8 pm and 10:30 pm) **$$**

Kellogg Park. *8200 Camino Del Oro, La Jolla (92037). At La Jolla Shores Beach, foot of Avenida de la Playa. Phone 619/235-1169.* Swimming, snorkeling, surfing, bathing beach, small-boat landing; boardwalk, picnic areas. (Daily dawn-dusk)

⭐ **La Jolla Cove.** *1100 Coast Blvd, La Jolla (92037). Phone 619/221-8901. www.sannet.gov/lifeguards/ beaches/cove.shtml.* La Jolla Cove is at the southern edge of the San Diego-La Jolla Underwater Park, an ecologically protected area. The tiny beach, with its coarse sand and extraordinary beauty, is a great place to sunbathe, snorkel, or scuba dive. The cove's curious and show-offy harbor seals are popular with divers and landlubbers alike. Divers can enjoy visibility of more than 30 feet—the waters are ideal for photography and videography—as well as diverse plant and animal life within caves, reefs, and kelp forests. ("Look but don't Touch" is the operative phrase here.) More experienced divers can explore the nearby La Jolla submarine canyons. And, unknown to many, scubas a festive sport. Every year around Halloween, divers participate in an underwater pumpkin carving contest held by local diving company Ocean Enterprises (phone 858/565-6054). (Daily)

La Jolla Playhouse. *Revelle College Dr, La Jolla (92037). Phone 858/550-1010. www.lajollaplayhouse.com.* Sometimes, it seems like the term *hobnobbing* was invented here. On any given night, you will find the gracious créme de la créme of La Jolla and surrounding areas standing on the lush, tree-dense, floodlit lawn before the show or between acts, living up to the theaters illustrious pedigree. This Tony Award-winning venue has been one of America's premier regional theaters since its 1947 founding by Gregory Peck, Dorothy McGuire, and Mel Ferrer. Located on the campus of the University of California, San Diego, the playhouse puts on six shows per season. Although *Thoroughly Modern Millie* premiered here and *Rent* took its West Coast bow here, the playhouse is best known for taking chances on new works. (Performances Mon noon-6 pm, Tues-Sat noon-8 pm, Sun noon-7 pm) **$$$$**

Museum of Contemporary Art. *700 Prospect St, La Jolla (92037). Phone 858/454-3541. www.mcasd.org.* Permanent collection and changing exhibits of contemporary painting, sculpture, design, photography, and architecture. Sculpture garden; bookstore; films, lecture programs. (Mon-Tues, Fri-Sun 11 am-5 pm, Thurs to 7 pm; closed Jan 1, Thanksgiving, Dec 25) **$$**

⭐ **Temecula Wine Region Bike Tour.** *PO Box 840, La Jolla (92038). Company provides transportation to and from San Diego. Phone 858/551-9510.* Southern California wines? Yes, you're reading the compass right. Over the last decade, Temecula's wine industry and tours for aficionados have sprouted up almost simultaneously. Local vintners have samples of everything from sparkling wine to cabernet. Proving that this is as much a destination as an industry, however, several offer extras like restaurant dining and Sunday jazz concerts. HBK San Diego provides a day-long tour that covers your bike and helmet, tasting fees at three stops, a private tasting at the Wilson Creek Winery & Vineyards, and a catered lunch and snacks. (The bikes go on the racks for the afternoon session, and you tour in a van.) Other tours with varying activities and costs are out there, including Gravity Activated Sports (phone 760/742-2294 or toll-free 800/985-4427) and the Sierra Club (phone 619/282-0425). (Phone ahead for reservations; closed holidays) **$$$$**

Torrey Pines Gliderport. *2800 Torrey Pines Scenic Dr, La Jolla (92037). Phone 858/452-9858. www.flytorrey. com.* If you're interested in rising above it all, there's no better place to soar than the Torrey Pines Gliderport in La Jolla. Here, paragliders and hang gliders take off from the cliffs above the Pacific Ocean and sweep onto a breathtaking natural canvas. The 1,750-acre Torrey Pines State Reserve was established to protect the world's rarest pine tree, the gnarly, malformed Torrey Pine, which, hundreds of years ago, covered Southern California. Today, they are found only on Santa Rosa Island off the coast of Santa Barbara and in the Torrey Pines State Reserve. You'll be 50 to 150 feet above the pinetops during your paragliding experience. If the thought of paragliding tempts you but you've never tried it, don't worry: the Gliderport gives you 20 minutes of ground instruction before sending you up in tandem with a certified instructor. Hang gliding is offered as well, but it takes longer to learn; you'll need eight lessons to earn a beginner rating before you can take flight. (Daily) **$$$$**

Torrey Pines State Reserve. *12000 N Torrey Pines Rd, La Jolla. Phone 858/755-2063. www.torreypine.org.* Wilderness park on 2,000 acres. Home to the rare and elegant Torrey Pine trees, miles of unspoiled beaches, and a lagoon that is vital to migrating seabirds. Includes 8 miles of hiking trails, a visitor center and museum (daily 9 am-sunset), guided nature walks (weekends and holidays, 10 am and 2 pm), and educational programs. (Daily 8 am-sunset) **$$**

University of California, San Diego. *9500 Gilman Dr, La Jolla (92093). Near I-5. Phone 858/534-2230. www. ucsd.edu.* (1960) (18,000 students) Scattered around campus is an outdoor collection of contemporary sculpture. Campus tours.

Wind 'n' sea Beach. *At the foot of Palomar St. Phone 619/221-8901.* Surfing area; also a bathing beach. (Daily)

Windansea surfing. *6800 Neptune Pl, La Jolla (92083). From San Diego, take I-5 north to Ardath Rd. Continue on Ardath Rd as it becomes Torrey Pines Rd. Follow Torrey Pines Rd and turn right at Pearl St. Follow Pearl St and turn right at La Jolla Blvd. Follow La Jolla Blvd and turn right on Nautilus. Phone 619/221-8874. www.sannet.gov/ lifeguards/beaches/windan.shtml.* In San Diego, surfing is the only sport that matters. When the big waves roll in, even those who don't partake should get to the shore to watch. For those who do enjoy surfing, Windansea boasts intense veterans-only breaks created by underwater reefs. (The steepness of the beach also causes hard-breaking surf right at the shoreline, so as silly as it sounds, beware getting in and out of the water.) Windansea offers excellent waves at any time of year, but summer, when the swells come from the south, tends to be a better bet. The only drawback: everyone knows it. On the best days, Windansea's concentrated surf breaks get crowded very quickly. Even ambitious amateurs are advised to stay out of the way. But whether you can participate passively or actively, *participate*—surfing is a genuine, joyously American phenomenon. **FREE**

Special Event

Wine and Roses Dinner. *The Westgate Hotel,1055 2nd Ave, La Jolla (92122). Phone 858/229-7582. www. wineandroses.net.* Each year, the largest wine competition in the United States is held in San Diego. Alas, it is judged by professionals, not regular people. But after the competition ends, you can grab your wallet and a nicely dressed companion and head for La Jolla, the location of the San Diego National Wine Competition's Wine and Roses Dinner. Here, you can not only taste the gold, silver, and bronze medal winners, but buy them, too. Proceeds from the event go to charity, making the drinking, the eating, and the buying seem absolutely necessary. Mid-June. **$$$$**

Limited-Service Hotels

★ ★ **BEST WESTERN INN BY THE SEA.** *7830 Fay Ave, La Jolla (92037). Phone 858/459-4461; toll-free 800/462-9732; fax 858/456-2578. www.bestwestern.com.* 134 rooms, 8 story. Complimentary continental breakfast. Check-in 2 pm, check-out noon. Restaurant. Tennis. **$$**

★ ★ **EMBASSY SUITES HOTEL SAN DIEGO-LA JOLLA.** *4550 La Jolla Village Dr, San Diego (92122). Phone 858/453-0400; toll-free 800/362-2779; fax 858/453-4226. www.embassysuites.hilton.com.* This all-suite hotel is located in La Jolla, across from a large shopping center and minutes to UCSD, the Birch Aquarium, theaters, and restaurants. 335 rooms, 12 story, all suites. Complimentary full breakfast. Check-in 4 pm, check-out noon. High-speed Internet access. Restaurant, bar. Fitness room. Outdoor pool, whirlpool. Credit cards accepted. **$$**

★ ★ **GRANDE COLONIAL HOTEL.** *910 Prospect St, La Jolla (92037). Phone 858/454-2181; toll-free 888/530-5766; fax 858/454-5679. www.thegrandecolonial.com.* 75 rooms, 5 story. Check-in 3 pm, check-out noon. Restaurant. Outdoor pool. **$$**

★ ★ **HOTEL LA JOLLA.** *7955 La Jolla Shores Dr, La Jolla (92037). Phone 858/459-0261; toll-free 800/666-0261; fax 858/459-7649. www.hotellajolla.com.* 108 rooms, 11 story. Complimentary continental breakfast. Check-in 3 pm, check-out noon. Restaurant, bar. Fitness room. Outdoor pool, whirlpool. **$$**

★ ★ ★ **SEA LODGE ON LA JOLLA SHORES BEACH.** *8110 Camino Del Oro, La Jolla (92037). Phone 858/454-7126; toll-free 800/640-7702; fax 858/456-3805. www.sealodge.com.* 129 rooms, 3 story. Check-in 3 pm, check-out noon. Restaurant, bar. Fitness room. Outdoor pool, children's pool, whirlpool. Tennis. **$$**

Full-Service Hotels

★ ★ ★ **EMPRESS HOTEL OF LA JOLLA.** *7766 Fay Ave, La Jolla (92037). Phone 858/454-3001; toll-free 888/369-9900; fax 858/454-6387. www.empress-hotel. com.* 77 rooms, 5 story. Complimentary continental breakfast. Check-in 4 pm, check-out noon. Restaurant, bar. Fitness room. **$$**

★ ★ ★ **HOTEL PARISI.** *1111 Prospect, La Jolla (92037). Phone 858/454-1511; toll-free 877/472-7474; fax 858/454-1531. www.hotelparisi.com.* La Jolla's Hotel Parisi has a Dalai Lama-meets-Giorgio Armani appeal. This temple of peace is a decorator showpiece, with darkened interiors guided by the design principles of feng shui. Seductively cool, the accommodations are havens from the outside world with abundant creature comforts. From the all-natural bath products created especially for the hotel to the psychologist on call 24 hours a day, the experience here is far from the ordinary. This hotel satisfies the Zen quotient, where guests dial in for holistic services ranging from Eastern-inspired bodywork and massage to relaxation techniques. Of course, the ocean views from this La Jolla hideaway might just be the perfect therapy for many guests. 20 rooms, 2 story. Complimentary continental breakfast. Check-in 4 pm, check-out noon. **$$$**

★ ★ ★ **HYATT REGENCY LA JOLLA.** *3777 La Jolla Village Dr, San Diego (92122). Phone 858/552-1234; fax 858/552-6066. www.hyatt.com.* 419 rooms, 16 story. Check-in 3 pm. Check-out noon. Restaurant, bar. Fitness room, spa. Outdoor pool, children's pool, whirlpool. Tennis. Business center. **$$$**

★ ★ ★ **LA VALENCIA.** *1132 Prospect St, La Jolla (92037). Phone 619/454-0771; toll-free 800/451-0772; fax 619/456-3921. www.lavalencia.com.* La Valencia is the pride of La Jolla. Perched on a bluff overlooking the Pacific in the center of town, the "pink lady" is a classic choice in this popular resort village. The hotel effortlessly blends old-world charm with modern-day conveniences. European elegance defines the rooms and suites, where large windows open out to views of the flourishing gardens or sparkling sea. Guests lounge by the shimmering pool or luxuriate with an in-room spa treatment, while others head for the diversions of the beach and town. Dining is always a pleasure here. Locals adore the Whaling Bar and Grill; romantics head for the tiny 12-table Sky Room (see) with 180-degree ocean views; and the Mediterranean Room and Tropical Patio remains a good choice throughout the day. 115 rooms, 11 story. Pets accepted; fee. Check-in 3 pm, check-out noon. High-speed Internet access. Three restaurants, two bars. Fitness room. Beach. Outdoor pool, whirlpool. Business center. **$$$$**

★ ★ **RADISSON HOTEL LA JOLLA.** *3299 Holiday Ct, La Jolla (92037). Phone 858/453-5500; toll-free 800/333-3333; fax 858/453-5550. www.radisson.com.* 252 rooms, 4 story. Check-in 3 pm, check-out noon. Restaurant, bar. Fitness room. Outdoor pool, whirlpool. Airport transportation available. Business center. **$$**

Full-Service Resorts

★ ★ ★ **HILTON LA JOLLA TORREY PINES.** *10950 N Torrey Pines Rd, La Jolla (92037). Phone 858/558-1500; toll-free 800/762-6160; fax 858/450-4584. www.hilton.com.* The Hilton La Jolla Torrey Pines is a favorite choice among sophisticated travelers for its golf course views and privileged address. This full-service resort enjoys a majestic setting overlooking the famed oceanfront links of the Torrey Pines Golf Course in the heart of the exclusive San Diego resort community of La Jolla. The rooms and suites are tastefully appointed and enhanced with thoughtful touches. Balconies or patios add to the serene settings with views of the emerald course and the sapphire sea. Whether enjoying the resort's on-site activities or venturing beyond to explore the area's many treasures, guests are sure to have an enjoyable visit while staying at the Hilton. All-day dining is available at the Torreyana Grille, where an open kitchen entertains patrons. 394 rooms, 4 story. Check-in 3 pm, check-out noon. Restaurant, bar. Children's activity center. Fitness room. Outdoor pool, whirlpool. Golf. Tennis. Business center. **$$**

★ ★ ★ ★ **LODGE AT TORREY PINES.** *11480 N Torrey Pines Rd, La Jolla (92037). Phone 858/453-4420; fax 858/453-0691. www.lodgetorreypines.com.* The Lodge at Torrey Pines arguably has cornered the market on enviable locations, from its rocky clifftop spot overlooking the Pacific Ocean to the protected forest and unspoiled beaches of Torrey Pines State Reserve just beyond its well-tended grounds. Adjacent to the 18th green of one of the world's most acclaimed courses, it is also a veritable nirvana for golfers. Tee times are guaranteed for guests who try their hand at this championship course. Others flock to the full-service spa, where elements from the sea blend with ancient traditions. The resort is a celebration of the American Craftsman period, from its stained glass and handcrafted woodwork to its Stickley-style furnishings. The guest rooms convey a rustic sophistication, many with fireplaces, and all with breathtaking vistas of the legendary course or the crashing surf. Befitting this first-class resort, two restaurants offer casual or refined dining to match any mood. 170 rooms. Check-in 4 pm, check-out noon. High-speed Internet access. Two restaurants, two bars.

Fitness room, fitness classes available, spa. Outdoor pool, whirlpool. Golf, 36 holes. Tennis. Airport transportation available. Business center. **$$$**

Full-Service Inn

★ ★ ★ **BED AND BREAKFAST INN AT LA JOLLA.** *7753 Draper Ave, La Jolla (92037). Phone 858/456-2066; toll-free 800/582-2466; fax 858/456-1510. www.innlajolla.com.* Constructed in 1913 using "Cubist" architecture, this inn offers airy and sunny guest rooms. All rooms offer views of the tranquil garden and ocean. Complimentary seasonal fruits and flowers will be found in your room along with terry robes and fine sherry in crystal decanters. 16 rooms, 2 story. Children over 12 years only. Complimentary full breakfast. Check-in 3-5 pm. Check-out 11 am. Beach nearby. **$$**

Specialty Lodgings

LA JOLLA INN. *1110 Prospect St, La Jolla (92037). Phone 858/454-0133; toll-free 888/855-7829; fax 858/454-2056. www.lajollainn.com.* 22 rooms, 4 story. Complimentary continental breakfast. Check-in 3 pm, check-out 11 am. **$$**

SCRIPPS INN. *555 Coast Blvd S, La Jolla (92037). Phone 858/454-3391; fax 858/456-0389. www.scrippsinn.com.* 14 rooms. Complimentary full breakfast. Check-in 3 pm, check-out noon. Beach. **$$**

Spa

★ ★ ★ ★ **THE SPA AT TORREY PINES.** *11480 N Torrey Pines Rd, La Jolla (92037). Phone 858/777-6690; toll-free 800/656-0087. www.lodgetorreypines.com.* The oceanfront setting adjacent to the protected forest of Torrey Pines State Preserve accounts for this 9,500-square-foot spa's focus, with seawater and botanicals influencing many of the treatments. Hydrotherapy works wonders here, from balneotherapy and underwater massage to the aromatic water bath and the California grape seed tea bath. Fourteen treatment rooms invite you to enjoy quiet reflection as you are massaged, cleansed, exfoliated, and rebalanced. Massages range from traditional Swedish and therapeutic to stone, shiatsu, table Thai, and reflexology. The signs of aging are no match for the rejuvenating facials available. The champagne facial fights free radicals

with yeast extracts from French champagne, while the Q-10 facial is a proven wrinkle fighter. Deep-cleansing sea mud, antiaging aqua, vitamin C, and natural botanicals create youthful and vibrant skin. Wonderful body treatments wrap you in vitamins, honey, foaming seaweed, and remineralizing gel to detoxify and renew your skin, while body scrubs use grape seeds, coastal sage, and pine for effective exfoliation. The rituals at The Spa at Torrey Pines are particularly rewarding and offer fascinating insight into ancient cultures. The Ayoma ritual is influenced by centuries-old Ayurvedic principles, the San Tao ritual borrows from the Orient, and the Litya sacred earth ritual takes its inspiration from the Aborigines. These unusual treatments offer a blend of bodywork and massage to achieve balance and well-being.

Restaurants

★ **ASHOKA.** *8008 Girard Ave, La Jolla (92037). Phone 858/454-6263.* Indian menu. Dinner. Closed Mon. Casual attire. Outdoor seating. **$$**

★ ★ ★ **AZUL.** *1250 Prospect St, La Jolla (92037). Phone 858/454-9616; fax 858/454-0934. www.brigantine. com.* Step into this grottolike space and experience the best of the California markets. A great combination of good food, friendly service, attractive ambience, and a fantastic view of the cove. California menu. Lunch, dinner. Closed holidays. Bar. Children's menu. Casual attire. Valet parking. Outdoor seating. **$$$**

★ ★ **BROCKTON VILLA.** *1235 Coast Blvd, La Jolla (92037). Phone 858/454-7393; fax 858/454-2895. www. brocktonvilla.com.* American menu. Breakfast, lunch, dinner. Closed Thanksgiving, Dec 25. Casual attire. Outdoor seating. **$$$**

★ ★ **CAFE JAPENGO.** *8960 University Center Ln, La Jolla (92122). Phone 858/450-3355; fax 858/552-6104. www.lajolla.hyatt.com.* Delightful cuisine is served in this minimalist, high-tech environment by young and eager staff. Located in the Hyatt Regency, the adjacent bar has a great grazing menu and is a popular after-work place for local professionals. Japanese menu. Lunch, dinner. Closed Jan 1, Dec 25. Bar. Casual attire. Valet parking. Outdoor seating. **$$$**

★ **THE COTTAGE.** *7702 Fay Ave, La Jolla (92037). Phone 858/454-8409; fax 858/454-8204. www.cottage-lajolla.com.* California menu. Breakfast, lunch, dinner. Closed holidays. Children's menu. Casual attire. **$$**

★ **DAILY'S FIT AND FRESH.** *8915 Towne Centre Dr, La Jolla (92122). Phone 858/453-1112; fax 858/453-1393. www.dailysrestaurant.com.* Vegetarian menu. Lunch, dinner. Closed Sun, holidays. Children's menu. Casual attire. Outdoor seating. **$$**

★ ★ **ELARIOS.** *7955 La Jolla Shores Dr, La Jolla (92037). Phone 858/459-0541; fax 858/454-3871. www.clayslajolla.com.* California menu. Breakfast, lunch, dinner, Sun brunch. Bar. Casual attire. **$$**

★ ★ **FLEMING'S PRIME STEAKHOUSE & WINE BAR.** *8970 University Center Ln, La Jolla (92122). Phone 858/535-0078; fax 858/535-0096. www.flemingssteakhouse.com.* In addition to the usual New York strip, ribeye, and porterhouse steaks, you'll find some real gems hidden in the menu, such as the smoked salmon flatbread with goat cheese and dill spread, or the Australian lamb chops. American, steak menu. Dinner. Closed July 4, Thanksgiving, Dec 25. Bar. Casual attire. Outdoor seating. Reservations accepted. **$$$**

★ ★ **GEORGE'S AT THE COVE.** *1250 Prospect Pl, La Jolla (92037). Phone 858/454-4244; fax 858/454-5458. www.georgesatthecove.com.* Overlooking the scenic La Jolla Cove and located 15 minutes from downtown San Diego, this three-story restaurant offers superb selections. The views are unsurpassed, and the atmosphere is one of understated elegance. California menu. Lunch, dinner. Casual attire. Valet parking. Outdoor seating. **$$**

★ ★ **MANHATTAN.** *7766 Fay Ave, La Jolla (92037). Phone 858/459-0700; fax 858/454-4741.* Five saltwater aquariums; singing waiter. Italian menu. Lunch, dinner. Closed Sat-Mon, holidays. Bar. Casual attire. **$$$**

★ ★ **MARINE ROOM.** *2000 Spindrift Dr, La Jolla (92037). Phone 858/459-7222; fax 858/551-4673. www.marineroom.com.* Ocean views, fabulous sunsets, and crashing waves create a meal with drama. In operation since 1941, the restaurant is now owned by the La Jolla Beach & Tennis Club. French, International menu. Dinner. Bar. Casual attire. **$$**

★ ★ **PIATTI RISTORANTE.** *2182 Avenida de la Playa, La Jolla (92037). Phone 858/454-1589; fax 858/454-1799. www.piatti.com.* This energetic country-style restaurant serves homey but refined fare. Sit in the terra-cotta and Chianti bottle-filled dining room or out by the fountain patio. Italian menu. Lunch, dinner. Closed holidays. Bar. Casual attire. Outdoor seating. **$$**

★ ★ ★ **ROPPONGI.** *875 Prospect St, La Jolla (92037). Phone 858/551-5252; fax 858/551-7712. www.roppongiusa.com.* Restaurateur Sami Ladeki has hit the jackpot again with this popular dining spot. The 23-item roster of tapas is irresistible; diners make a whole meal off of it. The food is exciting and the décor is adventurous. Asian fusion menu. Lunch, dinner. Bar. Reservations recommended. Valet parking. Outdoor seating. **$$$**

★ ★ **SAMMY'S CALIFORNIA WOOD-FIRED PIZZA.** *702 Pearl St, La Jolla (92037). Phone 858/456-5222; fax 858/456-9334. www.sammyspizza.com.* California menu. Lunch, dinner. Closed Thanksgiving, Dec 25. Casual attire. Outdoor seating. **$$**

★ ★ ★ **SANTE.** *7811 Herschel Ave, La Jolla (92037). Phone 858/454-1315; fax 858/454-6744. www.santeristorante.com.* Tony Buonsante brings touches from his native Italy and former New York restaurant to this intimate, elegant space. Choose to dine on the sidewalk terraces, in the courtyard, in the white-tableclothed dining room, or at the cozy bar where you can browse the celebrity photographs. Italian menu. Lunch, dinner. Closed Jan 1, Thanksgiving, Dec 25. Bar. Casual attire. Outdoor seating. **$$**

★ ★ ★ **SKY ROOM RESTAURANT.** *1132 Prospect St, La Jolla (92037). Phone 858/454-0771; fax 858/456-3921. www.lavalencia.com.* French menu. Dinner. Jacket required. **$$$**

★ ★ ★ **TAPENADE.** *7612 Fay Ave, La Jolla (92037). Phone 858/551-7500; fax 858/551-9913. www.tapenaderestaurant.com.* The first item to arrive at your table is, not surprisingly, tapenade. What follows is expertly prepared southern French food. French menu. Lunch, dinner. Closed holidays. Bar. Casual attire. Outdoor seating. **$$$**

★ ★ ★ **TOP O' THE COVE.** *1216 Prospect St., La Jolla (92037). Phone 858/454-7779; fax 858/454-3783. www.topofthecove.com.* Overlooking the marina, this restaurant offers diners a place to meet and relax while enjoying a menu of pastas and prime steaks. If the scenic cove and fine cuisine is not enough to relax you, the bar offers cocktails, as well as Cuban cigars from their walk-in humidor. In converted cottage (1896); rare Moreton fig trees at front entrance. American, seafood menu. Lunch, dinner. Bar. Casual attire. Valet parking. Outdoor seating. **$$$**

★ ★ **TRATTORIA ACQUA.** *1298 Prospect St, La Jolla (92037). Phone 858/454-0709; fax 858/454-0710. www.trattoriaacqua.com.* Italian, seafood menu. Lunch, dinner. Closed Thanksgiving, Dec 25. Casual attire. **$$**

★ ★ ★ **TUTTO MARE.** *4365 Executive Dr, La Jolla (92121). Phone 858/597-1188; fax 858/597-0248. www. tuttomare.com.* In a contemporary but elegant setting, this restaurant features fresh seafood and authentic homemade pasta. It is located in the business and financial area of La Jolla and is also close to a major shopping center. Italian, seafood menu. Lunch, dinner. Closed July 4, Thanksgiving, Dec 25. Bar. Children's menu. Casual attire. Outdoor seating. **$$**

La Quinta

See also Carlsbad, Del Mar, Escondido, San Diego

Web Site www.la-quinta.org

Restaurants

★ ★ ★ **AZUR BY LE BERNARDIN.** *49-499 Eisenhower Dr, La Quinta (92253). Phone 760/564-4111. www.laquintaresort.com.* Trading on the success of their New York temple of refined French food, the team behind Le Bernardin ups the ante in the California desert at Azur by Le Bernardin. This first-rate restaurant puts a new spin on resort dining at Palm Springs La Quinta Resort & Spa with its masterful seafood and meat creations. A quiet elegance pervades the dining room, where vaulted, beamed ceilings; distinctive artwork; and decorative accents set a decidedly Mediterranean villa style. Refined yet casual, the dining room attracts a stylish crowd with a penchant for gourmet dining. Behind the scenes, chef de cuisine Jasper Schneider works magic with highly creative dishes infused with international flavors. Artfully prepared and presented, the dishes are perfectly complemented by the well-rounded wine list. Seafood menu. Dinner. Closed in summer. Bar. Jacket required. **$$$$**
🅳

★ **THE FALLS PRIME STEAKHOUSE.** *78-430 Hwy 111, La Quinta (92253). Phone 760/777-9999. www.thefallsprimesteakhouse.com.* Steak menu. Dinner. Closed Sun in summer. Bar. Outdoor seating. **$$$**

★ ★ **LA QUINTA CLIFFHOUSE.** *78-250 Hwy 111, La Quinta (92260). Phone 760/360-5991; fax 760/360-8654. www.hulapie.com.* Situated on a hillside. Seafood, steak menu. Dinner. Closed July 4, Dec 25. Bar. Children's menu. Casual attire. Valet parking. Outdoor seating. **$$**

Laguna Beach (J-3)

See also Avalon (Catalina Island), Costa Mesa, Irvine, Laguna Niguel, Newport Beach, San Clemente, San Juan Capistrano

Population 23,727
Information Chamber of Commerce, 357 Glenneyre St, 92651; phone 949/494-1018
Web Site www.lagunabeachchamber.org

Artists have contributed to the quaint charm of this seaside town. Curio, arts and crafts, and antique shops make leisurely strolling a pleasure. There is swimming and surfing at beautiful beaches.

What to See and Do

Laguna Playhouse. *606 Laguna Canyon Rd, Laguna Beach (92651). Phone 949/497-2787. www.laguna-playhouse.com.* Theater company presents dramas, comedies, musicals, children's theater. Main stage (mid-July-June, Tues-Sun; closed Jan 1, Dec 25).

Special Events

Festival of Arts and Pageant of the Masters. *650 Laguna Canyon Rd, Laguna Beach (92652). Phone 949/494-1145; toll-free 800/487-3378. www.foapom. com.* All pageant seats reserved. Exhibits by 160 artists; *tableaux vivants;* entertainment; restaurant. Grounds: daily. For information on ticket prices and reservations, contact festival box office. Mid-July-Aug. **$$$$**

Sawdust Fine Arts and Crafts Festival. *935 Laguna Canyon Rd, Laguna Beach (92651). Phone 949/494-3030. www.sawdustfestival.org.* Showcases paintings, photographs, sculptures, jewelry, ceramics, hand-blown glass, and other works of art created by over 175 Laguna Beach artists. Daily, July-early Sept.

Limited-Service Hotels

★ ★ **ALISO CREEK INN.** *31106 S Pacific Coast Hwy, Laguna Beach (92677). Phone 949/499-2271; toll-free 800/223-3309; fax 949/499-4601. www.aliso-creekinn.com.* In secluded area of Aliso Canyon near the beach. 60 rooms, 2 story, all suites. Pets accepted, some restrictions; fee. Check-in 3 pm, check-out noon. High-speed Internet access. Restaurant. Fitness room. Outdoor pool, whirlpool. Golf, 9 holes. Business center. **$$**
🐾 🏋 🏊 🏌 🏃

★ **BEST WESTERN LAGUNA REEF INN.**
*30806 Pacific Coast Hwy, Laguna Beach (92651). Phone
949/499-2227; toll-free 800/922-9905; fax 949/499-
5575. www.bestwestern.com.* 43 rooms, 2 story.
Complimentary continental breakfast. Check-in 3 pm,
check-out noon. High-speed Internet access. Outdoor
pool, whirlpool. Business center. **$$**

★ ★ **HOLIDAY INN.** *25205 La Paz Rd, Laguna Hills
(92653). Phone 949/586-5000; toll-free 800/282-1789;
fax 949/457-0610. www.holidayinn.com.* 147 rooms, 4
story. Complimentary continental breakfast. Check-in
3 pm, check-out 1 pm. Restaurant, bar. Fitness room.
Outdoor pool. **$**

Full-Service Hotel

★ ★ ★ **SURF & SAND HOTEL.** *1555 S Coast Hwy,
Laguna Beach (92651). Phone 949/497-4477; toll-free
888/869-7569; fax 949/494-2897. www.surfandsan-
dresort.com.* Guests are treated to a taste of California
beach living while staying at the Surf & Sand Hotel.
This resort blends coastal elegance with West Coast
cool, and its sun-kissed shoreline and crashing waves
beckon beach lovers. Sophisticated yet unpretentious,
this resort welcomes couples breaking away from the
daily grind or families seeking to spend quality time
together. Life revolves around the beach here, where
guests while away the afternoons soaking up the
famous sunshine at the beach or the oceanfront pool. A
fabulous fitness center and yoga studio help keep guests
bikini-ready, and the Aquaterra Spa is the answer to any
primping and pampering needs. Splashes restaurant
and lounge serves up signature Southern California
views with a Mediterranean-inspired menu. 165 rooms,
9 story. Check-in 4 pm, check-out noon. High-speed
Internet access. Restaurant, bar. Fitness room, spa. Out-
door pool, whirlpool. Business center. **$$$$**

Full-Service Resort

★ ★ ★ ★ **MONTAGE RESORT & SPA.** *30801
S Coast Hwy, Laguna Beach (92651). Phone 949/715-
6000; toll-free 866/271-6953; fax 949/715-6130. www.
montagelagunabeach.com.* Reigning over Laguna
Beach from its rugged clifftop location overlook-
ing the crashing surf of the Pacific Ocean, Montage
is the ultimate California beach house. This stylish
getaway seamlessly blends Arts and Crafts style with
breezy coastal elegance, all while paying homage to

Laguna Beach's strong artistic roots. Rooms, suites,
and bungalows encourage lingering with a variety of
creature comforts, from flat-screen televisions and
DVD players to 400-thread-count bed linens and
five-fixture marble bathrooms, while private balconies
with impressive ocean views never cease to enchant.
Sybarites make their way to the innovative spa, where
more than 20 treatment rooms await weary souls.
Sun worshipers take their pick from three pools and
relax in poolside cabanas complete with audiovisual
equipment, while others dig their toes in the sand at
the golden beach. Three restaurants suit every mood,
from casual poolside dining to gourmet cuisine with
stunning 280-degree ocean views. 262 rooms, 5 story.
Pets accepted, some restrictions; fee. Check-in 4 pm,
check-out noon. High-speed Internet access, wireless
Internet access. Three restaurants, four bars. Fitness
room, fitness classes available, spa. Beach. Three out-
door pools, whirlpool. Business center. **$$$$**

Specialty Lodgings

CASA LAGUNA INN. *2510 S Pacific Coast Hwy,
Laguna Beach (92651). Phone 949/494-2996; toll-free
800/233-0449; fax 949/494-5009. www.casalaguna.
com.* 22 rooms. Pets accepted; fee. Complimentary full
breakfast. Check-in 3 pm, check-out 11 am. High-speed
Internet access. Outdoor pool. Business center. **$$**

EILER'S INN. *741 S Coast Hwy, Laguna Beach
(92651). Phone 949/494-3004; toll-free 866/617-2696;
fax 949/497-2215. www.eilersinn.com.* 12 rooms, 2
story. No children allowed. Complimentary full break-
fast. Check-in 2 pm, check-out 11 am. **$$**

INN AT LAGUNA BEACH. *211 N Pacific Coast
Hwy, Laguna Beach (92651). Phone 949/497-9722;
toll-free 800/544-4479; fax 949/497-9972. www.innat-
lagunabeach.com.* Relax as the warm sea breeze rustles
the palm leaves and the waves crash. Enjoy the ocean
view and sunsets but don't forget to take advantage
of the many village shops, restaurants, and renowned
art galleries, all within walking distance of the guest
rooms. 70 rooms, 5 story. Complimentary continental
breakfast. Check-in 4 pm, check-out noon. Wireless
Internet access. Outdoor pool, whirlpool. **$$**

Spa

★ ★ ★ ★ ★ **SPA MONTAGE AT MONTAGE RESORT.** *30801 S Coast Hwy, Laguna Beach (92651). Phone 949/715-6000; toll-free 866/271-6953. www. spamontage.com.* Spa Montage is a stunning facility that takes advantage of its superior beachfront setting. An indoor-outdoor structure and floor-to-ceiling windows framing 160-degree views alleviate any guilt you may feel for opting to leave the outdoors behind for a day at the spa. The spa's holistic, get-back-to-nature approach is evident in its design, as well as in the products it uses. Custom-mixed lotions and oils blend natural ingredients, including eucalyptus, lavender, orange blossoms, and citrus. Wrap yourself in one of the spa's sinful cashmere robes and breathe in the fresh ocean air as you begin your spa experience. The natural surroundings influence many of the treatments here, including the thalasso bath, marine wrap, sea salt body scrub, and algae cellulite massage. Vichy showers harness the healing powers of water, while botanical baths and hydrotherapy sessions ease aches and pains. The mineral-enriched mud used in clay body sculpting helps eliminate toxins, while the clay wrap draws out impurities with a rosemary and eucalyptus exfoliation followed by an application of warm clay. The powerful antioxidants in lemons, limes, and oranges serve as the basis for the California citrus polish. Facials deliver supple skin with marine-based treatments, toning stones, and seasonal fruits and vegetables, and the spa offers a variety of massage techniques in 30-, 60-, and 90-minute sessions. Spa Montage's signature treatments offer the opportunity to experience different healing traditions in one spa appointment. The elements of life therapy covers you in warm mud, bathes you in rose and jasmine, exfoliates your skin, and massages you into utter ecstasy, while the aroma-balancing therapy blends bathing, massage, antiaging techniques, and lymph drainage into one treatment. If all this relaxation makes you hungry, find a spot by the lap pool, where you can order healthy snacks and meals from the Mosaic Grille.

Restaurants

★ **A LA CARTE.** *1915 S Coast Hwy, Laguna Beach (92651). Phone 949/497-4927; fax 949/497-4927. www.alacarteworldfusioncatering.com.* This cute and friendly spot in downtown Laguna Beach offers gourmet salads and sandwiches. Most customers take their food to go, but you can eat in if you like. Order at the counter, and don't expect beer or wine with your meal. American menu. Lunch, dinner. Closed holidays. Casual attire. **$**

★ ★ **BEACH HOUSE INN.** *619 Sleepy Hollow Ln, Laguna Beach (92651). Phone 949/494-9707; fax 949/494-7597. www.thebeachhouse.com.* Offering the kind of casual beachside dining experience that once prevailed along the Southern California coast, Beach House Inn is—as its name suggests—an old, restored former residence on the water's edge with an expansive and romantic view of the Pacific. A lively crowd of gabby tourists, preening surfers, and nonchalant locals find the well-prepared, primarily seafood and steak fare a good excuse to stick near the sand, and the ingratiating waitstaff does everything it can to keep them happy. Early birds drifting in at 5 pm can enjoy hearty entrées at nearly half off. Seafood, steak menu. Breakfast, lunch, dinner. Closed Thanksgiving, Dec 25. Bar. Children's menu. Casual attire. Reservations recommended. Valet parking. Outdoor seating. **$$$**

★ ★ **CEDAR CREEK INN.** *384 Forest Ave, Laguna Beach (92651). Phone 949/497-8696; fax 949/376-3108. www.cedarcreekinn.com.* Convenient to the Laguna Moulton Playhouse and one of three so-named eateries in greater Los Angeles, Cedar Creek Inn is family run—a fact evident in its homey décor (elegant beige hues and hardwood furnishings, plus a big hearth), hospitable waitstaff, and free lot parking (a rarity in this town). The value-priced, marvelously fulfilling menu—featuring fresh fish, specialties like scampi with beef medallions, and standby starters including ahi sashimi—is such a mover-and-shaker magnet that locals consider the restaurant a City Hall annex. Don't miss the oyster bar, which delivers beaucoup shucks along with plenty of mollusk-fueled camaraderie. California menu. Lunch, dinner. Closed holidays. Bar. Children's menu. Casual attire. Reservations recommended. Outdoor seating. **$$**

★ **THE COTTAGE.** *308 N Pacific Coast Hwy, Laguna Beach (92651). Phone 949/494-3023; fax 949/497-5183. www.thecottagerestaurant.com.* This turn-of-the-20th-century landmark home with sweeping Oriental roof lines overlooks the Pacific. The home functioned as a Café in the 1930s and 1940s; after being closed due to war shortages, it reopened under its current name in 1964. Ever since, The Cottage has been serving home-style cooking in a homey environment, with Tiffany lamps, vintage sideboards, and theater seats from the Old Laguna Playhouse in the lobby giving it an antiquey character. The menu options range from omelettes to cioppino to filet mignon, ensuring that all diners can find something to tempt their taste buds. American menu. Breakfast, lunch, dinner. Closed holidays. Children's menu. Casual attire. Reservations recommended. Outdoor seating. **$$**

★ ★ **FIVE FEET RESTAURANT.** *328 Glenneyre St, Laguna Beach (92651). Phone 949/497-4955; fax 949/497-4186. www.fivefeetrestaurant.com.* Just a stone's throw from the beach, you'll find Five Feet, a funky, upscale restaurant featuring unique and spirited Californian-Chinese cuisine. The swanky room is modern and minimalist, slickly styled with urban accents like exposed pipes and air vents and a hip, trendy crowd to match. As for the food, be prepared to take some of it to go—the portions are enormous. Plates arrive piled high with vibrantly flavored Chinese classics tweaked with a smart dose of modern California sensibility. Served with passion and flair, this is Chinese food like you've never tasted before. The whole catfish, a house special, is prepared in a bright, spicy tomato-ginger-citrus sauce. A significant risk is that you may find it hard to go back to greasy takeout. Chinese menu. Dinner. Closed holidays. Casual attire. Reservations recommended. **$$$**

★ ★ **KING'S FISH HOUSE.** *24001 Avenida de la Carlota, Laguna Hills (92653). Phone 949/586-1515; fax 949/586-8932. www.kingsfishhouse.com.* This local chain prides itself on having restored the tradition of the "all-American roadside seafood restaurant." Simple preparations of fresh seafood, including a nice selection of raw and cooked oysters, dominate the menu; whether you prefer your fish grilled, fried, poached, or in a salad, you're sure to find something to please. Sauces are made at the table, adding an element of fun to the experience. Seafood menu. Lunch, dinner. Closed holidays. Bar. Children's menu. Casual attire. Outdoor seating. **$$$**

★ **LAGUNA THAI BY THE SEA.** *31715 S Coast Hwy, Laguna Beach (92651). Phone 949/415-0924. www.lagunathai.com.* Thai menu. Lunch, dinner. Closed holidays. Casual attire. Outdoor seating. No credit cards accepted. **$$**

★ ★ **LAS BRISAS DE LAGUNA.** *361 Cliff Dr, Laguna Beach (92651). Phone 949/497-5434; fax 949/497-9210. www.lasbrisaslagunabeach.com.* A fair amount of hubbub accompanies dinner at this popular, tourist-intensive Mexican eatery. In light of the jaw-dropping Pacific panorama provided by the blufftop location, you can forgive the clienteles boisterousness—which is only exacerbated by the gorgeous, excellent entrées emerging from the kitchen. Among the top dishes: the 12-ounce Black Angus New York steak mesquite-grilled with tequila-truffle glaze and the tomato-saf-

fron bouillabaisse of lobster tail, scallops, prawns, crab, green mussels, and fresh fish. An amazing selection of specialty margaritas and an unhurried pace encouraged by the capable, congenial waitstaff lend immeasurably to the relaxed atmosphere. Continental menu. Breakfast, lunch, dinner, Sun brunch. Closed holidays. Bar. Casual attire. Reservations recommended. Valet parking. Outdoor seating. **$$$**

★ **SAN SHI GO.** *1100 S Pacific Coast Hwy, Laguna Beach (92651). Phone 949/494-1551; fax 949/497-5660.* Some consider the "star" rolls at this unassuming sushi restaurant to be the best in Laguna Beach. Fresh-fish delicacies are cut and arranged like mini-masterpieces for diners delectation—and with flavor to match their splendid visual presentation, they are enough to divert ones attention from the room's generally mirthful air, if not the awesome bay view. The California roll, a word-of-mouth favorite with its spicy snap, may well have you dreaming. Japanese, sushi menu. Lunch Tues-Fri, dinner. Closed July 4, Thanksgiving, Dec 25. Casual attire. **$$**

Laguna Niguel

Web Site www.ci.laguna-niguel.ca.us

Restaurant

★ ★ **SAVANNAH STEAK & CHOP HOUSE.** *32441 Golden Lantern St, Laguna Niguel (92677). Phone 949/493-7107; fax 949/493-7346. www.culinary-adventures.com.* Perched atop a bluff that affords a fantastic Laguna vista, Savannah Steak & Chop House creates an appealingly clubby, contemporary atmosphere with big, cozy horseshoe-shaped booths, stone fireplaces, vaulted ceilings, and elegantly subdued lighting that makes the largely A-list clientele look its best. But executive chef Jose Colin's sumptuous lineup of Southern-accented steak, poultry, and seafood entrées is the main draw, and whether you go for plate-overlapping specialties like hickory-smoked, slow-roasted bone-in prime rib; buttermilk-fried chicken; or jumbo Alaskan king crab legs, you are unlikely to leave unsatisfied. (The wide selection of California and Oregon wines only cinches it.) Polished service, full-menu availability at the bar, and a romantic, heated outdoor patio with fire pit—plus live entertainment on most evenings—help make this steakhouse a gastronome's home away from home. American, steak menu. Dinner. Closed holidays. Bar. Business casual attire. Reservations recommended. Valet parking. Outdoor seating. **$$$**

Lake Arrowhead

See also Big Bear Lake, Crestline, Redlands, San Bernardino, Victorville

Population 8,934
Elevation 5,191 ft
Area Code 909
Zip 92352
Information Chamber of Commerce, PO Box 219; phone 909/337-3715
Web Site www.lakearrowhead.net

Wonderful outdoor recreation and year-round beauty draw people to this mountainous lake region in the San Bernadino National Forest. Unfortunately, the lake itself is private and reserved for use by homeowners and their guests. Visitors can only tour it on the *Arrowhead Queen* (see), take water-skiing lessons, or use the beach at Lake Arrowhead Resort (see) if they're staying there. But everyone can enjoy all the other outdoor pursuits—hiking, biking, horseback riding, camping, and the like. You'll also find shops, restaurants, and other attractions, including the ice skating rink where Michelle Kwan mastered her sport. In winter, skiers and snowboarders take to the powdery slopes.

What to See and Do

Arrowhead Queen. *28200 Hwy 189 # C 100, Lake Arrowhead. On the waterfront at Lake Arrowhead Village. Phone 909/336-6992.* Enjoy a 50-minute narrated boat cruise on Lake Arrowhead, past architectural points of interest and historical sites. (Call for hours; hourly departures) **$$$**

Lake Arrowhead Children's Museum. *Suite T-100, 28200 Hwy 189, Lake Arrowhead. Lower peninsula, Lake Arrowhead Village. Phone 909/336-3093. www.mountaininfo.com/kids.* Offers a hands-on interactive setting for children; learning through play and activities. (Daily; closed Thanksgiving, Dec 25) **$**

Snow Valley Ski Resort. *Hwy 18, Running Springs. 14 miles SE on Hwy 18, 30; 5 miles E of Running Springs. Phone 909/867-2751. www.snow-valley.com.* Five triple, eight double chairlifts; patrol, school, rentals; snowmaking; cafeteria, restaurant, bar. Twenty-five runs; longest run 1 1/4 miles; vertical drop 1,141 feet. (Mid-Nov-Apr) Snowboarding. Summer activities include hiking, mountain biking, backpacking, camping, outdoor concerts. Indoor playland for children. **$$$$**

Limited-Service Hotel

★ **LAKE ARROWHEAD TREE TOP LODGE.** *27992 Rainbow Dr, Lake Arrowhead (92352). Phone 909/337-2311; toll-free 800/358-8733; fax 909/337-1403. www.arrowheadtreetop.com.* 20 rooms, 2 story. Pets accepted, some restrictions; fee. Check-in 11 am, check-out 11 am. Outdoor pool. **$**

Full-Service Resort

★ ★ ★ **LAKE ARROWHEAD RESORT.** *27984 Hwy 189, Lake Arrowhead (92352). Phone 909/336-1511; toll-free 800/800-6792; fax 909/744-3040. www.laresort.com.* This resort is found in the majestic forest of San Bernardino, on the crystal blue water of Arrowhead Lake. 177 rooms, 3 story. Check-in 4 pm, check-out noon. Restaurant, bar. Children's activity center. Fitness room. Outdoor pool, whirlpool. Tennis. **$**

Specialty Lodgings

CHATEAU DU LAC. *911 Hospital Rd, Lake Arrowhead (92352). Phone 909/337-6488. www.chateau-du-lac.com.* 5 rooms, 3 story. Complimentary full breakfast. Check-in 2 pm, check-out 11 am. **$$**

ROMANTIQUE LAKEVIEW LODGE. *28051 Hwy 189, Lake Arrowhead (92352). Phone 909/337-6633; toll-free 800/358-5253; fax 909/337-5966. www.lakeviewlodge.com.* Reconstructed lodge that was once a private home; antique furnishings; Victorian-style décor. 9 rooms, 2 story. Complimentary continental breakfast. Check-in 2 pm, check-out 11 am. **$$**

Restaurant

★ ★ **ROYAL OAK.** *27187 Hwy 189, Blue Jay (92317). Phone 909/337-6018; fax 909/337-2212.* Dinner. Closed Easter, Thanksgiving, Dec 25. Bar. **$$**

Lancaster (H-4)

See also Palmdale

Population 118,718
Elevation 2,355 ft
Area Code 661
Information Chamber of Commerce, 554 W Lancaster Blvd, 93534; phone 661/948-4518
Web Site www.lancasterchamber.org

What to See and Do

Edwards Air Force Base. *Rosamond Blvd, Rosamond. 10 miles N via Hwy 14 to Rosamond Blvd, then 10 miles E. Phone 661/277-3510. www.edwards.af.mil.* Landing site for the NASA space shuttle program. Public tours the first and third Friday of each month. Reservations required.

Special Events

Antelope Valley Fair and Alfalfa Festival. *Antelope Valley Fairgrounds, 2551 W Ave H, Lancaster (93535). Phone 661/948-6060. www.avfair.com.* The fair features Freddy's Camp with friendly Belgian mules, rural Olympics including events like hay baling and tractor races, and concerts starring big name country singers. Eleven days in late Aug-early Sept. **$$**

Wildflower Season. *Antelope Valley California Poppy Reserve,15101 Lancaster Rd, Lancaster (93534). Phone 661/724-1180. www.parks.ca.gov.* Seven miles of walking trails meander through the 1,745-acre park that becomes a beautiful medley of colors and fragrance each spring when the poppies, lupines, and owls clovers bloom. Mid-Mar-mid-May.

Limited-Service Hotel

★ ★ **BEST WESTERN ANTELOPE VALLEY INN.** *44055 Sierra Hwy, Lancaster (93534). Phone 661/948-4651; toll-free 800/780-7234; fax 661/948-4532. www.bestwestern.com.* 148 rooms, 3 story. Pets accepted, fee. Complimentary full breakfast. Check-in 3 pm, check-out 11 am. Restaurant, bar. Outdoor pool, whirlpool. **$**

Lawndale

Restaurant

★ **AL-NOOR.** *15112 Inglewood Ave, Lawndale (90260). Phone 310/675-4700. www.alnoor-restaurant.com.* Pakistani menu. Lunch, dinner. Closed Mon. Casual attire. **$**

Lompoc(H-2)

See also Santa Maria, Solvang

Settled 1874
Population 41,103
Elevation 104 ft
Area Code 805
Zip 93436
Information Chamber of Commerce, 111 South I St; phone 805/736-4567
Web Site www.lompoc.com

Lompoc is known as "The City of Murals in the Valley of Flowers." More than two dozen murals showcase the works of internationally acclaimed muralists such as Roberto Delgado and Dan Sawatsky. Lompoc is also the flower seed capital of the world; most of the world's flower seeds come from here. From May through September, the city is bordered by over a thousand acres of vivid zinnias, marigolds, sweet peas, petunias, stock, and other blossoms. Vandenberg AFB is 10 miles west of here.

What to See and Do

La Purisima Mission State Historic Park. *2295 Purisima Rd, Lompoc (93436). 3 miles NE at the jct of Purisima and Mission Gate rds. Phone 805/733-3713. www.lapurisimamission.org.* The 11th in a chain of 21 Franciscan missions. Founded in 1787, moved in 1812. Restored in current setting. Native American artifacts, mission relics. Guide map at museum. Craft demonstrations in summer. Picnicking. Living history tours summer and fall; write for schedule, fees. (Daily 9 am-5 pm; closed Jan 1, Thanksgiving, Dec 25) **$**

Mural Walk. More than 24 giant murals, painted by world-class artists, adorn the exterior walls of buildings in old downtown. Contact the Chamber of Commerce for a brochure.

Special Events

Greenhouse Tour. *Phone 805/736-5118.* Spectacular display of flowers by Bodger Seed Company. Apr.

Lompoc Valley Flower Festival. *Ocean and O St, Lompoc. Phone 805/735-8511. www.flowerfestival.org.* Floral parade, flower exhibits, arts and craft show, entertainment, bus tours of 1,200 acres of flower fields. June. **FREE**

Limited-Service Hotels

★ ★ **EMBASSY SUITES.** *1117 N H St, Lompoc (93436). Phone 805/735-8311; toll-free 800/362-2779; fax 805/735-8459. www.embassysuites.com.* 155 rooms, 3 story. Complimentary full breakfast. Check-in 3 pm, check-out noon. Fitness room. Outdoor pool, whirlpool. **$**
🛅 🖼

★ **QUALITY INN.** *1621 N H St, Lompoc (90802). Phone 805/735-8555; toll-free 800/638-7949; fax 805/735-8566. www.qualitysuiteslompoc.com.* 218 rooms, 4 story. Pets accepted, some restrictions; fee. Complimentary full breakfast. Check-in 3 pm, check-out noon. Outdoor pool, whirlpool. **$**
🖼 🖼

Lone Pine (G-4)

See also Santa Maria, Solvang

Population 1,655
Elevation 3,733 ft
Area Code 760
Zip 93545
Information Chamber of Commerce, 126 S Main, PO Box 749; phone 760/876-4444
Web Site www.lone-pine.com

Dating from the early 1860s, Lone Pine caters to tourists and outfits hiking trips to nearby Mount Whitney (14,495 feet, tallest peak in the contiguous United States). A 13-mile drive due west to the base of Mount Whitney leads through the unusual Alabama Hills.

A Ranger District office of the Inyo National Forest (see) is located here.

What to See and Do

Alabama Hills Recreation Area. *798 N Main St E, Bishop (93514). 2 miles W via Whitney Portal Rd. Phone 760/873-2500.* Site of Indian Wars in the 1860s; named for Southern warship *Alabama.* These hills are a favorite film location for TV and movie companies because of the unique rock formations and Sierra backdrop.

Eastern California Museum. *155 N Grant St, Independence (93526). 16 miles N via Hwy 395, W on Center St. Phone 760/878-0364. www.ecmuseum.inyocounty.us.* Little Pine Village; Native American baskets and artifacts; pioneer artifacts, photographs; natural history. (Wed-Sun 10 am-4 pm; closed holidays) **FREE**

Special Event

Lone Pine Film Festival. *126 S Main St, Lone Pine. www.lonepinefilmfestival.org.* Celebration of movies made on location in Lone Pine. Friday evening concert; bus tour of movie locations; films; movie memorabilia; arts and crafts. Mid-Oct.

Long Beach (J-4)

See also Anaheim, Avalon (Catalina Island), Buena Park, Los Angeles, Newport Beach, Santa Ana

Founded 1881
Population 461,552
Elevation 29 ft
Area Code 562
Information Long Beach Area Convention & Visitors Bureau, One World Trade Center, 3rd Floor, 90831; phone 562/436-3645 or toll-free 800/452-7829
Web Site www.visitlongbeach.com

A multibillion dollar redevelopment program helped Long Beach become one of Southern California's most diverse waterfront destinations, recapturing the charm it first attained as a premier California seaside resort in the early 1900s. Projects involving hotels and major attractions, along with shopping, commercial, and residential area development, contributed to the revitalization of both the downtown and the waterfront. A 21 1/2-mile light rail system, the Metro Blue Line, connects Long Beach and Los Angeles.

Founded by British-born W. E. Willmore as the "American Colony" of Willmore City, the name change to Long Beach was prompted by a desire to advertise its 5 1/2-mile-long, 500-foot-wide beach. Earlier in the 20th century, prosperity came with the elegant hotels and summer houses of the wealthy and, later, with the discovery of oil. Today, the state's largest beach city derives its economic security from the aerospace, harbor, oil, and tourism industries. McDonnell Douglas is its largest employer.

What to See and Do

Alamitos Bay. *205 Marina Dr, Long Beach. Phone 562/570-3215.* Seven miles of inland waterways for swimming, sunning, windsurfing, and boating.

Alamitos Bay Marina has slips for 2,005 pleasure craft; guest docking. On the grounds is Seaport Village; restaurants, shops. (Daily)slips

Aquarium of the Pacific. *100 Aquarium Way, Long Beach (90802). Phone 562/590-3100. www.aquariumofpacific.org.* With more than 12,000 animals in 50 exhibits, you and your family won't have trouble finding breathtaking creatures to marvel at here. From anemones to zebra sharks, the aquarium gives you a glimpse into the animals that call the three major regions of the Pacific home. In the hands-on Shark Lagoon exhibit, you can get up close and personal with these much misunderstood ocean animals—one experience you won't soon forget! The museums new Animal Vision 3-D exhibit is an interactive animated film giving visitors the chance to experience marine habitats in a way that's fun for everyone. (Daily 9 am-6 pm; closed Apr 1, weekend of the Toyota Grand Prix of Long Beach, Dec 25) **$$$$**

California State University, Long Beach. *1250 Bellflower Blvd, Long Beach (90840). Phone 562/985-4111. www.csulb.edu.* (1949) (32,000 students) On the 320-acre campus are monumental sculptures created by artists, from here and abroad, who participated in the first International Sculpture Symposium held in the United States (1965); an art museum with displays and exhibits; the Earl Burns Miller Japanese Garden. Campus tours (Mon-Fri, by appointment).

Catalina Express. *Berth 95, San Pedro (90731). Phone toll-free 800/481-3470. www.catalinaexpress.com.* Catalina advertises itself as "another world", and that's why so many people get away from it all and go ashore on this lovely island that sits 22 miles off the Los Angeles coast. Catalina Express makes getting to and from the isle easy and pleasant with its fleet of eight state-of-the-art catamarans specially designed to provide a smooth, stable ride through the Catalina Channel. To ensure an even more comfortable trip, the boats come with airline-style seating, panoramic viewing windows, and on-deck seating. And you're basking in Catalina's sunshine before you know it—in just about an hour. **$$$$**

El Dorado Regional Park East and Nature Center. *7550 E Spring St, Long Beach. At I-605. Phone 562/570-1745.* A 450-acre park with four fishing lakes, boat rentals; archery range, nature and hiking trails, picnicking. Museum and visitor center (FREE). Nature center (Tues-Sun). (Daily 7 am-dusk) **$**

General Phineas Banning Residence Museum. *401 E M St, Wilmington (90744). Phone 310/548-7777. www.banningmuseum.org.* Restored Greek Revival house (1864); exhibits tell of Banning's role in the development of Los Angeles. Docent-led tours (Tues-Thurs, Sat 12:30, 1:30, and 2:30 pm, Sat-Sun 12:30, 1:30, 2:30, and 3:30 pm). **DONATION**

Long Beach Convention & Entertainment Center. *300 E Ocean Blvd, Long Beach (90802). At end of Long Beach Frwy. Phone 562/436-3636. www.longbeachcc.com.* A 111-acre multipurpose complex houses a major sporting arena, convention/exhibition complex, and two traditional performing theaters. Terrace Theater has a proscenium stage and Center Theater. Resident companies include the Long Beach Symphony, Long Beach Opera, Civic Light Opera, and Classical Ballet.

Long Beach Museum of Art. *2300 E Ocean Blvd, Long Beach (90803). Phone 562/439-2119. www.lbma.org.* Changing contemporary exhibitions. Permanent collection includes American art, German expressionists, and video art. Facilities include a contemporary sculpture garden and an education gallery. A café and gift shop are housed in a 1912 mansion overlooking the Pacific Ocean. (Tues, Sat-Sun 11 am-5 pm, Wed-Fri 11 am-9 pm; closed holidays) **$**

Long Beach Sport Fishing. *555 Pico Ave, Long Beach. In port of Long Beach. Phone 562/432-8993. www.longbeachsportfishing.com.* Entertainment/fishing complex with full range of sportfishing vessels for half-day, three-quarter-day, full-day, and night fishing excursions; restaurants, fish market, bar. Whale-watching (Nov-Feb). **$$$$**

Los Alamitos Race Course. *4961 Katella Ave, Los Alamitos (90720). Phone 714/820-2800. www.losalamitos.com.* Located about 30 minutes south of downtown Los Angeles, near Long Beach, you can find Quarter Horse, Arabian, Thoroughbred, Paint, and Appaloosa racing at Los Alamitos. Spend the day in Long Beach and head to the tracks for some racing action as the sun goes down. (Thurs-Sun; closed Super Bowl Sun, Sept 11, Thanksgiving) **$**

Municipal Beach. *Cherry and Ocean sts, Long Beach (90803). S of Ocean Blvd from Alamitos Marina. Phone 562/436-3645.* Lifeguards at many areas in summer. (Daily)

⭐ *Queen Mary* **Seaport.** *1126 Queens Hwy, Long Beach (90802). Located at the S end of the Long Beach Frwy (710). Phone 562/435-3511. www.queenmary.com.* For 25 years, the rich and famous boarded this 12-deck luxury ocean liner to cross the Atlantic in grand style. But since 1967, this 81,237-ton beauty of a ship has been docked in Long Beach, where ordinary folks board it every day for tours, weddings, special events, shipboard dining, or an overnight hotel stay in one of its 365 staterooms. The price of admission includes a ghosts and legends tour (supposedly the vessel is haunted), but for $5 extra, you can also get a behind-the-scenes guided tour or a World War II tour, which gives insight into the role the ship played in transporting our military personnel from 1940 to 1946. For $10, you can also board a Foxtrot submarine the Russians used to track enemy forces in the Pacific during the Cold War. (Mon-Thurs 10 am-5 pm, Fri-Sun 10 am-6 pm) **$$$$**

Rancho Los Alamitos. *6400 Bixby Hill Rd, Long Beach (90815). Phone 562/431-3541. www.rancholosalamitos. com.* Guided tours on the half hour of an adobe ranch house (circa 1800) with antique furnishings; six barns and outbuildings, including a blacksmith shop; 5 acres of gardens. (Wed-Sun 1-5 pm; closed holidays) **FREE**

Rancho Los Cerritos. *4600 Virginia Rd, Long Beach (90807). Phone 562/570-1755. www.rancholoscerritos. org.* (1844) One of the original California land grants that became Long Beach. Renovated Monterey colonial-style adobe building served as a headquarters for sheep ranchers in the 1870s; historic garden; orientation exhibit. Special events throughout the year (fee). Picnic area. (Wed-Sun 1-5 pm; closed holidays; guided tours on the hour, weekends) **FREE**

Shoreline Village. *429 Shoreline Village Dr, Long Beach (90802). Adjacent to the Downtown Shoreline Marina at the foot of Pine Ave, just S of the Long Beach Convention Center. Phone 562/435-2668. www.shorelinevillage. com.* This 7-acre shopping, dining, and entertainment complex recaptures the look and charm of a turn-of-the-century California seacoast village. Special features include a collection of unique shops, galleries, and restaurants; a historic carousel; and a complete marine center with daily harbor cruises and seasonal whale-watching excursions. Alternative transportation to Shoreline Village is available via the free Promenade Tram from downtown Long Beach, the Runabout Shuttle (also from downtown Long Beach), and the Water Taxi that transports passengers between Shoreline Village and the downtown marina. (Daily) **FREE**

Special Events

Boat parades. *Phone 562/570-5333. www.longbeach. gov.* Festively decorated boats wind through the canals of Naples Island and along the water by Shoreline Village each year. Dec.

Long Beach Jazz Festival. *Rainbow Lagoon Park,1288 N Bellflower Blvd, Long Beach (90815). Phone 562/424-0013. www.longbeachjazzfestival.com.* Held every year on a comfortable, grassy knoll, this annual event features top artists, delicious food, and fabulous art. Mid-Aug. **$$$$**

Toyota Grand Prix. *3000 Pacific Ave, Long Beach. Phone 562/981-2600. www.longbeachgp.com.* International race held on downtown streets. Usually three days in Apr. **$$$$**

Limited-Service Hotels

★ ★ **BEST WESTERN GOLDEN SAILS HOTEL.** *6285 E Pacific Coast Hwy, Long Beach (90803). Phone 562/596-1631; toll-free 800/762-5333; fax 562/594-0623. www.bestwestern.com.* 173 rooms, 4 story. Check-in 2 pm, check-out noon. Restaurant, bar. Fitness room. Outdoor pool, whirlpool. Airport transportation available. **$**
🛉 ⛫

★ ★ **THE COAST HOTEL.** *700 Queensway Dr, Long Beach (90802). Phone 562/435-7676; toll-free 800/716-6199; fax 562/437-0866. www.coasthotels.com.* 195 rooms, 5 story. Pets accepted, fee. Check-in 3 pm, check-out noon. Restaurant, bar. Outdoor pool. Tennis. Airport transportation available. **$**
🐾 ⛫ 🎾

★ ★ **GUESTHOUSE INTERNATIONAL HOTEL.** *5325 E Pacific Coast Hwy, Long Beach (90804). Phone 562/597-1341; fax 562/597-5171. www. guesthouse.net.* 143 rooms, 2 story. Pets accepted; fee. Check-in 3 pm, check-out noon. Restaurant, bar. Outdoor pool. Airport transportation available. **$**
🄳 🐾 ⛫

Full-Service Hotels

★ ★ ★ **HILTON LONG BEACH.** *701 W Ocean Blvd, Long Beach (90831). Phone 310/983-3400; toll-free 800/345-6565; fax 310/983-3478. www.longbeach. hilton.com.* Located in downtown Long Beach, this hotel is within four blocks of the beach, convention center, and the Catalina Island landing. 393 rooms, 15 story. Pets accepted, some restrictions. Check-in 3 pm, check-out noon. Restaurant, bar. Fitness room. Outdoor pool, whirlpool. Business center. **$$**
🐾 🛉 ⛫ 🛉

★ ★ ★ **HYATT REGENCY LONG BEACH.** *200 S Pine Ave, Long Beach (90802). Phone 562/491-*

1234; fax 562/432-1972. www.longbeach.hyatt.com. Within walking distance of the Aquarium of the Pacific, a 1,700-slip marina, and a shoreline village. Also a convenient location for vacationers planning a trip to Disneyland and Universal Studios. 521 rooms, 17 story. Check-in 3 pm, check-out noon. Restaurant, bar. Fitness room. Outdoor pool, whirlpool. Business center. **$$**

★ ★ ★ **RENAISSANCE LONG BEACH HO-TEL.** *111 E Ocean Blvd, Long Beach (90802). Phone 562/437-5900; toll-free 800/228-9898; fax 562/499-2509. www.renaissancehotels.com.* Situated in the heart of Long Beach, this hotel is centered around popular attractions, upscale boutiques, and eateries. 374 rooms, 12 story. Pets accepted, fee. Check-in 3 pm, check-out noon. Restaurant, bar. Fitness room. Outdoor pool, whirlpool. Airport transportation available. Business center. **$$**

Full-Service Inn

★ ★ ★ **SEAL BEACH INN AND GARDENS.** *212 5th St, Seal Beach (90740). Phone 562/493-2416; toll-free 800/443-3292; fax 562/799-0483. www.seal-beachinn.com.* This delightfully appointed, restored inn (1924) is filled with fine antiques and historical pieces to make your stay unforgettable. Experience the old-world charm with an attentive staff, elegant suites, gourmet breakfasts, and lavish décor. 23 rooms, 2 story. Complimentary full breakfast. Check-in 4 pm. Check-out 11 am. Restaurant, bar. Outdoor pool. **$$**

Specialty Lodging

THE TURRET HOUSE VICTORIAN BED AND BREAKFAST. *556 Chestnut Ave, Long Beach (90802). Phone 562/624-1991; toll-free 888/488-7738; fax 562/432-8204. www.turrethouse.com.* Built in 1906; Victorian décor. 5 rooms, 3 story. Complimentary full breakfast. Check-in 3 pm. Check-out 11 am. **$**

Restaurants

★ ★ **KING'S FISH HOUSE.** *100 W Broadway Ave, Long Beach (90802). Phone 562/432-7463; fax 562/436-5432. www.kingsfishhouse.com.* This local chain prides itself on having restored the tradition of the "all-American roadside seafood restaurant."

Simple preparations of fresh seafood—including a nice selection of raw and cooked oysters—dominate the menu; whether you prefer your fish grilled, fried, poached, or in a salad, you're sure to find something to please. Sauces are made at the table, adding an element of fun to the experience. Seafood menu. Lunch, dinner, brunch. Closed holidays. Bar. Children's menu. Outdoor seating. **$$**

★ ★ ★ **L'OPERA RISTORANTE.** *101 Pine Ave, Long Beach (90802). Phone 562/491-0066; fax 562/436-1108. www.lopera.com.* This local favorite serves up modern northern Italian cuisine with classic influences—think pappardelle rather than spaghetti, ravioli stuffed with duck rather than beef. The menu is divided into first and second courses, as in a traditional Italian restaurant, with pasta dominating the former and meat and fish selections filling out the latter. Massive marble columns grace the lovely dining room, and the service is warm and attentive. Italian menu. Lunch, dinner, late-night. Bar. Children's menu. Business casual attire. Reservations recommended. **$$$**

★ ★ **PARKER'S LIGHTHOUSE.** *435 Shoreline Village Dr #1, Long Beach (90802). Phone 562/432-6500; fax 562/436-3551. www.parkerslighthouse.com.* It's hard to miss this landmark three-story restaurant, which sits in a prime spot on the Long Beach Marina. Wall-to-wall windows and a 280-degree view ensure that diners can enjoy the sight of the water, the lighthouse, and the *Queen Mary.* As you might expect, the menu matches the setting, offering fresh seafood selections. Seafood menu. Lunch, dinner. Closed Dec 25. Bar. Children's menu. Casual attire. Outdoor seating. **$$**

★ ★ **THE YARD HOUSE.** *401 Shoreline Village Dr, Long Beach (90802). Phone 562/628-0455; fax 562/435-5544. www.yardhouse.com.* Beer is the headliner at Yard House—the restaurant claims to have the worlds largest selection on draft, 250 in all. Its location right on the Long Beach Marina encourages lingering over a few pints, as do food selections ranging from a classic cheeseburger to pan-seared ahi tuna. California menu. Lunch, dinner, late-night. Closed Dec 25. Bar. Children's menu. Casual attire. Outdoor seating. **$$$**

Los Angeles (J-4)

See also Anaheim, Arcadia, Beverly Hills, Hollywood, Long Beach, Los Angeles International Airport Area, Marina del Rey, San Marino, San Pedro, Santa Monica, Thousand Oaks, Valencia, Westwood and Westwood Village, West Hollywood

Founded 1781
Population 3,694,820
Elevation 330 ft
Area Code 213, 310, 323, 569 or 818 (San Fernando Valley)
Information Convention and Visitors Bureau, 633 W Fifth St, 90071; phone 213/624-7300
Web Site www.lacvb.com

Occupying a land area of 463 1/2 square miles, Los Angeles has spilled over from the plain into the canyons and foothills. Like an empire in miniature, it boasts mountains and deserts, canyons formed by skyscrapers and by rock, a Mediterranean climate, and working ranches. The city has spread out and around the independent communities of Beverly Hills, Santa Monica, Culver City, Universal City, and Inglewood. The Los Angeles city limits are twisting and confusing, so make sure to keep a street map handy.

Imagine a sprawling formation made up of a thousand pieces from a thousand different jigsaw puzzles. Illuminate it with klieg lights and flashing neon signs, garnish it with rhinestones, oranges, and oil wells, and you have Los Angeles.

The city has many faces: excitement, tranquility, tall buildings, cottages, ultramodern electronics plants, offbeat religious sects, health fads, sunshine, smog, movie stars and would-be stars, artists, writers, libraries, museums, art galleries, superhighways, and real estate booms.

Los Angeles presents a distilled, concentrated picture of the United States. People are drawn to its glamour, riches, excitement, and sunshine—all of which have encouraged a general informality. Beneath the glitter and salesmanship there is a pioneer spirit. Although no further geographic frontiers exist, many writers, researchers, scientists, and artists have settled in this area to explore scientific and intellectual frontiers.

Los Angeles is a young city with ancient roots. Along with modern architecture, exuberant growth, and a cultural thirst, it has retained a Spanish serenity and historical interest. On September 4, 1781, Don Felipe de Neve, governor of California, marched to the site of the present city and with solemn ceremonies founded El Pueblo de Nuestra Seora la Reina de Los Angeles de Porciuncula—"The Town of Our Lady the Queen of the Angels of Porciuncula"—now popularly shortened to "Los Angeles."

Los Angeles Fun Facts

- The first motion picture theater opened in Los Angeles on April 2, 1902.

- Los Angeles is the only city in the world divided in two by a mountain range, the Santa Monica Mountains, and thus it is also the only city divided by a national park.

- Los Angeles County is the world's 18th largest economy.

- With about 200,000 small businesses, Los Angeles is the entrepreneurial capital of the world.

- Los Angeles's full name is "El Pueblo de Nuestra Señora la Reina de Los Angeles de Porciuncula."

The little pueblo slumbered until 1846, when the seizure of California by the United States converted it into a vigorous frontier community. The gold rush of 1849 fanned its growth; for a time, lawlessness became so prevalent that the city was referred to as "Los Diablos"—The Devils. The railroads reached it in 1885 and 1886 and, helped by a fare war, brought a tidal wave of new settlers. By 1890, a land boom developed, and the population figure reached 50,000, with oil derricks appearing everywhere. The piping in of water from the Owens Valley in 1913 paved the way for expansion and doubling of the population in the 1920s. In the half century between 1890 and 1940, the city grew from 50,395 to 1,504,277—a gain of more than 2,000 percent. The war years added new industries and brought new waves of population that continued throughout the 1980s. Currently, the city's economic assets are invested in "growth" industries such as electronics, machinery, chemicals, oil, printing, publishing, tourism, and entertainment.

Historic District and Olvera Street

Though Los Angeles isn't known as a walking city, the only way to see the historic district where the city was born, El Pueblo de Los Angeles State Historic Park, is on foot. The historic area is located in the heart of downtown LA, west of Alameda Street, south of Cesar Chavez Avenue, and north of Arcadia Street and the Hollywood Freeway. This is the place to discover that Los Angeles really does have a history that predates the 20th century-all the way back to 1781, when Spaniards and Mexicans settled here. Much of the area has been or is being restored. The tour continues to adjacent pedestrian-only Olvera Street, where you'll find Mexican-style street markets, restaurants, cafés, and occasional festivals.

Start at the visitor center in the 1887-vintage Sepulveda House (622 N Main St) to pick up free self-guided walking tour brochures. Now, walk a short distance down Main Street and cross east into the Pueblos historic focal point, the Plaza de Los Angeles, located between Main and Los Angeles streets. In the early 1800s, the plaza was the site of bullfights and bear fights; folkloric performances now take place there on Sundays. The city's first firehouse, dating from 1884, is located on the south side of the plaza; it now serves as a small fire-fighting museum of the era. The Pico House, once known as Southern California's finest hotel, stands nearby. Walking northeast from the Plaza, you'll enter Olvera Street. Continue on Olvera to the Avila Adobe (10 Olvera St), LA's oldest surviving house (built in 1818), which has been restored in an 1840s style. Then browse the markets of Olvera Street and stop to eat at one of the Mexican restaurants. La Golondrina (17 Olvera St), housed in the city's first brick building, is particularly atmospheric with an open-air patio and mariachi music. For a smaller meal, you can find delicious tacos at one of several casual stands. Allow at least two hours for the walk, assuming a few stops to tour historic sites, but distances are fairly short. If you want to extend your walking tour of downtown, you can head north up Spring Street (west of Main St), to nearby Chinatown, which is centered along North Broadway.

The city's geographic scope makes it almost essential that visitors drive their own car, or rent one, for sightseeing in areas other than the downtown section and Westwood. Parking facilities are ample.

Additional Visitor Information

Los Angeles magazine, available at newsstands, has up-to-date information about cultural events and articles of interest to visitors.

The Los Angeles Convention and Visitors Bureau, 633 W Fifth St, Suite 6000, 90071, phone 213/624-7300, handles written inquiries and has general information brochures available in English, French, German, Japanese, and Spanish. Printed tourist guides are available at two visitor information centers: Downtown at 685 S Figueroa St, phone 213/689-8822; and in Hollywood, 6541 Hollywood Blvd, phone 213/236-2311. In addition, multilingual counselors are on staff at each information center to assist visitors.

Public Transportation

Buses (Metropolitan Transit Authority), phone 213/626-4455.

What to See and Do

Amateur Athletic Foundation. *2141 W Adams Blvd, Los Angeles (90018). 5 miles SW via Santa Monica Frwy, Western Ave exit. Phone 323/730-4600. www.aafla.com.* Resource center contains more than 35,000 print and nonprint volumes, audio and video exhibits, Olympic awards and memorabilia; multipurpose pavilion. (Mon-Fri; closed holidays) **FREE**

Beach areas. There are miles of oceanfront in Los Angeles County within 35 miles of downtown Los Angeles. Beaches include Malibu, Santa Monica, Ocean Park, Venice, Manhattan, Redondo, Long Beach, and others. Redondo Beach has a horseshoe pier and yacht harbor.

Beverly Center. *8500 Beverly Blvd, Los Angeles (90048). Phone 310/854-0071. www.beverlycenter.com.* The Beverly Center has 160 stores ranging from Bloomingdale's and Macy's to DKNY and Betsey Johnson. The mall also has a movie theater with 13 screens, as well as a range of restaurants, including California Pizza Kitchen, P. F. Chang's, and Hard Rock Cafe. The mall claims dozens of celebrity shoppers, including the likes of Ben Affleck, Halle Berry, Leonardo DiCaprio, Paul McCartney, and Julianne Moore, so keep your eyes peeled for more than just bargains. (Mon-Fri 10 am-9 pm, Sat 10 am-8 pm, Sun 11 am-6 pm; closed Easter, Thanksgiving, Dec 25)

Central Library. *630 W 5th St, Los Angeles (90071). Phone 213/228-7000. www.lapl.org/central.* (1926) A classic, Egyptian-style structure renovated after a 1986 fire. Includes a children's story theater inside and a 1 1/2-acre garden outside. (Mon-Thurs 10 am-8 pm, Fri-Sat 10 am-6 pm, Sun 1-5 pm) **FREE**

Downtown. Contains, among others, these facilities:

ARCO Plaza. *505 S Flower St, Los Angeles (90071).* Bilevel, subterranean shopping center; art shows, exhibits; restaurants, specialty and service shops.

Broadway Plaza. *2611 E Broadway, Los Angeles (90803). 7th and Hope sts.* Designed after an Italian Renaissance shopping galleria.

Chinatown. *900 N Broadway, Los Angeles (90012). Phone 213/680-0243.* Since this Chinatown was originally built as a tourist attraction, it's not as big or authentic as it's better-known counterpart up Highway 1 in San Francisco. But you still feel like you've stepped out of the LA scene and into another world when you wander through it, especially since many of the buildings have that distinctive Chinese look with their tiled roofs. Dine at a dim sum restaurant, check out the curio shops selling jade and gold jewelry, eye the Chinese treasures available at antique dealers, learn about natural remedies at herb shops, and more. Before leaving, toss a few coins in the wishing well in the central plaza on Broadway—especially if you're looking for love, good health, or wealth.

City Hall. *200 N Spring St, Los Angeles. Phone 213/978-8011.* The first tall building constructed in Southern California.

Grand Central Market. *317 S Broadway, Los Angeles (90013). Phone 213/624-2378.* Since 1917, the Grand Central Market has been a favorite among Angelenos. At this open-air market, you'll find more than 38 vendors selling everything from fresh fruits and vegetables to meat and poultry to herbs and spices from far and wide. Grab a burrito or a Cuban sandwich and take in the sights and sounds as you eat. Pick up a bouquet of fresh flowers to take with you to remind you of the experience. Parking at Hill and 3rd streets. (Daily 9 am-6 pm; closed Jan 1, Thanksgiving, Dec 25) **FREE**

Hall of Justice. *211 W Temple St, Los Angeles.* County law enforcement headquarters.

Little Tokyo. *1st St between Main and San Pedro sts.* On these 67 downtown acres, immerse yourself in Japanese culture in the heart of Los Angeles. Stroll through Japanese Village Plaza and enjoy traditional Japanese fare at the noodle and sushi shops of Ebun Market. After lunch, visit LA's premier modern art museum, the Geffen Contemporary, to see work by artists such as Jackson Pollock and Andy Warhol. Shop for silk kimonos, tableware, and other Japanese goods in the stores. Visit Buddhist temples. Relax and meditate in calming gardens. Join in the merrymaking during annual events, such as the LA Tofu Festival each July and Nesei Week each August. The latter, a colorful nine-day celebration, features Japanese folk dancing, Taiko drummers, sumo wrestlers, and more.

Los Angeles Mall. *500 W Temple St, Los Angeles (90012). Spring St across from City Hall.* Mall complex; shops, restaurants; triforium; music and light presentation.

Museum of Contemporary Art (MOCA). *250 S Grand Ave, Los Angeles (90012). Phone 213/621-1741.* This eye-pleasing tribute to modern-day art focuses solely on works from the 1940s to present, the only Los Angeles institution to do so. Visitors are treated to changing exhibitions of regional, national, and international importance, as well as specially selected pieces from the internationally renowned permanent collection. The latter includes works by John Baldessari, Lee Krasner, Jackson Pollock, Andy Warhol, and many other distinguished artists. (Mon, Fri 11 am-5 pm, Thurs to 8 pm, Sat-Sun to 6 pm; closed holidays) Free admission on Thurs. **$$**

Music Center of Los Angeles County. *135 N Grand Ave, Los Angeles (90012). Phone 213/972-7211.* The Music Center in downtown LA is home to four separate venues—the Dorothy Chandler Pavilion, the Ahmanson Theater, the Mark Taper Forum, and the new Frank Gehry designed Walt Disney Concert Hall (see). Home to the Los Angeles Philharmonic, the Los Angeles Opera, the Los Angeles Master Chorale, and the Center Theatre Group, the Music Center is one of the largest performing-arts centers in the United States. Event prices vary. Tours of the Walt Disney

Concert Hall ($$$) and the Symphonian Music Center (FREE) are available.

Wells Fargo History Museum. *333 S Grand Ave, Los Angeles (90071). Phone 213/253-7166.* Since 1852, Wells Fargo has offered banking services to the public. But more than just a bank, Wells Fargo is part of the history of America's westward expansion, and this museum captures it all, from an original Concord Coach to the gold the miners were after (including the 100-ounce Challenge Nugget). For full effect, sing the famous lyrics from *The Music Man* ("Oho, the Wells Fargo Wagon is a-comin' down the street, oh please let it be for me..."). (Mon-Fri 9 am-5 pm; closed holidays) **FREE**

World Trade Center. *350 S Figueroa St, Los Angeles (90071). Phone 213/680-1888.* Retail stores, restaurants, banks, golf driving ranges, tennis center, and travel and tour services. A concourse mural depicts the history of world trade.

El Pueblo de Los Angeles Historic Monument and Olvera Street. *125 Paseo de la Plaza, Los Angeles (90012). Phone 213/628-3562. www.ci.la.ca.us/elp.* If you're looking to dispel the myth that nothing in Los Angeles is older than the newest strip mall, El Pueblo and Olvera Street are the answer. El Pueblo is where it all began. Here you'll find 27 historic buildings, four of which are open to the public free of charge as historic museums: Avila Adobe is the oldest house in the city, dating back to 1818; Sepulveda House dates back to 1887 and is home to the monument's visitor center; the Fire House Museum, built in 1884, was in service as a fire station for 13 years before evolving into a saloon and a boarding house; and the Masonic Hall, built in 1858, is the oldest building south of the plaza. A big part of the fun is Olvera Street, dating back to 1877 and now a Mexican marketplace where you can find everything from cheap tourist-trap shops to authentic Mexican clothing and food. Several annual celebrations take place here, including the Blessing of the Animals (Sat before Easter), Cinco de Mayo (May 5), the city's birthday (Sept 4), Mexican Independence Day (Sept 15), and Los Posadas (Dec 16-24). As you walk through the narrow street, with mariachi bands playing and the smell of salsa in the air, you'll swear you've been transported south of the border. (Daily) **FREE** The park includes

Avila Adobe. *10 Olvera St, Los Angeles (90012). Phone 213/628-1274.* The oldest existing house in Los Angeles (circa 1820), damaged by an earthquake in 1971, now restored as an example of 1840s lifestyle in honor of Los Angeles's Hispanic heritage. (Daily 9 am-3 pm)

Guided walking tours. *622 N Main St, Los Angeles.* Tours leave from Sepulvada House (see). **FREE**

Nuestra Señora la Reina de Los Angeles. *535 N. Main St, Los Angeles (90012). Phone 213/629-3101.* (1818-1822) Our Lady Queen of the Angels. The restored Old Plaza Catholic Church is still an active parish and contains fine old statuary. (Daily)

Old Plaza Firehouse. *134 Paseo de la Plaza, Los Angeles.* Built as Los Angeles's first firehouse in 1884; restored as a museum with photographs and fire-fighting equipment of the 19th century. (Tues-Sun)

Sepulveda House. *622 N Main St, Los Angeles. Phone 213/628-1274.* (1887) Partially restored Victorian business block; also houses a visitor center (Mon-Sat 10 am-3 pm). Offers an 18-minute film on the early history of Los Angeles and the park (shown upon request). **FREE**

Elysian Park. *Pasadena and Golden State frwys, Los Angeles (90012). Near the intersection of Pasadena and Golden State frwys.* Covers 575 acres with beautiful landscaping. Picnicking, playground, tennis courts, and ballfields. Dodger Stadium, home of the Los Angeles Dodgers baseball team (see), is located here. (Daily dawn-dusk) **FREE**

Exposition Park. *701 State Dr, Los Angeles (90037). Figueroa St and Exposition Blvd. Phone 213/748-4772.* Park includes a sunken rose garden, picnic grounds, a sports arena, and the Los Angeles Swimming Stadium. (Daily 9 am-5 pm) The park is also the setting for

California Science Center. *Exposition Park, 700 State Dr, Los Angeles (90037). Phone 323/724-3623.* The California Science Center offers hands-on exhibits dealing with communication, transportation, building design, biology, and space exploration, among other things. Kids will love the Whisper Dishes, which allow them to whisper messages to be heard by friends on the other side of the room. Be sure to catch the Earthquake Experience so you can see what the real thing feels like in case the ground doesn't shake while you're in Los Angeles. (Daily 10 am-5 pm; closed Jan 1, Thanksgiving, Dec 25) **FREE**

Los Angeles Memorial Coliseum and Sports Arena. *3911 S Figueroa St, Los Angeles (90037). Phone 213/747-7111.* Home field for University of Southern California (USC) teams. Also scene of soccer games, concerts, track events, and many others. Seating capacity of 92,516.

Natural History Museum of Los Angeles County.
*900 Exposition Blvd, Los Angeles (90007). Phone
213/763-3466.* Permanent science exhibits feature
mammal, bird, insect, and marine life as well as
dinosaurs, other prehistoric fossils, and extinct
creatures. The minerals and metals display includes an extensive collection of cut gems. History
gallery includes features on US history, 400 years
of life in California, displays of pre-Columbian
cultures. Docent tours (one tour every afternoon
except first Tues of each month). Cafeteria. Parking fee. (Mon-Fri 9:30 am-5 pm, Sat-Sun from 10
am; closed holidays) Free admission the first Tues
of each month. **$$**

Fowler Museum of Cultural History, UCLA. *405 Hilgard
Ave, Los Angeles (90024). Located near the center of the
UCLA campus. Enter campus from Sunset Blvd, at the
Westwood Plaza entrance, and inquire about parking
availability at the information kiosk. Phone 310/825-
4361. www.fowler.ucla.edu.* This museum features
changing exhibits on cultures around the world. A
museum store is also on-site. (Wed-Sun noon-5 pm,
Thurs to 8 pm) Parking (fee). **FREE**

⭐ **Getty Center.** *1200 Getty Center Dr, Los Angeles
(90049). Phone 310/440-7300. www.getty.edu.*
Established by the trust of oil magnate J. Paul Getty,
the Getty Center exhibits Greek and Roman antiqui-
ties and European and American art and photographs.
Free docent-led gallery talks, architecture tours, and
garden tours are given daily. But just as impressive as
the art collection (if not more so) is the complex of
buildings itself. Designed by architect Richard Meier,
the Getty Center, located on 110 acres in the Santa
Monica Mountains overlooking the Pacific Ocean
and Los Angeles, is a complex of what are perhaps the
most breathtaking buildings in the city. Even if you
don't count yourself an art lover, a trip to the Getty is
worth your time — you can grab a cup of coffee and a
snack and gaze at the incredible views, getting a real
sense (on a relatively clear day) of the layout of Los
Angeles. (Tues-Thurs, Sun 10 am-6 pm, Fri-Sat to 9
pm; closed holidays) Parking (fee). **FREE**

Japanese American National Museum. *369 E 1st St,
Los Angeles (90012). Phone 213/625-0414. www.janm.
org.* Permanent exhibits document Japanese life in
America; temporary exhibits focus on Japanese-Amer-
ican culture, such as World War II internment camps.
(Tues-Sun 11 am-5 pm, Thurs to 8 pm; closed Jan 1,
Thanksgiving, Dec 25) **$$**

Los Angeles Clippers (NBA). *Staples Center,1111 S
Figueroa St, Los Angeles (90015). Professional basketball
team. Phone 213/742-7555. www.nba.com/clippers.*

Los Angeles County Museum of Art. *5905 Wilshire
Blvd, Los Angeles (90036). Phone 323/857-6000. www.
lacma.org.* Located within blocks of several other Los
Angeles museums, including the Petersen Automotive Museum and the La Brea Tar Pits, the Los Angeles
County Museum of Art (LACMA) is one of the
leading art museums in the United States. Known in
particular for its Japanese art collection, LACMA is
home to everything from costumes and textiles dating
from 900 BC to nearly 5,000 photographs dating from
the invention of photography in 1839 to the present.
(Mon-Tues, Thurs noon-8 pm, Friday noon-9 pm,
Sat-Sun 11 am-8 pm; closed Thanksgiving, Dec 25)
Free admission the second Tues of each month. **$$**

Los Angeles Dodgers (MLB). *Dodger Stadium, 1000
Elysian Park Ave, Los Angeles (90012). Phone 323/224-
1500. www.dodgers.com.* Professional baseball team.

Dodger Stadium. *1000 Elysian Park Ave, Los Angeles
(90012). Phone 323/224-1500.* This more than 40-year-
old stadium is the home of Major League Baseball's
Los Angeles Dodgers.

Los Angeles Farmers' Market. *6333 W Third St, Los
Angeles (90036). Phone 323/933-9211. www.farmersmar-
ketla.com.* When visitors think of Los Angeles, a farmers'
market may be the farthest thing from their minds. But
the Los Angeles Farmers' Market has been a much-loved
part of the city since 1934, at the same location where it
exists today. Here, you can find 70 shops (90 percent of
which are owner-operated), and among the employees
of the market, at least 20 different languages are spoken.
Whether you're looking for the freshest fruits and
vegetables or you just want to experience a piece of Los
Angeles history, the Farmers' Market won't let you down.
(Mon-Fri 9 am-9 pm, Sat 9 am-8 pm, Sun 10 am-7 pm;
closed Jan 1, Thanksgiving, Dec 25) **FREE**

Los Angeles Fashion District. *5th and San Pedro sts,
Los Angeles. From 5th and 16th sts between Main and
San Pedro sts. Phone 213/488-1153. www.fashiondis-
trict.org.* Bargain hunters won't find needless markups
here. More than 1,000 of the nearly 2,000 wholesalers
in this bustling 82-block district sell their samples and
extras to the general public every Saturday, at prices
40 to 70 percent off retail. What a deal! And 220 of
them are always open to everyone. You'll bag even bet-
ter buys in Santee Alley, an open-air bazaar where you
might pay as little as $20 for a prom dress. No wonder

Touring the Stars' Homes

Touring the stars' homes has been a ritual of Los Angeles visitors since the days when Lucy and Ethel tried to get a grapefruit from Richard Widmark's garden on *I Love Lucy*. If you want to tour the stars' homes, you have several options. If you like the idea of doing your own driving and being able to stop off at other attractions throughout your drive, you can buy your own map of the stars' homes on the street and serve as your own tour guide. Maps are available everywhere from the Santa Monica Pier to the side of the road. If you buy more than one map, the first thing you'll notice is that the addresses aren't always the same from one map to the next. To find the most reliable maps (remember, we can't guarantee the accuracy), head to Sunset Boulevard east of UCLA. Along the side of the road, you'll see large signs advertising the sale of star maps. Before you fork over the $6 or so that they charge, check to see whether the map lists the date it was last updated. If the idea of navigating the palm treelined streets of Beverly Hills and Bel-Air sounds daunting and you'd rather leave the driving to someone else, numerous companies offer tours of the stars' homes on air-conditioned buses or vans. Check for brochures at your hotel to see which tours appeal to you. A reliable operator is StarLine Tours of Hollywood, which has been in business since 1935. You can join the tour in front of Grauman's Chinese Theatre on Hollywood Boulevard or have the tour bus pick you up at your LA hotel (phone toll-free 800/959-3131 to see whether your hotel is in their pickup area).

Hollywood stylists and costume designers often come to this downtown shopping district for accessories, jewelry, and fabric. And you thought all those well-dressed celebrities paid a fortune to look so fabulous.

Los Angeles Galaxy (MLS). *Home Depot Center, 18400 Avalon Blvd, Carson (90746). Phone toll-free 877/342-5299. www.lagalaxy.com.* The team opened the Home Depot Center in Carson, California, for the 2003 season, moving them out of the Rose Bowl and into a 21st-century facility.

Los Angeles Kings (NHL). *Staples Center, 1111 S Figueroa St, Los Angeles (90015). Phone toll-free 888/546-4752. www.lakings.com.*

Los Angeles Lakers (NBA). *Staples Center, 1111 S Figueroa St, Los Angeles (90015). Phone 213/742-7333. www.nba.com/lakers.* Professional basketball team.

Los Angeles Sparks (WNBA). *Staples Center, 1111 S Figueroa St, Los Angeles (90015). Phone 310/426-6031. www.wnba.com/sparks.* Women's professional basketball team.

Lummis Home and Garden State Historical Monument. *200 E Ave 43, Los Angeles (90042). Phone 323/222-0546.* Charles Lummis—the noted writer, photographer, historian, and archaeologist—spent 14 years (1896-1910) building this L-shaped home out of concrete and granite boulders. One look at this residential piece of art, now the headquarters for the Historical Society of Southern California, and you sense this eccentric man had a keen interest in pueblos and missions (indeed, he founded the Southwest Museum). Lummis named the house El Elisal, the Spanish word for sycamore, after the large tree that once grew beside it. Many drought-tolerant plants native to Southern California flourish in the gardens, offering a lesson in regional horticulture. (Tours, Fri-Sun noon-4 pm; closed holidays) **FREE**

Museum of Tolerance. *Simon Wiesenthal Center, 9786 W Pico Blvd, Los Angeles (90035). Phone 310/553-8403. www.museumoftolerance.com.* Opened in 1993, the Museum of Tolerance is devoted to exploring not only the Holocaust of World War II, but also the topic of prejudice in the United States. You can see a re-creation of a 1930s Berlin street and listen to people's concerns about the Nazis; hear survivors of the Holocaust describe their experiences; and look at artifacts from the period, including original letters written by Anne Frank. (Mon-Thurs 11:30 am-6:30 pm; Fri 11:30 am-5 pm, until 3 pm Nov-Mar; Sun 11 am-7:30 pm; closed holidays) **$$**

Page Museum at the La Brea Tar Pits. *5801 Wilshire Blvd, Los Angeles (90036). Phone 323/934-7243. www.tarpits.org.* In this museum located at the famous La Brea Tar Pits, you can get a glimpse of the kinds of creatures—like saber-toothed cats and mammoths—that called Los Angeles home 10,000 to 40,000 years ago. In the past century, more than a million bones have been removed from these tar pits, which still spurt out 8 to

12 gallons of hot asphalt a day. Don't get too close—unless you want to be the next fossil on display! (Mon-Fri 9:30 am-5 pm, Sat-Sun from 10 am; closed holidays) Free admission the first Tues of each month. **$$**

Petersen Automotive Museum. *6060 Wilshire Blvd, Los Angeles (90036). Phone 323/930-2277. www.petersen. org.* Who can resist the temptation of a cool car? You'll find plenty at the Petersen Automotive Museum, the world's largest of its kind. Dedicated to the history and cultural impact of the automobile, it contains more than 150 rare and classic vehicles—everything from Ford Model Ts and vintage motorcycles to muscle cars and movie wheels, like Fred Flinstones Rockmobile. Exhibits have included "Tuner Revolution: A New Generation of Speed" and "French Curves: The Automobile as Sculpture." Plus, adult visitors gain practical knowledge by learning the history of our car insurance system, while children master the mechanics of autos in the Children's Interactive Discovery Center (Tues-Fri 10 am-4 pm, Sat-Sun 10 am-5 pm). (Tues-Sun and Mon holidays 10 am-6 pm; closed Jan 1, Thanksgiving, Dec 25) **$$**

Rancho Park Golf Club. *10460 W Pico Blvd, Los Angeles (90064). Phone 310/839-9812. www.rpgc.org.* Rancho Park has a lot of straight, deceptive holes with greens that are challenging, to say the least. It may be hard to find straight putts, but the fairways are wide enough that it should be easy not to run up your score too high. The 18th hole offers the only real bunker challenge, guarding the back of the green. The courses Web site boasts that Arnold Palmer once took a 12 on the 18th. The course is beautiful in the fall, as all the fairways are lined with tall oaks and other deciduous foliage. If only the red on the leaves would transfer over to your scorecard.... **$$$$**

Rustic Canyon Golf Course. *15100 Happy Camp Canyon Rd, Moorpark (93021). Phone 805/530-0221. www. rusticcanyongolfcourse.com.* Opened for play in November 2001, Rustic Canyon needed very little earth to be moved to make way for the eventual route of the course. Course designers Geoff Shackelford and Gil Hanse let nature take its course, and it provided such interesting features as a natural alley to the 16th green and swales of up to 4 feet on greens like numbers six and nine. The greens have a tendency to be shaped uniquely, often like a boomerang or with bunkers covering just one side, forcing players to be inventive and courageous to reach them in regulation. All this for less than $50 a round makes it perhaps the best course in the LA area. **$$$$**

San Antonio Winery. *737 Lamar St, Los Angeles (90031). Phone 323/223-1401. www.sanantoniowinery.*

com. Winery, gift shop, wine tasting; restaurant. Self-guided tours. (Daily; closed holidays) **FREE**

Sony Pictures Studio Tour. *10202 W Washington Blvd, Culver City (90232). Phone 310/520-8687.* This storied lot used to be MGM Studios, the stomping grounds of MGM's honcho Louis B. Mayer, one of Hollywood's most feared bosses during his iron-fisted reign. It's also where movie legends Judy Garland and Clark Gable showcased their acting talent in those two classics everyone loves, *The Wizard of Oz* and *Gone with the Wind*. But Sony has owned the lot since 1989, and it's now home to Columbia Pictures and Columbia Tri Star, which produces popular television shows such as *Jeopardy!* and *Wheel of Fortune*. On a two-hour tour, you get an eye-opening behind-the-scenes look at the image-conscious industry that put LA on the map. You'll see a wardrobe department, visit movie and TV sets, and more. (Mon-Fri; closed holidays) Photo ID required for entrance. **$$$$**

South Coast Botanic Garden. *26300 Crenshaw Blvd, Palos Verdes Peninsula (90274). 1 mile S of Pacific Coast Hwy in Palos Verdes Peninsula. Phone 310/544-6815. www.south-coastbotanicgarden.org.* Hillside and coastal plants on 87 acres of filled land. (Daily 9 am-5 pm; closed Dec 25) **$$**

Southwest Museum. *234 Museum Dr, Los Angeles (90065). At Marmion Way, Pasadena Frwy, Ave 43 exit. Phone 323/221-2164. www.southwestmuseum.org.* The oldest museum in Los Angeles, which dates to 1907, offers immense insight into the life and culture of the American Indian. Its 17,000 square feet of exhibit space features four main exhibit halls in which visitors learn about the native people of the Southwest, California, the Great Plains, and the Northwest Coast. See a Cheyenne tepee, prehistoric painted pottery, basketry, and much more. The museum recently merged with the Autry Museum of Western Heritage, forming the Autry National Center of the American West, which also includes the Institute for the Study of the American West. (Tues-Sun 10 am-5 pm; closed holidays) **$$**

Sur La Table. *6333 W Third St, Los Angeles (90036). Phone 323/954-9190. www.surlatable.com.* In the 1970s, Seattle spawned this clearinghouse for hard-to-find kitchen gear, and it soon became known as a source for cookware, small appliances, cutlery, kitchen tools, linens, tableware, gadgets, and specialty foods. Sur La Table has since expanded to include cooking classes ($$$$), chef demonstrations, and cookbook author signings, as well as a catalog and online presence. Cooking connoisseurs discover such finds as cool oven mitts, zest graters, cop-

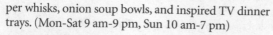

per whisks, onion soup bowls, and inspired TV dinner trays. (Mon-Sat 9 am-9 pm, Sun 10 am-7 pm)

Tijeras Creek Golf Club. *29082 Tijeras Creek, Rancho Santa Margarita (92688). Phone 949/589-9793. www.tijerascreek.com.* In the suburb of Rancho Santa Margarita in northern Orange County is Tijeras Creek. Like many other courses in the area, Tijeras Creek is set in a gradually sloping canyon, which lends its natural backdrop to sometimes intimidating but challenging and fun golf. Hole 16, a 172-yard par-three, requires quite a shot (over water to a green guarded by bunkers and deep rough) to leave a chance to make even par, let alone a birdie. The best bet for affordability? Be over 55 years old. Then a round costs just $55 Monday through Thursday. Otherwise, expect to spend around $100. **$$$$**

Tustin Ranch Golf Club. *12442 Tustin Ranch Rd, Tustin (92782). Phone 714/730-1611. www.tustinranchgolf.com.* Tustin Ranch is located near Anaheim, just a short drive from LA. The course sports some interesting features, like its truly beautiful 11th hole, a par-three over a lake with waterfalls on either side. When your front nine is coming to a close, order your lunch from the 9th tee box and it'll be waiting for you by the time you've finished the hole. The front nine plays through a suburban housing development, while the back nine is a little more wide open. This public course also offers caddies and a helpful staff that will be glad to fetch food or drinks during a round on a hot summer day. **$$$$**

UCLA Mildred Mathias Botanical Garden. *Hilgard and Le Conte aves, Los Angeles (90095). Phone 310/825-1260. www.botgard.ucla.edu.* Collection of plants, trees, and shrubs. Parking (fee). (Mon-Fri 8 am-5 pm, Sat-Sun to 4 pm; closed school holidays, also Jan 2, day after Thanksgiving, Dec 24) Guided tour of campus from Nest Ampitheater (weekdays). **FREE**

University of California, Los Angeles (UCLA). *405 Hilgard Ave, Los Angeles (90095). Phone 310/825-4321. www.ucla.edu.* (1919) (34,000 students) Tours (Mon-Fri). Art gallery, botanical garden, Franklin D. Murphy Sculpture Garden. Parking (fee).

University of Southern California. *3800 S Figueroa St, Los Angeles. Phone 213/740-2311. www.usc.edu.* (1880) (28,800 students) This is the oldest and largest private university in the Western United States. Points of interest on campus include Fisher Gallery, 823 Exposition Boulevard (Sept-Apr: Tues-Sat; May-Aug: by appointment, phone 213/740-4561) and the Hancock Memorial Museum (phone 213/740-5144).

Walt Disney Concert Hall. *111 S Grand Ave, Los Angeles (90012). wdch.laphil.com.* With a dramatic-looking exterior featuring curved stainless-steel panels, this concert hall designed by Frank Gehry promises to be quite a conversation piece. Opened in the downtown area in October 2003, the striking 293,000-square-foot facility features performances by the Los Angeles Philharmonic Orchestra, the Los Angeles Master Chorale, and other noted ensembles and orchestras from around the world. The main auditorium seats 2,265 people; two outdoor amphitheaters, 300 and 120 each. The 3.6-acre site also includes an inviting urban park with lush public gardens and ornamental landscaping. Event prices vary.

Watts Towers. *1765 E 107th St, Los Angeles (90002). S of Century Blvd, E of Harbor Frwy. Phone 213/847-4646. www.parks.ca.gov.* If the first thing that comes to mind when you hear the name Watts is the 1965 Watts riots, a visit to Watts Towers is sure to change that. In 1921, Italian immigrant Simon Rodia began building what are now known as the Watts Towers around his home in Los Angeles. Using steel rods and concrete and decorating the towers (the tallest of which stands at almost 100 feet) with pieces of broken glass and ceramics, Rodia spent 33 years constructing this masterpiece of folk art. (Tues-Fri 11 am-3 pm, Sat 10:30 am-3 pm, Sun 12:30-3 pm; closed Mon, rainy days) **$**

Westfield Shoppingtown Century City. *10250 Santa Monica Blvd, Los Angeles (90067). Phone 310/277-3898. www.westfield.com.* This high-end shopping mall, with 141 shops and restaurants, is one of the nicer outdoor shopping areas in Los Angeles. With Bloomingdale's and Macy's as anchors, it also features everything from Crate & Barrel and Restoration Hardware to Crabtree & Evelyn and Coach. The restaurants are a cut above the typical mall food court fare; you'll find such favorites as Baja Fresh Mexican Grill, Johnny Rocket's, and Ben & Jerry's. The malls movie theater often features movies on their opening weekends, before the rest of the country has a crack at them. (Mon-Sat 10 am-9 pm, Sun 11 am-6 pm; closed Easter, Thanksgiving, Dec 25)

Westside Pavilion. *10800 W Pico Blvd, Los Angeles (90064). Between Westwood Blvd and Overland Ave on Pico Blvd. Phone 310/474-6255. www.westsidepavilion.com.* With more than 160 stores and restaurants, including anchor department stores Nordstrom and Robinson's-May, Westside Pavilion is sure to have just about everything you're looking for. Located in the prestigious Westside community, this three-level, glass-ceiling mall was a hangout for the well-to-do shop-aholics in the movie *Clueless*. The movie theater usually features a good selection of movies that lean toward the artsy side. (Mon-Fri 10 am-9 pm, Sat 10 am-8 pm, Sun 11 am-6 pm; closed Thanksgiving, Dec 25)

Special Events

Chinese New Year Festival. *Contact Chamber of Commerce, 977 N Broadway # E, Los Angeles. Phone 213/617-0396.* Just when it seems that all the holiday fun is over, Los Angeles kicks up its heels for Chinese New Year somewhere between late January and mid-February. Known as a time to have fun and enjoy fresh starts, Chinese New Year gives Angelenos and visitors alike something to celebrate. Watch Chinatown come alive with two weeks of festivities to usher in the the spring, including the annual Golden Dragon Parade, a dazzling display of costume and revelry; the Miss LA Chinatown Pageant; and the Chinese New Year Banquet.

Cinco de Mayo Celebration. *El Pueblo de Los Angeles Historic Monument, Los Angeles.* There is no better place to celebrate Cinco de Mayo than Los Angeles. Known to attract even more celebrants than Mexico City, LA hosts numerous public festivals in honor of the Mexican victory at the Battle of Puebla. The party starts the last Sunday in April with the downtown Fiesta festival and continues on May 2 on historic Olvera Street with a free three-day celebration that includes traditional music, dance, food, and live entertainment.

Fiesta Broadway. *Downtown, Los Angeles. Phone 310/914-0015. www.fiestabroadway.la.* Given its large Latino population, Los Angeles observes Cinco de Mayo in a mucho grande way, with rousing celebrations throughout the area. The largest of the parties, Fiesta Broadway, kicks off the festivities each year on the Sunday before May 5. More than half a million fun-lovers crowd into 36 blocks of downtown to celebrate the Mexican armys defeat of the French at a key battle in Puebla, Mexico, in 1862. The cultural merrymaking features lots of top-name Latin entertainment (lively music and colorful dancers) and plenty of sizzlin south-of-the-border food and ice-cold drinks.

Los Angeles Opera. *Music Center of Los Angeles County, Dorothy Chandler Pavilion, 1st and Hope sts, Los Angeles (90012). Phone 213/972-8001. www.losangelesopera.com.* Directed by Plácido Domingo and conducted by Maestro Kent Nagano, the Los Angeles Opera has a long history of excellence has hosted several world premiere productions, never ceasing to "wow" its audiences. Early Sept-June.

Lotus Festival. *Echo Park Lake, Park and Glendale aves, Los Angeles (90039). www.laparks.org.* Celebrates various Asian and Pacific island cultures. Mid-July.

Nisei Week. *Little Tokyo, 244 S San Pedro St #303, Los Angeles (90012). Phone 213/687-7193. www.niseiweek. org.* First held in 1934 to brighten the dark days of The Depression, Nisei Week is one of the oldest Japanese-American festivals in the country. Commencing with the crowning of the queen at the coronation ball, the festival features a variety of sporting and martial arts events, stage performances, a 5K run, and parade. Aug.

Limited-Service Hotels

★ ★ **BEST WESTERN CARLYLE INN.** *1119 S Robertson Blvd, Los Angeles (90035). Phone 310/275-4445; toll-free 800/322-7595; fax 310/859-0496. www. carlyle-inn.com.* 32 rooms, 5 story. Complimentary full breakfast. Check-in 3 pm, check-out noon. Wireless Internet access. Fitness room. Whirlpool. **$**

★ ★ **COURTYARD BY MARRIOTT.** *10320 W Olympic Blvd, Los Angeles (90064). Phone 310/556-2777; toll-free 800/321-2211; fax 310/203-0563. www. courtyard.com.* 135 rooms, 5 story. Check-in 3 pm, check-out noon. High-speed Internet access. Restaurant, bar. Fitness room. Whirlpool. **$$**

Full-Service Hotels

★ ★ ★ **HILTON CHECKERS LOS ANGELES.** *535 S Grand Ave, Los Angeles (90071). Phone 213/624-0000; toll-free 800/445-8667; fax 213/891-0531. www. hiltoncheckers.com.* A downtown landmark, the Art Deco-era Hilton Checkers (opened 1927) offers modern amenities within a smartly maintained vintage façade. Checkers guest rooms sport warm neutral tones, plush bedding, and flat-screen TVs. The house dining room, Checkers Downtown, is a favorite for California-meets-the-classics food. One of the best benefits of residency here is the rooftop pool surrounded by LA's soaring skyscrapers. Another is its convenient location near the convention center, financial district, theaters, and Staples Center, home of the NBA's Lakers. 188 rooms, 12 story. Check-in 3 pm, check-out noon. High-speed Internet access. Restaurant, bar. Fitness room, spa. Outdoor pool, whirlpool. **$$$**

★ ★ ★ HYATT REGENCY CENTURY PLAZA.

2025 Avenue of the Stars, Los Angeles (90067). Phone 310/277-2000; toll-free 888/591-1234; fax 310/551-3355. www.hyatt.com. Given that the Hyatt Regency Century Plaza is adjacent to Beverly Hills, it's no wonder that it resonates star power. This glitzy contemporary hotel is situated on 7 acres dotted with reflecting pools and lush tropical plants. All guest rooms have balconies with views of the Los Angeles cityscape and the tree-lined boulevards of Beverly Hills. The accommodations are styled handsomely with Asian decorative objects and warm tones, while leather headboards and striking light fixtures enhance the contemporary feel. Asian influences abound at Spa Mystique, from the feng shui design principles used in the 27 treatment rooms and 4 outdoor cabanas to the popular treatments on the menu. Surrounded by manicured grounds, the heated outdoor pool provides yet another urban oasis. All tastes are suited at the Hyatt Regency Century Plaza, whether at the signature Breeze Restaurant or at the casual and light alternatives of the Lobby Court. 728 rooms, 19 story. Pets accepted, some restrictions; fee. Check-in 3 pm, check-out noon. High-speed Internet access. Two restaurants, bar. Fitness room (fee), spa. Outdoor pool, whirlpool. Business center. **$$**

★ ★ ★ LE MERIDIEN AT BEVERLY HILLS. 465

S La Cienega Blvd, Los Angeles (90048). Phone 310/247-0400; toll-free 800/645-5624; fax 310/246-2166. www. lemeridienbeverlyhills.com. Le Meridien expertly blends European panache with the lively spirit of its famous neighborhood. Centrally located on Restaurant Row in Beverly Hills, the hotel provides a convenient base for visitors soaking up the glamour of Rodeo Drive or conducting business in nearby Wilshire. The guest rooms show off the flair of French architect Pierre Yves Rochon. Spacious and stylish, the accommodations offer the latest and most luxurious amenities. Many rooms include terraces overlooking peaceful courtyard gardens. Business and fitness centers round out the experience at this cool contemporary hotel, and the heated outdoor pool provides a respite from working, touring, or shopping. The hip design of the Café Noir Bar & Lounge makes it a happening spot, and the star-studded Cannes Film Festival is celebrated at Le Festival, where vintage photographs line the walls, and Mediterranean dishes top the tables. 297 rooms, 6 story. Pets accepted, some restrictions; fee. Check-in 3 pm, check-out noon. High-speed Internet access. Restaurant, bar. Fitness room, spa. Outdoor pool. Business center. **$$**

★ ★ ★ LOEWS BEVERLY HILLS HOTEL.

1224 S Beverwil Dr, Los Angeles (90035). Phone 310/277-2800; toll-free 800/235-6397; fax 310/277-5470. www.loewshotels.com. Perched on a knoll adjacent to Beverly Hills and affording city, mountain, and ocean views, this boutique hotel delivers luxurious yet playful European-style sophistication to a discriminating leisure and business clientele. Plush furnishings, private balconies, pricey lithographs, and pastel hues—accented by tropical plantings and granite bathroom vanities—highlight the guest rooms, some of which feature spa tubs. High-speed Internet, secretarial services, and concierge service are available, and the continental-flavored on-site restaurant, Lot 1224, makes for a cozy social hub. Close to Rodeo Drive, Hillcrest Country Club, and Twentieth Century Fox studios, the Loews offers complimentary sedan service to downtown Beverly Hills. 137 rooms, 12 story. Pets accepted. Check-in 3 pm, check-out noon. High-speed Internet access. Restaurant, bar. Fitness room. Outdoor pool. Business center. **$$**

★ ★ ★ LUXE HOTEL SUNSET BOULEVARD.

11461 W Sunset Blvd, Los Angeles (90049). Phone 310/476-6571; toll-free 866/589-3411; fax 310/471-6310. www.luxehotels.com. A sophisticated, contemporary property terraced on a hillside bordering the tony Bel-Air district below the Getty Museum (see), the Luxe Summit boasts seven lushly landscaped acres just off Sunset Boulevard. A shuttle bus plies the hill transporting patrons between two guest room buildings. The lower one shelters the lobby, restaurant, and fitness center, while the upper house encompasses a full-service spa with an outdoor pool and adjacent tennis court. Guest quarters are notably spacious, decorated in understated colors with residential style furnishings. 164 rooms, 2 story. Pets accepted, some restrictions; fee. Check-in 3 pm, check-out noon. Restaurant, bar. Fitness room. Outdoor pool. Tennis. Airport transportation available. **$$**

★ ★ ★ MARRIOTT LOS ANGELES

DOWNTOWN. *333 S Figueroa St, Los Angeles (90071). Phone 213/617-1133; toll-free 800/228-9290; fax 213/613-0291. www.marriott.com.* This marvelously self-contained hotel in the heart of the downtown financial district is connected to the World Trade Center by skywalks and is within a short walk or drive of the Convention Center, Staples Center sports arena, Dodger Stadium, and Walt Disney Concert Hall, as well as various theaters and restaurants. Spacious rooms and suites are fully equipped for comfort and wired for business travelers, and all guests will enjoy the heated outdoor pool, health club, and dynamic skyline views. Meeting space abounds, and three on-site restaurants, plus the continental-themed Lobby Bar and Lounge, offer savory meals and spirits. 469 rooms, 13 story. Check-in 3 pm, check-out noon. Wireless Internet access. Three restaurants, bar. Fitness room. Outdoor pool. Business center. **$$**

★ ★ ★ MILLENNIUM BILTMORE HOTEL LOS ANGELES. *506 S Grand Ave, Los Angeles (90071). Phone 213/624-1011; toll-free 800/245-8673; fax 213/612-1545. www.thebiltmore.com.* The original home of the Academy Awards, the 1923 vintage Millennium Biltmore brings out the magnate in every patron. Frescoes, decorative pillars, and other old-world flourishes distinguish this hotel from the downtown convention pack. Best-loved amenities include the Roman-style tiled swimming pool and the Gallery lounge, complete with period chandeliers and a baby grand. Its "Black Dahlia" drink pays homage to the mysteriously murdered starlet who was last sighted at the Biltmore. As befits a Gatsby-era hotel, guest quarters are classic and roomy. 682 rooms, 12 story. Check-in 3 pm, check-out noon. High-speed Internet access. Two restaurants, two bars. Fitness room. Indoor pool, whirlpool. Business center. **$$**

★ ★ ★ NEW OTANI HOTEL & GARDEN. *120 S Los Angeles St, Los Angeles (90012). Phone 213/629-1200; toll-free 800/639-6826; fax 213/622-0980. www.newotanihotels.com.* A Japanese oasis in the heart of Los Angeles, this high-rise hotel edges downtown's Little Tokyo district. The hotel has a tranquil plant-filled two-story lobby and a manicured Japanese roof garden. Traditional Japanese restaurants serve Kobe beef, sushi, and tempura; the health spa specializes in shiatsu massage; and the bar offers state-of-the-art karaoke. Guest rooms are largely configured in Western style, although Japanese rooms with sunken futons and tatami mats are also available. 434 rooms, 21 story. Check-in 3 pm, check-out noon. High-speed Internet access. Three restaurants, two bars. Fitness room. Whirlpool. Business center. **$**

★ ★ ★ OMNI LOS ANGELES HOTEL AT CALIFORNIA PLAZA. *251 S Olive St, Los Angeles (90012). Phone 213/617-3300; toll-free 800/442-5251; fax 213/617-3399. www.omnihotels.com.* Located in the heart of downtown Los Angeles atop Bunker Hill, this hotel is part of a plaza complex with an outdoor courtyard displaying contemporary sculptures. The Museum of Contemporary Art is next door, and and the Walt Disney Concert Hall is two blocks away. 453 rooms, 17 story. Pets accepted, some restrictions; fee. Check-in 3 pm, check-out noon. Wireless Internet access. Two restaurants, bar. Fitness room, spa. Outdoor pool. Business center. **$$**

★ ★ ★ PARK HYATT LOS ANGELES. *2151 Avenue of the Stars, Los Angeles (90067). Phone 310/277-1234; toll-free 800/233-1234; fax 310/785-9240. www.parkhyattlosangeles.com.* Located at Century City near West Side studios and financiers, the Park Hyatt Los Angeles gives guests a slick, urban LA stay. Rooms are spacious and comfortable, sporting neutral colors and cherry wood furniture. Though largely a business hotel, the Park Hyatt makes a great getaway, too, with an indoor pool, outdoor sundeck, complimentary limo service to nearby Rodeo Drive shops and golf outings arranged at several area courses. 362 rooms, 17 story. Check-in 3 pm, check-out noon. High-speed Internet access. Restaurant, bar. Fitness room, spa. Outdoor pool, whirlpool. Business center. **$$$**

★ ★ ★ SHERATON LOS ANGELES DOWNTOWN HOTEL. *711 S Hope St, Los Angeles (90017). Phone 213/488-3500; fax 213/488-4110. www.sheraton.com/losangeles.* 485 rooms. Pets accepted, some restrictions; fee. Check-in 3 pm, check-out noon. High-speed Internet access. Two restaurants, bar. Fitness room. Business center. **$**

★ ★ ★ SOFITEL LOS ANGELES. *8555 Beverly Blvd, Los Angeles (90048). Phone 310/278-5444; toll-free 800/763-4835; fax 310/657-2816. www.sofitella.com.* Directly opposite the chic Beverly Center shopping mall and convenient to Melrose Avenue, Beverly Hills, and the nightlife of West Hollywood, this contemporary hotel features a blend of French and Californian cultures that appeals to business travelers and discerning guests. Bright blue awnings adorn glassed-in balconies, which extend from rooms and suites outfitted in French country luxury and well stocked with comforting amenities, including fresh flowers. The classy but casual indoor/outdoor brasserie Gigi offers exquisite French fare all day, with breads and pastries made fresh in an on-site bakery. Free shuttle service to the airport and Union Station is available. 297 rooms, 10 story, all suites. Pets accepted.

Check-in 3 pm, check-out noon. High-speed Internet access. Restaurant, bar. Fitness room. Outdoor pool. Business center. **$$$**

★ ★ ★ **THE ORLANDO.** *8384 W Third St, Los Angeles (90404). Phone 323/658-6600; toll-free 800/624-6836; fax 323/653-3464.ww.theorlando.com.* 98 rooms. Pets accepted, some restrictions. Complimentary full breakfast. Check-in 3 pm, check-out noon. High-speed Internet access. Restaurant, bar. Fitness room. Whirlpool. **$$**

★ ★ ★ **THE WESTIN BONAVENTURE HOTEL AND SUITES.** *404 S Figueroa St, Los Angeles (90071). Phone 213/624-1000; toll-free 800/937-8461; fax 213/612-4800. www.westin.com.* If you're looking for a hotel that has it all, look no farther than the Westin Bonaventure, an icon of downtown LA. The mega-hotel houses more than 1,300 rooms in five gleaming metal towers. Enter the six-story lobby and wind through the indoor gardens and waterfalls to one of 12 elevators that whisk you to your pie-shaped room featuring one entire wall of windows overlooking the city. Among the hotel's 20-some restaurants and bars is a rooftop steakhouse and revolving lounge. 1,354 rooms, 35 story. Pets accepted, some restrictions. Check-in 3 pm, check-out noon. High-speed Internet access. Three restaurants, two bars. Fitness room. Outdoor pool, whirlpool. **$**

★ ★ ★ **WYNDHAM COMMERCE.** *5757 Tele-graph Rd, Commerce (90040). Phone 323/887-8100; fax 213/887-4343. www.wyndham.com.* Located ten minutes southeast of downtown in the landmark Citadel outlet mall, which features an Assyrian-style castle wall used as a backdrop in the 1959 film *Ben-Hur,* this neoclassical hotel is ideal for fans of tax-free shopping and travelers seeking a convenient midpoint between the area's big theme parks. Lushly landscaped grounds and a cozy, fireplace-accented lobby give way to spacious accommodations featuring pillow-top mattresses and stylish furnishings. The Wyndham sponsors "Women on Their Way," a program offering security measures and amenities for female travelers, and allows children 18 years and under accompanied by a parent to stay free. 201 rooms, 7 story. Pets accepted; fee. Check-in 3 pm, check-out noon. High-speed Internet access. Restaurant, bar. Outdoor pool, whirlpool. Business center. **$$**

Spa

★ ★ ★ **SPA MYSTIQUE AT THE CENTURY PLAZA HOTEL.** *2025 Avenue of the Stars, Los Angeles (90067). Phone 310/556-2256; toll-free 877/544-2256. www.spamystique.com.* Designed according to feng shui principles, this Asian-influenced spa is the ultimate urban retreat. With 27 indoor treatment rooms, 4 outdoor treatment cabanas, 2 Japanese furo baths, Vichy and Swiss showers, saunas, and a meditation garden, this facility is 35,000 square feet of pure bliss. From an Asian-inspired treatment menu and pampering at the salon to a full-service fitness center and a café, Spa Mystique offers guests a well-rounded spa experience. Benefit from the yoga, Pilates, sculpt, stretch, and cardiovascular classes offered at the fitness center, where personal trainers are available to assist you with the free weights and exercise machines. Celebrating Asian customs, the spa's treatment menu invites you to delight in traditions from Korea, Japan, and Thailand. Simple yet luxurious, the therapies deliver results, whether you are seeking total relaxation or softer, younger-looking skin. Reawaken your senses with an invigorating ginger wrap or renew yourself with a sugar scrub, which uses unrefined cane sugar and Babassu palm oil to exfoliate skin. The serenity bath is inspired by the Japanese Sento, or community bath, where individuals wash before bathing. This treatment begins with a therapist scrubbing your back and ends with a soak in a cypress tea, seaweed, or milk bath. The akasuri treatment scrubs your skin before covering you in warm oil, followed by the soothing application of ground cucumber. Skin care services include marine spring water, seaweed, yin, yang, enzyme, and aromatherapy facials. Traditional Asian massage techniques, including Thai, shiatsu, reiki, and reflexology, are available, and the sleeping tiger massage is not to be missed. The long strokes and kneading of this massage are sure to relieve your tension. The stylish haircuts from Yamaguchi at Spa Mystique are a nod to the hotel's chic location, yet the salon's innovative practice of applying the principles of feng shui to beauty services is distinctly Eastern. For a unique experience, book a manicure or pedicure—in varieties such as hayaku, centering, or tea.

Restaurants

★ ★ **ABC SEAFOOD.** *205 New High St, Los Angeles (90012). Phone 213/680-2887; fax 218/680-0121.* Dim sum devotees descend regularly on this casual Chinatown favorite, where a virtual rainbow of the sweet and savory snacks enlivens a somewhat austere, mirrored-ceiling dining room. Patrons need not remain seated to select entrées–they can press their noses to several large saltwater display tanks to inspect tilapia fish and other live dishes-to-be. Swift, congenial service, modest prices (banquet specials are offered for parties of four or more) and authentic Hong Kong-style fare are ABCs hallmarks. And from the Peking duck to the sautéed geoduck clam, the portions are grand. Seafood menu. Lunch, dinner. Casual attire. **$**

★ **ALEGRIA ON SUNSET.** *3510 W Sunset Blvd, Los Angeles (90026). Phone 323/913-1422; fax 323/913-1422.* Never mind its nondescript strip-mall setting. Step inside this family-run Silver Lake institution and discover a minor Mexi-Cali marvel. Walls adorned with colorful Mexican and Southwestern art telegraph the featured flavors, whether they are in the form of fish tacos, baked-chicken enchiladas or vegan tostadas filled with marinated cactus. Casual diners and critics have been known to say ole! to the homemade molea zesty sauce that can enrich any of Alegrias fresh-cooked, largely grease-free entrées. For dessert, the one-of-a-kind chocolate chimichangaa chocolate bar bundled and fried in a tortilla, then given a dollop of fruit sauce or whipped creamshould sate any sweet tooth. Mexican menu. Lunch, dinner. Closed Sun. Children's menu. Casual attire. No credit cards accepted. **$**

★ **ANNA'S.** *10929 W Pico Blvd, Los Angeles (90064). Phone 310/474-0102; fax 310/470-8018. www.annaitalian.com.* With the closing of Bruno's Ristorante, whose cathedral-like décor doubled as a film and TV backdrop for decades, the West Side has turned to Anna's for authentic Sicilian atmosphere. From the lamps and the poster-covered walls to the tablecloths and the rich sauces ladled generously over lovingly prepared pasta, the color red prevails; its copious use here announces "wholly appetizing" (and "somewhat pricey"). Featuring pepperoni pizza, whitefish piccata, and everything in-between, the selection is impressive, and the waitstaff—apropos to the culture—is warm and very family oriented. Italian menu. Lunch, dinner. Closed Thanksgiving, Dec 25. Bar. Casual attire. Valet parking. **$$**

★ **THE APPLE PAN.** *10801 W Pico Blvd, Los Angeles (90064). Phone 310/475-3585.* This historic burger joint is simply a horseshoe-shaped counter with a baffling seating policy (fend for yourself!) and minimal frills. What you get in return are cheap and juicy sirloin burgers that many swear are the best in town. Sure, ham sandwiches are offered, but aficionados go for the hickory cheeseburger, a drippy treat wrapped in paper (no plates!), and a pile of crispy fries. Don't miss the transcendent banana cream pie for dessert. Down-home dining never felt so decadent. American menu. Lunch, dinner. Closed Mon. Casual attire. **$**

★ **BATTAMBANG.** *648 New High St, Los Angeles. Phone 213/620-9015.* Pacific-Rim/Pan-Asian menu. Breakfast, lunch. **$**

★ ★ **C2 CAFE & KITCHEN.** *2039 Century Park E, Los Angeles (90067). Phone 310/551-1600. www.patinagroup.com/c2.* Comprised of a full-service restaurant/bar and a gourmet grab-and-go counter, this dual eatery within the landmark Century Towers office complex caters primarily to the spit-polished business crowd that wheels and deals in the immediate vicinity. The chic, bright café features a flavorful andas befits the clientelefinely presented lunch menu of California-Mediterranean cuisine; the offerings expand and the full bar opens after 4 pm. The side counter includes a variety of savory soups, sandwiches, and side dishes that also incorporate Mexican and Asian influences, as well as a lively salad bar stocked with antipasti and fresh vegetables from the famous nearby Farmers' Market. California menu. Breakfast, lunch. **$$**

★ ★ **CA'BREA.** *346 S La Brea Ave, Los Angeles (90036). Phone 323/938-2863; fax 323/938-8659. www.cabrearestaurant.com.* More traditional than trendy, this bustling northern Italian eatery is a favorite for family gatherings with its warm terra-cotta-washed dining room, gracious service, and homey atmosphere. A balcony dining area is perched above a theatrical open kitchen, while a long marble bar with backlit bottles is the perfect spot for a pre-dinner drink. The rustic-chic vibe extends to the menu, which can offer fennel lamb fritters or agnolotti stuffed with veal or prosciutto. At Ca'Brea, you get the comfort of a home-cooked meal—without having to do the dishes. Italian menu. Lunch, dinner. Closed holidays. Bar. Casual attire. Reservations recommended. Valet parking. **$$$**

★ **CAFE BRAZIL.** *10831 Venice Blvd, Los Angeles (90034). Phone 310/837-8957.* Latin American, Brazilian menu. Lunch, dinner. Bar. Casual attire. Outdoor seating. **$**

★ ★ **CAFÉ PINOT.** *700 W 5th St, Los Angeles (90071). Phone 213/239-6500; fax 213/239-6514. www.patinagroup.com.* One of LA celebrity chef Joachim Splichal's restaurants, Café Pinot delivers romance amid the downtown business setting largely void of quality eateries. His California fare has a country French accent that draws desk jockeys in at lunch and destination diners—especially theatergoers and special-occasion celebrants—in for dinner. But for all its worldliness, Café Pinot is a relaxing spot. Glimpse dramatically lit skyscrapers by night from a perch on the pleasant patio. California menu. Lunch, dinner. Closed holidays. Bar. Business casual attire. Reservations recommended. Valet parking. Outdoor seating. **$$**

★ **CAFE STELLA.** *3932 W Sunset Blvd, Los Angeles (90029). Phone 323/666-0265.* This quaint French restaurant is tucked away in the back corner of the rust-colored Sunset Junction strip mall—and this joints intimate funkiness meshes well with its artsy neighborhood. A tiny dining room holds only six tables; other diners are seated on the dark yet charming patio. The menu is full of hearty French bistro classics, like French onion soup with a crust of molten cheese, chicken with herbaceous tarragon sauce, and a silky pot au chocolat. Romance is always in the airthis is a popular date spot for trendy locals. French menu. Dinner. Closed Sun-Mon. Casual attire. Reservations recommended. Outdoor seating. **$$**

★ ★ ★ **CAMPANILE.** *624 S La Brea Ave, Los Angeles (90036). Phone 323/938-1447; fax 323/938-5840. www.campanilerestaurant.com.* Chefs Mark Peel and Nancy Silverton have scaled culinary highs with Campanile, a California-Mediterranean restaurant with LA legend status. Charlie Chaplin once owned the historic building, but since 1989 it has adopted a Southern European grace with red tile floors, a fountain, and a skylit atrium in the dining room. Menus change frequently, but always rely on seasonal ingredients in dishes like dandelion salad, battered soft-shell crab, charred baby lamb, and seared spot prawns. Come Monday night for convivial family-style dinners and Thursdays for sandwiches on bread from neighboring venture La Brea bakery. California, Mediterranean menu. Lunch, dinner. Closed July 4, Labor Day. Bar. Business casual attire. Reservations recommended. Valet parking. Outdoor seating. **$$$**

★ **CASA BIANCA PIZZA PIE.** *1650 Colorado Blvd, Los Angeles (90041). Phone 323/256-9617.* This friendly pizza joint seems frozen in time, with its flashing neon blue sign, linoleum floors, red vinyl booths, and serious red-sauce-Italian vibe. Large families, couples young and old, punkers, and local artists flood the place nightly for what most claim are the best pies in town. Although pastas and salads are of-

fered, the house pizza is legendary—with a crisp thin crust, sweet tomato sauce, mountains of gooey stringy cheese and clumps of homemade sausage that burst with juicy flavor. Pizza. Dinner. Closed Sun-Mon. Bar. Children's menu. Casual attire. **$**

★ **CASSELL'S.** *3266 W 6th St, Los Angeles (90020). Phone 213/480-5000; fax 213/480-8668.* Blue-collar workers, business suits and stray tourists alike crowd the stark-white confines of Cassell's. The big attraction? Fresh-ground, 100-percent USDA Prime beef hamburgers double-broiled to well-done yet sublimely juicy perfection. Amiable kitchen staff and a shockingly well-stocked toppings bar are welcome garnishes in this no-frills eat-mosphere. But its bleak 1970s cafeteria chic, replete with Formica tabletops, orange food trays, and even a faded, signed cast photo from *The Love Boat,* keeps customers focused on what countsa burger that many claim is the city's best. American menu. Lunch. Closed holidays. Casual attire. No credit cards accepted. **$**

★ ★ **CHIN CHIN.** *206 S Beverly Dr, Beverly Hills (90212). Phone 310/248-5252.www.chinchin.com.* This sunny Chinese bistro is always abuzz with young executives taking quick business lunches, post-yoga beauties munching on salads, and shoppers refueling for the next boutique. The interior is pure SoCal, with lots of peach and green appointments surrounding the blonde wood tables and the model-like waitstaff. From mu shu pork to fried rice, hot-and-sour soup to chow fun, classic Chinese fare gets a healthy twist with light preparations and fresh ingredients. Chinese menu. Lunch, dinner. Casual attire. Outdoor seating. **$$**

★ ★ **CIAO TRATTORIA.** *815 W 7th St, Los Angeles (90017). Phone 213/624-2244; fax 213/624-7788. www. ciaotrattoria.com.* Close to the Staples Center, the Walt Disney Concert Hall, and other vibrant attractions, downtown's landmark Fine Arts Building—with its burnished wood accents and high, ornate ceilings—is a cozy, appropriately Romanesque and decidedly romantic setting for this pre-performance hot spot. Lobster ravioli and seared ahi salad dishes are standouts among the traditional Italian fare, which includes savory chicken and beef entrées alongside flavorful (and family-friendly) pasta standards. From Archery Summit to San Guido Sassicaia, the award-winning wine list boasts some of the best producers and vintages from California and Italy. Shuttles to select major local venues are available—call for details. Italian menu. Lunch, dinner. Closed Sun, holidays. Bar. Casual attire. Reservations recommended. Valet parking. **$$**

★ ★ **CICADA.** *617 S Olive St, Los Angeles (90014). Phone 213/488-9488; fax 213/488-9032. www.cicadarestaurant.com.* Famed as the site where Richard Gere romanced Julia Roberts in the film *Pretty Woman*, Cicada is equally renowned for its own beauty. Lodged in a classic Art Deco Oviatt Building downtown, the restaurant places elegantly dressed tables under stunning 30-foot gold ceilings, awing all but the most jaded of diners. The northern Italian menu is highlighted by duck ravioli, tiger shrimp risotto, filet with foie gras, and osso buco. A lengthy after-dinner drink menu encourages you to savor the special-occasion surroundings. Italian menu. Lunch, dinner. Closed Sat, Sun; holidays. Bar. Business casual attire. Reservations recommended. Valet parking. **$$$**

★ ★ **CIUDAD.** *445 S Figueroa St, Los Angeles (90071). Phone 213/486-5171; fax 213/486-5172. www.ciudad-la.com.* This bright and whimsical dining room is more South Beach (Florida) than downtown LA, with apricot and yellow tones, Miró-like sketches on the walls, and lots of energy. The upscale eatery, brought to us by the ladies behind the popular Border Grill, offers eclectic twists on a plethora of Latin American specialties. Expect the delectably unusual, like butternut squash empanadas and tamarind-glazed salmon. A happening happy hour draws in local executives who nosh on tapas and drain glasses of sangria. Latin menu. Lunch, dinner. Closed holidays. Bar. Children's menu. Casual attire. Outdoor seating. **$$$**

★ ★ **EL CHOLO.** *1121 S Western Ave, Los Angeles (90006). Phone 323/734-2773; fax 323/734-7565. www.elcholo.com.* This historic landmark is the foundation of LA's love affair with Mexican food. The enormous ranch-style restaurant is replete with tile floors, arched entryways, and lots of south-of-the-border accoutrements, and the torso-sized combination platters pack diners in. Traditional rolled beef tacos, blue corn enchiladas, and sizzling fajitas are popular, but the star of the menu is the green corn tamales—available only from May through October. Families with children, couples on casual dates, fraternity boys, and yuppie birthday parties all congregate here. As expected, the perennially popular margaritas are powerful, keeping everyone rowdy. Mexican menu. Lunch, dinner. Closed holidays. Bar. Casual attire. Reservations recommended. Valet parking. **$$**

★ **EL COYOTE.** *7312 Beverly Blvd, Los Angeles (90036). Phone 323/939-2255; fax 323/939-7766. www.elcoyotecafe.com.* This massive taco and tequila emporium is always jam-packed with a lively young crowd slugging down high-octane margaritas and generally getting the party started. A heated patio keeps smokers happy, a crowded bar plays televised sports, and a maze of dining rooms is crammed with bad Mexican art, fake birds, and Christmas lights dangling from the rafters. No unique ethnic specialties here, just football-sized burritos, mountainlike fajita platters, and surprisingly delicate tamales. El Coyote also has the creepy distinction of having served Sharon Tate her last meal. Mexican menu. Lunch, dinner. Bar. Children's menu. Casual attire. Valet parking. **$$**

★ ★ **ENGINE CO. NO. 28.** *644 S Figueroa St, Los Angeles (90017). Phone 213/624-6996. www.engineco.com.* This beautifully preserved firehouse-turned-restaurant is one of Los Angeles's historic architectural treasures. The original brick façade, tile floors, and pressed-tin ceilings now surround clubby high-backed booths and a long wooden bar. Luxurious comfort food matches the classic surroundings, with specialties like chicken pot pie and grilled bone-in pork chops. This is a popular business spot, as well as a great place for Lakers fans to grab a pre-game bite. Shuttles are available to the Staples Center and the Music Hall; call for further information. American menu. Lunch, dinner. Closed holidays. Bar. Casual attire. Reservations recommended. Valet parking (dinner). **$$**

★ ★ **EUROCHOW.** *1099 Westwood Blvd, Los Angeles (90024). Phone 310/209-0066; fax 310/209-0055. www.eurochow.com.* One of the most architecturally stunning dining rooms in the city, this whitewashed two-story cathedral has a circular martini lounge, a massive mirrored dining table for large parties, and twin floating staircases that seem to hover magically above it all. Cuisines of two different cultures, Italian and Chinese, seem like odd partners, but one taste of the glazed walnut prawns or the filet mignon prosciutto washed down with a lychee martini will make anyone a believer. A terminally hip crowd approves. Chinese, Italian menu. Dinner. Bar. Business casual attire. Reservations recommended. Valet parking. Outdoor seating. **$$$**

★ **FRED 62.** *1850 N Vermont Ave, Los Angeles (90027). Phone 323/667-0062; fax 323/665-3621. fred62.com.* This lime green 24/7 diner is ground zero for East Side hipstersmusicians, artists, and vintage-wearing club kids flock here for inexpensive gourmet diner fare. The interior is retro-chic, the servers tattooed, and the menu full of offbeat twists on old standards with terribly clever names. The Hunka Burnin Love pancake stuffed with peanut butter, bananas, and chocolate and the French toast dusted with cornflakes are popular breakfast treats. Seoul-food can be found in the Noo-deli menu, full of international soups and starches. Super-juicy burgers, crisp onion rings, and tuna melts are available for purists. American menu. Breakfast, lunch, dinner, late-night. **$$**

★ ★ ★ **GRACE.** *7360 Beverly Blvd, Los Angeles (90036). Phone 323/934-4400. www.gracerestaurant. net.* Neal Fraser is the new darling of LA's dining scene with his original twist on contemporary American cuisine at the much-hyped Grace. The sexy dining room is appointed with orchids floating in vases, massive fish-eyed mirrors, squash-colored booths, and chandeliers that seem to drip with seashells. Despite its unmistakably trendy crowd and ultra-fashionable atmosphere, the kitchen solidly delivers excellent cuisine, like pumpkin and sea urchin risotto and skate in a raisin-caper emulsion. Striking entrées, such as bacon-wrapped saddle of rabbit and wild boar with violet mustard sauce, impress even the most world-weary foodies. American menu. Dinner. Closed Mon; holidays. Bar. Business casual attire. Reservations recommended. Valet parking. **$$$**

★ **GUELAGUETZA.** *3337 1/2 W 8th St, Los Angeles (90005). Phone 213/427-0601.* In a city rife with Mexican-American restaurants, this institution is a rare shining example of authentic Oaxacan cuisine. The large dining room is clean and bright, with yellow walls, colorful tables, and simple plastic chairs. Mexican families and commuting foodies clamor for a table and a taste of nearly a dozen legendary moles. From the spicy-sweet red mole on tamales to the inky-dark mole negro on chicken, these intensely flavored and complex sauces are as unique as they are addictive. Mexican menu. Breakfast, lunch, dinner. Bar. Casual attire. **$**

★ ★ **HAMASAKU.** *11043 Santa Monica Blvd, Los Angeles (90025). Phone 310/479-7636. www.hamasakula.com.* Hidden in the back corner of a mini-mall, HamaSaku may seem like an unlikely spot for star sightings, but this sushi stronghold is frequented by everyone from Harrison Ford to Calista Flockhart to Christina Aguilera, who even has a roll named after her. The décor is minimalist chic, with a requisite sushi bar, wooden tables, and screens that act as privacy shields. Raw fish is exquisitely fresh, and the chefs turn out amazing sculptural towers of salads and imaginative hand rolls that utilize cucumber instead of seaweed. Japanese, sushi menu. Lunch, dinner. Closed Sun. Casual attire. Reservations recommended. **$$$**

★ **HIDE SUSHI.** *2040 Sawtelle Blvd, Los Angeles (90025). Phone 310/477-7242.* There is always a line snaking out the door of this popular sushi joint in Sawtelle's Little Japan neighborhood. Fish fans know that the freshest catch of the day is here, and its a bargain. Sure, the décor isn't much, you sign yourself in and wait your turn, and credit cards are a no-no, but in return, you will be rewarded with generous platters of albacore sashimi and sweet shrimp sushi. Japanese, sushi menu. Lunch, dinner. Closed Mon. Casual attire. No credit cards accepted. **$$** 🅳

★ ★ **THE IVY.** *113 N Robertson Blvd, Los Angeles (90048). Phone 310/274-8303.* Any avid tabloid reader will recognize The Ivy's star-studded patio from the hundreds of published celebrity photos. West Hollywood's country-chic café is a favorite haunt for Hollywood elite, who do movie deals and power breakfasts over the famed grilled vegetable salad or the blue crab omelet. (Santa Monica's modish beach outpost, at 1541 Ocean Ave, also attracts a stylish crowd.) The Shore's bar is a sophisticated spot to watch the sun set and grab an Ivy gimlet, a potent concoction of vodka, mint, and lime. California menu. Lunch, dinner. Casual attire. Reservations recommended. Valet parking. Outdoor seating. **$$$**

★ **THE KITCHEN.** *4348 Fountain Ave, Los Angeles (90029). Phone 323/664-3663; fax 323/664-3663.* Despite its cramped, weathered, generally themeless interior and sometimes blaring music, The Kitchen is a haven for hearty home cookingas an eclectic adult crowd of club-oers, foodies and ravening locals has discovered. Delightfully presented delectables such as grilled tofu, roasted chicken soup, and cioppino bolster a tasty traditional line-up that includes burgers, stews, and salads. The efficient waitstaff steers vegetarians toward a variety of meat-free specialties. American menu. Lunch, dinner, late-night. Casual attire. Outdoor seating. **$$**

★ ★ **KOUTOUBIA.** *2116 Westwood Blvd, Los Angeles (90025). Phone 310/475-0729; fax 310/475-0720. www.koutoubiarestaurant.com.* Live music and belly dancing (sometimes hilariously enhanced by patron participation) may be the flashier attractions of this popular Moroccan eatery. But the traditional setting and menu hold their own considerable charms. Lit softly by candles and chandeliers, brass tables surrounded by plush seating and vivid tapestries form an intimate ambience for mouthwatering cuisine—including merguez sausage with couscous, lamb tagine and b'stia au poulet, a chicken pie textured with almonds and encased in a delicate crust. Children are welcomed warmly, while adults are greeted with a smile—and a well-stocked wine list. Middle Eastern menu. Dinner. Closed Mon. Bar. Casual attire. Reservations recommended. **$$**

★ **LA BREA BAKERY.** *624 S La Brea Ave, Los Angeles (90036). Phone 323/964-8594; fax 323/938-7440. www.labreabakery.com.* Although Nancy Silverton's famed baguettes and brioches have made their way into gourmet grocery stores across the city—food fans continue to travel to the source, an artisanal bakery attached to the famed restaurant, Campanile. Besides turning out original loaves with flavors like roasted garlic or chocolate sour cherry, the full-service café offers exquisite sandwiches and paninis, which utilize rare cheeses, imported meats, and naturally, the best bread in town. This is a perfect spot to stop by for a picnic to go. Sandwiches, bakery. Breakfast, lunch, dinner. Closed holidays. Casual attire. Outdoor seating. **$**

★ ★ **LA CACHETTE.** *10506 Santa Monica Blvd, Los Angeles (90025). Phone 310/470-4992; fax 310/470-7451. www.lacachetterestaurant.com.* This classic French restaurant has long been a favorite for Beverly Hills' quiet elite. During the day, ladies who lunch nosh on exquisite salads and discuss charity events, and at night, refined couples dress up to dine on chef Jean Franois Meteigners haute cuisine. The dining room is elegant in peach and gold hues, with a nice view above the bustling street. Caviar, foie gras, duck confit, farm-raised squabthe menu reads like a gourmand's dream. And vegans will be delighted to find suitable dishes on the regular menu, as well as a weekly tasting menu. French menu. Lunch, dinner. Closed holidays. Bar. Casual attire. **$$$**

★ ★ **LA SERENATA GOURMET.** *10924 W Pico Blvd, Los Angeles (90064). Phone 310/441-9667; fax 310/441-0597.* Mexican menu. Lunch, dinner. Bar. Casual attire. Reservations recommended. Outdoor seating. **$$**

★ **LUNA PARK.** *672 S La Brea Ave, Los Angeles (90036). Phone 323/934-2110; fax 323/934-2010. www.lunapark.com.* This northern California transplant has become a hip oasis for the terminally trendy, an urbane dining outpost for those who are sophisticated and young at heart. The intimate bar is always abuzz with locals swilling the finest mojitos in town. Scarlet walls and funky chandeliers envelope the dim dining room, where diners nosh on eclectic fare like silky goat cheese fondue

with green apples. Channel your inner child for the do-it-yourself s'mores dessert. American menu. Lunch, dinner, brunch. Closed holidays. Bar. Casual attire. **$$**

★ **MEXICO CITY.** *2121 Hillhurst Ave, Los Angeles (90027). Phone 323/661-7227.* This ultra-hip Mexican restaurant is where the local club kids and young professionals go to slug margaritas and dine on eclectic fare before painting the town red. The large, diner-like room is festive with lots of folk art tchotchkes and always bustling, especially on the weekends. The food is more Tex-Mex than the real deal: green corn tamales are sweet and savory, the queso fundido rich and salty, and the shrimp on tomatillo sauce appropriately fiery. Mexican menu. Lunch, dinner. Children's menu. Casual attire. **$$**

★ ★ **MORI SUSHI.** *11500 W Pico Blvd, Los Angeles (90064). Phone 310/479-3939.* There's no sign to mark this superlative sushi bar, just a drawing of a fish above the diminutive spot. The interior is classic minimalism, with hanging paper lanterns, soft lighting, and lots of glossy blond wood. Inventive sushi appetizers like spicy tuna tacos are served on one-of-a-kind ceramicware, hand-painted by the master chef. Try the meltingly fresh sashimi or put yourself in the kitchens hands and order the omakase tasting menu. This is the spot where local chefs get their sushi fix, so you know it's something special. Japanese menu. Lunch, dinner. Closed holidays. Casual attire. **$$**

★ ★ **NICK & STEF'S.** *330 S Hope St, Los Angeles (90071). Phone 213/680-0330; fax 213/680-0052. www.patinagroup.com.* This dramatic room boasts a circular bar, a lively dining patio, sleek candlelit seating, and a glassed-in cooler used for aging massive hunks of red meat. The carnivore's menu works in dozens—choose from a dozen appetizers (classics like oysters), steaks (porterhouse is the house specialty), vegetables, and starches (mashed potatoes whipped into silk). Businessmen in nifty suits, dolled-up theatergoers, and large parties celebrating birthdays make this a glamorous and festive spot to dine in style. Steak menu. Lunch, dinner. Bar. Children's menu. Casual attire. Reservations recommended. Valet parking. Outdoor seating. **$$$**

★ **THE ORIGINAL PANTRY.** *877 S Figueroa St, Los Angeles (90017). Phone 213/972-9279; fax 213/972-0187.* Not much has changed at this historic corner diner since it opened dozens of years ago—and it hasn't closed its doors since. There isn't even a key anymore for this 24/7 joint, which boasts that it is never, ever without a customer. Rickety tables, harsh lighting, and greasy food don't detract from the charm of this placewhere else does a steak dinner run you less than $15? American menu. Breakfast, lunch, dinner, brunch. Casual attire. No credit cards accepted. **$**

★ ★ ★ ★ **ORTOLAN** *8338 W 3rd St, Los Angeles (90012). Phone 323/653-3300; fax 323/653-3327. www. ortolanrestaurnt.com.* Ortolan may be named after a small songbird, but have no fear; you certainly won't be eating like one at this Southern California French sensation. French chef Christophe Eme, formerly of L'Orangerie, has ventured out on his own with Ortolan and created an exquisite menu of hearty haute cuisine that blends classic French style with contemporary elements. Signature dishes include crispy langoustines with basil, chickpeas, and minestrone; and roasted squab breast and leg with a gratin of macaroni and tapenade salad. A modernized provincial restaurant with cream-colored booth and banquettes, floor-to-ceiling velvet drapes, crystal chandeliers, and antique mirrors, Ortolan dazzles the eye as well as the palate. Glamorous yet contemporary and casual, Ortolan has become the place for French dining in Los Angeles. With its relaxing ambience, visually stunning room, and artfully presented plates, it's sheer perfection. French menu. Dnner. Closed Sun. Bar. Business casual attire. Reservations recommended. Valet parking. **$$$**

★ ★ **PACIFIC DINING CAR.** *1310 W 6th St, Los Angeles (90017). Phone 213/483-6000. www.pacificdiningcar.com.* This downtown landmark is straight out of *LA Confidential* a swanky, shadowy kind of place where deals go down. Its sister restaurant in Santa Monica (2700 Wilshire Blvd, phone 310/453-4000) is more modern and massive, but the classic menu is the same. Think meat. The cowboy steak is a massive charred rib steak, while the baseball steak is a cut of filet that's as tall as it is wide. This is an ever-popular spot for politicians and captains of industry who hunger 'til all hours: the Santa Monica location serves customers until 2 am, and the downtown restaurant is open 24 hours. Steak menu. Breakfast, lunch, dinner, late-night. Bar. Children's menu. Casual attire. Reservations recommended. Valet parking. **$$$**

★ ★ ★ ★ **PATINA.** *141 S Grand Ave, Los Angeles (90012). Phone 323/972-3331; fax 323/972-3531. www. patinagroup.com.* LA celebrity chef Joachim Splichal moved his celebrated Patina restaurant into the new Walt Disney Concert Hall downtown, making the Frank Gehry-designed landmark, home to the Los Angeles Philharmonic, a culinary—as well as a design—destination. Splichal's signature French-by-way-of-California cooking, interpreted here by executive chef Theo Schoenegger, celebrates local and regionally sourced foodstuffs in dishes such as foie gras with Ranier cherry jam, Wild River salmon with heirloom tomatoes, and olive-oil poached squab with truffles from Umbria. The polished dining room, with walnut wood-paneled walls and curvy ceilings, echoes the hall itself, prepping concertgoers for events ahead. To make a night of it at the restaurant solely, gather the gang and reserve the kitchen table to indulge in a six-course market-tasting menu while spying behind the scenes. The bar serves nibbles and drinks after the show, and a lunch menu caters to tourists visiting the Hall as well as downtown business folk. California menu. Lunch, dinner. Closed holidays. Bar. Business casual attire. Reservations recommended. Valet parking. Outdoor seating. **$$$**

★ ★ **PECORINO.** *11604 San Vicente Blvd, Los Angeles (90049). Phone 310/571-3800. www.pecorinorestaurant.com.* Italian menu. Lunch, dinner. Closed holidays. Bar. Casual attire. Reservations recommended. Valet parking. **$$**
🄳

★ **PHILIPPE THE ORIGINAL.** *1001 N Alameda St, Los Angeles (90012). Phone 213/628-3781; fax 213/628-1812. www.philippes.com.* Since 1908, this counter-service sandwich shop has had sawdust on the floors, communal tables, throngs of customers, and the bragging rights of having invented the French dip sandwich. Choose beef, lamb, turkey, or ham on a French roll dipped in pan juices, served with fiery hot mustard, tart macaroni salad, and scalding mugs of coffee (which cost only a dime). Angelenos from all walks of life dine here—and there is camaraderie among the Dodger fans, Union Station workers, Chinatown shoppers, and yuppies on jury duty. American menu. Breakfast, lunch, dinner. Closed Thanksgiving, Dec 25. Casual attire. No credit cards accepted. **$**

★ ★ **PRADO.** *244 N Larchmont Blvd, Los Angeles (90004). Phone 323/467-3871; fax 323/467-2119.* This charming eatery in Larchmont Village serves up zesty Caribbean and Latin American fare in a graceful and feminine setting. Kitschy sparkling chandeliers hang from the faux-frescoed ceiling, where painted cherubs peer down from the clouds, creating a whimsical and romantic atmosphere. The lighthearted baroque style is offset by the bold flavors of specialties like grilled shrimp in black pepper sauce, corn tamales with caviar, and steak with melted tomatoes and onions. This neighborhood gem is coveted by locals, who flock to this hidden spot for sultry dinner dates. Caribbean menu. Lunch, dinner. Casual attire. Outdoor seating. **$$**

★ ★ **R-23.** *923 E 2nd St, Los Angeles (90012). Phone 213/687-7178. www.r23.com.* This hidden gem is difficult to find, but it's worth the adventure. This SoHo-like loft has exposed-brick walls, minimalist art, and a giant sushi bar along the back wall. Have a seat in a Frank Gehry-designed cardboard chair (surprisingly comfortable) and prepare to be dazzled by exotic raw specialties. The ever-changing menu offers some of the freshest fish in town, prepared with impeccable precision. Foodies make frequent pilgrimages to this white-hot spot, so reservations are essential. Japanese, sushi menu. Lunch, dinner. Closed Sun. Casual attire. Reservations recommended. **$$$**

★ ★ **THE RESTAURANT GETTY CENTER.**
1200 Getty Center Dr, Los Angeles (90049). Phone 310/440-6810. www.getty.edu. This architectural masterpiece is a marriage of the Getty family's wealth and passion for culture and Richard Meir's stunning design talent. Towering over Los Angeles, offering unparalleled panoramic views, and housing a fortune of fine art—why not dine here? Amid the marble and limestone courtyards, the sleek and modern dining room is a swell setting to enjoy creamy lobster risotto or Muscovy duck after viewing the collections. Make reservations for parking and meals. California menu. Lunch. Closed Mon. Reservations recommended. **$$$**

★ **SEOUL GARDEN.** *1833 W Olympic Blvd, Los Angeles (90006). Phone 213/386-8477.* Shabu-shabu is the irresistible draw of this busy K-town barbecue—so much so that its hungry customer base, which is about 90 percent Korean, is willing to forgive a décor that's a tad shabby. Whether you go for the main-attraction entrée (wonderfully thin-sliced beef tossed into boiling broth with tofu, mushrooms and watercress), grilled eel, or raw crab marinated in chili paste, the efficient, cook-it-yourself burners installed at the granite tables can make this a gratifying gustatory adventure. Korean menu. Lunch, dinner. Bar. Casual attire. **$**
Ⓓ

★ ★ **SEOUL JUNG.** *930 Wilshire Blvd, Los Angeles (90017). Phone 213/688-7880; fax 213/612-3976.* Its executive chef may be Austrian, but Seoul Jung is virtually unmatched in Los Angeles for authentic gourmet Korean food. The culinary "Seoul" of the elegant Wilshire Grand Hotel, situated on the lower lobby level, it offers sumptuous fare and a contemporary, granite-and-marble décor highlighted by floral settings, striking tapestries, and genuine Korean furnishings. Business-attired professionals and elegantly dressed gourmands tend to dominate the dining

room, indulging in aromatic dishes like dea ju gui (spicy lean pork capped with shredded beef, scallions, vermicelli noodles, and gi-dan) or cooking their own delicacies on smokeless tabletop barbecues. On purely olfactory terms, breathing here almost beats eating here. Korean menu. Lunch, dinner. Bar. Casual attire. Reservations recommended. Valet parking. **$$**

★ ★ **SONORA CAFE.** *180 S La Brea Ave, Los Angeles (90063). Phone 323/857-1800; fax 323/857-1601. www.sonoracafe.com.* This upscale Southwestern eatery's décor is a wild intersection of old-world luxury and modern, resortlike breeziness. Imposing iron chandeliers dangle from the towering wood-beam ceiling, thatched and linen-draped tables are plenty roomy, and the service is fittingly attentive. Luxurious takes on south-of-the-border fare, like the jalapeo-cilantro smoked salmon and the barbecued pork chop, are decadent meals. A hip bar area is a popular spot for tequila fanatics, who sip rare shots at tables with sail-like umbrellas straight out of a *Mad Max* flick. Southwestern menu. Lunch, dinner. Closed holidays. Bar. Casual attire. Reservations recommended. Valet parking. **$$**

★ ★ ★ **TANINO RISTORANTE BAR.**
1043 Westwood Blvd, Los Angeles (90024). Phone 310/208-0444; fax 310/208-2344. www.tanino.com. Tanino stands out as a classy Italian option in the trendy Westwood area. Operated by chef and Sicilian native Tanino Drago, the handsome restaurant occupies historic digs with frescoed ceilings, wall murals, and artisan plaster treatments that recall the great palaces of Italy. Among the pasta and second-plates are bold and creative dishes such as risotto with sea urchins and red peppers, pumpkin and sage lasagna, and pheasant with prosciutto and fontina. Italian menu. Lunch, dinner. Closed Jan 1, Easter, Dec 25. Bar. Casual attire. Outdoor seating. **$$**

★ ★ **TANTRA.** *3705 W Sunset Blvd, Los Angeles (90026). Phone 323/663-9090; fax 323/666-5522. www.tantrasunset.com.* This wild and wondrous dining room is draped in orange and magenta tones, dripping in glowing lanterns, and full of sexy surprises, like a small pond with floating candles. The dreamy atmosphere lends itself well to the excellent Indian fare, which is creatively executed, delicately spiced, and perfect for sharing. Try the spinach samosas and the coconut shrimp curry. DJs spin in the adjacent cocktail lounge, where hipsters mingle and sip the signature drink, the Tantrini. Indian menu. Dinner. Closed Mon. Bar. Casual attire. Reservations recommended (six or more people). Valet parking. **$$**

★ ★ **TENGU.** *10853 Lindbrook Dr, Los Angeles (90024). Phone 310/209-0071. www.tengu.com.* This spacious sushi den caters to the next generation—with dark stone walls, colorful cocktails, and a DJ spinning soft trance music next to the master chefs who carve up fresh fish. Although the toro and yellowtail sashimi are sublime, composed dishes like the fire garlic sprouts with shrimp will satisfy non-raw fans. Don't forget to pair your spicy tuna hand roll with a sake tasting flight—an intoxicating way to sample exotic rice wines. This is a sexy spot for a date, yet it's upbeat enough to make it a party destination with your pals. Asian menu. Lunch, dinner. Bar. Casual attire. Reservations recommended. Valet parking. Outdoor seating. **$$$** 🄳

★ ★ **TRAXX.** *800 N Alameda, Los Angeles (90012). Phone 213/625-1999; fax 213/625-2999. www.traxxrestaurant.com.* Beautifully restored to its Art Deco grandeur, Union Station is home to the small and elegant Traxx restaurant and bar. This polished wooden jewel box of a dining room has white linen tablecloths, dramatic lighting, and a view of the throngs of train travelers swishing by. Contemporary American fare is the norm, such as a killer steak sandwich and some of the best crab cakes in the city. Downtown shoppers and traveling executives dine here and harken back to a time when train travel was glitzy. American menu. Lunch, dinner. Closed Sun; holidays. Bar. Casual attire. Reservations recommended. Outdoor seating. **$$$**

★ ★ **VERMONT.** *1714 N Vermont Ave, Los Angeles (90027). Phone 323/661-6163; fax 323/661-6206. www.vermontrestaurantonline.com.* This stylish restaurant is vast, but the pleasing maze of interconnected small rooms keeps it intimate, each space retaining its own cool character. Post-grunge hipsters nosh on upscale American comfort food, like roasted free-range chicken and poached salmon. Couples can enjoy a romantic dinner by candlelight, while large groups party in the front cocktail lounge, where a DJ spins. A tangle of sleek patios out back can be packed with revelers and hosts elite private parties. American menu. Lunch, dinner. Bar. Casual attire. Reservations recommended. Valet parking. Outdoor seating. **$$$**

★ **VERSAILLES.** *1415 S La Cienega Blvd, Los Angeles (90035). Phone 310/289-0392; fax 310/289-8408.* This casual Cuban café never seems to slow down; there's always a line of hungry families, young couples, and party-bound college kids waiting for a seat. Although the menu is vast, 99 percent of the clientele is here for one thing: the legendary garlic-roasted chicken. Half a bird comes lacquered in a citrusy garlic sauce that oozes onto the pile of rice and fried plantains below. Wash it down with a beer or a Cuban pineapple soda, and you've got a feast for around $10. Seafood menu. Lunch, dinner. Casual attire. **$$**

★ ★ ★ **WATER GRILL.** *544 S Grand Ave, Los Angeles (90071). Phone 213/891-0900; fax 213/629-1891. www.watergrill.com.* Often considered one of LA's best restaurants, long-standing favorite Water Grill serves flawlessly prepared seafood. Options include prix fixe, à la carte, and raw bar samplings. The Art Deco setting models a luxury liner that transmits a just-right tone given the pricey seafood and fine wine list. Consequently, Water Grill is the place to take a business colleague or romantic partner you aim to impress with your refinement. Its downtown location makes it a good pre-theater option. Seafood menu. Lunch, dinner. Closed Memorial Day. Bar. Business casual attire. Reservations recommended. Valet parking. **$$$**

★ **YANG CHOW.** *819 N Broadway, Los Angeles (90012). Phone 213/625-0811; fax 213/625-7901. www.yangchow.com.* There's always a line snaking out the door of this happening spot, which is packed with Angelenos of every culture. Blame it on the slippery shrimp, the house specialty of deep-fried prawns in a sweet and spicy sauce that packs a ton of flavor. Excellent classics like won'ton soup, cold sesame noodles, and green beans with ground chicken distract from the dull and dated décor. Chinese menu. Lunch, dinner. Casual attire. Valet parking. **$**

★ ★ **YONGSUSAN.** *950 S Vermont Ave, Los Angeles (90006). Phone 213/388-3042.* The initial impression of YongSuSans layout and color scheme is that of a funhouse maze—the pleasant surprise is that cozily appointed private dining room lie around every corner. Ideal for family gatherings or romantic outings, these intimate spaces foster personalized service that's rare in Koreatown. Prix fixe meals—including the barbecued meat mainstay, galbee—are served fully prepared in courses, and they are distinguished by their milder, more delicate North Korean flair. Beef-stuffed vegetables and mini hand-rolled crepes are scrumptious specialties. Korean menu. Lunch, dinner. Bar. Casual attire. **$$** 🄳

★ ★ **ZUCCA.** *801 S Figueroa St, Los Angeles (90017). Phone 213/614-7800; fax 213/614-7887. www.patinagroup.com.* One of the finest establishments for top-notch Italian fare is merely a stone's throw from the Staples Center. This lovely dining room has a barrel-vaulted ceiling, dramatic chandeliers, a massive mirrored bar, and large, comfy booths done in warm orangey tones. The menu includes house-made pastas, fresh seafood, and imported delicacies. This stunning experience is superb for business diners and romantic evenings or to glam up an evening at a Lakers game. Italian menu. Lunch, dinner. Closed holidays. Bar. Casual attire. Reservations recommended. **$$$**

Los Angeles International Airport Area (J-4)

See also Los Angeles, Manhattan Beach

Web Site www.lawa.org

Information Phone 310/646-5252

Lost and Found Phone 310/417-0440

Airlines Aer Lingus, Aero California, Aeroflot, Aerolitoral, Air Canada, Air China, Air France, Air Jamaica, Air New Zealand, Air Pacific, Air Tahiti Nui, Alaska Airlines, American Airlines, American Eagle, America West, ANA (All Nippon Airways), Asiana Airlines, ATA, Aviacsa Airline, Avianca, British Airways, Cathay Pacific Airways, Champion Air, China Airlines, China Eastern, China Southern, Copa Airlines, CORSAIR International, Delta Air Lines, EL AL, EVA Air, Frontier Airlines, Hawaiian Airlines, HMY Airlines, Horizon Air, Japan Airlines, KLM Royal Dutch, Korean Air, LACSA Airlines, Lan Chile, LTU International Airways, Lufthansa, Malaysia Airline, Mexicana Airlines, Midwest Express Airlines, Northwest Airlines, Omni Air International, Philippine Airlines, Quantas, Singapore Airlines, Song Airlines, Sun Country, TACA International, Thai Airways, Varig Brazillian Airlines, VG Airlines, Virgin Atlantic Airlines

Limited-Service Hotels

★ ★ **COURTYARD BY MARRIOTT.** *6161 W Century Blvd, Los Angeles (90045). Phone 310/649-1400; toll-free 800/321-2211; fax 310/649-0965. www. courtyard.com.* 178 rooms, 7 story. Check-in 4 pm, check-out noon. High-speed Internet access. Restaurant, bar. Fitness room. Whirlpool. Airport transportation available. Business center. **$$**

★ ★ ★ **EMBASSY SUITES.** *1440 E Imperial Ave, El Segundo (90245). Phone 310/640-3600; toll-free 800/362-2779; fax 310/322-0954. www.embassysuites. com.* 349 rooms, 5 story, all suites. Pets accepted, some restrictions; fee. Complimentary full breakfast. Check-in 3 pm, check-out noon. High-speed Internet access. Restaurant, bar. Fitness room. Indoor pool, whirlpool. Airport transportation available. **$$**

★ **SUMMERFIELD SUITES.** *810 S Douglas Ave, El Segundo (90245). Phone 310/725-0100; fax 310/725-0900. www.wyndham.com.* 122 rooms, 3 story, all suites. Pets accepted, some restrictions; fee. Complimentary continental breakfast. Check-in 4 pm, check-out noon. High-speed Internet access. Fitness room. Outdoor pool, whirlpool. **$**

Full-Service Hotels

★ ★ ★ **RENAISSANCE MONTURA HOTEL.** *9620 Airport Blvd, Los Angeles (90045). Phone 310/337-2800; toll-free 800/468-3571; fax 310/216-6681. www. renaissancelosangeles.com.* This 499-room lodge—a modernist-meets-French Manor landmark—is half a mile from Los Angeles International Airport and convenient to freeways, the West Side, and Santa Monica Bay's beach cities. Room and suite décor is tastefully ultra-contemporary, with amenities including work desks, refrigerators, and complimentary weekday newspapers. The Conservatory, with a continental menu, serves breakfast, lunch, and dinner, while the Library Steakhouse offers dinner only. The hotel is soundproofed, and wireless high-speed Internet is accessible in all rooms and public areas. Concierge, secretarial, and childcare services are available. There's also a free shuttle to and from LAX. 499 rooms, 11 story. Pets accepted. Check-in 4 pm, check-out noon. High-speed Internet access. Two restaurants, bar. Fitness room. Outdoor pool. Airport transportation available. Business center. **$$**

★ ★ ★ **SHERATON GATEWAY HOTEL LOS ANGELES AIRPORT.** *6101 W Century Blvd, Los Angeles (90045). Phone 310/642-1111; toll-free 800/325-3535; fax 310/645-1414. www.sheratonlosangeles.com.* This sleek, welcoming hotel is for business travelers and vacationers seeking a convenient, centrally-located refuge from the airport and its bustling environs. The rooms—spacious and contemporary—are outfitted with custom plush-top mattresses, fleece blankets, extra-fluffy pillows, and large desks, along with practical features like safes, irons, and two-line phones. The seaside pleasures of Marina del Rey and Venice Beach are within a few miles. 802 rooms, 15 story. Pets accepted, some restrictions. Check-in 3 pm, check-out noon. High-speed Internet access. Two restaurants, bar. Fitness room. Outdoor pool, whirlpool. Airport transportation available. Business center. **$$**

★ ★ ★ WESTIN LOS ANGELES AIRPORT.

5400 W Century Blvd, Los Angeles (90045). Phone 310/216-5858; toll-free 800/937-8461; fax 310/417-4545. www.westin.com/losangelesairport. Charming ambience, state-of-art technology, and trademark Westin efficiency draw business travelers, conventioneers, and families to this distinctive hotel, just four blocks from Los Angeles International Airport. All guest rooms feature signature Heavenly Beds with pillow-top mattresses and down blankets, and many include fax machines, printers, and high-speed Internet access. Close to the freeway and within an easy drive of Santa Monica, Venice Beach, Manhattan Beach, and the entire West Side, the hotel also offers a heated outdoor pool, a well-equipped weight room, and concierge service for on-site convenience. A kids' club provides coloring books, bath toys, and a phone line dedicated to bedtime stories. 740 rooms, 12 story. Pets accepted, some restrictions. Check-in 3 pm, check-out noon. Wireless Internet access. Restaurant, bar. Fitness room. Outdoor pool, whirlpool. Airport transportation available. Business center. **$$**

Restaurant

★ ★ CHARISMA CAFE. *5400 W Century Blvd, Los Angeles (90045). Phone 310/216-5858; fax 310/417-4569. www.westin.com.* International menu. Breakfast, lunch, dinner. Bar. Children's menu. Casual attire. Valet parking. **$$**

Malibu (J-3)

See also Santa Monica

Population 12,575
Elevation 25 ft
Area Code 310
Zip 90265
Web Site www.ci.malibu.ca.us

This coastal community stretches along Pacific Coast Highway, a picturesque stretch of road that skirts along the water's edge, along the base of steep hills. Most of Malibu is located right on this highway, in houses that dangle off the cliffs or hover on the hillsides above. The sweeping vistas provide many camera-worthy views, and it comes as no surprise that this is where many movie stars have chosen this spot to call home.

Several small shopping centers are found along the highway, mostly catering to locals for the bare necessities, however there are a few choice destinations for visitors. Fresh seafood can be enjoyed seaside, from the funky fish shack, The Reel Inn, to the classy Chart House. Naturally, beaches are a major destination, and every local seems to have his or her own secret spot, but Zuma and Will Rogers are always popular.

What to See and Do

Beach areas. *Phone 310/457-9891.* Surfrider, Malibu Lagoon, Topanga Canyon, and Zuma beaches offer surfing and swimming.

Pepperdine University. *24255 Pacific Coast Hwy, Malibu (90263). Phone 310/506-4000. www.pepperdine.edu/arts/museum.* (1937) (2,300 students) On 830 acres, campus includes School of Law as well as college of arts, sciences, and letters; cultural arts center and Weisman Museum of Art (Tues-Sun).

Santa Monica Mountains National Recreation Area. *401 W Hillcrest Dr, Thousand Oaks (91360). Phone 805/370-2301.* (See SANTA MONICA)

Full-Service Inns

★ MALIBU BEACH INN. *22878 Pacific Coast Hwy, Malibu (90265). Phone 310/456-6444; toll-free 800/462-5428; fax 310/456-1499. www.malibubeachinn.com.* A Mission-style retreat tucked within the moneyed bluffs of Hollywood's exclusive seaside

colony, this tile-roofed lodge offers privacy and luxury to match its awesome ocean views. Large, individually appointed rooms and suites feature private balconies along with Jacuzzis, fireplaces, private bars, beamed ceilings, VCRs, and hair dryers—plus warm details like theme names (e.g., Beachcomber, Surfrider) and hand-painted bathroom tile. Guests can enjoy a stroll on the nearby Malibu Pier or engage in activities ranging from kayaking and surfing to dolphin-watching. 47 rooms, 3 story. Complimentary continental breakfast. Check-in 3 pm, check-out noon. **$$$**

★ ★ ★ **MALIBU COUNTRY INN.** *6506 Westward Beach Rd, Malibu (90265). Phone 310/457-9622; toll-free 800/386-6787; fax 310/457-1349. www.malibu-countryinn.com.* This cozy, romantic Cape Cod-style inn, built in 1943, is set on three well-tended acres atop a bluff above spectacular Zuma Beach. The uniquely decorated guest rooms have private patios overlooking magnificent gardens; several have ocean views and Jacuzzis. Most accommodations feature fireplaces, refrigerators, and coffee makers. Fine local dining is in abundance, and the many retail, restaurant, and entertainment options of Santa Monica are within a short drive. 16 rooms, 1 story. Complimentary continental breakfast. Check-in 3 pm, check-out noon. Restaurant, bar. Outdoor pool. **$$**

Restaurants

★ ★ **ALLEGRIA.** *22821 Pacific Coast Hwy, Malibu (90265). Phone 310/456-3132; fax 310/456-0492. www.allegriamalibu.com.* Tucked away on the side of Pacific Coast Highway, this Italian spot is a destination for Malibu's social set and courting couples. Paneled windows frame the Pacific, bougainvillea drapes the outdoor patio, and hammered copper lamps cast a sexy glow over it all. Salads and appetizers, like the superlative eggplant Parmesan, are large enough to share. Gourmet pizzas dressed with fine cheeses and specialty meats are the standouts on the menu, a perfect pairing with a bottle of Chianti and a coastline view. Italian menu. Lunch, dinner. Bar. Casual attire. Reservations recommended. Valet parking. **$$$**

★ ★ **GEOFFREY'S.** *27400 Pacific Coast Hwy, Malibu (90265). Phone 310/457-1519; fax 310/457-7885. www.geoffreysmalibu.com.* Perched on the high cliffs above the Malibu coastline, this sprawling patio dining destination has been the sight of many movie scenes, marriage proposals, and special celebrations. With 180-degree coastline views, sounds of crash-

ing waves and bubbling waterfalls, and a backdrop of wildflowers, it's no wonder local celebrities frequently choose to dine here. The cuisine matches the luxe Southern California environs, with lobster in puff pastry, ahi with wasabi, and gourmet brunch offerings. Make reservations and bring a coat to combat chilly ocean breezes. California menu. Lunch, dinner. Bar. Casual attire. Reservations recommended. Valet parking. Outdoor seating. **$$$**

★ ★ **MOONSHADOWS.** *20356 W Pacific Coast Hwy, Malibu (90265). Phone 310/456-3010; fax 310/456-7718. www.moonshadowsmalibu.com.* This oceanfront dining destination practically pours off the side of a cliff into the crashing Pacific Ocean below. During the day, umbrellaed patio seats offer unparalled views of coastline. Dinnertime is all about romance in the shadowy dining room with paneled windows and shell-shaped lanterns that casts a sexy glow on the crowd. California cuisine gets an Asian twist here—and naturally seafood is featured. Ahi tuna tartare and shrimp cocktail are classic starters, and regulars swear by the pineapple chocolate upside-down cake for dinner. American menu. Lunch, dinner. Bar. Casual attire. Valet parking. Outdoor seating. **$$$**

★ ★ ★ **NOBU.** *3835 Cross Creek Rd, Malibu (90265). Phone 310/317-9140; fax 310/317-9136.* Enjoy the picturesque drive up the coast to this smaller outpost of the big-time Nobu. Its plain wooden interior may not look spectacular, but its minimalist style serves not to overshadow the superior sushi and the namesake Chilean-Japanese dishes that made an empire. Nobu takes the concept of freshness seriously—some of the seafood arrives live. Foodies, celebrities, and high society fill the room to nosh on sushi, sashimi, or the omakase tasting menu, the ultimate indulgence for gourmands. Japanese, sushi menu. Dinner. Closed Jan 1, Thanksgiving, Dec 25. Reservations recommended. **$$$$**

★ **REEL INN.** *18661 Pacific Coast Hwy, Malibu (90265). Phone 310/456-8221; fax 310/456-3568.* The scenic drive up the coast alone is worth the trip to this funky little beach shack with communal outdoor picnic tables, a view of the Pacific, and a soundtrack of the crashing surf, although the 3rd Street outpost in Santa Monica offers the same daily fresh fish specials. Choose from mountains of just-pulled-from-the-water seafood, pick a preparation, and sip pitchers of beer with other sandy beachcombers indulging in shrimp tacos and sunbeams. Seafood menu. Lunch, dinner. Children's menu. Casual attire. Outdoor seating. **$$**

Manhattan Beach (J-4)

See also Los Angeles International Airport

Web Site www.ci.manhattan-beach.ca.us

This once-quiet residential beach enclave has become a vibrant neighborhood that is constantly buzzing with new construction, and an influx of increasingly wealthy inhabitants. The rolling hills mere blocks from the beach are graced with quaint homes and mini-mansions of such luminaries as Tiger Woods.

The mellow beach atmosphere is still prevalent—it is not unusual to spot groups of surfers walking down the street, or sandy families shopping in the local markets. The main zone of activity is Manhattan Beach Boulevard and the Pier, which is crammed with trendy nightclubs, surf shops, and restaurants from sushi bars to Mexican dives. Along the strand, in-line skaters, beach volleyball players, bikers, and dog lovers make for an active pickup scene.

Limited-Service Hotel

★ **SPRINGHILL SUITES LOS ANGELES LAX/ MANHATTAN BEACH.** *14620 Aviation Blvd, Manhattan Beach (90250). Phone 310/727-9595; toll-free 800/228-9290; fax 310/727-0896. www.springhill-suites.com.* 164 rooms, 6 story. Complimentary continental breakfast. Check-in 3 pm, check-out noon. High-speed Internet access. Fitness room. Outdoor pool, whirlpool. Business center. **$**

Full-Service Hotel

★ ★ ★ **MANHATTAN BEACH MARRIOTT.** *1400 Parkview Ave, Manhattan Beach (90266). Phone 310/546-7511; toll-free 800/228-9290; fax 310/939-1486. www.marriott.com.* Located 3 miles from Los Angeles International Airport, 26-acre property is self-contained for the business traveler, yet also offers vacationers a South Bay resort location close to Manhattan Beach's warm sands and eclectic eateries. Deluxe rooms and suites come equipped with coffee makers, hair dryers, and Web TV. 385 rooms, 7 story. Check-in 4 pm, check-out noon. High-speed Internet access. Restaurant, bar. Fitness room. Outdoor pool, whirlpool. Golf, 9 holes. Business center. **$$**

Restaurants

★ **BACK HOME IN LAHAINA.** *916 N Sepulveda Blvd, Manhattan Beach (90266). Phone 310/374-0111. www.backhomeinlahaina.com.* Hawaiian menu. Breakfast, lunch, dinner. Bar. Children's menu. Casual attire. **$**

★ ★ ★ **MANGIAMO.** *128 Manhattan Beach Blvd, Manhattan Beach (90266). Phone 310/318-3434. www.mangiamorestaurant.com.* This quiet, romantic restaurant is just steps from the Pier 9 beach. For even more atmosphere, try to snag a table in the intimate wine cellar, or sit up front to catch a view of the sun setting over the Pacific. The northern Italian menu features many seafood selections, as well as dishes like osso buco and three-mushroom farfalle. Italian menu. Dinner. Bar. Business casual attire. Reservations recommended. **$$$**

★ ★ **REED'S RESTAURANT.** *2640 N Sepulveda Blvd, Manhattan Beach (90266). Phone 310/546-3299; fax 310/546-1869.* This quaint, charming South Bay restaurant defies its storefront location. A good-sized wine list accompanies the California-French menu, which features entrées like scallops with curry sauce and duck with raspberry sauce. A piano player sets a romantic mood on weekend evenings, and attentive service ensures that diners feel adequately pampered. California, French menu. Lunch, dinner. Casual attire. Reservations recommended. Outdoor seating. **$$**

★ **UNCLE BILL'S PANCAKE HOUSE.** *1305 Highland Ave, Manhattan Beach (90266). Phone 310/545-5177; fax 310/545-7278.* Converted 1908 house. American menu. Breakfast, lunch. Children's menu. Casual attire. Outdoor seating. **$**

Marina del Rey (J-3)

See also Los Angeles, Santa Monica

Population 8,176
Elevation 10 ft
Area Code 310
Zip 90292
Information Marina del Rey Convention & Visitors Bureau, 4701 Admiralty Way, phone 310/305-9545
Web Site www.visitthemarina.com

With its name, could this community next to Venice be anything but boat oriented? The 5,300-slip facility attracts many boating and sport fishing enthusiasts. Sail and power boat rentals, ocean cruises, and fishing

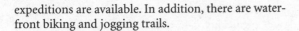

expeditions are available. In addition, there are waterfront biking and jogging trails.

What to See and Do

Fisherman's Village. *13755 Fiji Way, Marina del Rey (90292). Phone 310/823-5411. www.visitthemarina. com.* Modeled after a turn-of-the-century New England fishing town and located on the main channel of the largest man-made small craft harbor in the country, this area and its well-known lighthouse have appeared in many television and movie productions. Cobblestone walks complement the nautical atmosphere and provide a panoramic view of the marina; boat rentals, fishing charters, harbor cruises; shops, boutiques, and restaurants. Entertainment throughout the year (weather permitting), including free jazz concerts (Sat-Sun). (Daily)

Limited-Service Hotel

★ **BEST WESTERN JAMAICA BAY INN.**
4175 Admiralty Way, Marina Del Rey (90292). Phone 310/823-5333; toll-free 888/823-5333; fax 310/823-1325. www.bestwestern.com. 42 rooms. Check-in 3 pm, check-out noon. Bar. Beach. Outdoor pool, whirlpool. Business center. **$**

Full-Service Hotels

★ ★ **COURTYARD BY MARRIOTT.** *13480 Maxella Ave, Marina del Ray (90292). Phone 310/822-8555; toll-free 800/321-2211; fax 310/823-2996. www.marriott. com/laxcm.* 276 rooms, 5 story. Check-in 3 pm, check-out noon. High-speed Internet access. Restaurant, bar. Fitness room. Outdoor pool, whirlpool. **$**

★ ★ ★ **MARINA DEL REY MARRIOTT.** *4100 Admiralty Way, Marina del Rey (90292). Phone 310/301-3000; toll-free 800/228-9290; fax 310/448-4870. www.marriott.com/laxmb.* Notable for its scenic location between the popular Los Angeles shore districts of Marina del Rey and Venice Beach, as well as for its convenience to Los Angeles International Airport, this newly renovated hotel is a favorite of business travelers and conventioneers who enjoy playing outdoors between meetings. Jogging, biking, swimming, and all manner of water-related activities are available across the street at the world's largest man-made harbor. A variety of shops and fine restaurants are within walking distance. 370 rooms, 10 story.

Check-in 3 pm, check-out noon. High-speed Internet access. Restaurant, bar. Fitness room. Outdoor pool, whirlpool. Business center. **$$**

★ ★ ★ **THE RITZ-CARLTON, MARINA DEL REY.** *4375 Admiralty Way, Marina del Rey (90292). Phone 310/823-1700; toll-free 800/241-3333; fax 310/823-2403. www.ritzcarlton.com.* Moments from central Los Angeles, The Ritz-Carlton, Marina del Rey, introduces guests to a different side of this West Coast capital. Situated on 5 acres on the world's largest man-made marina, this hotel is a waterside resort within a city. An instant calm washes over visitors who daydream while watching yachts bob on gentle waves. Joggers rejoice in the hotels location along the 21-mile coastal Promenade, running from Malibu to Manhattan Beach. The guest rooms are gracefully appointed, with picture-perfect views of the marina adding to the soothing ambience. Sprinkled with art and antiques, the accommodations are refreshingly elegant. A heated outdoor pool is only steps from the ocean, and seasonal dining service is available at the poolside grill, Wave. Capturing the sophistication of nautical design with light woods and white walls, Jer-ne takes diners on a satisfying culinary journey. 304 rooms, 12 story. Pets accepted; restrictions, fee. Check-in 3 pm, check-out noon. High-speed Internet access. Two restaurants, two bars. Fitness room. Outdoor pool, whirlpool. Tennis. Business center. **$$$**

Specialty Lodging

INN AT PLAYA DEL REY. *435 Culver Blvd, Playa Del Rey (90293). Phone 310/574-1920; fax 310/574-9920. www.innatplayadelrey.com.* Described as an oasis in Los Angeles, this inn is close to the beach and overlooks the main channel of Marina del Rey and the Ballona Wetlands bird sanctuary. 25 rooms, 4 story. Complimentary full breakfast. Check-in 3 pm. Check-out noon. **$$**

Restaurant

★ ★ **BALLONA FISH MARKET.** *13455 Maxella Ave, Marina del Rey (90292). Phone 310/822-8979; fax 310/823-7832. www.ballonamdr.com.* You wouldn't expect to find a funky independent fish house anchored in the bottom level of a mall, yet that's exactly where you will find picket fence-lined Ballona. The décor meshes the hipness of Venice with the charm of New

England, with red overhead lanterns, seashell-strewn tables, and royal blue awnings. The kitchen veers from the traditional seafood preparations in favor of fusion dishes like salmon spring rolls and scallop pot pie. This laid-back spot is a perfect companion to a night at the movies or an alternative family destination. Seafood, sushi menu. Lunch, dinner. Bar. Casual attire. Reservations recommended. **$$$**

Morro Bay (G-2)

See also Atascadero, Cambria, Paso Robles, Pismo Beach, San Luis Obispo, San Simeon

Population 10,350
Elevation 200 ft
Area Code 805
Zip 93442
Information Chamber of Commerce, 845 Embarcadero, PO Box 876; phone 805/772-4467 or toll-free 800/231-0592
Web Site www.morrobay.org

At the harbor entrance to this seaport town is Morro Rock, a 576-foot-high volcanic dome discovered by Juan Rodriguez Cabrillo in 1542. A large commercial fishing fleet sails from here, and many boats dock along the Embarcadero. Morro Bay is a designated State and National Estuary; other natural features are Morro Bay Heron Rookery, Montana de Oro State Park, Morro Strand State Beach, and Los Osos Oaks Reserve.

What to See and Do

Harbor cruises. *1205 Embarcadero, Morro Bay (93442). Phone 805/772-2257.* One-hour narrated tours of bay on sternwheeler *Tiger's Folly II,* departing from Harbor Hut Dock. **$$$**

Montana de Oro State Park. *350 Pecho Valley Rd, Los Osos (93402). 8 miles S on Pecho Valley Rd. Phone 805/528-0513. www.parks.ca.gov.* Spectacular scenery along 7 miles of shoreline, with tidepools, beaches, and camping. Hikers enjoy trails up the 1,350-foot Valencia Peak. The park is popular for whale-watching and viewing harbor seals and sea otters along the shore. **$$**

Morro Bay Aquarium. *595 Embarcadero, Morro Bay (93442). Phone 805/772-7647. www.morrobay.com/morrobayaquarium.* Displays 300 live marine specimens. (Daily) **$**

Morro Bay State Park. *S of town. Phone 805/772-7434. www.parks.ca.gov.* Approximately 2,400 acres on Morro Bay. Fishing, boating; 18-hole golf course (fee), picnicking, café; hiking, tent and trailer camping (showers, dump station, water and electric hook-ups). (Daily 10 am-5 pm) On White Point is

Museum of Natural History. *State Park Rd, Morro Bay (93442). Phone 805/772-2694.* Films, slide shows, displays; nature walks. (Daily 10 am-5 pm; closed Jan 1, Thanksgiving, Dec 25) **$**

Morro Rock. *Embarcadero and Coleman Dr, Morro Bay (93442). Phone 805/772-4467.* A 576-foot-high volcanic boulder often called "The Gibraltar of the Pacific," now a bird sanctuary. Drive to the base of the rock for optimum viewing. (Daily)

Special Event

Winter Bird Festival. *880 Main St, Morro Bay (93442). Phone toll-free 800/231-0592. www.morro-bay.net/birds.* Celebration of migrating birds includes birding and natural history field trips; workshops, guest speakers; banquet, ice cream social; art exhibit. Four days in mid-Jan.

Limited-Service Hotels

★ **BLUE SAIL INN.** *851 Market Ave, Morro Bay (93442). Phone 805/772-7132; toll-free 888/337-0707; fax 805/772-8406. www.bluesailinn.com.* 48 rooms, 2 story. Check-in 3 pm, check-out 11 am. Whirlpool. **$**

★ ★ ★ **INN AT MORRO BAY.** *60 State Park Rd, Morro Bay (93442). Phone 805/772-5651; toll-free 800/321-9566; fax 805/772-4779. www.innatmorrobay.com.* Located halfway between Los Angeles and San Francisco, Morro Bay is a peaceful, slow-paced retreat, and the Inn at Morro Bay is no exception. Made up of Cape Cod-style buildings, it's located within the 4,000 acres of Morro Bay State Park. The hotel makes for a relaxing getaway on its own, but it's also located just a short drive from the National Estuary, vineyards, historic missions, and the famed Hearst Castle. After a day of sightseeing, golf, or bike riding, you'll love falling into the feather bed or dining in one of the inn's two restaurants. 97 rooms, 2 story. Check-in 4 pm, check-out noon. High-speed Internet access. Two restaurants, bar. Spa. Outdoor pool. **$$**
🛏

★ **LA SERENA INN.** *990 Morro Ave, Morro Bay (93442). Phone 805/772-5665; toll-free 800/248-1511; fax 805/772-1044. www.laserenainn.com.* 38 rooms, 3 story. Complimentary continental breakfast. Check-in 3 pm, check-out noon. Whirlpool. **$**

Specialty Lodging

BEACHWALKER INN. *501 S Ocean Ave, Cayucos (93430). Phone 805/995-2133; toll-free 800/750-2133; fax 805/995-3139. www.beachwalkerinn.com.* The individually designed rooms are cozy, but don't miss this quaint town's beaches, magnificent gardens, and other attractions. Enjoy water sports, golfing, whale- and seal-watching, and winery tours nearby. 24 rooms, 2 story. Pets accepted; fee. Complimentary continental breakfast. Check-in 2 pm, check-out 11 am. Opposite beach. **$$**

Restaurant

★ **HOFBRAU.** *901 Embarcadero, Morro Bay (93442). Phone 805/772-2411. www.hofbraurestaurant.com.* American menu. Lunch, dinner. Children's menu. Casual attire. Outdoor seating. **$**

Needles (H-6)

Also see Bullhead City, Lake Havasu City, Laughlin, NV

Founded 1882
Population 4,830
Elevation 488 ft
Area Code 760
Zip 92363
Information Chamber of Commerce, 100 G St; phone 760/326-2050

Founded as a way station for the Santa Fe Railroad, this town took its name from the needlelike peaks visible 15 miles away in Arizona. The town has a variety of trees and desert plant life. Nearby are many mines and ghost towns. With marinas on the Colorado River and recreational areas under development, the area is attracting anglers, boaters, and campers.

What to See and Do

Moabi Regional Park. *100 Park Moabi Rd, Needles (92363). 11 miles SE via I-40, on the Colorado River. Phone 760/326-3831. www.moabi.com.* Swimming beach and lagoon, water-skiing, fishing, boating (boat rentals, launches, marina); camping (fee; hook-ups, hot showers), laundry, general store. Peninsula, riverfront camping. Pets on leash only. Water, restrooms only. Fee per vehicle.

Providence Mountains State Recreation Area. *40 miles W on I-40, then 17 miles NW on Essex Rd. Phone 760/928-2586. www.parks.ca.gov.* Spectacular scenery includes a 300-square-mile area of desert. Two of the Mitchell Caverns are open to the public—El Pakiva and Tecopa; both contain fine examples of stalactites and stalagmites. El Pakiva has rare shields or palettes (round platelike protrusions from the walls). Cavern tours (Labor Day-Memorial Day, daily; rest of year, weekends; fee). Visitors are advised to bring adequate clothing, food, and water. There are trails to the surrounding area near the visitor center. Developed and RV camping (fee). Park open all year. Contact the Ranger Office, Box 1, Essex 92332. **$$$**

Restaurant

★ **HUNGRY BEAR.** *1906 Needles Hwy, Needles (92363). Phone 760/326-2988.* American menu. Breakfast, lunch, dinner, late-night. Closed Dec 25. Bar. Casual attire. **$**

Newport Beach (J-4)

See also Avalon (Catalina Island), Costa Mesa, Huntington Beach, Irvine, Laguna Beach, Long Beach, Santa Ana

Population 70,032
Elevation 25 ft
Area Code 949
Zip 92660
Information Newport Harbor Area Chamber of Commerce, 1470 Jamboree Rd; phone 949/729-4400
Web Site www.newportbeach.com

This seaside community, sometimes referred to as the American Riviera, is famous for elegant waterfront villas, smart shops and restaurants, and beautiful Pacific Coast scenery. With a 6-mile-long beach and a fine harbor, it offers a variety of water activities. Vacation attractions are largely clustered around the Balboa peninsula, a 6-mile finger of land running east and west. Behind it is Newport Harbor, with 12 miles of waterways and eight islands.

What to See and Do

Balboa Fun Zone. *600 E Bay Ave, Newport Beach (92661). Phone 949/673-0408. www.thebalboafunzone. com.* Amusement area at the pier. Ferris wheel, kiddie rides, video games, arcade. Fee for rides. (Sun-Thurs 11 am-9 pm, Fri-Sat until 10 pm) **FREE**

Orange County Museum of Arts. *850 San Clemente Dr, Newport Beach (92660). Phone 949/759-1122. www.ocma.net.* Permanent and changing exhibits of modern and contemporary art, with an emphasis on California art since World War II. Bookshop; Sculpture Garden Cafe (Tues-Fri). Museum (Tues-Sun 11 am-5 pm, Thurs until 8 pm; closed holidays). Admission free on Tues. **$$**

Sherman Library & Gardens. *2647 E Pacific Coast Hwy, Corona del Mar (92625). 5 miles S via Pacific Coast Hwy, Dahlia Ave exit. Phone 949/673-2261. www.sl-gardens.org.* Botanical gardens set amid fountains and sculptures. Historical library has a research center for the study of Pacific Southwest. (Daily 10:30 am-4 pm; closed Jan 1, Thanksgiving, Dec 25) **$**

Special Events

Christmas Boat Parade. *Newport Beach Harbor, Newport Blvd, Newport Beach (92663). Phone 949/729-4400. www.christmasboatparade.com.* Hundreds of lighted yachts, boats, kayaks, and canoes sail around the harbor. Many are decorated with Christmas scenes and feature music or costumed carolers. Mid-Dec.

Taste of Newport. *Newport Center Dr, Newport Beach. Phone 949/729-4400. www.tasteofnewport.com.* If you love to eat, you'll definitely want to catch this festival—after all, how can 75,000 people be wrong? For three days, you can taste countless culinary creations from some of the area's best-loved restaurants. In addition to pizza, tacos, gyros, and ribs, you'll find a number of, shall we say, more refined options that may include prime rib, crab cakes, and sushi. And while your taste buds dance with delight, so can your ears—the Sound Stage features live music throughout the festival. But what would a California food festival be without wine? Don't forget to taste a sampling of wines from premium California wineries. Mid-Sept. **$$$**

Limited-Service Hotel

★ **BEST WESTERN BAY SHORES INN.** *1800 W Balboa Blvd, Newport Beach (92663). Phone 949/675-3463; toll-free 800/222-6675; fax 949/675-4977. www.bestwestern.com.* 25 rooms, 3 story. Complimentary full breakfast. Check-in 3 pm, check-out 11 am. High-speed Internet access. **$**

Full-Service Hotels

★ ★ **FAIRMONT NEWPORT BEACH.** *4500 MacArthur Blvd, Newport Beach (92660). Phone*

949/476-2001; fax 949/476-0153. www.fairmont.com. 435 rooms, 10 story. Pets accepted; fee. Check-in 3 pm, check-out noon. High-speed Internet access, wireless Internet access. Two restaurants, bar. Fitness room. Outdoor pool, whirlpool. Tennis. Airport transportation available. **$**

★ ★ ★ **HYATT NEWPORTER.** *1107 Jamboree Rd, Newport Beach (92660). Phone 949/729-1234; toll-free 800/633-7313; fax 949/759-3253. www.newporter.hyatt.com.* 403 rooms, 3 story. Check-in 4 pm, check-out noon. Restaurant, bar. Fitness room. Three outdoor pools. Airport transportation available. Business center. **$$**

★ ★ ★ ★ **THE ISLAND HOTEL NEWPORT BEACH.** *690 Newport Center Dr, Newport Beach (92660). Phone 949/759-0808; toll-free 800/819-5053; fax 949/720-1718. www.theislandhotel.com.* In the heart of Southern California, this 20-story tower is angled toward the Pacific Ocean and only minutes from the glorious beaches. Guests here reap the rewards of a refreshing sleep, a delicious meal, or a perfectly lazy day spent by the pool. All rooms have private balconies overlooking the beautiful grounds. The accommodations are West Coast casual blended with European lan; shades of lemon, lime, and peach enhance the restful appearance. The pool sparkles, and its 17-foot fireplace warms visitors on chilly evenings. Guests can stay in touch poolside, where dataports and telephone jacks are available. The nearby Pelican Hill Golf Club and Grill provide leisure and culinary diversions, while the hotels signature Pavilion restaurant (see) is a lovely spot for dining at any time of day. 295 rooms, 20 story. Pets accepted, some restrictions. Check-in 3 pm, check-out noon. High-speed Internet access. Two restaurants, bar. Fitness room, spa. Outdoor pool, whirlpool. Tennis. Airport transportation available. Business center. **$$$**

★ ★ ★ **MARRIOTT SUITES NEWPORT BEACH.** *500 Bayview Cir, Newport Beach (92660). Phone 949/854-4500; toll-free 800/228-9290; fax 949/854-3937. www.marriott.com.* 254 rooms, 9 story, all suites. Check-in 4 pm, check-out noon. Restaurant, bar. Fitness room. Outdoor pool, whirlpool. Airport transportation available. Business center. **$$**

Full-Service Resorts

★ ★ ★ BALBOA BAY CLUB & RESORT.
1221 W Coast Hwy, Newport Beach (92663). Phone 949/630-4200; fax 949/630-4111. www.balboabayclub. com. 132 rooms. Check-in 3 pm, check-out noon. Wireless internet access. Restaurant, bar. Fitness room. Spa. Outdoor pool, whirlpool. Business center. Credit cards accepted. **$$$**

★ ★ ★ NEWPORT BEACH MARRIOTT HOTEL AND SPA.
900 Newport Center Dr, Newport Beach (92660). Phone 949/640-4000; toll-free 800/228-9290; fax 949/640-5055. www.marriott.com. A recent $70 million renovation of the Newport Beach Marriott Hotel and Spa offers coastal living with sleek, modern style. Conveniently located between Los Angeles and San Diego amid the attractions of Orange County, this hotel is just blocks from Newport Harbor and for shopping and entertainment, the high-end Fashion Island mall is next door. 532 rooms. Check-in 4 pm, check-out noon. High-speed internet access. Restaurant, bar. Fitness room. Spa. Outdoor pool, whirlpool. Tennis. Airport transportation available. Business center. **$$**

Specialty Lodgings

DORYMAN'S INN BED & BREAKFAST.
2102 W Oceanfront, Newport Beach (92663). Phone 949/675-7300; fax 949/673-2101. www.dorymansinn.com. This quaint bed-and-breakfast—confined to the second-story of a Victorian landmark built in 1921—charms adventurous vacationers and romantics with its classic design and historic, wharf-side Old Newport location. French and American antiques are sprinkled liberally throughout the guest rooms, which feature fireplaces, sunken marble tubs, and old-fashioned window seats from which the harbor's boating and fishing activities can be observed. 10 rooms. Complimentary continental breakfast. Check-in 3-7 pm, check-out 11 am. **$$**

PORTOFINO BEACH HOTEL.
2306 W Oceanfront Blvd, Newport Beach (92663). Phone 949/673-7030; toll-free 800/571-8749; fax 949/723-4370. www.thenewportbeachhotel.com. This restored oceanfront hotel has apartments as well as standard guest rooms, all of which are distinct. The Italian Renato Restaurant next door provides room service.

20 rooms, 2 story. Complimentary continental breakfast. Check-in 3 pm, check-out noon. **$$**

Restaurants

★ ★ 21 OCEANFRONT.
2100 W Oceanfront, Newport Beach (92663). Phone 949/673-2100; fax 949/673-2101. www.21oceanfront.com. This landmark eatery's prime spot adjacent to the Newport Pier makes it the envy of its competition. But 21 Oceanfront earns its reputation and upscale repeat patronage—singles flock to the candlelit, burnished-mahogany bar to spark romance, while business types slip into the Victorian-themed dining room's black leather banquettes to cut deals—with a marvelous menu. Although the pasta, poultry, and meat entrées exceed most expectations for presentation and flavor, seafood is king: fresh lobster, swordfish, mahi mahi, and abalone (an expensive, one-of-a-kind specialty) are among the highlights. A well-stocked wine cellar and jazz standards performed nightly further stir the luxe seaside air. Seafood, steak menu. Dinner. Closed holidays. Bar. Valet parking. Outdoor seating. **$$$**

★ ★ EL TORITO GRILL.
951 Newport Center Dr, Newport Beach (92660). Phone 949/640-2875; fax 949/640-4625. www.eltorito.com. "Grill" is the key word in the name of this colorful chain eatery (one of six in greater Los Angeles), which differentiates itself from the average El Torito restaurant by adding distinctive Southwestern flair and flavor to its array of Mexican dishes, courtesy of a wood-fired mesquite grill. Specialties like grilled-chicken fajita salad and baby-back ribs basted in tamarind barbecue sauce thrive alongside hearty, generously portioned combination platters, and an impressive selection of oak-aged tequilas makes for potent margaritas. Best of all are the waiters who cheerfully provide tableside guacamole-making service and ample servings of warm tortillas. Mexican menu. Lunch, dinner, Sun brunch. Closed Thanksgiving. Bar. Children's menu. Casual attire. Valet parking. Outdoor seating. **$$**

★ ★ NEWPORT BEACH BREWING COMPANY.
2920 Newport Blvd, Newport Beach (92663). Phone 949/675-8449; fax 949/675-4562. www. nbbrewco.com. As its name suggests, this bustling brewery/restaurant—housed in a landmark building in the historic cannery district—is less prized for its large, no-holds-barred, perfectly passable American

menu than the assortment of house brews it has on tap: Newport Beach Blonde, Kirk's Wicked Wheat, and John Wayne Imperial Stout are among the more enigmatic favorites. The hip, upbeat music and rustic saloon-style décor rate highly with locals, tourists, and especially singles, and the free high-speed Internet access is impressive as well. Notable side draws: weeknight happy hours, monthly beer-tasting seminars, and plentiful onsite parking. American menu. Lunch, dinner. Closed Easter, Thanksgiving, Dec 25. Bar. Children's menu. Casual attire. Outdoor seating. **$$**

★ ★ ★ **PASCAL.** *1000 Bristol St, Newport Beach (92660). Phone 949/263-9400; fax 949/261-9041. www. pascalnewportbeach.com.* The famed signature dining experience of much-lauded chef/restaurateur Pascal Olhats, who has built something of an epicurean empire with several eateries in Newport Beach and visited *The Oprah Winfrey Show,* this extraordinarily lovely, rose-filled, farmhouse-style space showcases French countryside cuisine with a light, herb-enhanced touch. Local old money and nouveau riche alike congregate here, and for good reason: they can afford Olhats's penchant for perfection, which is evident in every facet of flavor and presentation—from the delectable distribution of apples and walnuts in the lamb salad, to the charming tableau of brandied cherries and dandelion greens surrounding the duo of foie gras, to the choice cuts and tasty application of apricot and Spanish chorizo garnishes of the grilled pork rack. A lavish five-course prix fixe meal is available, and the waitstaff is no-nonsense professional—the appropriate tone for an establishment of this pedigree. French menu. Lunch, dinner. Closed Sun; holidays. **$$$**

★ ★ ★ **PAVILION.** *690 Newport Center Dr, Newport Beach (92660). Phone 949/760-4920; fax 949/759-0568. www.islandhotel.com.* Pavilion delivers all you would expect from a dining experience at the Island Hotel Newport Beach: impeccable service, brilliant cuisine, and a well-chosen wine list to match. The formal, European-style dining room is decked out in creamy camel tones, with deep cushioned banquettes; tall, tan, veneered columns; ornate Versailles-styled mirrors; magnificent fresh floral arrangements; and a tented terrace with heat lamps for cozy outdoor dining. The kitchen puts a gentle Mediterranean spin on contemporary seasonal California cuisine, ensuring an exciting culinary journey. If you crave formal dining and simple, elegant food, seek out a table at

Pavilion. California menu. Breakfast, lunch, dinner. Bar. Valet parking. Outdoor seating. **$$$**

★ ★ ★ **THE RITZ.** *880 Newport Center Dr, Newport Beach (92660). Phone 949/720-1800; fax 949/720-1886. www.ritzrestaurant.com.* The Ritz earns its reputation with its luxurious and varied facilities alone. No fewer than five distinctive, richly appointed indoor and outdoor dining spaces grace the premises—ranging from the Escoffier Room, a pavilion-style space with Georgian accents and portraits of the renowned Paris Ritz Hotel chef Auguste Escoffier, to the Wine Cellar, a vaulted brick chamber accessed through an oval tunnel and illuminated by antlered chandeliers. The spectacle would be for naught without cuisine to match, and the outstanding contemporary menu encompassing French, Italian, and American influences meets the task. A clientele laden with deal-makers and lovebirds indulges in entrées like almond-crusted halibut, grilled ahi and swordfish, and carmelized onion and pepper top sirloin—all served with sophisticated, elegant flair by a caring waitstaff. The inspired desserts, many of which incorporate liqueurs, include a homey warm pear cheesecake and a decadent martini made with coffee- and vanilla-flavored vodka and Godiva chocolate. American, French menu. Lunch, dinner. Closed holidays. Bar. Valet parking. **$$$**

★ ★ **ROUGE BISTRO & BAR.** *327 Newport Center Dr, Newport Beach (92660). Phone 949/640-2700; fax 940/640-1186. www.culinaryadventures.com.* This hot new French eatery from noted local restaurateur David Wilhelm (it's actually located on the former site of Wilhelm's Southwestern-themed Chimayo Grill) has a romantic atmosphere modeled on French "Café Society." Tunes by the likes of Edith Pilaf, Louis Armstrong, and Billie Holiday waft across the tasteful, contemporary dining area, which is redolent of flavorful basic French and American bistro classics including crepes, chilled shellfish dishes, and onion soup. Foodies can wash this all down with one of the many French and California wines in stockor order up one of Rouge's signature martinis or aperitifs. American, French bistro menu. Lunch, dinner, Sun brunch. Business casual attire. **$$**

★ ★ **SAPORI.** *1080 Bayside Dr, Newport Beach (92660). Phone 949/644-4220; fax 949/644-1932.* Family-friendly alfresco dining and scenic views of Balboa Island and Newport Harbor are among the highlights at Sapori, a casually intimate Italian eatery. Plenty of delicious wood-fired pizzas and splendid pasta dishes supplement a specialty-studded menu that includes fettuccine with scallops and asparagus, sage cream-sauced ravioli with ham and mushrooms, and the signature insalata mista—arugula, radicchio, and Belgian endive tossed with walnuts. An attentive wait-staff and an excellent wine list foster the truly flavorful fun. Italian menu. Lunch, dinner. Closed holidays. Bar. Reservations recommended. Outdoor seating. **$$$**

★ ★ **TUTTO MARE.** *545 Newport Center Dr, Newport Beach (92660). Phone 949/640-6333; fax 949/640-1752. www.tuttomare.com.* Peach marble floors, burnished mahogany columns and beams, and expansive windows framing a classy Fashion Island location set the stage for casual upscale dining at Tutto Mare, where Mediterranean-style Italian meals hit their mark. Choice mains of mesquite-grilled fish and rotisserie meats join a variety of homemade pastas and oak-fired pizzas in the eatery's quest to satisfy everyone from families to foodies. Sunday brunch is a big hit here, presented to the soothing live sounds of classical guitar. Italian menu. Lunch, dinner, Sun brunch. Closed holidays. Bar. Outdoor seating. **$$$**

★ ★ **VILLA NOVA.** *3131 W Coast Hwy, Newport Beach (92663). Phone 949/642-7880; fax 949/642-0674. www.villanovarestaurant.com.* A local landmark since 1967, this award-winning eatery—originated in Hollywood by a native Italian who was an actor/stuntman—attracts rather large, adult crowds with its stunning harbor views and cavernous, old-world-themed interior stuffed with paintings and nautical artifacts. The miles-long menu catalogues marvelously prepared variations on every kind of classic Italian cuisine: homemade pastas, fresh seafood, juicy steaks, and tender veal, to name a few. Romantics love the stellar wine list and intimate lighting, and patrons of all income levels enjoy arriving by land or by sea: the valet parking is free, and boat slips are available just outside the door. Italian menu. Dinner. Closed Jan 1, Thanksgiving, Dec 25. Bar. Children's menu. Valet parking. Outdoor seating. **$$**

Oceanside (K-4)

See also Carlsbad, Escondido, San Clemente

Population 161,029
Elevation 47 ft
Area Code 760
Information Chamber of Commerce, Visitor Information Center, 928 N Coast Hwy, 92054; phone toll-free 800/350-7873
Web Site www.oceansidechamber.com

Camp Pendleton, a US Marine base, borders this city on the north. Interstate 5 goes through the camp property for about 18 miles.

What to See and Do

Antique Gas & Steam Engine Museum. *2040 N Santa Fe Ave, Vista (92083). 7 miles E via Oceanside Blvd. Phone 760/941-1791; toll-free 800/587-2286; fax 760/941-0690. www.agsem.com.* Nestled in Guajome Regional Park in north San Diego County, this combination museum, working farm, and restoration area educates the public about the agriculture, construction, and early industrial trades of 1849-1949 through exhibits, ongoing restoration projects, and demonstrations. Much of the 40 acres is a working farm, where visitors can see crops being harvested with decades-old equipment and prepared in the kitchen for cooking. (Daily 10 am-4 pm; closed Jan 1, Dec 25) **$**

California Surf Museum. *223 N Coast Hwy, Oceanside (92054). Phone 760/721-6876. www.surfmuseum.org.* Learn about the sport and lifestyle of the surfer through various exhibits and presentations. Tours (by appointment). (Daily 10 am-4 pm; closed holidays) **FREE**

Mission San Luis Rey de Francia. *4050 Mission Ave, Oceanside (92057). 4 1/2 miles E on Hwy 76. Phone 760/757-3651. www.sanluisrey.org.* (1798) Founded by Father Lasuén, it was named for Louis IX, crusader and ruler of France from 1226 to 1270. "King of Missions," the 18th and the largest of the 21 early California missions, has a large collection of Spanish vestments, cloister gardens, Native American cemetery, first pepper tree (1830), and other historic artifacts. Picnicking. Self-guided tours. Museum (daily 10 am-4:30 pm; closed Jan 1, Thanksgiving, Dec 25). **$**

Oceanside Harbor and Marina. *1540 Harbor Dr N, Oceanside. Phone 760/435-4000.* Mecca for sportfishing, whale-watching, boating, and other water-oriented activities. Marina has slips ranging in length from 26 to 51 feet. Transient moorings and limited RV beach camping available. Cape Cod Village offers restaurants and gift shops.

Limited-Service Hotels

★ **BEST WESTERN MARTY'S VALLEY INN.** *3240 E Mission Ave, Oceanside (92054). Phone 760/757-7700; toll-free 800/747-3529; fax 760/439-3311. www.bestwestern.com.* 111 rooms, 2 story. Complimentary continental breakfast. Check-in 3 pm, check-out 11 am. Bar. Fitness room. Outdoor pool, whirlpool. Business center. **$**

★ BEST WESTERN OCEANSIDE INN.
1680 Oceanside Blvd, Oceanside (92054). Phone 760/722-1821; toll-free 800/443-9995; fax 760/967-8969. www.bestwestern.com. 80 rooms, 2 story. Complimentary continental breakfast. Check-in 2 pm, check-out noon. Fitness room. Outdoor pool, whirlpool. **$**

Restaurant

★ LA PALOMA.
116 Escondido Ave, Vista (92084). Phone 760/758-7140; fax 760/758-3915. Mexican menu. Lunch, dinner. Closed holidays. Bar. Children's menu. Casual attire. Reservations recommended. Outdoor seating. **$$**

Ojai (H-3)
See also Oxnard, Santa Barbara, Ventura

Population 7,862
Elevation 746 ft
Area Code 805
Zip 93023
Information Ojai Valley Chamber of Commerce & Visitors Center, 150 W Ojai Ave; phone 805/646-8126
Web Site www.ojaichamber.org

The Ojai Valley was first farmed by citrus and cattle ranchers after the Civil War. In the 1870s, publicity in Eastern newspapers initiated its popularity as a tourist haven and winter resort. Attracted by its quiet, rural beauty and proximity to urban centers, many artists, writers, and other creative people make their home in the Ojai Valley.

A Ranger District office of the Los Padres National Forest (see SANTA BARBARA) is located here.

What to See and Do

Lake Casitas Recreation Area. *11311 Santa Ana Rd, Ojai (93001). 5 miles W on Hwy 150. Phone 805/649-2233.* Fishing, boating (rentals, trailer rentals); picnicking, concession; camping (fee; for reservations phone 805/649-1122; hook-ups), trailer storage (fee). Pets on leash only (fee); no firearms. Nearby are beaches, golf courses, and tennis courts. (Daily)

Ojai Center for the Arts. *113 S Montgomery, Ojai (93023). Phone 805/646-0117. www.ojaiartcenter.org.* Rotating exhibitions of local artists; live theater productions. (Tues-Sun noon-4 pm)

Ojai Valley Museum. *130 W Ojai Ave, Ojai (93023). Phone 805/640-1390. www.ojaivalleymuseum.org.* Permanent and changing exhibits explore environmental, cultural, and historical factors that shaped the Ojai Valley; research library. (Thurs-Fri 1-4 pm, Sat from 10 am, Sun from noon; closed holidays) **$**

Special Events

Ojai Music Festival. *Libby Bowl, 201 S Signal St, Ojai (93023). Phone 805/646-2053. www.ojaifestival.org.* For four days in early June, the Libby Bowl is host to some of the most talented classical musicians who perform pieces from composers such as Mozart, Stravinsky, and Beethoven. Early June. **$$$$**

Ojai Shakespeare Festival. *Matilija JHS Auditorium, 703 El Paseo St, Ojai (93023). Phone 805/646-9455. www.ojaishakespeare.org.* Outdoor evening and matinee performances of Shakespeare plays. July-Aug.

Ojai Studio Artists Tour. *Chamber of Commerce, 150 W Ojai Ave, Ojai (93023). Phone 805/646-8126. www.ojaistudioartists.com.* Recognized artists open their studios to the public. Two days in mid-Oct. **$$$$**

Ojai Valley Tennis Tournament. *1467 Grand Ave, Ojai. Phone 805/646-7241. www.ojaitourney.org.* Held since 1895, this is the oldest amateur tennis tournament in the United States. Games take place at a variety of venues, including Libby Park, the Ojai Valley Athletic Club, high schools, and colleges. Late Apr. **$$**

Limited-Service Hotels

★ BEST WESTERN CASA OJAI.
1302 E Ojai Ave, Ojai (93023). Phone 805/646-8175; toll-free 800/255-8175; fax 805/640-8193. www.bestwestern.com. 44 rooms, 2 story. Pets accepted, some restrictions; fee. Complimentary continental breakfast. Check-out noon. Outdoor pool, whirlpool. **$**

★ HUMMINGBIRD INN.
1208 E Ojai Ave, Ojai (93023). Phone 805/646-4365; toll-free 800/228-3744; fax 805/646-0625. www.hummingbirdinnofojai.com. 31 rooms, 2 story. Complimentary continental breakfast. Check-in 3 pm, check-out 11 am. Outdoor pool, whirlpool. **$**

Full-Service Resort

★ ★ ★ **OJAI VALLEY INN & SPA.** *905 Country Club Rd, Ojai (93023). Phone 805/646-1111; fax 805/646-7969. www.ojairesort.com.* The Ojai Valley Inn & Spa is a superb destination for the discriminating traveler. This luxurious resort rests on 220 acres in the beautiful Ojai Valley, near Santa Barbara. Lavish accommodations, championship golf and tennis, children's programming, and horseback riding are among the many reasons this resort wins rave reviews. This resort takes the business of relaxation very seriously, and this is perhaps best seen at its award-winning spa. The treatment menu at this extensive facility goes beyond the ordinary to include seasonally inspired services, water therapy, physical fitness, and treatments designed especially for men and pregnant clients. From delicious California cuisine and American grill favorites to indulgent-tasting spa food, the resort's five restaurants are sure to please. 209 rooms, 3 story. Pets accepted; fee. Check-in 4 pm, check-out noon. Five restaurants, bar. Children's activity center. Fitness room. Three outdoor pools, whirlpool. Golf. Tennis. Business center. **$$$**

Spa

★ ★ ★ ★ **SPA OJAI.** *905 Country Club Rd, Ojai (93023). Phone 805/646-1111.* With its gorgeous Spanish architecture and picture-perfect location across the hills from Santa Barbara, it's no wonder that the Ojai Valley Inn has been used as a backdrop for several films throughout the years. But even this flawless exterior can't prepare you for the luxury that awaits inside at Spa Ojai. Hikers, golfers, and couples on romantic getaways all flock to this sophisticated 31,000-square-foot sanctuary of health and well-being for a spa experience like no other. Face and body treatments customized for both men and women are designed to spoil and pamper, as well as to cleanse and detoxify. Massage therapies range from the traditional Swedish massage to the spa's own Ojai Stone Massage and utilize only the highest quality oils and lotions made from the finest natural products. Spa Ojai encourages guests to enjoy one of its magnificent signature treatments, which includes Kuyama treatment that combines the therapeutic effects of cleansing mud, dry heat, inhalation therapy, and guided meditation. This communal experience (kuyam means a place to rest together) accommodates up to eight men or eight women and is the only treatment of its kind available in the United States. Mothers-to-be will appreciate the treatments that The Spa has created especially for them. The Mothers Joy Body Treatment features a full-body exfoliation, warm shower, and shea and cocoa body butter application, while the Pregnancy Massage relaxes and nurtures both mother and baby. But because Spa Ojai believes that the well-being of the mind is just as important as that of the body, they have created Mind/Body Programs. Here, you can find out which foods and activities can keep you in balance or determine your level of muscular strength, flexibility, and endurance. Truly an experience for the mind, body, and spirit, you'll feel on top of the world after a visit to Spa Ojai.

Restaurants

★ ★ ★ **L'AUBERGE.** *314 El Paseo Rd, Ojai (93023). Phone 805/646-2288. www.laubergeatojai.com.* Continental, French menu. Dinner, brunch. Outdoor seating. **$$**

★ ★ ★ **RANCH HOUSE.** *102 Besant Rd, Ojai (93023). Phone 805/646-2360; fax 805/646-1292. www.theranchhouse.com.* American menu. Dinner, Sun brunch. Closed Mon; Jan 1, July 4, Dec 24-25. Children's menu. Outdoor seating. **$$$**

Ontario (J-4)

See also Claremont, Corona, Pomona, Rancho Cucamonga, Redlands

Founded 1882
Population 158,007
Elevation 988 ft
Area Code 909
Information Convention and Visitors Authority, 2000 Convention Center Way, 91764; phone 909/937-3000 or toll-free 800/455-5755
Web Site www.ontariocc.com

What to See and Do

Air Museum: Planes of Fame. *7000 Merrill Ave, Chino (91710). Phone 909/597-3722. www.planesoffame.org.* Exotic collection of more than 60 operable historic military aircraft, including Japanese Zero, ME-109G, B-17. Aircraft rides. (Daily 9 am-5 pm; closed Thanksgiving, Dec 25) **$$**

California Speedway. *9300 Cherry Ave, Fontana (92335). I-10 W to Cherry Ave, N to Randall Ave* entrance. *Phone 909/429-5000; toll-free 800/944-7223. www.californiaspeedway.com.* Two-mile asphalt track is home to professional auto racing, including NASCAR Nextel Cup Series and PPG CART World Series races. (Dates vary)

Fontana Skate Park. *Juniper Park,Juniper Ave and Filbert St, Fontana (92335). Phone 909/428-8360. www. fontana.org/main/public_serv/skate_park.htm.* Rated among the top ten of skate parks at www. socalskateparks.com, the Fontana facility has street action, intermediate bowl/banks, and a three-bowl clover with an 8- to 9-foot vertical. Protective gear must be worn at all times. (Fri-Wed 9 am-9:30 pm, Thurs noon-9:30 pm) **FREE**

Graber Olive House Tour. *315 E 4th St, Ontario (91762). Phone 909/983-1761. www.graberolives.com.* Tour of sorting, canning, packaging areas. Mini-museum, gourmet food, and gift shop. (Daily; closed holidays) **FREE**

Museum of History and Art, Ontario. *225 S Euclid Ave, Ontario (91762). Phone 909/983-3198.* Regional history and fine arts exhibits. (Wed-Sun noon-4 pm; closed holidays) **FREE**

Ontario Mills. *One Mills Cir, Ontario (91764). Phone 909/484-8300. www.ontariomills.com.* This is California's largest entertainment and outlet mall—1.5 million square feet (that's nearly 30 football fields) of retail entertainment under one roof. It's the kind of place where busloads of tourists troop in to make mass souvenir purchases. Retail outlets include Nordstrom Rack, Off 5th Saks Fifth Avenue, JCPenney, and the small but comfortable LoveSac shop. Attractions include an enormous Dave & Buster's with a Million Dollar Midway, billiards, golf simulator, and dining room. (Mon-Sat 10 am-9:30 pm, Sun 10 am-8 pm) **FREE**

Prado Regional Park. *16700 Euclid Ave, Ontario (91710). 8 miles S via Euclid Ave; 6 miles S of Pomona Frwy. Phone 909/597-4260. www.co.san-bernardino. ca.us/parks/prado.htm.* Fishing, nonpower boat rentals; horseback riding (rentals; fee); golf; picnicking; camping. (Daily; closed Dec 25) **$**

Raging Waters. *Dr. Frank G. Bonelli Regional Park, 111 Raging Waters Dr, San Dimas (91773). Phone 909/802-2200. www.ragingwaters.com.* Huge 50-acre water park with 50 million gallons of water in use. Largest flume ride in the United States; highest two-person tube ride. Million-gallon wave cove. Separate waterplay area for young kids. (Late Apr-late May: Sat-Sun 10

am-6 pm; July-Aug: daily 10 am-8 pm; Sept: 10 am-5 pm, days vary) **$$$$**

Limited-Service Hotels

★ ★ **AYRES SUITES ONTARIO AIRPORT CONVENTION CENTER.** *1945 E Holt Blvd, Ontario (91761). Phone 909/390-7778; toll-free 800/706-4881; fax 909/937-9718. www.ayreshotels.com.* 167 rooms, 3 story. Complimentary full breakfast. Check-in 3 pm, check-out noon. Restaurant. Fitness room. Outdoor pool, whirlpool. Airport transportation available. **$**

★ ★ **DOUBLETREE HOTEL.** *222 N Vineyard Ave, Ontario (91764). Phone 909/937-0900; toll-free 800/222-8733; fax 909/937-1999. www.doubletree.com.* This hotel is located 2 miles from Ontario International Airport and next to the city's convention center, in the heart of the "Inland Empire." 484 rooms, 4 story. Pets accepted, some restrictions; fee. Check-in 3 pm, check-out noon. Restaurant, bar. Fitness room. Outdoor pool, whirlpool. Airport transportation available. **$$**

Full-Service Hotels

★ ★ ★ **HILTON ONTARIO AIRPORT.** *700 N Haven, Ontario (91764). Phone 909/980-0400; toll-free 800/654-1379; fax 909/948-9309. www.hilton.com.* This property offers easy access to the airport and major freeways. The Café Catalina offers California cuisine; the lobby lounge serves the full restaurant menu. 309 rooms, 10 story. Pets accepted. Complimentary continental breakfast. Check-in 3 pm, check-out noon. Restaurant, bar. Fitness room. Outdoor pool, whirlpool. Airport transportation available. **$$**

★ ★ ★ **MARRIOTT ONTARIO AIRPORT.** *2200 E Holt Blvd, Ontario (91761). Phone 909/986-8811; toll-free 800/228-8811; fax 909/391-6151. www. marriott.com.* This hotel is convenient to California Speedway and Ontario Mills shopping area; it's also an hour drive away from local beaches, Palm Springs, and snow skiing. 299 rooms, 3 story. Check-in 3 pm, check-out noon. High-speed Internet access, wireless Internet access. Restaurant, bar. Fitness room. Outdoor pool, whirlpool. Tennis. Airport transportation available. **$**

Restaurant

★ ★ ★ **ROSA'S.** *425 N Vineyard Ave, Ontario (91764). Phone 909/937-1220; fax 909/937-7022. www. rosasitalian.com.* Italian menu. Lunch, dinner. Closed Sun. Bar. Reservations recommended. **$$$**

Orange(J-4)

See also Anaheim, Disneyland, Garden Grove, Santa Ana,

Founded 1868
Population 128,821
Elevation 187 ft
Area Code 714
Information Chamber of Commerce, 439 E Chapman Ave, 92866; phone 714/538-3581
Web Site www.orangechamber.org

What to See and Do

Tucker Wildlife Sanctuary. *29332 Modjeska Canyon Rd, Orange. Phone 714/649-2760. www.tuckerwildlife. org.* Twelve-acre refuge for native plants and animals, including several species of hummingbirds (seasonal); observation porch, nature trails; museum displays; picnic areas. (Tues-Sun 9 am-4 pm) **FREE**

Limited-Service Hotels

★ ★ **COUNTRY INN BY AYRES ORANGE.** *3737 W Chapman Ave, Orange (92868). Phone 714/978-9168; toll-free 800/706-4885; fax 714/385-1528. www.countrysuites.com.* 130 rooms, 6 story. Complimentary full breakfast. Check-in 3 pm, check-out noon. Restaurant. Fitness room. Outdoor pool, whirlpool. **$**

★ ★ **DOUBLETREE HOTEL.** *100 The City Dr, Orange (92868). Phone 714/634-4500; toll-free 800/528-0444; fax 714/978-2370. www.doubletree.com.* 454 rooms, 20 story. Check-out noon. Restaurant, bar. Fitness room. Outdoor pool, whirlpool. Tennis. Business center. **$$**

★ **HAWTHORN SUITES.** *720 The City Dr S, Orange (92668). Phone 714/740-2700; toll-free 800/278-4837; fax 714/971-1692. www.hawthorn.com.* 123 rooms, 3 story, all suites. Complimentary full breakfast. Check-out noon. Outdoor pool, whirlpool. Business center. **$$**

Full-Service Hotel

★ ★ **HILTON SUITES ANAHEIM/ORANGE.** *400 N State College Blvd, Orange (92868). Phone 714/938-1111; fax 714/938-0930. www.anaheimsuites. hilton.com.* This property is located within walking distance of the Anaheim Stadium and minutes from Disneyland. 230 rooms, 10 story. Complimentary full breakfast. Check-in 4 pm, check-out 11 am. Restaurant, bar. Fitness room. Indoor pool, whirlpool. Business center. **$$**

Restaurants

★ ★ ★ **THE HOBBIT.** *2932 E Chapman Ave, Orange (92869). Phone 714/997-1972; fax 714/997-3181. www.hobbitrestaurant.com.* American menu. Dinner. Closed Mon; holidays. Bar. Jacket required. Reservations recommended. **$$$**

★ ★ **LA BRASSERIE.** *202 S Main St, Orange (92868). Phone 714/978-6161; fax 714/978-1806. www.774food.com.* French menu. Lunch, dinner. Closed Sun; holidays. Bar. **$$**

★ ★ **YEN CHING.** *574 S Glassell St, Orange (92866). Phone 714/997-3300; fax 714/997-8889. www. yenchingoc.com.* Chinese menu. Lunch, dinner. **$$**

Oxnard(H-3)

See also Camarillo, Ojai, Ventura

Population 170,358
Elevation 52 ft
Area Code 805
Zip 93030
Information Tourism Bureau, 200 W Seventh St; phone 805/385-7545 or toll-free 800/269-6273
Web Site www.visitoxnard.com

What to See and Do

Carnegie Art Museum. *424 South C St, Oxnard (93030). Phone 805/385-8157. www.vcnet.com/ carnart/default.html.* Features quarterly changing exhibits of regional and international visual and fine arts. (Thurs-Sat 10 am-5 pm, Sun 1-5 pm; closed holidays) **$**

CEC/Seabee Museum. *Naval Base Ventura County, Building 99, Port Hueneme (93043). Channel Islands Blvd and Ventura Rd, SW off Hwy 101 in Port*

Hueneme. Enter on Ventura Rd at Sunkist St, S of Channel Islands Blvd. Phone 805/982-5165. www.sea-beehf.org. Memorabilia of the US Navy Seabees, who are the construction battalions of the Navy. Uniforms, Antarctic display, South Pacific artifacts, underwater diving display, outrigger canoes, World War II dioramas, weapons, flags. By appointment. **FREE**

Channel Islands Harbor. *Visitor Center, 2741 S Victoria Ave, Suite F, Oxnard (93035). Phone 805/985-4852. www.channelislandsharbor.org.* Public recreation includes boating, fishing, swimming, beaches; parks, barbecue and picnic facilities, playgrounds; tennis courts; charter boat and bicycle rentals. Also here is

> **Fisherman's Wharf.** *Phone 805/985-4852; toll-free 800/269-6273.* A New England-style village with specialty shops, restaurants, and transient docking for pleasure boaters.

Gull Wings Children's Museum. *418 W 4th St, Oxnard (93030). Phone 805/483-3005. www.gullwingsmuseum.org.* Hands-on interactive exhibits encourage children to learn by doing. Young visitors can explore the cockpit of a space shuttle, dig for fossils, or put on their own puppet show. (Tues-Sat 10 am-5 pm) **$**

Heritage Square. *715 S A St, Oxnard (93030). Phone 805/483-7960.* Created in 1985, Heritage Square in downtown Oxnard, about an hour north of Los Angeles, is a quaint block of historic homes and buildings. Dating from 1876 to 1912, the buildings include several homes, a church, a water tower, a pump house, and a storehouse. Tours of the homes, offered through the visitor center on Saturdays from 10 am to 2 pm, are free of charge, although donations are welcome. **FREE**

Ventura County Maritime Museum. *2731 S Victoria Ave, Oxnard (93035). Phone 805/984-6260.* Nautical exhibits and model ships illustrate maritime history. (Daily 11 am-5 pm) **DONATION**

Special Events

California Strawberry Festival. *Strawberry Meadows of College Park, 3250 S Rose Ave, Oxnard (93033). Phone 805/385-4739; toll-free 888/288-9242. www.strawberry-fest.org.* Waiters' race, wine tasting, entertainment, crafts, strawberry foods. Third weekend in May. **$$**

NAS Point Mugu Air Show. *521 9th St, Oxnard (93030). Pacific Coast Hwy (Hwy 1) or I-101 (Ventura Frwy) W to Las Posas exit. Phone 805/989-8786. www.nbvc.navy.mil.* Military aircraft demonstration, parachutists, displays; civilian/foreign acrobatics. Oct.

Limited-Service Hotels

★ ★ **CASA SIRENA HOTEL & MARINA.** *3605 Peninsula Rd, Oxnard (93035). Phone 805/985-6311; toll-free 800/447-3529; fax 805/278-4329. www.casasi-renahotel.com.* 273 rooms, 3 story. Pets accepted, some restrictions; fee. Check-out noon. Restaurant, bar. Fitness room. Outdoor pool, whirlpool. Tennis. Airport transportation available. **$**
🏄 🏋 🏊 🎿

★ **COUNTRY INN & SUITES BY CARLSON.** *350 E Hueneme Rd, Port Hueneme (93041). Phone 805/986-5353; toll-free 800/456-4000; fax 805/986-4399. www.countryinns.com.* 135 rooms, 3 story. Complimentary full breakfast. Check-out noon. Outdoor pool, whirlpool. **$**
🏊

★ ★ **EMBASSY SUITES.** *2101 Mandalay Beach Rd, Oxnard (93035). Phone 805/984-2500; toll-free 800/362-2779; fax 805/984-8339. www.mandalaybeach.embassysuites.com.* 250 rooms, 3 story. Complimentary full breakfast. Check-out noon. Restaurant, bar. Fitness room. Beach. Outdoor pool, whirlpool. Tennis. Airport transportation available. Business center. **$$**
🏋 🏊 🎿 🏃

Restaurant

★ **MONEY PANCHO.** *155 E 7th St, Oxnard (93030). Phone 805/483-1411.* Mexican menu. Breakfast, lunch, dinner. Children's menu. **$$**

Palm Desert (J-5)

See also Desert Hot Springs, Idyllwild, Indian Wells, Indio, Joshua Tree National Park, Palm Springs,

Population 41,155
Elevation 243 ft
Area Code 760
Zip 92260
Information Chamber of Commerce, 73710 Fred Waring Dr Suite 114; phone 760/346-6111 or toll-free 800/873-2428
Web Site www.palmdesert.org

What to See and Do

Living Desert. *47-900 S Portola Ave, Palm Desert (92260). Phone 760/346-5694. www.livingdesert.org.* This 1,200-acre wildlife and botanical park contains interpretive exhibits from the world's deserts. Animals include mountain lions, zebras, bighorn sheep, coyotes, cheetas, reptiles, and birds. Native American exhibits; picnic areas, nature trails; gift shop; café; nursery. Special programs on weekends. (Sept-mid-June: daily 9 am-5 pm; mid-June-late Aug 31: daily 8 am-1:30 pm; closed Dec 25) **$$$**

Palms to Pines Highway. *47-900 S Portola Ave, Palm Desert.* Scenic Hwy 74 goes S and W toward Idyllwild and Hemet (see both).

Special Event

Bob Hope Chrysler Classic. *73000 Fred Waring Dr, Palm Desert (92260). Phone 760/346-8184. www.bhcc. com.* Golf pros and celebrities play at four country clubs at Bermuda Dunes, La Quinta, Palm Desert, and Indian Wells. Mid-Jan. **$$$$**

Limited-Service Hotels

★ ★ **COURTYARD BY MARRIOTT.** *74895 Frank Sinatra Dr, Palm Desert (92211). Phone 760/776-4150; fax 760/776-1816. www.courtyard.com.* 151 rooms, 3 story. Check-in 4 pm, check-out noon. High-speed Internet access. Restaurant, bar. Fitness room. Outdoor pool. **$**

★ **HOLIDAY INN EXPRESS.** *74-675 Hwy 111, Palm Desert (92260). Phone 760/340-4303; fax 760/340-3723. www.sixcontinentshotel.com.* 129 rooms, 3 story. Complimentary full breakfast. Check-in 3 pm. Check-out noon. Fitness room. Outdoor pool, whirlpool. Tennis. **$**

Full-Service Resort

★ ★ ★ **JW MARRIOTT DESERT SPRINGS RESORT AND SPA.** *74855 Country Club Dr, Palm Desert (92260). Phone 760/341-2211; toll-free 800/255-0848; fax 760/341-1872. www.desertspringsresort. com.* The JW Marriott Desert Springs Resort and Spa captures the spirit of the islands. Calypso bands play poolside, and tropical birds chirp melodies at this paradise in the California desert. Set against the majesty of the Santa Rose Mountains, this resort is a true oasis with its world of water. Gondolas greet guests at the lobby level, pools beckon swimmers and sun worshipers, and golfers weave their way through dramatic waterscapes on 36 championship holes. Spacious and comfortable, the guest rooms have a contemporary flavor, while the bathrooms of granite, limestone, and marble are exceedingly luxurious. Activities are plentiful, from tennis and golf to a fitness center and an elaborate spa with salon. Dining is elevated to an activity here, with restaurants spanning the globe from Italy and Japan to the Americas. 884 rooms, 8 story. Check-in 4 pm, check-out noon. High-speed Internet access. Five restaurants, two bars. Fitness room, spa. Outdoor pool, whirlpool. Golf, 36 holes. Tennis. Business center. **$$$**

Restaurants

★ ★ **BIG FISH.** *74-225 Hwy 111, Palm Desert (92260). Phone 760/779-1988; fax 760/779-1031. www. restaurantsofpalmsprings.com.* Seafood. Dinner. Closed holidays. Bar. Business casual attire. Reservations recommended. Valet parking. Outdoor seating. **$$**

★ ★ **CUISTOT.** *72595 El Paseo, Palm Desert (92260). Phone 760/340-1000; fax 760/340-1254.* California, French menu. Lunch, dinner. Closed Mon; also July-Aug. Bar. Business casual attire. Reservations recommended. Valet parking. Outdoor seating. **$$$**

★ ★ ★ **JILLIAN'S.** *74-155 El Paseo, Palm Desert (92260). Phone 760/776-8242; fax 760/776-8247. www. jilliansfinedining.com.* International/Fusion menu. Dinner. Closed Sun; mid-June-early Sept. Bar. Business casual attire. Reservations recommended. Valet parking. Outdoor seating. **$$$**

★ **LE DONNE CUCINA ITALIANA.** *72624 El Paseo, Palm Desert (92260). Phone 760/773-9441; fax 760/779-8664.* Italian menu. Dinner. Closed early July-mid-Sept. Children's menu. Casual attire. Outdoor seating. **$$**

★ ★ ★ **LE PAON.** *45640 Hwy 74, Palm Desert (92260). Phone 760/568-3651; toll-free 800/428-7414; fax 760/568-2394.* Elegant dining; rose garden. Continental, French menu. Dinner. Closed Sun-Wed in summer. Bar. Children's menu. Business casual attire. Reservations recommended. Valet parking. Outdoor seating. **$$$**

★ ★ **LG'S PRIME STEAKHOUSE.** *74-225 Hwy 111, Palm Desert (92260). Phone 760/779-9799; fax 760/779-1979. www.lgsprimesteakhouse.com.* Steak menu. Dinner. Closed holidays. Bar. Business casual attire. Reservations recommended. Valet parking. Outdoor seating. **$$$**

★ ★ **RISTORANTE MAMMA GINA.** *73-705 El Paseo, Palm Desert (92260). Phone 760/568-9898; fax 760/568-6639. www.mammagina.com.* Italian menu. Dinner. Bar. Casual attire. Reservations recommended. Outdoor seating. **$$$**

★ ★ ★ RUTH'S CHRIS STEAK HOUSE.
74-740 Hwy 111, Palm Desert (92260). Phone 760/779-1998; fax 760/773-5490. Consistently considered Southern California's top-rated chop shop, this chain's Palm Desert location features cherry wood paneling, subdued theatrical lighting, and, of course, outstanding cuts of beef sizzling in butter. Steak menu. Dinner. Closed Thanksgiving, Dec 25. Bar. Business casual attire. Reservations recommended. Valet parking. **$$$**

★ ★ TUSCANY.
74855 Country Club Dr, Palm Desert (92260). Phone 760/341-1839. www. desertspringsresort.com. Italian menu. Dinner. Bar. Children's menu. Business casual attire. Valet parking. Outdoor seating. **$$$**

Palm Springs (J-5)

See also Beaumont, Desert Hot Springs, Hemet, Idyllwild, Indio, Palm Desert, Rancho Mirage

Founded 1876
Population 42,807
Elevation 466 ft
Area Code 760
Information Palm Springs Desert Resort Convention and Visitors Bureau, 70-100 Hwy 111, Rancho Mirage, 92270; phone 760/770-9000 or toll-free 800/967-3763
Web Site www.palmspringsusa.com

Discovered in 1774 by a Spanish explorer, this site was dubbed Agua Caliente (hot water). One hundred years later, it was the location of a stagecoach stop and a drowsy, one-store railroad town. Today, after a second hundred years, Palm Springs is known as "America's premier desert resort." Originally the domain of the Cahuilla, the city has been laid out in a checkerboard pattern, with nearly every other square mile still owned by the tribe.

What to See and Do

Indian Canyons. *38-500 S Palm Canyon Dr, Palm Springs (92264). Phone 707/581-3025. www. indian-canyons.com.* The remains of the ancient Cahuilla people include rock art, mortars ground into the bedrock, pictographs, and shelters built atop high cliff walls. Hiking trails throughout the canyons are also home to bighorn sheep and wild ponies. Rangers give interpretive walks. (Daily 8 am-5 pm) **$$**

Knott's Soak City USA. *1500 Gene Autry Trail, Palm Springs (92264). 5 miles S off I-10. Phone 760/325-7873. www.knotts.com.* This 22-acre water park has 13 water slides, inner tube ride, and wave pool. (Late Mar-Labor Day: daily; early Sept-late Oct: weekends; hours vary, call or visit Web site for schedule) **$$$$** Also here is

Uprising Rock Climbing Center. *, Palm Springs. Phone 760/382-1452; toll-free 888/254-6266.* The only outdoor rock-climbing gym in the United States. Offers training and climbing for all ages. Night climbing. **$$$$**

Moorten's Botanical Garden. *1701 S Palm Canyon Dr, Palm Springs (92264). Phone 760/327-6555. www. moplants.com.* Approximately 3,000 varieties of desert plants; nature trails. World's first "cactarium" contains several hundred species of cactus and desert plants from around the world. Guide maps to desert wildflowers. (Mon-Tues, Thurs-Sat 9 am-4:30 pm, Sun 10 am-4 pm; closed holidays) **$$**

Palm Canyon. *6 1/2 miles S on S Palm Canyon Dr, in the Palm Springs Indian Canyons. Phone toll-free 800/790-3398.* Approximately 3,000 native palm trees line a stream bed. Magnificent views from the canyon floor or from points above the canyon. Picnic tables. (Daily 8 am-5 pm) **$$$**

★ **Palm Springs Aerial Tramway.** *1 Tramway Rd, Palm Springs (92262). 2 miles N on Hwy 111, then 4 miles W on Tramway Rd. Phone 760/325-1449. www.pstramway. com.* World's longest double-reversible, single-span aerial tramway. Two 80-passenger cars make 2 1/2-mile trip ascending to 8,516-foot elevation on Mount San Jacinto. Picnicking, camping in summer; cafeteria at summit. (Mon-Fri every half hour from 10 am, Sat-Sun from 8 am) **$$$$**

Palm Springs Air Museum. *745 N Gene Autry Trail, Palm Springs (92262). Phone 760/778-6262. www. air-museum.org.* Vintage, World War II aircraft on display. Also period photographs and video documentaries. (June-Sept: 9 am-3 pm, Oct-May: 10 am-5 pm; closed holidays) **$$**

Palm Springs Desert Museum. *101 Museum Dr, Palm Springs (92262). Phone 760/325-7186. www.psmuseum. org.* Enjoy diverse art collections of world-renowned artists; science exhibitions with interactive elements; educational programs for the whole family; the Annenerg Performing Arts Theater with jazz, classical, dance, and Broadway and off-Broadway performances; the Tour Gallery Cafe and its unique menu, as well as handcrafted treasures at the museum store.(Tues-Wed, Fri-Sun 10 am-5 pm, Thurs noon-8 pm; closed Jan 1, Thanksgiving, Dec 25) Free admission Thurs 4-8 pm. **$$$**

Palm Springs Historical Society on Village Green.
221 S Palm Canyon Dr, Palm Springs (92262). Phone 760/323-8297. www.palmspringshistoricalsociety.org. Consists of two 19th-century houses exhibiting artifacts from early Palm Springs. McCallum Adobe (circa 1885) is the oldest building in the city and houses an extensive collection of photographs, paintings, clothes, tools, books, and Native American ware. The Cornelia White House(circa 1893) was partially constructed of rail ties from the defunct Palmdale Railway and is furnished with authentic antiques. (Mid-Oct-late May, Wed, Sun noon-3 pm; Thurs-Sat 10 am-4 pm) **$**

Tahquitz Creek Golf Resort. *1885 Golf Club Dr, Palm Springs (92264). 3 miles SE on Hwy 111. Phone 760/328-1956; toll-free 877/598-6921. www.tahquitzcreek.com.* The resort consists of two 18-hole courses: the Legend course and the Resort course. There are 87 other courses within a 15-mile radius of the city, making this area the "Winter Golf Capital of the World." (Daily) **$$$$**

Limited-Service Hotels

★ **BALLANTINES HOTEL.** *1420 N Indian Canyon Dr, Palm Springs (92262). Phone 760/320-1178; toll-free 800/485-2808; fax 760/320-5308. www.ballantinesoriginalhotel.com.* This circa-1940s modernist-style hideaway once attracted the celebrated likes of Gloria Swanson and Marilyn Monroe. Today, its well-preserved mid-century accommodations draw romantics and escape-seeking adults. The rooms, done up in individual Old Hollywood themes (including '50s Musicals, Douglas Fairbanks, and Audrey Hepburn), feature private patios, high-end retro furnishings, and kitschy kitchenettes with functional period appliances. A day spa and a massage room are available, and the party-ready pool area is replete with a bar, a fire pit, and a hot tub. 14 rooms. No children allowed. Check-in 3 pm, check-out noon. Outdoor pool, whirlpool. **$$**

★ **BEST WESTERN LAS BRISAS.** *222 S Indian Canyon Dr, Palm Springs (92262). Phone 760/325-4372; toll-free 800/346-5714; fax 760/320-1371. www.bestwestern.com.* 90 rooms, 3 story. Pets accepted; fee. Complimentary full breakfast. Check-in 3 pm, check-

out noon. Wireless Internet access. Outdoor pool, whirlpool. **$**

★ ★ **CASA CODY INN.** *175 S Cahuilla Rd, Palm Springs (92262). Phone 760/320-9346; toll-free 800/231-2639; fax 760/325-8610. www.casacody.com.* Located within walking distance of the Palm Springs Desert Museum and the dynamic Palm Canyon Drive shopping and dining district, this quiet adobe hacienda property—founded in the early 1900s by a cousin of Wild West legend Buffalo Bill Cody—is a romantic retreat comprised of several buildings surrounded by flowering trees and shrubs. Spacious rooms, suites, and cottages feature Samta Fe-style furnishings, refrigerators, private phones, data ports, and private entrances. Many units also have fireplaces, fully equipped kitchens, and microwave ovens. 27 rooms. Pets accepted; fee. Complimentary continental breakfast. Check-in 2 pm, check-out 11 am. Outdoor pool. **$**

★ **COMFORT SUITES.** *69151 E Palm Canyon Dr, Cathedral City (92234). Phone 760/324-5939; fax 760/324-3034. www.choicehotels.com.* 97 rooms, 3 story. Pets accepted, some restrictions; fee. Complimentary continental breakfast. Check-out noon. Outdoor pool, whirlpool. **$**

★ ★ **RAMADA RESORT.** *1800 E Palm Canyon Dr, Palm Springs (92264). Phone 760/323-1711; toll-free 800/245-6907; fax 760/322-1075. www.ramada.com.* Popular with business travelers and vacationing families, this courtyard-style property is conveniently located just 10 minutes from the airport—and within walking and short driving distance of shopping centers, restaurants and nightclubs. Rooms feature contemporary décor and mountain or pool views. In-house dining choices include Leon's Bar & Grill, specializing in seafood, and Tonys Café, offering American fare. 255 rooms, 3 story. Pets accepted, some restrictions; fee. Check-in 3 pm, check-out noon. Two restaurants, bar. Fitness room. Outdoor pool, whirlpool. Tennis. Airport transportation available. **$**

Full-Service Hotels

★ ★ ★ **HILTON PALM SPRINGS RESORT.**
400 E Tahquitz Canyon Way, Palm Springs (92262). Phone 760/320-6868; toll-free 800/522-6900; fax 760/320-2126. www.hiltonpalmsprings.com. A dra-

matic setting at the foot of the steeply rising San Jacinto Mountains is just one of the highlights of this sprawling resort, whose clientele consists primarily of business travelers and vacationing families. The guest rooms feature Italian travertine flooring, contemporary furnishings, and cozy sitting areas. Less than two miles from the airport, the resort is within walking distance of cafes, galleries, boutiques, a casino, and the Palm Springs Desert Museum. 260 rooms, 3 story. Pets accepted; fee. Check-in 3 pm, check-out noon. High-speed Internet access. Two restaurants, bar. Fitness room (fee), spa. Outdoor pool, whirlpool. Business center. **$**

★ ★ ★ **HYATT REGENCY SUITES PALM SPRINGS.** *285 N Palm Canyon Dr, Palm Springs (92262). Phone 760/322-9000; toll-free 800/223-1234; fax 760/322-6009. www.palmsprings.hyatt.com.* 193 rooms, 6 story, all suites. Check-in 3 pm, check-out noon. High-speed Internet access, wireless Internet access. Restaurant, bar. Fitness room. Outdoor pool. Business center. **$$**

★ ★ ★ **MARRIOTT RANCHO LAS PALMAS RESORT.** *41000 Bob Hope Dr, Rancho Mirage (92270). Phone 760/568-2727; toll-free 800/909-6019; fax 760/568-5845. www.rancholaspalmas.com.* 450 rooms, 2 story. Check-in 4 pm, check-out noon. High-speed Internet access. Two restaurants, bar. Fitness room, spa. Three outdoor pools, whirlpool. Tennis. Business center. **$$**

★ ★ ★ **SPA RESORT CASINO.** *100 N Indian Canyon Dr, Palm Springs (92262). Phone 760/325-1461; toll-free 800/854-1279; fax 760/325-5635. www.sparesortcasino.com.* This is the only full-service resort/casino in Palm Springs, so if gambling is your thing, you won't find a better option. But the "Resort" part of Spa Resort Casino shouldn't be overlooked. You'll find a full-service spa, a fitness center (where you can hire a personal trainer if you need someone to help you get moving), and a large palm tree-surrounded pool. The resort offers two Asian restaurants, a New York-style deli, a large buffet-style restaurant, and several bars. Located in downtown Palm Springs, the hotel is only a block from Palm Canyon Drive, where you'll find numerous shopping and dining options. Although the entire resort underwent a renovation in 2003, the rooms are less luxurious than those found in some of the other resorts in the area. The focus here is on gaming and nightlife—making it great for adults and less appealing for kids. 228 rooms, 5 story. Check-in 4 pm, check-out 11 am. Wireless Internet access. Two restaurants, bar. Fitness room, spa. Outdoor pool, whirlpool. Casino. **$**

★ ★ ★ **THE LODGE AT RANCHO MIRAGE.** *68-900 Frank Sinatra Dr, Rancho Mirage (92270). Phone 760/321-8282; toll-free 800/518-6870; fax 760/321-6928. www.rockresorts.com.* The Lodge at Rancho Mirage is a stylish desert retreat. Located only minutes from the world-class shopping of Rancho Mirage and Palm Desert, this serene resort, perched 650 feet above the Coachella Valley, enjoys a spectacular setting. Distant views of the San Jacinto Mountains instantly soothe frayed nerves, and relaxation is the ultimate draw here. The Avanyu Spa is the centerpiece of the resort, and many of its 30 treatments include products indigenous to the desert. The rooms and suites are a sensual blend of Mediterranean-inspired furnishings and neutral colors. Feather beds and Frette linens heighten comfort, and balconies and patios focus attention on the panoramas. Dining at the breezy Café and the clifftop Mirada allows guests to further enjoy the sights, while the mahogany-paneled Lobby Lounge exudes elegance. Adults build their day around tennis, croquet, and relaxation at the pool, and children enjoy the fun-filled activities at Camp Little Bighorn. 240 rooms, 3 story. Pets accepted; fee. Check-in 3 pm, check-out noon. Wireless Internet access. Two restaurants, bar. Fitness room, spa. Outdoor pool, whirlpool. Tennis. Business center. **$$**

★ ★ ★ **VICEROY PALM SPRINGS.** *415 S Belardo Rd, Palm Springs (92262). Phone 760/320-4117; toll-free 800/237-3687; fax 760/323-3303. www.viceroypalmsprings.com.* Built in 1929 and updated to reflect the Hollywood Regency style popular during the city's original glamour era, this centrally located property lures a primarily adult clientele with exquisite landscaping and a decidedly exclusive air. Luxurious rooms, suites, and villas surround several courtyards, fountains, and pools. On-site, the full-service Estrella Spa offers aromatherapy and an array of body treatments in a private setting, while the distinctive gourmet restaurant Citron dishes up California cuisine. Athletic guests can enjoy a state-of-the-art fitness center, expert yoga training and guided hikes, or test their swing on one of the PGA-quality golf courses nearby. 68 rooms, 2 story. Pets accepted, some restrictions. Check-in 3 pm, check-out noon. High-speed Internet access. Restaurant, bar. Fitness room, spa. Outdoor pool, whirlpool. **$$**

★ ★ ★ WYNDHAM PALM SPRINGS HOTEL.
888 Tahquitz Canyon Way, Palm Springs (92262). Phone 760/322-6000; toll-free 800/996-3426; fax 760/322-5351. www.wyndham-palmsprings.com. Just eight blocks from the airport and connected directly to the convention center, this business-oriented yet family-friendly hotel anchors a 40-acre commercial development that lies within a short walk of the Palm Springs Desert Museum and fashionable Palm Canyon Drive. The hotels Spanish-colonial exterior gives way to the more contemporary, newly refurbished décor of the guest rooms, which feature oversized desks, high-speed Internet access and scenic mountain views. Recreational and leisure amenities include a professionally equipped health club, a complete body spa, and a large pool area with adjacent bar and barbecue. 410 rooms, 5 story. Pets accepted; fee. Check-in 4 pm, check out noon. High speed Internet access. Restaurant, bar. Fitness room, spa. Outdoor pool, two whirlpools. Business center. **$$**

Full-Service Resorts

★ ★ ★ DORAL PALM SPRINGS.
67-967 Vista Chino at Landau Blvd, Cathedral City (92234). Phone 760/322-7000; toll-free 888/386-4677; fax 760/322-6817. www.doralpalmsprings.com. On 347 acres; panoramic mountain view. 285 rooms, 4 story. Pets accepted; restrictions, fee. Check-in 4 pm, check-out noon. Restaurant, bar. Fitness room. Outdoor pool, whirlpool. Golf. Tennis. Airport transportation available. **$**

★ ★ ★ LA MANCHA RESORT AND SPA.
400 N Avenida Caballeros, Palm Springs (92263). Phone 760/320-0398; toll-free 800/593-9321; fax 760/320-7155. www.la-mancha.com. Centrally located yet secluded, this Mediterranean-style resort is a getaway for romantics and an oasis of pampered privacy for leisure-seekers. Deluxe villas with up to three bedrooms feature kitchens, living rooms, and one bath for each bedroom. Some larger villas also include fireplaces, wet bars, Jacuzzis, and private pools—plus the optional private use of one of the property's eight tennis courts. Indoor/outdoor dining and an American menu are on tap at the on-site Don Quixote Restaurant and Tapas Bar. The resort's Spa Aldonza offers massage, facial, manicure, and pedicure services.

47 rooms, 2 story. Pets accepted, some restrictions. Check-in 3 pm, check-out 11 am. Restaurant, bar. Spa. Outdoor pool, whirlpool. Tennis. Airport transportation available. **$$**

★ ★ ★ MIRAMONTE RESORT AND SPA.
45-000 Indian Wells Ln, Indian Wells (92210). Phone 760/341-2200; fax 760/568-541. Miramonte Resort brings the romance and charm of Tuscany to the California desert. Located just 15 minutes from Palm Springs, this stylish resort is nestled at the base of the Santa Rosa Mountains in the exclusive resort community of Indian Wells. A quiet elegance and gentle pace pervade this resort, defined by its intimate courtyards and manicured rose gardens. Room service arrives via bicycle here, adding to the unique charm. Many choose to spend their afternoons gently swaying in one of the many hammocks found throughout the property, while others opt to golf on one of the three surrounding courses, play tennis at the nearby Indian Wells Tennis Garden, or shop at El Paseo, just minutes away. 222 rooms, 3 story. Check-in 4 pm, check-out noon. Restaurant. Fitness room, spa. Outdoor pool, whirlpool. Tennis. Business center. **$$$**

★ ★ ★ THE WESTIN MISSION HILLS RESORT.
71333 Dinah Shore Dr, Rancho Mirage (92270). Phone 760/328-5955; toll-free 888/625-5144; fax 760/770-2199. www.westin.com/missionhills. 512 rooms, 2 story. Pets accepted, some restrictions. Check-in 4 pm, check-out noon. High-speed Internet access. Two restaurants, bar. Fitness room, spa. Outdoor pool, whirlpool. Business center. **$$$**

Full-Service Inns

★ ★ ★ INGLESIDE INN.
200 W Ramon Rd, Palm Springs (92264). Phone 760/325-0046; toll-free 800/772-6655; fax 760/325-0710. www.inglesideinn. com. Fashioned from an early-1900s estate, this romantic landmark and longtime celebrity magnet—everyone from Rita Hayworth to Arnold Schwarzenegger has lodged here—is tucked within a residential neighborhood, yet located just one block from the city's heart. Luxurious suites and villas, which combine period décor with modern amenities, feature steam baths, whirlpool tubs, fireplaces, refrigerators, and private terraces. On-site dining and entertainment are provided by the award-winning Melvyn's Restaurant, specializing in continental cuisine, and the Casablanca

Room, an intimate piano bar. Mountain hiking is available just outside the door and a short drive away in the majestic Indian Canyons. 30 rooms. Check-in 2 pm, check-out noon. Restaurant, bar. Outdoor pool, whirlpool. **$$**

★ ★ ★ **THE VILLA ROYALE INN.** *1620 Indian Trail, Palm Springs (92264). Phone 760/327-2314; toll-free 800/245-2314; fax 760/327-2314. www.villaroyale. com.* Set dramatically against a panoramic mountain backdrop just a mile from downtown, this adult-oriented property combines the pampered privacy of a bed-and-breakfast with the amenities of a full-service hotel to create an ideal weekend or romantic getaway. Individually appointed Mediterranean-style suites and villas—nestled around tranquil, lushly landscaped courtyards and two heated pools—are decorated with European antiques and feature down duvets, luxuriant robes, and herbal toiletries. Larger accommodations also have fireplaces, open-beam ceilings, kitchens, and private patios. The intimate, elaborately themed Europa restaurant (see) and bar serves award-winning continental cuisine on the premises—both indoors and under the stars. 30 rooms. Complimentary full breakfast. Check-in 3 pm, check-out noon. Restaurant, bar. Two outdoor pools, whirlpool. **$$**

★ ★ ★ **THE WILLOWS HISTORIC PALM SPRINGS INN.** *412 W Tahquitz Canyon Way, Palm Springs (92262). Phone 760/320-0771; fax 760/320-0780. www.thewillowspalmsprings.com.* If only the walls could talk. This legendary inn has hosted Albert Einstein, Marion Davies, and Clark Gable and Carole Lombard, who spent part of their honeymoon here. This historic Mediterranean villa in the heart of Old Palm Springs is a delightful place firmly rooted in history, yet thoroughly modern. Seclusion and privacy are guaranteed here, with only eight lovely guest rooms. At once historic and fashion-forward, the rooms are seductive in spirit, with luscious fabrics and sleigh beds. Each room is unique, yet all share a flair for romance. Claw-foot bathtubs add old-fashioned charm in some rooms, while a giant boulder takes center stage in the Rock Room's bathroom. Guests choosing to leave their gracious shelters enjoy gourmet cuisine, lounge poolside, or marvel at the sweeping views of the Coachella Valley and Little San Bernardino Mountains from the hillside gardens. 8 rooms, 2 story. Check-in 4-7 pm, check-out noon. Outdoor pool. **$$$**

Restaurants

★ ★ **BLUE COYOTE BAR & GRILL.** *445 N Palm Canyon Dr, Palm Springs (92262). Phone 760/327-1196; fax 760/325-3876.* Southwestern menu. Lunch, dinner. Closed Aug. Bar. Casual attire. Reservations recommended. Outdoor seating. **$$**

★ ★ **CEDAR CREEK INN.** *1555 S Palm Canyon Dr, Palm Springs (92264). Phone 760/325-7300; fax 760/325-2592. www.cedarcreekinn.com.* Continental menu. Breakfast, lunch, dinner, brunch. Bar. Children's menu. Casual attire. Reservations recommended. Outdoor seating. **$$**

★ ★ ★ **EUROPA.** *1620 Indian Trail, Palm Springs (92264). Phone 760/327-2314. www.villaroyale.com.* Housed in the Villa Royale Inn (see), this restaurant provides a romantic setting in which to enjoy continental dishes inspired by the flavors of France, Italy, Spain, and Greece. Dine poolside by the fountains or fireside in the cozy dining room. Continental menu. Dinner. Closed Mon. Bar. Business casual attire. Reservations recommended. Outdoor seating. **$$$**

★ **GREAT WALL.** *362 S Palm Canyon Dr, Palm Springs (92262). Phone 760/322-2209.* Chinese menu. Lunch, dinner. Casual attire. **$$**

★ ★ **KAISER GRILL.** *233 E Palm Canyon Dr, Palm Springs (92264). Phone 760/327-1551.* California, Mediterranean menu. Lunch, dinner. Bar. Children's menu. Casual attire. Reservations recommended. Outdoor seating. **$$**

★ ★ **LAS CASUELAS TERRAZA.** *222 S Palm Canyon Dr, Palm Springs (92262). Phone 760/325-2794; fax 760/327-4174.* Mexican menu. Lunch, dinner. Bar. Children's menu. Casual attire. Reservations recommended. Outdoor seating. **$$**

★ ★ ★ **LE VALLAURIS.** *385 W Tahquitz Canyon Way, Palm Springs (92262). Phone 760/325-5059; fax 760/325-7602. www.levallauris.com.* French menu. Lunch, dinner. Closed July-Aug. Bar. Business casual attire. Reservations recommended. Valet parking. Outdoor seating. **$$$**

★ ★ **MELVYN'S.** *200 W Ramon Rd, Palm Springs (92264). Phone 760/325-2323; toll-free 800/772-6655; fax 760/325-0710. www.inglesideinn.com.* Historic building; two main dining areas. Continental menu. Lunch, dinner. Bar. Business casual attire. Reservations recommended. Valet parking. Outdoor seating. **$$$**

★ ★ **PALMIE.** *44491 Town Center Way, Palm Springs (92260). Phone 760/341-3200.* French menu. Dinner. Closed Sun. Bar. Business casual attire. Reservations recommended. Valet parking. **$$**

★ **ROCK GARDEN CAFE.** *777 S Palm Canyon Dr, Palm Springs (92264). Phone 760/327-8840.* American menu. Breakfast, lunch, dinner. Closed holidays. Bar. Children's menu. Casual attire. Outdoor seating. **$**

★ ★ ★ **ST. JAMES AT THE VINEYARD.** *265 S Palm Canyon Dr, Palm Springs (92262). Phone 760/320-8041; fax 760/416-5446. palmsprings.com/ dine/stjames.* International menu. Dinner. Bar. Business casual attire. Outdoor seating. **$$$**

Palm Springs Area (J-5)

Web Site www.palm-springs.org

What was once one of the country's favorite vacation towns has become one of America's most popular resort regions. Tourism experienced a remarkable boom in the years since the first Hollywood celebrities built their winter houses here. The beautiful scenery and ideal weather that attracted those first vacationers are still present, but as the area's popularity has increased, they have been accompanied by an ever-growing number of hotels, inns, resorts, shopping malls, golf courses, recreation sites, and performing arts facilities. No longer is the area solely a retreat for the famous and wealthy. Although there are more luxurious restaurants, resorts, and stores than ever before, it is now also quite easy to take full advantage of the area's attractions while on a restricted budget. The more than 3 million people who visit each year come mostly to relax, soak up the sun, and enjoy the climate. It is also possible to enjoy everything from cross-country skiing atop Mount San Jacinto to camping among the tall cactus at Joshua Tree National Park (see). The following towns, all within a short distance of the city of Palm Springs, provide this great variety of recreation: Desert Hot Springs, Idyllwild, Indio, Palm Desert, and Palm Springs (see all).

Palmdale (H-4)

See also Lancaster

Population 116,670
Elevation 2,659 ft
Area Code 661
Zip 93550

Information Chamber of Commerce, 38260 10th St E; phone 661/273-3232
Web Site www.cityofpalmdale.org

The Angeles National Forest is west and south of town (see PASADENA).

Limited-Service Hotel

★ ★ **RAMADA INN.** *300 W Palmdale Blvd, Palmdale (93551). Phone 661/273-1200; toll-free 800/272-6232; fax 661/947-9593. www.ramada.com.* 131 rooms, 4 story. Pets accepted; fee. Complimentary continental breakfast. Check-in 3 pm, check-out noon. Restaurant. Fitness room. Outdoor pool, whirlpool. **$**

Pasadena (J-4)

See also Arcadia, Claremont, Glendale, Pomona, San Marino

Founded 1874
Population 133,936
Elevation 865 ft
Area Code 626
Information Convention & Visitors Bureau, 171 S Los Robles, 91101; phone 626/795-9311
Web Site www.pasadenacal.com

Home of the world-famous Tournament of Roses, Pasadena was first chosen as a health refuge for weary Midwesterners and, later, as a winter retreat for Eastern millionaires. Today, it is a cultural center and scientific and industrial frontier because of its many research, development, and engineering industries, including NASA's Jet Propulsion Laboratory. The name Pasadena comes from the Ojibwa language; it means "Crown of the Valley."

What to See and Do

Angeles National Forest. *701 N Santa Anita Ave, Arcadia (91006). N, E, and S via Hwys 210, 2, 118, and 39 and I-5. Phone 626/574-5200. www.fs.fed.us/r5/angeles.* Since 1892, the Angeles National Forest has been "Los Angeles's backyard playground." More than 650,000 acres of beautiful chaparral and pine-covered terrain, ranging from 1,200 to 10,064 feet, provide endless opportunities for every imaginable outdoor activity. Enjoy fishing and jet-skiing on Pyramid Lake, more than 500 miles of hiking trails, skiing, horseback riding, hunting, and more. Plus, spending the night is convenient with more than 110 camping and picnicking sites in the area. This is truly a nature lover's paradise. **$** Also here is

Crystal Lake Recreation Area. *0 N San Gabriel Canyon Rd, Pasadena.* Fishing; nature and hiking trails; picnicking, store; tent and trailer camping (fee). Amphitheater programs (summer). Visitor center has maps and interpretive materials (Sat-Sun). Long trailers (over 22 feet) and recreational vehicles not recommended (steep roads).

Arroyo Seco Trail. *Ventura St and Windsor Ave, Altadena (91001). Take the 210 Frwy to the Windsor Ave exit. Drive about 1 mile N on Windsor Ave to the intersection of Ventura St. Park in the paved lot on the S side of the intersection. Take the paved road to the right, leading N into the canyon. Go around the locked gate, and you're on the trail.* This 7.5-mile trail leads through a thick forest along the Arroyo Seco River in the foothills near Pasadena. The first part of the trail is a paved fire road, with easy biking for less-experienced riders. As it winds farther north, however, the trail narrows and you'll cross the river—expect to carry your bike across the rocky riverbed. Continue into the Angeles National Forest for a longer ride.

Brookside Golf Course. *1133 N Rosemont Ave, Pasadena (91103). Phone 626/796-8151.* In the shadow of football's Rose Bowl, Brookside has two 18-hole courses: the Koiner and the Nay. The Koiner course is the better but more difficult of the two. It plays considerably longer and features vistas not to be missed. The Rose Bowl itself sits beyond hole 16, which is a medium-length dogleg par-four, and hole 8 offers a challenge off the tee with a par-three over a large water hazard. A little expensive for the golf itself, but the ambience makes up the difference. **$$$$**

Descanso Gardens. *1418 Descanso Dr, La Caada (91011). Phone 818/949-4200. www.descansogardens. org.* For a natural high, wander through this lush attraction, often described as a 165-acre oasis. Many types of beautiful plants thrive here, but Descanso is especially known for growing the most camellias outdoors, more than 100,000. And it gets potfuls of praise for its radiant roses. Significant international roses bloom brightly in the Rose History Garden, and its All-America Rose Selections Garden showcases every variety that has won this coveted designation. In addition, the gardens are alive with music in summer, thanks to a performing arts program that hits all the

right notes. (Daily 9 am-5 pm; tram tours Tues-Fri 1 pm, 2 pm, 3 pm, Sat-Sun 11 am, 1 pm, 2 pm, 3 pm; closed Dec 25) **$$**

Gamble House. *4 Westmoreland Pl, Pasadena (91103). Phone 626/793-3334. www.gamblehouse.org.* (1908) Exemplary of the mature California bungalow designs of American architects Greene and Greene; interiors of teakwood, mahogany, maple, and cedar; gardens. One-hour guided tour. (Thurs-Sun noon-3 pm; closed holidays) **$$**

Kidspace Children's Museum. *480 N Arroyo Blvd, Pasadena (91103). Phone 626/449-9144. www.kidspacemuseum. org.* The museum features tons of indoor and outdoor exhibits. Kids can climb aboard raindrops as they travel through the precipitation cycle, or they can dig up fossils and dinosaur eggs. (Daily 9:30 am-5 pm) **$$**

Norton Simon Museum of Art. *411 W Colorado Blvd, Pasadena (91105). Phone 626/449-6840; fax 626/796-4978. www.nortonsimon.org.* Many art lovers will tell you this stellar museum in Pasadena outclasses the better-known, more-hyped Getty in Los Angeles. In this 85,000-square-foot facility, you'll be awed by one of the world's finest private collections of European, American, and Asian art spanning more than 2,000 years. Paintings, sculptures, works on paper, photography—it has it all. Of particular note are rare etchings by Rembrandt and Goya, and a collection of Picasso graphics. Much of what you see belonged to the museum's wealthy namesake, who died in 1993. A wildly successful entrepreneur, his companys holdings included Avis Car Rental, Hunt-Wesson Foods, and McCall's Publishing. (Mon, Wed-Thurs noon-6 pm, Fri to 9 pm, Sat-Sun to 6 pm; closed Jan 1, Thanksgiving, Dec 25) **$$**

Pacific Asia Museum. *46 N Los Robles Ave, Pasadena (91101). Phone 626/449-2742; fax 626/449-2754. www. pacificasiamuseum.org.* Changing exhibits of traditional and contemporary Asian and Pacific Basin art; Chinese Imperial Palace-style building and Chinese courtyard garden; research library; bookstore. Docent tours available. (Wed-Thurs, Sat-Sun 10 am-5 pm) **$$**

Pasadena Museum of History. *470 W Walnut St, Pasadena (91103). Phone 626/577-1660. www.pasadenahistory.org.* Housed in the 18-room Fenyes Estate (1905); contains original furnishings, antiques, paintings, and accessories. The mansion gives a glimpse of the elegant lifestyle that existed on Orange Grove Boulevard at the turn of the century. Mansion, Finnish Folk Art Museum, and library archives that have extensive photo collections and San Gabriel Valley historic collections. Tours. (Wed-Sun noon-5 pm; closed holidays) **$**

Rose Bowl. *1001 Rose Bowl Dr, Pasadena (91103). Rosemont Ave off Arroyo Blvd between I-210 and Hwy 134. Phone 626/577-3100; fax 626/405-0992. www.rosebowlstadium.com.* Although no longer the home of the annual bowl game between the winners of the Pac-10 and the Big Ten conferences, the Rose Bowl still hosts Bowl Championship Series games every year and the national championship game every fourth year. During the regular season, UCLA's Bruins football team calls the venue home. Don't miss the annual New Year's Day Tournament of Roses Parade in Pasadena that runs concurrently with the football festivities. Millions of visitors turn out each year to watch floats made entirely of flowers and high school bands from around the country parade through the streets of Pasadena.

Special Event

Tournament of Roses. *391 S Orange Grove Blvd, Pasadena (91184). Phone 626/449-4100; fax 626/449-9066. www.tournamentofroses.com.* Gorgeous floral floats. High-stepping marching bands. Strikingly beautiful equestrian units. No wonder this colorful spectacle staged annually on New Year's Day for more than 100 years ranks as one of the worlds finest parades. But, ironically, the genteelness of this flower-show-on-wheels stands in stark contrast to the follow-up event, the Rose Bowl gridiron duel. The floral procession lasts for two splendid hours and covers a 5 1/2-mile route. Before the big day, for $5, the curious can view some of the wondrous floats while they're still being decorated petal by petal, leaf by leaf. After the parade, you can get an up-close look at all of the natural beauties in the Showcase of Floats, which continues through January 2. Tickets for the aprs event cost just $6.

Full-Service Hotels

★ ★ ★ **HILTON PASADENA.** *168 S Los Robles Ave, Pasadena (91101). Phone 626/577-1000; toll-free 800/445-8667; fax 626/584-3148. www.hilton.com.* The polished-marble lobby of this hotel welcomes dignitaries and professional athletes as well as vacationers. The Pasadena Convention Center and Old Town Pasadena—with its hundreds of dining, shopping, and entertainment options—are steps away. Spacious guest rooms are equipped with dataports, high-speed Internet access, and comfortable ergonomic chairs, and the hotel's self service business center is open

24 hours. Also on-site are Trevo's Restaurant, which serves up considerable atmospheric charm along with California cuisine, and the Sports Edition, a lively bar with a pool table, and multiple video screens. 296 rooms, 14 story. Pets accepted; restrictions, fee. Check-in 3 pm, check-out noon. High-speed Internet access, wireless Internet access. Restaurant, bar. Fitness room. Outdoor pool, whirlpool. Business center. **$$**

★ ★ ★ **SHERATON PASADENA HOTEL.** *303 E Cordova St, Pasadena (91101). Phone 626/449-4000; toll-free 800/457-7940; fax 626/584-1390. www.sheratonpasadena.com.* Customary Sheraton comfort and efficiency combined with walking-distance proximity to many of the city's attractions make this hotel ideal for business and leisure travelers. In addition to plush-top mattresses and large desks, guest rooms feature two-line phones, dataports, voice mail, and complimentary newspapers. 317 rooms, 5 story. Check-in 3 pm, check-out noon. Restaurant, bar. Fitness room. Outdoor pool. Tennis. Business center. **$$**

★ ★ ★ **WESTIN PASADENA.** *191 N Los Robles Ave, Pasadena (91101). Phone 626/792-2727; fax 626/792-3755. www.westin.com/pasadena.* This beautifully appointed hotel in the heart of downtown appeals to both business travelers and families. The cozy Oaks Restaurant and more adult-oriented 191 North Bar and Grill are two of three on-site dining options, while the restaurants and attractions of historic Old Town Pasadena are a short walk away. An in-house kid's club supplies coloring books, bath toys, and a phone line dedicated to bedtime stories. Office rooms come with fax and printer, and all accommodations feature signature Heavenly Beds with pillow-top mattresses. Services include a concierge and a business center. 350 rooms, 12 story. Check-in 3 pm, check-out noon. Two restaurants, bar. Fitness room. Outdoor pool, whirlpool. Airport transportation available. **$$**

Full-Service Resort

★ ★ ★ ★ **THE RITZ-CARLTON, HUNTINGTON HOTEL & SPA.** *1401 S Oak Knoll Ave, Pasadena (91106). Phone 626/568-3900; fax 626/568-3700. www.ritzcarlton.com.* The Ritz-Carlton, Huntington Hotel & Spa has been painting a rosy picture for lucky guests since 1907. This historic hotel, acquired by Ritz-Carlton in 1991, is nestled at the foothills of the San Gabriel Mountains on 23 beautiful acres. Its relaxed, rural setting defies its convenient location in Pasadena, near Los Angeles. Oriental carpets, crystal chandeliers, and antique furniture comprise the resolutely classic interiors. The guest rooms reflect the great tradition of this hotel while incorporating modern necessities. Dining at the Terrace Restaurant is a treat, from its alfresco setting with a view of the Picture Bridge to its appetizing dishes. The Grill specializes in seafood and meats in a casual environment, while the lounge and pool bar entertain day and night. From refreshing spa treatments and bike rentals to tennis lessons and tee times at nearby golf courses, this resort has it covered. 392 rooms, 8 story. Pets accepted, some restrictions; fee. Check-in 3 pm, check-out noon. Two restaurants, two bars. Fitness room, spa. Outdoor pool, whirlpool. Tennis. Business center. **$$$$**

Specialty Lodging

ARTISTS' INN AND COTTAGE. *1038 Magnolia St, South Pasadena (91030). Phone 626/799-5668; toll-free 888/799-5668; fax 626/799-3678. www.artistsinns.com.* 1890s Victorian style; antiques. 10 rooms, 2 story. Children over 9 years only. Complimentary full breakfast. Check-in 4-6 pm, check-out 11 am. **$$**

Restaurants

★ **BECKHAM GRILL.** *77 W Walnut St, Pasadena (91103). Phone 626/796-3399; fax 626/796-7875. www.beckhamgrill.com.* You can't miss this English pub: just look for the red phone booth and the black London taxicab out front. In the Crown Pub, guests can sit by the fire, play a game of backgammon or darts, and enjoy a pint or two. The restaurant serves up a meat-focused menu, with classic fish and chips available for lunch. At dinner, try the roast prime rib of beef or pork—with a side of Yorkshire pudding, of course. American, steak menu. Lunch, dinner. Closed holidays. Bar. Casual attire. Reservations recommended. Valet parking. Outdoor seating. **$$$**

★ ★ ★ **BISTRO 45.** *45 S Mentor Ave, Pasadena (91106). Phone 626/795-2478; fax 626/792-2676. www.bistro45.com.* Consistently ranked among the top dining experiences in greater Los Angeles, Bistro 45 maintains a low profile in upscale Pasadena. And that suits its generally well-heeled customers, who find the usually hushed, always high-class atmosphere and generously spaced tables perfect for sealing business deals or stoking romance—even if such amenities come

at a premium. Decorated in shades of yellow, with bamboo accents and twinkling lights, the dining areas maintain an intimate ambience despite their event-friendly capacity (200 total). The French-influenced menu, focused on fresh ingredients, is an impressive scroll of more than a dozen appetizers and nearly 20 entrées. Notable specialties include a luscious lobster bisque, roasted prime rib au jus with a mousseline of horseradish and potatoes, and grilled salmon drizzled with sun-dried tomato vinaigrette—all presented with refined service and a wine list that should humble the most discerning connoisseur. California, French menu. Lunch, dinner. Closed Mon; holidays. Bar. Casual attire. Reservations recommended. Valet parking. Outdoor seating. **$$$**

★ ★ **CAFE SANTORINI.** *64 W Union St, Pasadena (91103). Phone 626/564-4200; fax 626/564-4227. www.cafesantorini.com.* Café Santorini is a Mediterranean oasis in the midst of popular Old Town Pasadena—and if you're unfamiliar with its location, you may accidentally overlook its alfresco charms (the intersection is Delancey). The art-filled, loft-style dining space and romantic, brick-walled patio elevate diners well above the street bustle while providing a view of the action. But the more immediate attractions are superior martinis, a reasonably priced wine list, and a menu chockablock with choice Italian, Greek, and multiethnic dishes like souvlaki, red-curry paella, and oven-roasted chicken marinated in Dijon mustard and rosemary. A lively downstairs lounge offers dancing and entertainment. Mediterranean menu. Lunch, dinner. Closed holidays. Bar. Casual attire. Reservations recommended. Valet parking. Outdoor seating. **$$$**

★ **CROCODILE CAFE.** *140 S Lake Ave, Pasadena (91101). Phone 626/449-9900; fax 626/449-6969. www.crocodilecafe.com.* Fast, friendly service and a huge menu are hallmarks of Los Angeles's Crocodile mini-chain (another nearby location is at 626 N Central Ave in Glendale). From the three-section pizza—incorporating barbecued chicken, sausage, and pepperoni—to tortilla soup and grilled salmon in guajillo chile pepper sauce, it's a bonus that virtually all of the fare is prepared with flair. Add trendy décor, and you've got a reliably fun, relaxing family food spot. California menu. Lunch, dinner. Closed Thanksgiving, Dec 25. Bar. Children's menu. Casual attire. Outdoor seating. **$$**

★ ★ ★ **THE DINING ROOM.** *1401 S Oak Knoll Ave, Pasadena (91106). Phone 626/568-3900; fax 626/568-3700. www.ritzcarlton.com.* Dine on perfectly prepared grilled meats and seafood at this clubby dining room located within the excellent Ritz-Carlton, Huntington Hotel & Spa (see). The service is top-notch, and the waitstaff and kitchen will gladly accommodate any special request. A perfect spot for entertaining clients. Mediterranean menu. Dinner. Closed Sun-Mon. Bar. Jacket required. Reservations recommended. Valet parking. Outdoor seating. **$$$$**

★ ★ **MAISON AKIRA.** *713 E Green St, Pasadena (91101). Phone 626/796-9501; fax 626/796-0061. www. maisonakira.com.* Per its moniker, French-Japanese fusion is the featured cuisine here, and chef Akira Hirose—late of hot eateries like Citrus and L'Orangerie—has devised a winning mix. Foodies and sophisticated fun-seekers flock to this red-draped, chandelier-lit collection of intimate dining rooms, prepping for a show at the nearby Pasadena Playhouse or a night of Old Town people-watching with one of Hirose's impeccably presented specialties. Best known is the Chilean sea bass, marinated in miso and grilled to perfection; pan-fried venison wrapped in bacon and ladled with red currant-peppercorn sauce is another hit. Several waiters dote on each table, and they will patiently explain the la carte and prixe fixe options (available with or without wine). French, Japanese menu. Lunch, dinner, Sun brunch. Closed Mon. Bar. Business casual attire. Reservations recommended. Outdoor seating. **$$$**

★ ★ **MI PIACE.** *25 E Colorado Blvd, Pasadena (91105). Phone 626/795-3131; fax 626/795-9698. www. mipiace.com.* This Italian restaurant and bakery, whose name means, "I like it," is the place to see and be seen in Old Town Pasadena. From the kitchen come generous portions of standard Italian fare, along with some more interesting twists, like pumpkin ravioli in brown butter with sage and Parmesan. Italian menu. Breakfast, lunch, dinner. Closed holidays. Bar. Children's menu. Casual attire. Valet parking. Outdoor seating. **$$**

★ ★ **THE RAYMOND RESTAURANT.** *1250 S Fair Oaks Ave, Pasadena (91105). Phone 626/441-3136; fax 626/441-4770. www.theraymond.com.* This turn-of-the-20th-century caretakers cottage on the grounds of the historic Raymond Hotel is set amid lavish gardens, from which the kitchen harvests herbs and seasonal fruits. Three shaded patios enable diners to enjoy the carefully tended flora, and bouquets of flowers grace the white linen-topped tables inside. The kitchen focuses on classic cooking methods and straightforward presentations of dishes like boneless pork chops and grilled sea bass. Seasonal prix fixe dinner menus are available, and

a quaint afternoon tea is served daily. American menu. Lunch, dinner, brunch. Closed Mon; Jan 1, July 4, Dec 25. Bar. Casual attire. Outdoor seating. **$$$**

★ **SALADANG SONG.** *383 S Fair Oaks Ave, Pasadena (91105). Phone 626/793-5200; fax 626/793-2225.* Set in a former warehouse within walking distance of Old Pasadena, Saladang Song is a great option for large groups, with ample outdoor seating and reasonable prices. Some argue that the Thai cuisine served here is less than authentic, but that doesn't stop the crowds from coming, so be prepared for a wait. Thai menu. Breakfast, lunch, dinner. Closed holidays. Casual attire. Outdoor seating. **$**

★ ★ **SHIRO.** *1505 Mission St, South Pasadena (91030). Phone 626/799-4774; fax 626/799-9560. www. restaurantshiro.com.* An imaginative fusion of French and Asian culinary influences makes a colorful splash in this virtually ambience-free dining space. Shiro's palate-pleasing pièce de résistance—sizzling catfish stuffed with ginger, fried whole, and then garnished with cilantro and steeped in ponzu sauce—easily distracts customers from the lacking décor; its the only constant on a menu that rotates chicken, duck, and lamb entrées. Pan-Asian menu. Dinner. Closed Mon-Tues; holidays; also Sept. **$$**

★ ★ **TWIN PALMS.** *101 W Green St, Pasadena (91105). Phone 626/577-2567; fax 626/577-1306. www. twin-palms.com.* By day, canvas sails form a ceiling over the space; at night, the sails are removed to reveal the stars and allow guests to dine in the open air. The kitchen focuses on light and flavorful preparations of locally produced ingredients, with pizzas, rotisserie meats, and seafood selections dominating the menu. Live jazz and other types of music create a festive atmosphere. California menu. Lunch, dinner, Sun brunch. Closed Dec 25. Bar. Children's menu. Business casual attire. Reservations recommended. Outdoor seating. **$$**

★ **VILLA SOMBRERO.** *6101 York Blvd, Los Angeles (90042). Phone 323/256-9014.* Located in the Highland Park neighborhood northeast of Downtown, this traditional Mexican eatery is a favorite of locals and foodies who love settling into its high-backed red banquettes and absorbing the fiesta-style atmosphere. Massive margaritas and delectable carnitas have been mainstays here for three decades, but the traveling guacamole cart—a waiter tosses chopped tomatoes, avocado, and other fresh ingredients into a molcajete and grinds them into a tasty condiment before your eyes—is one of the best tableside shows around. The portions are huge, the prices reasonable. Mexican menu. Lunch, dinner. Bar. Casual attire. **$**

★ ★ **XIOMARA.** *69 N Raymond Ave, Pasadena (91103). Phone 626/796-2520; fax 626/796-2750. www.xiomararestaurant.com.* The Pasadena outpost of Xiomara glitters with modish white walls and black leather seating. A second location, at 6101 Melrose Avenue in Hollywood, is an airy two-story space reminiscent of a Spanish hacienda, with tile floors, wrought-iron railings, arched windows, and seductive candlelight. At both locations, the bar specializes in mojitos with sugar canes freshly juiced from a nifty machine. The sweet, cool drinks pair well with the bold menu choices, like steamed mussels in orange juice, spicy swordfish with fried plantains and yucca, and Nicaraguan skirt steak with blue cheese mashed potatoes. Latin American menu. Lunch, dinner. Closed Easter. Bar. Casual attire. Reservations recommended. Valet parking. Outdoor seating. **$$**

★ ★ **YUJEAN KANG'S.** *67 N Raymond Ave, Pasadena (91103). Phone 626/585-0855; fax 626/565-0856.* This isn't a General Tso's chicken kind of Chinese restaurant. Although the kitchen demonstrates its traditional Cantonese and Mandarin roots, the dishes served here are much more international in nature, showing French, Thai, and other influences. Menu options include surprising ingredients like Louisiana prawns, as well as creatively named dishes like "Ants on a Tree" (noodles dotted with black sesame seeds). There's a second location in West Hollywood (8826 Melrose Ave, phone 310/288-0806). Chinese menu. Lunch, dinner. Closed holidays. Casual attire. Reservations recommended. **$$**

Paso Robles (G-2)

See also Atascadero, Morro Bay, San Simeon

Population 18,600
Elevation 721 ft
Area Code 805
Zip 93446
Information Chamber of Commerce, 1225 Park St; phone 805/238-0506 or toll-free 800/406-4040
Web Site www.pasorobleschamber.com

Franciscan Fathers named this city for the great oak trees in the area at the southern end of the fertile Salinas River Valley. Lying between mountains on the west and barley and grape fields on the east, Paso Robles is also noted for its almond tree orchards.

What to See and Do

Lake Nacimiento Resort. *10625 Nacimiento Lake Dr, Bradley (93426). 17 miles NW on Lake Nacimiento Dr (G14), off Hwy 101. Phone 805/238-3256; toll-free 800/323-3839. www.nacimientoresort.com.* Swimming, water-skiing, fishing, boating (dock, landing, dry storage, rentals), marina (all year, daily); picnicking, lodge, cafe, general store, camping (fee). Park (daily). **$$$$**

Lake San Antonio Recreation Area. *2610 San Antonio Rd, Bradley (93426). 28 miles NW off Hwy 101, between Nacimiento and Lockwood on Interlake Rd. Phone 805/472-2311. www.lakesanantonio.net.* Swimming, water-skiing, fishing, boating (marina, launching, rentals); picnicking, snack bar; grocery, laundry; camping (fee), trailer facilities (off-season rates mid-Sept–mid-May). Pets on leash only; fee. Fee for activities. (Daily) **$$**

Wineries. For a brochure describing many of the 35 wineries in the Paso Robles appellation, tours, and tasting rooms, contact the Chamber of Commerce.

Special Events

California Mid-State Fair. *2198 Riverside Ave, Paso Robles (93447). Phone 805/239-0655; fax 805/238-5308. www.midstatefair.com.* Rodeo, horse show, amusements, entertainment. Late July–early Aug.

Wine Festival. *Phone 805/239-8463; fax 805/237-6439. www.pasowine.com.* Wine tasting, winemaker dinner concerts, and open houses. Third Sat in May.

Limited-Service Hotels

★ **ADELAIDE INN.** *1215 Ysabel Ave, Paso Robles (93446). Phone 805/238-2770; toll-free 800/549-7276; fax 805/238-3497. www.adelaideinn.com.* 67 rooms, 2 story. Check-out noon. Outdoor pool, whirlpool. Airport transportation available. **$**

★ ★ **BEST WESTERN BLACK OAK MOTOR LODGE.** *1135 24th St, Paso Robles (93446). Phone 805/238-4740; toll-free 800/780-7234; fax 805/238-0726. www.bestwestern.com.* 110 rooms, 2 story. Check-out noon. Restaurant. Outdoor pool, children's pool, whirlpool. Airport transportation available. Business center. **$**

Restaurant

★ **F. MCCLINTOCK'S SALOON.** *1234 Park St, Paso Robles (93446). Phone 805/238-2233; fax 805/238-2912. www.mclintocks.com.* Steak menu. Lunch, dinner. Closed Jan 1, Thanksgiving, Dec 24- 25, Dec 31. Bar. Children's menu. **$$**

Pauma Valley

Web Site www.paumavalley.net

What to See and Do

Palomar Plunge. *Mount Palomar is approximately two hours from San Diego. Take I-15 to State Hwy 76 E and follow for 25 miles. Turn left on County Rd S-6. Phone 760/742-2294; toll-free 800/985-4427.* For astronomy buffs, the Palomar Observatory is a can't-miss destination. But if you hop on a bike for the Palomar Plunge, you won't need the scientists to explain gravity. The plunge is a winding 16-mile descent down a 5,000-foot vertical drop. The company supplies the guides, a bike, equipment, and a support van. All skill levels are welcome, and you don't even have to pedal. Lunch is offered afterward. (Daily) **$$$$**

Pebble Beach (G-7)

See also Atascadero, Carmel, Monterey, Pacific Grove

Population 5,000
Elevation 0-37 ft
Area Code 831
Zip 93953
Web Site www.pebblebeach.com

Pebble Beach is noted for its scenic beauty, the palatial houses of its residents, and its golf courses, where the annual National Pro-Amateur Golf Championship and other prestigous tournatments are held.

What to See and Do

Pebble Beach Golf Links. *1700 Seventeen Mile Dr, Pebble Beach (93953). Phone 831/625-8518; fax 831/622-8795. www.pebblebeach.com.* You can't talk about California golf without mentioning Pebble Beach. Although it's quite a drive from San Francisco, any opportunity to play on one of the nation's most exclusive courses is not to be missed. To get a tee time, call well in advance (at least a month is a good idea) and be prepared to spend well in excess of $400 per person. The course goes over the Pacific Ocean at times, and the sounds and views of the waves lapping at the edges of the course are what make the trip worthwhile, as is the thought that you're playing in the footsteps of many of golf's elite. **$$$$**

Full-Service Resorts

★ ★ ★ **CASA PALMERO AT PEBBLE BEACH.** *1518 Cypress Drive, Pebble Beach (93953). Phone 831/622-6650; toll-free 800/654-9300; fax 831/622-7955. www.pebblebeach.com.* The path to Casa Palmero may be lined with verdant fairways, but it is certainly a gilded route. With its villa-style architecture and gentle intimacy, Casa Palmero feels like a grand European estate. This gracious hideaway overlooks the first and second fairways of Pebble Beach, one of the most lauded golf courses in the world. Old-world charm and first-class service make this hotel a favorite of luxury-loving golfers. With overstuffed furniture and neutral tones interspersed with soft plaids, the guest rooms echo the resorts sophistication. Visitors are invited to enjoy the serene pool area or venture beyond to take advantage of the larger Pebble Beach complex's four restaurants, shops, private Oceanside Beach & Tennis Club, spa, and, of course, world-renowned golf. Offering the best of all worlds, this quietly romantic hotel brings many guests back for repeat visits. 24 rooms, 2 story. Complimentary full breakfast. Check-in 3 pm, check-out noon. High-speed Internet access. Bar. Spa. Outdoor pool. Airport transportation available. **$$$$**

★ ★ ★ **INN AT SPANISH BAY.** *2700 Seventeen Mile Dr, Pebble Beach (93953). Phone 831/647-7500; toll-free 800/654-9300; fax 831/644-7955. www.pebblebeach.com.* The Inn at Spanish Bay is the essence of contemporary elegance at Pebble Beach. Direct access to the revered links makes it popular with golfers, while the splendid natural setting overlooking the Pacific Ocean and Spanish Bay has a universal appeal. Views of the Del Monte Forest, golf course, and ocean are striking, especially when enjoyed from the privacy of a splendid guest room or suite. A gallery of shops showcases fine sportswear and resort apparel along with tennis and golf equipment. From an expertly staffed tennis and fitness facility to the wonderful outdoor pool, the amenities are top notch. Massages are offered, and self-guided tours through the windswept dunes prove therapeutic. Distinctive dining establishments tease taste buds with an array of offerings. All diners will find something here, from comfort food and Tuscan dishes to casual American fare and exuberant Hawaiian fusion cuisine. 269 rooms, 4 story. Check-in 4 pm, check-out noon. High-speed Internet access. Three restaurants, three bars. Fitness room, fitness classes available, spa. Beach. Outdoor pool, whirlpool. Golf, 18 holes. Tennis. Airport transportation available. Business center. **$$$$**

★ ★ ★ LODGE AT PEBBLE BEACH.

1700 Seventeen Mile Dr, Pebble Beach (93953). Phone 831/624-3811; toll-free 800/654-9300; fax 831/625-8598. www.pebblebeach.com. Distinguished by its impressive architecture and spectacular oceanside setting, The Lodge at Pebble Beach is the jewel in the crown of the world-class Pebble Beach resort. Exclusive and refined, the fashionably appointed rooms and suites are supremely comfortable. All feature balconies, and the spa rooms even feature private gardens with outdoor whirlpools. In addition to its famous golf, the Lodge encourages its guests to unwind by the pool, enjoy a vigorous workout in the fitness center, or play a tennis match in its state-of-the-art facility. Its four restaurants offer a variety of casually elegant settings and run the gamut from casual American fare and succulent seafood to updated, lightened versions of French classics. The Lodges spa celebrates the diversity of natural resources indigenous to the Monterey Peninsula in its treatments and therapies, and the shops tantalize visitors with an array of apparel, jewelry, and art. 161 rooms, 3 story. Pets accepted, some restrictions. Check-in 4 pm, check-out noon. High-speed Internet access. Four restaurants, four bars. Fitness room, fitness classes available, spa. Beach. Outdoor pool, children's pool, whirlpool. Golf, 18 holes. Tennis. Airport transportation available. Business center. **$$$$**

Spa

★ ★ ★ ★ THE SPA AT PEBBLE BEACH.

1700 Seventeen Mile Dr, Pebble Beach (93953). Phone 831/624-3811. Blending California's Spanish-colonial heritage with Pebble Beachs gloriously rugged natural setting, the Spa at Pebble Beach is a perfect blend of exotic elegance. From its terra cotta-hued exterior to its in-room fireplaces, this spa knows how to harness the power of décor to relax and soothe guests. The Spa at Pebble Beach goes far beyond simple body treatments and massage therapies to offer a well-rounded therapeutic experience. From water therapies and sig-

nature services to the renowned Keller Skin Institute, this spa covers all the bases. Relaxation is paramount here, where water rituals revive, replenish, and restore energy with seaweed and rose petals, and body treatments nourish and polish the skin with grapeseeds, chai soy mud, and sea salt. The massage menu is particularly thorough, offering everything from classic, light touch massages and Eastern-inspired Shiatsu and Thai therapies to massages designed specifically with the golfer in mind. The spas signature treatments are worth noticing, from wild strawberry body scrubs to seductive milk baths a la Cleopatra. The Keller Skin Institute is a full-service facility within the spa, where Botox injections, laser hair removal, photo facelifts, microdermabrasion, and vascular laser therapy are among the available beautification procedures.

Restaurant

★ ★ ★ CLUB XIX.

1700 Seventeen Mile Dr, Pebble Beach (93953). Phone 831/625-8519; fax 831/644-7960. www.pebblebeach.com. Located in the Lodge at Pebble Beach (see), just off the famous 18th green of the championship Pebble Beach Golf Links, Club XIX is a luxurious restaurant with glorious views of Carmel Bay. Featuring the clean flavors of the season and accented with California style, the food here is prepared with refined French technique. Even the most addicted golfers slow down for a lavish meal at Club XIX. The indoor dining room is small and intimate, while the cozy, outdoor brick patio is warmed by the glow of a blazing fireplace, making either choice ideal for romance. The only problem is that seasoned golfers may find it difficult to focus on romance or food, because the mind tends to wander to the next morning's tee time. It is Pebble Beach, after all. French menu. Dinner. Bar. Business casual attire. Reservations recommended. Valet parking. Outdoor seating. **$$$$**

Pinnacles National Monument (F-2)

See also King City, Salinas

35 miles S of Hollister, off Hwy 25 or 35 miles NE of King City, off Hwy 101; also 11 miles E of Soledad, off Hwy 101.

Geologic activity formed a large volcano 23 million years ago—Pinnacles is the eroded remnant. The volcano formed where two plates of the earth's crust grind together along the San Andreas fault; one portion has remained near the point of origin, while the other has shifted 195 miles northward. The former section now lies between Gorman and Lancaster; the latter section, traveling at a rate of two centimeters a year, is the Pinnacles—an area of 3 square miles eroded by wind, rain, heat, frost, and chemical action. Also here are the canyons of Bear Gulch and Chalone Creek, containing talus caves, or "covered canyons," formed by large blocks of rock that have slipped from the steep walls. In all, the monument covers 25 square miles, is 4 miles wide, and 7 miles long.

It has a variety of bird life, including the prairie falcon, turkey vulture, and golden eagle. Hiking is the main activity, with well-defined trails (some strenuous). High Peaks Trail follows the spectacular cliffs and pinnacles; the North Chalone Peak Trail reaches 3,305 feet, the highest point in the monument. Trails in the caves area are shorter but equally interesting.

There are picnic areas with barbecue grills on both the east and west sides. Visitors must bring their own fuel. No wood fires permitted during high fire season (usually June-Oct). Pets on leash only; not permitted on trails. There is limited camping on west side (June-Jan only), and there is a private campground outside east entrance (phone 831/389-4462). A service station and camper store are also available there. Interpretive programs on east side (mid-Feb-Memorial Day, weekends). There is no through road; access to the east entrance is via Hollister, off Highway 25 or via King City, off Highway 101. The west entrance is reached via Soledad, off Highway 101. Visitor center on east side. For campground and visitor information, phone 831/389-4485. Golden Eagle Passport (see MAKING THE MOST OF YOUR TRIP). Per vehicle fee.

Pismo Beach (G-2)

See also Morro Bay, San Luis Obispo, Santa Monica

Population 8,551
Elevation 33 ft
Area Code 805
Zip 93449
Information Conference & Visitors Bureau, 760 Mattie Rd; phone 805/773-7034 or toll-free 800/443-7778
Web Site www.pismobeach.org

This town is famous for its 23 miles of scenic beach. Ocean fishing, dunes, swimming, surfing, diving, golf, horseback riding, and camping make the area popular with vacationers. Pismo Beach is also in a growing wine region. It is the last Pacific oceanfront community where autos can still be driven on the beach (access ramps are at two locations along the beach). A more dramatic and rugged coastline is found at Shell Beach, to the north, which has been incorporated into Pismo Beach.

What to See and Do

Lopez Recreational Area. *6800 Lopez Dr, Arroyo Grande (93420). 12 miles SE via Hwy 101, Grand Ave exit. Phone 805/788-2381.* On lake created by Lopez Dam. Swimming, water-skiing, water slide, windsurfing, fishing, boating; hiking; picnicking; primitive camping, tent and trailer sites (hook-ups, dump station; fee). Summer campfire programs, boat tours. **$$**

Monarch Butterfly Grove. *Dolliver St, Pismo Beach. Pismo State Beach, 1 mile S via Hwy 1, North Beach Campground exit. Phone toll-free 800/443-7778. www. monarchbutterfly.org.* The state's largest winter site for Monarch butterflies; they can be seen in the grove located at the North Beach Campground (Oct-Feb, daily; dependent on butterfly migration). **FREE**

Oceano Dunes State Vehicular Recreation Area. *Hwy 1 and Pier Ave, Pismo Beach. Phone 805/473-7220. www.parks.ca.gov.* Operated by the state park system to provide a location for off-highway vehicle use (vehicle access to the beach is not common in California). (Daily) **$$$**

Wineries of the Edna Valley & Arroyo Grande Valley. *5828 Orcutt Rd, Petaluma. Phone toll-free 800/443-7778.* Several wineries, many with public tasting rooms and offering tours, may be found along the county roads of Edna Valley and Arroyo Grande Valley; approximately

5-8 miles northeast and southeast via Highway 227 off Highway 101. Many are free; fee at some. Contact the Chamber of Commerce for winery maps.

Special Event

Pismo Beach Clam Festival. *581 Dolliver St, Pismo Beach (93449). Phone 805/773-4382; toll-free 800/443-7778.* Well-known festival held annually at Pismo Beach pier. Includes parade, clam chowder contest, sand sculpture contest, rubber duckie regatta, a clam dig, carnival rides, and food booths. Mid-Oct. **$$**

Limited-Service Hotels

★ **OXFORD SUITES RESORT - PISMO BEACH.** *651 Five Cities Dr, Pismo Beach (93449). Phone 805/773-3773; toll-free 800/722-7915; fax 805/773-5177. www.oxfordsuites.com.* 133 rooms, 2 story, all suites. Pets accepted, some restrictions; fee. Complimentary full breakfast. Check-in 3 pm, check-out 11 am. Bar. Outdoor pool, whirlpool. Business center. **$**

★ **SANDCASTLE INN.** *100 Stimson Ave, Pismo Beach (93449). Phone 805/773-2422; toll-free 800/822-6606; fax 805/773-0771. www.sandcastleinn.com.* 75 rooms, 3 story. Pets accepted; fee. Complimentary continental breakfast. Check-in 3 pm, check-out 11 am. Whirlpool. **$$**

★ ★ **SEA VENTURE RESORT.** *100 Ocean View Ave, Pismo Beach (93449). Phone 805/773-4994; toll-free 800/760-0664; fax 805/773-0924. www.seaventure. com.* 50 rooms, 3 story. Complimentary continental breakfast. Check-in 4 pm, check-out noon. Restaurant, bar. Beach. Whirlpool. **$$**

★ ★ **SPYGLASS INN.** *2705 Spyglass Dr, Shell Beach (93449). Phone 805/773-4855; toll-free 800/824-2612; fax 805/773-5298. www.spyglassinn.com.* 82 rooms, 2 story. Pets accepted; fee. Check-in 3 pm, check-out 11 am. Outdoor pool, whirlpool. **$**

Full-Service Hotel

★ ★ ★ **THE CLIFFS RESORT.** *2757 Shell Beach Rd, Pismo Beach (93449). Phone 805/773-5000; toll-free 800/826-5838; fax 805/773-0764. www.cliffsresort. com.* It's no wonder business and leisure travelers find this lodge near the historic Mission town of San Luis

Obispo, just off scenic Highway 101, so inviting: its cliff-top location overlooking the Pacific, inn-style hospitality, and proximity to the local airport make it a comfortable and convenient retreat. Guest rooms, having recently undergone a $2 million refurbishing, are luxuriously contemporary in décor and feature work desks, Italian marble baths, and private balconies or patios with coastal or mountain views. Activities such as surfing, kayaking, hiking, and golf are available on-site or nearby, and dozens of wineries are within driving distance. 165 rooms, 5 story. Pets accepted, some restrictions, fee. Check-in 3 pm, check-out noon. Wireless Internet access. Restaurant, bar. Fitness room. Outdoor pool, two whirlpools. Airport transportation available. Business center. **$$**

Restaurants

★ ★ **F. MCLINTOCK'S.** *750 Mattie Rd, Pismo Beach (93449). Phone 805/773-1892; fax 805/773-5813. www.mclintocks.com.* Old-fashioned mercantile, souvenir shop, and butcher shop. Steak menu. Dinner. Closed holidays. Bar. Children's menu. Casual attire. Reservations recommended (Sun-Thurs). **$$**

★ ★ **ROSA'S.** *491 Price St, Pismo Beach (93449). Phone 805/773-0551; fax 805/773-6529. www.rosas-restaurant.com.* Extensive floral display. Italian menu. Lunch, dinner. Bar. Children's menu. Casual attire. Reservations recommended. **$$**

Pomona (J-4)

See also Claremont, Ontario, Pasadena, Rancho Cucamonga, West Covina

Population 149,473
Elevation 850 ft
Area Code 909
Information Pomona Chamber of Commerce, 101 W Mission Blvd, Suite 223, 91767; phone 909/622-1256
Web Site www.pomonachamber.org

What to See and Do

California State Polytechnic University, Pomona. *3801 W Temple Ave, Pomona (91768). Phone 909/869-7659. www.csupomona.edu.* (1938) (19,000 students) Kellogg West Continuing Education Center has conference facilities (daily). On campus is the renowned

Kellogg Arabian Horse Center. *Phone 909/869-2224; fax 909/869-4856.*Also houses Equine Research Center. One-hour performances (Oct-May, first Sun each month; no shows Easter). Stable (daily; free). **$**

Fairplex. *1101 W McKinley Ave, Pomona (91768). Phone 909/623-3111; fax 909/865-3602. www.fairplex.com.* Fairplex hosts the Los Angeles County Fair each September, but something fun is always going on here, whatever the month. Dog shows. Horse sales. Antique auto shows. Computer fairs. Boat shows. Collector-car auctions. Fourth of July celebrations. Arts and crafts fairs. Its a busy, busy venue with ample room for the 300-plus events that take place on its 487-acre grounds every year. It has 325,000 square feet of indoor exhibit space in eight exhibit halls, an equine complex, scenic plazas, picnic areas, and carnival grounds.

Historical Society of Pomona Valley. *491 E Arrow Hwy, Pomona (91767). 1 mile N on Garey Ave off San Bernardino Frwy. Phone 909/623-2198. www.osb.net/pomona.* (1850-1854) Grounds, furnished 13 room adobe house illustrate romantic "Days of the Dons." Native American artifacts, baskets. (Sun 2-5 pm or by appointment; closed holidays) **DONATION** Located here are

Adobe de Palomares. *1 mile N on Garey Ave off San Bernardino Frwy. Phone 909/623-2198.*

La Casa Primera. *Corner of Park and McKinley aves, Pomona (91766). Phone 909/623-2198.*

Pomona School of Fine Arts. *244 S Garey Ave, Pomona. Phone 909/868-0900.* Classes in fine arts, exhibits.

Special Event

Los Angeles County Fair. *Fairplex, 1101 W McKinley Ave, Pomona (91768). Phone 909/623-3111; fax 909/865-3602. www.lacountyfair.com.* Bigger doesn't necessarily mean better, unless you're talking about the Los Angeles County Fair. The world's largest county fair delivers 17 exciting days filled with all the usual traditions of a fair, plus unique and elaborate exhibits such as the Flower and Garden Pavilion, one of the most impressive floral displays out there, and even thoroughbred horse racing. Los Angeles is known for its stellar live music scene, so it's not surprising that the fair also attracts world-famous musical acts. Sept. **$$$**

Limited-Service Hotels

★ **BEST WESTERN DIAMOND BAR HOTEL & SUITES.** *259 Gentle Springs Ln, Diamond Bar (91765). Phone 909/860-3700; toll-free 800/780-7234; fax 909/348-0319. www.bestwestern.com.* 97 rooms, 2 story. Complimentary continental breakfast. Check-in 3 pm, check-out noon. Fitness room. Outdoor pool, whirlpool. Business center. **$**

★ ★ **HOLIDAY INN.** *21725 E Gateway Dr, Diamond Bar (91765). Phone 909/860-5440; toll-free 800/988-3587; fax 909/860-8224. www.holiday-inn.com.* 175 rooms, 6 story. Check-out noon. Restaurant, bar. Outdoor pool, whirlpool. **$**

Restaurant

★ ★ **D'ANTONIO'S RISTORANTE.** *808 N Diamond Bar Blvd, Diamond Bar (91765). Phone 909/860-3663; fax 909/860-8051.* Italian menu. Lunch, dinner. Closed holidays. Outdoor seating. **$$**

Poway (K 4)

Web Site www.ci.poway.ca.us

What to See and Do

Poway Center for the Performing Arts. *15498 Espola Rd, Poway (92064). From San Diego, take I-15 N and turn right at Ted Williams Pkwy exit. Turn right at Twin Peaks. Turn left at Espola Rd. Building is at the corner of Espola Rd and Titan Way. Phone 858/748-0505. www.powayarts.org.* Open since 1990, this venue, just northeast of San Diego, offers theater, concerts, and an array of short-run entertainments. Although you should check the newspaper or the Internet in advance to see whats playing, the Poway Center usually offers solid entertainment. In recent years, acts have ranged from the New Shanghai Circus to big bands and from musical Marines to the Girls Choir of Harlem. For lovers of the just-hand-me-a-mike style, the likes of Betty Buckley, Jack Jones, and Manhattan Transfer have made visits. The Poway is a good option for holiday visitors in particular—like many midrange venues, it always features holiday-themed shows on its schedule.

Rancho Cucamonga (J-4)

See also Claremont, Ontario, Pomona

Population 127,743
Elevation 1,110 ft
Area Code 909
Zip 91730
Information Chamber of Commerce, 7945 Vineyard Ave, Suite D-5; phone 909/987-1012
Web Site www.ranchochamber.org

The original residents, the Serrano, called this area Cucamonga or "sandy place." Later, it was part of the vast Rancho de Cucamonga. Violent deaths and long legal battles caused the eventual sale of the land to several wine and citrus industries in 1871.

What to See and Do

Casa de Rancho Cucamonga (Rains House).
8810 Hemlock St, Rancho Cucamonga (91730). Just N of Vineyard. Phone 909/989-4970. Oldest burned-brick house in San Bernardino County (circa 1860); was home to wealthy and socially prominent John and Merced Rains. (Tues-Sat 10 am-3 pm) **DONATION**

Special Event

Grape Harvest Festival. *Rancho Cucamonga Epicenter, Rochester Ave between Arrow Rte and Foothill Blvd, Ontario (91764).* Wine tasting, grape stomping contest, carnival, displays, entertainment. Early Oct.

Limited-Service Hotel

★ **BEST WESTERN HERITAGE INN.**
8179 Spruce Ave, Rancho Cucamonga (91730). Phone 909/466-1111; toll-free 800/682-7829; fax 909/466-3876. *www.bestwestern.com.* 115 rooms, 6 story. Complimentary continental breakfast. Check-in 3 pm, check-out noon. Fitness room. Outdoor pool, whirlpool. **$**
🧍 ⊠

Restaurant

★ ★ **MAGIC LAMP INN.** *8189 E Foothill Blvd, Rancho Cucamonga (91730).* Phone 909/981-8659; fax 909/981-2039. American menu. Lunch, dinner. Closed Mon; Dec 25. Bar. Children's menu. **$$$**

Rancho Mirage (J-5)

See also Palm Springs

Web Site www.ci.rancho-mirage.ca.us

Restaurant

★ ★ ★ **WALLY'S DESERT TURTLE.** *71-775 Hwy 111, Rancho Mirage (92270).* Phone 760/568-9321; fax 760/558-9713. *www.wallysdesertturtle.com.* Built in 1979 by Wally Botello, Wally's Desert Turtle in the Rancho Mirage desert is a uniquely Palm Springs kind of place. The interior is elaborately decorated with beveled mirrored ceilings, cushy furniture, and faux frescoes. A pianist plays nightly, skillfully dancing through songs from an era long past. The extensive continental menu offers dishes familiar to many, with an option for everyone. A specialty of the house is roasted rack of lamb, served with potato gratin, cannelloni bean pure, and rosemary-thyme sauce. A 200-bottle wine list concentrates on California but ventures abroad as well, for a healthy variety of choices to accompany dinner. If you're in town on a Friday, stop by at lunchtime, when the restaurant hosts its weekly fashion show. Continental menu. Dinner. Closed mid-June-mid-Sept. Bar. Business casual attire. Reservations recommended. Valet parking. **$$$$**

Rancho Santa Fe (K-4)

See also Del Mar

Population 3,252
Elevation 245 ft
Area Code 858
Zip 92067

Full-Service Resorts

★ ★ ★ **MORGAN RUN RESORT & CLUB.**
5690 Cancha de Golf, Rancho Santa Fe (92091). Phone 858/756-2471; toll-free 800/378-4653; fax 858/756-3013. *www.morganrun.com.* As its name suggests, the Morgan Run Resort & Club is both a club for area residents and a resort that plays host to guests from all over the world. When you stay here, you can take full advantage of the club and its facilities, including its 27-hole championship golf course, tennis courts, and fitness center, offering Pilates and yoga classes. The guest rooms are traditional and elegant, and each has its own private patio or balcony. The resort is only 5

miles from the beach community of Del Mar, where you can lounge on the beach, browse the many shops and boutiques, or bet on the horses at the Del Mar Race Track. 90 rooms, 2 story. Check-in 4 pm, check-out noon. Restaurant, bar. Fitness room, spa. Outdoor pool, whirlpool. Golf, 27 holes. Tennis. **$$**

★ ★ ★ ★ **RANCHO VALENCIA RESORT.**
5921 Valencia Cir, Rancho Santa Fe (92067). Phone 858/756-1123; toll-free 800/548-3664; fax 858/756-0165. www.ranchovalencia.com. Rancho Valencia carries on the regions Spanish colonial tradition in a rural setting only 25 miles north of downtown San Diego. Nestled in the canyon of Rancho Santa Fe on 40 manicured acres of rolling hills, fragrant blossoms, and giant palm trees, this relaxing retreat is just minutes from the charming boutiques and cafés of La Jolla. Guests relish the independence and secluded location of this romantic resort, where 20 pink casitas house only 49 suites. Whitewashed beams, hand-painted tiles, cathedral ceilings, and tile-bordered fireplaces create an enchanting atmosphere. The open-air setting of the restaurant perfectly suits the mood of this resort, while the Pacific Rim cuisine tickles the fancy of gourmets. With privileges at local golf courses, a fitness center complete with a sensational spa, and one of the best tennis facilities in the country, boredom is never an issue. 49 rooms, all suites. Pets accepted, fee. Check-in 4 pm, check-out noon. High-speed Internet access. Restaurant, bar. Fitness room, fitness classes available, spa. Outdoor pool, whirlpool. Tennis. Business center. **$$$$**

Full-Service Inn

★ ★ ★ **INN AT RANCHO SANTA FE.** *5951 Linea Del Cielo, Rancho Santa Fe (92067). Phone 858/756-1131; toll-free 800/843-4661; fax 858/759-1604. www.theinnatranchosantafe.com.* A member of the Historic Hotels of America, the Inn at Rancho Santa Fe isn't what you might expect when you see the word "inn." Located primarily in many small cottages dotting the 20-acre property, guest accommodations are available in three varieties: deluxe rooms, suites, and private cottages, all featuring Aveda beauty and bath products. The deluxe rooms have patios or decks; many have fireplaces, wet bars, kitchenettes, or sitting areas; and some of the older rooms have hardwood floors. Suites are one- or two-bedroom cottages, each with its own living room, kitchen, and fireplace, plus a patio or deck. The one-, two-, and three-bedroom private cot-

tages have a full-sized kitchen and guest bath. If you can pull yourself away from your room, you'll find a full-service spa, a fitness program (offering guided runs and walks, swim lessons, water aerobics, and weight-training classes), tennis courts (private lessons available), a croquet lawn, and walking and jogging trails. 89 rooms. Pets accepted, some restrictions; fee. Check-in 4 pm, check-out noon. Restaurant. Fitness room. Outdoor pool, whirlpool. Tennis. **$$**

Restaurants

★ ★ ★ **DELICIAS.** *6106 Paseo Delicias, Rancho Santa Fe (92067). Phone 858/756-8000; fax 858/759-1739.* California menu. Dinner. Closed holidays. Bar. Outdoor seating. **$$$**

★ ★ ★ **MILLE FLEURS.** *6009 Paseo Delicias, Rancho Santa Fe (92067). Phone 858/756-3085; fax 858/756-9945. www.millefleurs.com.* This charming, well-admired restaurant is perfect for special occasions. Grab a romantic table by the fireplace or step outside to the courtyard. French menu. Lunch, dinner. Closed Jan 1, Dec 25. Bar. Reservations recommended. Outdoor seating. **$$$**

★ ★ ★ **VALENCIA.** *5921 Valencia Cir, Rancho Santa Fe (92067). Phone 858/759-6216; fax 858/756-0105. www.ranchovalencia.com.* Seafood menu. Breakfast, lunch, dinner, Sun brunch. Bar. Casual attire. Reservations recommended. Valet parking. Outdoor seating. **$$$$**

Redlands (J-4)

See also Beaumont, Big Bear Lake, Lake Arrowhead, Ontario, Riverside, San Bernardino

Founded 1888
Population 63,591
Elevation 1,302 ft
Area Code 909
Information Chamber of Commerce, 1 E Redlands Blvd, 92373; phone 909/793-2546
Web Site www.redlandschamber.org

Named for the color of the earth in the area and known for many years as the Navel Orange Center, Redlands still handles a large volume of citrus fruits, but has diversified its industry in recent years to achieve greater economic prosperity and stability.

What to See and Do

Asistencia Mission de San Gabriel. *26930 Barton Rd, Redlands. Phone 909/793-5402.* (1830) Restored adobe with Native American and early pioneer exhibits, historic scenes of the valley; cactus garden; wishing well, bell tower, wedding chapel, and reception room. (Tues-Sat 10 am-3 pm; closed Jan 1, Thanksgiving, Dec 25) **FREE**

Kimberly Crest House and Gardens. *1325 Prospect Dr, Redlands (92373). Phone 909/792-2111. www.kimberly-crest.org.* (1897) French chteau-style house and accompanying carriage house on 6.5 acres. Former house of John Kimberly, founder of the Kimberly-Clark Corporation. Structure is representative of the "Mansion Era" of Southern California; 1930s furnishings. Italian gardens and citrus grove on grounds. Guided tours. (Sept-July, Thurs-Sun 1-4 pm; closed holidays, also Aug) **$$**

Lincoln Memorial Shrine. *125 W Vine St, Redlands (92373). In Smiley Park. Phone 909/798-7632. www.lincolnshrine.org.* George Grey Barnard's Carrara marble bust of Lincoln; murals by Dean Cornwell; painting by Norman Rockwell; manuscripts, books, artifacts relating to Lincoln and the Civil War. (Tues-Sat 1-5 pm; closed holidays) **FREE**

Pharaoh's Lost Kingdom. *1101 California St, Redlands (92374). At I-10. Phone 909/335-7275. www.pharaohslostkingdom.com.* Family theme park features race car complex with Indy, Grand Prix, and kiddy cars; water park with wave pools, multiple water slides, and flumes; 16 amusement rides; miniature golf; arcade, indoor playground; gift shop; restaurant; amphitheater. (Daily; schedule varies, call or visit Web site for information) **$$$$**

Redlands Bowl. *Eureka and Vine sts, Redlands (92373). Phone 909/793-7316. www.redlandsbowl.org.* The free concerts held here every Tuesday and Friday in summer have earned it the name Little Hollywood Bowl.

San Bernardino County Museum. *2024 Orange Tree Ln, Redlands (92374). Phone 909/307-2669. www.co.san-bernardino.ca.us/museum.* Mounted collection of birds and bird eggs of Southern California; reptiles, mammals. Pioneer and Native American artifacts; rocks and minerals; paleontology. Changing art exhibits. On grounds are steam locomotive, garden of cacti and succulents. (Tues-Sun 9 am-5 pm; closed Jan 1, Thanksgiving, Dec 25) **$$**

Limited-Service Hotel

★ **BEST WESTERN SANDMAN MOTEL.** *1120 W Colton Ave, Redlands (92374). Phone 909/793-2001; toll-free 800/780-7234; fax 909/792-7612. www.bestwestern.com.* 65 rooms, 2 story. Pets accepted, some restrictions; fee. Complimentary continental breakfast. Check-in 2 pm, check-out 11 am. Outdoor pool, whirlpool. **$**

Restaurant

★ ★ ★ **JOE GREENSLEEVES.** *220 N Orange St, Redlands (92374). Phone 909/792-6969; fax 909/792-0402.* Seafood, steak menu. Lunch, dinner. Closed Jan 1, July 4, Dec 25. **$$$**

Redondo Beach

Population 63,261
Elevation 59 ft
Information Chamber of Commerce and Visitors Bureau, 200 N Pacific Coast Hwy, 90277; phone 310/376-6911 or toll-free 800/282-0333
Web Site www.visitredondo.com

This recreation and vacation center just south of LAX airport features a 2-mile beach and the popular King Harbor, which houses hundreds of watercraft. Once a commercial port, the historic beach town's pier now features shops, restaurants, and marinas. Biking, fishing, surfing, and all sorts of water sports are popular here.

What to See and Do

Galleria at South Bay. *1815 Hawthorne Blvd, Redondo Beach (90278). Phone 310/371-7546. www.southbaygalleria.com.* Located just 15 minutes from LAX, The Galleria at South Bay is an easy stop on your way into or out of town if you have a little time to spare. With Mervyn's, Nordstrom, and Robinson's-May anchoring this mall, you'll also find the standard mall shops (such as Abercrombie & Fitch, Banana Republic, and Gap) and restaurants, plus some nicer food fare, such as California Pizza Kitchen. (Mon-Fri 10 am-9 pm, Sat 10 am-8 pm, Sun 11 am-7 pm; closed Easter, Thanksgiving, Dec 25)

Redondo Beach Pier. *Torrance Blvd, Redondo Beach (90277). W end of Torrance Blvd, just W of the Pacific Coast Hwy. Phone 310/318-0631; toll-free 800/280-0333. www.redondopier.com.* With its laid-back atmosphere and white sandy beaches, Redondo is a beach bum's paradise. Surfing and volleyball are local favorites here, but catching rays and enjoying the area's mild weather are acceptable alternatives. All that surfing and tanning may work up an appetite, so be sure to hit one of the many funky and fun beach restaurants and bars that have sprung up along the pier, which is the perfect place to catch the sunset after dinner. (Daily 24 hours)

Limited-Service Hotels

★ **BEST WESTERN SUNRISE AT REDONDO BEACH MARINA.** *400 N Harbor Dr, Redondo Beach (90277). Phone 310/376-0746; toll-free 800/334-7384; fax 310/376-7384. www.bestwestern.com.* 111 rooms, 3 story. Complimentary continental breakfast. Check-in 3 pm, check-out noon. Fitness room. Outdoor pool, whirlpool. Business center. **$**

★ ★ **PORTOFINO HOTEL & YACHT CLUB.** *260 Portofino Way, Redondo Beach (90277). Phone 310/379-8481; toll-free 800/468-4292; fax 310/372-7329. www.hotelportofino.com.* Panoramic, sunset-and-sailboat-accented views of Santa Monica Bay and Catalina Island highlight this boutique-style ocean-front hotel, which is perched on a beautifully land-scaped peninsula in King Harbor near the Redondo Beach Pier. Private balconies and floor-to-ceiling windows allow the scenery and sea breezes to flow indoors, where relaxation and a romantic seaside ambience reign. The indoor/outdoor Breakwater restaurant, overlooking the tranquil Portofino marina, offers jazz music, candlelight, and glowing fireplaces along with a selection of steak and seafood dishes. Guests can explore the 27-mile beach bike path—which runs from Palos Verdes all the way to Malibu—on complimentary bicycles. 200 rooms, 3 story. Check-in 3 pm, check-out noon. High-speed Internet access. Restaurant, bar. Fitness room. Outdoor pool, whirlpool. **$$**

Full-Service Hotel

★ ★ ★ **CROWNE PLAZA.** *300 N Harbor Dr, Redondo Beach (90277). Phone 310/318-8888; toll-free 800/368-9760; fax 310/376-1930. www.crowneplaza. com.* 339 rooms, 5 story. Check-in 3 pm, check-out noon. High-speed Internet access. Restaurant. Fitness room. Outdoor pool, whirlpool. Tennis. Business center. **$$**

Restaurants

★ ★ ★ **CHEZ MELANGE.** *1716 S Pacific Coast Hwy, Redondo Beach (90277). Phone 310/540-1222; fax 310/316-9283.* Often dubbed the "Spago of the South Bay," Chez Melange raised the bar for fine California cuisine in the beach cities years ago, and the upscale clientele is fiercely loyal to this day. With warm peach walls and modern art, the dining room harkens back to the 1980s. The menu, however, is contemporary, offering a full sushi list as well as modern twists on classics like rabbit three ways, spicy fried oysters, and steak tartare. The restaurant is open 365 days a year; keep an eye out for the whimsical holiday menus. California menu. Breakfast, lunch, dinner, brunch. Bar. Casual attire. Reservations recommended. **$$$**

★ ★ **KINCAID'S BAY HOUSE.** *500 Fisherman's Wharf, Redondo Beach (90277). Phone 310/318-6080.* This chain restaurant flagship, a popular stop for tourists and locals, is docked spectacularly at a local pier—affording one of the most romantic Pacific views in the South Bay. The seafood-intensive fare is a sight in its own right, and whether you belly up the raw bar for fresh shellfish or order a well-portioned entrée (black tiger prawns stuffed with blue crab and macadamia nuts is a favorite), your taste buds will be in the swim. Done in shades of red and filled with booth seating, the dining room accommodates the crowds without compromising comfort. The servers are professional and family friendly—and, weather permitting, they will steer patrons toward the lovely outdoor waterfront tables. Seafood, steak menu. Lunch, dinner, Sun brunch. Bar. Casual attire. Reservations recommended. Outdoor seating. **$$$**

★ ★ **ZAZOU.** *1810 S Catalina Ave, Redondo Beach (90277). Phone 310/540-4884.* A hot spot amid the art galleries and boutiques of this shore towns picturesque Riviera Village, Zazou soothes its clientele of sophisticated locals and hopeful romantics with an intimate, orange-hued, contemporary décor enhanced by soft jazz music and plenty of candles and Mediterranean artwork. Even finicky foodies are impressed by the menu's California twist on French and Mediterranean fare—delicacies like sautéed frog legs and roasted rabbit are listed alongside pan-roasted veal sweetbreads and seared, peppered ahi tuna with tasty couscous. The superior (if pricey) martinis, outstanding wine list, and excellent service support the cuisines zesty sense of adventure. Mediterranean menu. Lunch, dinner. Bar. Reservations recommended. Outdoor seating. **$$**

Riverside (J-4)

See also Beaumont, Big Bear Lake, Claremont, Corona, Hemet, Redlands, San Bernardino

Founded 1870
Population 255,166
Elevation 858 ft
Area Code 951
Information Greater Riverside Chambers of Commerce, 3985 University Ave, 92501; phone 951/683-7100
Web Site www.riverside-chamber.com

In 1873, a resident of the new town of Riverside obtained from the US Department of Agriculture two cuttings of a new type of orange, a mutation that had suddenly developed in Brazil. These cuttings were the origin of the vast navel orange groves that make this the center of the "Orange Empire."

What to See and Do

California Museum of Photography. *3824 Main St, Riverside (92501). Phone 951/827-4787. www.cmp. ucr.edu.* Large collection of photographic equipment, prints, stereographs, memorabilia. Interactive gallery, walk-in camera; library. (Tues-Sat noon-5 pm; closed holidays) **$**

Castle Amusement Park. *3500 Polk St, Riverside (92505). Hwy 91 between Tyler and La Sierra exits. Phone 951/785-3000. www.castlepark.com.* Features 80-year-old Dentzel carousel with hand-carved animals; antique cars. Park with 30 rides and attractions (Mon-Thurs 11 am-9 pm, Fri-Sat 11 am-11 pm, Sun 11 am-10 pm). Four 18-hole miniature golf courses and video arcade (Mon-Thurs 10 am-10 pm, Fri-Sat 11 am-midnight, Sun 11 am-10 pm). Fee for activities.

Chinese Memorial Pavilion. *3581 Mission Inn Ave, Riverside. On Riverside Public Library grounds.* Dedicated to Chinese pioneers of the West and those who contributed to the growth of Riverside.

Heritage House. *8193 Magnolia Ave, Riverside (92503). Phone 951/689-1333.* (1891) Restored Victorian mansion. (Sept-June, Fri noon-3 pm, Sat-Sun to 3:30 pm) **FREE**

March Field Air Museum. *22550 Van Buren Blvd, Riverside (92518). Phone 951/697-6602. www. marchfield.org.* Located just off the Van Buren Boulevard exit of Interstate 215, this museum houses more than 60 historic aircraft, including the first operational jet used by the US Air Force and the speed record-breaking SR-71 Blackbird. Take a spin in the g-force flight simulator or explore the collection of 2,000 artifacts dating back to 1918. (Daily 9 am-4 pm; closed holidays) **$$**

Mount Rubidoux Memorial Park. *4393 Riverview Dr, Riverside.* According to legend, the mountain was once the altar of Cahuilla and Serrano sun worship. A cross rises on the peak in memory of Fray Junipero Serra, founder of the California missions. The World Peace Tower stands on the side of the mountain. Hiking. (Daily, weather permitting; vehicular traffic prohibited) **FREE**

Orange Empire Railway Museum. *2201 South A St, Perris (92570). 14 miles S via I-215. Phone 951/943-3020. www. oerm.org.* This free museum features more than 150 rail vehicles and pieces of off-rail equipment, railroad and trolley memorabilia. Trolley rides ($$) run from 11 am to 5 pm on Saturday, Sunday, and holidays. (Daily 9 am-5 pm; closed Thanksgiving, Dec 25) **FREE**

Parent Washington Navel Orange Tree. *Magnolia and Arlington aves, Riverside (92501).* Propagated from one of the two original trees from Bahia, Brazil. Planted in 1873, all navel orange trees stem from this tree or from its offspring.

Riverside Art Museum. *3425 Mission Inn Ave, Riverside (92501). Corner of Lime St and Mission Inn Ave. Phone 951/684-7111. www.riversideartmuseum.org.* Changing exhibits of historical and contemporary sculpture, painting, and graphics; lectures, demonstrations, juried shows, sales gallery. Housed in 1929 Mediterranean-style YWCA building designed by Julia Morgan. (Mon-Sat 10 am-4 pm; closed holidays) **DONATION**

Riverside Metropolitan Museum. *3580 Mission Inn Ave, Riverside (92501). Phone 951/826-5273.* Area history, anthropology, and natural history displays; changing exhibits. (Tues-Fri 9 am-5 pm, Sat 10 am-5 pm, Sun 11 am-5 pm; closed holidays) **FREE**

Rubidoux Drive-In. *3770 Opal St, Riverside (92509). Phone 951/683-4455. www.rubidoux.icyspicy.com.* The Rubidoux opened in 1948 and has three screens, each showing double features year round. Call for listings and times. No oversided vehicles, RVs, or bicycles. Leave skateboards and pets at home. **$**

University of California, Riverside. *900 University Ave, Riverside (92521). Phone 951/787-1012. www.ucr.edu.* (1954) (16,000 students) The campus centers around a 161-foot Carillon Tower, with a botanic garden featuring flora from all parts of the world.

Special Event

Easter Sunrise Pilgrimage. *Mount Rubidoux Memorial Park, Riverside.* First nonsectarian sunrise service in the United States; continuous since 1909. Easter Sun.

Limited-Service Hotels

★ **COMFORT INN.** *1590 University Ave, Riverside (92507). Phone 951/683-6000; toll-free 800/228-5150; fax 951/782-8052. www.choicehotels.com.* Near the University of California-Riverside, this clean, comfortable hotel features easy access to the highway. 115 rooms, 2 story. Complimentary continental breakfast. Check-in 3 pm, check-out noon. Outdoor pool. **$**
🔁

★ ★ **COURTYARD BY MARRIOTT.** *1510 University Ave, Riverside (92507). Phone 951/276-1200; toll-free 800/321-2211; fax 951/787-6783. www.court-yard.com.* Convenient to area shopping, dining, and the University of California-Riverside campus, visitors will appreciate this hotels location and amenities. 163 rooms, 6 story. Check-in 3 pm, check-out noon. High-speed Internet access. Restaurant. Fitness room. Outdoor pool, whirlpool. **$**
🚶🔁

★ **DYNASTY SUITES.** *3735 Iowa Ave, Riverside (92507). Phone 951/369-8200; toll-free 800/842-7899; fax 951/341-6486. www.dynastysuites.com.* Featuring a surprising array of amenities and thoughtful touches like freshly baked cookies and fresh fruit upon arrival, this budget-friendly hotel is close to area shopping and dining. 34 rooms, 2 story. Complimentary continental breakfast. Check-in 2 pm, check-out noon. High-speed Internet access. Outdoor pool. **$**
🔁

Full-Service Hotels

★ ★ **MARRIOTT RIVERSIDE.** *3400 Market St, Riverside (92501). Phone 951/784-8000; toll-free 800/228-9290; fax 951/369-7127. www.marriott.com.* This hotel adjacent to the Riverside Convention Center and within a shuttle ride of Ontario International Airport attracts business and leisure travelers looking for a range of amenities. Spacious, casually elegant guest rooms offer comfort and practical business connections; features include work desks, speaker phones, and complimentary coffee. On-site, Olio Ristorante specializes in Italian fare, while Martini's Lounge serves an eclectic menu. Antique stores, museums, shops, and other attractions are within walking dis-

tance. 292 rooms, 12 story. Check-in 3 pm, check-out noon. High-speed Internet access. Two restaurants, bar. Fitness room. Outdoor pool, whirlpool. Airport transportation available. Business center. **$$**
🚶🔁🚶

★ ★ ★ **MISSION INN.** *3649 Mission Inn Ave, Riverside (92501). Phone 909/784-0300; fax 909/341-6730. www.missioninn.com.* A National Historic Landmark, the Mission Inn is one hotel you won't forget. The hotel had its beginnings in the late 19th century and played host to such guests as Theodore Roosevelt and Andrew Carnegie in the early 20th century. It went through a period of decline mid-century but was restored and reopened in the 1990s, in full glory. Today, the hotel impresses from the moment you step into the expansive, ornately decorated lobby, with its dark wood floors, columns, and accents. The hotel features two chapels, perfect for weddings and other occasions; Tiffany stained-glass windows adorn the larger of the two. The restaurants are sure to have something to suit any craving—from steak to seafood to authentic Mexican fare. None of the hotel rooms are exactly like the others, but all are elegantly appointed. With its Spanish architecture and beautiful outdoor spaces, occupying a full city block, the hotel transports you to another time and place—you'll have a hard time remembering that you're less than an hour from downtown Los Angeles. 239 rooms, 5 story. Check-in 3 pm, check-out noon. Three restaurants, three bars. Fitness room. Outdoor pool, whirlpool. Airport transportation available. **$$**
🚶🔁

Restaurants

★ ★ **CIAO BELLA.** *1630 Spruce St, Riverside (92507). Phone 951/781-8840; fax 951/781-1970.* With understated décor and warm, mellow colors, this airy restaurant serves a variety of unique Italian dishes. Diners spend quiet afternoons and evenings amid aromas from the open kitchen and lots of natural light from the multipaned windows. Italian menu. Lunch, dinner. Closed Sun. Bar. Casual attire. Reservations recommended. Outdoor seating. **$$**

★ ★ **GERARD'S.** *9814 Magnolia Ave, Riverside (92503). Phone 951/687-4882; fax 909/687-2433. www.dineatgerards.com.* Enjoy classic French cuisine in a relaxed setting. This restaurant is set in a renovated house just outside of Riverside, and diners are encouraged to take their time, savor their meals, and sample from a menu featuring traditional French mainstays like bouillabaisse and tournedos of beef. French menu. Dinner. Closed Mon-Wed. Casual attire. Reservations recommended. **$$**

★ **MARKET BROILER.** *3525 Merrill Ave, Riverside (92506). Phone 951/276-9007; fax 951/276-1963. www.marketbroiler.com.* For fresh fish, a fun atmosphere, and friendly service, locals come to this California mini-chain to choose from 18 varieties of fish and shellfish. All of the fish is mesquite-broiled and served in pretty much any form and flavoring you could imagine. However, the menu also includes wood-fired pizzas and a "dishes without fishes" section, featuring chicken, pasta, and steak entrees. Seafood menu. Lunch, dinner. Bar. Casual attire. **$$**

San Bernardino (J-4)

See also Anaheim, Beaumont, Big Bear Lake, Lake Arrowhead, Redlands, Riverside

Founded 1810
Population 185,401
Elevation 1,049 ft
Area Code 909
Information San Bernardino Area Chamber of Commerce, 546 W 6th St, 92410; or PO Box 658, 92402; phone 909/885-7515
Web Site www.ci.san-bernardino.ca.us

Set amid mountains, valleys, and deserts, San Bernardino is a mixture of Spanish and Mormon cultures. The city takes its name from the valley and mountains discovered by a group of missionaries in 1810 on the feast of San Bernardino of Siena. In 1851, a group of Mormons bought the Rancho San Bernardino and laid out the city, modeled after Salt Lake City. The group was recalled by Brigham Young six years later, but the city continued to thrive. The area has a vast citrus industry. In April, the fragrance and beauty of orange blossoms fill the nearby groves.

What to See and Do

Glen Helen Regional Park. *2555 Glen Helen Pkwy, San Bernardino (92407). 10 miles N, 1 mile W of I-215. Phone 909/887-7540. www.co.san-bernardino.ca.us/ parks/glen.htm.* Approximately 500 acres. Swimming ($), two flume water slides ($); fishing ($); nature trail; picnicking; playground. Group camping ($$). (Daily; closed Jan 1, Dec 25) **$$**

Mountain High Ski Area. *24510 Hwy 2, Wrightwood (92397). 20 miles N on I-215 (Hwy 395), then 9 miles NW on Hwy 138, then 8 miles SW, off Hwy 2. Phone toll-free 888/754-7878. www.mthigh.com.* Three quad, three triple, six double chairlifts; patrol, school, rentals, snowmaking; concession areas, cafeterias. Longest run 1 1/2 miles; vertical drop 1,600 feet. Night skiing. Free shuttle bus operates between east and west areas. (Mid-Nov-late Apr, daily) **$$$$**

✪ **Rim of the World Highway.** Scenic 45-mile mountain road leading to Big Bear Lake, Snow Summit, Running Springs, Lake Arrowhead, Blue Jay, and Skyforest. Beaches on the lakes, fishing; hiking and riding trails; picnic grounds.

San Bernardino National Forest. *602 S Tippecanoe, San Bernardino (92408). 10 miles N via I-215, Hwy 18, 30, 38, 330. Phone 909/382-2600. www.fs.fed.us/r5/ sanbernardino.* One of the most heavily used national forests in the country; stretches east from San Bernardino to Palm Springs. Includes the popular San Gorgonio Wilderness at the forest's east edge by Redlands, the small Cucamonga Wilderness in the west end of the San Bernardino Mountains, and the San Jacinto Wilderness in the San Jacinto Mountains (permits required for wildernesses). Fishing, boating; hunting, hiking, horseback riding, skiing; off-road vehicle trails; picnicking; camping (fees charged; reservations for camping accepted, as well as first-come, first-served basis). **$$$$**

Special Events

National Orange Show. *Fairgrounds, 689 S E St, San Bernardino (92408). Mill and E sts. Phone 909/888-6788. www.nationalorangeshow.com.* Marks completion of winter citrus crop harvest. Held annually since 1915. Exhibits, sports events, entertainment. Memorial Day weekend. **$**

Renaissance Faire. *Santa Fe Dam Recreation Area,15501 E Arrow Hwy, Irwindale (91706). E of where the 605 San Gabriel River Frwy and the 210 Foothill Frwy cross. Phone 626/969-4750. www.renfair. com.* Re-creates an Elizabethan experience with costumed performers, booths, food, and games. Mid-Apr-mid May, weekends. **$$$$**

Stater Brothers Route 66 Rendezvous. *Downtown, San Bernardino. Phone 909/889-3980; toll-free 800/867-8366. www.route-66.org.* Go cruisin' down memory lane at this smokin' car show that celebrates the historic road that runs right through San Bernardino.

During this annual four-day auto rally, more than 2,400 cool-as-heck cars that rolled off the assembly line before 1974 rule the streets in a 35-block area of downtown. All these classic cars and hot rods share the blacktop with any year's Corvette, Viper, or Prowler. These spiffy wheels attract more than 500,000 spectators, who come for the parades, contests, lively entertainment, and festival food. Mid-Sept. **FREE**

Limited-Service Hotel

★ **LA QUINTA INN.** *205 E Hospitality Ln, San Bernardino (92408). Phone 909/888-7571; toll-free 800/687-6667; fax 909/884-3864. www.laquinta.com.* 153 rooms, 3 story. Pets accepted, some restrictions. Complimentary continental breakfast. Check-out noon. Outdoor pool. **$**

Full-Service Hotel

★ ★ **CLARION HOTEL & CONVENTION CENTER.** *295 North E St, San Bernardino (92401). Phone 909/381-6181; fax 909/381-5288. www.choice-hotels.com.* 231 rooms, 12 story. Check-in 3 pm, check-out noon. Restaurant, bar. Fitness room. Whirlpool. Airport transportation available. Business center. **$$**

Restaurant

★ ★ **LOTUS GARDEN.** *111 E Hospitality Ln, San Bernardino (92408). Phone 909/381-6171; fax 909/381-1757.* Chinese menu. Lunch, dinner. Bar. Children's menu. **$**

San Clemente (J-4)

See also Anaheim, Laguna Beach, Oceanside, San Juan Capistrano

Population 49,936
Elevation 200 ft
Area Code 949
Zip 92672
Information Chamber of Commerce, 1100 N El Camino Real; phone 949/492-1131
Web Site www.scchamber.com

What to See and Do

San Clemente State Beach. *Califia Ave, off I-5. Phone 949/492-3156. www.parks.ca.gov.* Swimming, lifeguard, fishing; hiking trail; picnicking; trailer hook-ups,

camping. Camping reservations necessary. (Daily) **$$$$**

Swimming. Municipal pier and beach. *100 Avenida Presidio, San Clemente (92672). 1/2 miles W of I-5. Phone 949/361-8219.* Swimming, surfing; picnicking; playground; fishing, bait and tackle shop at the end of the pier. (Daily; lifeguards) **FREE**

Special Event

San Clemente Fiesta Street Festival. *Ave Del Mar, San Clemente (92672). Phone 949/492-1131. www.scchamber.com/html/fiesta.htm.* This giant block party is designed to provide fun for the entire family: food, games, a classic car and motorcycle show, and the Salsa Challenge. Second Sun in Aug.

Limited-Service Hotel

★ ★ **HOLIDAY INN.** *111 S Avenida De La Estrella, San Clemente (92672). Phone 949/361-3000; toll-free 800/469-1161; fax 949/361-2472. www.ichotelsgroup.com.* Conveniently located an hour from Los Angeles International Airport, an hour from San Diego Airport, and only 45 minutes from Disneyland, this Holiday Inn is a great place from which to base your explorations of Southern California. Even if you don't plan to travel far, the city of San Clemente has a lot to offer—from its beautiful beaches to its Mediterranean architecture. Many of the hotels guest rooms have ocean views, and some have private hot tubs. 72 rooms, 3 story. Pets accepted; fee. Check-in 3 pm, check-out noon. Restaurant. Outdoor pool, whirlpool. **$$**

San Diego (K-4)

See also Carlsbad, Del Mar, Escondido, La Jolla, Pacific Beach, Julian

Founded 1769
Population 1,223,400
Elevation 42 ft
Area Code 619
Information Convention & Visitors Bureau, 401 B St, Suite 1400, 92101; phone 619/236-1212
Web Site www.sandiego.org

There are no catchy phrases or cute nicknames for San Diego. No one has written a song or poem that has snuggled its way into our collective consciousness: it's up to you, San Diego, San Diego? San Diego, that toddlin' town? The other city by the bay? No; it simply has to be enough that once you've been here, you'll never quite get it out of your system. The best weather in the country is here, as is world-class theater, great shopping, quirky museums, and an ocean where sea lions crawl onto the shore to sun themselves. There's a terrific zoo, a fantastic wildlife park, wonderful restaurants serving, among other things, the city's world-famous fish tacos, great snorkeling, great surfing, great fishing, great biking, and great hiking.

This is San Diego, a vacationer's paradise, ideal for those who like variety and for those who can't decide between the city and the beach. It is one of the few areas of the country where the weather is given for the mountains, desert, inland, and sea, since all are within a couple of hours of the city. The joke is that meteorologists are forced to report the weather outside of San Diego because the most boring job in the world is to report the weather in San Diego: "Today will be 70 and sunny." "Today will be 70 and sunny." "Today will be 70 and sunny."

It wasn't too long ago that San Diego was a sleepy little town, peaceful but devoid of much culture, a place where movie stars came to get away from it all. In the past 10 to 15 years, however, the city has grown by leaps and bounds; it now has a population of 1.3 million (2.8 million county-wide) and is the seventh-largest city in the United States. Much of the growth has come from people tired of unpredictable weather and winter coats who want to live where they can go holiday shopping in shorts and T-shirts. Other growth has come from companies that relocate here partly because of the ease of recruiting workers. The area is also filled with Navy and Marine personnel from the bases here who retire from the military and don't want to leave.

San Diego is where California began. In 1542, explorer Juan Rodriguez Cabrillo was commissioned by the governor of Guatemala to take a voyage up the California coast under the flag of Spain. He reached "a very good enclosed port," which is what we now know as San Diego Bay; Cabrillos statue stands at the edge of Cabrillo Park on the spot where he is believed to have anchored his boat. In the mid-18th century, when it was feared that Russian interest in Alaska was a prelude to Southern expansion, Spanish missionaries came to California, and Father Junipera Serra built the first of his 31 famous California missions in San Diego. All around San Diego there are tributes to the city's rich past.

And yet San Diego's focus is very much on the present. It is a city in which the arts flourish. Balboa Park, the largest urban cultural park in the country, features 15 museums, numerous art galleries, free outdoor concerts, the Tony Award-winning Globe Theatres, and the San Diego Zoo. The upscale community of La Jolla, a few miles up the coast, is the site of the La Jolla Playhouse, another Tony Award-winning theater. This one was begun in 1947 by Gregory Peck, Dorothy McGuire, and Mel Ferrer. Quirky museums, like the Museum of Making Music, flood the county. Art exhibits are plentiful. And the kids won't know what to do first—swim in the ocean, visit SeaWorld, pan for gold in an old hard-rock gold mine, go to LEGO-LAND (see CARLSBAD), explore the tidepools, or visit the Aerospace Museum and Hall of Fame, where they can go on a motion simulator ride that takes them on different planes throughout time.

But really, it won't matter, because whatever you don't have a chance to do this time, you can do next time. Or the next. Or the one after that.

Additional Visitor Information

The San Diego Convention & Visitors Bureau, International Visitor Information Center, 401 B St, Suite 1400, 92101, phone 619/236-1212, offers general information brochures in English, French, German, Japanese, Portuguese, and Spanish. *San Diego Magazine,* available at newsstands, has up-to-date information about cultural events and articles of interest to visitors.

Public Transportation

Buses and trolleys downtown, to East County, and to Tijuana (San Diego Transit), phone 619/233-3004.

Airport San Diego International Airport; weather, phone 619/289-1212; cash machines, East Terminal.

Information phone 619/231-2100

Lost and Found phone 619/686-8002

What to See and Do

Aerospace Museum and Hall of Fame. *2001 Pan American Plz, San Diego (92101). Phone 619/234-8291. www.aerospacemuseum.org.* This museum tells the story of aviation and spaceflight. In its hall of fame—the only one of its kind in the nation—visitors learn about the extraordinary accomplishments of the world's leading aviation pioneers, from the Wright Brothers and Amelia Earhart to Neil Armstrong, Yuri Gagarin, and Benjamin O. Davis Jr, a Tuskegee airman and the first African-American graduate of West Point. Don't miss "Wings," a motion simulator ride that takes you on different planes through time. (Memorial Day-Labor Day: 10 am-5:30 pm; rest of year: to 4:30 pm; closed Jan 1, Thanksgiving, Dec 25) **$$**

★ **Balboa Park.** *1549 El Prado, San Diego (92101). Phone 619/239-0512. www.balboapark.org.* On 1,200 acres, center of city. Art galleries, museums, theaters, restaurants, recreational facilities, and miles of garden walks, lawns, flowers, subtropical plants, and ponds. Off Park Boulevard are

House of Pacific Relations. *10410 Corporal Way, San Diego (92101). Phone 619/234-0739.* Thirty-one nations offer cultural and art exhibits in 15 California/Spanish-style cottages. (Sun noon-4 pm) **FREE**

Mingei International Museum of World Folk Art. *1439 El Prado, San Diego (92101). In Plaza de Panama. Phone 619/239-0003.* Six galleries contain art exhibits of people from all cultures of the world. Many art forms, such as costumes, jewelry, dolls and toys, utensils, painting, and sculpture are shown in different collections and changing exhibitions. Also here is a theater, library, collections research center, and educational facilities. (Tues-Sun 10 am-4 pm; closed holidays) **$$**

Museum of Man. *1350 El Prado, San Diego (92101). Phone 619/239-2001.* At the base of the 200-foot Spanish Renaissance California Tower—built in Balboa Park as the centerpiece of the 1915 Panama-California Exposition—is the San Diego Museum of Man. A must-see for anthropology buffs, the museum has collections of artifacts, folk art, and archaeological finds that help unfold stories of hunters creating the first spears and arrows, artisans blending forms and symbols, and the cultures in which American Indians lived and died. One of the newest and most popular exhibits is "Footsteps Through Time," which takes visitors through 4 million years of human evolution. And don't miss the ever-popular Children's Discovery Center, where children can experience aspects of royal and ordinary Egyptian life in the 18th Dynasty by bartering in an Egyptian market, "navigating" a small boat on the Nile, and dressing up in costumes of royalty or faithful subjects

of the pharaohs. (Daily 10 am-4:30 pm; closed Jan 1, Thanksgiving, Dec 25) **$$**

Museum of Photographic Arts. *1649 El Prado, San Diego (92101). Phone 619/238-7559.* Changing exhibitions featuring 19th-century, early-mid-20th century, and contemporary works by world-renowned photographers. (Mon-Wed, Fri-Sun 10 am-5 pm, Thurs to 9 pm; closed holidays) Free guided tours Sun. **$$**

Old Globe Theatre. *1363 Old Globe Way, San Diego (92101). Phone 619/239-2255.* The first time anyone saw five naked men doing "the full Monty" before a live audience was in this thatched-roof replica of Shakespeare's Globe, behind the Museum of Man in Balboa Park (see). This superb 581-seat venue (it won a Tony in 1984 for excellence in regional theater) is frequently used for pre-Broadway tryouts, as was the case with Stephen Sondheim's *Into the Woods,* but produces plenty of new works and Shakespearean productions as well. It is one of three associated theaters on a grassy complex in Balboa Park, the other two being the Cassius Carter Center, an intimate 225-seat theater, and the 612-seat Lowell Davies Festival Theater, used in the summer primarily for Shakespeare. Tours (Sat-Sun 10:30 am; $). **$$$$**

Reuben H. Fleet Science Center. *1875 El Prado, San Diego (92101). On Park Blvd at Bay Theater Way. Phone 619/238-1233.* A science museum specializing in space-related topics, the Fleet Science Center offers the latest in bang-zoom interactive and virtual reality exhibits. What better way to learn astronomy than to stand in the middle of a meteor storm or rocket toward a comet? More contemplative types may prefer the planetarium shows or—for those who love old technologies—a collection of astronomical photography. But the Fleet explains earthly science, too. The Explorazone 3 area offers a hands-on experience with such concepts as wind, illusion, and (most enjoyably) turbulence. For pre-schoolers, there's a Little Learners Lab, and AIBO, Sony's famous robot dog, makes the rounds several times a day. You may need to sit down after all this. Rest assured, the museum boasts a state-of-the-art IMAX domed theater, too. Maybe a quiet movie about coral reefs will be playing. (Mon-Thurs 9:30 am-5 pm, Fri to 9 pm, Sat to 8 pm, Sun to 6 pm) **$$$**

San Diego Hall of Champions Sports Museum. *2131 Pan American Plz, San Diego (92101). Phone*

619/234-2544. Exhibits on more than 40 sports in the area; theater, gift shop, Breitbard Hall of Fame, and San Diego sports archives. (Daily 10 am-4:30 pm; closed Jan 1, Thanksgiving, Dec 25) **$$**

San Diego Museum of Art. *1450 El Prado, San Diego (92101). Phone 619/232-7931.* European and American paintings and decorative arts; Japanese, Chinese, and other Asian art; and contemporary sculpture. (Tues-Wed, Fri-Sun 10 am-6 pm, Thurs to 9 pm; closed Jan 1, Thanksgiving, Dec 25) Free admission the third Tues of each month. **$$**

San Diego Natural History Museum. *1788 El Prado, San Diego (92101). Phone 619/232-3821.* Exhibits of flora and fauna and minerology of southwestern United States and Baja California; Foucault pendulum; traveling exhibits; classes, nature outings. (Daily 10 am-5 pm; closed Jan 1, Thanksgiving, Dec 25) **$$**

San Diego Zoo. *2920 Zoo Dr, San Diego (92103). Off of Park Blvd. Phone 619/234-3153.* More than 4,200 rare and exotic animals representing 800 species, many of which are displayed in natural habitats such as Polar Bear Plunge, Hippo Beach, Tiger River, Sun Bear Forest, and Gorilla Tropics. The children's zoo features a petting paddock, animal nursery, and animal exhibits at children's eye level. Walk-through aviaries. Animal shows daily; 40-minute guided tour aboard double-deck bus; aerial tramway. (Daily 9 am-4 pm; to 9 pm in summer; to 5 pm for two weeks in Apr) **$$$$**

Spanish Village Center. *1770 Village Pl, San Diego (92101). Phone 619/233-9050.* Visitors can observe artists and craftspeople working here. Studios surround the patios. (Daily 11 am-4 pm; closed Jan 1, Thanksgiving, Dec 25) **FREE**

Spreckels Organ Concerts. *Spreckels Organ Pavilion, Pan American Way, San Diego (92101). Phone 619/702-8138.* The magnificent Spreckels organ, nestled in its ornate pavilion in the heart of Balboa Park, is a sight to see. With 4,446 individual pipes ranging from less than 1/2 inch to more than 32 feet in length, its something to hear as well. With a few brief respites, the organ has been in continuous use since brothers John and Adolph Spreckels gave it to San Diego's citizens in 1914. Free hour-long concerts are held on Sundays at 2 pm, with seating for 2,400. In summer, a 12-week

Organ Festival takes place on Monday evenings. (Sun 2 pm) **FREE**

Starlight Bowl/Starlight Theatre. *2005 Pan American Dr, San Diego (92101). Phone 619/544-7827.* Since the first strands of *The Naughty Marietta* played in 1946, the San Diego Civic Light Opera Association has been staging musicals in the open-air Starlight Theatre in Balboa Park. The company employs union actors, musicians, and stagehands, but also hires local actors and technicians who are able to get a start in Starlight's apprentice and internship programs. The season runs from mid-June through September, and since 1946, the company has performed 120 different musicals. If you attend a performance, be sure to look for the legendary red box: on opening night in 1946, the costumer took her red sewing box, tied it with a gold tassel, and gave it to the stage manager as something regal for the bride to carry when she ran off to get married in *The Mikado*. The performance was so successful that the red box has been on stage every night since. (Thurs-Sun 8 pm; box office: Mon-Wed 10 am-4 pm, Thurs-Fri 10 am-9:30 pm, Sat-Sun noon-9:30 pm) **$$$$**

Timken Museum of Art. *1500 El Prado, San Diego (92101). Phone 619/239-5548.* Collection of European Old Masters, 18th- and 19th-century American paintings, and Russian icons. (Tues-Sat 10 am-4:30 pm, Sun from 1:30 pm; closed holidays, Sept) **FREE**

Veterans Memorial Center Museum. *2115 Park Blvd, San Diego (92101). Phone 619/239-2300.* One of the things that makes this veterans memorial particularly interesting is how far back its materials go: it displays historical objects, artifacts, documents, and memorabilia dating back to the Civil War. The memorial/museum is housed in a building that was once the chapel of the US Naval Hospital. After a victorious battle to save it from becoming a parking lot extension for the San Diego Zoo, it is now on the National Register of Historic Places. (Tues-Sat 9:30 am-3 pm) **DONATION**

Balboa Park Golf Course. *2600 Golf Course Dr, San Diego (92102). Balboa Park, near 26th and A sts. Phone 619/239-1660. www.sannet.gov/park-and-recreation/ golf/bpgolf.shtml.* Municipal courses, 18 and 9 holes; pro shop, driving range, three putting greens; restaurant. (Daily) **$$$$**

Barona Casino. *1932 Wildcat Canyon Rd, Lakeside (92040). Phone 619/443-2300; toll-free 888/722-7662. www.barona.com.* Located amid rolling hills 25 miles north of San Diego and designed by the creative forces behind Las Vegas's Mirage Hotel and Casino, the Barona Casino is one of the most popular gaming destinations in California. It has everything gamblers could want: 310,000 square feet of Vegas-style casino, including slots, tables, and a poker room, plus an off-track betting facility, and a bingo hall. Whatever your game, the Barona's service is legendary: management, for example, aims to solve any problem with the slots within two minutes. If the cards are treating you coldly, warm up at a centrally located rock fireplace that's open on four sides. Eating choices range from a food court to a dinner-only steakhouse with buffalo on the menu. Note that, due to the difficulty of the roads and the Barona Indian's cultural sensitivity to alcohol, no liquor is allowed in the casino. (Daily) **FREE**

Beach areas. Ocean Beach *(off I-8 and Sunset Cliffs Blvd);* **Mission and Pacific beaches** *(adjacent to each other off I-5 at Garnet Ave exit);* **Coronado Beach** *(off Orange Ave on Coronado); and* **Silver Strand Beach** *(Palm Ave exit on I-5, then W to Hwy 75; follow signs).* Mission Beach also includes

> **Belmont Park.** *3190 Mission Blvd, San Diego (92109). Phone 858/488-1549.* Seaside amusement park includes a vintage wooden roller coaster and other rides, as well as the largest indoor swimming pool in Southern California. (Hours vary by season) **$**

Cabrillo National Monument. *1800 Cabrillo Memorial Dr, San Diego (92106). From I-5 S or I-8 W: exit at Rosecrans St, right on Caon St, left on Catalina Blvd. From I-5 N: exit and left on Hawthorne St, right on N Harbor Dr, left on Rosecrans St, right on Caon St, left on Catalina Blvd. Phone 619/557-5450. www.nps.gov/cabr.* In late autumn of 1542, explorer Juan Rodrguez Cabrillo and his crew arrived at what he called "a very good enclosed port," San Diego Harbor. Today, his statue looks out over one of the most beautiful views in all of San Diego. In addition to enjoying the scenery, there are many other things to do in this national park overlooking the Pacific. Its grounds include a historic lighthouse and much military history, including base end-stations, fire control stations, searchlight bunkers, and the remains of coastal defenses built to protect the approaches to San Diego Bay during the two World Wars. Many excellent walking paths guide you or simply allow you to explore. From late De-

cember through mid-March, natives flock to this site to watch the annual migration of Pacific gray whales. Don't miss the coastal tide pools, particularly exciting during winter's low tides, when the sea pushes back to reveal a unique world of marine plants and animals in little pockets of the earth. (Daily) **$**

Café Sevilla. *555 4th Ave, San Diego (92101). Phone 619/233-5979. www.cafesevilla.com.* Latin is the beat at this tapas bar, restaurant, and nightclub. Have some paella as you watch a flamenco dinner show or a little shrimp empañada as you enjoy a tango show. On certain nights of the week, free salsa and samba lessons are offered. On other nights, Latin music lovers can listen to rock en Espaol played by Latin bands. The restaurant of Café Sevilla is "casual-elegant," and the tapas bar, which features live flamenco music every night, has been known to attract celebrities such as the Gipsy Kings. Weekend dinner shows fill up quickly; make reservations in advance. (Daily 5 pm-1 am) **$$$**

Corporate Helicopters of San Diego. *3753 John J Montgomery Dr, San Diego (92123). Phone 858/505-5650. www.corporatehelicopters.com.* Sky tours offer views of the city's attractions and natural beauty. **$$$$**

Fashion Valley Mall. *7007 Friars Rd, San Diego (92108). Off Hwy 163, take Friars Rd W exit. Phone 619/297-3381. www.shopfashionvalleymall.com.* One of the more upscale malls in San Diego, this is a multilevel outdoor shopping fantasy. Among its anchor stores are Neiman Marcus, Saks Fifth Avenue, Robinson's-May, and Lord & Taylor, and its remaining shops consist of well-known specialty chains and unique, one-of-a-kind boutiques. There are several restaurants as well, both indoor and outdoor. (Mon-Sat 10 am-9 pm, Sun 11 am-7 pm)

Gaslamp Quarter. *Downtown. Phone 619/233 1692. www.gaslamp.org.* A 16 1/2-block national historic district bordered by Broadway on the north, 6th Avenue on the east, Harbor Drive on the south, and 4th Avenue on the west. This area formed the city's business center at the turn of the century. Many Victorian buildings under restoration. Walking tours (Sat).

Horton Plaza. *324 Horton Plz, San Diego (92101). Bounded by Broadway, G St, and 1st and 4th aves. Phone 619/238-1596. www.westfield.com.* They say that Horton Plaza has been a catalyst for a regenerated downtown San Diego, and it's not difficult to see why. Sixteen years of research went into the design of this whimsical, multilevel shopping mall. The black concrete and narrow walkways were patterned after those found in European marketplaces. Many merchants display their goods on carts. The building is covered in 1 million 1-inch tiles, laid individually by hand, and the ornate lights on level three are replicas of the city's turn-of-the-century gas lamps. The interlocking levels are lined with 140 specialty shops, department stores, and several sit-down restaurants. Thankfully, there are also many cookie and ice cream stores, perfectly placed for taking a break when your feet plead for a rest from walking the 11 1/2-acre plaza. (Mon-Fri 10 am-9 pm, Sat to 8 pm, Sun 11 am-7 pm)

Humphrey's Concerts by the Bay. *2241 Shelter Island Dr, San Diego (92106). Take I-5 S to the Rosecrans exit. Take Rosecrans W 5 miles to Shelter Island Dr and turn left. Humphreys is on the right. Phone 619/224-3577. www.humphreysconcerts.com.* Palm trees to one side, a harbor to the other, California weather all around, and a concert in the middle of it all; if that's your idea of entertainment, Humphrey's is the place for you. For more than ten years, Humphrey's has been offering a who's who of comedy and musical acts that cover all tastes and genres, from Paul Anka to Smokey Robinson, and from Jay Leno to Ladysmith Black Mambazo. No matter whos performing, the 1,295-seat venue itself is worth the price of admission. **$$$$**

Ken Cinema. *4061 Adams Ave, San Diego (92116). Phone 619/819-0236. www.landmarktheatres.com.* Seeing a film at the Ken means hard seats and subtitles. For movie buffs, though, that's an invitation, not a threat. They know that surfers have the ocean, but anyone wanting to catch a different kind of wave (the French New Wave, say) has this San Diego landmark, long *the* local place for art films, foreign cinema, and revivals. The locals try to keep it hidden from tourists, whom they consider unworthy of such fare. So try to blend in with the crowd.

Kobey's Swap Meet. *3500 Sports Arena Blvd, San Diego (92110). Phone 619/226-0650. www.kobeyswap. com.* Kobey's is San Diego's largest and most popular open-air market, featuring everything from furniture, crafts, antiques, and fashion to electronics, sporting goods, and fresh produce. The faithful come frequently and are usually in place when the doors open at 7 am. The back section with its secondhand goods is a bargain hunter's delight. Vendors sell food and beverages, and live entertainment will keep you humming between negotiations. (Fri-Sun 7 am-3 pm) **$**

Lake Cuyamaca. *From San Diego, take I-8 E to State Hwy 79 N until you see the lake. Once you leave the freeway, you are 15 minutes away. Phone toll-free 877/581-9904. www.lakecuyamaca.org.* There are plenty of fish that didn't get away at this beautiful 110-acre lake, surrounded on three sides by the Lake Cuyamaca Rancho State Park. Lake Cuyamaca is stocked with 440,000 pounds of fish—Florida bass, smallmouth bass, channel catfish, crapple, bluegill, and sturgeon—and it's the only lake in San Diego that is able to stock trout all year long. The lake's Web site provides a wealth of information, including telling you just "How to Bag a Bucket of Bullhead Catfish" and "The Best Method for Catching Trout at Lake Cuyamaca." **$$**

Mission Bay Park. *2688 E Mission Bay Dr, San Diego (92109). N of San Diego River, reached via I-5. Phone 619/276-8200.* Aquatic park on 4,600 acres. Swimming, water-skiing in Fiesta and Sail bays, fishing, boating, sailing (rentals, ramps, landings, marinas), sportfishing fleet; golf; picnicking; camping. (Daily) **FREE** In the park is

SeaWorld San Diego. *500 SeaWorld Dr, San Diego (92109). SeaWorld Dr, exit W off I-5. Phone toll-free 800/257-4268.* Take a simulated helicopter ride and come face to face with beluga whales, polar bears, and walruses at a research station in the Arctic. Or put on your tux and watch 400 other tuxedoed guys strut around the Penguin Encounter. Or just sit and watch in amazement as Shamu, Baby Shamu, and Namu entertain you with astonishing behaviors and tricks. Whatever you choose to do in this 190-acre marine park on Mission Bay, you're bound to have fun. Open since 1964, SeaWorld has continued to add attractions and animals and has even ventured beyond the sea: its newest section, Pets Rule!, is devoted to dogs and cats. The park has four different shows, four rides, and more than 20 exhibits and attractions. If you're there during the summer, don't miss Cirque de la Mer, an over-water acrobatic performance of mystical creatures. (Daily; hours vary by season) **$$$$**

Mission San Diego de Alcala. *10818 San Diego Mission Rd, San Diego (92108). Phone 619/281-8449. www.missionsandiego.com.* San Diego de Alcala marks the birthplace of Christianity in the Far West. It was California's first church and the first of the 21 great California missions. This remarkable shrine, still an active Catholic parish, provides an interesting look

Old Town San Diego

This short walk leads you through intriguing Old Town, an amalgam of Old Town State Historic Park and adjacent areas containing restored or replicated 19th-century historic structures, small museums, and lively restaurants and shops. The area—which has the flavor of a low-key historic theme park (but without the rides and tacky touristy elements)—pays homage to San Diego's first settlers from the Mexican and early American eras. It lies north of downtown San Diego at Juan Street, near the intersection of Interstate 5 and Interstate 8. You could spend an hour or a day here, depending on how long you wish to linger at the museums and shops; on certain days, you may encounter living history presentations, with demonstrations of blacksmithing and tortilla-making. From the parking lot at Juan and Mason streets, walk down Mason a block or so to Old Town Plaza in the middle of the State Historic Park. The dirt streets that line the plaza help transport you back to the days before San Diego became known for surfers and the US Navy. At the Robinson-Rose House on the north side of the plaza, you can pick up brochures and view depictions of Old Town in the early 1800s. Turn right and head along the southwestern edges of the plaza to view some old adobes dating from the 1820s and

1830s. Back on Mason Street, don't miss the Mason Street School, a one-room schoolhouse dating from 1865, where you can sit at the wooden desks and assess the punishments listed on the board for acting up. Nearby is the McKinstry Dentist Office, where the primitive dental tools will make you glad for the invention of floss. At the Wells Fargo History Museum, you can view an 1868 stagecoach, a telegraph machine, and gold samples. A bit farther up Mason Street is the Casa de Estudillo, Old Towns largest original adobe, which is furnished in the mid-19th-century style of a wealthy rancher. At Calhoun Street, go right to see the Casa de Bandini, which dates from 1829 and now houses a good Mexican restaurant. Just down the street is the Seeley Stable, with a nice stagecoach exhibit. Turning right on Twiggs Street, you'll come upon the old office of the *San Diego Union* newspaper. Take a left turn on San Diego Avenue to the Whaley House Museum, which has a nice collection of early California artifacts. Complete your walk around Old Town by going back on San Diego Avenue to Old Town Plaza and walking northwest to Calhoun Street. There you'll come upon the Bazaar del Mundo, a colorful collection of Mexican-flavored shops and open-air restaurants, including the festive Casa de Pico.

into San Diego's Spanish heritage, as well as an understanding of the beginning of Catholicism in this corner of the world. The San Diego Trolley makes a stop just half a block from the mission, which is a National Historic Landmark. Gift shop, visitor center (daily 9 am-4:45 pm; closed Thanksgiving, Dec 25),

Mount Woodson rock climbing. *Mount Woodson lies along Hwy 67 between Poway and Ramona. Park about 3 miles N of the Hwy 67/Poway Rd junction in the vicinity of the state forestry fire station. A short dirt trail passes through the trees until it hits a paved road, which winds all the way to the top of Mount Woodson. Phone 760/789-1311.* With its millions of boulders and perfect weather, Southern California is a fantastic place to boulder, and Mount Woodson may be the best place in Southern California to do it. You'll find super-thin cracks, super-wide ones, mantles, edging, low-angle climbs, friction climbing—just about anything you want to do in the way of climbing, you can find here.

You can bring your own equipment and practice leading cracks or climb walls with problems ranging in difficulty levels. For simpler climbs, bring a chalk bag and you're off. But if you want to explore, make sure that you're with someone who knows these routes; many are hidden, and most aren't in any guide

Museum of Contemporary Art San Diego. *1001 Kettner Blvd, San Diego (92101). Phone 619/234-1001. www.mcasandiego.org.* Permanent and changing exhibits of contemporary painting, sculpture, design, photography, and architecture. Bookstore. (Mon-Tues, Thurs-Sun 11 am-5 pm; closed Jan 1, Thanksgiving, Dec 25) **FREE**

Ocean Beach Farmers' Market. *4900 block of Newport Ave, San Diego. Phone 619/224-4906. www.oceanbeach-sandiego.com.* You like farmers' markets but would rather ride a llama. Whoever said you couldnt do both? Head for this weekly wonder in Ocean Beach, where the pickings are ripe and the llamas are, well, rideable. Llama rides aren't the only reason this market differs

Gaslamp Quarter and Harborfront

This tour combines the best aspects of San Diego's downtown area, a historic area now thriving with shops and restaurants, with the scenic waterfront—all best appreciated on foot. Start at Horton Plaza, a multilevel open-air complex of shops and snack bars. The colorful architecture alone is worth a look. Walk east down F Street to 4th Avenue, where you'll come upon the Gaslamp Quarter, a 16 1/2-block historic district with renovated Victorian-era architecture. Bounded by 4th Avenue, 6th Avenue, Broadway, and L Street, the Gaslamp Quarter is just two blocks wide and eight blocks long. This is a good place to wander among antique shops, art galleries, cafés, restaurants, and nightspots (in the evening, especially on weekends, it can be quite lively; you may want to return to experience some of the nightlife). Walk east for two blocks on F Street, turning right at 6th Avenue; walk three blocks south to Island Avenue and make another right so you're walking west. Now, walk north a block to Market Street and cross West Harbor Drive to Kettner Boulevard, where you'll find Seaport Vil-

lage, an attractive open-air complex of shops and other entertainment, including an old-fashioned carousel. There are good seaside views here, which continue as you walk south on Kettner to Embarcadero Marina Park—a lovely area filled with sights of green grass, kites flapping in the breeze, and sailboats skimming across the bay. Continue back up to Harbor Drive and follow it north along the waterfront, also known as the Embarcadero. At the Broadway Pier, near the intersection of North Harbor Drive and Broadway, you'll see the San Diego-Coronado ferry port (ferries leave hourly for Coronado, which is just across the ways). Harbor cruise boats also depart from here. A bit past the pier is the Maritime Museuma collection of three historic ships berthed in the harbor, including the striking *Star of India*, an 1863 windjammer that is the oldest iron sailing ship still afloat. The ships are available for tours. Depending on stops, the entire walking tour can take anywhere from two to four hours or more.

from others in the area (there are no fewer than two dozen in San Diego County alone; the county produces more than $1 billion worth of fruits, flowers, and other crops annually). Whereas other markets typically end by noon, this one favors those who prefer to pick their fruits, vegetables, avocados, fresh-cut flowers, and exotic fruits and foods, much of which is laid out for sampling, in the late afternoon to early evening. (Winter: Wed 4-7 pm; summer: Wed 4-8 pm)

Old Mission Dam Historical Site. *1 Father Junipero Serra Trail, San Diego (92119). Phone 619/668-3275. www.desertusa.com/mistrail/mtrails.html.* The Old Mission Dam was constructed to provide water for the residents of the San Diego Mission de Alcala. It is 44 feet long, 13 feet thick, and 13 feet wide, built of stone and cement on exposed bedrock. Approximately 6 miles away is Mission Trails Regional Park, where the history of habitants goes back 10,000 years. More than 30 archaeological sites have been identified within the park, including dwelling sites, work areas, and spiritually significant areas. Walking trails in both areas lead to magnificent vistas. (Daily 9 am-5 pm; closed Jan 1, Thanksgiving, Dec 25) **FREE**

Old Town. *Mason St and San Diego Ave, San Diego. Around the plaza.* Historic section of city with many restored or reconstructed buildings; old adobe structures; restaurants, shops. Guided walking tours (daily). Old Town includes Old Town San Diego State Historic Park and

Presidio Park. *2811 Jackson St, San Diego (92110). Presidio Dr off Taylor St.* Inside is site of the first mission in California. Mounds mark the original presidio and fort. (Daily 6 am-10 pm) **$**

Serra Museum. *2727 Presidio Dr, San Diego (92121). Phone 619/297-3258.* Landmark of San Diego; the museum stands on top of the hill recognized as the site where California's first mission and presidio were established in 1769. The museum interprets the Spanish and Mexican periods of San Diego's history. (Daily 10 am-4:30 pm; closed holidays) **$**

The Whaley House. *2482 San Diego Ave, San Diego (92110). At Harney St. Phone 619/297-9327.* In the mid-19th century, New Yorker Thomas Whaley came to San Diego via San Francisco, where the scent of fresh gold beckoned. This home, which was built for him and his family in 1856, was the first brick building in San Diego County. In part, the house was also built by him; the bricks were made in his own kiln, while the walls were finished with plaster made from ground seashells. The inside of the house has an illustrious heritage as well. Not only have five generations of the Whaley family lived here, but apparently so have a few spirits. This is one of two authenticated haunted houses in California. (Thurs-Tues 10 am-4 pm; closed holidays) **$**

Old Town San Diego State Historic Park. *Visitor Center, 4002 Wallace St, San Diego (92110). Use I-5 and I-8. Phone 619/220-5422. www.parks.ca.gov.* This is an area within Old Town that is bounded by Congress, Wallace, Twigg and Juan streets. (Daily 10 am-5 pm; closed Jan 1, Thanksgiving, Dec 25) **FREE** The park includes

> **Casa de Estudillo.** *4001 Mason St, San Diego (92110). Phone 619/220-5422.* (1820-1829) Restored example of a one-story adobe townhouse; period furnishings. (Daily 10 am-5 pm; closed Jan 1, Thanksgiving, Dec 25)

> **San Diego Union Museum.** *2626 San Diego Ave, San Diego.* Restored birthplace of the San Diego newspaper that first came off the press in 1868. (Daily 10 am-5 pm; closed Jan 1, Thanksgiving, Dec 25) **FREE**

San Diego Bay and the Embarcadero. *1300 N Harbor Dr, San Diego (92101).* Port for active Navy ships, cruise ships, commercial shipping, and tuna fleet. Sailing, powerboating, water-skiing, and sportfishing at Shelter Island, Harbor Island, the Yacht Harbor, and America's Cup Harbor.

San Diego Chargers (NFL) *Qualcomm Stadium, 9449 Friars Rd, San Diego (92108). Phone 858/874-4500; toll-free 877/242-7437. www.chargers.com.* Playing from August through December, the "Bolts," as they're nicknamed because of the lightning strikes on their helmets and uniforms, regularly play in front of more than 71,000 home fans.

San Diego-Coronado Ferry. *1050 N Harbor Dr, San Diego (92101). Phone 619/234-4111. www.sdhe.com.* Hourly departures from San Diego Harbour Excursion dock to Ferry Landing Marketplace in Coronado. (Daily) **$**

San Diego Early Music Society. *3510 Dove Ct, San Diego (92103). Phone 619/291-8246. www.sdems.org.* The setting is almost impossibly perfect: a church called St. James-by-the-Sea, in La Jolla, one of the most beautiful parts of San Diego County. Six times a year, the church plays host to international concerts of the San Diego Early Music Society, and out of this picture-perfect setting, drift strains of a harpsichord or a baroque guitar, or the melodious voices of a quartet performing medieval and Renaissance work. The San Diego Early Music Society, a group dedicated to preserving European medieval, Renaissance, and baroque music, brings musicians from all over the world to play, frequently on authentic instruments; the group also holds concerts featuring local musicians six Sundays each year at the San Diego Museum of Art in Balboa Park. Dates are scheduled but can change; check the Web site for updates. **$$$$**

San Diego Gulls. *3500 Sports Arena Blvd, San Diego (92110). Phone 619/224-4171. www.sandiegogulls.com.* Put down the surfboard and head to the ice. The four-time Taylor Cup champions are moving into a new conference with the merger of the West Coast and East Coast Hockey Leagues. This will give hockey fans a better chance to spot a future National Hockey League player while he's still developing his skills and, hopefully, before he gets hurt.

San Diego Harbor Excursion. *1050 N Harbor Dr, San Diego (92101). Phone 619/234-4111; toll-free 800/442-7847. www.sdhe.com.* One-hour (12-mile) narrated tour highlights Harbor Island, Coronado, and the Navy terminals at North Island and 32nd Street. Two-hour (25-mile) narrated tour includes the above plus Shelter Island, Ballast Point (where Cabrillo is believed to have first landed in 1542), the harbor entrance, the ship yards, and the Navy's submarine base. (Daily) **$$$$**

San Diego Junior Theatre at the Casa del Prado Theater. *1650 El Prado, San Diego (92101). Phone 619/239-1311. www.juniortheatre.com.* Few children's theater groups have entertained a million people or boast alums like Raquel Welch. This San Diego institution, founded in 1947 and performing behind the heavy oak doors of the Casa del Prado Theater, always aims big. In recent seasons, the group has put up Broadway standards like *Guys and Dolls* and *Oliver!,* has adapted kids' literature like *Nancy Drew* and *James and the Giant Peach,* and—as any troupe must—has risen to the challenge of the real bears of the British tradition (Pooh, Paddington, and William Shakespeare). Most unique of all is that children not only perform the plays but also work on costumes and lighting, serve as the stage crew, and even staff the ticket windows. (Fri 7 pm, Sat-Sun 2 pm) **$$$**

San Diego Maritime Museum and *Star of India*. *1492 N Harbor Dr, San Diego (92101). Embarcadero. Phone 619/234-9153. www.sdmaritime.com.* Restored bark *Star of India* (1863) built at Ramsey on the Isle of Man and launched as the *Euterpe;* sailed under the British, Hawaiian (before it was part of the United States), and United States flags. It sailed for the first time in 50 years on July 4, 1976. Also here are the steam ferry *Berkeley* (1898), with nautical exhibits, and the luxury steam yacht *Medea* (1904). (Daily 9 am-8 pm) **$$**

San Diego Opera. *202 B St, San Diego (92101). Phone 619/533-7000. www.sdopera.com.* The San Diego Opera Company was born in 1965 and has grown to become one of the most respected opera companies in America. Between January and May, the company presents five grand opera productions and several concerts and special recitals. Performers are internationally known opera stars and the best young American singers. And happily for opera neophytes, brief English translations of the operas lyrics are projected onto the stage. **$$$$**

San Diego Padres (MLB). *Qualcomm Stadium, 9449 Friars Rd, San Diego (92108). Phone 619/795-5000; toll-free 877/374-2784. www.padres.com.* Sure, throughout their history, the Padres have usually been battling to get out of last place. And, yes, sometimes the rest of the country rolls its eyes at the "California cuisine" offered at the concession stands. However, whether you're relaxing in the pleasant San Diego sun or feeling a cool evening breeze, you'll enjoy the national pastime under ideal conditions at a Padres game. Just keep in mind that if the Dodgers or Giants are in town, Southern California isn't always mellow. Game tickets are available by telephone, online, at the Padres Ticket Office at Qualcomm Stadium, or at any San Diego County Office Depot store.

San Diego scenic tours. *Phone 858/273-8687. www.sandiegoscenictours.com.* Narrated bus and harbor tours. Choose from the four-hour San Diego City Tour, City and Harbor Tour, or the Tijuana Tour. Also offered are the full-day Tijuana Tour and the ultimate full-day San Diego, Harbor, and Tijuana Tour or the San Diego-Tijuana Tour. (Daily) **$$$$**

San Diego Trolley. *707 F St, San Diego. www.sdcommute.com.* The 47-mile light rail system goes from downtown east to Santee and north through Old Town, serving many major shopping centers in Mission Valley and Qualcomm Stadium for easy access to San Diego Padres and Chargers games. (Daily) **$**

Scenic drive. This 59-mile loop, marked by blue and yellow seagull signs, takes 2 1/2 to 3 hours and includes the waterfront, Shelter Island, Cabrillo National Monument, Point Loma, Old Town, and the top of Mount Soledad, which has a magnificent view of the entire area.

Seaport Village. *849 W Harbor Dr, San Diego (92101). Market St at Kettner Blvd, adjacent to Embarcadero Marina Park. Phone 619/235-4014. www.spvillage.com.* Seaport Village presents one of the city's more delightful oxymorons: it was designed to look like a 100-year-old fishing village, yet you can sit at the water's edge and sip a glass of wine or stroll to one of the specialty stores and purchase a necklace of imported amber. Seventy-five stores make their home here, many with a specific audience ("Southpaw Shoppe," "Whiskers, The Ultimate Cat Shoppe," "Kite Flite") and some of a more general nature, plus four restaurants. In between stores, don't miss the Broadway Flying Horses Carousel with its jumping and standing horses, goats, and dogs, originally built at Coney Island in 1890. (Daily 10 am-10 pm)

Tavern Brick by Brick. *1130 Buenos Ave, San Diego (92110). Phone 619/275-5483. www.brickbybrick.com.* Unless you're looking for jazz or swing, there's a lot to please the over-21 crowd at this live-music neighborhood club. In the front is the music: everything from local bands, techno, rock, and pop to heavy metal (buy tickets in advance for the music). In the back is a more relaxing element: a lounge with round, white cocktail tables and matching swivel stools; low, cushioned bench seating; overhanging ice-blue light fixtures; and a small bar. (Daily 8 pm-2 am)

Villa Montezuma/Jesse Shepard House. *1925 K St, San Diego (92102). Phone 619/239-2211.* (1887) Lavish Victorian mansion built for Jesse Shepard, musician and author, during the city's "Great Boom" (1886-1888). More than 20 stained-glass windows reflect Shepard's interest in art, music, and literature; includes restored kitchen, antiques. (Fri-Sun 10 am-4:30 pm) **$**

Whale-watching trips. For three months each year (mid-Dec-mid-Feb), California gray whales make their way from Alaska's Bering Sea to the warm bays and lagoons of Baja, passing only a mile or so off the

San Diego shoreline. As many as 200 whales a day have been counted during the peak of the migration period. Trips to local waters and Baja lagoons are scheduled by the San Diego Natural History Museum. For information on other whale-watching trips, inquire at local sportfishing companies (like San Diego Harbor Excursion; phone 619/234-4111; www.sdhe.com), or at the International Visitors Information Center; phone 619/236-1212. **$$$$**

Wild Animal Park. *15500 San Pasqual Valley, Escondido (92027). 30 miles NE via I-15 to Via Rancho Pkwy exit, follow signs. Phone 760/747-8702; toll-free 800/934-2267. www.wildanimalpark.org.* More than 3,500 exotic animals wander in herds and packs through this 1,800-acre wild animal preserve as if they were in their native Africa or Asia—and we are lucky observers of their world. In 1972, the park opened to the public, and today it still operates as a preservation area for endangered species. You can wander through the Heart of Africa, traverse botanical gardens on the Kilimanjaro Safari Walk, or discover what's in the Epiphyllum House (hint: it's not an animal). Several different tours are conducted daily, such as the highly popular Photo Caravan Tours, and special events are held all summer long, including Roar and Snore, in which you sleep under the stars and see what happens in the zoo after dark. Don't miss Condor Ridge, an educational tribute to one of America's endangered species. Upon entering the area, you receive a self-guided tour journal; begin your walk to the ridge past roosting places for endangered thick-billed parrots and a ground for western great roadrunners. (Winter and spring: daily 9 am-4 pm, to 8 pm in early and late Dec; summer: daily 9 am-8 pm) **$$$$**

William Heath Davis Home. *410 Island Ave at 4th Ave, San Diego (92101). Phone 619/233-4692. www.gaslampquarter.org.* Today, the idea of "moving" is generally that you pack up and the house stays behind. But 150 years ago, it often meant taking the house with you. In 1850, the William Heath Davis House—the oldest structure in the Gaslamp Quarter—arrived in San Diego after being shipped by boat from Portland, Maine. The structure of the house has remained unchanged for 120 years and is an excellent example of a historic, prefabricated "saltbox" family home—a small, square house with two stories in front and one in back. A museum occupies the first and second floors. The house is also home to the Gaslamp Quarter Historical Foundation, which gives daily walking tours of the historic area. Call ahead for tour times. (Tues-Sun 10 am-6 pm) **$**

Special Events

Artwalk. *734 W Beech St, San Diego (92101). Phone 619/615-1090. www.artwalkinfo.com.* If you're in town in April, be sure to check out this lively self-guided multimedia tour that takes you into artists' studios; through galleries; and to exhibits of stained glass, sculpture, photography, electronic imaging, and works of architecture and design. Musical performances, short plays, dances, and poetry readings are also staged for visitors' enjoyment. Year after year, a particularly popular exhibit is "Refrigerator Art," in which student artists use refrigerators as canvases for their projects, after which the refrigerators are sold to benefit local school art programs. Last weekend in Apr. **FREE**

Balboa Park December Nights-The Annual Celebration of Christmas on the Prado. *Balboa Park, 1549 El Prado, San Diego (92103). Phone 619/239-0512. www.balboapark.org.* Balboa Park itself is a San Diego treasure, but if you're lucky enough to be visiting on the first Friday or Saturday in December, you're in for a unique delight. The park is transformed into a winter wonderland—sans snow, of course—with walkways and buildings adorned with beautiful lights and genteel decorations. All the museums are open until 9 pm, and all are free. Entertainment includes an eclectic mix of bell choirs, Renaissance and baroque music, African drums, and barbershop quartets. Unusual crafts, sweets, hot cider, and ethnic treats abound. And everyone acts as though their days are indeed merry and bright. Early Dec. **FREE**

Cabrillo Festival. *Cabrillo National Monument, 1800 Cabrillo Memorial Dr, San Diego (92106). Phone 619/557-5450.* Celebration of discovery of the West Coast. Early Oct.

Christmas on the Prado. Spreckels Outdoor Organ Pavilion and throughout Balboa Park. Fifty-foot-tall lighted tree, nativity scenes; special programs. First weekend in Dec.

Corpus Christi Fiesta. *Mission San Antonio de Pala, San Diego. 41 miles N via Hwy 163, I-15, then 7 miles E on Hwy 76.* Open-air mass, procession; games, dances, entertainment; Spanish-style pit barbecue; held annually since 1816. First Sun in June.

Ethnic Food Fair. *10410 Corporal Way, San Diego (92124). Phone 619/234-0739.* If ethnic food is what you're after, but you can't decide whether you're in the mood for Hungarian or Israeli—or Austrian or Finnish or Lithuanian or Irish or Ukrainian—head for the International Cottages at Balboa Park's House of Pacific

Relations. Each of these tiny cottages belonging to a single nation is decorated in the style of that nation and staffed by a volunteer who will explain things to you and answer your questions. On Memorial Day weekend, the normally staid scene comes alive with music, dancing, and the ethnic foods of 32 countries. The treats are plentiful, recipes are handed out, and each cottage is staffed with at least two people, one inside to explain customs and such, and the other outside to talk about food. Memorial Day weekend. **FREE**

Festival of Bells. *Mission Basilica San Diego de Alcala, 10818 San Diego Mission Rd, San Diego. Phone 619/283-7319.* Commemorates the July 16, 1769, founding of the mission. Weekend in mid-July.

Movies Before the Mast. *1492 N Harbor Dr, San Diego (92103). Phone 619/234-9153. www.sdmaritime.org.* Try this in a landlocked city! During July and August, one of San Diego's most unique movie venues is the 19th-century ship *Star of India,* anchored in the bay. It is also the Maritime Museum's 140-year-old centerpiece of its historic ship collection. Movies are shown on a special sail, and the theme is always nautical. Features have included films like *Captain Blood, Mutiny on the Bounty,* and *The Muppets Treasure Island.* And, yes, of course there's popcorn. July-Aug. **$$$**

San Diego Bay Parade of Lights. *www.sdparadeoflights.org.* For two Sunday evenings each December, the pitch-black San Diego Bay is flooded with color and light. Anywhere from 75 to 200 boats ranging from kayaks to yachts follow one another on a semicircular path through the calm waters of the bay. Some boats string lights in intricate patterns, and other simply string them in lines. Every once in a while, Santa makes an appearance on a mast. Early Dec.

Limited-Service Hotels

★ **BEST WESTERN AMERICANA INN.**
815 W San Ysidro, San Diego (92173). Phone 619/428-5521; toll-free 800/553-3933; fax 619/428-0693. www.bestwestern.com. 120 rooms, 2 story. Check-in 3 pm, check-out noon. Outdoor pool, whirlpool. **$**

★ ★ **BEST WESTERN CABRILLO GARDEN INN.** *840 A St, San Diego (92101). Phone 619/234-8477; toll-free 866/260-0402; fax 619/615-0422. www.bestwestern.com.* 30 rooms. Complimentary full breakfast. Check-in 3 pm, check-out noon. High-speed Internet access. Restaurant, bar. **$$**

★ ★ **COURTYARD BY MARRIOTT.** *530 Broadway, San Diego (92101). Phone 619/446-3000; toll-free 800/321-2211; fax 619/446-3010. www.courtyard.com/sancd.* Located in the heart of downtown San Diego in a historic bank building, this hotel is particularly well suited to business travelers. Each room is furnished with a large desk, two phones with voicemail, and free high-speed Internet access; a fax machine, copier, PC, and printer are also available to guests. Unwind or entertain in the hotel bar, or enjoy the hotel's Mediterranean restaurant, which serves breakfast, lunch, and dinner. The hotel, just a half-mile from the San Diego Convention Center, is also convenient to the bay, shopping, and entertainment. The historic Gaslamp District is just a few blocks away; Balboa Park and the San Diego Zoo are within 3 miles; and Coronado Island is just 4 miles from the hotel. 246 rooms. Check-in 3 pm, check-out noon. High-speed Internet access. Restaurant, bar. Fitness room. Whirlpool. **$$**

★ ★ **DANA INN AND MARINA.** *1710 W Mission Bay Dr, San Diego (92109). Phone 619/222-6440; toll-free 800/445-3339; fax 619/222-5916. www.thedana.net.* Providing the closest accommodations to SeaWorld, this value-priced hotel boasts a private marina on Mission Bay and is popular with families seeking convenience (and a free shuttle) to the park. Guest rooms feature modern bayside décor and are equipped with refrigerators, dataports, and video games. Shuffleboard, Ping-Pong, and an outdoor heated pool are among the on-site activities; beaches, playgrounds, shops, and restaurants are within walking distance. Parent-accompanied children 17 and under stay free. 196 rooms, 2 story. Check-in 4 pm, check-out noon. Restaurant. Outdoor pool, whirlpool. Airport transportation available. **$**

★ ★ **DOUBLETREE CLUB HOTEL.** *1515 Hotel Cir S, San Diego (92108). Phone 619/881-6900; toll-free 800/222-8733; fax 619/260-0147. www.doubletreeclubsd.com.* 217 rooms, 8 story. Pets accepted, some restrictions; fee. Check-in 3 pm, check-out noon. High-speed Internet access. Restaurant, bar. Fitness room. Outdoor pool, whirlpool. Business center. **$**

★ ★ **EMBASSY SUITES.** *601 Pacific Hwy, San Diego (92101). Phone 619/239-2400; toll-free 800/362-2779; fax 619/239-1520. www.essandiegobay.com.* 337 rooms, 12 story, all suites. Complimentary full breakfast. Check-in 3 pm, check-out noon. High-speed

Internet access. Restaurant, bar. Fitness room. Indoor pool, whirlpool. Airport transportation available. Business center. **$$**

★ HAMPTON INN DOWNTOWN. *1531 Pacific Hwy, San Diego (92101). Phone 619/233-8408; fax 619/233-8418. www.hamptoninn.com.* Geared toward business travelers, this hotel also offers recreational options that are sure to please. In addition to the obvious benefits of high-speed Internet access in every room, a large work desk, and a refrigerator and microwave, some rooms come with Jacuzzi tubs. You'll find a rooftop pool and sundeck here, with a view of the San Diego Bay only two blocks away. The color scheme of the Art Deco-inspired lobby, decorated in navy blue, black, and gray, is mimicked in the rooms themselves. A trolley around the corner from the hotel will carry you to several popular areas in San Diego, including the Gaslamp District, Old Town, and the Convention Center. 177 rooms. Check-in 4 pm, check out noon. Outdoor pool. Business center. **$**

★ ★ HOLIDAY INN. *1617 First Ave, San Diego (92101). Phone 619/239-9600; toll-free 800/366-3164; fax 619/233-6228. www.holiday-inn.com.* 220 rooms, 16 story. Check-in 3 pm, check-out noon. High-speed Internet access. Restaurant, bar. Fitness room. Outdoor pool. Business center. **$$**

★ ★ HOLIDAY INN SELECT-HOTEL CIRCLE. *595 Hotel Cir, San Diego (92108). Phone 619/291-5720; toll-free 800/465-4329; fax 619/297-7362. www.holiday-innselect.com.* 318 rooms. Check-in 3 pm, check-out noon. High-speed Internet access. Restaurant, bar. Fitness room. Outdoor pool, whirlpool. Business center. **$**

★ ★ HORTON GRAND HOTEL. *311 Island Ave, San Diego (92101). Phone 619/544-1886; toll-free 800/542-1886; fax 616/239-3823. www.hortongrand. com.* Centrally located downtown in the Gaslamp Quarter, this elegant, 132-room historic Victorian hotel, built in 1886, is the city's oldest building. Accommodations combine modern amenities with period décor: each individually furnished room or suite features a queen-size bed, a hand-carved armoire, lace curtains, antiques, a gas fireplace, and a balcony or bay window with city or courtyard views. The hotel's award-winning restaurant, Ida Bailey's, specializes in healthier American cuisine. 132 rooms, 4 story.

Pets accepted, some restrictions; fee. Check-in 3 pm, check-out noon. Restaurant, bar. Airport transportation available. **$$**

★ ★ HUMPHREY'S HALF MOON INN & SUITES. *2303 Shelter Island Dr, San Diego (92106). Phone 619/224-3411; toll-free 800/345-9995; fax 619/224-3478. www.halfmooninn.com.* Nestled amid tropical gardens on romantic Shelter Island, this waterfront hotel appeals to families and leisure travelers seeking convenience without the hustle and bustle. Elegantly appointed guest rooms with bay or city views include dataports, free HBO, and free in-room coffee. Just minutes from fine restaurants, stores, and entertainment options, the hotel also offers the intimate piano-bar pleasures of Humphrey's Backstage Lounge—a local favorite known for its lively happy hour. 182 rooms, 2 story. Check-in 4 pm, check-out noon. High-speed Internet access. Restaurant, bar. Fitness room. Outdoor pool, whirlpool. Airport transportation available. **$$**

★ ★ PACIFIC TERRACE HOTEL. *610 Diamond St, San Diego (92109). Phone 858/581-3500; toll-free 800/344-3370; fax 858/274-3341. www.pacificterrace. com.* This seaside hotel in northern San Diego is the perfect place to revel in the Southern California beach atmosphere. Old Spanish style characterizes the exterior and the common areas. The upscale guest accommodations feature cheery prints and rattan furnishings, with private patios or balconies and fully stocked minibars. Some rooms have fully equipped kitchenettes, and most have fabulous views of the ocean. Within walking distance are the shops and restaurants of Pacific Beach; SeaWorld, tidepools, and the famous Seal Rock are just five minutes away. 74 rooms, 3 story. Complimentary continental breakfast. Check-in 4 pm, check-out 11 am. High-speed Internet access. Beach. Outdoor pool, whirlpool. Business center. **$$$**

★ QUALITY SUITES SAN DIEGO. *9880 Mira Mesa Blvd, San Diego (92131). Phone 858/530-2000; toll-free 800/822-6692; fax 858/530-0202. www. qualitysuitessandiego.com.* 132 rooms, 4 story, all suites. Complimentary continental breakfast. Check-in 3 pm, check-out noon. Outdoor pool, whirlpool. **$**

★ ★ RADISSON SUITE HOTEL RANCHO BERNARDO. *11520 W Bernardo Ct, San Diego (92127). Phone 858/451-6600; toll-free 866/593-4267;*

fax 858/592-0253. www.radissonranchobernardo.com. 180 rooms, 3 story, all suites. Complimentary full breakfast. Check-out noon. Restaurant. Fitness room. Outdoor pool, whirlpool. **$$**

★ ★ ★ **SHELTER POINTE HOTEL AND MARINA.** *1551 Shelter Island Dr, San Diego (92106). Phone 619/221-8000; toll-free 800/566-2524; fax 619/222-5953. www.shelterpointe.com.* Just five minutes from SeaWorld and downtown and a mere 3 miles from the airport, this Mediterranean-themed hotel on the tip of Shelter Island strikes a balance between convenience and quiet retreat for travelers of all types. Rooms feature bright, elegant, contemporary décor, with amenities including dataports and coffeemakers as well as patios or balconies with bay or coastal views. Recreational options encompass a fitness club, a sunning beach with volleyball courts, jogging paths, and bicycle, boat, and tennis court rentals. A. J.'s Grill, the hotels on-site eatery, offers American fare along with great scenery and a Sunday brunch. 206 rooms, 2 story. Pets accepted. Check-in 4 pm, check-out noon. High-speed Internet access. Restaurant, bar. Fitness room, spa. Outdoor pool. **$$**

★ ★ **SHERATON MISSION VALLEY HOTEL.** *1433 Camino Del Rio S, San Diego (92108). Phone 619/260-0111; fax 619/497-0813. www.sheraton.com.* 261 rooms, 12 story. Pets accepted, some restrictions; fee. Check-in 4 pm, check-out noon. Restaurant, bar. Fitness room. Outdoor pool, whirlpool. **$**

★ ★ **SHERATON SUITES SAN DIEGO.** *701 A St, San Diego (92101). Phone 619/696-9800; tol l-free 800/962-1367; fax 619/696-1555. www.sheraton.com.* Sharing a roof with Symphony Hall, this downtown hotel is an all-suite property that offers rapid access to the convention center, Petco Park baseball stadium, and the historic Gaslamp District. It's also within minutes of the airport, the San Diego Zoo, and other major attractions. Spacious accommodations feature living rooms, minibars, and custom-designed beds with plush-top mattresses. The on-site restaurant, Renditions, serves breakfast, lunch, and dinner daily, and the serene Sky Lobby lounge offers sparkling skyline views along with refreshing beverages. 264 rooms, 27 story, all suites. Pets accepted; fee. Check-in 3 pm, check-out noon. High-speed Internet access. Restaurant, bar. Fitness room. Indoor pool, whirlpool. Business center. **$$**

Full-Service Hotels

★ ★ **BEST WESTERN HACIENDA SUITES-OLD TOWN.** *4041 Harney St, San Diego (92110). Phone 619/298-4707; toll-free 800/888-1991; fax 619/298-4771. www.haciendahotel-oldtown.com.* Romantic California tradition and relaxing hillside seclusion characterize this lodge—just minutes from SeaWorld, the San Diego Zoo, downtown, and the beaches. Guest accommodations feature hand-crafted Santa Fe furnishings, private balconies or courtyards, and sweeping views of Old Town and the bay. Social hours are hosted Monday through Thursday, and lodgers have two on-site dining options: Acapulco, serving Mexican fare, and Zocalo, specializing in Pacific Rim dishes. Concierge, business, and courtesy car services are available. 199 rooms, 3 story, all suites. Check-in 3 pm, check-out noon. High-speed Internet access, wireless Internet access. Restaurant, bar. Fitness room. Outdoor pool, whirlpool. Business center. **$$**

★ ★ ★ **DOUBLETREE HOTEL MISSION VALLEY.** *7450 Hazard Center Dr, San Diego (92108). Phone 619/297-5466; toll-free 800/222-8733; fax 619/688-4088. www.doubletree.com.* Close to SeaWorld, the San Diego Zoo, and other major attractions hotel appeals to travelers of all types with its immediate proximity to the Hazard Center retail/entertainment complex and the San Diego Light Rail Trolley, which offers service to downtown and to shopping opportunities at the Mexican border. Stylishly appointed guest accommodations include dataports, bathrobes, and turn-down service. Tennis and indoor and outdoor pools are among the recreational amenities, and the on-site Fountain Café provides a relaxed mealtime setting with Mediterranean flair. 300 rooms, 11 story. Pets accepted, some restrictions; fee. Check-in 3 pm, check-out noon. High-speed Internet access, wireless Internet access. Restaurant, bar. Fitness room. Indoor pool, outdoor pool, whirlpool. Airport transportation available. **$$**

★ ★ ★ **HILTON AIRPORT/HARBOR ISLAND.** *1960 Harbor Island Dr, San Diego (92101). Phone 619/291-6700; toll-free 800/774-1500; fax 619/293-0694. www.sandiegoairport.hilton.com.* 211 rooms, 9 story. Check-in 4 pm, check-out noon. High-speed Internet access. Restaurant, bar. Fitness room. Outdoor pool, whirlpool. Airport transportation available. Business center. **$$**

★ ★ ★ HILTON SAN DIEGO GASLAMP

QUARTER. *401 K St, San Diego (92101). Phone 619/231-4040; toll-free 800/774-1500; fax 619/231-6439. www.hilton.com.* Located in the historic Gaslamp Quarter (where you'll find a nearly endless array of shopping, restaurants, and nightclubs) and across the street from the San Diego Convention Center, the Hilton San Diego Gaslamp Quarter offers a host of amenities for both business and leisure travelers. With large desks perfect for your computer and papers, high-speed Internet access, and a speaker phone with voicemail, you can use your room as an office and conduct meetings with ease. Whether you choose a standard guest room or a one-bedroom suite, the décor is modern and sophisticated, and your bed will have a pillow-top mattress and down comforter. At the spa, you can enjoy a massage or other salon services. From the fitness room to the outdoor heated pool and hot tub, you'll find many ways to relax without leaving the hotel. The hotel has two restaurants—the New Leaf Restaurant features California cuisine with indoor and outdoor seating for breakfast, lunch, and dinner; Lou & Mikey's serves steak and seafood for dinner in a more casual atmosphere—plus a coffeehouse that offers lighter fare. The beach is less than a mile away, and whether you're in the mood for golf, tennis, fishing, or scuba diving, you'll find it with just a short drive. 282 rooms. Check-in 4 pm, check-out noon. High-speed Internet access. Restaurant, bar. Fitness room. Outdoor pool, whirlpool. Business center. **$$$**

★ ★ ★ HILTON SAN DIEGO MISSION

VALLEY. *901 Camino del Rio S, San Diego (92108). Phone 619/543-9000; toll-free 800/733-2332; fax 619/543-9358. www.sandiegomissionvalley.hilton.com.* 351 rooms, 14 story. Check-in 4 pm, check-out noon. High-speed Internet access. Restaurant, bar. Fitness room. Outdoor pool. Business center. **$$**

★ ★ ★ HYATT REGENCY ISLANDIA.

1441 Quivira Rd, San Diego (92109). Phone 619/224-1234; fax 619/224-0348. www.hyattregencyislandia.com. Whether the venue is SeaWorld or the Pacific Ocean, whale-watching is always in season at this towering landmark surrounded by gardens in Mission Bay Park. In addition to offering easy SeaWorld access and panoramic harbor, marina, and sea views, the Hyatt Regency Islandia features tasteful contemporary accommodations with amenities that include dataports, bathrobes, and coffeemakers. Guests can exercise in the fitness room, enjoy free use of a nearby Gold's Gym, or

engage in recreational activities from biking to boating. Downtown and the airport are just 6 miles away, while myriad dining, shopping, and entertainment options are within a short drive. 421 rooms, 17 story. Check-in 4 pm, check-out noon. Restaurant, bar. Fitness room. Outdoor pool, whirlpool. Business center. **$$**

★ ★ ★ MANCHESTER GRAND HYATT SAN

DIEGO. *One Market Pl, San Diego (92101). Phone 619/232-1234; toll-free 800/223-1234; fax 619/233-6464. www.manchestergrandhyatt.com.* Combining a resortlike atmosphere with the convenience of a downtown location, this luxury property on San Diego Bay attracts business and leisure travelers with its next-door proximity to the convention center and the Seaport Village retail/restaurant complex. Graciously appointed guest rooms and suites feature dataports, high-speed Internet access, coffeemakers, and express check-out, among other amenities. The full-service Regency Spa and Salon staffs skilled therapists, estheticians, and stylists. The hotel is 3 miles from the airport and provides easy access to San Diego Zoo, SeaWorld, Old Town, Balboa Park, the beaches, and other attractions. 1,625 rooms, 40 story. Check-in 3 pm, check-out noon. High-speed Internet access. Six restaurants, two bars. Fitness room (fee), spa. Outdoor pool, whirlpool. Tennis. Business center. **$$$**

★ ★ ★ MARRIOTT SAN DIEGO HOTEL &

MARINA. *333 W Harbor Dr, San Diego (92101). Phone 619/234-1500; toll-free 800/228-9290; fax 619/234-8678. www.marriott.com/sandt.* Adjacent to the convention center and the Seaport Village retail/restaurant complex and just 2 miles from the airport, this waterfront hotel is conveniently situated for guests pursuing business or pleasure. Accommodations offer bay and marina views along with comfort-inducing amenities and options like complimentary coffee, work desks, refrigerators, and full kitchens. The property boasts 110,00 square feet of meeting space as well as several ballrooms, restaurants, and boutiques. The unique shops of Horton Plaza are an easy walk, and attractions including SeaWorld and the San Diego Zoo are within a short drive. Concierge, secretarial, and limousine services are available. 1,358 rooms, 25 story. Pets accepted, some restrictions. Check-in 4 pm, check-out noon. High-speed Internet access. Four restaurants, bar. Fitness room. Outdoor pool, whirlpool. Tennis. Business center. **$$**

★ ★ ★ **MARRIOTT SAN DIEGO MISSION VALLEY.** *8757 Rio San Diego Dr, San Diego (92108). Phone 619/692-3800; toll-free 800/842-5329; fax 619/692-0769. www.sandiegomarriottmissionvalley. com.* Featuring a host of amenities for both business travelers and fun-seeking vacationers, this hotel is about 7 miles northwest of downtown and less than 2 miles from Qualcomm Stadium—home of the San Diego Chargers and the San Diego Padres. Dataports, high-speed Internet access (in select units), and an optional flat-rate local/long-distance calling plan augment the practicality and comfort of the guest rooms, many of which overlook the hotel's beautiful courtyard pool and tropical landscaping. A relaxing on-site eatery, Café del Sol, offers continental cuisine. Concierge, secretarial, and childcare services are available. 352 rooms, 17 story. Check-in 4 pm, check-out 11 am. High-speed Internet access. Restaurant, bar. Fitness room. Outdoor pool, whirlpool. Business center. **$$**

★ ★ ★ **SHERATON SAN DIEGO HOTEL AND MARINA.** *1380 Harbor Island Dr, San Diego (92101). Phone 619/291-2900; toll-free 877/734-2726; fax 619/692-2337. www.sheraton.com.* Leisure seekers and business travelers alike are lured by the panoramic waterfront and skyline views afforded by this dual-tower landmark, which is within a ten-minute drive of SeaWorld, the San Diego Zoo, historic Old Town, Balboa Park, and Seaport Village. Guest rooms and suites, recently renovated with contemporary décor, have custom-designed beds with plush-top mattresses, oversized desks, high-speed Internet access, and private patios or balconies. The East Tower has four restaurants and lounges—including Tapatini's, which serves a tapas menu and signature martinis. The West Tower features an outdoor heated pool and the restaurant Alfiere's, specializing in Mediterranean cuisine. 1,044 rooms, 12 story. Pets accepted, some restrictions. Check-in 3 pm, check-out noon. High-speed Internet access. Three restaurants, three bars. Fitness room, spa. Outdoor pool, whirlpool. Airport transportation available. Business center. **$$**

★ ★ ★ **WESTGATE HOTEL.** *1055 Second Ave, San Diego (92101). Phone 619/238-1818; toll-free 800/221-3802; fax 619/557-3737. www.westgatehotel. com.* Guests step inside the distinguished Westgate Hotel and are immediately transported to the grace and elegance of a bygone era. This sumptuous hotel rivals many European palaces with its treasure trove of antiques, French tapestries, crystal chandeliers, and Persian carpets. It is the picture of refinement in the heart of San Diego. The accommodations are appointed with stunning Richelieu furniture, distinctive artwork, and bountiful fresh flowers. The Westgate's tradition of excellence extends to its dining, where guests are treated to a series of fantastic restaurants and cafés. Le Fontainebleau (see) is a favorite choice for special occasions, with its romantic, formal dining room and refined nouveau cuisine, and afternoon tea is a particularly delightful tradition here. 223 rooms, 19 story. Pets accepted, some restrictions; fee. Check-in 3 pm, check-out noon. Two restaurants, bar. Fitness room, spa. **$$$**

★ ★ ★ **WESTIN HORTON PLAZA.** *910 Broadway Cir, San Diego (92101). Phone 619/239-2200; fax 619/239-0509. www.westin.com/hortonplaza.* 450 rooms, 16 story. Pets accepted, some restrictions. Check-in 3 pm, check-out noon. High-speed Internet access, wireless Internet access. Two restaurants, bar. Fitness room, spa. Outdoor pool, whirlpool. Business center. **$$**

★ ★ ★ **WYNDHAM EMERALD PLAZA HOTEL.** *400 W Broadway, San Diego (92101). Phone 619/239-4500; fax 619/239-3274. www.wyndham.com.* 436 rooms, 25 story. Check-in 3 pm, check-out noon. High-speed Internet access, wireless Internet access. Two restaurants, bar. Fitness room, spa. Outdoor pool, whirlpool. Business center. **$$**

Full-Service Resorts

★ ★ **CATAMARAN RESORT HOTEL.** *3999 Mission Blvd, San Diego (92109). Phone 858/488-1081; toll-free 800/422-8380; fax 858/488-1619. www. catamaranresort.com.* A huge waterfall greets you when you enter the lobby of this casually elegant resort. The tropical-themed rooms feature Hawaiian-print linens and décor and each has either a balcony or patio. And acres of lush grounds surround the pool and whirlpools. The fun atmosphere continues with a luau and torch lighting on Friday nights (seasonal). 315 rooms, 13 story. Check-in 4 pm, check-out noon. High-speed Internet access. Restaurant, bar. Fitness room. Spa. Beach activities. Outdoor pool, whirlpool. Business center. Credit cards accepted. **$$**

★ ★ DOUBLETREE GOLF RESORT.

14455 Penasquitos Dr, San Diego (92129). Phone 858/672-9100; toll-free 800/622-9223; fax 858/672-9166. www.sandiegogolfresort.doubletree.com. Situated on 130 rolling acres about 25 minutes north of downtown, this secluded resort offers relaxation and recreation amid the manicured greens of an Arnold Palmer-managed, 18-hole championship golf course. Recently renovated guest rooms feature contemporary décor and spectacular countryside views; dual-line phones, dataports, and coffeemakers are included. Leisure seekers can enjoy two outdoor heated pools, five lighted tennis courts, and basketball and volleyball courts, as well as a fully equipped fitness center. For business travelers, there's a business center and complimentary transportation to nearby Rancho Bernardo and Poway business parks. A sports lounge and restaurant complete the amenities. 174 rooms, 3 story. Check-in 3 pm, check-out noon. Restaurant, bar. Fitness room. Two outdoor pools, whirlpool. Golf, 18 holes. Tennis. Airport transportation available. Business center. **$$**

★ ★ ★ HILTON SAN DIEGO RESORT. *1775 E Mission Bay Dr, San Diego (92109). Phone 619/276-4010; toll-free 800/345-6565; fax 619/275-7991. www.sandiegoresort.com.* This full-service resort is located on Mission Bay and is adjacent to SeaWorld. Old Town and the historic Gaslamp District are nearby. Beaches and secluded islands surround this property, which is decorated in bright colors of blue, orange, and green. And there are plenty of activities (jet ski, bicycle, and rollerblade rentals; kids' club; spa; pools; tennis) here to keep everyone in the family busy. 357 rooms, 8 story. Check-in 4 pm, check-out noon. High-speed Internet access. Restaurant, two bars. Children's activity center. Fitness room. Spa. Beach. Outdoor pool, whirlpool. Tennis. Business center. Credit cards accepted. **$$**

★ ★ ★ PARADISE POINT RESORT & SPA.

1404 W Vacation Rd, San Diego (92109). Phone 858/274-4630; toll-free 800/344-2626; fax 858/581-5929. www.paradisepoint.com. Ideal for a leisure getaway or a business conference, this 44-acre island oasis in the middle of Mission Bay offers an environment comprised of tropical gardens, lagoons, and beaches just 7 miles from downtown and the airport. Cabana-style accommodations feature contemporary décor, with amenities including dataports and coffeemakers as well as garden and water views. The state-of-the-art Spa Terre, incorporating gentle Indonesian body

treatments, offers a private sanctuary for relaxation and renewal, and recreation enthusiasts can enjoy the tennis and basketball courts and marina rentals. SeaWorld, the historical Gaslamp District, and many other attractions are within a short drive. 462 rooms. Check-in 4 pm, check-out noon. High-speed Internet access. Two restaurants, three bars. Children's activity center. Fitness room, fitness classes available. Spa. Beach. Outdoor pool, whirlpool. Tennis. Business center. Credit cards accepted. **$$**

★ ★ ★ RANCHO BERNARDO INN. *17550 Bernardo Oaks Dr, San Diego (92128). Phone 858/675-8500; fax 858/675-8501. www.ranchobernardoinn.com.* This resort—located just 30 minutes from SeaWorld and the Wild Animal Park and 45 minutes from LEGOLAND, Balboa Park, and the world-renowned San Diego Zoo—has so much to offer that you may have trouble pulling yourself away to see these nearby attractions. All the guest rooms are decorated with antiques and original artwork; suites also have wood-burning fireplaces. Whether your room has a view of the surrounding valley, the on-site 18-hole championship golf course, or one of the hotel's gardens, you'll be able to enjoy it on your balcony or patio. The hotel offers two excellent options for dining—the Veranda Grill, an outdoor restaurant that overlooks the golf course, and El Bizcocho (see), known by the locals for its French cuisine. 287 rooms, 3 story. Pets accepted, some restrictions; fee. Check-in 4 pm, check-out noon. Bar. Fitness room, spa. Outdoor pool, children's pool, whirlpool. Golf, 18 holes. Tennis. Airport transportation available. Business center. **$$**

Full-Service Inn

★ ★ ★ BRISTOL HOTEL. *1055 First Ave, San Diego (92101). Phone 619/232-6141; toll-free 800/662-4477; fax 619/232-1948. www.thebristolsandiego.com.* Contemporary décor accented by gerbera daisies and soft jazz music graces the lobby of this downtown boutique hotel, where young professionals and romantics can wander amid a pop art collection that includes works by Andy Warhol, Roy Lichtenstein, and Keith Haring. Bold lines and color strokes continue through the guest rooms, which include dataports, bathrobes, and a selection of pillows. A retractable roof highlights the top-floor Starlight Ballroom, and a signature martini—the Craizi Daizi—is a major draw at Daisies Bistro, the hotels restaurant. The Bristol is conveniently located near the city's convention center and the Gaslamp Quarter. 102

rooms, 9 story. Pets accepted, some restrictions. Check-in 3 pm, check-out noon. High-speed Internet access. Restaurant, bar. Fitness room. **$$**

Specialty Lodgings

BALBOA PARK INN. *3402 Park Blvd, San Diego (92103). Phone 619/298-0823; toll-free 800/938-8181; fax 619/294-8070. www.balboaparkinn.com.* Located in a quiet neighborhood bordering Balboa Park, a short walk from the San Diego Zoo and Hillcrest's museums and nightlife, this inn features changeable themed rooms ranging from the escapist ("Aruba," "Paris in the 30s") to the erudite ("Monets," "Nouveau Ritz") to the exceedingly romantic ("Harlequin," "Victorias Secret"). Amenities include refrigerators, free local telephone calls, and free coffee, tea, and hot chocolate help anchor the fantasy settings in comfortable reality. 26 rooms, 2 story. Complimentary continental breakfast. Check-in 2 pm, check-out noon. **$**

ELSBREE BEACH AREA BED & BREAKFAST. *5054 Narragansett Ave, San Diego (92107). Phone 619/226-4133; fax 619/223-4133. www.bbinob.com.* New England architecture and hospitality characterize this charming country house, a romantic getaway located in a quiet seaside neighborhood just half a block from the beach. Victorian-style décor prevails in the guest rooms, which overlook beautiful gardens and offer the soothing sound of rolling surf. Antiques enthusiasts can browse among more than 250 local dealers, while foodies can graze at a number of fine restaurants within walking distance. A farmers' market is held nearby each week. 6 rooms, 2 story. Complimentary continental breakfast. Check-in 2 pm, check-out 11 am. **$**

HERITAGE PARK INN. *2470 Heritage Park Row, San Diego (92110). Phone 619/299-6832; toll-free 800/995-2470; fax 619/299-9465. www.heritageparkinn. com.* Victorian house (1889) moved to this site. 12 rooms, 2 story. No children allowed. Complimentary full breakfast. Check-in 11 am, check-out noon. **$$**

Restaurants

★ ★ **3RD CORNER WINE SHOP & BISTRO.** *2665 Bacon St, San Diego (92107). Phone 619/223-2700. www.the3rdcorner.com.* Continental, French menu, wine bar. Lunch, dinner. Closed Mon; holidays.

Bar. Casual attire. Outdoor seating. **$$**

★ ★ **AFGHANISTAN KHYBER PASS.** *523 University Ave, San Diego (92103). Phone 619/294-7579. www.khyberpasscuisine.com.* Interior designed as an Afghan cave. Middle Eastern menu. Lunch, dinner. Closed holidays. Bar. Casual attire. Outdoor seating. **$$**

★ **ATHENS MARKET TAVERNA.** *109 W F St, San Diego (92101). Phone 619/234-1955. www.athensmarkettaverna.com.* Greek menu. Lunch, dinner. Closed Sun; holidays. Bar. Casual attire. Reservations recommended. Outdoor seating. **$$$**

★ ★ **BACI.** *1955 W Morena Blvd, San Diego (92110). Phone 619/275-2094; fax 619/275-3004. www.bacicucina.com.* Impressive in-house baking makes this intimate space with great service a notch above. Many art pieces and prints adorn the walls. Italian menu. Lunch, dinner. Closed Sun; Dec 25. Bar. Children's menu. Business casual attire. Reservations recommended. Valet parking. **$$$**

★ ★ **BELLA LUNA.** *748 Fifth Ave, San Diego (92101). Phone 619/239-3222; fax 619/239-1202. www.bellaluna.com.* Italian menu. Lunch, dinner. Closed holidays. Bar. Children's menu. Business casual attire. Reservations recommended. Outdoor seating. **$$$**

★ ★ **BLUE POINT.** *565 Fifth Ave, San Diego (92101). Phone 619/233-1931; fax 619/233-1931. www.cohnrestaurants.com.* The prized catch is on the wall and on your plate at this historic Gaslamp Quarter seafood and oyster bar. Sink into black banquette seating inside, or step outside and enjoy specialties from the "Hook," "Line," and "Sinker" sections of the menu. Seafood menu. Dinner. Closed Thanksgiving, Dec 25. Bar. Children's menu. Reservations recommended. Valet parking. Outdoor seating. **$$$**

★ ★ **BUSALACCHI'S.** *3683 Fifth Ave, San Diego (92103). Phone 619/298-0119; fax 619/298-7942. www.busalacchis.com.* One of the gems in the Busalacchi family-owned group of Italian eateries. This particular site occupies a Victorian-style home. The Sicilian menu is authentic and well prepared, and the cheerful service makes it all the better. Italian menu. Lunch, dinner. Closed holidays. Bar. Business casual attire. Reservations recommended. Valet parking. **$$$**

★ **CAFE COYOTE.** *2461 San Diego Ave, San Diego (92110). Phone 619/291-4695; fax 619/291-0715. www.cafecoyoteoldtown.com.* Mexican menu. Breakfast, lunch, dinner. Closed Thanksgiving, Dec 25. Bar.

Children's menu. Casual attire. Reservations recommended. Outdoor seating. **$$**

★ ★ **CAFE PACIFICA.** *2414 San Diego Ave, San Diego (92110). Phone 619/291-6666; fax 619/291-0122. www.cafepacifica.com.* Seafood menu. Dinner. Closed holidays. Bar. Children's menu. Business casual attire. Reservations recommended. Valet parking. Outdoor seating. **$$$**

★ ★ ★ **CALIFORNIA CUISINE.** *1027 University Ave, San Diego (92103). Phone 619/543-0790; fax 619/543-0106. www.californiacuisine.cc.* California menu. Dinner. Closed holidays. Business casual attire. Reservations recommended. Outdoor seating. **$$$**

★ ★ **CHATEAU ORLEANS.** *926 Turquoise St, San Diego (92109). Phone 858/488-6744; fax 858/488-6745. www.chateauorleans.com.* Sit back, relax, and enjoy the Mardi Gras atmosphere at Chateau Orleans, where dishes of down home Southern cooking are served atop tables decorated with confetti and colorful carnival masks. Cajun/Creole menu. Dinner. Closed Sun; holidays. Children's menu. Casual attire. **$$**

★ **CITY DELICATESSEN.** *535 University Ave, San Diego (92103). Phone 619/295-2747; fax 619/295-2129.* Jewish-style delicatessen. Deli menu. Breakfast, lunch, dinner. Bar. Children's menu. Casual attire. Outdoor seating. **$$**

★ **CORVETTE DINER.** *3946 Fifth Ave, San Diego (92103). Phone 619/542-1476; fax 619/542-1001. www.corvettediner.com.* Corvette in center of room. American menu. Lunch, dinner. Children's menu. Casual attire. **$**

★ ★ **CROCE'S RESTAURANT & BAR.** *802 Fifth Ave, San Diego (92101). Phone 619/233-4355; fax 619/232-2891. www.croces.com.* Ingrid Croce opened this restaurant/jazz club as a tribute to her singer-husband, Jim Croce, after his death. Guitars, photos, and music memorabilia line the walls, but it's hardly a shrine; the music emanating from its two clubs is enough to make anyone feel terrific. Seven nights a week, one club, Top Hat, pumps out rhythm and blues, while the Jazz Clubs cool strands make you dream of the Roaring Twenties. Diners at Croce's restaurant receive complimentary admission to the clubs. American menu. Lunch, dinner. Closed holidays. Bar. Business casual attire. Reservations recommended. Valet parking. Outdoor seating. **$$$**

★ **D.Z. AKIN'S.** *6930 Alvarado Rd, San Diego (92120). Phone 619/265-0218; fax 619/265-8186. www.dzakinsdeli.com.* Deli menu. Breakfast, lunch, dinner. Children's menu. Casual attire. **$$**

★ ★ **DAKOTA GRILL AND SPIRITS.** *901 5th Ave, San Diego (92101). Phone 619/234-5554. www.cohnrestaurants.com.* Found on the bottom floor of the Gaslamp Plaza Suite Hotel, this spot offers a tasty mix of eclectic Southwestern fare, as well as delicious desserts. Southwestern menu. Lunch, dinner. Closed holidays. Bar. Casual attire. Reservations recommended. Valet parking. Outdoor seating. **$$$**

★ ★ **DOBSON'S.** *956 Broadway Cir, San Diego (92101). Phone 619/231-6771; fax 619/696-0861. www.dobsonsrestaurant.com.* California menu. Lunch, dinner. Closed Sun; holidays. Bar. Casual attire. Reservations recommended. Valet parking. **$$**

★ **EDGEWATER GRILL.** *861 W Harbor Dr, San Diego (92101). Phone 619/232-7581. www.edgewater.com.* Seafood, steak menu. Breakfast, lunch, dinner. Closed holidays. Bar. Children's menu. Casual attire. Reservations recommended. Outdoor seating. **$$**

★ ★ **EL BIZCOCHO.** *17550 Bernardo Oaks Dr, San Diego (92128). Phone 858/487-1611; fax 858/675-8443. www.ranchobernardoinn.com.* This restaurant in the Rancho Bernardo Inn (see) has attracted attention since the 1970s. The menu is balanced between classics and seasonal specials offering intricate preparations. French menu. Dinner, Sun brunch. Bar. Jacket required. Reservations recommended. Valet parking. **$$$**

★ **EL INDIO MEXICAN.** *3695 Indian St, San Diego (92103). Phone 619/299-0333. www.el-indio.com.* Tortilla factory. Mexican menu. Breakfast, lunch, dinner. Casual attire. Outdoor seating. No credit cards accepted. **$**

★ **FAIROUZ CAFE AND GALLERY.** *3100 Midway Dr, San Diego (92110). Phone 619/225-0308. www.alnashashibi.com.* Mediterranean menu. Lunch, dinner. Closed Jan 1, July 4, Thanksgiving. Bar. Children's menu. Casual attire. **$$**

★ ★ **FRENCH MARKET GRILLE.** *15717 Bernardo Heights Pkwy, San Diego (92128). Phone 858/485-8055; fax 858/673-5471. www.frenchmarketgrille.com.* French menu. Breakfast, lunch, dinner. Closed holidays. Casual attire. Reservations recommended. Outdoor seating. **$$$**

★ **GREEN FLASH.** *701 Thomas Ave, Pacific Beach (92109). Phone 858/270-7715; fax 858/270-7793. www.*

greenflashrestaurant.com. American, seafood, steak menu. Breakfast, lunch, dinner. Bar. Children's menu. Casual attire. Outdoor seating. **$$$**

★ ★ ★ **GREYSTONE - THE STEAKHOUSE.** *658 Fifth Ave, San Diego (92101). Phone 619/232-0225; fax 619/233-3606. www.greystonesteakhouse.com.* In a historical theater building in the Gaslamp district. Steak menu. Dinner. Closed holidays. Bar. Business casual attire. Reservations recommended. Valet parking. Outdoor seating. **$$$**

★ ★ **HARBOR HOUSE.** *831 W Harbor Dr, San Diego (92101). Phone 619/232-1141. www.harbor-house-sandiego.com.* Seafood menu. Lunch, dinner. Bar. Children's menu. Casual attire. Reservations recommended. Outdoor seating. **$$**

★ ★ **HOB NOB HILL.** *2271 1st Ave, San Diego (92101). Phone 619/239-8176; fax 619/239-5856. www.hobnobhill.com.* American menu. Breakfast, lunch, dinner. Closed Dec 25. Children's menu. Casual attire. Outdoor seating. **$$**

★ ★ **IMPERIAL HOUSE.** *505 Kalmia St, San Diego (92101). Phone 619/234-3525; fax 619/239-5406. www.imperialhouse.net.* Continental menu. Lunch, dinner. Closed holidays. Bar. Children's menu. Business casual attire. Reservations recommended. Valet parking. **$$$**

★ **JACK AND GIULIO'S.** *2391 San Diego Ave, San Diego (92110). Phone 619/294-2074; fax 619/294-4188. www.jackandgiulios.com.* Italian menu. Lunch, dinner. Closed holidays. Bar. Casual attire. Reservations recommended. Outdoor seating. **$$**

★ ★ **JASMINE.** *4609 Convoy St, San Diego (92111). Phone 858/268-0888; fax 858/268-7729. www.jasmineseafoodrestaurant.com.* Large dining room with movable walls. Chinese menu. Lunch, dinner. Bar. Casual attire. **$$**

★ ★ **KARL STRAUSS' BREWERY AND GRILL.** *1157 Columbia St, San Diego (92101). Phone 619/234-2739; fax 619/234-2773. www.karlstrauss.com.* The fun and lively atmosphere of this downtown San Diego brewery makes it the perfect spot to meet friends for drinks or watch the big game. The main bar area features stainless steel fermenters for brewing beer. American menu. Lunch, dinner. Closed holidays. Bar. Children's menu. Casual attire. Outdoor seating. **$$**

★ ★ **KELLY'S STEAKHOUSE.** *500 Hotel Cir N, San Diego (92108). Phone 619/291-7131; fax 619/291-3584.* Steak menu. Dinner. Closed holidays. Bar. Children's menu. Casual attire. Reservations recommended. Valet parking. Waterfalls. **$$$**

★ ★ **LA VACHE AND COMPANY.** *420 Robinson Ave, San Diego (92103). Phone 619/295-0214. www.lavacheandco.com.* French menu. Lunch, dinner, brunch. Closed holidays. Casual attire. Reservations recommended. Outdoor seating. **$$**

★ ★ **LAMONT STREET GRILL.** *4445 Lamont St, San Diego (92109). Phone 858/270-3060. www.lamontstreetgrill.com.* Converted bungalow with intimate dining; garden courtyard. Seafood, steak menu. Dinner. Closed Jan 1, July 4, Dec 24-25. Bar. Outdoor seating. **$$**

★ ★ ★ **LAUREL.** *505 Laurel St, San Diego (92101). Phone 619/239-2222; fax 619/239-6822. www.sdurbankitchen.com.* If Scarlet O'Hara were alive today, she would dine at Laurel. First, she would love making the entrance down a grand, sweeping, wrought-iron staircase into the sleek and sexy 3,200-square-foot dining room and packed bar, where all eyes inevitably stray to the door as it opens. In addition to the entrance, she would adore the chic, glamorous crowd that fills the room; the rustic, contemporary French comfort food that graces the menu (signature dishes include an onion and Roquefort tart and chicken cooked in a clay pot); and the restaurant's stellar wine list assembled by partner Gary Parker. (The 200-bottle list emphasizes the Rhone region of France.) It's safe to say that Scarlet would also be wooed by the music. Laurel hosts some of the best live jazz musicians in town, making the bar a lively spot to unwind and make new friends. French, Mediterranean menu. Dinner. Bar. Casual attire. Valet parking. **$$$**

★ ★ ★ **LE FOUNTAINEBLEAU.** *1055 Second Ave, San Diego (92101). Phone 619/238-1818; fax 619/557-3737. www.westgatehotel.com.* This downtown, European-designed dining room in the Westgate Hotel (see) is all romance, with creamy colors, a harpist at lunch, and a pianist at dinner. California, French menu. Lunch, dinner. Bar. Jacket required. Reservations recommended. Valet parking. Outdoor seating. **$$$**

★ ★ **NICK'S AT THE BEACH.** *809 Thomas Ave, San Diego (92109). Phone 858/270-1730; fax 858/270-1781. www.nicksatthebeach.com.* Seafood menu. Breakfast, lunch, dinner. Bar. Children's menu. Casual attire. Reservations recommended. Outdoor seating. **$$**

★ **OLD TOWN MEXICAN CAFE AND CANTINA.** *2489 San Diego Ave, San Diego (92110).*

Phone 619/297-4330; toll-free 888/234-9823; fax 619/297-8002. www.oldtownmexcafe.com. Mexican menu. Breakfast, lunch, dinner. Closed holidays. Bar. Children's menu. Casual attire. Reservations recommended. **$$**

★ ★ ★ **THE PRADO AT BALBOA PARK.** 1549 El Prado, San Diego (92101). Phone 619/557-9441; fax 619/557-9442. In a historic building in Balboa Park. Italian, Latin American menu. Lunch, dinner. Closed holidays. Bar. Children's menu. Jacket required. Reservations recommended. Outdoor seating. **$$$**

★ ★ **PANDA INN.** 506 Horton Plz, San Diego (92101). Phone 619/233-7800; fax 619/233-5632. www.pandainn.com. Several dining areas, all with Chinese art, one with a whole-ceiling skylight; pandas depicted in stained-glass windows. Chinese menu. Lunch, dinner. Closed Thanksgiving. Bar. Casual attire. Outdoor seating. **$$**

★ ★ **PREGO.** 1370 Frazee Rd, San Diego (92108). Phone 619/294-4700; fax 619/294-5722. www.pregoristoranti.com. Italian menu. Lunch, dinner. Bar. Children's menu. Business casual attire. Reservations recommended. Valet parking. Outdoor seating. **$$$**

★ ★ ★ **RAINWATER'S.** 1202 Kettner Blvd, San Diego (92101). Phone 619/233-5757; fax 619/233-6722. www.rainwaters.com. American, steak menu. Lunch, dinner. Closed holidays. Bar. Business casual attire. Reservations recommended. Valet parking. Outdoor seating. **$$$$**

★ **RED SAILS INN.** 2614 Shelter Island Dr, San Diego (92106). Phone 619/223-3030; fax 619/222-8230. www.theredsails.com. Located on Shelter Island, just minutes from downtown San Diego, Red Sails Inn is a cute and casual restaurant with nautical décor. Seafood menu. Breakfast, lunch, dinner. Closed Dec 25. Bar. Children's menu. Casual attire. Outdoor seating. **$$**

★ ★ **REGION.** 3671 5th Ave, San Diego (92103). Phone 619/299-6499; fax 619/291-9973. www.region-restaurant.com. California menu. Dinner. Closed Mon; holidays. Bar. Casual attire. **$$$**
▣

★ ★ ★ **RUTH'S CHRIS STEAK HOUSE.** 1355 N Harbor Dr, San Diego (92101). Phone 619/233-1422; fax 619/233-1530. www.ruthschris.com. The San Diego location of this famous chain serves up the usual steakhouse fare, but all of it is incredible; however, like its counterparts, it can be noisy and pricey. Be advised: reservations should be made at least a

week in advance. Steak menu. Dinner. Bar. Business casual attire. Reservations recommended. Valet parking. **$$$**

★ **SAFFRON.** 3731 India St, San Diego (92103). Phone 619/574-7737. www.sumeiyu.com. Thai menu. Lunch, dinner. Closed holidays. Children's menu. Casual attire. Outdoor seating. Picnic baskets available. **$$**

★ ★ ★ **SALLY'S.** One Market Pl, San Diego (92101). Phone 619/358-6740. www.manchestergrand.hyatt.com. American menu. Lunch, dinner. Bar. Casual attire. Reservations recommended. Valet parking. Outdoor seating. **$$$**

★ ★ ★ **SALVATORE'S.** 750 Front St, San Diego (92101). Phone 619/544-1865; fax 619/544-1871. www.salvatoresdowntown.com. Italian menu. Dinner. Closed holidays. Bar. Business casual attire. Valet parking. **$$$**

★ **SAN DIEGO PIER CAFE.** 885 W Harbor Dr, San Diego (92101). Phone 619/239-3968; fax 619/232-7981. www.piercafe.com. On harbor pier. Seafood menu. Lunch, dinner. Closed holidays. Bar. Children's menu. Casual attire. Reservations recommended. Outdoor seating. **$$**

★ ★ ★ **TAKA.** 555 Fifth Ave, San Diego (92101). Phone 619/338-0555; fax 619/338-0898. www.takasushi.com. Japanese, sushi, fusion menu. Dinner. Closed holidays. Bar. Children's menu. Casual attire. Reservations recommended. Outdoor seating. **$$**

★ ★ ★ **THEE BUNGALOW.** 4996 W Point Loma Blvd, San Diego (92107). Phone 619/224-2884; fax 619/224-3563. www.theebungalow.com. The menu seems to change concepts as often as the tides, but it's all for good reason as chef/owner Ed Moore strives to please his loyal Ocean Beach following. American, French menu. Dinner. Closed holidays. Bar. Business casual attire. Reservations recommended. Outdoor seating. **$$$**
▣

★ ★ **TOM HAM'S LIGHTHOUSE.** 2150 Harbor Island Dr, San Diego (92101). Phone 619/291-9110. www.tomhamslighthouse.com. Seafood menu. Lunch, dinner. Closed holidays. Bar. Casual attire. Reservations recommended. Outdoor seating. **$$$**

★ ★ ★ **TOP OF THE MARKET.** 750 N Harbor Dr, San Diego (92101). Phone 619/234-4867; fax 619/232-8648. www.thefishmarket.com. Pictures of turn-of-the-century fishing scenes. Retail fish market lower floor. Seafood menu. Lunch, dinner. Closed holidays. Bar.

Children's menu. Business casual attire. Reservations recommended. Valet parking. Outdoor seating. **$$$**

★ ★ **TRATTORIA FANTASTICA.** *1735 India St, San Diego (92101). Phone 619/234-1735. www.trattoriafantastica.com.* Italian menu. Lunch, dinner. Closed holidays. Casual attire. Valet parking. Outdoor seating. **$$**

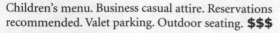

★ ★ ★ **WINESELLAR AND BRASSERIE.** *9550 Waples St, San Diego (92121). Phone 858/450-9576; fax 858/558-0928. www.winesellar.com.* With crisp white linens and a candlelit atmosphere, Winesellar and Brasserie is the perfect destination for a romantic dinner of fine French cuisine. Don't forgot to stop at the lower level wine shop to browse the large selection of fine wines. French menu. Dinner. Closed Sun; holidays. Bar. Casual attire. **$$$**

★ ★ **ZOCALO GRILL.** *2444 San Diego Ave, San Diego (92110). Phone 619/298-9840; fax 619/298-0601. www.zocalogrill.com.* California menu. Lunch, dinner, Sun brunch. Closed holidays. Bar. Children's menu. Casual attire. Reservations recommended. Outdoor seating. **$$$**

San Fernando (H-3)

Population 23,564
Elevation 1,061 ft
Area Code 818
Information Chamber of Commerce, 519 S Brand Blvd, 91340; phone 818/361-1184
Web Site www.ci.san-fernando.ca.us

A Ranger District office of the Angeles National Forest (see PASADENA) is located here.

What to See and Do

Mission San Fernando Rey de España. *15151 San Fernando Mission Blvd, Mission Hills (91345). Phone 818/361-0186. www.missiontour.org/sanfernando.* Ornate and strikingly beautiful best describes the altar at this 18th-century mission, the 17th of 21 built by Franciscans in California. As you gaze at the altar, you'll be reminded of Spain's richness and appreciation for the finest of things back then, especially in its houses of God. One caveat: you're not really visiting an 18th-century church, but an exact replica built after the 1971 Sylmar earthquake destroyed the original. If you want to worship here, priests still say Mass daily. The convent building, which dates back to the early days, houses an impressive museum of religious artifacts, some quite valuable. (Daily 9 am-5 pm; closed Thanksgiving, Dec 25) **$** Also here, and included in admission, is the

Archival Center. *15151 San Fernado Mission Blvd, Mission Hills (91345). Phone 818/365-1501.* Located in the west garden of the mission, the center houses ecclesiastical and historical documents, medals and mitres, relics of early California missionaries; changing exhibits. (Archival center: Mon-Fri 8:30 am-noon, 1-4:30 pm; Museum: Mon, Thurs 1-3 pm) **$**

San Fernando Valley Area (H-3)

North and west of Los Angeles (see) and bounded by the Santa Monica, Santa Susana, and San Gabriel mountains is the area known as the San Fernando Valley. The Los Angeles River, which flows through the valley, has its source in the mountains. Once primarily an agricultural area, the San Fernando Valley has diversified into a haven for light industry and commuters to Los Angeles.

The valley was explored by the Spanish in 1769; they found "a very pleasant and spacious valley... with many live oaks and walnuts." The arrival of the Southern Pacific railroad in 1876, linking Los Angeles to San Francisco, temporarily boosted agricultural production. However, production decreased following World War II, when the land was divided into housing tracts. At one time, the valley gained 15,000-20,000 new residents per year, rivaling the spectacular growth of Los Angeles.

The following towns and Los Angeles neighborhoods in the San Fernando Valley area are included in this book. For additional information on any of them, see the individual listing: San Fernando, Studio City, Woodland Hills.

San Gabriel (J-4)

Another of the so-called bedroom communities, San Gabriel is a personable enclave a scant 20 miles from downtown Los Angeles. Slightly south of the upscale suburbs of San Marino, it is bound on the west by Alhambra and on the east by El Monte. Home of one of the original California missions, often called "the pride of California Missions," founded by Junipero Serra, San Gabriel refers to itself as the Mission City and is pleasantly aggressive about maintaining, displaying, and reveling in its early Spanish/Indian history. Spectacular views of the nearby San Gabriel Mountains are plentiful toward the north and north-west. The Civic Auditorium, on South Mission Drive just south of West Las Tunas Drive, is an outstanding example of Mission-style architecture. The Perform-ing Arts Center, also on South Mission Drive, has a statewide reputation for comfort, architecture, and ambience. It is often compared favorably with the venerable Lobero Theater in Santa Barbara. Check the Plaza Park for historical relics and commemorative landscaping. An equally impressive historical walk, featuring exciting historical sites in the California his-tory, radiates outward from the Mission.

Restaurants

★ **GOLDEN DELI.** *815 W Las Tunas Dr, San Gabriel (91776). Phone 626/308-0803.* Golden Deli is one of the best places in San Gabriel to enjoy wonderful Vietnamese classics. The décor may not be much, and the location in a mini-mall is deceiving, but the per-petual crowds waiting in line for seats agree that this is among the best to be found. For a tiny sum, you can enjoy a wide variety of Vietnamese specialties, includ-ing excellent renditions of crispy pork-filled spring rolls (cha gio), beef noodle soup (pho bo), shrimp on sugar cane (chao tom), or barbecued pork with rice noodles (bun thit nuong). There are so many delicious items to choose from that one must visit Golden Deli frequently to enjoy the vibrant flavors that are surely one of the closest matches to the real thing we've found. Vietnamese menu. Lunch, dinner. No credit cards accepted. **$**

★ **MEI LONG VILLAGE.** *301 W Valley Blvd #112, San Gabriel (91776). Phone 626/284-4769.* The differ-ences in regional cuisines of China are more pro-nounced than most anywhere, even in the vast United States. Chinese and non-Chinese alike feel strongly about which regional cuisine is paramount, as the Brit-ish with their football teams. Shanghaiese gets many votes as a favorite, and Mei Long Village is one of the better spots—among the many in San Gabriel—to determine your stand on the issue. A good place to start testing the waters is with dumplings, one of the

Shanghai's claims to fame. The diversity offered at Mei Long Village—in soup, steamed, baked, or fried—is mind-boggling. A feast could be made of dumplings alone, perhaps with a side of sautéed greens (whatever they have that day) to help cut the starch. Of course, once you've sampled these, you'll want to move on to the many other specialties of Shanghai, but avoid the generic Chinese basics or you won't truly experience Mei Long Village or one of the most elegant cuisines of China. Chinese menu. Lunch, dinner. **$$**

San Juan Capistrano (J-4)

See also Anaheim, Carlsbad, Laguna Beach, San Clemente

Founded 1776
Population 33,826
Elevation 104 ft
Area Code 949
Zip 92675
Information Chamber of Commerce, 31781 Camino Capistrano, Suite 306; phone 949/493-4700
Web Site www.sanjuanchamber.com

Because of its colorful mission and its euphoni-ous name, this town has been romanticized in song, legend, short stories, and movies. Perched between mountains and ocean, San Juan Capistrano developed around the mission and today is occupied, in part, by descendants of early Mexican settlers. At one time, the village declared war on Mexico.

What to See and Do

Mission San Juan Capistrano. *Ortega Highway & Camino Capistrano, San Juan Capistrano (92675). 2 blocks W of I-5, Ortega Hwy exit. Phone 949/234-1300. www.missionsjc.com.* Famous for its swallows, which depart each year on St. John's Day (October 23) and return on St. Joseph's Day (March 19). Founded by Fray Junipero Serra in 1776 and named for St. John of Capistrano, the crusader, the church was built in the form of a cross and was one of the most beautiful of all California missions. The arched roof, five domes, nave, cloister, and belfry collapsed during the 1812 earthquake. Pillars, arches, the garden, and quadrangle remain. Self-guided tour includes the Serra Chapel (still in use), oldest building in California, ruin of the Great Stone Church, padres' living quarters, soldiers' barracks, and three museum rooms exhibiting artifacts from Native American and early Spanish culture. Also the site of a major archaeological dig. (Daily 8:30 am-5 pm; closed Good Fri afternoon, Thanksgiving, Dec 25) **$$**

O'Neill Museum. *31831 Los Rios St, San Juan Capistrano (92675). Phone 949/493-8444. www.sjchistoricalsociety.com/museum.html.* Housed in a restored Victorian house, museum features collections of historical photographs, rare books, period furniture and clothing, Native Americans artifacts; also genealogical information. (Tues-Fri 9 am-4 pm; Sat-Sun noon-3 pm; closed holidays) **DONATION**

Ronald W. Caspers Wilderness Park. *33401 Ortega Hwy, San Juan Capistrano (92675). Phone 949/923-2210. www.ocparks.com/caspers.* Wilderness on 8,060 acres. Riding and hiking trails, nature center. Camping (fee). Inquire in advance for camping and trail use information and restrictions. No pets. (Daily 7 am-sunset)

San Juan Capistrano Regional Library. *31495 El Camino Real, San Juan Capistrano (92675). Phone 949/493-1752. www.ocpl.org/15brnch.asp.* Architecturally noteworthy postmodern building, designed by Michael Graves, combines Spanish, Egyptian, Greek, and pre-Columbian American influences in its design. (Mon-Wed 10 am-8 pm, Thurs to 6 pm, Sat to 5 pm, Sun noon-5 pm; tours by appointment) **FREE**

Tour of old adobes. *31831 Los Rios St, San Juan Capistrano (92675). Phone 949/493-8444. www.sjchistoricalsociety.com/tour.html.* Sponsored by the San Juan Capistrano Historical Society. (Sun 1 pm)

Special Events

Festival of Whales. *Dana Point Harbor, 34675 Golden Lantern, San Juan Capistrano (92629). Phone 949/472-7888; toll-free 888/440-4309. www.dpfestivalofwhales.com.* Educational and entertainment events saluting visit of California gray whales. Mid-Mar, weekends.

Fiesta de las Golondrinas. *31831 Camino Capistrano, San Juan Capistrano. Phone 949/493-1976. www.sanjuancapistrano.net/fiesta.* Mission San Juan Capistrano. Celebrates the return of the swallows to the mission; dance pageant, art exhibits, parade. Mid-Mar.

Limited-Service Hotel

★ **BEST WESTERN CAPISTRANO INN.** *27174 Ortega Hwy, San Juan Capistrano (92675). Phone 949/493-5661; toll-free 800/441-9438; fax*

949/661-8293. www.bestwestern.com. 108 rooms, 2 story. Pets accepted; fee. Check-in 3:30 pm, check-out noon. Outdoor pool, whirlpool. **$**

Restaurants

★ ★ **EL ADOBE DE CAPISTRANO.** *31891 Camino Capistrano, San Juan Capistrano (92675). Phone 949/493-1163; fax 949/493-4565. www.eladobedecapistrano.com.* Spanish adobe courthouse (1778). Mexican menu. Lunch, dinner, Sun brunch. Bar. Children's menu. Outdoor seating. **$$**

★ ★ **L'HIRONDELLE.** *31631 Camino Capistrano, San Juan Capistrano (92675). Phone 949/661-0425; fax 949/661-3405.* French menu. Lunch, dinner, Sun brunch. Closed Mon; Jan 1, Dec 25. Outdoor seating. **$$**

San Luis Obispo (G-2)

See also Atascadero, Morro Bay, Pismo Beach, Santa Maria

Founded 1772
Population 44,174
Elevation 315 ft
Area Code 805
Information Chamber of Commerce, 1039 Chorro St, 93401; phone 805/781-2777
Web Site www.visitslo.com

Father Fray Junipero Serra, who established the mission in 1772, saw a resemblance to a bishop's mitre in two nearby volcanic peaks and named the mission San Luis Obispo de Tolosa (St. Louis, Bishop of Toulouse). After the thatched mission roofs burned several times, a tile-making technique was developed that soon set the style for all California missions. Located in a bowl-shaped valley, the town depends on government employment, tourism, agriculture, retail trade, and its university population.

What to See and Do

Ah Louis Store. *800 Palm St, San Luis Obispo (93401).* (1874) Leader of the Chinese community, Ah Louis was an extraordinary man who achieved prominence at a time when Asians were given few opportunities. The two-story building, which served as the Chinese bank, post office, and general merchandise store, was the cornerstone of the Chinese community. (Mon-Sat; closed holidays)

California Polytechnic State University. *1 Grand Ave, San Luis Obispo (93407). N edge of town. Phone 805/756-5734. www.calpoly.edu.* (1901) (17,000 students) On the campus are three art galleries; working livestock and farm units; and horticultural, architectural, and experimental displays. Campus tours (Mon-Fri, 11:10 am-12:30 pm; reservations required). **FREE** Also here are

> **Performing Arts Center of San Louis Obispo.** *1 Grand Ave, San Luis Obispo (93407). Phone 805/756-2787.* Center (91,500 square feet) offers professional dance, theater, music, and other performances all year. The 1,350-seat Harmon Concert Hall is JBL Professional's exclusive North American test and demonstration site.

> **Shakespeare Press Museum.** *California Polytechnic State University, Graphic Communications Bldg, San Luis Obispo (94301). Phone 805/756-1108.* Features a collection of 19th-century printing presses, type, and related equipment; demonstrations for prearranged tours. (Mon, Wed; closed holidays) **FREE**

Mission San Luis Obispo de Tolosa. *751 Palm St, San Luis Obispo (93401). Phone 805/543-6850. www.missionsanluisobispo.org.* Fifth of the California missions, founded in 1772, still serves as the parish church. Eight-room museum contains extensive Chumash collection and artifacts from early settlers. First olive orchard in California planted here; two original trees still stand. (Daily 9 am-5 pm; closed holidays) **DONATION**

San Luis Obispo County Museum and History Center. *696 Monterey St, San Luis Obispo (93406). Near mission. Phone 805/543-0638. www.slochs.org.* (1905) Local history exhibits; decorative arts. (Wed-Sun 10 am-4 pm; closed holidays) **FREE**

Special Events

Madonnari Italian Street Painting Festival. *Mission Plaza, Monterey and Chorro sts, San Luis Obispo (93401). Phone 805/781-2777.* Local artists decorate the streets around the mission with chalk drawings. Also music, Italian cuisine, and open-air market. Mid-Sept. **$**

Mozart Festival. *1160 Marsh St, San Luis Obispo (93401). Phone 805/781-3008. www.mozartfestival.com.* Recitals, chamber music, orchestra concerts, and choral music. Held at various locations throughout the county, including Mission San Luis Obispo de

Tolosa and California Polytechnic State University campus. Mid-July-early Aug. **$$$$**

Renaissance Festival. *1087 Santa Rosa St, San Luis Obispo (93408). Phone 707/864-5706.* Celebration of the Renaissance; period costumes, food booths, entertainment, arts and crafts. July.

SLO International Film Festival. *817 Palm St, San Luis Obispo. Phone 805/546-3456. www.slofilmfest.org.* This festival showcases the history and art of filmmaking with screenings of new releases, classics, short and long films, and documentaries. Additional events include seminars, a film competition, and the annual sing-along, where moviegoers dress up as characters from the featured musical and—you guessed it—sing along to the soundtrack. Early-mid-Mar. **$$$$**

Limited-Service Hotels

★ **BEST WESTERN ROYAL OAK HOTEL.** *214 Madonna Rd, San Luis Obispo (93405). Phone 805/544-4410; toll-free 800/545-4410; fax 805/544-3026. www.bestwestern.com.* 99 rooms, 2 story. Pets accepted; restrictions, fee. Complimentary continental breakfast. Check-in 3 pm, check-out noon. Outdoor pool. **$**

★ ★ **EMBASSY SUITES.** *333 Madonna Rd, San Luis Obispo (93405). Phone 805/549-0800; toll-free 800/864-6000; fax 805/543-5273. www.embassysuites-lo.com.* 196 rooms, 4 story, all suites. Complimentary full breakfast. Check-in 3 pm, check-out noon. High-speed Internet access. Restaurant, two bars. Fitness room. Indoor pool, outdoor pool, whirlpool. **$$**

★ **HOLIDAY INN EXPRESS.** *1800 Monterey St, San Luis Obispo (93401). Phone 805/544-8600; toll-free 800/465-4329; fax 805/541-4698. www.hiexpress.com.* 100 rooms, 3 story. Pets accepted, fee. Complimentary continental breakfast. Check-in 3 pm, check-out noon. Outdoor pool, whirlpool. **$**

★ ★ **QUALITY SUITES.** *1631 Monterey St, San Luis Obispo (93401). Phone 805/541-5001; toll-free 800/228-5151; fax 805/546-9475. www.qualitysuites.com.* 138 rooms, 3 story, all suites. Complimentary continental breakfast. Check-in 3 pm, check-out noon. High-speed Internet access. Outdoor pool, whirlpool. Business center. **$**

★ **SANDS SUITES & MOTEL.** *1930 Monterey St, San Luis Obispo (93401). Phone 805/544-0500; toll-free 800/441-4657; fax 805/544-3529. www.sandssuites.com.* 70 rooms, 2 story. Pets accepted; fee. Complimentary continental breakfast. Check-in 3 pm, check-out 11 am. Outdoor pool, whirlpool. **$**

Full-Service Hotel

★ ★ ★ **APPLE FARM TRELLIS COURT.** *2015 Monterey St, San Luis Obispo (93401). Phone 805/544-2040; toll-free 800/255-2040; fax 805/544-2452. www. applefarm.com.* 69 rooms, 3 story. Check-in 4 pm, check-out noon. Restaurant. Outdoor pool, whirlpool. Airport transportation available. **$**

Specialty Lodgings

GARDEN STREET INN. *1212 Garden St, San Luis Obispo (93401). Phone 805/545-9802; toll-free 800/488-2045; fax 805/545-9403. www.gardenstreet-inn.com.* Restored Victorian house (1887) furnished with antiques. 13 rooms, 2 story. Complimentary full breakfast. Check-in 3-7 pm, check-out 11 am. **$$$**

MADONNA INN. *100 Madonna Rd, San Luis Obispo (93405). Phone 800/543-9666; toll-free 800/543-9666; fax 805/543-1800. www.madonnainn.com.* Odds are, you've never seen anything quite like the Madonna Inn, conveniently located halfway between Los Angeles and San Francisco. The hotel and its restaurants are shameless kitsch at its finest, and you may feel like you've stepped back in time to the 1940s or '50s. Flowers figure largely into the décor, as does ornately carved hardwood, brightly colored leather, and gold plating. Photographs of each uniquely decorated room are available for viewing on the inn's Web site, so you can decide exactly which color combination you want to wake up to. (Will it be the hot-pink carpeting and gold-and-crystal chandelier of Room 215, "Morning Star," or the solid-rock floors, walls, ceilings, and shower plus animal-print upholstery and bedding of Room 137, "Caveman Room"?) Even if you decide not to stay the night in San Luis Obispo, the Madonna Inn is worth a stop as you drive by it on Highway 101, if only to use the restroom and walk past the famed horseshoe-shaped bar and the Copper Café. 109 rooms, 4 story. Check-in 4 pm, check-out noon. Restaurant, bar. Airport transportation available. **$$**

Restaurants

★ ★ **1865 RESTAURANT.** *1865 Monterey St, San Luis Obispo (93401). Phone 805/544-1865; fax 805/541-5259. www.1865.com.* Seafood, steak menu. Lunch, dinner. Closed Sun. Bar. Business casual attire. Reservations recommended. **$$**

★ **APPLE FARM.** *2015 Monterey St, San Luis Obispo (93401). Phone 805/544-6100; fax 805/544-6890. www.applefarm.com.* American menu. Breakfast, lunch, dinner. Children's menu. Casual attire. **$$**

★ ★ **CAFE ROMA.** *1020 Railroad Ave, San Luis Obispo (93401). Phone 805/541-6800; fax 805/786-2522. www.caferomaslo.com.* Italian menu. Lunch, dinner. Closed Sun; holidays. Bar. Casual attire. Reservations recommended. **$$**

★ **CISCO'S.** *778 Higuera St, San Luis Obispo. Phone 805/543-5555.* American menu. Lunch, dinner. Children's menu. Casual attire. Outdoor seating. **$**

★ **SLO BREWING CO.** *1119 Garden St, San Luis Obispo (93401). Phone 805/543-1843. www.slobrew.com.* American menu. Lunch, dinner, late-night. Bar. Children's menu. Casual attire. **$**

San Marino (J-4)

See also Arcadia, Los Angeles, Pasadena

Population 12,945
Elevation 566 ft
Area Code 626
Zip 91108
Information Chamber of Commerce, 2304 Huntington Dr, Suite 202; phone 626/286-1022
Web Site www.sanmarinochamber.com

What to See and Do

El Molino Viejo. *1120 Old Mill Rd, San Marino (91108). Phone 626/449-5458. www.old-mill.org.* (Circa 1816) The first gristmill to be operated by water in Southern California. Changing exhibits of paintings and prints of California and the West. (Tues-Sun 1-4 pm; closed holidays) **FREE**

Huntington Library, Art Collections, and Botanical Gardens. *1151 Oxford Rd, San Marino (91108). Phone 626/405-2100. www.huntington.org.* The Huntington Library, Art Collections, and Botanical Gardens opened to the public in 1928 and have been a draw ever since. Situated on 150 acres, the gardens feature more than 14,000 species of plants, with a series of themed gardens. The library houses many rare manuscripts, including a Gutenberg Bible. The Huntington Art Collections are particularly strong in British and French art from the 18th and 19th centuries. Have a traditional English tea in the Rose Garden Tea Room to round out your day. (Tues-Fri noon-4:30 pm, Sat-Sun 10:30 am-4:30 pm; closed holidays) $$$

San Pedro (LA) (J-4)

See also Avalon (Catalina Island), Los Angeles

Elevation 20 ft
Area Code 310
Information Chamber of Commerce, 390 W 7th St, 90731; phone 310/832-7272
Web Site www.sanpedrochamber.com

Nestled in the Palos Verdes hills, this community is a neighborhood of Los Angeles but is regarded by many as a separate entity.

What to See and Do

Cabrillo Marine Aquarium. *3720 Stephen White Dr, San Pedro (90731). Phone 310/548-7562. www.cabrilloaq.org.* Extensive marine life displayed in 34 seawater aquariums; interpretive displays, environmental conservation, multimedia shows, "Touch Tank." Seasonal grunion programs, whale-watching, tidepool tours. Access to beaches, picnic areas, fishing pier, and launching ramp (beach parking, $$). (Tues-Fri noon-5 pm, Sat-Sun 10 am-5 pm; closed Thanksgiving, Dec 25) **DONATION**

Los Angeles Maritime Museum. *Berth 84, San Pedro (90731). Foot of 6th St at Los Angeles Harbor. Phone 310/548-7618. www.lamaritimemuseum.org.* A truly educational museum featuring scale models of ships and numerous displays and artifacts from sailing vessels of all types. Models include the *Titanic* and movie studio models from the films *The Poseidon Adventure* and *Mutiny on the Bounty*. Past exhibits have been dedicated to submarines on film and maritime history through popular art. Also housed on-site is the Los Angeles Maritime Institute, which takes pride in its TopSail Youth Program, which gives thousands of hours of free sailing lessons and trips to schoolchildren each year. (Tues-Sat 10 am-5 pm, Sun noon-5 pm; closed holidays) $

Ports O' Call Village. *Berths 76 and 77, Sampson Way, San Pedro (90731). Phone 310/732-7696. www.spirit-dinnercruises.com.* Yes, it's in Southern California, but a visit to this quaint seaside village takes you back East to the New England coast. As you wander along its cobblestone streets, duck into the many small shops, which sell goods from around the world. If you get hungry, take your pick from numerous restaurants, any of which will gladly fill you up with something tasty. Take time to enjoy the views, too; the 15-acre village overlooks the Los Angeles Harbor, a busy port with cruise ships and other types of seagoing vessels used for commercial fishing, sailing, whale-watching, deep-sea fishing, and more. (Daily from 11 am; some restaurants open earlier)

Limited-Service Hotel

★ **BEST WESTERN SUNRISE HOTEL.** *525 S Harbor Blvd, San Pedro (90731). Phone 310/548-1080; toll-free 800/356-9609; fax 310/519-0380. www.bestwestern.com.* Harbor view. 110 rooms, 3 story. Complimentary continental breakfast. Check-in 3 pm. Check-out noon. Outdoor pool, whirlpool. $

Full-Service Hotels

★ ★ **CROWNE PLAZA HARBOR HOTEL.** *601 S Palos Verdes St, San Pedro (90731). Phone 310/519-8200; fax 310/519-8421. www.crowneplaza.com/laharbor.* 246 rooms, 10 story. Complimentary continental breakfast. Check-in 3 pm, check-out noon. Restaurant, bar. Fitness room. Outdoor pool, whirlpool. $$

★ ★ ★ **MARINA HOTEL SAN PEDRO.** *2800 Via Cabrillo Marina, San Pedro (90731). Phone 310/514-3344; fax 310/514-8945. www.marinahotel-sanpedro.com.* Just 19 miles from LAX and 6 miles from downtown Long Beach, this hotel overlooks Cabrillo Marina and is convenient to the World Cruise Center and Catalina Island. 226 rooms, 3 story. Pets accepted; fee. Check-in 3 pm. Check-out noon. Restaurant, bar. Fitness room. Outdoor pool, whirlpool. Tennis. Business center. $$

Restaurant

★ ★ **22ND STREET LANDING SEAFOOD.** *141A W 22nd St, San Pedro (90731). Phone 310/548-*

4400; fax 310/548-5194. www.22ndstreet.com. Seafood menu. Dinner. Closed Dec 25. Bar. Children's menu. Casual attire. Outdoor seating. **$$$**

San Simeon (G-2)

See also Cambria, Hearst-San Simeon State Historical Monument (Hearst Castle), Morro Bay, Paso Robles

Population 250
Elevation 20 ft
Area Code 805
Zip 93452
Information Chamber of Commerce, 9255 Hearst Dr; phone 805/927-3500
Web Site www.sansimeon-online.com

San Simeon is a historical old whaling village. About 100 years ago, death-defying forays took place off these rocky shores when whales were spotted. Sea lion, sea otter, and whale-watching are popular during northward migration in March-May, and also during December-January, when southward migration occurs. Deep-sea fishing is especially popular all year.

Limited-Service Hotel

★★ **BEST WESTERN CAVALIER OCEANFRONT RESORT.** *9415 Hearst Dr, San Simeon (93452). Phone 805/927-4688; toll-free 800/826-8168; fax 805/927-6472. www.cavalierresort. com.* 90 rooms, 2 story. Pets accepted. Check-out noon. Restaurant, bar. Fitness room. Two outdoor pools, whirlpool. **$**

Santa Ana (J-4)

See also Anaheim, Costa Mesa, Garden Grove, Irvine, Long Beach, Newport Beach, Orange

Population 337,977
Elevation 110 ft
Area Code 714
Information Chamber of Commerce, 2020 N Broadway, 2nd Floor, 92706; phone 714/541-5353
Web Site www.santaanacc.com

Originally a valley site chosen in the 1760s for its mild weather, its readily available water, and its suitability for ranching and farming, Santa Ana quickly became populated, citified, and influential. By 1889, when Or-

ange County was carved out of the southern portion of Los Angeles County, Santa Ana was named county seat. Slightly over 27 square miles, it is the largest city in Orange County, the ninth-largest city by population in California.

Home to a number of theatrical companies, art galleries, and museums, Santa Ana's thriving downtown business district comes alive on the first Saturday of each month with an elaborate open house in which artists, actors, and musicians perform for the public at the Artists Village (Second St at Broadway). The zoo, at 1801 East Chestnut, specializes in rare and endangered species. The Centennial Regional Park, at 3000 Centennial Road, has excellent playground equipment, a historical feature bike path following the original path of the Santa Ana River, and a 10-acre lake stocked with fish.

What to See and Do

Bowers Kidseum. *1802 Main St, Santa Ana (92706). Phone 714/480-1520. www.bowers.org/kidseum/ kidseum.asp.* For children ages 6-12. Focuses on art and culture of the Americas, Pacific Rim, and Africa. (Tues-Sun 11 am-4 pm; closed holidays) **$**

Bowers Museum of Cultural Art. *2002 N Main St, Santa Ana (92706). Phone 714/567-3600. www.bowers.org.* Over 80,000 objects in its collection, which focuses on the artwork of pre-Columbian, Oceanic, Native American, African, and Pacific Rim cultures. (Tues-Sun 10 am-4 pm; closed Jan 1, Thanksgiving, Dec 25) **$$$$**

Centennial Heritage Museum. *3101 W Harvard St, Santa Ana (92704). Phone 714/540-0404. www. centennialmuseum.org.* A hands-on museum, geared toward families, that helps make the history of Orange County come alive. Visitors can talk through a hand-cranked telephone, play a pump organ, try on Victorian clothing, wash clothes on a scrub board, and more. (Wed-Fri 1-5 pm, Sun 11 am-3 pm) **$**

Discovery Science Center. *2500 N Main St, Santa Ana (92705). Phone 714/542-2823. www.discoverycube.org.* Features more than 100 hands-on, interactive exhibits with emphasis on math, science, and technology for kids and their parents. (Daily 10 am-5 pm; closed Jan 1, Thanksgiving, Dec 25) **$$$**

Santa Ana Zoo at Prentice Park. *1801 E Chestnut, Santa Ana (92701). I-5 to 1st St exit. Phone 714/836-4000.santaanazoo.org.* Playgrounds, picnic area, zoo.

(Mon-Fri 10 am-4 pm; also Sat-Sun from Memorial Day-Labor Day; closed Jan 1, Dec 25) **$$**

Limited-Service Hotels

★ ★ **DOUBLETREE HOTEL.** *7 Hutton Centre Dr, Santa Ana (92707). Phone 714/751-2400; toll-free 800/528-0444; fax 714/662-7935. http://www. dtclluborangeco.com.* 167 rooms, 6 story. Check-out noon. Restaurant, bar. Fitness room. Outdoor pool, whirlpool. Airport transportation available. **$**

★ ★ **HOLIDAY INN.** *2726 S Grand Ave, Santa Ana (92705). Phone 714/481-6300; toll-free 800/522-6478; fax 714/966-1889. www.holiday-inn.com.* 178 rooms, 3 story. Complimentary continental breakfast. Check-in 3 pm, check-out noon. Restaurant, bar. Fitness room. Outdoor pool. Business center. **$**

★ **QUALITY SUITES.** *2701 Hotel Terrace Dr, Santa Ana (92705). Phone 714/957-9200; toll-free 800/638-7949; fax 714/641-8936. www.qualityinns.com.* 177 rooms, 3 story, all suites. Pets accepted, some restrictions; fee. Complimentary continental breakfast. Check-in 3 pm, check-out noon. Bar. Outdoor pool. Airport transportation available. **$**

Restaurant

★ ★ ★ **ANTONELLO.** *3800 Plaza Dr, Santa Ana (92704). Phone 714/751-7153; fax 714/751-8650. www. antonello.com.* Antonello's restaurant prides itself in offering a taste of northern Italy in sunny California. While the restaurant is a perfect choice for a romantic evening, with alfresco seating under the stars, Antonellos is also a power lunch spot for celebs, foodies, and others who fancy themselves as part of the super-fabulous set. Whatever camp you fall into, you'll be satisfied with a terrific menu of antipastos, soups, salads, and fresh pasta dishes, as well as a variety of exceptional fish, poultry, veal, and beef entrées. To keep your thirst quenched, Antonello's wine list boasts more than 300 foreign and domestic labels. Italian menu. Lunch, dinner. Closed Sun; holidays. Bar. Jacket required. Reservations recommended. Valet parking. **$$$**

Santa Barbara (H-3)

See also Ojai, Solvang, Ventura

Founded 1769
Population 92,325
Elevation 37-850 ft
Area Code 805
Information Conference and Visitors Bureau & Film Commission, 1601 Anacapa St, 93101; phone 805/966-9222 or toll-free 800/676-1266
Web Site www.santabarbaraca.com

Spanish charm hangs over this city, with its colorful street names, Spanish- and Moorish-style architecture, adobe buildings, and beautiful houses and gardens on the slopes of the Santa Ynez Mountains. It faces east and west on the Pacific Ocean along the calmest stretch of the California coast. Although the Spanish explorer Vizcaino entered the channel on Saint Barbara's Day, December 4, 1602, and named the region after the saint, a Portuguese navigator, Juan Rodriguez Cabrillo, is credited with the discovery of the channel in 1542. Its large harbor and breakwater can accommodate many boats and offers boat rentals and excursions. A Ranger District office of the Los Padres National Forest is located in Santa Barbara.

What to See and Do

Beach areas. East Beach *(E Cabrillo Blvd, next to Stearns Wharf)*, **West Beach** *(W Cabrillo Blvd, between Stearns Wharf and Harbor)*, and **Ledbetter Beach** *(Shoreline Dr and Loma Alta Dr)* are some of the outstanding beaches in Santa Barbara, known for great sand and surf, plus bike paths, picnicking, and play areas. (Daily)

Carpinteria State Beach. *5361 6th St, Carpintoria (93013). 12 miles SE on Hwy 101. Phone 805/684-2811. www.parks.ca.gov.* Swimming, lifeguard (summer), fishing; picnicking; camping (some hook-ups, dump station; fee). (Daily dawn-dusk)

El Paseo. *Central Ave and Main St, Santa Barbara (93015). Opposite City Hall, de la Guerra St.* Courtyards and passageways similiar to old Spain. Shops, art galleries, and restaurants.

El Presidio de Santa Barbara State Historic Park. *123 E Caon Perdido St, Santa Barbara (93101). Phone 805/965-0093. www.sbthp.org/presidio.htm.* Original and reconstructed buildings of the last presidio (military and government outpost) built by Spain in the New World. Museum displays, slide show. (Daily; closed holidays) **$**

Island and coastal fishing trips. *301 W Cabrillo Blvd, Santa Barbara (93101). Phone 805/963-3564.* Scuba diving trips, fishing, dinner cruises; whale-watching in season. **$$$$**

Los Padres National Forest. *3505 Paradise Rd, Santa Barbara (93105). N of town. Phone 805/967-3481. www.fs.fed.us/r5/lospadres.* Forest of 1,724,000 acres encompassing the La Panza, Santa Ynez, San Rafael, Santa Lucia, and Sierra Madre mountains. The vegetation ranges from chaparral to oak woodlands to coniferous forests, which include the Santa Lucia fir, the rarest and one of the most unusual firs in North America. Also contains the mountainous 149,000-acre San Rafael Wilderness, the 64,700-acre Dick Smith Wilderness, and the 21,250-acre Santa Lucia Wilderness. There is also the Sespe Condor Refuge. Fishing for trout in 485 miles of streams; hunting, hiking, and riding on 1,750 miles of trails; camping.

Mission Santa Barbara. *2201 Laguna St, Santa Barbara (93105). E Los Olivos and Upper Laguna sts, 2 miles N. Phone 805/682-4149. www.sbmission.org.* Founded in 1786, the present church was completed in 1820. Known as "Queen of the Missions" because of its architectural beauty, the tenth California mission stands on a slight elevation and at one time served as a beacon for sailing ships. Its twin-towered church and monastery represent the earliest phase of Spanish Renaissance architecture. Self-guided tours. Display rooms exhibit mission building arts, mission crafts, and examples of Native American and Mexican art. (Daily 9 am-5 pm; closed holidays) **$$**

Moreton Bay fig tree. *Chapala St and Hwy 101, Santa Barbara.* Believed to be the largest of its kind in the United States. Planted in 1877, it is considered possible for the tree to attain a branch spread of 160 feet. A Santa Barbara city engineer estimated that 10,450 persons could stand in its shade at noon.

Santa Barbara Botanic Garden. *1212 Mission Canyon Rd, Santa Barbara. 1 1/4 miles N of Mission. Phone 805/682-4726. www.sbbg.org.* Native trees, shrubs, and wildflowers of California on 65 acres; Old Mission Dam (1806). Guided tours. (Mar-Oct: daily 9 am-5 pm; Nov-Feb: Mon-Fri 9 am-4 pm, Sat-Sun to 5 pm; closed holidays) **$$**

Santa Barbara County Courthouse. *1100 Anacapa St, Santa Barbara (93121). Phone 805/962-6464. www.*

sbcourts.org. Resembles a Spanish-Moorish palace. Considered one of the most beautiful buildings in the West. (Daily; closed Dec 25) Guided tours (Mon-Tues, Fri 10:30 am; Mon-Sat 2 pm). **FREE**

Santa Barbara Historical Museum. *136 E de la Guerra St, Santa Barbara (93101). Phone 805/966-1601. www.santabarbaramuseum.com.* Rich collections interpret the city's artistic and multicultural history from Native American period to Spanish settlement to present day. Large, gilded Chinese *Tong* shrine. Library (Tues-Fri). Museum (Tues-Sat 10 am-5 pm, Sun noon-5 pm; closed holidays). **FREE**

Santa Barbara Maritime Museum. *113 Harbor Way, Santa Barbara (93109). Phone 805/962-8404. www.sbmm.org.* Museum at the harbor with interactive maritime-related exhibits, including historic vessels, whales, shipwrecks, and a virtual-reality submarine ride. (Labor Day-Memorial Day: daily 10 am-5 pm; rest of year: to 6 pm) **$$**

Santa Barbara Museum of Art. *1130 State St, Santa Barbara (93101). Phone 805/963-4364. www.sbma.net.* Collections of ancient and Asian art, 19th-century French art, American and European paintings and sculpture, 20th-century art, photography; changing exhibits; lectures; guided tours. (Tues-Sun 11 am-5 pm; closed holidays) **$$**

Santa Barbara Museum of Natural History. *2559 Puesta del Sol Rd, Santa Barbara (93105). Phone 805/682-4711. www.sbnature.org.* Exhibits of fauna, flora, geology, and prehistoric life of the Pacific coast; lectures, shows, planetarium. (Daily 10 am-5 pm; closed Jan 1, Thanksgiving, Dec 25; also first Fri in Aug) **$$**

Santa Barbara Zoo. *500 Nios Dr, Santa Barbara (93103). Off Hwy 101. Phone 805/962-6310. www.santabarbarazoo.org.* Zoo with walk-through aviary, monkeys, big cats, elephants, and other exhibits; miniature railroad (fee); snack bar and picnic, barbecue sites. (Daily 10 am-5 pm; closed Thanksgiving, Dec 25) **$$**

Stearns Wharf. *219 Stearns Wharf, Santa Barbara (93101). Three-block extension of State St. www.stearnswharf.org.* Oldest operating wharf on the West Coast. Restaurants, shops, sportfishing pier, beautiful view of harbor and city. Wharf open 24 hours.

Truth Aquatics. *301 W Cabrillo Blvd, Santa Barbara (93101). Phone 805/962-1127. www.truthaquatics.com.* Direct boat service to Channel Islands National Park

Downtown Santa Barbara

Providing ample evidence that Santa Barbara is more than a series of beautiful beaches, this easy walk offers samplings of history, art, and distinctive architecture, as well as chances to shop and eat. If you stop to see some of the museums along the way, you could spend the better part of a day finishing the tour; if you stick mainly to walking, you can complete it in an hour or two. Starting in the 1100 block of Anacapa Street, you'll come upon what looks like a Spanish-Moorish palace. This building is actually the Santa Barbara County Courthouse, a wonderland of Moorish tiles, arched doorways, and tropical gardens that was built in 1929. You can ride the elevator to the deck of its clock tower for a panoramic view of the city. Across the street is the Spanish-style public library. Now, walk about two blocks southeast down Anacapa Street (toward the harbor) to Caon Perdido Street; go left a short distance to find El Presidio de Santa Barbara State Historic Park, located at 123 East Canon Perdido Street. Dating to 1782, the reconstructed presidio was a Spanish fort and Santa Barbaras birthplace. At Santa Barbara Street, take a right and then another right at de la Guerra Street. At the Santa Barbara Historical Museum (136 East de la Guerra St), you can view artifacts ranging from Spanish fans to silver saddles and a Chinese temple that reflect the city's surprisingly varied history. (To view two historic adobes dating to 1817 and 1836, go around the corner from the museum to 715 Santa Barbara St.) Continue down de la Guerra until you reach State Street; across State is the Paseo Nuevo, an attractive open-air mall, where you can browse among specialty shops or stop at a café for lunch or a snack. On the other side of State, mid-block, is El Paseo ("street" in Spanish), a shopping arcade constructed around the 1827 adobe of the prominent de la Guerra family. Walk northwest along State Street (away from the harbor) for about three blocks until you reach the Santa Barbara Museum of Art (1130 State Street), which has a nice collection of European paintings and exceptional displays of Asian art and artifacts. To extend your tour, walk back down State Street toward the harbor. Turn right at Montecito Street and walk to the intersection of Chapala Street (near Hwy 101) to behold the 1877-vintage Moreton Bay fig tree. The largest of its kind in the United States, its 160-foot breadth may leave you breathless. But save your remaining breath for the walk back to State Street, where you'll turn right to find Stearns Wharf, the West Coasts oldest operating wharf. It's lined with shops, marine exhibits, and restaurants with harbor views.

(one departure daily). Call for fee information and reservations.

University of California, Santa Barbara. *552 University Rd, Goleta (93106). Approximately 10 miles N on Hwy 101. Phone 805/893-2485. www.ucsb.edu.* (1944) (20,000 students) An 815-acre seaside campus. Tours (Mon-Fri). For current performing arts activities on campus, phone 805/893-3535. On campus is

> **Art Museum.** *Arts Bldg. Phone 805/893-7564.* Sedgwick collection of Old Master and baroque period paintings; Morgenroth collection of Renaissance medals and plaques; Dreyfus collection of Mid-Eastern and pre-Columbian artifacts; changing exhibits. (Wed-Sun noon-5 pm) **FREE**

Special Events

Old Spanish Days Fiesta. *Carriage Western Art Museum, 129 Castillo St, Santa Barbara (93101). City-*wide. *Phone 805/962-8101. www.oldspanishdays-fiesta. org.* Re-creates the city's history from Native American days to arrival of American troops. Early Aug.

Santa Barbara International Orchid Show. *Earl Warren Fairgrounds, 3400 Calle Real, Santa Barbara (93105). www.sborchidshow.com.* Growers from around the world display their orchids. Mar.

Santa Barbara National Horse Show. *Earl Warren Fairgrounds, 3400 Calle Real, Santa Barbara (93105). Phone 805/687-0766. www.earlwarren.com.* One of the most impressive and well known horse shows in the United States, the Santa Barbara National Horse Show features champion jumpers as well as American Saddle Breds, Tennessee Walking horses, and Welsh ponies. Mid-July.

Summer Sports Festival (Semana Nautica). *www. semananautica.com.* No matter what your age or level of athletic ability, you can be sure that Semana Nautica has a competition for you. Chose from more than 50 land and water sports, including water polo, beach volleyball, softball, running, and canoeing. Late June or early July.

Limited-Service Hotels

★ ★ **BEST WESTERN ENCINA LODGE AND SUITES.** *2220 Bath St, Santa Barbara (93105). Phone 805/682-7277; toll-free 800/526-2282; fax 805/563-9319. www.bestwestern.com.* Built around a swimming pool and graceful gardens, just blocks from the California coastline and the historic Queen of the Missions, this affordable and charming hotel boasts amenities from spa services to cocktail hour and barbers and babysitters, creating an atmosphere of casual convenience and unpretentious comfort. Rooms reflect the rural country theme, with exposed beamed ceilings, quilted beds, floral walls, and homey touches like flower baskets. For economy travelers, this luxe-hotel provides the finer things, without the sticker-shock. 121 rooms, 2 story. Check-in 3 pm, check-out noon. High-speed Internet access. Restaurant, bar. Outdoor pool, whirlpool. **$$**

★ ★ **BEST WESTERN PEPPER TREE INN.** *3850 State St, Santa Barbara (93105). Phone 805/687-5511; toll-free 800/338-0030; fax 805/682-2410. www.bestwestern.com.* Guests are greeted by a stone fountain, red-tile roofs, and courtyard gardens, reflecting the area's historic Spanish architecture. Just across the street from Le Cumbre Shopping Plaza, a top-notch open-air mall, this tranquil and delightful hotel is a miniature escape within itself, with two large courtyard pools that seem to block out the entire sprawling city beyond. Each room in this two-story spread has a private balcony, and on-site amenities include a fitness center, restaurant, and massage center. An amiable staff is ever-ready with suggestions for local beaches, restaurants, and tourist destinations. 150 rooms, 2 story. Check-in 3 pm, check-out noon. Wireless Internet access. Restaurant, bar. Fitness room. Two outdoor pools, whirlpool. **$$**

★ ★ **COAST VILLAGE INN.** *1188 Coast Village Rd, Santa Barbara (93108). Phone 805/969-3266; toll-free 800/257-5131; fax 805/969-7117. www.coastvillageinn. com.* Located near the heart of the exclusive coastal community of Montecito, the Inn is a small two-story hotel that offers privacy, ocean breezes, and Pacific views from some rooms. Cape Cod-style architecture with lush California gardens create a crisp atmo-

sphere, and the appealing Peabody restaurant offers fine dining in an enchanting log cabin. After a day at nearby Butterfly Beach, guests may relax around the heated pool or enjoy a cocktail on the alfresco patio before retiring in serene country-chic bedrooms. 28 rooms, 2 story. Complimentary continental breakfast. Check-in 3 pm, check-out noon. High-speed Internet access. Restaurant. Outdoor pool. **$$**

★ **FRANCISCAN INN.** *109 Bath St, Santa Barbara (93101). Phone 805/963-8845; fax 805/564-3295. www.fransicaninn.com.* This historic Inn was a ranch house in the 1920s and has since evolved into a sweet country style hotel—secluded, intimate, and sweet. Exterior grounds reflect the significant past, while the interior rooms are awash in pastel, floral prints, and brass lighting fixtures. A short walk away, the marina, downtown, and Stern's Wharf are prime attractions, making this a convenient starting point for tourists. Back at the hotel awaits a personable staff, heated whirlpool and pool, and even a lending library of books and videos. 53 rooms, 2 story. Complimentary continental breakfast. Check-in 3 pm, check-out noon. Outdoor pool, whirlpool. **$**

★ ★ **HOTEL OCEANA.** *202 W Cabrillo Blvd, Santa Barbara (93101). Phone 805/965-4577; toll-free 800/965-9776; fax 805/965-9937. www.hoteloceana. com.* Rising up from Santa Barbara's popular West Beach, this beach-chic resort is modern and crisp, mere steps to the water and touristy Stearn's Wharf. Sun-dappled patios sporting bright yellow umbrellas provide perfect Pacific vistas. The grounds include landscaped parks, two swimming pools, a fitness center, and whirlpools, while the staff provides the excellent service one could expect from a high-end resort. Rooms reflect casual coastal elegance, with sleek canopied beds sporting Frette linens. 122 rooms, 2 story. Complimentary full breakfast. Check-in 4 pm, check-out 11 am. Wireless Internet access. Fitness room, spa. Two outdoor pools, whirlpools. **$$**

★ **HOTEL SANTA BARBARA.** *533 State St, Santa Barbara (93101). Phone 805/957-9300; toll-free 888/259-7700; fax 805/962-2412. www.hotelsantabarbara.com.* Located in the epicenter of historic State Street, this spot can't be beat for a convenience to restaurants, shopping, and the energetic nightlife of downtown. This European-style hotel still has a naturally lit Mediterranean-style lobby, and tastefully decorated rooms that are laid-back and luxe at the same time. Meeting rooms are popular for traveling executives and salespeople. An excellent choice for young travelers looking for nightlife, business travelers on working retreats, or anyone who values a central location, this grand hotel is a relaxing retreat in the heart of it all. 75 rooms, 4 story. Complimentary continental breakfast. Check-in 3 pm, check-out noon. **$$**

★ **MARINA BEACH MOTEL.** *21 Bath St, Santa Barbara (93101). Phone 805/963-9311; toll-free 877/627-4621; fax 805/564-4102. www.marinabeach-motel.com.* This charming little motor lodge looks straight out of the 1950s, and you can literally drive right up to your door. Rooms may be small but are packed with conveniences like a kitchenette, fresh flower bouquets, and extra pillows. Bicycles are available for exploring the area, which is a mere half block to the beach. Although it's a bit small for traveling families and lacks a swimming pool, it can't be beat in terms of location and value. 32 rooms. Pets accepted, some restrictions; fee. Complimentary continental breakfast. Check-in 1 pm, check-out noon. **$**

★ **PACIFICA SUITES.** *5490 Hollister Ave, Santa Barbara (93111). Phone 805/683-6722; toll-free 800/338-6722; fax 805/683-4121. www.pacificasuites. com.* This magnificent hotel is an ideal retreat for any discerning traveler, whether in town for business or pleasure. Reflecting a tradition of the grand hotels of Europe, the grounds are dramatic and sprawling, meeting and dining rooms lavish and striking, and the service impeccable. Tucked away between the University and downtown, this secluded resort offers alfresco fine dining, a long, stylish lap pool, world-class business facilities, and a full-service spa. 87 rooms, 2 story, all suites. Pets accepted; fee. Complimentary full breakfast. Check-in 3 pm, check-out noon. Spa. Outdoor pool, whirlpool. Business center. **$**

★★ **SANTA BARBARA INN.** *901 E Cabrillo Blvd, Santa Barbara (93103). Phone 805/966-2285; fax 805/966-6584. www.santabarbarainn.com.* This boutique hotel sits right across the highway from the Pacific, affording stunning ocean views. The sleek architecture evokes Santa Barbaras Mission style with a touch of modern, minimalist California chic, with an airy and sun-drenched lobby, breezy open air hallways, and crisp, neutral bedroom suites. The grounds boast a swimming pool, verdant parks, and one of the area's finest restaurants, Citronelle, famed

for their modern Cal-French cuisine. There are even batting cages for the kids. 71 rooms, 5 story. Check-in 3 pm, check-out noon. Restaurant, bar. Outdoor pool, whirlpool. Business center. **$$**

Full-Service Hotels

★★★ **EL ENCANTO HOTEL & GARDEN VILLAS.** *1900 Lasuen Rd, Santa Barbara (93103). Phone 805/687-5000; toll-free 800/346-7039; fax 805/687-3903. www.elencantohotel.com.* Since 1915, these grounds have been a vacation destination for celebrities and business titans seeking a quiet refuge in this exclusive locale. More than 80 individual bungalows are nestled in these grounds, and each of the accommodations is unique, from Spanish revival to California Craftsmen. Expect fireplaces, living rooms, and homey niceties like swanky bath products. Located in the upscale Rivera neighborhood above Mission Santa Barbara, the resort offers unparallel panoramic views of the Pacific and the Channel Islands. 77 rooms. Pets accepted; fee. Check-in 3 pm, check-out noon. Wireless Internet access. Restaurant, bar. Outdoor pool, whirlpool. Tennis. Business center. **$$**

★★★ **FESS PARKER'S DOUBLETREE RESORT.** *633 E Cabrillo Blvd, Santa Barbara (93103). Phone 805/564-4333; toll-free 800/222-8733; fax 805/962-8198. www.fpdtr.com.* Beautiful and elegant, this grand resort is located where the ocean meets the sand, a unique beachfront location that is only surpassed by it's world-class services. Luxuries like complimentary airport transportation, lighted tennis courts, a sparkling swimming pool, attentive concierges, and health clubs make leaving the resort seem unnecessary. Whitewashed with red-tile roofs, lush gardens, arched walkways, and old California charm, this sprawling villa has become one of the premiere coastal destinations for honeymooners and discerning travelers. 360 rooms, 3 story. Pets accepted. Check-in 4 pm, check-out 11 am. High-speed Internet access, wireless Internet access. Two restaurants, bar. Fitness room. Outdoor pool, whirlpool. Tennis. Business center. **$$$**

★★★ **FOUR SEASONS RESORT SANTA BARBARA.** *1260 Channel Dr, Santa Barbara (93108). Phone 805/969-2261; fax 805/565-8323. www.fourseasons.com.* Perfectly situated on 20 lush acres facing the Pacific Ocean, the Four Seasons Resort Santa Barbara is a veritable Eden. Nicknamed "America's Riviera" because of its temperate climate and golden beaches, Santa Barbara offers a wonderful getaway. The resort pays tribute to the region's Spanish colonial history with its red-tiled roof and arches in the hacienda-style main building. The guest rooms, located in the main building and also in separate cottages, are warm and inviting retreats imbued with international design influences and local flavor. Crisp white cabanas line the sparkling pool at this full-service resort, where the beach is only steps away and the spa is a sybarite's fantasy. The lovely garden setting of the Patio is matched by its delicious Mediterranean and Pacific Rim cuisine, while La Marina (see) is a visual and culinary wonder with dramatic ocean views and artful regional dishes. 211 rooms, 2 story. Pets accepted, some restrictions. Check-in 4 pm, check-out 1 pm. High-speed Internet access. Two restaurants, bar. Fitness room, spa. Outdoor pool, whirlpool. Tennis. Business center. **$$$$**

★ ★ ★ **SAN YSIDRO RANCH.** *900 San Ysidro Ln, Montecito (93108). Phone 805/969-5046; toll-free 800/368-6788; fax 805/565-1995. www.sanysidroranch. com.* It is entirely possible that Cupid himself is the force behind the scenes at San Ysidro Ranch. This resort (550 acres) is a posh love nest, tucked away in the Montecito foothills of Santa Barbara. Lushly planted acres are filled with fragrant flowers and plants, and stunning vistas of the Pacific Ocean and the Channel Islands flirt in the distance. Scattered among the paths are the bungalows, which provide a secreted-away ambience. All of the little luxuries have been added to the accommodations, including wood-burning fireplaces or stoves and Frette linens. Extraordinarily gifted cuisine is a hallmark of this resort, and the resort's two restaurants provide charming settings for the imaginative food. 40 rooms. Pets accepted; fee. Check-in 3 pm, check-out noon. High-speed Internet access. Restaurant, bar. Fitness room. Outdoor pool, whirlpool. Tennis. **$$$$**

★ ★ ★ **SANTA YNEZ VALLEY MARRIOTT.** *555 McMurray Rd, Buellton (93427). Phone 805/688-1000; toll-free 800/638-8882; fax 805/688-0380. www.marri-ott.com.* 149 rooms, 4 story. Pets accepted; restrictions. Check-in 4 pm, check-out noon. Restaurant, bar. Fitness room. Outdoor pool. Golf. Business center. **$$**

Full-Service Resort

★ ★ ★ ★ **BACARA RESORT & SPA.** *8301 Hollister Ave, Santa Barbara (93117). Phone 018/059-6801; toll-free 877/422-4245; fax 805/968-1800. www.bacararesort.com.* Bacara Resort & Spa, with its spectacular setting and a dash of old-time Hollywood glamour, is a jet-setter's fantasy. This resort sparkles from its majestic location atop a bluff overlooking the Pacific Ocean. It is truly a delight for the senses, with its magnificent stretch of beach, three infinity-edge pools, and romantic Spanish colonial architecture. Rustic tiles set a relaxed elegance in the accommodations, where luxurious amenities are de rigueur. Fresh sea breezes attest to the notion that serenity is paramount here, and the spectacular spa is no exception. From citrus-avocado body polishes to earth crystal therapies, this spa is sublime. Guests adopt a healthy lifestyle while staying here; golf, tennis, yoga, and meditation are just some of their passions. Mediterranean flavors and feelings mingle at The Bistro; Miro amazes with its Californian cuisine; and the Spa Café breathes new life into healthy eating. 360 rooms, 4 story. Pets accepted, some restrictions; fee. Check-in 4 pm, check-out noon. Restaurant, bar. Children's activity center. Fitness room, spa. Three outdoor pools. Whirlpool. Golf. Tennis. Business center. **$$$$**

Full-Service Inns

★ ★ ★ **HARBOR VIEW INN.** *28 W Cabrillo Blvd, Santa Barbara (93101). ; toll-free 800/755-0222; fax 805/963-7967. www.harborviewinnsb.com.* It would be hard to beat the location of this upscale motor inn, which is nestled right where the city meets the shore near Stern's Wharf. Just steps from the ocean, this complex includes a swimming pool, adults-only fitness center, and gardens perfect for soaking up the sun and ocean air. Well-decorated rooms have sweeping views and private patios, and the hotel is perfect for vacationing couples or beach-loving families on a road trip, looking for a scenic stop. 96 rooms, 3 story. Check-in 4 pm, check-out noon. High-speed Internet access, wireless Internet access. Restaurant, bar. Fitness room. Beach. Outdoor pool, whirlpool. Business center. **$$$**

★ ★ ★ **MONTECITO INN.** *1295 Coast Village Rd, Santa Barbara (93108). Phone 805/969-7854; toll-free 800/843-2017; fax 805/969-0623. www.montecitoinn. com.* Originally built by Charlie Chaplin as a vacation spot for his Hollywood cronies, the tradition of the silver screen legend lives on here with photos, memorabilia, and an entire video library available for rental. This aging hotel is a mere two blocks from gorgeous Butterfly Beach, and convenient to local galleries and restaurants. The rooms reflect the building's history—tiles are beautifully hand crafted but the bathrooms small, and the grounds are graced by a pool, sauna, and gym. Luxury suites include a living area and modern media technology. 61 rooms. Complimentary continental breakfast. Check-in 4 pm, check-out noon. Wireless Internet access. Restaurant, bar. Fitness room. Business center. **$$$**

Specialty Lodgings

CHESHIRE CAT INN. *36 W Valerio St, Santa Barbara (93101). Phone 805/569-1610; fax 805/682-1876. www.cheshirecatinn.com.* This adorable and intimate inn is rife with old-world Victorian charm. The main complex resembles a multi-leveled doll house, with towering bay windows and an open front porch. Each room is unique, with private balconies, whirlpools, fireplaces, and shabby chic décor. This cozy alternative to larger hotels is convenient to downtown as well as beaches, and massage therapist will provide services within the privacy of your own room. Laura Ashley appointments and antique furniture make for a romantic destination perfect for vacationing couples. 17 rooms, 2 story. No children allowed in main house, only cottages. Complimentary continental breakfast. Check-in 3 pm, check-out noon. Wireless Internet access. Whirlpool. **$$**

INN ON SUMMER HILL. *2520 Lillie Ave, Summerland (93067). Phone 805/969-9998; toll-free 800/845-5566; fax 805/565-9946. www.innonsummerhill.com.* Tucked away between Montecito and Santa Barbara, this inn, with its New England-style hospitality, offers suites with views of the Pacific Ocean and sunrises and sunsets you are sure to enjoy. 16 rooms, 2 story. Complimentary continental breakfast. Check-in 3 pm, check-out 11 am. Whirlpool. **$$$**

OLD YACHT CLUB INN. *431 Corona Del Mar Dr, Santa Barbara (93103). Phone 805/962-1277; toll-free 800/676-1676; fax 805/962-3989. www.oldyachtclubinn. com.* A perfect retreat for a romantic weekend, this huge California Craftsman Inn is shaded by trees and surrounded by lush gardens and a white picket fence. Each room is individually decorated with unique touches such as the canopied four-poster bed in

the Portofino Suite, to the private deck off the Belle Caruso Suite. After a gourmet breakfast prepared individually by innkeepers, guests enjoy the one block walk to the beach. Evening cocktails can be enjoyed on the large patio, studded with lounge tables and umbrellas—a perfect way to socialize and unwind at days end. 15 rooms, 2 story. Complimentary full breakfast. Check-in 4-8 pm, check-out 11 am. **$$**

PRUFROCK'S GARDEN INN BY THE BEACH. *600 Linden Ave, Carpinteria (93013). Phone 805/566-9696; toll-free 877/837-6257; fax 805/566-9404. www. prufrocks.com.* 8 rooms. No children allowed. Complimentary full breakfast. Check-in 4-8 pm, check-out 11 am. Built in 1904; seaside village. **$$$**

SIMPSON HOUSE INN. *121 E Arrellaga St, Santa Barbara (93101). Phone 805/963-7067; toll-free 800/676-1280; fax 805/564-4811. www.simpsonhouseinn.com.* Only a five-minute walk from Santa Barbara's restaurants and shops, the Simpson House welcomes guests to a world of gracious English country gardens and Victorian-era accommodations. This lovely bed-and-breakfast provides guests with a historic and charming alternative in this fashionable resort town. Delicious country breakfasts are a highlight, and early-evening wine and hors doeuvres are a thoughtful touch. Period furnishings and antiques characterize the rooms in the mansion, while updated country décor characterizes the barn and cottage rooms. The English gardens, filled with towering oaks, blooming magnolias, and tranquil fountains, are the centerpiece of this East Lake-style Victorian estate. 15 rooms. Check-in 3 pm, check-out 11 am. Wireless Internet access. **$$$$**

TIFFANY COUNTRY HOUSE. *1323 de la Vina St, Santa Barbara (93101). Phone 805/963-2283; toll-free 800/999-5672; fax 805/962-0994. www.tiffanycountry-house.com.* Originally built in 1898, this painstakingly restored Victorian beauty is now one of the most unique bed-and-breakfasts in the area. Located within walking distance to downtown shops and galleries, this is a quiet retreat perfect for couples that are looking for a privacy and peace. Antique furnishings grace every room; most have fireplaces, and some even provide modern luxuries like whirlpool tubs. Breakfast is served outdoors in the lush garden, while cocktails and hors d oeuvres are served by the roaring fire every evening. 7 rooms, 3 story. Complimentary full breakfast. Check-in 3 pm, check-out 11 am. **$$**

WHITE JASMINE INN. *1327 Bath St, Santa Barbara (93101). Phone 805/966-0589; toll-free 800/966-0589; fax 805/962-7343. www.*

whitejasmineinnsantabarbara.com. Located in the heart of downtown Santa Barbara, this Inn is a complex of large bed-and-breakfasts (with breakfast delivered to your room every morning). Guests can choose from individually decorated rooms, like the pink and flowery French Rose, the wooden-beamed Craftsman, or the sea-foam green nautical-themed Captains Quarters. A large living room acts as a common parlor, and a gazebo graces the private grounds. This romantic retreat offers champagne room service, massages and body wraps, and a secluded alfresco hot tub. 14 rooms, 2 story. Complimentary full breakfast. Check-in 3-6 pm, check-out 11 am. Whirlpool. **$$**

Spa

★ ★ ★ ★ SPA AT FOUR SEASONS RESORT SANTA BARBARA. *1260 Channel Dr, Santa Barbara (93108). Phone 805/969-2261; toll-free 800/819-5053. www.fourseasons.com.* Definitively California cool, this spa captures the essence of its flower-filled, oceanfront location with treatments bursting with marine and botanical ingredients. Good enough to eat, the avocado-citrus wrap is a spa signature that combines fruit extracts with sea salts and clays to hydrate and heal your body. Designed to moisturize and revitalize skin, the decadent-sounding perle de caviar facial is another signature therapy. Revitalize with a detoxifying sea mud body wrap or reap the purifying rewards of a volcanic earth clay ritual. Aromatic coconut and rice are the perfect exfoliants in a Thai coconut scrub, which also includes a heavenly Thai foot massage. Enjoy an aromatherapy salt glow and let the intoxicating scent of vetiver (grass from tropical regions in India that is known for its fragrant roots), magnolia, green tea, or woods work their wonders. Feel like a new you with a Swedish, shiatsu, deep tissue, reflexology, or stone therapy massage. Boost your energy with a JAMU massage, which combines Chinese, Hindu, and European techniques of acupressure, long strokes, and rolling motions to create a sensational experience. If you prefer to relax in your own accommodations, book an in-room massage. Relish a deluxe hydrating facial, well suited for mature or sun-damaged skin. For additional beauty needs, hair styling services, manicures, pedicures, and makeup applications are available at the Kevin Charles Salon. A fitness center complete with a whirlpool, sauna, and steam room beckons you to unwind.

Restaurants

★ ★ ★ BOUCHON. *9 W Victoria St, Santa Barbara (93101). Phone 805/730-1160. www.bouchonsantabar-bara.com.* Critically lauded and beloved by locals, this lively dining room is turning out penultimate California wine country cuisine. The room is rustic-chic, with an open line kitchen, homey farmhouse touches, and a gracious staff. Chef Josh Brown has taken advantage of the bounty of fresh ingredients from local farmers and has created a menu that is sophisticated, simple, and pleases even the most discerning palate. Lemon- and thyme-glazed sea scallops or bourbon- and maple-glazed duck are fantastic complements to the wide selection of local Santa Barbara wines. California, French menu. Dinner. Closed holidays. Business casual attire. Reservations recommended. Outdoor seating. **$$$**

★ ★ ★ DOWNEY'S. *1305 State St, Santa Barbara (93101). Phone 805/966-5006; fax 805/966-5000. www.downeyssb.com.* This unpretentious restaurant is housed in a converted storefront, providing a relaxing backdrop for the seasonal fare. John Downey changes the menu each day to reflect the best of what the market has to offer. Expect simple dishes that let the ingredients speak for themselves, like porcini soup and grilled local swordfish. Well-selected California wines round out the meal. California, French menu. Dinner. Closed Mon; holidays. Bar. Casual attire. Reservations recommended. **$$$**

★ ★ ★ EL ENCANTO DINING ROOM. *1900 Lasuen Rd, Santa Barbara (93103). Phone 805/687-5000; fax 805/687-3903. www.elencantohotel.com.* This exclusive resort hideaway is home to what *Gourmet* magazine calls "the most beautiful dining room in Santa Barbara." On the patio, diners can enjoy the spectacle of the sun setting into the Pacific Ocean, and the city lights twinkling below. The food is equally remarkable as the view—Chef Mark Kropyzynski strikes a perfect balance between luxurious cuisine and the simplicity of fresh local delicacies. The frothy floating island dessert is a must try, and a walk around the lovely and historic hotel grounds a perfect finale. California, French menu. Breakfast, lunch, dinner. Bar. Business casual attire. Reservations recommended. Valet parking. Outdoor seating. **$$$**

★ ★ EL PASEO. *10 El Paseo Pl, Santa Barbara (93101). Phone 805/962-6050; fax 805/962-8277.* This restaurant was originally built in 1922, part of a historic adobe building complex that dates back to 1826. Plenty of old-world charm and ambience remains, with bubbling fountains, beautiful tiled details, and intricate wrought iron work. The dining is indoors and outdoors in a courtyard, sometimes shaded, and

sometimes drenched with sun. The Mexican food is delightful—with guacamole prepared tableside to your taste and lots of massive combo platters. A great place to split a couple of pitchers of margaritas and carouse with friends or enjoy a simple dinner with the whole family. Mexican menu. Lunch, dinner. Closed holidays. Bar. Children's menu. Casual attire. Reservations recommended. Valet parking. Outdoor seating. **$$**

★ ★ **HARBOR.** *210 Stearns Wharf, Santa Barbara (93101). Phone 805/963-3311; fax 805/962-9021.* You can't get much closer to oceanfront dining than here—this ever-popular dining destination is perched on Stearns Wharf, providing diners with breathtaking views of the Channel Islands, the marina, and mountains that frame the coastline. With all the scenery, food takes a back seat, but diners can expect classic American surf-and-turf fare, like clam chowder, juicy steaks, and ahi tuna served with theatrical California flare. Clientele ranges from locals celebrating special occasions, to traveling families who cap the meal off with a seaside stroll. Seafood menu. Breakfast, lunch, dinner. Bar. Children's menu. Casual attire. Reservations recommended. Valet parking. **$$$**

★ ★ **OPAL'S RESTAURANT & BAR.** *1325 State St, Santa Barbara (93101). Phone 805/966-9676. www.opalrestaurantandbar.com.* This romantic little spot serves up the kind of Italian food that Southern Californians lovesure its wood-fired pizza, but its swathed in organic vegetables or duck confit. This whimsical and elegant take on comfort food has been packing in the date crowd for years, while singles enjoy cocktails at the bar. The room is cast with an amber glow, couples canoodle across tiny tables, and the sound of big band music hangs in the air. Perfect for a romantic night without any fussiness. California menu. Lunch, dinner. Closed holidays. Bar. Casual attire. Reservations recommended. Valet parking. **$$**
D

★ ★ **PALACE GRILL.** *8 E Cota St, Santa Barbara (93101). Phone 805/963-5000. www.palacegrill.com.* This neighborhood institution has been a lively dining destination for locals and traveling dignitaries alike— everyone from Kevin Costner to Regan's secret service squad has feasted here. Dedicated to delivering superb Creole and Cajun cooking, the menu offers regional delicacies like crawfish cakes, flash-fried soft-shell crabs, and sweet potato pecan pie. The attentive staff serves diners as a team, which enhances the social atmosphere. Prepare to drop your forks and sing for

your supper during the group sing-along. Cajun, Creole menu. Lunch, dinner. Closed holidays. Bar. Casual attire. Outdoor seating. **$$**

★ ★ **PALAZZIO DOWNTOWN.** *1026 State St, Santa Barbara (93101). Phone 805/564-1985; fax 805/564-2022. www.palazzio.com.* In the heart of State Street, this romantic eatery is aglow with twinkling lights, and filled with diners spilling from the loft-like space onto tables on the sidewalk. A replica of the Sistine Chapel ceiling hovers above the open-air dining room, quite a spot for a leisurely dinner over plates of world-class pasta preparations, like capellini with grilled chicken and brie. Wine is on the honors system—diners wander around the room to communal decanters, serving themselves, and marking their intake with crayons at the table. Solo diners are especially welcome and offered a complimentary glass of wine. Italian menu. Lunch, dinner. Closed Thanksgiving, Dec 25. Bar. Children's menu. Casual attire. Outdoor seating. **$$**
D

★ ★ ★ **SAGE & ONION.** *34 E Ortega St, Santa Barbara (93101). Phone 805/963-1012; fax 805/963-8584. www.sageandonion.com.* A rising star on the Central Coast, this upscale bistro in downtown Santa Barbara opened in the fall of 1999 with a winning combination of good food from the kitchen of co-owner/chef Steven Giles and friendly, attentive service under the amiable direction of his partner, Norbert Furnee. Seasonal menus take full advantage of the freshest local and regional ingredients, and the wine bar is a popular gathering place. American, European menu. Lunch, dinner. Closed holidays. Bar. Casual attire. Reservations recommended. Outdoor seating. **$$$**

★ ★ ★ **WINE CASK.** *813 Anacapa St, Santa Barbara (93101). Phone 805/966-9463; fax 805/568-0664. www.winecask.com.* An outgrowth of the neighboring wine shop in downtown Santa Barbara, Wine Cask serves vine-friendly fare alongside 40 by-the-glass pours and a 65-page wine list. The contemporary American menu offers something to match every varietal, from duck confit salad and seared foie gras (think hearty reds) to wasabi-crusted salmon (an ask-the-sommelier choice). In addition to the handsome dining room, which sports an oversized fireplace and hand-painted beams, the restaurant also serves meals on its secluded patio. American menu. Lunch, dinner. Closed holidays. Bar. Casual attire. Reservations recommended. Outdoor seating. **$$$**

Santa Monica (J-3)

See also Beverly Hills, Buena Park, Fullerton, Los Angeles, Malibu, Marina del Rey, Pismo Beach

Founded 1875
Population 84,084
Elevation 101 ft
Area Code 310
Information Visitor Center, 1400 Ocean Ave, 90401; phone 310/393-7593
Web Site www.santamonica.com

Santa Monica is one of the more diverse and interesting of the so-called "beach cities" that rim the western terminus of Los Angeles County. For great surfing conditions, you'd look north to some of the Malibu coves or south toward Hermosa Beach. But if you want an immaculate strand of beach, dramatic palisades, oceanfront parks, a variety of dining options, a world-class farmers' market, shopping, celebrity spottings, and living conditions with high-approval ratings from locals and tourists alike, this 8.3-square-mile city to the west of Los Angeles and Beverly Hills is it. Thrown in as a bonus is the Santa Monica Civic Auditorium on Main Street, home to book fairs, rock concerts, antique shows, theater, and a variety of jazz and classical music events.

Two blocks south of Santa Monica Boulevard, at the corner of Ocean and Colorado, is the famed Santa Monica Pier, with amusements and restaurants. Yes, the fabled South Coast Shopping Center is farther south, but Santa Monica is not exactly a poor relative. Take, for instance, the Montana Avenue shopping area, starting at 13th Street. More than 150 small stores and boutiques line this well-manicured east-west traffic artery with ample parking. Montana has enough coffee and nosh bars to make browsing more than comfortable. The Main Street shopping area, running from Pico Boulevard south toward Marine, provides a funkier, more eclectic approach to shopping. And don't forget the Big Daddy, perhaps the most famous of the Santa Monica shopping areas, the Third Street Promenade. Known as the "3-Prom" by locals, this cornucopia is a nearly 24/7 experience of theaters, boutiques, restaurants, curbside vendors, and street performers. The exciting venue runs adjacent to Third Street from Wilshire south to Broadway. The Third Street Promenade is often the first place locals bring out-of-towners.

To introduce yourself to the pulse and variety of Santa Monica, approach it for the first time on Wilshire Boulevard. Head west until you appear to dead-end at Ocean Avenue and then move down the California Incline, which puts you on the Pacific Coast Highway (the PCH, to locals). Make a 180-degree turn when you get tired of looking at the beach and head south toward the pier. Return to town through the McClure Tunnel, which will send you careening onto the Santa Monica (I-10) freeway.

What to See and Do

California Heritage Museum. *2612 Main St, Santa Monica (90405). Phone 310/392-8537. www.californiaheritagemuseum.org.* Located on charming Main Street, the California Heritage Museum adds culture and flair to the neighborhood with its unique displays of American decorative art, fine art, and folk art. This renovated Victorian house, built along the palisades in 1894, was moved to its present site and restored to represent four decades of design. The museum features unusual and entertaining themes and exhibits, such as "Aloha Spirit—Hawaii's Influence on the California Lifestyle." Afterward, enjoy the many restaurants and galleries in the neighborhood. (Wed-Sun 11 am-4 pm; closed holidays) **$**

Douglas Park. *1155 Cheslea Ave, Santa Monica (90403). Between Wilshire Blvd, Chelsea Ave, California Ave, and 25th St.* Santa Monica's Douglas Park offers two free lighted tennis courts in a quiet residential neighborhood just off busy Wilshire Boulevard. Palm trees and a playground surround the courts. Trees near three reflecting pools shade picnic tables. And you may even catch members of the Santa Monica Lawn Bowling Club clad all in white and strutting their stuff. (Daily)

Main Street. *Main St, Santa Monica. From Los Angeles, take the Santa Monica (10) Frwy W to Santa Monica and exit at Fourth St. Turn left (S); turn right onto Pico Blvd. Turn left onto Main St. From Ocean Ave in Santa Monica, go S on Ocean and turn left onto Pico. Turn right onto Main St. www.mainstreetsm.com.* The Third Street Promenade (see) is not the only shopping district Santa Monica calls its own. If you're looking for a slightly edgier, more urban feel, head just a few blocks south to Main Street. Here, you'll find dozens of restaurants ranging from Joe's Diner to the California-French cuisine at the Frank Gehry-designed Rockenwagner. Shops include everything from the Gap to Betsey Johnson, Patagonia to Armani Exchange—plus all kinds of locally owned specialty shops and boutiques. If you tire of shopping, you can walk a few blocks west to the beach and lie in the sand to rejuvenate.

⭐ **Palisades Park.** *851 Alma Real Dr, Santa Monica (90272). Ocean Ave from Colorado Ave to Adelaide Dr. Phone 310/458-8974.* Even with all the glitz and glamour of Hollywood, Los Angeles is known for its natural beauty. Palisades Park, a beautiful stretch of blufftop lawn and walkways overlooking the Pacific, offers some of the best views you'll find of the West Coast's most prized natural wonder, the California sunset. As a bonus, the park is within walking distance of Santa Monica's Third Street Promenade (see), a lively outdoor mall full of shops and eateries, and the Santa Monica Pier. **FREE**

Santa Monica Mountains National Recreation Area. *401 W Hillcrest Dr, Thousand Oaks (91360). Phone 818/597-9192. www.nps.gov/samo.* A huge park incorporating both federal lands (with a number of old ranch sites) and four state parks ranging from Will Rogers State Historic Park to Point Mugu (also Topanga and Malibu Creek state parks) and state beaches (Topanga and Will Rogers among them). Surfing; hiking, horseback riding, and mountain biking trails. (Daily 9 am-5 pm; closed holidays)

Santa Monica Pier. *Ocean and Colorado aves, Santa Monica (90401). Phone 310/458-8900. www.santamonicapier.org.* Opened in 1909, the Santa Monica Pier is a landmark in Los Angeles, seen in television shows and movies the world over. Today, you can ride the Ferris wheel, the roller coaster, or the antique carousel; test your skills in the Playland video arcade; or simply stroll the piers 1,600 feet and marvel at the views of the Santa Monica Bay. Vendors hawk everything from sunglasses to T-shirts to souvenirs to bring home to your friends. Restaurants range from food court-style snacks to sit-down fare. Tickets are required for all the rides. (Daily) **FREE** Also here are

Pacific Park. *Phone 310/260-8744.* Two-acre amusement park with 11 rides, including a nine-story Ferris wheel and a roller coaster. (schedule varies by season; call or visit Web site for information)

Santa Monica Pier Aquarium. *1600 Ocean Front Walk, Santa Monica (90401). Phone 310/393-6149.* An innovative, interactive aquarium that's popular with local families. (Hours vary seasonally) **$**

Santa Monica Place. *Fourth and Broadway, Santa Monica (90401). On Broadway at the S end of the Third Street Promenade. Phone 310/394-1049. www.santa-monicaplace.com.* With almost 150 shops, including anchor stores Macy's and Robinsons-May, the three-level Santa Monica Place is located just a few blocks from the famous Santa Monica Pier (see). In addition to the many shops, there are pushcart vendors throughout the mall and a food court with many international eateries bound to please everyone's palate. This mall has everything, but on the rare occasion that you can't find what you're looking for, the outdoor Third Street Promenade (see), conveniently located just to the north, will surely have it. (Mon-Sat 10 am-9 pm, Sun 11 am-6 pm; closed Easter, Thanksgiving, Dec 25)

Santa Monica State Beach. The natural beauty of Santa Monica and the many forms of entertainment available in the area make Santa Monica State Beach a favorite in California. The 3-mile-long beach provides opportunities for swimming (with lifeguards on duty), surfing, and sand volleyball, and there's a bike path as well. Kick back and enjoy the sun in this quintessential beach town and then stroll down the famous Santa Monica Pier (see), where you'll find arcades, shops, an interactive aquarium, and a 46-horse carousel. Free summertime concerts are also a local favorite and a perfect way to unwind after a hard day at the beach.

South Bay Bicycle Trail. *Temescal Canyon Rd, Santa Monica (90401). Between Will Rogers State Beach (on the Pacific Coast Hwy near Temescal Canyon Rd) and Torrance County Beach (W of Palos Verdes Blvd in Torrance).* Biking part or all of the South Bay Bicycle Trail, a paved trail that extends 22 miles along the beach from Will Rogers State Beach near Malibu to Torrance County Beach in Torrance, is great fun for cycling enthusiasts as well as casual riders. You can find bikes to rent at many places along the beach, but a good bet is to start in Santa Monica or Venice, where bike rentals are plentiful. No matter which part of the trail you ride, the views are unbeatable.

Third Street Promenade. *Third St, Santa Monica (90401). Between Broadway and Wilshire Blvd in downtown Santa Monica. Phone 310/393-8355. www.thirdstreetpromenade.com.* Get into the local sensibility at the promenade, a pedestrian-only street offering theaters, boutiques, restaurants, curbside vendors, and street performers. After the obligatory beach stop, this is often the first place locals bring out-of-towners for shopping, strolling, watching a movie, or grabbing a bite to eat. If you're visiting on a Wednesday or Saturday, check out the huge farmers' market, one of California's largest, on

Arizona between Second and Fourth streets (Wed 8:30 am-1:30 pm, Sat 8:30 am-1 pm).

Venice Beach and Boardwalk. *Pacific and Windward aves, Venice (90291). Phone 310/822-5425. www.venice. net.* People-watching just doesn't get any better than in this funkier-than-funky beach community. The boardwalk that fronts the ocean stretches for 2 miles, and every inch of it is packed with a colorful cast of characters, especially on weekends. In-line skaters, power-walkers, runners, and bikers share the surreal scene with street performers, local artists, massage therapists, street preachers, musclemen, panhandlers, tattoo artists, vendors selling sunglasses and other cheap goods, tourists, and anyone else who shows up for a day in the bright California sun. You get the picture—you'll see anything and everything here and have a heckuva lot of fun as you keep your eyes peeled. Head over to nearby Kinney Boulevard for upscale shopping and its art galleries.

Will Rogers State Historic Park. *1501 Will Rogers State Park Rd, Pacific Palisades (90272). 15 miles W off Sunset Blvd. Phone 310/454-8212. www.parks.ca.gov.* Yes, you can drive by the regal estates of many Hollywood celebrities, but you sure can't stop and tour them. One notable exception is the 186-acre hilltop ranch of Will Rogers, where the famed cowboy and humorist lived with his wife and family from the late 1920s until his death in 1935. Here, wide-eyed visitors roam freely, although the 31-room ranch house itself is undergoing a major renovation. But the visitor center and small museum remain open, and you can still enjoy the stunning ocean and mountain views and all the beautiful surrounding terrain. Hoof it on one of the hiking trails, go horseback riding, chow down on a picnic lunch, and, on weekends in season (Apr-Sept), watch all the galloping action on the polo field. For at least a few hours, live like one of Tinseltowns stars. (Daily 8 am-sunset; closed Jan 1, Thanksgiving, Dec 25) **FREE**

Ye Olde King's Head Pub. *116 Santa Monica Blvd, Santa Monica (90401). Phone 310/451-1402. www.yeoldekings-head.com.* If you're already planning your next trip and London is near the top of your list, head to Ye Olde King's Head Pub in downtown Santa Monica, just off the Third Street Promenade (see), where you'll get a feel for the authentic British pub scene (or at least as authentic as you can get on this side of the pond). Popular with everyone from British expatriates to tourists, Ye Old Kings Head is where to go if the term American beer seems like an oxymoron to you. Try a pint or three of Bass, Harp, Murphy's, McEwans, Newcastle Brown, Carlsberg, or Guinness Stout, among others—they may

have to scrape you up off the floor, but you'll fit right in. (Mon-Thurs 10 am-10 pm, Fri 10 am-midnight, Sat from 8 am, Sun 8 am-10 pm)

Limited-Service Hotel

★ ★ **FOUR POINTS BY SHERATON.** *530 W Pico Blvd, Santa Monica (90405). Phone 310/399-9344; fax 310/399-2504.* 314 rooms, 11 story. Pets accepted, some restrictions; fee. Check-in 3 pm, check-out noon. High-speed Internet access. Restaurant, bar. Fitness room. Outdoor pool, whirlpool. Business center. **$$**

Full-Service Hotels

★ ★ **DOUBLETREE GUEST SUITES.** *1707 Fourth St, Santa Monica (90401). Phone 310/395-3332; toll-free 800/222-8733; fax 310/452-7399. www.double-tree.com.* 253 rooms, 8 story, all suites. Check-in 3 pm, check-out noon. High-speed Internet access. Restaurant, bar. Fitness room. Outdoor pool, whirlpool. **$$**

★ ★ ★ **THE FAIRMONT MIRAMAR HOTEL.** *101 Wilshire Blvd, Santa Monica (90401). Phone 310/576-7777; toll-free 800/441-1414; fax 310/458-7912. www.fairmont.com.* Historic elegance, European sophistication, and tropical élan draw dignitaries and discriminating travelers to this century-old landmark, which sits atop Santa Monica's scenic beachfront bluffs just north of the city's world-famous pier. Guest accommodations, ranging from single- and double-story bungalows to tower suites, recently enjoyed a $14 million refurbishing; featured amenities include entertainment centers, oversized tubs, Japanese turbo-bidets, and (in some rooms) stunning ocean views. Exquisite landscaping abounds on the property, which also has extensive meeting facilities, a health club, and a day spa. The Third Street Promenade (see), with its upscale shops and nightlife, is around the corner. 302 rooms, 10 story. Pets accepted, some restrictions; fee. Check-in 3 pm, check-out noon. High-speed Internet access. Restaurant, bar. Fitness room. Outdoor pool, whirlpool. Business center. **$$$**

★ ★ ★ **GEORGIAN HOTEL.** *1415 Ocean Ave, Santa Monica (90401). Phone 310/395-9945; toll-free 800/538-8147; fax 310/260-9660. www.georgianhotel. com.* Popular with business travelers and vacationers seeking dramatic ocean sunsets, this Art Deco boutique hotel—built in 1933 and once the playground of celebrities like Clark Gable and Carole Lombard—is directly across from the beach, within a short walk of the Santa Monica Pier and the Third Street Promenade. Accommodations, most with views of the Pacific, feature goose down feather comforters, hand-woven carpets, custom draperies, and locally crafted furniture. Malibu and Los Angeles International Airport are within a short drive. 84 rooms, 8 story. Pets accepted, some restrictions; fee. Check-in 3 pm, check-out noon. High-speed Internet access, wireless Internet access. Restaurant. Fitness room. **$$**

★ ★ ★ **HOTEL CASA DEL MAR.** *1910 Ocean Way, Santa Monica (90405). Phone 310/581-5533; toll-free 800/898-6999; fax 310/581-5503. www.hotel-casadelmar.com.* Stylish and serene, Casa del Mar is a gracious hideaway. Fronting the Pacific Ocean on a stretch of Santa Monica's golden sand, this resort captures the essence of a 1920s Mediterranean villa with its graceful arches, tiled floors, and swaying palms. Tasteful and elegant, the European-style resort embodies the best of California beach living. Expansive views of the sparkling sea and beachfront pool serve as constant reminders of the idyllic location. A breezy, fresh style of understated luxury is evident throughout the property. The guest rooms are delightful, with mango-colored walls, gauzy curtains, and sumptuous linens. All rooms feature hydrothermal massage bathtubs, while the spa offers other wonderful ways to unwind. Detail-oriented and attentive, the service at Casa del Mar is superlative. Be sure to book a table at the Oceanfront restaurant (see), where the beautiful setting competes with the delicious California cuisine. 129 rooms, 7 story. Pets accepted; restrictions. Check-in 4 pm, check-out noon. High-speed Internet access. Restaurant, bar. Fitness room. Outdoor pool, whirlpool. Business center. **$$$$**

★ ★ ★ **HOTEL OCEANA.** *849 Ocean Ave, Santa Monica (90403). Phone 310/393-0486; toll-free 800/777-0758; fax 310/458-1182. www.hoteloceanas-antamonica.com.* You might be tempted to think that, with such a location, this all-suite hotel would skimp on everything else, but you'd be mistaken. Yes, its location—where Montana Avenue meets Ocean Boulevard—is about as good as it gets. You're only blocks from the Third Street Promenade (a major pedestrian street with shops and restaurants) and the Montana Avenue shopping district (smaller and more expensive than the Promenade). And Ocean Boulevard runs parallel to—you guessed it—the ocean. Palisades Park

is just across the street—whether you recognize the name or not, you've seen images of it in TV shows and movies. Think palm trees, a bike path, and kelly-green grass. All these things would be reason enough to choose this hotel, but the accommodations themselves are beautiful. Decorated in muted yellows, purples, and reds, with unique artwork and light wood furniture, it evokes the spirit of Southern California and the style of southern France. Fully stocked, full-size refrigerators, marble floors in the bathrooms, separate dining and living areas, and lanais that overlook the gorgeous pool will make you feel at home. Dozens of fine restaurants surround the hotel, all within walking distance, and the concierge will be happy to point you in the right direction. 63 rooms, all suites. Pets accepted; restrictions, fee. Check-in 3 pm, check-out noon. High-speed Internet access. Fitness room. Beach. Outdoor pool. **$$**

★ ★ ★ **LE MERIGOT, A JW MARRIOTT BEACH HOTEL AND SPA.** *1740 Ocean Ave, Santa Monica (90401). Phone 310/395-9700; toll-free 800/228-9290; fax 310/395-9200. www.lemerigothotel. com.* Recalling the grand hotels of the French Riviera, Le Merigot brings a bit of Europe to the Santa Monica coastline. Not far from the world-famous pier, the resort conveys quiet luxury. The guest rooms are at once classic and contemporary. Infused with a breath of fresh air, they reflect the elegance synonymous with European resorts. Frette linens dress the plush, oversized beds, while multi-line telephones, dataports, and high-speed Internet access make staying in touch with those back home easy and convenient. Creature comforts are plentiful here, especially at the spa, where guests unwind in the eucalyptus steam room or redwood sauna before surrendering to the fantastic treatments. Injected with bits of whimsy, Cézanne (see) has a bold and stunning décor. The artistic culinary creations, largely inspired by the bounty of local farmers' markets, delight hotel guests and locals alike. 175 rooms, 6 story. Pets accepted; fee. Check-in 3 pm, check-out 11 am. High-speed Internet access. Restaurant, bar. Fitness room, spa. Outdoor pool, whirlpool. Business center. **$$$**

★ ★ ★ **LOEWS SANTA MONICA BEACH HOTEL.** *1700 Ocean Ave, Santa Monica (90401). Phone 310/458-6700; toll-free 800/235-6397; fax 310/458-6761. www.loewshotels.com.* A classy, glass-walled beachfront haven affording magnificent sunset views of the Santa Monica Pier and walking proximity to the myriad shopping and dining options along Main Street and the Third Street Promenade, this contemporary landmark attracts romantics and business travelers alike. Whether dining by the palm-lined, Pacific-facing outdoor pool or indulging in the sensory delights of the spa (a favorite of West Side-dwelling celebrities), understated elegance is the running theme—and that extends to the comfortably muted guest room décor. The hotel is located conveniently at the convergence of Interstate 10 and the Pacific Coast Highway, midway between Malibu and downtown Los Angeles. 342 rooms, 8 story. Pets accepted. Check-in 3 pm, check-out noon. High-speed Internet access. Restaurant, two bars. Fitness room, fitness classes available, spa. Outdoor pool, whirlpool. Business center. **$$$**

★ ★ ★ **RENAISSANCE AGOURA HILLS HOTEL.** *30100 Agoura Rd, Agoura Hills (91301). Phone 818/707-1220; fax 818/707-6298. www.renaissance-hotels.com.* 280 rooms, 5 story. Check-in 3 pm. Check-out noon. Restaurant, bar. Fitness room. Outdoor pool. Business center. **$$**

★ ★ ★ **SHUTTERS ON THE BEACH.** *1 Pico Blvd, Santa Monica (90405). Phone 310/458-0030; toll-free 800/334-9000; fax 310/458-4589. www.shuttersonthebeach.com.* Shutters on the Beach is the beach cottage of your dreams. This luxurious hotel has a distinctly residential feel with cool, breezy interiors, unobstructed ocean views, and warm, professional service. Resting right on the sand in Santa Monica, this resort transports guests far from the everyday with its sparkling pool, beach activities, and creature comforts. The sunny rooms and suites are a study in contemporary California décor with white walls and country-chic furnishings. The amenities make the difference here, where beds are piled high with fine linens and oversized bathrooms feature Jacuzzi tubs. The beachfront pool attracts a stylish crowd with its lounge chair Internet connections and fantastic people-watching, and the two restaurants are among the best places to see-and-be-seen in Los Angeles. 198 rooms, 6 story. Check-in 4 pm, check-out noon. Wireless Internet access. Two restaurants, two bars. Fitness room. Outdoor pool, whirlpool. Business center. **$$$$**

★ ★ ★ **VICEROY.** *1819 Ocean Ave, Santa Monica (90401). Phone 310/451-8711; toll-free 800/670-6185; fax 310/394-6657. www.viceroysantamonica.com.* This cosmopolitan, yet decidedly coastal boutique hotel is sleek, chic, and intimate enough to lure sophisticated business types and adult pleasure-seekers from similar accommodations on the Sunset Strip. Close to the beach, the Third Street Promenade, and the scenic Santa Monica Pier, the Viceroy pampers its high-end clientele with a bold mix of British and contemporary designer touches, a cabana-ringed pool area, doting concierge service, and in-room massage and spa treatments by Fred Segal Beauty. The hotels fashionably retro Cameo Bar—where the city's elite mingle on weekend evenings—and award-winning restaurant, Whist (see), serve cocktails and cuisine on a par with Santa Monica's many great restaurants. (The Sunday champagne brunch is especially popular.) Amenity-packed guest rooms and suites include ocean or city views, Frette linens, 27-inch flat-screen TVs, CD and DVD players, and fully stocked minibars. Molton Brown of London Hair Care and Body Products are sold on-site. 163 rooms. Pets accepted, some restrictions; fee. Check-in 3 pm, check-out noon. High-speed Internet access. Restaurant, bar. Fitness room. Two outdoor pools. Business center. **$$$**

Specialty Lodging

CHANNEL ROAD INN. *219 W Channel Rd, Santa Monica (90402). Phone 310/459-1920; fax 310/454-9920. www.channelroadinn.com.* This historic home is tucked away in the rustic Santa Monica Canyon, just one block from the beach. 16 rooms, 3 story. Complimentary full breakfast. Check-in 3 pm, check-out noon. Whirlpool. **$$**

Restaurants

★ ★ **BORDER GRILL.** *1445 Fourth St, Santa Monica (90401). Phone 310/451-1655; fax 310/394-2049. www.bordergrill.com.* Susan Feniger and Mary Sue Milliken—aka "Two Hot Tamales"—ushered in a renaissance of upscale Southwestern cuisine with this flagship Mexican cantina. The atmosphere is decidedly hip, with colorful two-story murals on the high walls, wild and lively décor, and a crowd that's easy on the eyes. Atypical Latin American fare, such as plantain empanadas, halibut ceviche, and anchiote pork roasted in banana leaves, bursts with original flavor. Ruby red sangria and prickly pear margaritas pour out of the impressive and crowded bar, which is well stocked with top-shelf tequilas. Mexican menu. Lunch, dinner. Closed Jan 1, Thanksgiving, Dec 25. Bar. Children's menu. Casual attire. **$$**

★ **BROADWAY DELI.** *1457 Third St, Santa Monica (90401). Phone 310/451-0616; fax 310/451-0438.* This behemoth dining room frames the entrance to the popular Third Street Promenade (see) and is always packed with weary shoppers, loyal locals, and hungry tourists. The massive room has a modern flair, with high ceilings, a towering circular bar, walls of glass, and lots of iron and steel. The menu is more whimsical Los Angeles than classic New York, with deli standards like beef brisket intermixed with imaginative dishes like Rice Krispie French toast and duck enchiladas. Deli menu. Breakfast, lunch, dinner. Bar. Children's menu. Casual attire. Valet parking. **$$**

★ ★ **BUFFALO CLUB.** *1520 Olympic Blvd, Santa Monica (90404). Phone 310/450-8600.* Hidden in an industrial neighborhood, Buffalo Club looks like an unmarked speakeasy. Beyond the velvet rope, a swanky supper club awaits with mahogany wood, candlelight, and bottles of Dom chilling in silver buckets. Posh patrons who seem to have stepped from the pages of *GQ* and *Vogue* munch on steaks, mac and cheese, and the much-lauded lobster. The action is on the open-air back patio, where carousing parties dine under twinkle lights. Once the live band starts playing, the place becomes a swinging dance hall, and the mood is as celebratory as a wedding reception. American menu. Lunch, dinner. Closed Sun. Bar. Business casual attire. Reservations recommended. Valet parking. Outdoor seating. **$$$**

★ ★ **CAPO.** *1810 Ocean Ave, Santa Monica (90401). Phone 310/394-5550.* A rustic Italian farmhouse dropped right on the shores of the Pacific, Capo has become the definitive destination for gourmets when money is no object. Oil lanterns illuminate the linen-draped tables, prime cuts of meat sizzle over the roaring open fire, and men in coats and ties strive to impress their business partners or dressy dates. Hearty classics get a gourmet twist, like rigatoni with truffled meat sauce and polenta with lamb sausage, but the real draw is the King Kong—an $80 steak Fiorentina for two. This is serious food for serious diners. American menu. Dinner. Closed Sun-Mon; holidays. Bar. Business casual attire. **$$$$**

★ ★ ★ **CÉZANNE.** *1740 Ocean Ave, Santa Monica (90401). Phone 310/395-9700; fax 310/395-9200. www. lemerigothotel.com.* The signature restaurant of Santa Monicas Le Merigot hotel (see), Cézanne courts favor with its warm hues-of-Provence room, outdoor patio, and old-meets-new-world fare. Though ostensibly French, the kitchen brings West Coast style to the translation. As a result, dishes freely roam the globe from Mexican tortilla soup to Thai-spiced swordfish and Italian spaghetti with broccolini, all prepared with market-fresh ingredients. Try to snag one of the high-backed banquettes for the best people-watching. American, French menu. Breakfast, lunch, dinner. Bar. Casual attire. Reservations recommended. Valet parking. Outdoor seating. **$$$**

★ ★ ★ **CHINOIS ON MAIN.** *2709 Main St, Santa Monica (90405). Phone 310/392-9025; fax 310/396-5102. www.wolfgangpuck.com.* Wolfgang Pucks West Side outpost achieves a festive and vibrant atmosphere within a high-end restaurant. The décor is bright and wild, full of dragons and modern chinoiserie, and the place is always a roar of energy, with tables jammed full of dressed-up revelers celebrating birthdays. This party vibe meshes well with the family-style menu consisting of large servings of eclectic Asian fare. Shared dishes like lobster with spicy ginger curry and a whole sizzling catfish are as delicious as they are visually stunning. Chinese, French menu. Dinner. Closed holidays. Bar. Children's menu. Casual attire. Valet parking. **$$**

★ **CORA'S COFFEE SHOP.** *1802 Ocean Ave, Santa Monica (90401). Phone 310/451-9562.* This diminutive little spot serves up Olympian-sized breakfast fare to a casual and funky beach-loving crowd. The interior features a black-and-white-checked floor and a stainless steel counter for diners, while dog-owners and smokers take advantage of the sidewalk alfresco dining. Comfort food gets an eclectic twist, with flapjacks doused with orange zest, and omelets stuffed with burrata cheese. American menu. Breakfast, lunch, dinner. Closed holidays. Casual attire. Outdoor seating. **$**
🖼

★ ★ ★ **DRAGO.** *3628 Wilshire Blvd, Santa Monica (90405). Phone 310/828-1585, fax 310/582-2294. www. celestinodrago.com.* Modern impressionist paintings of Italian landscapes grace the cream-colored walls of this pleasant dining room, which oozes class. A sleek marble-and-wood bar with floating glass shelves of fine cognacs is a swell spot to grab a bite, and private dining rooms are perfect for working business meals. Reasonable pastas and salads depend on simple, high-quality ingredients, but the real star of the show is the encyclopedic wine list, one of the most comprehensive Italian collections in the city—at astronomical prices. Italian menu. Lunch, dinner. Closed holidays. Bar.

Children's menu. Casual attire. Reservations recommended. Valet parking. **$$$**

★ ★ **THE HUMP.** *3221 Donald Douglas Loop S, Santa Monica (90405). Phone 310/313-0977; fax 310/390-8032. www.thehump-sushi.com.* High in the tower of the Santa Monica airport, this sushi joint pays homage to Mount Everest (hence the odd name), which is etched into glass above its sushi bar. Walls of windows overlook private planes before, during, and after takeoff—quite a unique and fluid view. The fish is superlative, from hamachi sashimi to toro sushi, and hot entrées like flaming conch and fried soft-shell crab blend well with the endless carafes of hot sake that the fashionable crowd enjoys. Sushi menu. Lunch, dinner. Closed holidays. Reservations recommended. **$$$**

★ ★ **IL RISTORANTE DI GIORGIO BALDI.** *114 W Channel Rd, Santa Monica (90402). Phone 310/573-1660; fax 310/573-9007. www.giorgiobaldi.com.* Movie stars and captains of industry descend from their hillside mansions to this beachside Italian restaurant for classic fare and civilized service. The dining room is unpretentious and beachy, absent of the flowery frills of fussy restaurants, and that is just how the low-key patrons like it. Menu standards like homemade duck ravioli and bistecca Fiorentina always satisfy, and the daily fish and risotto specials impress. Owner Giorgio will likely pop by your table to see that all is to your liking—every diner here is a VIP. Italian menu. Dinner. Closed Mon. Bar. Casual attire. **$$$**
⒟

★ ★ **IVY AT THE SHORE.** *1535 Ocean Ave, Santa Monica (90401). Phone 310/393-3113; fax 310/458-9259.* Any avid tabloid reader will recognize the Ivy's star-studded patio from hundreds of published celebrity photo ops. Santa Monica's modish beach outpost and West Hollywood's country chic café (113 N Robertson Blvd, phone 310/274-8303) are favorite haunts for the Hollywood elite, who do movie deals and power breakfasts over the famed grilled vegetable salad or blue crab omelet. The bar is a sophisticated spot to watch the sun set and grab an Ivy Gimlet, a potent concoction of vodka, mint, and lime. American menu. Lunch, dinner. Bar. Casual attire. Reservations recommended. Valet parking. Outdoor seating. **$$**

★ ★ **JIRAFFE.** *502 Santa Monica Blvd, Santa Monica (90401). Phone 310/917-6671; fax 310/917-6677. www.jirafferestaurant.com.* Washed in golden hues, dripping with diminutive chandeliers, and appointed with gilded mirrors and wrought-iron railings, this cozy little dining room exudes grace and charm. The

place is always vibrant with the West Side's most tasteful clientele, who return time and again for the superb French fare—like roasted rabbit with herbed polenta and roasted chicken with sweet corn ragout. The best seats are on the railing of the second-story loft, with a view of the dining room and Santa Monica's shopping district outside. The three-course bistro menu on Mondays is a terrific bargain. French menu. Dinner. Closed holidays. Casual attire. Valet parking. **$$$**
⒟

★ ★ **JOSIE.** *2424 Pico Blvd, Santa Monica (90405). Phone 310/581-9888. www.josierestaurant. com.* Along an unmiraculous strip of Pico, Josie provides an elegant dining oasis. With dark walls, starched linen-covered tables, and a roaring stone fireplace, the dining room resembles a warm and graceful lodge. Chef Josie Le Balch aims to bring continental comfort food to new gastronomic heights, using exotic game in her entrées, like buffalo sirloin with Gruyére and venison with vegetable hash. Adventurous eaters from all corners of Los Angeles get dolled up to dine here for special occasions and romantic dates. Excellent selections of half bottles of wine are perfect for sharing and sampling. American menu. Dinner. Bar. Casual attire. **$$$**

★ ★ **LA SERENATA DE GARIBALDI.** *1416 Fourth St, Santa Monica (90401). Phone 310/656-7017; fax 310/656-7014.* This traditional Mexican restaurant full of authentic folk art is the dining destination for authentic south-of-the-border cuisine. Awash in pastel hues, it is frequented by upscale beachgoers who appreciate the simple and powerful food. The casual atmosphere seems appropriate for this seafood nirvana, where offerings of super-fresh fish are paired with complex house-made sauces, like smoky chipotle and mojo de ajo. A second location is on Los Angeles's East Side at 1842 E First St (phone 323/265-2887). Mexican menu. Lunch, dinner. Closed holidays. Bar. Children's menu. Casual attire. **$$**

★ ★ **THE LOBSTER.** *1602 Ocean Ave, Santa Monica (90401). Phone 310/458-9294; fax 310/458-9654. www.thelobster.com.* With staggering ocean views and spectacular seafood, there's no better place to catch a sunset than at this towering glass restaurant, which practically dangles off the Santa Monica Pier (see). During the day, sunlight and seawater permeate the chic industrial space; at night, the bar scene kicks up with swinging singles, while couples dine above the crashing surf. Plenty of champagne is poured as diners nosh on crab legs, sashimi, and, of course, lobster.

A favorite for special occasions, romantic dinners, and happy hours—it doesn't get more SoCal than this. American, seafood menu. Lunch, dinner. Bar. Casual attire. Valet parking. Outdoor seating. **$$$**
📖

★ ★ ★ ★ **MELISSE.** *1104 Wilshire Blvd, Santa Monica (90401). Phone 310/395-0881; fax 310/395-3810. www.melisse.com.* Classic French technique is the basis for the creative contemporary American menu at Melisse, an elegant, Provenal-style dining room. Warmed with fresh flower arrangements and paintings of rural French landscapes, the room at Melisse is lovely and intimate, with tabletops set in Egyptian cotton linens and beautiful hand-painted china. Chef/owner Josiah Citrin weaves intricate dishes from stunning, seasonal ingredients procured from regional farmers. His notable creations, served in four-, five-, seven-, or eight-course menus, include seared Hudson Valley foie gras, sweet corn ravioli, Dover sole roasted on the bone (filleted tableside), and dry-aged "Côte de Boeuf" for two, also carved tableside. French menu. Dinner. Bar. Casual attire. Reservations recommended. **$$$$**

★ ★ ★ **MICHAEL'S.** *1147 Third St, Santa Monica (90403). Phone 310/451-0843; fax 310/394-1830. www.michaelssantamonica.com.* No need to make a museum trip to view authentic Picassos, Diebenkorns, or Hockneys. At this beachside institution, you can gaze upon the works of modern masters over a supper of loup de mer or tarragon-roasted poussin. Touted as the birthplace of California cuisine, Michael's continues to assert itself as a spot for casual yet elegant dining and stimulating yet comforting meals. The heated back patio with retractable seating and lush greenery is the ultimate power lunch or special date spot—and the clientele of Malibu millionaires agrees. California, French menu. Lunch, dinner. Closed Sun; holidays. Bar. Children's menu. Casual attire. Valet parking. Outdoor seating. **$$$**

★ ★ **OCEAN AVENUE SEAFOOD.** *1401 Ocean Ave, Santa Monica (90401). Phone 310/394-5669; fax 310/394-7322. www.kingsseafood.com.* This upscale seafood emporium boasts not only a considerable menu but also a view of the Pacific Ocean and the Santa Monica Pier from its wall of windows. The interior glows with warm light and dark wood, creating an upscale, almost tropical ambience. Offerings change to highlight the freshest catch of the season—like king salmon or big-eye tuna. A fashionable and rowdy crowd packs the place, especially for happy hour around the oyster bar. Seafood menu. Lunch, dinner. Closed Thanksgiving. Bar. Children's menu. Casual attire. Reservations recommended. Valet parking. Outdoor seating. **$$$**
📖

★ ★ ★ **OCEANFRONT.** *1910 Ocean Way, Santa Monica (90405). Phone 310/581-7714; fax 310/581-5503. www.hotelcasadelmar.com.* Overlooking the wide, white sandy beach, you can practically feel the sand between your toes and the sunscreen on your skin while dining at Oceanfront, the flagship restaurant of the European château-style Casa Del Mar hotel (see). The dining room is steeped in rustic charm, with creamy walls, tile and hardwood floors, and floor-to-ceiling windows for optimal sea viewing. White linen-topped tables are appointed with pale blue goblets, bright flowers in copper pots, and frosted glass votives. The menu is of the California variety—straightforward seasonal ingredients prepared with global accents, served simply and deliciously with relaxed elegance. Before or after dinner, step out onto the veranda, relax under a star-blanketed sky, breathe in the salty sea air, and enjoy a cocktail or two. California menu. Breakfast, lunch, dinner. Bar. Casual attire. **$$$**

★ ★ **ONE PICO.** *1 Pico Blvd, Santa Monica (90405). Phone 310/458-0030; fax 310/458-4589. www.shuttersonthebeach.com.* Situated on the sand at the Shutters on the Beach hotel (see), this ocean-view dining room is reminiscent of the unfussy elegance of Cape Cod, with roaring fires, beamed ceilings, and table settings out of a magazine spread. The contemporary American fare has a slightly exotic Southern California twist, with kicked-up corn chowder, truffle-kissed salmon, and, for dessert, gourmet s'mores. This posh spot is a perfect place to impress either a loved one or a business associate who needs to be softened up. California menu. Lunch, dinner, Sun brunch. Bar. Children's menu. Casual attire. Valet parking. **$$$**

★ ★ ★ **SUSHI ROKU.** *1401 Ocean Ave, Santa Monica (90401). Phone 310/458-4771; fax 310/458-4746. www.sushiroku.com.* This ever-trendy sushi joint actually lives up to the hype—despite its fashionable clientele and never-ending reservation list. The interior looks like a sexy Zen rock garden, and the crowd is delectable eye candy. An extensive menu offers high-quality sushi, crisp tempura, and wonderful entrées like asparagus wrapped in filet mignon and miso-glazed black cod. don't miss out on the cold sake poured from giant stalks of bamboo. A longtime favorite spot for getting the party started, Roku seems to never go out of style. Additional locations include 3445 W Third St in West Hollywood (phone 323/655-6767) and 33 Miller Alley at 1 Colorado in Pasadena (phone 626/683-3000).

Pan-Asian, sushi menu. Lunch, dinner. Bar. Children's menu. Casual attire. Reservations recommended. Valet parking. Outdoor seating. **$$$**

★ ★ ★ **VALENTINO.** *3115 Pico Blvd, Santa Monica (90405). Phone 310/829-4313; fax 310/315-2791. www. pieroselvaggio.com.* For almost three decades, Valentino's owner, Piero Selvaggio, has been providing diners with premier Italian food accompanied by a startling wine list comprised of the best that both Italy and California have to offer. The food is classic, with dishes like linguini with clams and sweet garlic or veal chop with prosciutto, cream, and Marsala, providing satisfaction for those who are tired of the latest trends. Italian menu. Dinner. Closed Sun; holidays. Bar. Business casual attire. Reservations recommended. Valet parking. **$$$$**

★ ★ ★ **WHIST.** *1819 Ocean Ave, Santa Monica (90401). Phone 310/260-7511. www.viceroysanta-monica.com.* The Viceroy (see), Santa Monica's trendy boutique hotel, houses the clever hotspot Whist. Chef Tim Goodell of Orange County's rave Aubergine makes his first entry into the LA food scene with this stylish restaurant decked in limed green walls lined in English china. Goodells contemporary fare could stand on its own, however, distinguished by a respect for market produce, Asian-accented dishes, and fruit and savory combinations such as pineapple and foie gras. The fashion and film set favor Whist, so consider reservations—and a good look, your best entrée to the scene. California menu. Breakfast, lunch, dinner, Sun brunch. Bar. Casual attire. Outdoor seating. **$$$**

Sequoia and Kings Canyon National Parks

See also Porterville, Three Rivers

55 miles E of Fresno on Hwy 180; 35 miles E of Visalia on Hwy 198. www.nps.gov/seki.

Web Site www.nps.gov/seki/

Although independently established, Sequoia and Kings Canyon National Parks are geographically and administratively one. Lying across the heart of the Sierra Nevada in eastern central California, they comprise more than 1,300 square miles and include more than 25 isolated groves of spectacular giant sequoias, towering granite peaks, deep canyons, and hundreds of alpine lakes. Giant sequoias reach their greatest size and are found in the largest numbers here. Mount Whitney, 14,495 feet, is the highest point in the lower 48 states. Some rocks of the foothill and summit area indicate that this whole region once lay under the ocean.

Allow plenty of driving time due to the gradient into and out of the mountains. Limited groceries are available all year in both parks. Gasoline may not be available; inquire before entering. Camping (no trailer hook-ups) is restricted to designated areas. Many of the campgrounds are closed by snow, October-late May. Winter visitors should carry tire chains. Entry fee valid for seven days. For information, contact Sequoia and Kings Canyon National Parks, Three Rivers 93271; phone 559/565-3134.

What to See and Do

Boyden Cavern. *74101 E Kings Canyon Rd, Kings Canyon National Park (95222). Located in King's River Canyon in Sequoia National Forest between Grant Grove and Cedar Grove. Phone 209/736-2708. www.caverntours.com/boydenrt.htm.* A 45-minute tour on a lighted, handrail-equipped trail through ornate chambers with massive stalagmites, stalactites, and columns. (Summer: daily 10 am-5 pm; early Sept-Oct: daily 11 am-4 pm; early Oct to road closure: Sat-Sun 11 am-4 pm; closed mid-Nov-late Apr) **$$**

Cedar Grove. *Three Rivers. In canyon of South Fork of Kings River.* Towering peaks rise a mile high above the stream. Horses, pack animals. Hiking trails. Road closed Nov-Apr.

Fishing. *83918 Grant Grove Dr, Sequoia and Kings Canyon National Parks (93633).* Trout are abundant in a few lakes and streams; the most popular spots are along Kings River and the forks of the Kaweah River. Some stores in the park sell state fishing licenses.

Foothills, Lodgepole, and Grant Grove visitor centers. *Three Rivers. Foothills: located on the Generals Hwy, 1 mile from Sequoia Park entrance at Hwy 198. Lodge-pole: located on Lodgepole Rd, 21 miles from the Sequoia Park entrance on Hwy 198. Grant Grove: located 3 miles E on Hwy 80 from the Big Stump Entrance Station. Phone 559/565-3134.* Exhibits, photos, data about the parks; expert advice on how to organize sightseeing. Schedules of campfire talks and guided trips are posted here. (Daily)

General Grant Grove. *83918 Grant Grove Dr, Sequoia and Kings Canyon National Parks (93633).* Includes the General Grant Tree, 267 feet tall with a circumference of 108 feet. Saddle rides. Hiking trails.

⭐ **Giant Forest.** *83918 Grant Grove Dr, Sequoia and Kings Canyon National Parks (93633).* One of the finest groves of giant sequoias. The General Sherman Tree is the largest living thing on Earth. At 275 feet high and 103 feet in circumference, it is estimated to be 2,300-2,700 years old. Moro Rock, Crescent Meadow, Crystal Cave, and Tokopah Valley are in this section of the park. Horses, pack animals available at Wolverton Pack Station. Hiking trails.

High Country. *83918 Grant Grove Dr, Sequoia and Kings Canyon National Parks (93633).* A vast region of wilderness, mountains, canyons, rivers, lakes, and meadows; accessible by trail. The Sierra Crest forms the eastern boundary.

Redwood Mountain Grove. *83918 Grant Grove Dr, Sequoia and Kings Canyon National Parks (93633).* Includes the Hart Tree, a large sequoia; accessible by trail.

⭐ **Sequoia National Forest.** *1839 S Newcomb, Porterville (93257). 20 miles E via Hwy 190. Phone 559/784-1500. www.r5.fs.fed.us/sequoia.* Precipitous canyons, spectacular views of the Sierra Nevada, and more than 30 groves of giant sequoias on 1,139,000 acres. Largest tree of any national forest is here; the Boole Tree stands 269 feet and is 90 feet in circumference. (The General Sherman Tree in Sequoia National Park is a few feet taller.) The forest contains the 303,290-acre Golden Trout, 130,995-acre Dome Land, 10,610-acre Jennie Lake, 63,000-acre South Sierra, 88,290-acre Kiavah, and the 45,000-acre Monarch wilderness areas. Activities include swimming, lake and stream fishing for trout, white-water rafting in the Kern and Kings rivers; hunting; hiking, riding, and backpacking trails in wilderness areas (permit required). Cross-country skiing, snowshoeing, and snowmobiling in winter. Picnicking. Camping (for reservations, phone toll-free 877/444-6777) at 50 areas; 14-day/month limit, no electric hook-ups or other utility connections, campgrounds (fees vary).

Limited-Service Hotels

⭐ **CEDAR GROVE LODGE.** *Hwy 180, Kings Canyon National Park (93633). Phone 559/335-5507; fax 559/565-0101. www.kcanyon.com.* 21 rooms, 2 story. Closed Nov-Mar. Check-out 11 am. **$**

⭐ ⭐ **GRANT GROVE VILLAGE.** *5755 E Kings Canyon, Kings Canyon National Park (93633). Phone 559/335-5500; toll-free 866/522-6966; fax 559/335-5507. www.kcanyon.com.* 47 rooms. Check-in 4 pm, check-out 11 am. Restaurant. **$**

Sherman Oaks

A commercial and residential community starting on the north-facing slopes of the Santa Monica Mountains, Sherman Oaks bills itself as a gateway (from Los Angeles) to the San Fernando Valley. Close to two major freeways, 101 (eastbound/westbound) and 405 (northbound/southbound), Sherman Oaks is bound on the west by Haskell Avenue and gives up the ghost to Studio City eastward at Coldwater Canyon. Like much of this part of the Valley, Sherman Oaks is an amalgam of high-tone stores, restaurants, and specialty shops mixed with a liberal sprinkling of delicatessens, discount outlets, and mini-malls. It was here that Frank Zappa's daughter coined the term "Valley Girls," which, like all satire, has a germ of accurate truth. The main artery of Sherman Oaks is Ventura Boulevard, which will get you to Encino if you continue west or Studio City if you head east toward downtown Los Angeles.

What to See and Do

Fashion Square. *14006 Riverside Dr, Sherman Oaks (91423). Phone 818/783-0550. www.westfield.com/fashionsquare.* With more than 125 shops and restaurants and a location in the heart of the San Fernando Valley just off Ventura Boulevard, this mall just may be the Valley shopper's paradise. Anchored by Bloomingdale's and Macy's, Fashion Square also features such mall favorites as Abercrombie & Fitch, Banana Republic, Bath & Body Works, The Disney Store, Gap, J. Crew, and Victoria's Secret, as well as slightly offbeat finds like Betsey Johnson. (Mon-Fri 10 am-9 pm, Sat 10 am-7 pm, Sun 11 am-6 pm; closed Thanksgiving, Dec 25)

Restaurants

⭐ ⭐ **CAFE BIZOU.** *14016 Ventura Blvd, Sherman Oaks (91423). Phone 818/788-3536; fax 818/986-5550. www.cafebizou.com.* A contemporary adult atmosphere, abetted by an extremely professional waitstaff, pleasant jazz music and a stellar wine list, prevails in Café Bizous otherwise cozy country-style setting. Many consider this romantic, if typically crowded, bistro—the first of three similarly named, commonly owned establishments now open in the Los Angeles area—the very best in the city for moderately priced French provincial fare. And with substantial gourmet entrées like steak au poivre, roasted pork tenderloin, crab cakes and lobster ravioli topping out at around $20, you may be inclined to agree. California, French menu. Lunch, dinner, brunch. Closed Jan 1, Dec 25. Bar. Business casual attire. Reservations recommended. Valet parking. Outdoor seating. **$$**

★ **THE GREAT GREEK.** *13362 Ventura Blvd, Sherman Oaks (91423). Phone 818/905-5250; fax 818/905-8223. www.greatgreekcafe.com.* There's lots of Hellenic-raising fun to be had at this small restaurant and taverna, where during the evening waiters gyrate to bouzouki music as they whirl ravishing dishes such as shish kebab, moussaka, and oven-roasted lamb from kitchen to table. For the taste buds, the festivities begin with the fabulous pita bread, which arrives with hummus, tzatziki, and other zesty spreads. A fine selection of Greek wines and a dessert menu with baklava and Greek parfait complete the epicurean excursion. Families can select one of the budget-friendly feast options offering a cross-menu sampling. Greek menu. Lunch, dinner. Closed holidays. Bar. Casual attire. Outdoor seating. **$$**

★ ★ ★ **MAX.** *13355 Ventura Blvd, Sherman Oaks (91423). Phone 818/784-2915; fax 818/784-2918. www.maxrestaurant.com.* Max specializes in California-Asian fusion sans culinary confusion—refining some of the best elements of each category (and a few other ethnic genres), then combining them in smart, artfully flavorful ways. Chilean sea bass, served with wasabi-mashed potatoes, and mushroom risotto with duck and arugula are standouts among oft-requested entrées. The classy, uncluttered décor is colored cream, with adult sophistication reflected in mirrored walls that also add depth to the rather small, talky dining area; an outdoor patio provides a quieter setting for inspecting the lengthy wine list or indulging in a chocolate soufflé. Asian, California menu. Lunch, dinner. Closed holidays. Bar. Reservations recommended. Valet parking. Outdoor seating. **$$**

Solana Beach (K-4)

Web Site www.ci.solana-beach.ca.us

What to See and Do

Belly Up Tavern. *143 S Cedros Ave, Solana Beach (92075). Phone 858/481-8140. www.bellyup.com.* If you like your music in recycled Quonset huts with a side of hard rock ... or ... jazz or maybe accordion-based alterna-pop en Español, the Belly Up Tavern is for you. The eclectic mix of music played here ranges from Ladysmith Black Mambazo, Erykah Badu, and Lucinda Williams to the Neville Brothers and The Average White Band. Sundays are always Salsa Sundays; most Tuesdays focus on local bands. The mix of music and atmosphere creates an experience to write home about. Call in advance for tickets and schedule. (Shows begin anywhere from 7 to 9:15 pm) **$$$$**

Restaurant

★ ★ **PACIFIC COAST GRILL.** *437 S Hwy 101, Solana Beach (92075). Phone 858/794-4632; fax 858/793-2782. www.pacificcoastgrill.com.* Eclectic atmosphere; bright mosaic tiles in floor. California menu. Lunch, dinner, Sun brunch. Closed holidays. Bar. Casual attire. Outdoor seating. **$$$**

Solvang (H-2)

See also Lompoc, Santa Barbara, Santa Maria

Founded 1911
Population 5,332
Elevation 495 ft
Area Code 805
Zip 93463
Information Information Center, 1511-A Mission Dr, PO Box 70, 93464; phone toll-free 800/468-6765
Web Site www.solvangusa.com

Founded by Danes from the Midwest in 1911, a corner of Denmark has been re-created here. Solvang is a community of picturesque Danish-style buildings, which include four windmills. Rich Danish pastries and Danish imports are featured in its shops.

What to See and Do

Lake Cachuma Recreation Area. *Hwy 154, Solvang. 6 miles E on Hwy 246, then 6 miles S on Hwy 154. Phone*

805/686-5054. www.sbparks.org/docs/Cachuma.html. Swimming pool (summer), fishing, boating (rentals); camping (hook-ups). General store. Fees for some activities. (Daily) **$$**

Old Mission Santa Ines. 1760 Mission Dr, Solvang (93464). Phone 805/688-4815. www.missionsantaines. org. (1804) Established by Fray Estevan Tapis as the 19th mission. A gold adobe building with red-tiled roof, garden, and arched colonnade in front. Used as a church; many artifacts, manuscripts, and vestments on exhibit; recorded tour. (Daily 9 am-5:30 pm; closed holidays)

Special Events

Danish Days Festival. 1511 Mission Dr, Solvang (93463). Phone 805/688-6144. Danish folk dancing, singing, band concerts; parade on Sat. Third weekend in Sept.

Solvang Theaterfest. 420 Second St, Solvang (93456). Phone 805/922-8313. www.solvangtheaterfest.org. The Pacific Conservatory of the Performing Arts (PCPA) presents musicals, dramas, new works, and classics in an outdoor theater. Early June-early Oct. **$$$$**

Limited-Service Hotels

★ **BEST WESTERN PEA SOUP ANDERSEN'S.** 51 E Hwy 246, Buellton (93427). Phone 805/688-3216; toll-free 800/732-7687; fax 805/688-9767. www.peasoupandersens.com. 97 rooms, 2 story. Complimentary continental breakfast. Check-in 3 pm, check-out noon. Outdoor pool, whirlpool. **$**

★ **ROYAL COPENHAGEN INN.** 1579 Mission Dr, Solvang (93463). Phone 805/688-5561; toll-free 800/624-6604; fax 805/688-7029. www.royalcopenhageninn.com. 48 rooms, 2 story. Pets accepted. Complimentary continental breakfast. Check-in 2 pm, check-out 11 am. Outdoor pool. **$**

Full-Service Hotel

★ ★ ★ **ROYAL SCANDINAVIAN INN.** 400 Alisal Rd, Solvang (93464). Phone 805/688-8000; toll-free 800/624-5572; fax 805/688-0761. www.royalscandinavianinn.com. 133 rooms, 3 story. Check-in 4 pm, check-out 11 am. Restaurant, bar. Fitness room. Outdoor pool, whirlpool. **$$**

Full-Service Inns

★ ★ ★ **THE BALLARD INN.** 2436 Baseline Ave, Ballard (93463). Phone 805/688-7770; toll-free 800/638-2466; fax 805/688-9560. www.ballardinn.com. A romantic escape from the city to Santa Barbara wine country with plenty of warm hospitality. Accommodations are comfortable and elegant. 15 rooms, 2 story. Complimentary full breakfast. Check-in 3 pm. Check-out noon. Restaurant. **$$$**

★ ★ ★ **PETERSEN VILLAGE INN.** 1576 Mission Dr, Solvang (93463). Phone 805/688-3121; toll-free 800/321-8985; fax 805/688-5732. www.peterseninn.com. Replica of an old Danish village with 28 shops on the premises and a garden area. 39 rooms, 3 story. Complimentary full breakfast. Check-in 3 pm, check-out 1 pm. Restaurant. **$$$**

Specialty Lodgings

ALISAL GUEST RANCH AND RESORT. 1054 Alisal Rd, Solvang (93463). Phone 805/688-6411; toll-free 888/425-4725; fax 805/688-2510. www.alisal.com. What once was the homeland to the Chumash Indians in the heart of the Santa Ynez Valley, this horse and wine country ranch and resort is the hideway for romantics, families, and corporate clients to retreat and relax. 73 rooms. Check-in 4 pm, check-out noon. Restaurant, bar. Children's activity center. Outdoor pool, whirlpool. Golf. Tennis. **$$$$**

FESS PARKER'S WINE COUNTRY INN AND SPA. 2860 Grand Ave, Los Olivos (93441). Phone 805/688-7788; toll-free 800/446-2455; fax 805/688-1942. www.fessparker.com. 21 rooms, 2 story. Pets accepted, fee. Complimentary full breakfast. Check-in 3 pm, check-out noon. Outdoor pool, whirlpool. **$$$$**

WINE VALLEY INN & COTTAGES. 1564 Copenhagen Dr, Solvang (93463). Phone 805/688-2111; toll-free 800/824-6444; fax 805/688-8882. www.winevalleyinn.com. Located in a tranquil neighborhood just minutes from the Santa Barbara wine region, this inn oozes old-world charm. Rooms feature canopy beds and oversized tubs, and each is uniquely decorated. Outside, a gazebo and covered spa foster relaxation and romance. Or choose one of the cottages, which were inspired by those in the gardens of the Palace of Versailles. Each of the cottages has a kitchen, private patio, and spacious living room with wood-burning fireplace; some have lofts and private outdoor whirlpools. 56 rooms, 2 story. Pets accepted; restrictions, fee. Complimentary full breakfast. Check-in 3 pm, check-out 11 am. Whirlpool. **$$**

Restaurants

★ **MUSTARD SEED.** *1655 Mission Dr, Solvang (93463). Phone 805/688-1318.* American menu. Breakfast, lunch, dinner. Closed Mon; Thanksgiving, Dec 25. Children's menu. Casual attire. Outdoor seating. **$$**

★ ★ **PEA SOUP ANDERSEN'S.** *376 Avenue of the Flags, Buellton (93427). Phone 805/688-5581; fax 805/686-5670. www.peasoupandersens.net.* American menu. Breakfast, lunch, dinner. Bar. Children's menu. **$$**

★ ★ ★ **WINE CASK RESTAURANT.** *2860 Grand Ave, Los Olivos (93441). Phone 805/688-7788; fax 805/688-1942. www.fessparker.com/restaurant.* If you're in Santa Barbara wine country and don't mind waiting some time for (or rather between) a good meal, then this is the place. Its local ingredients, refreshing homemade sorbets, and a great selection of half-bottle wines make it worth your while. Mediterranean menu. Breakfast, lunch, dinner. Children's menu. **$$**

Studio City (LA) (H-3)

See also Lompoc, Santa Barbara, Santa Maria

Area Code 818
Zip 91604
Web Site www.studiocitychamber.com

Studio City, located between Sherman Oaks and Hollywood, grew up around and for the motion-picture industry. There are still a number of major and independent film studios in operation, but, like others of the 24 incorporated communities in the San Fernando Valley, Studio City is an amalgam of tourism (hotels), real estate (offices, single-dwelling homes, and apartment buildings), and commerce (restaurants, boutiques, and mom-and-pop businesses). It is some 12 miles northwest of downtown Los Angeles, making it an ideal commute to "The City" or some of the outlying areas such as downtown, the West Side, and the Valley. Convenient to the Santa Monica and Ventura freeways, Studio City maintains more of a bohemian atmosphere than other Valley communities. Check out the thriving ambience of Laurel Canyon and Ventura Boulevard for an accurate feel.

What to See and Do

Los Encinos. *16756 Moorpark St, Encino (91436). Phone 818/784-4849. www.parks.ca.gov.* Early California ranch; exhibits of ranch life contained in a nine-room adobe. Blacksmith shop, spring, and small lake. Picnicking. (Wed-Sun 10 am-5 pm) **FREE**

Limited-Service Hotel

★ ★ **SPORTSMEN'S LODGE HOTEL.** *12825 Ventura Blvd, Studio City (91604). Phone 818/769-4700; toll-free 800/821-8511; fax 818/769-4798. www.slhotel.com.* 200 rooms, 5 story. Pets accepted. Check-in 3 pm, check-out noon. Restaurant, bar. Outdoor pool, whirlpool. Airport transportation available. **$$**

Restaurants

★ ★ ★ **ASANEBO.** *11941 Ventura Blvd, Studio City (91604). Phone 818/760-3348.* Those who know superior sushi simply overlook the undercooked strip-mall ambience of Asanebo. Because what matters most here are the whip-fast, wonderfully helpful waiters and, especially, the jaw-dropping array of beautifully crafted delicacies they dispense for diner's delectation. Beyond the sushi, there are special dishes like Dungeness crab served sashimi-style and monkfish liver in ponzu sauce. Just be careful to keep a mental tab on the endless culinary seduction—the à la carte cost can run up quickly. Japanese. Lunch, dinner. Closed Mon; holidays. Casual attire. **$$**

★ ★ **FIREFLY.** *11720 Ventura Blvd, Studio City (91604). Phone 818/762-1833.* Casting its discreet light on a somewhat dreary stretch of the busy Ventura corridor, Firefly's clubby repute for luring celebrities, studio types and hip late-night noshers is confirmed by the task of locating its signless, ivy-covered exterior (Colfax Avenue is the cross street). Once past the doorman, you'll find two romantic dining areas—a comfortable, library-style bar/lounge and an outdoor patio surrounding a flickering fire pit. Drinks and delicious "chatter platters" of meat, cheese, or vegetables usually suffice, but a plurality of savory entrées—including filet mignon and grilled pancetta-wrapped shrimp—adds value to this vibrant singles scene. California menu. Dinner. Closed Sun. Bar. Casual attire. Reservations recommended. Outdoor seating. **$$**

★ ★ **LA LOGGIA.** *11814 Ventura Blvd, Studio City (91604). Phone 818/985-9222; fax 818/508-6877.*

Tantalizing traditional Italian fare served with flair by a super-polite waitstaff draws crowds to this romantic trattoria, which is wreathed in twinkling lights. Hollywood power brokers and locals alike press up to the bar and pack the outdoor patio, savoring gourmet pizzas and dishes such as duck-stuffed tortellini in porcini sauce, filet mignon with bordelaise wine reduction, and lasagna filled with pumpkin, spinach, zucchini, and ricotta. La Loggia's signature caramel-drizzled banana napoleon makes for a lovely finish. Italian menu. Lunch, dinner. Closed holidays. Bar. Casual attire. Reservations recommended. Valet parking. Outdoor seating. **$$**

★ ★ ★ **PINOT BISTRO.** *12969 Ventura Blvd, Studio City (91604). Phone 818/990-0500; fax 818/990-0540. www.patinagroup.com.* Los Angeles celebrity chef Joachim Splichal of Patina fame spins off Pinot Bistro, a less expensive, more accessible taste of his signature French cooking. The menu hews to bistro classics such as duck confit and roast chicken, while the extensive wine menu pleasingly defies French-only conventions. The Studio City favorite offers dining in several distinct areas, such as the Fireplace Room. Décor is uniformly warm and inviting throughout with wood accents, checkered floors, art-filled walls and cozy banquettes. California, French menu. Lunch, dinner. Closed Jan 1, July 4, Dec 25. Bar. Children's menu. Reservations recommended. Valet parking. **$$**

★ ★ **SUSHI KATSU-YA.** *11680 Ventura Blvd, Studio City (91604). Phone 818/985-6976.* Look for the line of BMWs in this otherwise ordinary mini-mall—this is where all the film executives take working lunches, closing deals over scrumptious sushi. The dining room is small and unremarkable, with a sushi bar wrapping around the front, and the décor comes mostly from schoolchildren's crayon creations. The creative sushi specials are on every table: spicy tuna on crispy rice, baked crab rolls, and albacore with crispy onions. The place is always packed with one token celebrity and lots of industry folk, who schmooze and air-kiss their way around the room. Japanese, sushi menu. Lunch, dinner. Closed holidays. Casual attire. **$$$**

★ ★ **TAMA SUSHI.** *11920 Ventura Blvd, Studio City (91604). Phone 818/760-4585; fax 818/760-4363.* With four decades of experience, Chef Michite Katsu is celebrated in the thriving local sushi scene for his magnificent omakase (chef's choice) selections. His dining room, painted white and tastefully outfitted with light wood furniture, is a color-popping showcase for Tama Sushi's sliced, diced, delightfully spiced,

and very reasonably priced treats. (Katsu himself spends four hours a day at markets buying the freshest possible fish, like island mackerel and yellowtail.) The artistry of the main attraction extends to the gorgeous handmade ceramic plates, while a bracing conch soup is served right in the shell. Japanese menu. Lunch, dinner. Closed Sun; holidays. Casual attire. **$$$**

★ ★ **WINE BISTRO.** *11915 Ventura Blvd, Studio City (91604). Phone 818/766-6233; fax 818/766-2465. www.winebistro.net.* Both nearby studio big shots and Laurel Canyon locals are among the regulars at Wine Bistro, a comfortable, casual French spot in Studio City. Bistro classics such as onion soup, duck confit, and peppered steak are supplemented by a blackboard of seasonal specials. Though the wine list is predominantly French (the restaurant annually fetes the Beaujolais Nouveau release), California vintages make an appearance. As in France, the prix fixe menu offers good value and ample food. French bistro menu. Lunch, dinner. Closed Sun; holidays. Bar. Casual attire. Reservations recommended. Valet parking. Outdoor seating. **$$$**

Tehachapi (H-4)

See also Bakersfield

Population 5,791
Elevation 3,973 ft
Area Code 661
Zip 93581
Information Greater Tehachapi Chamber of Commerce, 209 E Tehachapi, PO Box 401; phone 661/822-4180
Web Site www.tehachapi.com/chamber

Tehachapi was founded when the railroad made its way through the pass between the San Joaquin Valley and the desert to the east. The Tehachapi Pass, east of town, is one of the windiest areas in the world; of the approximately 15,000 wind turbines in the state, 5,000 are located here. The best time to see the turbines spinning is late afternoon, when heat on the nearby Mojave Desert is greatest. Historians believe the name Tehachapi is derived from a Native American word meaning "sweet water and many acorns," but others believe it means "windy place." Both are true of the area.

What to See and Do

Tehachapi Loop. *8 miles W of Tehachapi, near Hwy 58. www.tehachapi.com/loop.* Visitors and railroad buffs enjoy watching trains (with 85 or more boxcars) pass over themselves when rounding the "Tehachapi Loop." Built in 1875-1876, the loop makes it possible for trains to gain the needed elevation in a short distance. It can be seen by taking Woodford-Tehachapi Road to a viewpoint just above the loop.

Special Events

Indian PowWow. *Phone 661/822-1118.* Native American cultural and religious gathering of various tribes. Open to public viewing; dance competition, arts and crafts, museum display of artifacts. Usually last weekend in June.

Mountain Festival and PRCA Rodeo. *Phone 661/822-4180.* Includes arts and crafts, food booths, parade, events. Third weekend in Aug.

Limited-Service Hotels

★ **BEST WESTERN MOUNTAIN INN.** *418 W Tehachapi Blvd, Tehachapi (93561). Phone 661/822-5591; toll-free 800/780-7234; fax 661/822-6197. www.bestwestern.com.* 74 rooms, 2 story. Pets accepted; fee. Check-out noon. Restaurant. Outdoor pool. **$**

★ ★ **THE LODGE AT WOODWARD WEST.** *18100 Lucaya Way, Tehachapi (93561). Phone 661/822-5581; toll-free 800/244-0864; fax 661/822-4055. www.stallionsprings.com.* 63 rooms, 2 story. Check-in 3 pm, check-out noon. Restaurant, bar. Fitness room. Outdoor pool, whirlpool. Golf. Tennis. **$**

Temecula (J-4)

See also Fallbrook

Population 27,099
Elevation 1,006 ft
Area Code 909
Information Temecula Valley Chamber of Commerce, 26790 Ynez Rd, Suite 124, 92590; phone 951/676-5090
Web Site www.temeculacvb.com

The Temecula Valley, bordered on the west by Camp Pendleton Marine Corps Base and the Cleveland National Forest, is approximately midway between Los Angeles and San Diego. This area offers activities for everyone, from tours of local wineries to golfing on any of five championship courses.

What to See and Do

California Dreamin'. *33133 Vista Delmonte Rd, Temecula (92591). Phone toll-free 800/373-3359. www.californiadreamin.com.* Want to go up, up, and away? How about while drinking mimosas? This company offers sunrise balloon rides over the Temecula wine country east of San Diego, as well as spectacular daytime forays over the Pacific and the Del Mar bluffs. The baskets accommodate 6, 9, or 12 people, making it perfect for families. Adrenalin junkies may prefer to hop off the doghouse and schedule a ride in a World War I-style biplane, in which you can practice barnstorming, go screaming down the 5,000-foot-high Mount Palomar, or tour the wine country by air. For thrill seekers of another kind, California Dreamin offers romantic airplane flights at sunset, with the sea on one side, mountains on the other, and glasses of the local sparkling wine awaiting you on the ground. Wine country flights of both kinds take off from within the wine country itself, making it an easy complement to any tour. (Daily) **$$$$**

Callaway Vineyard and Winery. *32720 Rancho California Rd, Temecula (92589). Phone toll-free 800/472-2377. www.callawaywinery.com.* Located approximately two hours south of downtown Los Angeles, Callaway Winery makes a great escape for those looking to get out of the city. Have a taste of their coastal wines—cabernet sauvignon, chardonnay, chenin blanc, merlot, or sauvignon blan—call crisp, fresh wines typical of the area. Bring along a picnic lunch and you can eat outside under the trees. Or, if you'd rather leave the cooking to someone else, enjoy Allie's at Callaway, the on-site restaurant. (Daily 10 am-5 pm; closed holidays) **FREE**

Filsinger Winery. *39050 De Portola Rd, Temecula (92592). Phone 951/302-6363. www.filsingerwinery.com.* Started in 1980 by Kathy and Bill Filsinger in the beautiful Temecula Valley wine region, this family-owned and -operated winery produces about 7,000 cases of wine a year. Tours are available by appointment, but you can stop by for a tasting. (Fri 11 am-4 pm, Sat-Sun 10 am-5 pm) **FREE**

Stuart Cellars. *33515 Rancho California Rd, Temecula (92591). Phone toll-free 888/260-0870. www.stuartcellars.com.* A family-run winery two hours south of downtown Los Angeles, Stuart Cellars is a wonderful retreat from the city. Bring a picnic lunch and enjoy it on the winery grounds, with views of the Temecula Valley. Be sure to check out the gift shop—the tapestries for sale are beautiful. (Daily 10 am-5 pm; closed Thanksgiving, Dec 25) **FREE**

Temecula Valley Wineries. *Rancho California Rd, Temecula. Approximately 90 miles SE of LA County; take Hwy 91 E to I-15 S. Phone toll-free 800/801-9463. www.temeculawines.org.* Sure, most people associate winemaking in California with the celebrated Napa and Sonoma valleys east of San Francisco. But if you want to do some serious wine tasting in the Los Angeles area, head to the Temecula Valley, just about two hours away. There, Miramonte, Thornton, Wilson Creek, and 15 other wineries produce award-winning cabernet sauvignon, chardonnay, merlot, syrah, sauvignon blanc, and viognier wines. Each has a tasting room where you can sample the goods, and most offer tours, though not daily.

Special Event

Balloon and Wine Festival. *Lake Skinner, 37701 Warren Rd, Temecula. Phone 951/676-6713. www.tvbwf. com.* Wine tasting, hot air balloon race, musical entertainment, children's activities. Early June.

Limited-Service Hotel

★ **RAMADA INN OLD TOWN.** *28980 Front St, Temecula (92590). Phone 951/676-8770; toll-free 888/298-2054; fax 951/699-3400. www.ramada-temecula.com.* 70 rooms, 2 story. Complimentary continental breakfast. Check-out noon. Fitness room. Outdoor pool, whirlpool. **$**

Full-Service Hotels

★ ★ **EMBASSY SUITES.** *29345 Rancho California Rd, Temecula (92591). Phone 951/676-5656; toll-free 800/362-2779, fax 951/699-3928. www.embassysuites.com.* 136 rooms, 4 story, all suites. Complimentary full breakfast. Check-in 4 pm, check-out noon. Restaurant, bar. Fitness room. Outdoor pool, whirlpool. **$**

★ ★ ★ **PALA CASINO RESORT SPA.** *11154 Hwy 76, Pala (92059). Phone 760/510-2185; toll-free 877/725-2766; fax 760/510-2197. www.palacasino.com.* 425 rooms. Check-in 3 pm, check-out 11 am. Eight restaurants. Fitness room. Outdoor pool. Casino. **$$**

Full-Service Resorts

★ ★ ★ **PECHANGA RESORT & CASINO.** *45000 Pechanga Pkwy, Temecula (92592). Phone 909/719-8594; toll-free 888/732-4264; fax 909/303-2455. www.pechanga.com.* 522 rooms. Check-in 4 pm, check-out 11 am. High-speed Internet access. Seven restaurants, four bars. Fitness room. Outdoor pool, whirlpool. Airport transportation available. Business center. Casino. **$**

★ ★ ★ **TEMECULA CREEK INN.** *44501 Rainbow Canyon Rd, Temecula (92592). Phone 909/694-1000; toll-free 877/517-1823; fax 909/676-8961. www.temeculacreekinn.com.* This hotel offers the perfect combination of work and play, with ample meeting space and a 27-hole golf course with a Four Star rating from *Golf Digest.* Guest rooms are decorated in creams and tans, accented with natural wood. Whether your room overlooks the golf course or the mountains, you can enjoy the view on the patio or balcony, a standard feature. The hotel's Temet Grill offers cuisine to complement the area's many vineyards. 80 rooms, 2 story. Check-in 4 pm, check-out noon. Restaurant, bar. Outdoor pool, whirlpool. Golf, 27 holes. Tennis. **$**

Specialty Lodging

LOMA VISTA BED AND BREAKFAST. *33350 La Serena Way, Temecula (92591). Phone 951/676-7047; fax 951/676-0077. www.lomavistabb.com.* Mission-style house surrounded by citrus groves and vineyards. 10 rooms, 2 story. Complimentary full breakfast. Check-in 3 pm. Check-out 11 am. **$$**

Restaurants

★ ★ **BAILY'S.** *27644 Ynez Rd M-11, Temecula (92591). Phone 951/676-9567. www.baily.com.* American menu. Dinner. Closed holidays. Outdoor seating. **$$**

★ **THE BANK.** *28465 Front St, Temecula (92590). Phone 951/676-6160; fax 951/676-8075.* In refurbished bank building (1913). Mexican menu. Lunch, dinner. Closed Easter, Thanksgiving, Dec 25. Children's menu. Outdoor seating. **$$**

★ ★ **CAFE CHAMPAGNE.** *32575 Rancho California Rd, Temecula (92591). Phone 951/699-0088; fax 951/699-5536. www.thorntonwine.com.* Herb garden.

French menu. Lunch, dinner, Sun brunch. Bar. Outdoor seating. **$$$**

Thousand Oaks (H-3)

See also Camarillo, Los Angeles, Ventura

Population 117,005
Elevation 800 ft
Area Code 805
Information Thousand Oaks/Westlake Village Regional Chamber of Commerce, 600 Hampshire Rd, Suite 200, Westlake Village, 91361; phone 805/370-0035
Web Site www.towlvchamber.org

What to See and Do

Los Robles Golf Course. *299 S Moorpark Blvd, Thousand Oaks (91361). Phone 805/495-6171. www. golfthousandoaks.com.* Los Robles resides in the city of Thousand Oaks, about 40 miles from downtown Los Angeles. Redesigned three times since opening in 1963, the course is constantly changing for the better. Lots of native California wildlife can be found along the course, both flora and fauna. The course is only 6,304 yards from the back tees, so even the long shots should be accessible to most golfers. A new irrigation and drainage system ensures that even if nature provides little water in the summer, the fairways and greens are as verdant as always. **$$$$**

Stagecoach Inn Museum Complex. *51 S Ventu Park Rd, Newbury Park (91320). 1/2 mile S of Hwy 101. Phone 805/498-9441. www.stagecoachmuseum.org.* Reproduction of 1876 building with Victorian furnishings. Contains Chumash display, pioneer artifacts, changing exhibits, carriage house with antique vehicles, gift shop. Tri-Village consists of Chumash hut, Spanish adobe, and pioneer house representing three early cultures in Conejo Valley. One-room schoolhouse. Nature trail. (Wed-Sun 1-4 pm; closed Easter, Thanksgiving, Dec 25) **$**

Full-Service Hotels

★ ★ ★ **HYATT WESTLAKE PLAZA.** *880 S Westlake Blvd, Westlake Village (91361). Phone 805/557-1234; toll-free 800/633-7313; fax 805/379-9392. www. hyattwestlake.com.* Spanish mission-style architecture. 262 rooms, 5 story. Check-in 3 pm, check-out noon. Restaurant, bar. Fitness room. Outdoor pool, whirlpool. Business center. **$$**

★ ★ ★ **WESTLAKE VILLAGE INN.** *31943 Agoura Rd, Westlake Village (91361). Phone 818/889-0230; toll-free 800/535-9978; fax 818/879-0812. www. westlakevillageinn.com.* Located north of Malibu just off Highway 101, this hotel makes you feel like you're stepping into a European villa. The guest rooms are appointed in calming corals, blues, tans, and creams. With fountains, gardens (including a rose garden with more than 25 varieties), and trellised walkways, you'll want to spend as much time out of your room as you spend in it. Relax by the Mediterranean-style pool or hit the links (you can even take advantage of Westlake's only lighted driving range, in case you just can't wait until morning). Enjoy the live entertainment at Bogie's, the hotel's nightclub, or dine at Le Café, the well-known bistro and wine bar on site. The inn is the perfect retreat for those wanting a quieter pace outside the rush of Los Angeles. 144 rooms, 2 story. Pets accepted; restrictions, fee. Complimentary continental breakfast. Check-in 3 pm, check-out noon. Restaurant, bar. Fitness room. Outdoor pool, whirlpool. Golf. Tennis. **$$**

Restaurant

★ **CORRIGAN'S STEAK HOUSE.** *556 E Thousand Oaks Blvd, Thousand Oaks (91360). Phone 805/495-5234.* Seafood, steak menu. Breakfast, lunch, dinner. Closed Thanksgiving, Dec 25. Bar. **$$**

Three Rivers (G-4)

See also Sequoia and Kings Canyon National Parks, Visalia

Population 2,248
Elevation 1,200 ft
Area Code 559
Zip 93271
Web Site www.threerivers.com

Limited-Service Hotels

★ **BEST WESTERN HOLIDAY LODGE.** *40105 Sierra Dr, Three Rivers (93271). Phone 559/561-4119; toll-free 888/523-9909; fax 559/561-3427. www. bestwestern.com.* 54 rooms, 2 story. Pets accepted; fee. Complimentary continental breakfast. Check-in 3 pm, check-out 11 am. Outdoor pool, whirlpool. **$**

★ **HOLIDAY INN EXPRESS.** *40820 Sierra Dr, Three Rivers (93271). Phone 015/595-6190; toll-free 800/331-2140; fax 015/595-6190. www.hiexpress. com/3riversca.* 103 rooms, 3 story. Complimentary continental breakfast. Check-in 4 pm, check-out 11 am. Fitness room. Outdoor pool, whirlpool. **$**
🏃 ⛴

Torrance (J-3)

See also Visalia, Sequoia and Kings Canyon National Parks

Population 137,946
Elevation 84 ft
Information Chamber of Commerce, 3400 Torrance Blvd, Suite 100, 90503; phone 310/540-5858
Web Site www.torrancechamber.com

This middle-class South Bay community is the ethnically diverse model of day-to-day life in Southern California. Torrance was once the West Coast center of the aerospace industry and rapidly subdivided into suburban homes to house the families of engineers from around the world. Although other industries now dominate the area, the internationally mixed suburbia remains intact.

Driving along Crenshaw or Hawthorne boulevards, you can spot tiny sushi joints, Hawaiian restaurants, Peruvian chicken spots, Korean BBQs, and soul food diners. This is the kind of place where you might see a Beijing-Islamic restaurant nestled next to the Chuck E. Cheese, or an Ethiopian spot next to the Olive Garden.

The largest mall in Southern California calls Torrance home. The Del Amo shopping center is so huge that trekking from one end to the other is practically impossible if you're carrying shopping bags.

Restaurants

★ ★ **ASSAGGIO RISTORANTE ITALIANO.** *24215 Crenshaw Blvd, Torrance (90505). Phone 310/325-0543; fax 310/325-2207.* Savory Italian fare with a hint of Asian flair is the epicurean calling card of Assaggio, the sole mainland link in a popular Hawaii-based restaurant chain. Located in the Torrance Crossroads Shopping Center, this classy and contemporary cream-colored dining room has two distinct areas, each furnished with tables partitioned for privacy. Diners can choose from several fine meat specialties in addi-

tion to the more familiar, yet skillfully presented, pasta dishes—including a mouthwatering filet mignon with tangy Asian-spiced house sauce and a velvety-tender veal shank. A selection from the extra-sweet dessert selection makes for a perfect ending. Italian menu. Lunch, dinner. Casual attire. Outdoor seating. **$$**
🅿

★ ★ ★ **DEPOT.** *1250 Cabrillo Ave, Torrance (90501). Phone 310/787-7501. www.depotrestaurant. com.* This restored train station in Old Torrance has been renovated into a modern bistro where grateful locals gather for fine cuisine. The graceful dining room has high brick walls, white linen tablecloths, and chef Michael Schafer bustling about greeting diners. The eclectic international fare includes Asian-cured salmon with wasabi-infused caviar and Thai-dyed chicken on orzo pasta. To really kick-start a meal, don't miss the creative martinis, like the Tex Mex with Grey Goose vodka and a jalapeo olive. Top it all off with an apple crisp or a lemon tart brulee for dessert. International menu. Lunch, dinner. Closed Sun. Bar. Children's menu. Business casual attire. Reservations recommended. Valet parking. **$$$**

★ ★ **RESTAURANT CHRISTINE.** *24530 Hawthorne Blvd, Torrance (90505). Phone 310/373-1952; fax 310/373-8263. www.restaurantchristine.com.* This warm and cozy dining room is multileveled, with a loft for great people-watching and an open kitchen where all the action is. Servers bustle about, treating diners like cherished houseguests. The Pacific Rim-inspired bistro menu is eclectic and original. Starters like the crayfish and avocado tower with mango and napa cabbage is light and refreshing. The pork chop with carnitas enchilada swathed in a creamy chili sauce is exotic and hearty, while cioppino made with the day's freshest catch is pure seaside California. Pacific-Rim menu. Lunch, dinner. Bar. Business casual attire. Reservations recommended. Outdoor seating. **$$**

Universal City (LA) (J-4)

What to See and Do

Universal Amphitheatre. *100 Universal City Plz, Universal City (91608). 1/2 block N of Hollywood Frwy. Phone 818/622-4440. www.hob.com/venues/concerts/universal.* Even though this mammoth theater seats about 6,000, its well known for its good sight lines and good acoustics. It's also the home of many superstar concerts every year. Every chart-busting music act has entertained an appreciative crowd here at one time or another. Do you need any more reasons to buy a ticket and take in a show yourself? It's also part of the Universal City complex, so you're just steps from Universal Studios Hollywood and Universal CityWalk, a popular entertainment center bustling with restaurants, shops, and nightclubs.

⭐ **Universal Studios Hollywood.** *100 Universal City Plz, Universal City (91608). 1/2 block N of Hollywood Frwy. Phone 818/622-3801. www.universalstudios hollywood.com.* Universal Studios Hollywood opened its doors to the public in 1964, and since then, more than 90 million people have visited this movie studio and theme park. For those looking for a mix of Hollywood lore and amusement park thrills, Universal Studios has it all. Here, you can take a tour of the Universal Studios backlot, seeing not only the movie "streets" that will make you feel like you've stepped out of Southern California and into another time or place, but also how special effects make movies what they are today. Test your mettle on the rides, including ones centered around the movies *Jurassic Park* and *Back to the Future.* Take in the many amazing shows, including WaterWorld, Terminator 2: 3-D, and Animal Planet Live! Or, try out Shrek 4-D, an attraction that picks up where the popular animated film left off. And if that doesn't sound like enough, you can hang out at Universal CityWalk, where you'll find dozens of shops, restaurants, bars, and clubs, plus an IMAX 3-D theater. Universal Studios Hollywood is an essential part of the Los Angeles experience, especially to families and those who love movies. (Summer: Mon-Fri 9 am-9 pm, Sat-Sun 9 am-10 pm; rest of year: daily 9 am-6 pm; closed Thanksgiving, Dec 25) **$$$$** Also here is

> **NASCAR Silicon Motor Speedway.** *Universal CityWalk, 1000 Universal Studios Dr, Universal City (91608). Phone 818/763-7959. www.smsonline.com.* Experience centrifugal forces, turns, and crash impacts as you "drive" a full-motion NASCAR Silicon Motor Speedway simulator. **$$**

Full-Service Hotels

★ ★ ★ HILTON LOS ANGELES/UNIVERSAL CITY. *555 Universal Hollywood Dr, Universal City (91608). Phone 818/506-2500; toll-free 800/445-8667; fax 818/509-2058. http://www.losangelesuniversalcity.hilton. com.* Panoramic view of city. 483 rooms, 24 story. Check-in 3 pm, check-out noon. Restaurant, bar. Fitness room. Outdoor pool, whirlpool. Business center. **$$**
🏋 ⬛ 🚶

★ ★ ★ SHERATON UNIVERSAL HOTEL. *333 Universal Hollywood Dr, Universal City (91608). Phone 818/980-1212; toll-free 877/599-9810; fax 818/985-4980. www.sheraton.com.* Overlooks San Fernando Valley and Hollywood Hills. 436 rooms, 20 story. Check-in 3 pm, check-out noon. Restaurant, bar. Outdoor pool, whirlpool. Business center. **$**
⬛ 🚶

Valencia (J-4)

See also Los Angeles

Population 30,000
Area Code 661
Zip 91355
Information Santa Clarita Valley Chamber of Commerce, 28460 Avenue Stanford, Suite 100, Santa Clarita; phone 661/702-6977
Web Site www.scvchamber.org

What to See and Do

Pyramid Lake Recreation Area. *43000 Pyramid Lake Rd, Gorman. 20 miles N on I-5. Phone 661/257-2892.* Lake with swimming, water-skiing, windsurfing, fishing, boating (ramp); picnicking, concession; camping (fee). (Daily; closed holidays) **$$$**

Six Flags Magic Mountain. *26101 Magic Mountain Pkwy, Valencia (91355). Off I-5. Phone 661/255-4100. www.sixflags.com/parks/magicmountain.* Get your thrills on big, bold roller coasters at this 260-acre amusement park that bills itself as the world's only Xtreme Park. It now has 16 spine-chilling coasters, with one called Scream!, appropriately enough. The daring souls who ride this floorless megacoaster get strapped into flying chairs that move at intense speed up and over seven 360-degree inversions—all the while twisting and turning. Clearly not for the faint of heart. Neither are the 15 coasters that came before it, with names like Psyclone, Riddler's Revenge, and Viper. In all, the park has more than 100 rides, games, and attractions divided into nine themed lands, such as Colossus County Fair, Gotham City Backlot, and Samurai Summit. High Sierra Territory, the family-oriented section, includes Bugs Bunny World, an interactive wonderland that brings big smiles to little faces. The adjacent water park, Hurricane Harbor, features 75-foot-tall enclosed speed slides, pool and body slides, a 7,000-square-foot lagoon with water sports, and a children's Castaway Cove. (Sept-Mar: Fri-Sun 10 am-6 pm; Apr-May: Mon-Fri 10 am-6 pm, Sat-Sun to 8 pm; June-Aug: daily 10 am-10 pm) **$$$$**

Limited-Service Hotel

★ **HAMPTON INN.** *25259 The Old Rd, Santa Clarita (91381). Phone 661/253-2400; toll-free 800/426-7866; fax 661/253-1683. http://www.hampton-inn.com.* 130 rooms, 4 story. Complimentary continental breakfast. Check-in 3 pm, check-out noon. Fitness room. Outdoor pool, whirlpool. Business center. **$**

Full-Service Hotels

★ ★ **HILTON GARDEN INN VALENCIA SIX FLAGS.** *27710 The Old Rd, Valencia (91355). Phone 661/254-8800; toll-free 877/782-9444; fax 661/254-9399. www.hiltongardeninn.com.* 152 rooms, 2 story. Pets accepted; restrictions, fee. Check-in 3 pm, check-out noon. Restaurant, bar. Fitness room. Outdoor pool, whirlpool. Business center. **$**

★ ★ ★ **HYATT VALENCIA.** *24500 Town Center Dr, Valencia (91355). Phone 661/799-1234; toll-free 800/633-7313; fax 661/799-1233. www.hyatt.com.* 244 rooms, 6 story. Check-in 3 pm, check-out noon. Restaurant, bar. Fitness room. Outdoor pool, whirlpool. Business center. **$$**

Venice (J-4)

Venice Beach will forever be associated with the 1960s hippie-counterculture that still lives on in the hearts a few of its residents. A walk down the crammed Strand may feel like a freaky flashback—with dreaded hemp-wearing youngsters jamming in drum circles, passing out Greenpeace flyers, or just chilling. Amidst all the free love, vendors hawk T-shirts, knockoff designer sunglasses, and tattoos—so capitalism is not dead.

This upscale neighborhood is located along the Venice canals—actual canals accessible by foot and small boat that cut a watery maze through the city. Abbot Kinney Boulevard is the local center of town. This upscale and eclectic street is home to some of the best dining in Los Angeles, as well as art galleries, exclusive antique dealers, and fashionable boutiques.

Restaurants

★ ★ **AXE.** *1009 Abbot Kinney Blvd, Venice (90291). Phone 310/664-9787; fax 310/664-8994. www.axerestaurant.com.* Pronounced "ah-shay," this swanky and sparse space has gleaming polished concrete floors, strict angular furniture, tiny votives in simple dishes, and unadorned white walls—save for a drippy torso-sized candle, there is no décor to speak of. This minimalism serves the strictly organic menu, which uses the freshest ingredients to create dishes like coconut curry lamb stew and roasted trout with balsamic cabbage. The crowd consists of local couples on spontaneous dates, girlfriends playing catch-up, and toned folks on the way home from yoga. California menu. Lunch, dinner. Closed Mon; holidays. Children's menu. Casual attire. **$$**

★ ★ **CAPRI.** *1616 Abbot Kinney Blvd, Venice (90291). Phone 310/392-8777.* Traversing the heart of this world-famous artists' beach colony, trendy Abbot Kinney Boulevard offers an upscale, Uber-competitive culinary lineup, and Capri is no slouch. The eatery's sparse, whitewashed, pseudo-industrial interior—warmed by romantic candlelight and expensive-looking paintings—provides a canny counterpoint to its sumptuous northern Italian fare. Proud shore-dwellers, sneaker-clad tourists, and the occasional celebrity tend to linger over the handwritten menu, which, in addition to a selection of second-course pastas, features New Zealand rack of lamb, muscovy duck, and halibut steak with grilled red onion and radicchio. Italian menu. Dinner. Closed holidays. Casual attire. **$$$**

★ ★ **HAL'S BAR AND GRILL.** *1349 Abbot Kinney Blvd, Venice (90292). Phone 310/396-3105; fax 310/396-0011. www.halsbarandgrill.com.* Among trendy clothing boutiques, antique furniture stores, and yoga studios, Hal's stands out as the ultimate upscale neighborhood restaurant, where a hipster beach crowd dresses up to meet friends, family, and lovers. The loftlike white-washed space is adorned with commanding modern art pieces, dotted with spacious booths, and lined with an ever-crowded and lively bar. Sushi hand rolls and osso buco are glam offerings, but the turkey burger and Caesar salad have won national culinary acclaim. Live jazz on Saturdays and Sundays draws in the beautiful people. American menu. Lunch, dinner. Closed holidays. Bar. Casual attire. Valet parking. **$$$**

★ ★ **JAMES' BEACH.** *60 N Venice Blvd, Venice (90291). Phone 310/823-5396; fax 310/823-5397.* This sand-adjacent joint is a restaurant and a nightclub rolled into one. Like a swanky beach house, the décor is simple and chic, save for the illuminated boxer shorts hanging from the ceiling, which are rumored to have been left there over the years. A tan and toned crowd clad mostly in black swigs cocktails and flirts, but not before enjoying California comfort food like turkey burgers and fried calamari. Sinful homemade chocolate chip cookies cap off the meal before the party really begins. American menu. Lunch, dinner. Bar. Casual attire. Reservations recommended. Valet parking. Outdoor seating. **$$**

★ ★ **JOE'S.** *1023 Abbot Kinney Blvd, Venice (90291). Phone 310/399-5811; fax 310/829-7539. www.joesrestaurant.com.* Regarded as the culinary pinnacle of Abbot Kinney Boulevard, Joe's still retains a neighborhood charm, where beach-dwelling locals rub elbows with celebrities and gourmands who travel miles and miles to dine on excellent California/French country fare. Architecturally, Joe's runs the gamut from a mod blue-lit bar to a rustic provincial farmhouse to a Zen-like patio with a river-rock waterfall, united only by a distinctly Californian aura. Foie gras paired with ahi tuna and red snapper with "potato scales" are a couple of specialties of the eclectic and avant-garde menu. French, California menu. Lunch, dinner, brunch. Closed Mon; Jan 1, Dec 25. Bar. Casual attire. Reservations recommended. Valet parking. Outdoor seating. **$$**

★ ★ **PRIMITIVO.** *1025 Abbot Kinney Blvd, Venice (90291). Phone 310/396-5353.* Always teeming with eye-catching professionals, this wine bistro and tapas bar resembles an elegant swap meet, with candles resting in Depression-era glass, antiqued chandeliers, and bolts of fabric decoratively strewn about. The funky charm of the shabby-chic dining room is offset by the colorful and bold tapas, like zucchini blossoms stuffed with goat cheese and chorizo-stuffed quail. The high-energy bar is a great choice for impromptu dates and solo dinners. Wine fans take note: there is an excellent selection of half bottles for easy sampling. Mediterranean, Spanish, tapas menu. Lunch, dinner. Closed holidays. Bar. Casual attire. Reservations recommended. Valet parking. Outdoor seating. **$$$**

★ ★ **WABI-SABI.** *1635 Abbot Kinney Blvd, Venice (90291). Phone 310/314-2229.* This festive sushi restaurant is funky, Zen-like, modern, always packed, open late, and full of lookers. And it serves up great fish. In short, it's the ultimate neighborhood joint. A grand sushi bar graces the long dining room, which opens into an outdoor patio, which then becomes a glossy-white back dining room. Fresh sushi, sashimi, and oyster specials rotate daily, and entrées like miso black cod and tempura are favorites. An approachable cold sake list helps diners wash it all down. Japanese, sushi menu. Dinner. Bar. Casual attire. Valet parking. **$$**

Ventura (H-3)

See also Camarillo, Ojai, Oxnard, Santa Barbara, Thousand Oaks

Founded 1782
Population 93,483
Elevation 50 ft
Area Code 805
Information Visitor & Convention Bureau Information Center, 89 S California St, Suite C, 93001; phone 805/648-2075 or toll-free 800/333-2989
Web Site www.ventura-usa.com

What was once a little mission surrounded by huge stretches of sagebrush and mustard plants is now the busy city of Ventura. The sagebrush and mustard have been replaced by citrus, avocado, and other agriculture, but the mission still stands. With the Pacific shore at its feet and rolling foothills at its back, Ventura attracts a steady stream of vacationers. It is in the center of the largest lemon-producing county in the United States.

What to See and Do

Albinger Archaeological Museum. *113 E Main St, Ventura (93001). Phone 805/648-5823.* Preserved archaeological exploration site and visitor center in downtown area. Evidence of Native American culture 3,500 years old; Chumash village site, settled approximately AD 1500; foundation of original mission; Chinese and Mexican artifacts; audiovisual programs. (Wed-Sun 10 am-4 pm; closed holidays) **FREE**

Camping. *Access from W Pacific Coast Hwy, state beaches exit Hwy 101 N. Phone 805/968-1033. www.parks. ca.gov.* **Emma Wood State Beach** and **McGrath State Beach:** Swimming, fishing. Nature trail. 170 developed campsites. **North Beach:** Swimming, surfing, fishing; two RV group camping sites, 61 primitive camp sites. (Daily dawn-dusk)

Channel Islands National Park Visitors Center. *1901 Spinnaker Dr, Ventura (93001). Phone 805/658-5730. www.nps.gov/chis.* Displays, exhibits, and scale models of the five islands; marine life exhibit; observation tower; film of the islands (25 minutes). (Daily 8:30 am-5 pm; closed Thanksgiving, Dec 25) **FREE**

Island Packer Cruises. *1691 Spinnaker Dr, Ventura (93001). Phone 805/642-1393. www.islandpackers.com.* Boat leaves Ventura Harbor for picnic, sightseeing, and recreational trips to Channel Islands National Park. Reservations required. (Memorial Day-Sept, five islands; rest of year, two islands) **$$$$**

Mission San Buenaventura. *211 E Main St, Ventura (93001). Off Hwy 101. Phone 805/643-4318; fax 805/643-7831. www.sanbuenaventuramission.org.* (1782) Ninth California mission and the last founded by Father Junipero Serra. Massive, with a striped rib dome on the bell tower; restored. Garden with fountain. Museum (enter through the gift shop at 225 E Main St) features original wooden bell. Museum (Mon-Fri 10 am-5 pm, Sat from 9 am, Sun 10 am-4 pm; closed holidays). Church and gardens (daily). **$**

Olivas Adobe. *4200 Olivas Park Dr, Ventura (93003). Off Hwy 101, Victoria Ave exit. Phone 805/644-4346.* (1847) Restored with antique furnishings; displays; gardens; visitor center, video. Tours (by appointment). House open for viewing (Sat-Sun 10 am-4 pm). Grounds (daily; closed holidays). Special programs monthly. **FREE**

Ortega Adobe. *215 W Main St, Ventura (93001). Phone 805/658-4726.* (1857) Restored and furnished adobe built on the Camino Real. Furnished with rustic hand-made furniture from the 1850s. Tours (by appointment). Grounds (daily 9 am-4 pm). **FREE**

⭐ **Ronald Reagan Presidential Library and Museum.** *40 Presidential Dr, Simi Valley (93065). Phone 805/577-4000; toll-free 800/410-8354. www.reaganfoundation.org.* As the 40th president of the United States, the Great Communicator left his beloved California and took up residence in the White House from 1981 to 1989. This 150,000-square-foot tribute to his life and two-term presidency, built on 100 acres atop a hill with ocean views, includes 22,000 square feet of exhibit space packed with retrospective displays. It is also the site where the former president is buried. As you step back in time and relive the Reagan years in Washington, DC, you'll see a full-scale replica of the Oval Office and Cabinet Room, a nuclear missile that was deactivated after the President and Mikhail Gorbachev signed the INF treaty, a section of the Berlin Wall, more than 400 magazine covers of both the President and Mrs. Reagan, presidential memorabilia dating as far back as Andrew Jackson's administration, and many more interesting political treasures. (Daily 10 am-5 pm; closed Jan 1, Thanksgiving, Dec 25) **$$**

San Buenaventura State Beach. *Harbor Blvd and San Pedro, Ventura. Phone 805/968-1711. www.parks.ca.gov.* Approximately 115 acres on a sheltered sweep of coast. Offers swimming, lifeguard (summer), surf fishing; coastal bicycle trail access point; picnicking, concession. (Daily dawn-dusk) **$$**

Ventura County Museum of History and Art. *100 E Main St, Ventura (93001). Phone 805/653-0323; fax 805/653-5267. www.venturamuseum.org.* Collection of Native American, Spanish, and pioneer artifacts; George Stuart Collection of Historical Figures; changing exhibits of local history and art; outdoor areas depicting the county's agricultural history; educational programs, research library; gift shop. (Tues-Sun 10 am-5 pm; closed Jan 1, Thanksgiving, Dec 25) **$**

Ventura Harbor. *1603 Anchors Way Dr, Ventura (93001). Off Hwy 101. Phone 805/642-8538; toll-free 877/894-2726. www.venturaharbor.com.* Accommodates more than 1,500 boats; three marinas, launch ramp, mast up dry storage boat yard, dry dock and repair facilities, fuel docks, guest slips. Sportfishing and island boats, sailboat rentals, cruises. Swimming, fishing; hotel, shops, restaurants. Channel Islands National Park headquarters.

Special Events

Ventura County Fair. *Seaside Park, 10 W Harbor Blvd, Ventura (93001). Phone 805/648-3376. www.seaside-park.org/fair.* Parade, rodeo, carnival, entertainment, and livestock auction. Aug. **$$**

Whale-watching. *1691 Spinnaker Dr, Ventura (93001). Phone 805/642-1393; fax 805/642-6573. www.island-packers.com.* Gray whales, Dec-Mar; blue whales, July-Aug. **$$$$**

Limited-Service Hotels

★ ★ **CLOCKTOWER INN.** *181 E Santa Clara St, Ventura (93001). Phone 805/652-0141; toll-free 800/727-1027; fax 805/643-1432. www.clocktowerinn.com.* Near beach, downtown. Renovated firehouse in park setting. 49 rooms, 2 story. Complimentary continental breakfast. Check-out 11 am. Restaurant, bar. **$**

★ **COUNTRY INN & SUITES BY CARLSON.** *298 Chestnut St, Ventura (93001). Phone 805/653-1434; toll-free 800/456-4000; fax 805/648-7126. www.countryinns.com.* Featuring oversized guest rooms in a country motif, this hotel has its own footbridge to the beach. 120 rooms, 3 story. Complimentary full breakfast. Check-out noon. Beach. Outdoor pool, whirlpool. **$**

Full-Service Hotel

★ ★ ★ **MARRIOTT VENTURA BEACH.** *2055 Harbor Blvd, Ventura (93001). Phone 805/643-6000; toll-free 877/983-6887; fax 805/643-7137. www.marriott.com.* 284 rooms, 4 story. Pets accepted; fee. Check-in 3 pm, check-out noon. Restaurant, bar. Fitness room. Beach one block. Outdoor pool, whirlpool. **$**

Specialty Lodgings

THE BRAKEY HOUSE BED & BREAKFAST. *411 Poli St, Ventura (93001). Phone 805/643-3600; fax 805/653-7329. www.brakeyhouse.com.* 5 rooms, 2 story. Children over 13 years only. Complimentary full breakfast. Check-in 4 pm, check-out noon. **$**

PIERPONT INN. *550 SanJon Rd, Ventura (93001). Phone 805/643-6144; toll-free 800/285-4667; fax 805/643-9167. www.pierpontinn.com.* Established in 1928, this inn overlooks Pierpont Bay. 77 rooms, 3 story. Complimentary continental breakfast. Check-in 3 pm, check-out noon. Restaurant, bar. Indoor pool, outdoor pool. **$**

Victorville (H-4)

See also Barstow, Big Bear Lake, Lake Arrowhead

Founded 1878
Population 64,029
Elevation 2,715 ft
Area Code 760
Information Chamber of Commerce, 14174 Green Tree Blvd, 92392; phone 760/245-6506
Web Site www.vvchamber.com

You may never have been in Victorville, but you've probably seen the town before—it has been the setting for hundreds of cowboy movies. This aspect of the town's economy has waned, replaced by light industry. On the edge of the Mojave Desert, the town serves as a base for desert exploration. The presence of lime has attracted four major cement plants to the vicinity.

What to See and Do

California Route 66 Museum. *(Old Rte 66), 16825 D St, Victorville (92392). Phone 760/951-0436; fax 760/951-0509. www.califrt66museum.org.* A tribute to the first national highway to connect Chicago with Los Angeles. Exhibits on different artists' views of Route 66 and its history. (Thurs-Mon 10 am-4 pm) **FREE**

Mojave Narrows Regional Park. *18000 Yates Rd, Victorville (92392). 2 miles S on I-15, then 4 miles E on Bear Valley Rd, 3 miles N on Ridgecrest. Phone 760/245-2226; fax 760/245-7887. www.co.san-bernardino. ca.us/parks/mojave.htm.* Fishing, boating; hiking, bridle trails; picnicking, snack bar; camping (fee). Park (daily; closed Dec 25). **$$**

Special Events

Huck Finn Jubilee. *Mojave Narrows Regional Park, 18000 Yates Rd, Victorville (92392). Phone 760/245-2226. www.huckfinn.com.* River-raft building, fence painting, bluegrass and clogging activities, food. Father's Day weekend. **$$$**

San Bernardino County Fair. *14800 7th St, Victorville (92392). Phone 760/951-2200; fax 760/951-2419. www.sbcfair.com.* Rodeo, livestock and agricultural exhibits, carnival. May. **$**

Limited-Service Hotel

★ ★ **QUALITY INN & SUITES.** *14173 Green Tree Blvd, Victorville (92395). Phone 760/245-3461; toll-free 800/877-3644; fax 760/245-7745. www.choicehotels. com.* View of desert, mountains. 168 rooms, 3 story. Check-out 1 pm. Restaurant, bar. Outdoor pool, children's pool, whirlpool. Golf. Business center. **$**

Restaurant

★ ★ **CHATEAU CHANG.** *15425 Anacapa Rd, Victorville (92392). Phone 760/241-3040; fax 760/241-2775.* Chinese, French menu. Lunch, dinner. Closed Sun; holidays. Bar. **$$$**

Visalia (F-3)

See also Hanford, Porterville, Three Rivers

Population 91,565
Elevation 331 ft
Information Convention and Visitors Bureau, 303 E Acequia St; phone 559/713-4000
Web Site www.visalia.org

What to See and Do

Chinese Cultural Center. *500 S Akers Rd, Visalia (93277). Phone 559/625-4545.* Chinese artifacts, paintings, rare archaeological findings. Chinese garden. Confucius Temple. (Wed-Sun 8 am-4 pm; closed holidays) **FREE**

Tulare County Museum. *27000 S Mooney Blvd, Visalia (93277). Mooney Grove. Phone 559/733-6616. www.tularecountyhistoricalsociety.org.* Ten buildings sct in a 140 acre park house historical exhibits. Park features *End of the Trail* statue by James Earl Fraser. Museum has Native American artifacts, early farm equipment, antique guns, clocks, dolls; log cabin. (Thurs-Mon, admission times vary by season, call for information; closed holidays) **$**

Limited-Service Hotel

★ ★ **PRESIDIAN HOTEL VISALIA.** *300 S Court, Visalia (93291). Phone 559/636-1111; fax 559/636-8224. www.thepresidianhotel.com.* 201 rooms, 8 story. Check-out noon. Restaurant, bar. Fitness room. Outdoor pool, whirlpool. Airport transportation available. **$**

Specialty Lodging

THE SPALDING HOUSE. *631 N Encina, Visalia (93291). Phone 559/739-7877, fax 559/625-0902. www.spaldinghouse.com.* Colonial Revival house built 1901; fully restored. 3 rooms, 2 story. Complimentary full breakfast. Check-in 3 pm, check-out 11 am. **$**

Restaurant

★ ★ ★ **THE VINTAGE PRESS.** *216 N Willis, Visalia (93291). Phone 559/733-3033; fax 559/738-5262. www.thevintagepress.com.* French menu. Lunch, dinner, Sun brunch. Closed Dec 25. Bar. Children's menu. Reservations recommended. Outdoor seating. **$$$**

West Covina (J-4)

See also Pomona, Whittier

Population 105,080
Elevation 381 ft
Area Code 626
Web Site www.westcov.org

Limited-Service Hotels

★ **COMFORT INN.** *2804 E Garvey Ave S, West Covina (91791). Phone 626/915-6077; fax 626/339-4587. www.choicehotels.com.* 58 rooms, 3 story. Complimentary continental breakfast. Check-out 11 am. Outdoor pool, children's pool, whirlpool. **$**

★ ★ **HOLIDAY INN.** *3223 E Garvey Ave N, West Covina (91791). Phone 626/966-8311; fax 626/339-2850. www.holiday-inn.com.* 130 rooms, 5 story. Complimentary full breakfast. Check-out noon. Restaurant, bar. Fitness room. **$**

West Hollywood (LA) (J-4)

See also Beverly Hills, Hollywood, Los Angeles

Web Site www.visitwesthollywood.com

It doesn't get more fabulous than West Hollywood, or WeHo. This tiny city-within-the-city is home to the best home design shops, the most fashionable boutiques, and the finest restaurants.

West Hollywood's side streets are lined with sweet Spanish haciendas and trendy apartment complexes within walking distance of vibrant urban shopping streets. Robertson Boulevard features haute antiques, designer duds, and celeb-heavy lunch spots like The Ivy. La Cienega is home to "restaurant row" and the famed Beverly Center mall. Santa Monica Boulevard is the epicenter of the city's gay community, with hip fast-food joints, nightclubs, gyms, and crowded streets at all hours.

Hip locals take advantage of the breakfast spots, cheap manicures, tiny boutiques, and swanky cocktail lounges on Beverly Boulevard, and Third Street. Those with an unquenchable thirst for fashion flock to the famed Melrose Avenue, which is more couture west of Fairfax and more punk rock to the east.

Fairfax is the center of Los Angeles' Orthodox Jewish community, and historic Canter's Deli is beloved by all Angelenos. Nearby, The Grove shopping mall is parklike and gorgeous, and food fans shouldn't miss a trip to the adjacent Farmers Market.

What to See and Do

Forest Lawn and Hollywood Forever Memorial Parks. *6000 Santa Monica Blvd, West Hollywood (90038). Phone toll-free 800/204-3131. www.forestlawn.com.* To pay your respects to the movie industrys dearly departed, visit either of these two beautiful cemeteries with star quality. Forest Lawn (1712 S Glendale) in Glendale is the final resting place of greats such as Humphrey Bogart, George Burns (and his wife, Gracie Allen), Nat King Cole, Sammy Davis Jr., Carole Lombard, Red Skelton, Jimmy Stewart, and Spencer Tracy. At Hollywood Forever (6000 Santa Monica Blvd) in Hollywood, you'll find the graves of Cecil B. DeMille, Douglas Fairbanks Sr., Douglas Fairbanks Jr., Jayne Mansfield, Tyrone Power, Rudolph Valentino, and hundreds of other celebrities who entertained us. (Daily)

Paramount Film and Television Studios. *5555 Melrose Ave, West Hollywood (90038). Between Van Ness Ave and Gower St. Phone 323/956-1777. www.paramount. com/studio.* Tapings of situation comedies and talk shows (seasonal; usually Tuesday or Friday evenings). For television tapings, minimum age 18. For a taping schedule, write to Paramount Promotional Guest Relations. (Mon-Fri) **$$**

⭐ **Pink's Hot Dogs.** *709 N La Brea Blvd, West Hollywood (90038). Phone 323/931-4223. www.pinkshollywood.com.* In 1939, Paul Pink opened a hot dog cart at the exact location where Pink's hot dog stand sits today. Back then, you could eat your dog at Pinks surrounded by open fields, but, as you may suspect, times have changed. However, Pink's hot dog recipe and the loyalty of the clientele remain the same. The hot dogs are world famous, popular with everyone from typical Angelenos to those with celebrity status. You can eat inside (where you'll see dozens of autographed star photographs) or outside, under the shade of an umbrella. don't be deterred by the long line—it's a constant, but the people behind the counter move you through faster than you can say, "I'll have a Three-Peat LA Laker Dog, hold the onions." (Sun-Thurs 9:30-2 am, Fri-Sat to 3 am; closed Dec 25)

Saddle Ranch Chop House. *8371 Sunset Blvd, West Hollywood (90069). Phone 323/656-2007. www.srrestaurants.com.* Located on the Sunset Strip, the Saddle Ranch is a cheesy imitation of an Old West saloon that will leave you feeling like you've stepped onto the set of *Coyote Ugly.* Ride the mechanical bull for a cheap thrill (you've probably seen it in numerous movies and TV shows, including *Sex and the City*) or leave the riding to the rest of the crowd and watch as they make fools of themselves. Either way, the Saddle Ranch is an experience you won't soon forget. (Daily 8-2 am)

Sunset Plaza. *Sunset Blvd between La Cienega and San Vicente blvds, West Hollywood.* Though it spans just a two-block stretch of Sunset Boulevard, Sunset Plaza may have more people-watching potential than the rest of the Strip combined—especially if celebrity-watching is your thing. Here, you can dine at an outdoor café while you surreptitiously scan the passersby, who are either star-gawkers or the real deal out for a stroll. Stores include Armani A/X, Nicole Miller, and Oliver Peoples. Celebs spotted here have included Tom Cruise, Julia Roberts, Bruce Willis, Winona Ryder, Richard Gere...and the list goes on.

The Viper Room. *8852 Sunset Blvd, West Hollywood (90069). Phone 310/358-1881. www.viperroom.com.* Now owned by actor Johnny Depp, The Viper Room is a favorite nightclub of Hollywood celebrities and other Sunset Strip hipsters. You can hear live music at The Viper Room every night, sometimes from big-name performers who tend to drop by unannounced. The club gained national attention when actor River Phoenix died of a drug overdose on the sidewalk outside the club on Halloween night in 1993. (Daily 9 pm-2 am)

Limited-Service Hotels

★ **CHAMBERLAIN WEST HOLLYWOOD.** *1000 Westmount Dr, West Hollywood (90069). Phone 310/657-7400; toll-free 800/201-9652; fax 310/854-6744. www.chamberlainwesthollywood.com.* This hotel is close to Beverly Hills and only minutes from downtown Los Angeles. 111 rooms, 4 story, all suites. Pets accepted. Complimentary continental breakfast. Check-in 2 pm, check-out noon. Fitness room. Outdoor pool, whirlpool. **$$**

⊞ 🛉 ⊡

★ ★ **ELAN HOTEL MODERN.** *8435 Beverly Blvd, Los Angeles (90048). Phone 323/658-6663; toll-free*

888/611-0398; fax 323/658-6640. www.elanhotel.com. A stylishly futuristic construction of concrete and stained glass, this intimate boutique hotel is fitting for an establishment perched on the edge of culturally vibrant West Hollywood, just two blocks from the Pacific Design Center and the Beverly Center shopping mall. Trendy lodgers and business executives with an artistic bent enjoy its quiet, off-the-Sunset Strip ambience, while Web-wrangling hipsters come for the Cyber Lounge's free continental breakfast and high-speed Internet connections. Rooms and suites soothe with earth tones, designer amenities, and Egyptian cotton linens. Manager's evening wine-and-cheese receptions are held for guests Monday through Friday. 50 rooms, 2 story. Check-in 3 pm, check-out noon. High-speed Internet access. Fitness room. Business center. **$$**

Full-Service Hotels

★ ★ ★ **BEL AGE HOTEL.** *1020 N San Vicente Blvd, West Hollywood (90069). Phone 310/854-1111; toll-free 800/996-3426; fax 310/854-0926. www.luxuryresorts.com.* Tourists, business types and glitterati alike flock to this upscale Sunset Strip high-rise, which is steps from the fun, great food, and entertainment industry glitz that define West Hollywood and nearby Beverly Hills. All-suite accommodations—boasting balcony views of Los Angeles and the Hollywood Hills—feature California contemporary décor comprised of muted tones and tasteful artwork, and are outfitted with CD players and high-speed Internet access. Relaxation reigns in the rooftop garden and pool area. The hotels award-winning Diaghilev Restaurant (see) specializes in Franco-Russian cuisine, while the Ten20 piano bar serves up lively jazz. 200 rooms, 10 story, all suites. Pets accepted, some restrictions; fee. Check-in 3 pm, check-out noon. High-speed Internet access. Two restaurants, two bars. Fitness room. Outdoor pool, whirlpool. Business center. **$$**

★ ★ ★ **CHATEAU MARMONT.** *8221 Sunset Blvd, West Hollywood (90046). Phone 323/656-1010; toll-free 800/242-8328; fax 323/655-5311. www.chateaumarmont.com.* Sleep with a slice of Hollywood history at the classic Chateau Marmont, a hipster from the Greta Garbo era. Just above Sunset Boulevard, Chateau Marmont cossets the glitterati, particularly those who take one of its elite bungalows, within the heart of happening West Hollywood. It's favored by fashion photo shoots, starlet-toting publicists, and deal-making producers, so the poolside people-watching may

be worth the room price alone. The main castlelike building dates to 1929, but renovation efforts have kept amenities and décor contemporary. 63 rooms, 7 story. Pets accepted; fee. Check-in 2 pm, check-out noon. Wireless Internet access. Restaurant. Fitness room. Outdoor pool. **$$$**

★ ★ ★ **THE GRAFTON HOTEL.** *8462 W Sunset Blvd, West Hollywood (90069). Phone 323/654-4600; toll-free 800/821-3660; fax 323/654-5918. www.graftononsunset.com.* With an address on Sunset Boulevard, this hotel has a lot to offer those who want their stay in LA to be memorable. The décor, with soft yellows, rich reds, and deep greens, is Feng Shui reverential, and the bath products are organic. (Can you get more LA than that?) The swimming pool area has the feel of old Europe. A Mediterranean garden offers a respite from the plethora of boutiques, restaurant, and nightclubs (including the House of Blues and Sky Bar) just outside the hotel's door. If being in the heart of the action is what you want, the Grafton on Sunset will put you there. 108 rooms. Pets accepted; fee. Check-in 3 pm, check-out noon. Wireless Internet access. Restaurant, bar. Fitness room. Outdoor pool. **$$**

★ ★ ★ **HYATT WEST HOLLYWOOD.** *8401 Sunset Blvd, West Hollywood (90069). Phone 323/656-1234; toll-free 800/633-7313; fax 323/650-7024. www.hyatt.com.* 262 rooms, 14 story. Check-in 3 pm, check-out noon. Restaurant, bar. Fitness room. Outdoor pool. Business center. **$$**

★ ★ ★ **LE MONTROSE SUITE HOTEL.** *900 Hammond St, West Hollywood (90069). Phone 310/855-1115; toll-free 800/776-0666; fax 310/657-9192. www.lemontrose.com.* In West Hollywood, the Art Nouveau-styled Le Montrose furnishes its spacious suites with sunken living rooms, fireplaces, and refrigerators many with kitchenettes—and private balconies. Venture up to the roof for a dip in the pool and Jacuzzi or a set on the tennis court. The noteworthy restaurant, The Library, is reserved exclusively for guests and their friends. A well-equipped health club helps encourage residential stays. 133 rooms, 5 story, all suites. Pets accepted, fee. Check-in 3 pm, check-out noon. High-speed Internet access. Restaurant. Fitness room. Outdoor pool, whirlpool. Tennis. Business center. **$$**

★ ★ ★ **LE PARC SUITE HOTEL.** *733 N West Knoll Dr, West Hollywood (90069). Phone 310/855-*

8888; toll-free 800/578-4837; fax 310/659-7812. www. leparcsuites.com. Located in the heart of West Hollywood—a trendy area of restaurants, nightclubs, and shops—this hotel is just a block off Santa Monica Boulevard and Melrose Avenue (Santa Monica Blvd to the north, Melrose to the south). As the name suggests, the modernly appointed rooms aren't just "rooms," they're suites, which means that, at a minimum, you'll have 650 square feet in which to spread out. With a balcony, living room (with a sleeper sofa), fireplace, kitchenette (with microwave and refrigerator), two TVs, a VCR, a DVD player, and a CD player, you might not want to leave your room. If you do, you'll find a lighted tennis court, heated swimming pool, and sundeck on the roof of the building, all with astonishing views of the surrounding Hollywood Hills. You can arrange for a private tennis lesson, a massage, or an appointment with a personal trainer (all for a fee). For breakfast, lunch, or dinner, enjoy Café Le Parc, a Mediterranean-style restaurant. Although every suite has high-speed Internet access, you can use the computers (both PCs and Macs) in the hotel's business center if you're traveling without your computer. Laser printers and a copy machine are also available. If the thought of driving in Los Angeles (or finding parking in West Hollywood) makes you shudder, complimentary Town Car service will take you anywhere you want to go within a 3-mile radius. 154 rooms, all suites. Pets accepted; fee. Check-in 3 pm, check-out noon. High-speed Internet access. Restaurant, bar. Fitness room. Outdoor pool. Tennis. Business center. **$$$**

★ ★ ★ **MONDRIAN.** *8440 Sunset Blvd, West Hollywood (90069). Phone 323/650-8999; fax 323/650-5215. www.morganshotelgroup.com.* West Hollywood hipster Mondrian still holds its own among trendies, thanks to outre designer Philippe Starck, who filled the lobby with disproportionate props. For an urbanite, Mondrian manages to celebrate the outdoors, too. Its lobby, open to expansive views of LA, spans both indoor and outdoor plazas, as does its restaurant/lounge, Asia de Cuba (see). Rooms are furnished residentially with puffy, inviting beds and oversized bathrooms. Check out the artist-made light installations that illuminate the guest room corridors. It all looks like a nightclub but—surprise!—there's a kid's program at the hotel, too. 238 rooms, 12 story. Check-in 3 pm, check-out noon. High-speed Internet access. Restaurant, bar. Fitness room. Outdoor pool. Business center. **$$$**

★ ★ ★ **SUNSET MARQUIS HOTEL AND VILLAS.** *1200 N Alta Loma Rd, West Hollywood (90069). Phone 310/657-1333; toll-free 800/858-9758; fax 310/657-1330. www.sunsetmarquishotel.com.* An exclusive, ultra-cool, Mediterranean-style celebrity magnet since its debut in 1963, this hotel—secreted away on a quiet cul-de-sac just south of club-lined Sunset Boulevard—offers 3 1/2 acres of showy landscaping, shimmering koi ponds and shamelessly indulgent leisure. This boutique hotel's choice location and state-of-the-art recording studio have drawn top musical acts like the Rolling Stones and U2, and entertainment industry types can be found cutting deals and sharing gossip in the velvet-lined, lobby-adjacent Whiskey Bar any night of the week. Deluxe villas and suites feature king-size beds, marble bathrooms, refrigerators, plush bathrobes, an array of audiovisual electronics and twice-daily maid service, among many other amenities. Gourmet indoor/outdoor dining is available on-site, and fine restaurants and shops are within walking distance. A local guide assembled by the crack multilingual concierge staff, *Attention Deficit Sightseeing,* offers a crash course in the neighborhoods myriad attractions (plus a handy map). 114 rooms, 3 story, all suites. Check-in 3 pm, check-out noon. High-speed Internet access. Restaurant, bar. Fitness room. Two outdoor pools, whirlpool. Airport transportation available. Business center. **$$$**

★ ★ ★ **SUNSET TOWER HOTEL.** *8358 Sunset Blvd, West Hollywood (90069). Phone 323/654-7100; toll-free 800/225-2637; fax 323/654-9287. www. sunsettowerhotel.com.* This glamorous Art Deco tower has been a proud Sunset Boulevard landmark since Hollywood's Golden Age—when it corralled a galaxy of stars including Clark Gable, Marilyn Monroe, and Errol Flynn. From the elegant gold-and-black décor of the lobby to the luxe accommodations featuring custom furnishings, marble bathrooms, high-tech entertainment gadgets, and stunning city and Hollywood Hills views, discriminating guests and hardcore stargazers alike will find plenty to suit their tastes. The adjacent Fenix dining room, with its famous wrought-iron palm trees, is a frequent gathering spot for entertainment power-brokers and up-and-comers. 64 rooms, 15 story. Pets accepted; fee. Check-in 3 pm, check-out noon. Wireless Internet access. Restaurant, bar. Fitness room. Outdoor pool. Business center. **$$**

Restaurants

★ ★ **A.O.C.** *8022 W Third St, Los Angeles (90048). Phone 323/653-6359. www.aocwinebar.com.* This white-hot, critically acclaimed eatery is arguably the trendiest and tastiest joint in town for the "small plates" craze. The Mediterranean tapas menu rotates weekly and may include black rice with squid or pork cheeks with sweet potatoes. The open charcuterie bar with house-cured meats such as coppa and lomo is the best first-come, first-served spot in the golden, cathedral-like dining room. A long bar with 50 boutique wines by the glass is a fine accompaniment to the dozen rare cheeses available and is a classy spot for solo diners. Reservations are essential, the clientele savvy and stunning. California, Mediterranean menu. Dinner. Bar. Casual attire. Reservations recommended. Outdoor seating. **$$$**

★ ★ **AGO.** *8478 Melrose Ave, West Hollywood (90069). Phone 323/655-6333; fax 323/655-6640.*The parking lot is full of exotic cars, the bar is packed with modelesque babes, and the dining room is stuffed with Armani suits—would you expect anything less from a restaurant owned by Robert De Niro? This ritzy Italian joint has remained a powerhouse due to its superb cuisine, like the burrata cheese plate, blistered pizzas, and steaks and chops from the wood-burning oven. The bar is a sweet spot to take in the scene, sip a martini, and nosh on small insalate. Italian menu. Lunch, dinner. Bar. Casual attire. Reservations recommended. Valet parking. Outdoor seating. **$$**

★ ★ **ANGELI CAFFÉ.** *7274 Melrose Ave, Los Angeles (90046). Phone 323/936-9086; fax 323/938-9873. www.angelicaffe.com.* On a strip of Melrose that's better known for Johnny Rockets than fine cuisine, Angeli Caffé has been mounting a revolution for years—preaching the concept that good food is slow food. Chef Evan Kleinman takes the slow food concept into her kitchen, where she utilizes the finest organic seasonal ingredients to turn out deliciously simple rustic Italian fare. The dining room is unfussy, with exposed wooden beams and rickety tables, and kids are given pizza dough to sculpt while the kitchen slowly creates culinary perfection. Italian menu. Lunch, dinner. Bar. Casual attire. **$$**

★ ★ **ANGELINI OSTERIA.** *7313 Beverly Blvd, Los Angeles (90036). Phone 323/297-0070; fax 323/297-0072. www.angeliniosteria.com.* The stylish dining room may be diminutive, with diners seated elbow to elbow, but this charming little room turns out exciting Italian delicacies that pack a serious punch. The rotating seasonal menu offers specialties like grilled quail, tripe with cuttlefish, and breaded Dover sole. The theatrical house special is the whole roasted branzino in a heaping salt crust, cracked and served tableside. This popular joint is perpetually packed with swoony couples, executives doing business, and young Hollywood up-and-comers, so make reservations in advance. Italian menu. Lunch, dinner. Closed Mon. Casual attire. Reservations recommended. Outdoor seating. **$$**

★ ★ ★ **ASIA DE CUBA.** *8440 Sunset Blvd, West Hollywood (90069). Phone 323/848-6000. www. chinagrillmgt.com.* The sunglasses-after-dark crowd is drawn to this West Hollywood hotspot inside the Mondrian hotel (see). Part nightclub, part eatery, Asia de Cuba offers its star and star-wannabe clientele a chic backdrop against which to posture. The candlelit communal table is a great place for singles, and the outdoor patio plants tables between oversized pots. don't let the eye candy and the oversized martinis dumb down your culinary expectations. The kitchen does a good job with contemporary noshes like tuna tartare and fried calamari. Asian, Latin menu. Breakfast, lunch, dinner. Bar. Children's menu. Casual attire. Reservations recommended. Valet parking. Outdoor seating. **$$$$**

★ ★ **BALBOA RESTAURANT & LOUNGE.** *8462 W Sunset Blvd, West Hollywood (90069). Phone 323/650-8383; fax 323/650-8787.* If there is such a thing as a boutique steakhouse, this is it. Floating glass floors, artful screens of foliage, modern stained glass, and candlelit banquettes give this cozy dining room a sexy and intimate aura. Superb steaks grilled to perfection come with a choice of sauces, like pinot noir reduction, and sides, like a decadent creamed spinach. Don't miss the spectacle of the Caesar salad prepared tableside. For grape lovers, every wine on the impressive list is half price on Sunday nights. Steak menu. Breakfast, lunch, dinner. Bar. Casual attire. Reservations recommended. Valet parking. Outdoor seating. **$$$**

★ **CANTER'S DELICATESSEN.** *419 N Fairfax Ave, Los Angeles (90036). Phone 323/651-2030. www. cantersdeli.com.* Part deli, part bakery, and part institution, this historic restaurant is a special spot in Los Angeles culture. More than a Jewish landmark, Canter's has long been the nexus for comfort food, whether it be a bowl of matzo ball soup, a pastrami on rye, or a heap of eggs at 2 am. The two dining rooms are unremarkable in décor, and take diners on a trip back into time—except today, you can spot tattooed rockers noshing next to conservative families, with the full spectrum of LA culture in between. Deli menu. Breakfast, lunch, dinner, late-night. Bar. Children's menu. Casual attire. **$$**

★ ★ **CHAYA BRASSERIE.** *8741 Alden Dr, West Hollywood (90048). Phone 310/859-8833; fax 310/859-4991. www.thechaya.com.* Another branch of the trendy LA chain, this modern Embarcadero restaurant and bar doesn't quite attract the rich and famous, but it does attract crowds, especially for the weekday sushi happy hour. The open chrome kitchen serves a mix of French and Asian fare with a focus on sushi and seafood; the impressive wine list includes a number of wines by the glass, along with half bottles. Don't miss the views of the Bay Bridge and Treasure Island. French, Japanese menu. Lunch, dinner. Bar. Casual attire. Reservations recommended. Valet parking. Outdoor seating. **$$$**

★ ★ **CHIN CHIN.** *8618 Sunset Blvd, West Hollywood (90069). Phone 310/652-1818. www.chinchin.com.* This sunny Chinese bistro on the Sunset Strip is always abuzz with young executives taking quick business lunches, post-yoga beauties munching on salads, and shoppers refueling for the next boutique. The interior is pure SoCal, with lots of peach and green appointments surrounding the blond wood tables and a model-like waitstaff. From mu shu pork to fried rice, hot-and-sour soup to chow fun, classic Chinese fare gets a healthy twist with light preparations and fresh ingredients. Chinese menu. Lunch, dinner. Closed holidays. Casual attire. Outdoor seating. **$$**
🅳

★ ★ ★ **COBRAS & MATADORS.** *7615 W Beverly Blvd, Los Angeles (90036). Phone 323/932-6178.* Butcher paper lines the tables, sepia photos grace the walls, and piles of wine corks act as décor at this ever-popular tapas joint on trendy Beverly Boulevard. Hordes of chic young professionals and aspiring movie moguls flock here for the unpretentious attitude, party atmosphere, and cutting-edge tapas. An open kitchen turns out lentils with bacon and tiny fried croquettes that pair well with the beers and Spanish wines that diners may purchase at the adjacent wine store. Dining room and sidewalk tables are in demand, so reservations are essential. Spanish, tapas menu. Dinner. Closed July 4. Casual attire. Reservations recommended. **$$**

★ ★ **DAN TANA'S.** *9071 Santa Monica Blvd, West Hollywood (90069). Phone 310/275-9444; fax 310/274-2805.* When moguls like Steven Spielberg and David Geffen want to have a steak, they head to this venerable

Hollywood institution. At this unpretentious classic Italian eatery, impeccable tuxedo-clad servers shuttle bottles of Chianti and platters of chicken Parmesan and veal scaloppini through a maze of red-and-white-checked tablecloths. Although the restaurant can get crowded and raucous, affluent diners don't seem to mind the long wait or the impossible reservations because every customer is treated like a star here. Italian menu. Dinner. Closed Thanksgiving, Dec 25. Bar. Reservations recommended. Valet parking. **$$$**

★ ★ ★ ★ **DIAGHILEV.** *1020 N San Vincente Blvd, Los Angeles (90069). Phone 310/854-1111; fax 310/854-0926. www.wyndham-belage.com.* Named for a Russian dancer and choreographer, Diaghilev is the place to go if you find yourself craving the old-world opulence of pre-revolutionary Russia. This elegant restaurant pays homage to authentic Russian fare, supplying all the essential trimmings, from an array of spectacular caviars to a mind-numbing selection of house-infused flavored vodkas. Velvety loveseats, blood-red long-stemmed roses, and melodic balalaika music make this a perfect spot for romance and, often, the Big Question. (And by "Big Question," we mean not only "Will you marry me?" but also "Are you going to share your caviar with me?") The kitchen maintains true Russian influences but adds many French touches, so don't leave your sense of adventure at home. Signatures include eggshells filled with whipped eggs and chives and topped with sevruga caviar, and filet of Baltic salmon with sturgeon mousse in a light pastry with cabernet sauvignon sauce. While vodka abounds, the restaurant also carries a wonderful and extensive wine list. French, Russian menu. Dinner. Closed Sun-Mon; Jan 1. Bar. Jacket required. Reservations recommended. Valet parking. **$$$$**

★ ★ **DOLCE ENOTECA E RISTORANTE.** *8284 Melrose Ave, Los Angeles (90046). Phone 323/852-7174; fax 323/852-7187. www.dolceenoteca.com.* Perhaps more well known for its celebrity owner, Ashton Kutcher (star of television's *That '70s Show*), than its cuisine, this white-hot spot has been the ultimate destination for movie stars and those who love them. Packed since its opening, this place is pure 1980s, with black leather table covers, transparent Lucite chairs, and a bar with a wall of wildfire flames. Sure, Dolce turns out respectable Italian fare, like risotto with veal sauce, but with a crowd so happening, who cares? The most coveted seats can be found on the open-air back patio. Italian menu. Dinner. Closed holidays. Bar. Casual attire. Reservations recommended. Valet parking. Outdoor seating. **$$$**

★ ★ **FAT FISH.** *616 N Robertson Blvd, West Hollywood (90069). Phone 310/659-3882; fax 310/659-3873.* On one of the most dynamic intersections for LA nightlife, this Euro-Asian restaurant is always a favorite with club-bound locals. Red walls, a large sidewalk patio, and a whimsical projection of a fish tank on the wall give the space a free-spirited attitude. Imaginative and large martinis kick off the menu, which puts an eclectic spin on Asian fare, featuring, naturally, fish. Spider rolls are massive, tuna is done up in three creative ways, and regulars always save room for decadent desserts like chocolate truffle cake. Japanese, sushi menu. Lunch, dinner. Closed Mon; holidays. Bar. Casual attire. Outdoor seating. **$$**

★ **GREENBLATT'S DELICATESSEN.** *8017 W Sunset Blvd, West Hollywood (90046). Phone 323/656-0606.* This deli is the real deal, serving up classics like brisket on rye, creamy chopped liver, and matzo ball soup to an eclectic mix of customers—from club kids to oenophiles. The service is a bit laissez-faire, so grab a server and then grab a table for best results. The superior deli counter is a favorite late-night pit stop for patrons and performers of the adjacent comedy club. Newcomers will be pleasantly surprised by the outrageously vast wine collection and store, which sometimes hosts auctions of rare vintages. Deli menu. Breakfast, lunch, dinner. Casual attire. **$**

★ ★ **THE IVY.** *113 N Robertson Blvd, Los Angeles (90048). Phone 310/274-8303.* Any avid tabloid reader will recognize The Ivy's star-studded patio from the hundreds of published celebrity photos. West Hollywood's country-chic café is a favorite haunt for Hollywood elite, who do movie deals and power breakfasts over the famed grilled vegetable salad or the blue crab omelet. (Santa Monica's modish beach outpost, at 1541 Ocean Ave, also attracts a stylish crowd.) The Shore's bar is a sophisticated spot to watch the sun set and grab an Ivy gimlet, a potent concoction of vodka, mint, and lime. California, continental menu. Lunch, dinner. Casual attire. Reservations recommended. Outdoor seating. **$$$**

★ ★ ★ **JAR.** *8225 Beverly Blvd, Los Angeles (90048). Phone 323/655-6566. www.thejar.com.* Fronted by Campanile veteran Susan Tracht and Campanile co-owner Mark Peel, Jar fuses foodie and design appeal. The clean, minimalist setting near the Beverly Center modernizes the steakhouse standard. Also updated, the meat-centric menu features steaks, roasts, braises, and chops from top purveyors, many organic, prepared with a light hand and presented with stylish restraint. Starters contemporize classics including deviled eggs and iceberg wedge salad. Like old-school meateries, everything on the menu is à la carte, so do the math. Chophouse menu. Dinner, Sun brunch. Closed Jan 1, Dec 25; also Oscar night. Bar. Casual attire. Reservations recommended. **$$$**

★ ★ ★ **KATANA.** *8439 W Sunset Blvd, Los Angeles (90069). Phone 323/650-8585. www.sushiroku.com.* Located at the epicenter of the Sunset Strip, this modern Japanese eatery is lavishly adorned with hammered metal, roughly hewn stone, and flickering floating candles. Along the back wall, an army of chefs carve up flawless sashimi and grill robata-yaki—skewered meats like soy garlic lamb chops and king crab legs—over a charcoal grill. Hollywood power players appreciate the theatrical open kitchen, the wickedly potent cocktails, and the fact that they're at the most sizzling spot in town. Japanese, sushi menu. Dinner, late-night. Bar. Casual attire. Outdoor seating. **$$$**

★ ★ ★ **KOI.** *730 N La Cienega Blvd, Los Angeles (90069). Phone 310/659-9449. www.koirestaurant.com.* This swinging sushi sanctuary balances the elegance of a sleek Zen garden and the whimsy of a cocktail party. Bamboo terraces under the stars are reminiscent of an exotic resort, while the inner dining room's low lights, red walls, and fireplaces flatter the stunningly beautiful crowd clad mostly in black. Although the sushi is meltingly fresh, Koi is renowned for more unusual dishes, like a baked crab roll in soy paper and spicy tuna on crispy fried rice. It is also a famed launching spot for Hollywood club-goers. Japanese, sushi menu. Dinner. Bar. Casual attire. Reservations recommended. Outdoor seating. **$$$**

★ ★ ★ ★ **L'ORANGERIE.** *903 N La Cienega Blvd, Los Angeles (90069). Phone 310/652-9770; fax 310/652-8870. www.lorangerie.com.* This much is evident upon entering L'Orangerie: the place is stunning. You walk through an enclosed, candlelit terrace filled with square umbrella-topped tables to get to the formal, Versailles-style main dining room appointed with large murals, magnificent floral arrangements, linen- and porcelain-topped tables, and glowing hurricane lamps. During dinner, the extraordinary talent of the chefs working away behind closed doors is also apparent; they turn out plate after plate of eye-popping, modern, upscale French fare that borrows flavors from around the world, paying special attention to Asia. The extensive wine list offers many choices to match up with signatures such as eggs in the shell with sevruga caviar; hamachi marinated with blood orange juice, olive oil, and coriander; and roasted squab with braised legs, macaroni gratin, and herb salad with black olive paste. French menu. Dinner. Closed Sun-Mon; holidays. Bar. Jacket required. Reservations recommended. Valet parking. Outdoor seating. **$$$$**

★ ★ ★ **LA BOHEME.** *8400 Santa Monica, West Hollywood (90069). Phone 323/848-2360. www.cafe-laboheme.com.* The lavish West Hollywood La Boheme does its California-French fusion act with operatic flair. The various seating areas within the stone building could be considered individual acts: choose from the downstairs dining room with a wood-burning fireplace, the patio with gurgling fountains and another fireplace, or mezzanine balconies for prime people-watching. The menu ranges from forward tuna tataki salad and charred ahi to traditional filet mignon and duck breast with confit, satisfying both LA trendies and conservatives among the crowd. California, French menu. Dinner. Bar. Business casual attire. Reservations recommended. Valet parking. Outdoor seating. **$$$**

★ ★ **LA PAELLA.** *476 S San Vicente Blvd, Los Angeles (90048). Phone 323/951-0745.* Stepping into this hidden little spot is like entering the home of a friend, full of warm service and comfy surroundings—with Spanish knickknacks, drippy candles, and charming table settings. Start with a pitcher of cool, ruby-red sangria and sample exquisite tapas like sherried mushrooms and imported meats. Paella is the star of the meal, served in a huge cast-iron pan and studded with seafood and enough saffron rice to feed an army. The clientele is refined and pleased to be dining at one of the city's best-kept secrets. Spanish, tapas menu. Lunch, dinner. Closed Sun. Bar. Casual attire. **$$**
🄳

★ ★ **LE DOME.** *8720 Sunset Blvd, West Hollywood (90069). Phone 310/659-6919; fax 310/659-5429. www.ledomerestaurant.com.* This historic power-lunch hotspot can only be described as architecturally bizarre. The space features a strange marriage of shooting flames, gothic windows, stone walls, and a long red carpet. The clientele is studded with Hollywood heavy hitters, who await their tables around the glowing golden bar. Pricey entrées are equally flashy, like pheasant under glass, pan-roasted lobster, and caviar, whose price is listed merely as "expensive." (If you have to ask...) Industry rebels hang out on the smoker-friendly patio, while the old guard sticks to the private booths in back. Bring attitude. American menu. Dinner. Closed Sun-Mon; holidays. Bar. Casual

attire. Reservations recommended. Valet parking. Outdoor seating. **$$$**

★ **LE PETIT FOUR.** *8654 Sunset Blvd, West Hollywood (90069). Phone 310/652-3863; fax 310/652-1853. www.lepetitfour.com.* Along the stylish Sunset Junction shopping strip, this popular sidewalk Café is always a scene, jammed with jet-set shoppers, soccer moms, and European expats who crave a little piece of home. The alfresco dining is European in feel, as is the menu, which is heavy on classics like goat cheese salads, simple pastas, and a few continental entrées. Most everyone sips wine, no matter what the time of day, and watches the spectacle of the wealthy and privileged in transit. French menu. Lunch, dinner. Bar. Casual attire. Reservations recommended. Outdoor seating. **$$**

★ ★ **LOCANDA VENETA.** *8638 W Third St, Los Angeles (90048). Phone 310/274-1893; fax 310/274-4217. www.locandaveneta.com.* The tables are packed together, the room illuminated mostly by candlelight, the clientele full of celebrities—could you want anything more from an Italian restaurant? Notwithstanding the intimate atmosphere and lovely crowd, the kitchen turns out great northern Italian food, in particular grilled meats and seafood, which pair beautifully with exquisite pastas and fine wines. No wonder this classic joint is still one of the toughest reservations in town. Italian menu. Lunch, dinner. Casual attire. Reservations recommended. Valet parking. Outdoor seating. **$$**
🄳

★ ★ **LOLA'S.** *945 N Fairfax Ave, West Hollywood (90046). Phone 213/736-5652; fax 323/650-6591. www.lolasla.com.* The self-proclaimed "home of the apple martini," this cocktail institution is ever popular with the Hollywood party set. Locals who are truly in the know kick off the night at Lola's with its fantastic and affordable dinner menu, which features chicken satay, fish-and-chips, and linguine with clams. don't miss desserts like the fried bananas over ice cream or the famous and uber-creative martini menu. After dinner, mosey into the Moroccan-style bar and shoot pool, carouse, and table-hop with the other beautiful people. California menu. Dinner. Bar. Casual attire. Reservations recommended. Valet parking. **$$$**

★ **LOTERIA GRILL.** *6333 W Third St, Los Angeles (90036). Phone 323/930-2211; fax 323/930-2282. www.loteriagrill.com.* This colorful Mexican stand in the middle of the Farmers' Market has earned instant fame and acclaim for its exotic, unusual, and scrumptious tacos. Locals flocked here long before raves from *Bon Appétit* poured in, clamoring for smoky chicken mole, supple shredded beef, and pungent pork, all ladled into fat house-made tortillas. Breakfast dishes like chiliquilas are instant hangover cures, and the taquitos are the best in town. Grab a rickety table in the sun, a few beers from the adjacent bar, and you've got an instant fiesta. Mexican menu. Breakfast, lunch, dinner. Casual attire. Outdoor seating. No credit cards accepted. **$**

★ ★ ★ **LUCQUES.** *8474 Melrose Ave, West Holly-wood (90069). Phone 323/655-6277; fax 323/655-3925. www.lucques.com.* Much regarded LA chef Suzanne Goin launched the West Hollywood Lucques to national raves, cooking ground-breaking dishes that bridge California, France, and the Mediterranean. The setting, with brick walls, a fireplace, leather banquettes, and suspended light cubes, manages the welcome trick of looking trendy but feeling warm. Full flavors mark Goin's food in dishes like blood orange-date-Parmesan salad, sweetbreads and wild mushrooms, chorizo-stuffed rabbit, braised beef shortribs, and pancetta-wrapped sea bass. Menus change seasonally, but the Sunday night prix fixe served family-style is a weekly event. California menu. Lunch, dinner. Closed holidays. Bar. Casual attire. Reservations recommended. Valet parking. Outdoor seating. **$$$**

★ ★ **MIMOSA.** *8009 Beverly Blvd, Los Angeles (90048). Phone 323/655-8895; fax 323/655-9178. www.mimosarestaurant.com.* You have to love a French bistro whose motto is "No truffles, no caviar, no bizarre concoctions." What you can expect is classic bistro fare, like cassoulet of duck confit, mussels mariniere, and steak tartare, impeccably prepared without a trace of fussiness. The bright yellow dining room dotted with photos and flowers is always packed with swoony couples, foodies, and Francophiles. A lovely wine list is shockingly approachable and affordable. French bistro menu. Dinner. Closed Sun-Mon. Casual attire. Outdoor seating. **$$**

★ ★ **NISHIMURA.** *8684 Melrose Ave, West Hollywood (90069). Phone 310/659-4770; fax 310/659-4963.*This sushi restaurant looks like one of the trendy neighborhood houses in the chic design district. Through a Zen garden with burbling fountains, enter the simple white dining room, where master chefs carve up seafood behind a small sushi bar. Skip the sushi rolls and sample the sashimi specials, which are simply the finest, cleanest, tastiest cuts of fish—usu-ally thoughtfully garnished with a fleck of dried roe or a sliver of crispy garlic—the city has to offer. Shh, the cool crowd keeps it quiet about this amazing sushi find. Japanese menu. Lunch, dinner. Closed Sun;

holidays. Children's menu. Casual attire. Reservations recommended. Valet parking. **$$$**

★ **PAMPAS GRILL.** *6333 W Third St, Los Angeles (90036). Phone 323/931-1928; fax 323/937-9506.* There's always a line snaking out of this popular Brazilian churrascaria in the historic Farmers' Market. One look at the variety of meats spinning on swords over open flames and you'll see why. Grab a plate and a tray and pile up fried yucca and green salad before choosing from a variety of grilled sausages, chicken, and steak carved to order. Food cost is calculated by the pound— and then you're off to find a sunny spot to enjoy the feast. Brazilian menu. Lunch, dinner. Casual attire. Outdoor seating. No credit cards accepted. **$**

★ ★ ★ ★ **SONA.** *401 N La Cienega Blvd, West Hollywood (90048). Phone 310/659-7708; fax 310/360-7965. www.sonarestaurant.com.* This miraculous restaurant defies classification, dubbing its cuisine "seasonally spontaneous." But no matter; its discern-ing clientele have proclaimed it a world-class dining destination. In their spare eatery, adorned only with a 6-ton granite rock in the middle of the floor, chefs David and Michelle Meyers are creating a culinary stir. The fois gras terrine with apple butter is divine, as is the succulent duck breast. Don't miss the chocolate-banana brioche pudding for dessert. French menu. Dinner. Closed Sun-Mon. Bar. Business casual attire. Reservations recommended. Valet parking. **$$$$**

★ ★ ★ **TABLE 8.** *7661 Melrose Ave, Los Angeles (90046). Phone 323/782-8258; fax 323/782-8259. www.table8la.com.* You may not expect to find a chic restau-rant tucked under a Melrose tattoo parlor, but beyond the entrance, a honey-colored oasis with dark leather booths, curvy bars, tropical plants, and lots of flatter-ing light awaits. Market-fresh ingredients are creatively paired to form dishes like green bean salad with truffles, sweetbreads in torn pasta, and morsels of lamb done three ways. The polished clientele celebrates special occasions at linen-draped tables, while eye-catching cocktailers enjoy the bar menu featuring fondue, duck skewers, and pomegranate martinis. California menu. Dinner. Closed Sun; holidays. Bar. Business casual at-tire. Reservations recommended. **$$$**

★ **TOAST.** *8221 Third St, Los Angeles (90036). Phone 323/655-5018.* Movers, shakers, glamour girls, soccer moms, talent agents, and movie stars constantly pack this sceney breakfast and lunch spot. Although the in-terior is a lovely café with luscious desserts and fancy coffee drinks, the real action is outside on the sidewalk, where the beautiful clientele don shades, chat on cell phones, and feed scraps to their dogs. The vast menu includes decadent French toast with berries, chicken and avocado wraps, Southwest salads, turkey burgers, and just about any other simple dish one can imagine—done up with an LA twist. American menu. Breakfast, lunch. Casual attire. Outdoor seating. **$$**

Westwood and Westwood Village (LA) (J-4)

See also Los Angeles

Westwood is a cool college community in the midst of the big city—one place where walking in Los Angeles doesn't seem like a foolhardy notion. To the south of UCLA, Westwood Village is a casual campus within itself. The tree-lined streets have wide sidewalks and plenty of window shopping, so park the car and avoid confusing one-way streets.

This area caters to everything an undergrad would crave. Inexpensive and eclectic coffeehouses serve up a strong caffeine buzz, while cheap eats can be found from In n' Out Burger to a host of falafel stands and pizza parlors. This area has a dizzying number of movie theaters, each small and individual—a welcome change from multiplexes. The Hammer Museum provides some culture, as do the art galleries and theaters on the UCLA campus itself. Art lovers shouldn't miss the universitys stunning sculpture garden.

What to See and Do

Westwood Village Memorial Park. *1218 Glendon Ave, Los Angeles (90024). 1 block E of Westwood Blvd.* This is one place where you are sure to see a star or two. Located next to lively Westwood Village, this cemetery is one of the most famous resting places in the world. There is no charge to tour the beautifully groomed grounds, where you can pay your respects to the likes of Jack Lemmon, Walter Matthau, and the legendary Marilyn Monroe, who rests in a crypt on the north wall of the cemetery. **FREE**

Full-Service Hotel

★ ★ ★ **W LOS ANGELES WESTWOOD.** *930 Hilgard Ave, Los Angeles (90024). Phone 310/208-8765; toll-free 800/421-2317; fax 310/824-0355. www.whotels. com.* The in-crowd stays at the W Los Angeles Westwood. Synonymous with hip minimalism, this hotel rates high on the cool meter. The fashionable clientele frequents this place for its boutique-hotel ambience and its hotel chain amenities. From high-tech services in the rooms and suites to whatever/whenever attention from the courteous and professional staff, the W knows how to cosset the modern traveler. Hipsters stay fit at the hotel's SWEAT fitness center and leave the stress of the urban jungle behind at the AWAY spa. Whether lounging in the Living Room, sipping cocktails at Whiskey Blue, or savoring Latin fusion cuisine at Mojo, the scene here is positively sizzling. 257 rooms, 16 story. Pets accepted, some restrictions; fee. Check-in 3 pm, check-out noon. High-speed Internet access. Restaurant, bar. Fitness room, spa. Two outdoor pools. **$$**

Whittier (J-4)

See also Anaheim, Buena Park, La Habra, West Covina

Founded 1887
Population 83,680
Elevation 365 ft
Area Code 562
Information Chamber of Commerce, 8158 Painter Ave, 90602; phone 562/698-9554
Web Site www.whittierchamber.com

This Quaker-founded community was named for John Greenleaf Whittier, the Quaker poet. At the foot of the rolling Puente Hills, this residential city was once a citrus empire. It is the home of Whittier College.

What to See and Do

⭐ **Richard Nixon Library and Birthplace.** *18001 Yorba Linda Blvd, Yorba Linda (92886). Phone 714/993-5075. www.nixonlibrary.org.* Yes, the country's 37th president resigned in disgrace, but this 9-acre attraction still pays respect to the man and his presidential years, from 1969 to 1974. And, no, the Watergate scandal that forced him out of office isn't ignored. In the gallery devoted to the scandal, you can actually hear portions of the conversation Nixon had in which he first learns of John Dean's cover-up idea. Many other more positive exhibits fill the 52,000-square-foot main gallery. For example, the World Leaders section showcases priceless gifts the Nixons received from governments around the world. The Ambassador of Goodwill gallery focuses on First Lady Pat Nixon. And the Space exhibit heralds the role the President played in the country's space program. The complex also includes the farmhouse in which Nixon was born in 1913 and the memorial burial sites of both the President and his wife. (Mon-Sat 10 am-5 pm, Sun from 11 am; closed Thanksgiving, Dec 25) **$$**

Rose Hills Memorial Park and Morturary. *3888 S Workman Mill Rd, Whittier (90601). Phone 562/692-1212. www.rosehills.com.* Gardens and cemetery covering 2,500 acres. Pageant of Roses Garden has more than 7,000 rose bushes of over 600 varieties in bloom most of the year; Japanese gardens with a lake, arched bridge, and meditation house. (Daily sunrise-sunset) **FREE**

Full-Service Hotel

★ ★ ★ **RADISSON HOTEL WHITTIER.** *7320 Greenleaf Ave, Whittier (90602). Phone 562/945-8511; toll-free 800/333-3333; fax 562/945-6018. www.radisson.com.* 202 rooms, 8 story. Check-in 3 pm, check-out noon. Restaurant, bar. Fitness room. Outdoor pool, whirlpool. **$**

Woodland Hills (LA) (H-3)

Elevation 460 ft
Area Code 818
Web Site www.woodlandhillscc.net

This community, located in the San Fernando Valley, is a neighborhood of Los Angeles but is regarded by many as a separate entity.

Limited-Service Hotel

★ **COUNTRY INN & SUITES BY CARLSON CALABASAS.** *23627 Calabasas Rd, Calabasas (91302). Phone 818/222-5300; fax 818/591-0870. www.countryinns.com.* 122 rooms, 3 story. Complimentary continental breakfast. Check-in 3 pm, check-out noon. Fitness room. Outdoor pool, whirlpool. **$**

Full-Service Hotels

★ ★ ★ **HILTON WOODLAND HILLS & TOWERS.** *6360 Canoga Ave, Woodland Hills (91367). Phone 818/595-1000; toll-free 800/445-8667; fax 818/595-1090. www.hilton.com.* Located in suburban San Fernando Valley about 25 miles northwest of downtown Los Angeles, this property's proximity to the 101 Freeway, Warner Center, and attractions like The Getty Center, Universal Studios, and Six Flags California appeals to business and leisure travelers alike. The in-house Brasserie Restaurant specializes in California cuisine, and many restaurants, shops, and movie theaters are a short walk away. Welcome extras: free transportation within 3 miles and complimentary access to the adjacent L.A. Fitness Sports & Tennis Club. 325 rooms, 14 story. Check-in 3 pm, check-out noon. High-speed Internet access. Restaurant, bar. Fitness room. Outdoor pool, whirlpool. Business center. **$$**

★ ★ ★ **MARRIOTT WARNER CENTER WOODLAND HILLS.** *21850 Oxnard St, Woodland Hills (91367). Phone 818/887-4800; toll-free 800/228-9290; fax 818/340-5893. www.marriott.com.* This hotel is ideally located in the San Fernando Valley's Warner Center business park, adjacent to the 101 Freeway and within an easy drive of many of the Los Angeles area's major attractions. The on-site Parkside Bar and Grill, specializing in California cuisine, serves all day; other restaurants—as well as an array of shopping and entertainment options—are within walking distance. 476 rooms, 16 story. Pets accepted; fee. Check-in 4 pm, check-out noon. High-speed Internet access. Restaurant, bar. Fitness room. Indoor pool, outdoor pool, whirlpool. Business center. **$$**

Restaurant

★ ★ **LE SANGLIER FRENCH RESTAURANT.** *5522 Crebs, Tarzana (91356). Phone 818/345-0470.* French menu. Dinner. Closed Mon; holidays. Bar. Casual attire. Reservations recommended. **$$$**

Index

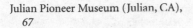

Chain Restaurants

California

Alameda

Chevy's, 2400 Mariner Sq, Alameda, CA, 94501, (510) 521-3768, 11 am-10 pm

Round Table Pizza, 2611 Blanding Ave, Alameda, CA, 94501, (510) 748-8600, 11:30 am-9 pm

Round Table Pizza, 901 Marina Village Pkwy, Alameda, CA, 94501, (510) 748-8600, 11:30 am-9 pm

Alhambra

Black Angus Steakhouse, 101 E Bay State St, Alhambra, CA, 91801, (626) 282-4100, 11 am-10 pm

Sizzler, 2201 W Commonwealth Ave, Alhambra, CA, 91801, (626) 570-9695, 11 am-10 pm

Tony Roma's, 68 W Main St, Alhambra, CA, 91801, (626) 300-6656, 11 am-10 pm

Aliso Viejo

Chili's, 26631 Aliso Creek Rd, Aliso Viejo, CA, 92656, (949) 448-9022, 11 am-10 pm

Romano's Macaroni Grill, 26641 Aliso Creek Rd, Aliso Viejo, CA, 92656, (949) 425-0180, 11 am-10 pm

Anaheim

Bakers Square, 2110 S Harbor Blvd, Anaheim, CA, 92802, (714) 750-2661, 7 am-11 pm

Benihana, 2100 E Ball Rd, Anaheim, CA, 92806, (714) 774-4940, 11:30 am-10 pm

Carrows, 915 S Harbor Blvd, Anaheim, CA, 92805, (714) 533-8630, 6 am-11 pm

Coco's Bakery, 1100 W Katella Ave, Anaheim, CA, 92802, (714) 772-0414, 6:30 am-10 pm

Hometown Buffet, Euclid Shopping Center, 1630 W Katella, Anaheim, CA, 92802, (714) 539-4664, 11 am-8:30 pm

Hooters, 2438 E Katella Ave, Anaheim, CA, 92806, (714) 634-9464, 11 am-midnight

Marie Callender's, 5711 E La Palma Ave, Anaheim, CA, 92807, (714) 779-0600, 11 am-10 pm

Marie Callender's, 540 N Euclid Ave, Anaheim, CA, 92801, (714) 774-1832, 11 am-10 pm

Sizzler, 888 S Brookhurst, Anaheim, CA, 92804, (714) 772-0010, 11 am-10 pm

Tony Roma's, 1640 S Harbor Blvd, Anaheim, CA, 92802, (714) 520-0200, 11 am-10 pm

Anaheim Hills

Chevy's, 8200 E Santa Ana Canyon Rd, Anaheim Hills, CA, 92808, (714) 974-6703, 11 am-10 pm

Coco's Bakery, 8188 E Santa Ana Canyon Rd, Anaheim Hills, CA, 92808, (714) 283-2394, 6:30 am-10 pm

Romano's Macaroni Grill, 8150 E Santa Ana Canyon Rd, Anaheim Hills, CA, 92808, (714) 637-6643, 11 am-10 pm

Arcadia

Coco's Bakery, 1150 W Colorado Blvd, Arcadia, CA, 91006, (626) 446-5611, 6:30 am-10 pm

Coco's Bakery, 1440 S Baldwin Ave, Arcadia, CA, 91006, (626) 447-4505, 6:30 am-10 pm

Dave and Buster's, 400 S Baldwin Ave, Ste 930-U, Arcadia, CA, (626) 802-6115, 11 am-midnight

Marie Callender's, 820 S Baldwin, Arcadia, CA, 91007, (626) 446-5229, 11 am-10 pm

Todai, 400 Baldwin Ave #L-440, Arcadia, CA, 91007, (626) 445-6155, 11:30 am-9 pm

Tony Roma's, 333 E Huntington Dr, Arcadia, CA, 91006, (626) 445-3595, 11 am-10 pm

Arroyo Grande

Round Table Pizza, 1412 Grand Ave, Arroyo Grande, CA, 93420, (805) 481-6996, 11:30 am-9 pm

Sizzler, 1170 W Branch, Arroyo Grande, CA, 93420, (805) 481-6404, 11 am-10 pm

Atascadero

Carrows, 7300 El Camino Real, Atascadero, CA, 93422, (805) 466-3861, 6 am-11 pm

Round Table Pizza, 7111 El Camino Real, Atascadero, CA, 93422, (805) 466-4030, 11:30 am-9 pm

Azusa

Marie Callender's, 1175 E Alosta Ave, Azusa, CA, 91702, (626) 963-9475, 11 am-10 pm

Sizzler, 900 E Alosta Ave, Azusa, CA, 91702, (626) 334-3443, 11 am-10 pm

Baker

Coco's Bakery, 72415 Baker Blvd, POBox 771, Baker, CA, 92309, (760) 733-4646, 6:30 am-10 pm

Bakersfield

Bakers Square, 3939 Ming Ave, Bakersfield, CA, 93309, (661) 832-9648, 7 am-11 pm

Black Angus Steakhouse, 3601 Rosedale Hwy, Bakersfield, CA, 93308, (661) 324-0814, 11 am-10 pm

Carrows, 2673 Mt Vernon Ave, Bakersfield, CA, 93306, (661) 872-3948, 6 am-11 pm

Carrows, 955 Oak St, Bakersfield, CA, 93304, (661) 322-8541, 6 am-11 pm

Carrows, 1300 Easton Dr, Bakersfield, CA, 93309, (661) 322-4644, 6 am-11 pm

Chili's, 8950 Rosedale Hwy, Bakersfield, CA, 93312, (661) 588-5872, 11 am-10 pm

Coco's Bakery, 7985 Rosedale Hwy, Bakersfield, CA, 93308, (661) 587-6487, 6:30 am-10 pm

Elephant Bar, 10100 Stockdale Hwy, Bakersfield, CA, (661) 663-3020, 11 amñ10 pm

Hometown Buffet, 4221 S H St, Bakersfield, CA, 93304, (661) 397-9363, 11 am-8:30 pm

Logan's Roadhouse, 3310 California Ave *, Bakersfield, CA, 93304, (661) 861-1830, 11 am-10 pm

Marie Callender's, 2631 Oswell St, Bakersfield, CA, 93306, (661) 872-1051, 11 am-10 pm

Marie Callender's, 3801 California Ave, Bakersfield, CA, 93309, (661) 327-0477, 11 am-10 pm

P.F. Changs, 10700 Stockdale Hwy, Bakersfield, CA, 93309, 11 am-10 pm

Romano's Macaroni Grill, 8850 Rosedale Hwy, Bakersfield, CA, 93312, (661) 588-2277, 11 am-10 pm

Sizzler, 3401 Chester Ave, Building A, Bakersfield, CA, 93301, (805) 322-2272, 11 am-10 pm

Sizzler, 2650 Mt Vernon Ave, Bakersfield, CA, 93306, (661) 871-9271, 11 am-10 pm

Sizzler, 900 Real Rd, Bakersfield, CA, 93309, (805) 325-2976, 11 am-10 pm

Baldwin Park

Sizzler, 14635-A Baldwin Park Towne Center, Baldwin Park, CA, 91706, (626) 472-6250, 11 am-10 pm

Banning

Carrows, 2034 W Ramsey St, Banning, CA, 92220, (951) 849-1450, 6 am-11 pm

Sizzler, 1750 W Ramsey, Banning, CA, 92220, (909) 849-6074, 11 am-10 pm

Barstow

Coco's Bakery, 1311 E Main St, Barstow, CA, 92311, (760) 256-8992, 6:30 am-10 pm

Sizzler, 1523 E Main St, Barstow, CA, 92311, (760) 256-2525, 11 am-10 pm

Carrows, 1200 E Main St, Barstow, CA, 92311, (760) 256-0415, 6 am-11 pm

Big Boy, 2860 Lenwood Rd, Barstow, CA, 92311, (760) 253-5107, 6:30 am-10 pm

Bell

Sizzler, 4941 E Florence Ave, Bell, CA, 90201, (323) 560-0218, 11 am-10 pm

Hometown Buffet, Bell Palm Pl, 6257 N Atlantic Av, Bell, CA, 90201, (323) 771-9091, 11 am-8:30 pm

Bellflower

Round Table Pizza, 15730 Bellflower Blvd, Bellflower, CA, 90706, (562) 866-7579, 11:30 am-9 pm

Sizzler, 10153 Artesia, Bellflower, CA, 90706, (562) 925-2582, 11 am-10 pm

Beverly Hills

Benihana, 38 N La Cienega Blvd, Beverly Hills, CA, 90211, (323) 655-7311, 11:30 am-10 pm

Cheesecake Factory, 364 N Beverly Dr, Beverly Hills, CA, 90210, (310) 278-7270, 11 am-11 pm

Big Bear Lake

Sizzler, 42137 Big Bear Blvd, PO Box 1552, Big Bear Lake, CA, 92315, (909) 866-1055, 11 am-10 pm

Blythe

Sizzler, 1101 W Hobson Way, Blythe, CA, 92225, (760) 922-3808, 11 am-10 pm

Brea

Cheesecake Factory, 120 Brea Mall Way, Brea, CA, 92821, (714) 255-0115, 11 am-11:30 pm

Yard House, 160 S Brea Blvd, Brea, CA, 92821, (714) 529-9273, 11 am-midnight

Round Table Pizza, 732 N Brea Blvd, Brea, CA, 92821, (714) 671-2821, 11:30 am-9 pm

Coco's Bakery, 1250 Imperial Hwy, Brea, CA, 92821, (714) 990-0671, 6:30 am-10 pm

Claim Jumper, 190 S State College Blvd, Brea, CA, (714) 529-9061, 11 am-10 pm

Brentwood

Round Table Pizza, 41 W Sand Creek Rd, Brentwood, CA, 94513, (925) 634-1700, 11:30 am-9 pm

Round Table Pizza, 2540 Sand Creek Rd, Brentwood, CA, 94513, (925) 240-8778, 11:30 am-9 pm

Buellton

Bakers Square, 321 McMurray Rd, Buellton, CA, 93427, (805) 688-3513, 7 am-11 pm

Buena Park

Black Angus Steakhouse, 7111 Beach Blvd, Buena Park, CA, 90620, (714) 670-2012, 11 am-10 pm

Carrows, 8650 Beach Blvd, Buena Park, CA, 90620, (714) 826-4280, 6 am-11 pm

Chili's, 8376 La Palma Ave, Buena Park, CA, 90620, (714) 252-9050, 11 am-10 pm

Claim Jumper, 7971 Beach Blvd, Buena Park, CA, (714) 523-3227, 11 am-10 pm

Fuddruckers, 7802 Orange Thorpe Ave, Buena Park, CA, 90621, 11 am-9 pm

Hometown Buffet, Lincoln Town Center, 8958 Knott Ave, Buena Park, CA, 90620, (714) 827-6116, 11 am-8:30 pm

Marie Callender's, 5960 Orangethorpe, Buena Park, CA, 90620, (714) 522-0170, 11 am-10 pm

Sizzler, 7902 Orangethorpe St, Buena Park, CA, 90260, (714) 521-8261, 11 am-10 pm

Burbank

Big Boy, 4211 Riverside Dr, Burbank, CA, 91505, (818) 843-9334, 6:30 am-10 pm

Black Angus Steakhouse, 235 S First St, Burbank, CA, 91502, (818) 848-8880, 11 am-10 pm

Chevy's, 701 N San Fernando Blvd, Burbank, CA, 91502, (818) 846-6999, 11 am-10 pm

Elephant Bar, 110 N First St, Burbank, CA, (818) 842-1334, 11 amñ10 pm

Fuddruckers, 221 N San Fernando Rd, Burbank, CA, 91501, 11 am-9 pm

Hometown Buffet, 1850 Empire Ave, Burbank, CA, 91504, (818) 955-5797, 11 am-8:30 pm

Hooters, 600 N 1st St, Burbank, CA, 92501, (818) 848-9464, 11 am-midnight

P.F. Changs, 201 E Magnolia Blvd, Burbank Town Center, Burbank, CA, 91502, (818) 391-1070, 11 am-10 pm

Romano's Macaroni Grill, 102 E Magnolia Blvd, Burbank, CA, 91502, (818) 729-9405, 11 am-10 pm

Round Table Pizza, 2408 W Victory Blvd, Burbank, CA, 91506, (818) 845-7613, 11:30 am-9 pm

Round Table Pizza, 321 E Alameda Ave, Ste A, Burbank, CA, 91502, (818) 842-9888, 11:30 am-9 pm

Sizzler, 1145 Hollywood Way, Burbank, CA, 91505, (818) 843-0281, 11 am-10 pm

Cabazon

Coco's Bakery, 49000 Seminole Dr, Cabazon, CA, 92230, (951) 922-3495, 6:30 am-10 pm

Calabasas

Coco's Bakery, 4895 N Las Virgenes Dr, Calabasas, CA, 91302, (818) 880-4085, 6:30 am-10 pm

Calexico

Carrows, 118 E Cole Rd, Calexico, CA, 92231, (760) 357-7811, 6 am-11 pm

Hometown Buffet, 222 Cole Rd, Calexico, CA, 92231, (760) 768-1440, 11 am-8:30 pm

Calimesa

Big Boy, 540 Sandalwood Dr, Calimesa, CA, 92323, (909) 446-8822, 6:30 am-10 pm

Camarillo

Tony Roma's, 1901 Daily Dr, Camarillo, CA, 93010, (805) 987-4939, 11 am-10 pm

Carrows, 301 E Daily Dr, Camarillo, CA, 93010, (805) 482-5176, 6 am-11 pm

Coco's Bakery, 259 W Ventura Blvd, Camarillo, CA, 93010, (805) 987-3534, 6:30 am-10 pm

Marie Callender's, 185 E Daily Dr, Camarillo, CA, 93010, (805) 987-5580, 11 am-10 pm

Round Table Pizza, 880 Arneill Rd, Camarillo, CA, 93010, (805) 484-8900, 11:30 am-9 pm

Sizzler, 1755 Daily Dr, Camarillo, CA, 93010, (805) 987-7995, 11 am-10 pm

Canoga Park

Coco's Bakery, 22200 Sherman Way, Canoga Park, CA, 91303, (818) 710-8081, 6:30 am-10 pm

Hometown Buffet, 6705 N Fallbrook Ave, Canoga Park, CA, 91307, (818) 713-1776, 11 am-8:30 pm

Canyon Country

Coco's Bakery, 16526 Soledad Canyon, Canyon Country, CA, 91351, (661) 251-7725, 6:30 am-10 pm

Round Table Pizza, 16612 Soledad Canyon Rd, Canyon Country, CA, 91387, (661) 252-8000, 11:30 am-9 pm

Carlsbad

Benihana, 755 Raintree Dr, Carlsbad, CA, 92009, (760) 929-8311, 11:30 am-10 pm

Marie Callender's, 5980 Avenida Encinas, Carlsbad, CA, 92008, (760) 438-3929, 11 am-10 pm

Claim Jumper, 5958 Avenida Encinas, Carlsbad, CA, (760) 431-0889, 11 am-10 pm

Carmel Mtn Rranch

Claim Jumper, 12384 Carmel Mountain Rd, Carmel Mtn Rranch, CA, (858) 485-8370, 11 am-10 pm

Carson

Chili's, 20760 S Avalon Blvd, Carson, CA, 90746, 11 am-10 pm

Sizzler, 20755 S Avalon Blvd, Carson, CA, 90746, (310) 532-5697, 11 am-10 pm

Tony Roma's, 20720 S Avalon Blvd, Carson, CA, 90746, (310) 329-5723, 11 am-10 pm

Cathedral City

Round Table Pizza, 31775 Date Palm Dr, Cathedral City, CA, 92234, (760) 321-1756, 11:30 am-9 pm

Sizzler, 31875 Date Palm Dr, Cathedral City, CA, 92234, (760) 202-6622, 11 am-10 pm

Ceres

Round Table Pizza, 1515 Mitchell Rd, Ceres, CA, 95307, (209) 541-1177, 11:30 am-9 pm

Cerritos

Black Angus Steakhouse, 11255 183rd St, Cerritos, CA, 90701, (562) 860-2582, 11 am-10 pm

Carrows, 19011 Bloomfield Ave, Cerritos, CA, 90703, (562) 865-1316, 6 am-11 pm

Coco's Bakery, 11510 E S St, Cerritos, CA, 90701, (562) 924-9487, 6:30 am-10 pm

Hometown Buffet, 11471 S St, Cerritos, CA, 90703, (562) 402-8307, 11 am-8:30 pm

Romano's Macaroni Grill, 12875 Towne Center Dr, Cerritos, CA, 90703, (562) 916-7722, 11 am-10 pm

Chatsworth

Carrows, 20557 Devonshire St, Chatsworth, CA, 91311, (818) 998-7423, 6 am-11 pm

Chino

Black Angus Steakhouse, 3968 Grand Ave, Chino, CA, 91710, (909) 627-7700, 11 am-10 pm

Carrows, 12325 Mountain Ave, Chino, CA, 91710, (909) 627-0271, 6 am-11 pm

Hometown Buffet, 3920 Grand Ave, Chino, CA, 91710, (909) 590-3377, 11 am-8:30 pm

Marie Callender's, 5455-A Philadelphia, Chino, CA, 91710, (909) 613-0434, 11 am-10 pm

Round Table Pizza, 12881 Mountain Ave, Chino, CA, 91710, (909) 591-9984, 11:30 am-9 pm

Chino Hills

Chili's, 3670 Grand Ave, Chino Hills, CA, 91709, (909) 364-9098, 11 am-10 pm

Round Table Pizza, 2545 Chino Hills Pkwy, Chino Hills, CA, 91709, (909) 597-6174, 11:30 am-9 pm

Chula Vista

Black Angus Steakhouse, 707 E St, Chula Vista, CA, 91910, (619) 426-9200, 11 am-10 pm

Carrows, 598 H St, Chula Vista, CA, 91910, (619) 426-1849, 6 am-11 pm

Chili's, 800 Paseo Del Rey, Chula Vista, CA, 91910, (619) 656-2910, 11 am-10 pm

Fuddruckers, 340 3rd Ave, Chula Vista, CA, 91910, 11 am-9 pm

Godfather's Pizza, 1187 BRdway, Chula Vista, CA, 91911, (619) 425-6760

Hometown Buffet, Hometown Square, 651 Palomar St, Chula Vista, CA, 91911, (619) 426-0505, 11 am-8:30 pm

Marie Callender's, 330 F St, Chula Vista, CA, 91910, (619) 420-0751, 11 am-10 pm

P.F. Changs, 2015 Birch Rd, Chula Vista, CA, 91915, 11 am-10 pm

Uno Chicago Grill, 555 BRdway, St 1076, Chula Vista, CA, 91910, (619) 420-8660, 11 am-12:30 am

City of Industry

Benihana, 17877 Gale Ave, City of Industry, CA, 91748, (626) 912-8784, 11:30 am-10 pm

Black Angus Steakhouse, 17615 Castleton St, City of Industry, CA, 91748, (626) 965-3488, 11 am-10 pm

Chili's, 17588 Castleton, City of Industry, CA, 91748, (626) 581-4769, 11 am-10 pm

Claim Jumper, 18061 Gale Ave, City of Industry, CA, (626) 964-1157, 11 am-10 pm

Hometown Buffet, Puente Hills E Commercial Center, 17500 Castleton St, City of Industry, CA, 91748, (626) 964-6393, 11 am-8:30 pm

Marie Callender's, 1560 Albatross Rd, City of Industry, CA, 91748, (626) 964-1094, 11 am-10 pm

Romano's Macaroni Grill, 17603 Colima Rd E, City of Industry, CA, 91748, (626) 581-8051, 11 am-10 pm

Todai, 1600 S Azusa Ave, #370, City of Industry, CA, 91748, (626) 913-8530, 11:30 am-9 pm

Claremont

Marie Callender's, 1030 W Foothill, Claremont, CA, 91711, (909) 621-3985, 11 am-10 pm

Round Table Pizza, 598 E Baseline Rd, Claremont, CA, 91711, (909) 621-6913, 11:30 am-9 pm

Round Table Pizza, 408 W Auto Center Dr, Claremont, CA, 91711, (909) 625-3856, 11:30 am-9 pm

Bakers Square, 710 S Indian Hill Blvd, Claremont, CA, 91711, (909) 621-4745, 7 am-11 pm

Colusa

Round Table Pizza, 1031 Bridge St, Colusa, CA, 95932, (530) 458-8151, 11:30 am-9 pm

Compton

Coco's Bakery, 1918 W Artesia, Compton, CA, 90220, (310) 639-8703, 6:30 am-10 pm

Corning

Round Table Pizza, 680 Edith Ave, Corning, CA, 96021, (530) 824-2134, 11:30 am-9 pm

Corona

Carrows, 493 N Main St, Corona, CA, 91720, (951) 734-5022, 6 am-11 pm

Chili's, 3579 Grand Oaks, Corona, CA, 92881, (951) 734-7275, 11 am-10 pm

Claim Jumper, 380 McKinley St, Corona, CA, (951) 735-6567, 11 am-10 pm

Coco's Bakery, 1300 El Sobrante Rd, Corona, CA, 92879, (951) 371-3300, 6:30 am-10 pm

Coco's Bakery, 4714 Green River Dr, Corona, CA, 92880, (951) 734-0981, 6:30 am-10 pm

Hometown Buffet, 390 Mckinley Ave, Corona, CA, 92879, (951) 273-0573, 11 am-8:30 pm

Marie Callender's, 160 E Rincon St, Corona, CA, 92879, (951) 735-4310, 11 am-10 pm

RA Sushi, 2785 Cabot Dr, Ste 101, Corona, CA, 92883

Romano's Macaroni Grill, 3591 Grand Oaks, Corona, CA, 92881, (951) 278-0999, 11 am-10 pm

Round Table Pizza, 2771 Green River Rd, #105, Corona, CA, 92882, (951) 736-4094, 11:30 am-9 pm

Round Table Pizza, 813 N Main St, Corona, CA, 91720, (951) 371-4841, 11:30 am-9 pm

Sizzler, 1461 S Rimpau, Corona, CA, 91719, (951) 272-8255, 11 am-10 pm

Corona del Mar

Coco's Bakery, 3446 E Coast Hwy, Corona del Mar, CA, 92625, (949) 673-7154, 6:30 am-10 pm

Coronado

Marie Callender's, 1300 Orange Ave, Coronado, CA, 92118, (619) 435-1798, 11 am-10 pm

Costa Mesa

Claim Jumper, 3333 Bristol St, Costa Mesa, CA, (714) 434-8479, 11 am-10 pm

Coco's Bakery, 2750 Harbor Blvd, Costa Mesa, CA, 92626, (714) 549-1289, 6:30 am-10 pm

Hooters, 1507 S Coast Dr, Costa Mesa, CA, 92626, (714) 427-0755, 11 am-midnight

Maggiano's, 3333 Bristol St, Costa Mesa, CA, 92626, (714) 546-9550, 11 am-10 pm

Marie Callender's, 353 E 17th St, Costa Mesa, CA, 92627, (949) 642-0822, 11 am-10 pm

Romano's Macaroni Grill, 595 Anton Blvd, Costa Mesa, CA, 92626, (714) 825-0345, 11 am-10 pm

Round Table Pizza, 1175 Baker St, Ste A, Costa Mesa, CA, 92626, (714) 549-2101, 11:30 am-9 pm

Round Table Pizza, 204 E 17th St, Ste 102, Costa Mesa, CA, 92627, (949) 722-8888, 11:30 am-9 pm

Yard House, 1875 Newport Blvd, Costa Mesa, CA, 92627, (949) 642-0090, 11 am-midnight

Ztejas Southwestern Grill, 3333 Bristol St #1876, Costa Mesa, CA, 92626, (714) 979-7469, 11 am-10 pm

Covina

Coco's Bakery, 306 N Azusa, Covina, CA, 91722, (626) 331-0955, 6:30 am-10 pm

Hometown Buffet, Covina Town Square, 1318 N Azusa Ave, Covina, CA, 91722, (626) 915-6066, 11 am-8:30 pm

Sizzler, 900 N Citrus, Covina, CA, 91722, (626) 967-2023, 11 am-10 pm

Crestline

Round Table Pizza, 565 Forest Shade Rd, Crestline, CA, 92325, (909) 338-5040, 11:30 am-9 pm

Culver City

Sizzler, 5801 Sepulveda Blvd, Culver City, CA, 90230, (310) 398-6111, 11 am-10 pm

Coco's Bakery, 5350 Sepulveda Blvd, Culver City, CA, 90230, (310) 397-7165, 6:30 am-10 pm

Cypress

Chili's, 10643 Valley View, Cypress, CA, 90630, (714) 229-0478, 11 am-10 pm

Round Table Pizza, 10101 Valley View St, Cypress, CA, 90630, (714) 995-2422, 11:30 am-9 pm

Dana Point

Round Table Pizza, 32525 B Golden Lantern, Dana Point, CA, 92629, (949) 496-9800, 11:30 am-9 pm

Del Mar

Chevy's, 2730 Via De La Valle, Del Mar, CA, 92014, (858) 793-8893, 11 am-10 pm

Tony Roma's, 2710 Via de la Valle, Del Mar, CA, 92014, (858) 794-7662, 11 am-10 pm

Diamond Bar

Big Boy, 21090 Golden Springs Dr, Diamond Bar, CA, 91789, (909) 595-9170, 6:30 am-10 pm

Coco's Bakery, 20955 Golden Springs Dr, Diamond Bar, CA, 91765, (909) 595-9811, 6:30 am-10 pm

Round Table Pizza, 1220 S Diamond Bar Blvd, Diamond Bar, CA, 91765, (909) 861-9432, 11:30 am-9 pm

Sizzler, 23525 E Palomino Dr, Diamond Bar, CA, 91765, (909) 861-2382, 11 am-10 pm

Downey

Bakers Square, 7954 Imperial Hwy, Downey, CA, 90242, (562) 923-4213, 7 am-11 pm

Carrows, 7900 Florence Ave, Downey, CA, 90240, (562) 927-6713, 6 am-11 pm

Chili's, 12030 Lakewood Blvd, Downey, CA, 90242, (562) 803-9151, 11 am-10 pm

Elephant Bar, 12002 Lakewood Blvd, Downey, CA, (562) 803-9910, 11 amñ10 pm

Hometown Buffet, 8432 Firestone Blvd, Downey, CA, 90241, (562) 861-5067, 11 am-8:30 pm

Marie Callender's, 7860 E Florence Ave, Downey, CA, 90240, (562) 927-3327, 11 am-10 pm

Sizzler, 10315 Lakewood Blvd, Downey, CA, 90241, (562) 861-8612, 11 am-10 pm

Eagle Rock

Sizzler, 2516 Colorado Blvd, Eagle Rock, CA, 90041, (323) 256-0255, 11 am-10 pm

East Anaheim

Hometown Buffet, East Anaheim Center, 2190 E Lincoln, East Anaheim, CA, 92806, (714) 774-6899, 11 am-8:30 pm

El Cajon

Black Angus Steakhouse, 1000 Graves Ave, El Cajon, CA, 92021, (619) 440-5055, 11 am-10 pm

Coco's Bakery, 1025 Fletcher Pkwy, El Cajon, CA, 92020, (619) 442-9271, 6:30 am-10 pm

Coco's Bakery, 1324 E Main St, El Cajon, CA, 92021, (619) 447-6852, 6:30 am-10 pm

Hometown Buffet, 390 W Main St, El Cajon, CA, 92020, (619) 441-6477, 11 am-8:30 pm

Round Table Pizza, 2650 Jamacha Rd, #143, El Cajon, CA, 92019, (619) 670-1808, 11:30 am-9 pm

Sizzler, 1030 Fletcher Park, El Cajon, CA, 92020, (619) 596-1695, 11 am-10 pm

El Centro

Sizzler, 707 N Imperial Hwy, El Centro, CA, 92243, (760) 353-3780, 11 am-10 pm

Carrows, 1002 N Imperial Ave, El Centro, CA, 92243, (760) 353-8206, 6 am-11 pm

Chili's, 3303 S Dogwood Rd, El Centro, CA, 92243, (760) 352-2116, 11 am-10 pm

Golden Corral, 2018 N Imperial Ave, El Centro, CA, 92243, (760) 336-0009, 11 am-9 pm

El Monte

Hometown Buffet, 3608 N Peck Rd, El Monte, CA, 91731, (626) 442-1422, 11 am-8:30 pm

El Segundo

Cozymel's Mexican Grill, 2171 Rosecrans Ave, El Segundo, CA, 90245, (310) 606-5505, 11 am-10 pm

P.F. Changs, 2041 Rosecrans Ave, El Segundo, CA, 90245, (310) 607-9062, 11 am-10 pm

Romano's Macaroni Grill, 2321 Rosecrans Ave, El Segundo, CA, 90245, (310) 643-0812, 11 am-10 pm

Sizzler, 600 N Sepulveda Blvd, El Segundo, CA, 90245, (310) 322-2532, 11 am-10 pm

El Toro

Bakers Square, 23515 El Toro Rd, El Toro, CA, 92630, (949) 770-8131, 7 am-11 pm

Elk Grove

Chevy's, 7401 Laguna Blvd #100, Elk Grove, CA, 95758, (916) 691-3400, 11 am-10 pm

Chili's, 7410 Laguna Blvd, Elk Grove, CA, 95758, (916) 478-2478, 11 am-10 pm

Hometown Buffet, 9089 Bruceville Rd, Elk Grove, CA, 95758, (916) 684-2771, 11 am-8:30 pm

Logan's Roadhouse, 9105 W Stockton Blvd *, Elk Grove, CA, 95758, (916) 684-8978, 11 am-10 pm

Marie Callender's, 9134 E Stockton Blvd, Elk Grove, CA, 95624, (916) 686-4589, 11 am-10 pm

Romano's Macaroni Grill, 8295 Laguna Blvd, Elk Grove, CA, 95758, (916) 478-2878, 11 am-10 pm

Round Table Pizza, 10054 Bruceville Rd, Elk Grove, CA, 95758, (916) 686-4009, 11:30 am-9 pm

Round Table Pizza, 5110 Laguna Blvd, #119, Elk Grove, CA, 95758, (916) 684-6200, 11:30 am-9 pm

Round Table Pizza, 8795 Elk Grove Blvd, Elk Grove, CA, 95624, (916) 685-2190, 11:30 am-9 pm

Round Table Pizza, 9117 E Stockton Blvd #150, Elk Grove, CA, 95624, (916) 714-5101, 11:30 am-9 pm

Encinitas

Chili's, 1004 N El Camino Real, Encinitas, CA, 92024, (760) 634-5488, 11 am-10 pm

Coco's Bakery, 407 Encinitas Blvd, Encinitas, CA, 92024, (760) 436-6023, 6:30 am-10 pm

Marie Callender's, 162 S Rancho Santa Fe Rd, Encinitas, CA, 92024, (760) 632-0204, 11 am-10 pm

Round Table Pizza, 1321 Encinitas Blvd, Encinitas, CA, 92024, (760) 753-8303, 11:30 am-9 pm

Encino

Benihana, 16226 Ventura Blvd, Encino, CA, 91436, (818) 788-7121, 11:30 am-10 pm

Chevy's, 16705 Ventura Blvd, Encino, CA, 91436, (818) 385-1905, 11 am-10 pm

Chili's, 17240 Ventura Blvd, Encino, CA, 91316, (818) 906-8469, 11 am-10 pm

Tony Roma's, 16575 Ventura Blvd, Encino, CA, 91436, (818) 461-8400, 11 am-10 pm

Escondido

Carrows, 510 W Valley Pkwy, Escondido, CA, 92025, (760) 738-9583, 6 am-11 pm

Chili's, 1105 W Valley Pkwy, Escondido, CA, 92025, (760) 737-5101, 11 am-10 pm

Coco's Bakery, 1280 W Valley Pkwy, Escondido, CA, 92029, (760) 745-2513, 6:30 am-10 pm

Marie Callender's, 515 W 13th Ave, Escondido, CA, 92025, (760) 741-3636, 11 am-10 pm

Romano's Macaroni Grill, 202 E Via Rancho Pkwy, Escondido, CA, 92025, (760) 741-6309, 11 am-10 pm

Round Table Pizza, 1161 E Washington Ave, Escondido, CA, 92025, (760) 489-0191, 11:30 am-9 pm

Round Table Pizza, 555 W Country Club Ln, #J, Escondido, CA, 92026, (760) 489-0955, 11:30 am-9 pm

Sizzler, 355 N Escondido Blvd, Escondido, CA, 92025, (760) 741-2568, 11 am-10 pm

Uno Chicago Grill, 890 W Valley Pkwy, St 450, Escondido, CA, 92025, (760) 480-8667, 11 am-12:30 am

Fontana

Chili's, 15252 Summit Ave, Fontana, CA, 92336, (909) 646-7779, 11 am-10 pm

Logan's Roadhouse, 13840 Baseline Ave *, Fontana, CA, 92335, (909) 463-2290, 11 am-10 pm

Round Table Pizza, 11617 Cherry Ave, Ste 2, Fontana, CA, 92337, (909) 357-3050, 11:30 am-9 pm

Round Table Pizza, 15002 Summit Ave, Fontana, CA, 92336, (909) 463-6500, 11:30 am-9 pm

Sizzler, 9860 Sierra Ave, Fontana, CA, 92335, (909) 829-4755, 11 am-10 pm

Foothill Ranch

Chili's, 26782 Portola Pkwy, Foothill Ranch, CA, 92610, (949) 830-6353, 11 am-10 pm

Fountain Valley

Black Angus Steakhouse, 17920 Brookhurst, Fountain Valley, CA, 92708, (714) 968-4477, 11 am-10 pm

Claim Jumper, 18050 Brookhurst St, Fountain Valley, CA, (714) 963-6711, 11 am-10 pm

Coco's Bakery, 18380 Brookhurst St, Fountain Valley, CA, 92708, (714) 962-5509, 6:30 am-10 pm

Marie Callender's, 18889 Brookhurst St, Fountain Valley, CA, 92708, (714) 963-6791, 11 am-10 pm

Round Table Pizza, 11095 Warner Ave, Fountain Valley, CA, 92708, (714) 839-0276, 11:30 am-9 pm

Sizzler, 16275 Harbor Blvd, Fountain Valley, CA, 92708, (714) 775-0974, 11 am-10 pm

Sizzler, 9480 Warner Ave, Fountain Valley, CA, 92708, (714) 962-4882, 11 am-10 pm

Fullerton

Black Angus Steakhouse, 205 E Imperial Hwy, Fullerton, CA, 92835, (714) 773-5101, 11 am-10 pm

Carrows, 1011 N Harbor Blvd, Fullerton, CA, 92832, (714) 992-1490, 6 am-11 pm

Round Table Pizza, 2506 E Chapman Ave, Fullerton, CA, 92831, (714) 871-4481, 11:30 am-9 pm

Round Table Pizza, CSU Fullerton - Pub, Fullerton, CA, 92631, (714) 278-7377, 11:30 am-9 pm

Sizzler, 2980 Yorba Linda Blvd, Fullerton, CA, 92831, (714) 993-6390, 11 am-10 pm

Sizzler, 1401 N Harbor Blvd, Fullerton, CA, 92635, (714) 738-5018, 11 am-10 pm

Tony Roma's, 1300 S Harbor Blvd, Fullerton, CA, 92832, (714) 871-4000, 11 am-10 pm

Garden Grove

Coco's Bakery, 12582 Valley View, Garden Grove, CA, 92845, (714) 898-9719, 6:30 am-10 pm

Coco's Bakery, 12032 Harbor Blvd, Garden Grove, CA, 92840, (714) 750-7477, 6:30 am-10 pm

Hometown Buffet, Garden Promenade Shopping Center, 9635 Chapman Ave, Garden Grove, CA, 92841, (714) 636-7550, 11 am-8:30 pm

Marie Callender's, 13252 Brookhurst St, Garden Grove, CA, 92843, (714) 537-0801, 11 am-10 pm

Round Table Pizza, 12829 Harbor Blvd, Garden Grove, CA, 92840, (714) 539-1934, 11:30 am-9 pm

Sizzler, 13265 Harbor Blvd, Garden Grove, CA, 92643, (714) 534-1234, 11 am-10 pm

Gardena

Carrows, 1638 W Redondo Beach, Gardena, CA, 90247, (310) 516-0495, 6 am-11 pm

Hometown Buffet, 1230-38 W Redondo Beach Blvd, Gardena, CA, 90247, (310) 515-5664, 11 am-8:30 pm

Marie Callender's, 15466 S Western Ave, Gardena, CA, 90249, (310) 516-9595, 11 am-10 pm

Sizzler, 15926 S Wern Ave, Gardena, CA, 90247, (310) 324-3544, 11 am-10 pm

Glendale

Big Boy, 1407 W Glenoaks Blvd, Glendale, CA, 91201, (818) 240-8130, 6:30 am-10 pm

Chevy's, 101 N Brand, Glendale, CA, 91203, (818) 291-9555, 11 am-10 pm

Marie Callender's, 707 N Pacific Ave, Glendale, CA, 91203, (818) 242-6836, 11 am-10 pm

Todai, 50 W BRdway, Glendale, CA, 91204, (818) 247-8499, 11:30 am-9 pm

Tony Roma's, 126 N Maryland, Glendale, CA, 91206, (818) 244-7427, 11 am-10 pm

Glendora

Coco's Bakery, 1317 S Lone Hill Ave, Glendora, CA, 91740, (909) 394-2025, 6:30 am-10 pm

Round Table Pizza, 407 W Foothill Blvd, Glendora, CA, 91741, (626) 963-5997, 11:30 am-9 pm

Round Table Pizza, 403 E Arrow Hwy, Glendora, CA, 91740, (626) 963-8576, 11:30 am-9 pm

Goleta

Sizzler, 5555 Hollister Ave, Goleta, CA, 93420, (805) 964-6769, 11 am-10 pm

Chili's, 6950 Market Pl Dr, Goleta, CA, 93117, (805) 968-8585, 11 am-10 pm

Gorman

Sizzler, 49713 Gorman Post Rd, Gorman, CA, 93243, (661) 248-3501, 11 am-10 pm

Granada Hills

Bakers Square, 17921 Chatsworth St, Granada Hills, CA, 91344, (818) 366-7258, 7 am-11 pm

Hacienda Heights

Round Table Pizza, 17170 Colima Rd, #H, Hacienda Heights, CA, 91745, (626) 965-8107, 11:30 am-9 pm

Hawthorne

Chili's, 2100 W Florida Ave, Hemet, CA, 92545, (951) 652-2777, 11 am-10 pm

Coco's Bakery, 3246 W Florida Ave, Hemet, CA, 92545, (951) 925-3040, 6:30 am-10 pm

Hometown Buffet, 12139 S Hawthorne Blvd, Hawthorne, CA, 90250, (310) 679-1373, 11 am-8:30 pm

Hometown Buffet, Village W Shopping Center, 3041 W Florida Ave, Hemet, CA, 92545, (951) 652-0282, 11 am-8:30 pm

Marie Callender's, 3969 W Florida Ave, Hemet, CA, 92545, (951) 925-7727, 11 am-10 pm

Sizzler, 1023 E Florida, Hemet, CA, 92543, (909) 658-2428, 11 am-10 pm

Hermosa Beach

Round Table Pizza, 2701 Pacific Coast Hwy, Hermosa Beach, CA, 90254, (310) 379-9277, 11:30 am-9 pm

Hesperia

Sizzler, 16988 E Main, Hesperia, CA, 92345, (760) 949-5505, 11 am-10 pm

Carrows, 17398 Main St, Hesperia, CA, 92345, (760) 948-1285, 6 am-11 pm

Big Boy, 12728 W Main, Hesperia, CA, 92345, (760) 947-2330, 6:30 am-10 pm

Highland

Coco's Bakery, 2442 Highland Ave, Highland, CA, 92346, (909) 862-8074, 6:30 am-10 pm

Highland Park

Carrows, 6040 York Blvd, Highland Park, CA, 90042, (323) 256-0563, 6 am-11 pm

Hollister

Round Table Pizza, 496 Tres Pinos, Hollister, CA, 95023, (831) 637-7444, 11:30 am-9 pm

Hollywood

Hooters, 6922 Hollywood Blvd, Hollywood, CA, 90028, (323) 962-3373, 11 am-midnight

Sizzler, 5310 Hollywood Blvd, Hollywood, CA, 90027, (323) 469-2657, 11 am-10 pm

Sizzler, 1323 N Highland Ave, Hollywood, CA, 90028, (323) 467-2353, 11 am-10 pm

Huntington Beach

Carrows, 16931 Magnolia Ave, Huntington Beach, CA, 92647, (714) 848-1995, 6 am-11 pm

Cheesecake Factory, 7871 Edinger Ave, Huntington Beach, CA, 92647, (714) 889-1500, 11 am-11 pm

Chili's, 17071 Beach Blvd, Huntington Beach, CA, 92647, (714) 841-6545, 11 am-10 pm

Coco's Bakery, 7311 W Edinger, Huntington Beach, CA, 92647, (714) 894-7940, 6:30 am-10 pm

Coco's Bakery, 6886 Bolsa Ave, Huntington Beach, CA, 92647, (714) 893-7020, 6:30 am-10 pm

Romano's Macaroni Grill, 7901 Edinger Ave, Huntington Beach, CA, 92647, (714) 901-4481, 11 am-10 pm

Round Table Pizza, 19750 Beach Blvd, Huntington Beach, CA, 92648, (714) 963-9877, 11:30 am-9 pm

Sizzler, 16122 Goldenwest Blvd, Huntington Beach, CA, 92647, (714) 848-2425, 11 am-10 pm

Huntington Park

Sizzler, 2111 E Florence Ave, Huntington Park, CA, 90255, (323) 583-8806, 11 am-10 pm

Indio

Round Table Pizza, 81637 Hwy 111, Indio, CA, 92201, (760) 347-6966, 11:30 am-9 pm

Sizzler, 81-760 Hwy 111, Indio, CA, 92201, (760) 347-6116, 11 am-10 pm

Inglewood

Chili's, 3490 W Century Blvd, Inglewood, CA, 90303, (310) 674-2505, 11 am-10 pm

Sizzler, 831 E Manchester, Inglewood, CA, 90301, (310) 672-5301, 11 am-10 pm

Irvine

Cheesecake Factory, 71 Fortune Dr, Irvine, CA, 92618, (949) 788-9998, 11 am-11 pm

Chili's, 3745 Alton Pkwy, Irvine, CA, 92606, (949) 250-8636, 11 am-10 pm

Claim Jumper, 3935 Alton Pkwy, Irvine, CA, (949) 851-5085, 11 am-10 pm

Dave and Buster's, 71 Fortune Dr, Irvine, CA, (949) 727-0555, 11 am-midnight

Elephant Bar, 14346 Culver Dr, Irvine, CA, (949) 651-6087, 11 amñ10 pm

Marie Callender's, 15363 Culver Dr, Irvine, CA, 92604, (949) 552-2101, 11 am-10 pm

Melting Pot, 2646 Dupont Dr , Irvine, CA, 92612, (949) 955-3242, 5 pm-10:30 pm

P.F. Changs, 61 Fortune Dr, The Irvine Spectrum Center, Irvine, CA, 92618, (949) 453-1211, 11 am-10 pm

Romano's Macaroni Grill, 13652 Jamboree Rd, Irvine, CA, 92602, (714) 508-7990, 11 am-10 pm

Round Table Pizza, 3953 Irvine Blvd, Irvine, CA, 92602, (714) 508-9800, 11:30 am-9 pm

Round Table Pizza, 3851 Alton Pkwy, Irvine, CA, 92606, (949) 476-3030, 11:30 am-9 pm

Yard House, 71 Fortune Dr, Irvine, CA, 92618, (949) 753-9373, 11 am-midnight

King City

Round Table Pizza, 500 B Canal St, King City, CA, 93930, (831) 385-0880, 11:30 am-9 pm

La Canada

Round Table Pizza, 502 Foothill Blvd, La Canada, CA, 91011, (818) 952-1100, 11:30 am-9 pm

La Habra

Carrows, 1000 Beach Blvd, La Habra, CA, 90631, (562) 691-8711, 6 am-11 pm

Chili's, 1600 W Imperial Hwy, La Habra, CA, 90631, (562) 690-7491, 11 am-10 pm

Hometown Buffet, 1901 W Imperial, La Habra, CA, 90631, (562) 690-0074, 11 am-8:30 pm

Marie Callender's, 340 E Whittier Blvd, La Habra, CA, 90631, (562) 691-0705, 11 am-10 pm

Round Table Pizza, 1240-B W Imperial Hwy, La Habra, CA, 90631, (562) 690-2205, 11:30 am-9 pm

La Jolla

Piatti Locali, 2182 Avenida de la Playa, La Jolla, CA, 92307, (858) 454-1589, 11:30 am-10 pm

Rock Bottom, 8980 Villa La Jolla Dr, La Jolla, CA, 92037, (858) 450-9277, 11 am-Close

Round Table Pizza, UCSD Price Center, La Jolla, CA, 92093, (858) 457-2060, 11:30 am-9 pm

La Mesa

Bakers Square, 5270 Baltimore Dr, La Mesa, CA, 91942, (619) 464-7833, 7 am-11 pm

Chili's, 8285 Fletcher Pkwy, La Mesa, CA, 91942, (619) 589-9890, 11 am-10 pm

Claim Jumper, 5500 Grossmont Center Dr, La Mesa, CA, (619) 469-3927, 11 am-10 pm

Coco's Bakery, 5550 Lake Murray Blvd, La Mesa, CA, 91942, (619) 464-1372, 6:30 am-10 pm

Fuddruckers, 5500 Grossmont Center, La Mesa, CA, 91941, 11 am-9 pm

Round Table Pizza, 5999 Severin Dr, La Mesa, CA, 91942, (619) 589-1510, 11:30 am-9 pm

Round Table Pizza, 8032 La Mesa Blvd, La Mesa, CA, 91941, (619) 462-1650, 11:30 am-9 pm

La Mirada

Elephant Bar, 14303 Firestone Blvd, La Mirada, CA, (714) 994-1474, 11 amñ10 pm

Round Table Pizza, 12820 La Mirada Blvd, La Mirada, CA, 90638, (562) 947-2557, 11:30 am-9 pm

Sizzler, 15252 Rosecrans Ave, La Mirada, CA, 90638, (714) 228-0153, 11 am-10 pm

La Puente

Sizzler, 1065 N Hacienda Blvd, La Puente, CA, 91744, (626) 934-8400, 11 am-10 pm

La Verne

Bakers Square, 1401 Foothill Blvd, La Verne, CA, 91750, (909) 593-1070, 7 am-11 pm

Chili's, 1912 Foothill Blvd, La Verne, CA, 91750, (909) 596-1666, 11 am-10 pm

Round Table Pizza, 2488 Foothill Blvd, La Verne, CA, 91750, (909) 596-9055, 11:30 am-9 pm

Laguna Hills

Carrows, 23952 Ave De La Carlota, Laguna Hills, CA, 92653, (949) 837-4963, 6 am-11 pm

Claim Jumper, 25322 McIntyre St, Laguna Hills, CA, (949) 768-0662, 11 am-10 pm

Coco's Bakery, 23000 Lake Forest Dr, Laguna Hills, CA, 92653, (949) 458-8389, 6:30 am-10 pm

Laguna Niguel

Coco's Bakery, 27360 Alicia Pkwy, Laguna Niguel, CA, 92677, (949) 643-0010, 6:30 am-10 pm

Round Table Pizza, 24012 Aliso Creek Rd, Laguna Niguel, CA, 92677, (949) 643-1636, 11:30 am-9 pm

Laguna Woods

Hometown Buffet, Laguna Woods Town Center, 24381 El Toro Rd, Laguna Woods, CA, 92653, (949) 595-0971, 11 am-8:30 pm

Lake Elsinore

Chili's, 29233 Central Ave, Lake Elsinore, CA, 92532, (951) 245-5101, 11 am-10 pm

Coco's Bakery, 31706 Casino Dr, Lake Elsinore, CA, 92530, (951) 245-5040, 6:30 am-10 pm

Sizzler, 31274 Casino Dr, Lake Elsinore, CA, 92330, (909) 674-8989, 11 am-10 pm

Lake Forest

Round Table Pizza, 22722 Lambert St, Ste #1705, Lake Forest, CA, 92630, (949) 859-8888, 11:30 am-9 pm

Black Angus Steakhouse, 23221 Lake Center Dr, Lake Forest, CA, 92630, (949) 837-4200, 11 am-10 pm

Fuddruckers, 26771 Rancho Pkwy, Lake Forest, CA, 92630, 11 am-9 pm

Fuddruckers, 23621 El Toro Rd, Lake Forest, CA, 92630, 11 am-9 pm

Lakewood

Bakers Square, 5520 S St, Lakewood, CA, 90713, (562) 804-2541, 7 am-11 pm

Black Angus Steakhouse, 5000 E Candlewood, Lakewood, CA, 90712, (562) 531-6921, 11 am-10 pm

Chili's, 4931 Candlewood, Lakewood, CA, 90712, (562) 602-1808, 11 am-10 pm

Coco's Bakery, 5809 Lakewood Blvd, Lakewood, CA, 90712, (562) 602-0275, 6:30 am-10 pm

Elephant Bar, 4630 Candlewood St, Lakewood, CA, (562) 529-3200, 11 amñ10 pm

Fuddruckers, 5229 N Clark St, Lakewood, CA, 90714, 11 am-9 pm

Hometown Buffet, 4700 Candlewood St, Lakewood, CA, 90713, (562) 633-8874, 11 am-8:30 pm

Marie Callender's, 4771 Candlewood St, Lakewood, CA, 90712, (562) 630-7600, 11 am-10 pm

Marie Callender's, 4419 Candlewood St, Lakewood, CA, 90712, (562) 634-3612, 11 am-10 pm

Round Table Pizza, 5250 Faculty, Lakewood, CA, 90712, (562) 408-1914, 11:30 am-9 pm

Lancaster

Black Angus Steakhouse, 44690 Valley Central Way, Lancaster, CA, 93534, (661) 942-5225, 11 am-10 pm

Carrows, 1650 W Ave K, Lancaster, CA, 93534, (661) 945-7059, 6 am-11 pm

Hometown Buffet, Toys R Us Shopping Center, 1317 W Ave K, Lancaster, CA, 93534, (661) 723-9477, 11 am-8:30 pm

Marie Callender's, 1649 W Ave K, Lancaster, CA, 93534, (661) 945-6958, 11 am-10 pm

Round Table Pizza, 44204 N 10th St W, Lancaster, CA, 93534, (661) 945-6677, 11:30 am-9 pm

Sizzler, 44430 20th St W, Lancaster, CA, 93534, (661) 948-4671, 11 am-10 pm

Lemon Grove

Godfather's Pizza, 7080 BRdway Ave, Lemon Grove, CA, 91945, (619) 698-7990

Loma Linda

Hometown Buffet, 24990 Redlands Blvd, Loma Linda, CA, 92354, (909) 796-6588, 11 am-8:30 pm

Lomita

Sizzler, 2421 W Pacific Coast Hwy, Lomita, CA, 90717, (310) 530-5642, 11 am-10 pm

Lompoc

Bakers Square, 936 N H St, Lompoc, CA, 93436, (805) 735-8330, 7 am-11 pm

Carrows, 1129 N H St, Lompoc, CA, 93436, (805) 736-0702, 6 am-11 pm

Round Table Pizza, 721 W Central Ave, Lompoc, CA, 93436, (805) 735-3333, 11:30 am-9 pm

Long Beach

Bubba Gump Shrimp, 87 Aquarium Way, Long Beach, CA, 90802, (562) 437-2434, 11 am-10 pm

Chili's, 30 Shoreline Dr West, Long Beach, CA, 90802, (562) 590-5103, 11 am-10 pm

Claim Jumper, 6501 E Pacific Coast Hwy, Long Beach, CA, (562) 431-1321, 11 am-10 pm

Hometown Buffet, City Pl, 290 E 4th St, Long Beach, CA, 90802, (562) 435-4006, 11 am-8:30 pm

Hooters, 130 Pine Ave, Long Beach, CA, 90802, (562) 983-1010, 11 am-midnight

P.F. Changs, 340 S Pine Ave, Long Beach, CA, 90802, (562) 308-1025, 11 am-10 pm

Rock Bottom, One Pine Ave, Long Beach, CA, (562) 308-2255, 11 am-12:30 am

Round Table Pizza, 1212 Bellflower Blvd, Long Beach, CA, 90815, (562) 494-1194, 11:30 am-9 pm

Round Table Pizza, 4007 E Ocean Blvd, Long Beach, CA, 90803, (562) 439-7799, 11:30 am-9 pm

Sizzler, 225 W 3rd St, Long Beach, CA, 90802, (562) 432-6433, 11 am-10 pm

Sizzler, 15 W Del Amo Blvd, Long Beach, CA, 90805, (562) 428-4967, 11 am-10 pm

Yard House, 401 Shoreline Village Dr, Long Beach, CA, 90802, (562) 628-0455, 11 am-midnight

Los Alamitos

Sizzler, 10471 Los Alamitos Blvd, Los Alamitos, CA, 90720, (562) 598-4497, 11 am-10 pm

Tony Roma's, 3642 Katella Ave, Los Alamitos, CA, 90720, (562) 598-0401, 11 am-10 pm

Los Angeles

Big Boy, 5050 Wilshire Blvd, Los Angeles, CA, 90036, (323) 939-3317, 6:30 am-10 pm

Cheesecake Factory, 189 The Grove Dr, K-90, Los Angeles, CA, 90036, (323) 634-0511, 11 am-11 pm

Cheesecake Factory, 11647 San Vicente Blvd, Los Angeles, CA, 90049, (310) 826-7111, 11 am-11 pm

Chili's, 1056 Westwood Blvd, Los Angeles, CA, 90024, (310) 401-2220, 11 am-10 pm

Coco's Bakery, 8731 Pico Blvd, Los Angeles, CA, 90035, (310) 858-0339, 6:30 am-10 pm

Fuddruckers, 10250 Santa Monica Blvd FC8, Los Angeles, CA, 90069, 11 am-9 pm

Maggiano's, 189 The Grove Dr Z80, Los Angeles, CA, 90036, (323) 965-9665, 11 am-10 pm

Marie Callender's, 5773 Wilshire Blvd, Los Angeles, CA, 90036, (323) 937-7952, 11 am-10 pm

Marie Callender's, 6081 Center Dr, Los Angeles, CA, 90045, 11 am-10 pm

P.F. Changs, 121 N La Cienega Blvd, Beverly Center, Los Angeles, CA, 90048, (310) 854-6467, 11 am-10 pm

Round Table Pizza, 2524 Glendale Blvd, Los Angeles, CA, 90039, (323) 663-8301, 11:30 am-9 pm

Sizzler, 400 S Vermont Ave, Los Angeles, CA, 90005, (213) 387-1647, 11 am-10 pm

Sizzler, 3701 Santa Rosalia, Los Angeles, CA, 90008, (323) 294-9927, 11 am-10 pm

Sizzler, 6145 Wilshire Blvd, Los Angeles, CA, 90048, (323) 936-4200, 11 am-10 pm

Sizzler, 5856 W Manchester Ave, Los Angeles, CA, 90045, (310) 641-1167, 11 am-10 pm

Sizzler, 2920 Los Feliz Blvd, Los Angeles, CA, 90039, (323) 660-1559, 11 am-10 pm

Sizzler, 3500 S Figueroa, Los Angeles, CA, 90007, (213) 747-4384, 11 am-10 pm

Sizzler, 710 S Wern Ave, Los Angeles, CA, 90005, (213) 385-4747, 11 am-10 pm

Todai, 8612 Beverly Blvd, Los Angeles, CA, 90048, (310) 659-1375, 11:30 am-9 pm

Los Osos

Round Table Pizza, 1050 Los Osos Valley Rd, Los Osos, CA, 93402, (805) 528-4780, 11:30 am-9 pm

Lynwood

Hometown Buffet, Plz Mexico, 3102 E Imperial Hwy, Lynwood, CA, 90262, (310) 537-6411, 11 am-8:30 pm

Manhattan Beach

Chili's, 2620 N Sepulveda Blvd, Ste B, Manhattan Beach, CA, 90266, (310) 546-5847, 11 am-10 pm

Coco's Bakery, 2620 N Sepulveda Blvd Ste A, Manhattan Beach, CA, 90266, (310) 545-8439, 6:30 am-10 pm

Marina Del Rey

Cheesecake Factory, 4142 Via Marina, Marina Del Rey, CA, 90292, (310) 306-3344, 11 am-11 pm

Mission Hills

Coco's Bakery, 10841 Sepulveda Blvd, Mission Hills, CA, 91345, (818) 365-3309, 6:30 am-10 pm

Mission Viejo

Carrows, 28502 Marguerite Pkwy, Mission Viejo, CA, 92692, (949) 364-5915, 6 am-11 pm

Cheesecake Factory, 42 The Shops at Mission Viejo, Mission Viejo, CA, 92691, (949) 364-6200, 11 am-11 pm

Chili's, 27407 Bellogente, Mission Viejo, CA, 92691, (949) 364-2207, 11 am-10 pm

Claim Jumper, 27845 Santa Margarita Pkwy, Mission Viejo, CA, (949) 461-7170, 11 am-10 pm

Coco's Bakery, 27750 Crown Valley Pkwy, Mission Viejo, CA, 92691, (949) 582-1463, 6:30 am-10 pm

P.F. Changs, 800 The Shops at Mission Viejo, Mission Viejo, CA, 92691, (949) 364-6661, 11 am-10 pm

Round Table Pizza, 25290 Marguerite Pkwy, #D, Mission Viejo, CA, 92692, (949) 951-3403, 11:30 am-9 pm

Monrovia

Black Angus Steakhouse, 560 W Huntington Dr, Monrovia, CA, 91016, (626) 303-2411, 11 am-10 pm

Chili's, 630 W Huntington Dr, Monrovia, CA, 91016, (626) 303-1604, 11 am-10 pm

Claim Jumper, 820 W Huntington Dr, Monrovia, CA, (626) 359-0463, 11 am-10 pm

Romano's Macaroni Grill, 945 W Huntington, Monrovia, CA, 91016, (626) 256-7969, 11 am-10 pm

Round Table Pizza, 626 W Huntington Dr, Monrovia, CA, 91016, (626) 303-1855, 11:30 am-9 pm

Montclair

Black Angus Steakhouse, 9415 Monte Vista, Montclair, CA, 91763, (909) 621-4821, 11 am-10 pm

Chili's, 9393 Monte Vista Ave, Montclair, CA, 91763, (909) 626-0171, 11 am-10 pm

Elephant Bar, 4949 S Plz Ln, Montclair, CA, (909) 621-3509, 11 amñ10 pm

Hometown Buffet, 5247 Arrow Hwy, Montclair, CA, 91763, (909) 624-3060, 11 am-8:30 pm

Romano's Macaroni Grill, 4955 S Plz Ln, Montclair, CA, 91763, (909) 621-2604, 11 am-10 pm

Sizzler, 5660 Holt Ave, Montclair, CA, 91763, (909) 626-0113, 11 am-10 pm

Tony Roma's, 9335 Monte Vista Ave, Montclair, CA, 91763, (909) 626-3391, 11 am-10 pm

Montebello

Bakers Square, 1322 W Beverly Blvd, Montebello, CA, 90640, (323) 722-6324, 7 am-11 pm

Carrows, 2501 W Via Campo, Montebello, CA, 90640, (323) 728-4690, 6 am-11 pm

Hometown Buffet, Montebello Shopping Center, 875-877 N Wilcox Ave, Montebello, CA, 90640, (323) 888-1181, 11 am-8:30 pm

Marie Callender's, 1852 Montebello Town Ctr, Montebello, CA, 90640, (323) 722-7437, 11 am-10 pm

Sizzler, 1908 W Beverly Blvd, Montebello, CA, 90640, (323) 722-8576, 11 am-10 pm

Montecito

Piatti Locali, 515 San Ysidro, Montecito, CA, 93108, (805) 969-7520, 11:30 am-9 pm

Monterey Park

Carrows, 2271 S Atlantic Blvd, Monterey Park, CA, 91754, (323) 264-5511, 6 am-11 pm

Marie Callender's, 220 S Atlantic Blvd, Monterey Park, CA, 91754, (626) 281-9548, 11 am-10 pm

Moorpark

Round Table Pizza, 239 W Los Angeles Ave, Moorpark, CA, 93021, (805) 529-2207, 11:30 am-9 pm

Moreno Valley

Chili's, 12525-A Frederick St, Moreno Valley, CA, 92553, (951) 653-1814, 11 am-10 pm

Coco's Bakery, 24949 Sunnymead Blvd, Moreno Valley, CA, 92553, (951) 924-2421, 6:30 am-10 pm

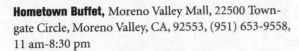

Hometown Buffet, Moreno Valley Mall, 22500 Towngate Circle, Moreno Valley, CA, 92553, (951) 653-9558, 11 am-8:30 pm

Sizzler, 25035 Sunnymead Blvd, Moreno Valley, CA, 92388, (909) 242-8012, 11 am-10 pm

Morro Bay

Round Table Pizza, 610 Quintana Rd, Morro Bay, CA, 93442, (805) 772-1800, 11:30 am-9 pm

Murrieta

Carrows, 24640 Maddison Ave, Murrieta, CA, 92562, (951) 461-2411, 6 am-11 pm

Chili's, 41070 California Oaks Rd, Murrieta, CA, 92562, (951) 698-8003, 11 am-10 pm

Sizzler, 40489 Murrieta Hot Springs, Murrieta, CA, 92362, (909) 698-5623, 11 am-10 pm

National City

Hometown Buffet, 1135 Highland Ave, National City, CA, 91950, (619) 477-7990, 11 am-8:30 pm

Sizzler, 1325 Plz Blvd, National City, CA, 91950, (619) 477-2590, 11 am-10 pm

Newport Beach

Benihana, 4250 Birch St, Newport Beach, CA, 92660, (949) 955-0822, 11:30 am-10 pm

Cheesecake Factory, 1141 Newport Center Dr, Newport Beach, CA, 92660, (949) 720-8333, 11 am-11 pm

Coco's Bakery, 900 N Bristol, Newport Beach, CA, 92660, (949) 752-2801, 6:30 am-10 pm

Coco's Bakery, 151 Newport Center Dr, Newport Beach, CA, 92660, (949) 644-1571, 6:30 am-10 pm

P.F. Changs, 1145 Newport Center Dr, Fashion Island, Newport Beach, CA, 92660, (949) 759-9007, 11 am-10 pm

Round Table Pizza, 4551 Jamboree Rd, Ste B, Newport Beach, CA, 92660, (949) 261-2222, 11:30 am-9 pm

Norco

Sizzler, 1750 Hamner Ave, Norco, CA, 91760, (951) 734-1787, 11 am-10 pm

North Hollywood

Coco's Bakery, 6601 Lankershim Blvd, North Hollywood, CA, 91606, (818) 764-7218, 6:30 am-10 pm

Sizzler, 6343 Laurel Canyon Blvd, North Hollywood, CA, 91606, (818) 509-3983, 11 am-10 pm

Northridge

Black Angus Steakhouse, 9145 Corbin Ave, Northridge, CA, 91325, (818) 701-1600, 11 am-10 pm

Carrows, 18521 Devonshire St, Northridge, CA, 91324, (818) 368-2911, 6 am-11 pm

Chili's, 9200 Reseda Blvd, Northridge, CA, 91324, (818) 886-2191, 11 am-10 pm

Claim Jumper, 9429 Tampa Ave, Northridge, CA, (818) 718-2882, 11 am-10 pm

Marie Callender's, 19310 Business Center Dr, Northridge, CA, 91324, (818) 993-0704, 11 am-10 pm

Romano's Macaroni Grill, 19400 Plummer St, Northridge, CA, 91324, (818) 725-2620, 11 am-10 pm

Sizzler, 8875 Tampa St, Northridge, CA, 91324, (818) 886-3344, 11 am-10 pm

Norwalk

Carrows, 10640 Rosecrans Ave, Norwalk, CA, 90650, (562) 868-1553, 6 am-11 pm

Sizzler, 11835 Imperial Hwy, Norwalk, CA, 90650, (562) 864-6622, 11 am-10 pm

Oceanside

Black Angus Steakhouse, 2471 Vista Way, Oceanside, CA, 92054, (760) 433-7712, 11 am-10 pm

Carrows, 936 N Coast, Oceanside, CA, 92054, (760) 722-9435, 6 am-11 pm

Chili's, 2627 Vista Way, Oceanside, CA, 92054, (760) 967-1064, 11 am-10 pm

Coco's Bakery, 3905 Mission Ave, Oceanside, CA, 92054, (760) 721-6462, 6:30 am-10 pm

Fuddruckers, 2320 S El Camino Real, Oceanside, CA, 92054, 11 am-9 pm

Hometown Buffet, Mission MarketPl, 491 College Blvd, Oceanside, CA, 92057, (760) 945-6080, 11 am-8:30 pm

Hooters, 3186 Vista Way Ste 100, Oceanside, CA, 92054, (760) 433-4668, 11 am-midnight

Romano's Macaroni Grill, 2655 Vista Way, Oceanside, CA, 92054, (760) 722-9905, 11 am-10 pm

Round Table Pizza, 455 College Blvd, #10, Oceanside, CA, 92057, (760) 945-3000, 11:30 am-9 pm

Sizzler, 3805 Plz Dr, Oceanside, CA, 92056, (760) 630-1551, 11 am-10 pm

Ojai

Carrows, 211 W Ojai Ave, Ojai, CA, 93023, (805) 646-5952, 6 am-11 pm

Ontario

Benihana, 3760 E Inland Empire Blvd, Ontario, CA, 91764, (909) 483-0937, 11:30 am-10 pm

Black Angus Steakhouse, 3640 Porsche Way, Ontario, CA, 91764, (909) 944-6882, 11 am-10 pm

Chevy's, 4551 E Mills Circle, Ontario, CA, 91764, (909) 481-4846, 11 am-10 pm

Coco's Bakery, 4360 Mills Circle Rd, Ontario, CA, 91764, (909) 481-8644, 6:30 am-10 pm

Dave and Buster's, Ontario Mills Mall, Ontario, CA, (909) 987-1557, 11 am-midnight

Fuddruckers, 4423 E Mills Circle, Ontario, CA, 91764, 11 am-9 pm

Hooters, 725 N Milliken Ave, Ontario, CA, 91764, (909) 989-2209, 11 am-midnight

Marie Callender's, 2149 Convention Center Way, Ontario, CA, 91764, (909) 937-0214, 11 am-10 pm

Round Table Pizza, 1020 No Mountain Ave, Ontario, CA, 91762, (909) 988-8444, 11:30 am-9 pm

Sizzler, 1865 E 4th St, Ontario, CA, 91764, (909) 984-0544, 11 am-10 pm

Sizzler, 2228 Mountain Ave, Ontario, CA, 91761, (909) 984-5059, 11 am-10 pm

Tony Roma's, 3550 Porsche Way, Ontario, CA, 91764, (909) 484-8444, 11 am-10 pm

Orange

Carrows, 2810 E Chapman Ave, Orange, CA, 92869, (714) 639-1297, 6 am-11 pm

Chili's, 1411 W Katella Ave, Orange, CA, 92867, (714) 771-4071, 11 am-10 pm

Dave and Buster's, I-5 Hwy 22, Orange, CA, (714) 769-1515, 11:30 am-12:30 am

Marie Callender's, 574 N Tusin Ave, Orange, CA, 92867, (714) 639-5054, 11 am-10 pm

Marie Callender's, 307 E Katella Ave, Orange, CA, 92867, (714) 633-3112, 11 am-10 pm

Round Table Pizza, 1737 E Katella Ave, Orange, CA, 92867, (714) 639-7344, 11:30 am-9 pm

Sizzler, 584 N Tustin Ave, Orange, CA, 92867, (714) 633-4485, 11 am-10 pm

Todai, 500 E Village Way #2203 , Orange, CA, 92865, (714) 974-0763, 11:30 am-9 pm

Oxnard

Bakers Square, 2420 E Vineyard Ave, Oxnard, CA, 93030, (805) 983-2232, 7 am-11 pm

Carrows, 1601 N Oxnard Blvd, Oxnard, CA, 93030, (805) 983-0655, 6 am-11 pm

Chili's, 2221 N Rose Ave, Oxnard, CA, 93030, (805) 278-0027, 11 am-10 pm

Hometown Buffet, 1901 Lockwood St, Oxnard, CA, 93030, (805) 983-8873, 11 am-8:30 pm

Palm Desert

Coco's Bakery, 78375 Varner Rd, Palm Desert, CA, 92211, (760) 360-9045, 6:30 am-10 pm

Palm Desert

Bakers Square, 73-075 Hwy 111, Palm Desert, CA, 92260, (760) 346-9811, 7 am-11 pm

Elephant Bar, 73833 Hwy 111, Palm Desert, CA, (760) 340-0456, 11 amñ10 pm

Hometown Buffet, Desert Crossing, 72-513C Hwy 111, Palm Desert, CA, 92260, (760) 341-6653, 11 am-8:30 pm

Marie Callender's, 72-840 Hwy111 Ste 399, Palm Desert, CA, 92260, (760) 773-4743, 11 am-10 pm

Romano's Macaroni Grill, 72920 Hwy 111, Palm Desert, CA, 92260, (760) 837-1333, 11 am-10 pm

Sullivan's Steakhouse, 73-505 El Paseo, Palm Desert, CA, 92260, (760) 341-3560, 11 am-11 pm

Tony Roma's, 73-155 Hwy 111, Palm Desert, CA, 92260, (760) 568-9911, 11 am-10 pm

Palm Springs

Bakers Square, 1596 N Palm Canyon Dr, Palm Springs, CA, 92262, (760) 325-1817, 7 am-11 pm

Carrows, 1243 E Palm Canyon, Palm Springs, CA, 92262, (760) 327-5150, 6 am-11 pm

Coco's Bakery, 1901 E Palm Canyon Dr, Palm Springs, CA, 92263, (760) 327-2666, 6:30 am-10 pm

Palmdale

Bakers Square, 350 W Palmdale Blvd, Palmdale, CA, 93550, (661) 273-1020, 7 am-11 pm

Carrows, 120 W Palmdale Blvd, Palmdale, CA, 93550, (661) 273-3335, 6 am-11 pm

Chili's, 1021 W Ave P, Palmdale, CA, 93551, (661) 267-1581, 11 am-10 pm

Hometown Buffet, Palmdale Promenade, 422 W Ave P, Palmdale, CA, 93551, (661) 267-6277, 11 am-8:30 pm

Sizzler, 853 W Palmdale Blvd, Palmdale, CA, 93550, (661) 273-4411, 11 am-10 pm

Pasadena

Bakers Square, 473 N Rosemead Blvd, Pasadena, CA, 91107, (626) 351-6579, 7 am-11 pm

Cheesecake Factory, 2 W Colorado Blvd, Pasadena, CA, 91101, (626) 584-6000, 11 am-11 pm

Coco's Bakery, 77 N Lake Ave, Pasadena, CA, 91106, (626) 449-3156, 6:30 am-10 pm

Hooters, 96-98 E Colorado Blvd, Pasadena, CA, 91105, (626) 395-7700, 11 am-midnight

Marie Callender's, 2300 E Foothill Blvd, Pasadena, CA, 91107, (626) 792-3109, 11 am-10 pm

Melting Pot, 88 W Colorado Blvd, 2nd Floor , Pasadena, CA, 91105, (626) 792-1941, 5 pm-10:30 pm

P.F. Changs, 260 E Colorado Blvd, Paseo Colorado, Pasadena, CA, 91101, (626) 356-9760, 11 am-10 pm

Sizzler, 730 S Arroyo Pkwy, Pasadena, CA, 91170, (626) 795-9024, 11 am-10 pm

Yard House, 330 E Colorado Blvd, Ste 230, Pasadena, CA, 91101, (626) 577-9273, 11 am-midnight

Paso Robles

Sizzler, 1111 Riverside Dr, #201, Paso Robles, CA, 93446, (805) 237-4050, 11 am-10 pm

Pedley

Sizzler, 6631 Clay St, Pedley, CA, 92509, (951) 681-4908, 11 am-10 pm

Perris

Round Table Pizza, 15 W Nuevo Rd, Ste C, Perris, CA, 92571, (951) 943-2268, 11:30 am-9 pm

Sizzler, 91 W Nuevo Rd, Perris, CA, 92370, (909) 940-4021, 11 am-10 pm

Pico Rivera

Chili's, 8890 Washington Blvd, Pico Rivera, CA, 90660, (562) 948-1876, 11 am-10 pm

Sizzler, 6730 Rosemead Blvd, Pico Rivera, CA, 90660, (562) 949-4511, 11 am-10 pm

Pismo Beach

Coco's Bakery, 411 Five Cities Dr, Pismo Beach, CA, 93449, (805) 773-3240, 6:30 am-10 pm

Marie Callender's, 2131 Price St, Pismo Beach, CA, 93449, (805) 773-0606, 11 am-10 pm

Placentia

Hometown Buffet, 620 N Rose Dr, Placentia, CA, 92670, (714) 528-2278, 11 am-8:30 pm

Marie Callender's, 126 E Yorba Linda Blvd, Placentia, CA, 92870, (714) 996-0500, 11 am-10 pm

Pomona

Carrows, 401 E Foothill Blvd, Pomona, CA, 91767, (909) 624-8470, 6 am-11 pm

Round Table Pizza, 3801 W Temple Ave, Bldg 55, Pomona, CA, 91768, (909) 869-5411, 11:30 am-9 pm

Round Table Pizza, 1101 W McKinley, Pomona, CA, 91769, (909) 629-0270, 11:30 am-9 pm

Sizzler, 2282 N Garey Ave, Pomona, CA, 91767, (909) 593-1439, 11 am-10 pm

Port Hueneme

Bakers Square, 747 W Channel Islands Blvd, Port Hueneme, CA, 93041, (805) 985-1937, 7 am-11 pm

Porterville

Round Table Pizza, 1138 W Henderson Ave, Porterville, CA, 93257, (559) 781-3602, 11:30 am-9 pm

Poway

Round Table Pizza, 13510 Poway Rd, Poway, CA, 92064, (858) 748-2333, 11:30 am-9 pm

Coco's Bakery, 13464 Poway Rd, Poway, CA, 92064, (858) 748-6118, 6:30 am-10 pm

Ramona

Sizzler, 344 Main St, Ramona, CA, 92065, (760) 789-3240, 11 am-10 pm

Rancho Bernardo

Coco's Bakery, 16759 Bernardo Center Dr, Rancho Bernardo, CA, 92128, (858) 485-9419, 6:30 am-10 pm

Elephant Bar, 17051 W Bernardo Dr, Rancho Bernardo, CA, (858) 487-7181, 11 amñ10 pm

Rancho Cucamonga

Carrows, 11669 Foothill Blvd, Rancho Cucamonga, CA, 91730, (909) 481-5644, 6 am-11 pm

Cheesecake Factory, Victoria Gardens Mall 12379 N MainSt, Rancho Cucamonga, CA, 91739, (909) 463-3011, 11 am-11 pm

Chili's, 10598 Foothill Blvd, Rancho Cucamonga, CA, 91730, (909) 948-5955, 11 am-10 pm

Claim Jumper, 12499 Foothill Blvd, Rancho Cucamonga, CA, (909) 899-8022, 11 am-10 pm

Coco's Bakery, 7269 H Aven Ave, Rancho Cucamonga, CA, 91730, (909) 948-5665, 6:30 am-10 pm

Hometown Buffet, 10910 Foothill Blvd, Rancho Cucamonga, CA, 91730, (909) 481-7730, 11 am-8:30 pm

P.F. Changs, 7870 Monticello Ave, Rancho Cucamonga, CA, 91739, (909) 463-4095, 11 am-10 pm

Romano's Macaroni Grill, 10742 Foothill Blvd, Rancho Cucamonga, CA, 91730, (909) 484-3200, 11 am-10 pm

Round Table Pizza, 7201 Archibald Ave, Ste 9, Rancho Cucamonga, CA, 91701, (909) 980-8040, 11:30 am-9 pm

Sizzler, 9588 Baseline Rd, Rancho Cucamonga, CA, 91701, (909) 987-8413, 11 am-10 pm

Yard House, 12473 N MainSt, Rancho Cucamonga, CA, 91739, (909) 646-7116, 11 am-midnight

Rancho Mirage

Black Angus Steakhouse, 69-640 Hwy 111, Rancho Mirage, CA, 92270, (760) 324-8407, 11 am-10 pm

Cheesecake Factory, The River at Rancho Mirage 71-800 Hwy 111, Rancho Mirage, CA, 92270, (760) 404-1400, 11 am-11 pm

Marie Callender's, 69-830 Hwy 111, Rancho Mirage, CA, 92270, (760) 328-0844, 11 am-10 pm

P.F. Changs, 71800 Hwy 111, Rancho Mirage, CA, 92270, (760) 776-4912, 11 am-10 pm

Yard House, 71800 Hwy 111, Rancho Mirage, CA, 92270, (760) 779-1415, 11 am-midnight

Redlands

Coco's Bakery, 1140 W Colton, Redlands, CA, 92373, (909) 792-3116, 6:30 am-10 pm

Marie Callender's, 1625 Industrial Park Ave, Redlands, CA, 92374, (909) 793-0988, 11 am-10 pm

Romano's Macaroni Grill, 27490 Lugonia Ave, Redlands, CA, 92374, (909) 798-4142, 11 am-10 pm

Sizzler, 110 W Redlands Blvd, Redlands, CA, 92373, (909) 792-3579, 11 am-10 pm

Redondo Beach

Cheesecake Factory, 605 N Harbor Dr, Redondo Beach, CA, 90277, (310) 376-0466, 11 am-11 pm

Marie Callender's, 1223 Pacific Coast Hwy, Redondo Beach, CA, 90277, (310) 316-1111, 11 am-10 pm

Marie Callender's, 2979 Artesia Blvd, Redondo Beach, CA, 90278, (310) 371-5583, 11 am-10 pm

Rialto

Carrows, 298 W Baseline Rd, Rialto, CA, 92376, (909) 874-4122, 6 am-11 pm

Coco's Bakery, 1683 S Riverside Ave, Rialto, CA, 92376, (909) 877-9270, 6:30 am-10 pm

Hometown Buffet, 127 W Valley Blvd, Rialto, CA, 92376, (909) 421-9688, 11 am-8:30 pm

Sizzler, 1236 Riverside Ave, Rialto, CA, 92376, (909) 874-4281, 11 am-10 pm

Ridgecrest

Sizzler, 1501 N Norma St, Ridgecrest, CA, 93555, (760) 446-0114, 11 am-10 pm

Riverside

Bakers Square, 3650 Tyler St, Riverside, CA, 92503, (951) 689-2160, 7 am-11 pm

Black Angus Steakhouse, 3610 Park Sierra Blvd, Riverside, CA, 92505, (951) 687-9190, 11 am-10 pm

Carrows, 11120 Magnolia Ave, Riverside, CA, 92505, (951) 354-6262, 6 am-11 pm

Carrows, 8800 Limonite Ave, Riverside, CA, 92509, (951) 681-6371, 6 am-11 pm

Coco's Bakery, 10098 Magnolia, Riverside, CA, 92503, (951) 687-3846, 6:30 am-10 pm

Coco's Bakery, 8845 Trautwein Rd, Riverside, CA, 92508, (951) 776-9053, 6:30 am-10 pm

Coco's Bakery, 3640 Central Ave, Riverside, CA, 92506, (951) 683-3962, 6:30 am-10 pm

Coco's Bakery, 1303 University Ave, Riverside, CA, 92507, (951) 683-5825, 6:30 am-10 pm

Marie Callender's, 3505 Merrill St, Riverside, CA, 92506, (951) 682-2504, 11 am-10 pm

P.F. Changs, Tyler Mall, Riverside, CA, 11 am-10 pm

Sizzler, 10355 Magnolia Blvd, Riverside, CA, 92505, (951) 359-1442, 11 am-10 pm

Rolling Hills

Marie Callender's, 550 Deep Valley Dr, Rolling Hills, CA, 90274, (310) 377-4449, 11 am-10 pm

Rosemead

Carrows, 1021 San Gabriel Blvd, Rosemead, CA, 91770, (626) 288-5633, 6 am-11 pm

Rubidoux

Round Table Pizza, 7732 Limonite Ave, Rubidoux, CA, 92509, (951) 681-0895, 11:30 am-9 pm

San Bernardino

Black Angus Steakhouse, 290 E Hospitality Ln, San Bernardino, CA, 92408, (909) 885-7551, 11 am-10 pm

Chili's, 475 E Hospitality Ln, San Bernardino, CA, 92408, (909) 885-6167, 11 am-10 pm

Claim Jumper, 1905 S Commercenter E, San Bernardino, CA, (909) 383-1818, 11 am-10 pm

Coco's Bakery, 284 E Highland Ave, San Bernardino, CA, 92404, (909) 882-1209, 6:30 am-10 pm

Coco's Bakery, 242 E Hospitality Ln, San Bernardino, CA, 92408, (909) 381-3513, 6:30 am-10 pm

Elephant Bar, 1050 E Harriman Pl, San Bernardino, CA, (909) 799-9177, 11 amñ10 pm

Marie Callender's, 800 E Highland Ave , San Bernardino, CA, 92404, (909) 882-1754, 11 am-10 pm

Sizzler, 1800 S Waterman Ave, San Bernardino, CA, 92408, (909) 381-4020, 11 am-10 pm

San Clemente

Round Table Pizza, 612 Camino de los Mares, San Clemente, CA, 92672, (949) 496-7701, 11:30 am-9 pm

Carrows, 620 Avenida Pico, San Clemente, CA, 92672, (949) 492-4290, 6 am-11 pm

Bakers Square, 610 Camino De Los Mares, San Clemente, CA, 92673, (949) 661-3100, 7 am-11 pm

San Diego

Bakers Square, 3711 Sports Arena Blvd, San Diego, CA, 92110, (619) 224-4454, 7 am-11 pm

Benihana, 477 Camino Del Rio So, San Diego, CA, 92108, (619) 298-4666, 11:30 am-10 pm

Black Angus Steakhouse, 10370 Friars Rd, San Diego, CA, 92120, (619) 563-5862, 11 am-10 pm

Black Angus Steakhouse, 10750 Camino Ruiz, San Diego, CA, 92126, (858) 693-3453, 11 am-10 pm

Black Angus Steakhouse, 5247 Kearny Villa Rd, San Diego, CA, 92123, (858) 279-3100, 11 am-10 pm

Black Angus Steakhouse, 3340 Sports Arena Blvd, San Diego, CA, 92110, (619) 223-5604, 11 am-10 pm

Carrows, 615 Saturn Blvd, San Diego, CA, 92154, (619) 424-6881, 6 am-11 pm

Cheesecake Factory, 7067 Friars Rd, San Diego, CA, 92108, (619) 683-2800, 11 am-11 pm

Chevy's, 11630 Carmel Mountain Rd, San Diego, CA, 92128, (858) 675-9292, 11 am-10 pm

Chevy's, 1202 Camino Del Rio N, San Diego, CA, 92108, (619) 297-5667, 11 am-10 pm

Chili's, 4060 Clairemont Mesa Blvd, San Diego, CA, 92117, (858) 273-3058, 11 am-10 pm

Chili's, 4252 Camino Del Rio N, San Diego, CA, 92108, (619) 280-7996, 11 am-10 pm

Chili's, 5969 Lusk Blvd, San Diego, CA, 92121, (858) 457-5962, 11 am-10 pm

Chili's, 3494 Sports Arena Blvd, San Diego, CA, 92110, (619) 223-1107, 11 am-10 pm

Chili's, 10184 Scripps Poway Pkwy, San Diego, CA, 92131, (858) 566-2096, 11 am-10 pm

Coco's Bakery, 7398 Clairemont Mesa Blvd, San Diego, CA, 92111, (858) 292-9030, 6:30 am-10 pm

Coco's Bakery, 10430 Friars Rd, San Diego, CA, 92120, (619) 280-6890, 6:30 am-10 pm

Coco's Bakery, 4280 Nobel Dr, San Diego, CA, 92122, (858) 597-0284, 6:30 am-10 pm

Coco's Bakery, 3444 College Ave, San Diego, CA, 92115, (619) 287-9010, 6:30 am-10 pm

Coco's Bakery, 3821 Sports Arena Blvd, San Diego, CA, 92110, (619) 222-6658, 6:30 am-10 pm

Coco's Bakery, 5955 Balboa Ave, San Diego, CA, 92111, (858) 279-5363, 6:30 am-10 pm

Coco's Bakery, 2644 El Cajon Blvd, San Diego, CA, 92104, (619) 291-5798, 6:30 am-10 pm

Cozymel's Mexican Grill, 4303 La Jolla Village Dr, San Diego, CA, 92122, (858) 658-0480, 11 am-10 pm

Dave and Buster's, 2931 Camino Del Rio N, San Diego, CA, (619) 280-7115, 11:30 am-midnight

Fuddruckers, 8285 Mira Mesa Blvd, San Diego, CA, 92126, 11 am-9 pm

Fuddruckers, 891 Camino de la Reina, San Diego, CA, 92108, 11 am-9 pm

Hometown Buffet, University Square, 5881 University Ave, San Diego, CA, 92115, (619) 583-7373, 11 am-8:30 pm

Hometown Buffet, 10660 Camino Ruiz, San Diego, CA, 92126, (858) 566-9848, 11 am-8:30 pm

Hometown Buffet, 3007 Clairemont Dr, San Diego, CA, 92117, (619) 275-4622, 11 am-8:30 pm

Hometown Buffet, Palm Promenage, 930 Dennery Rd, San Diego, CA, 92154, (619) 662-9181, 11 am-8:30 pm

Hooters, 4190 Mission Blvd, San Diego, CA, 92109, (858) 273-4668, 11 am-midnight

Hooters, 1400 Camino De La Reina, San Diego, CA, 92108, (619) 299-4668, 11 am-midnight

Hooters, 410 Market St, San Diego, CA, 92101, (619) 235-4668, 11 am-midnight

Marie Callender's, 5405 Balboa Ave, San Diego, CA, 92111, (858) 279-6604, 11 am-10 pm

Marie Callender's, 6950 Alvarado Rd, San Diego, CA, 92120, (619) 465-1910, 11 am-10 pm

Marie Callender's, 11122 Rancho Carmel Dr, San Diego, CA, 92128, (858) 675-9428, 11 am-10 pm

Melting Pot, 8980 University Center Ln, San Diego, CA, 92122, (858) 638-1700, 5 pm-10:30 pm

P.F. Changs, 4540 La Jolla Village Dr, La Jolla Village, San Diego, CA, 92122, (858) 458-9007, 11 am-10 pm

P.F. Changs, 7077 Friars Rd, Fashion Valley Mall, San Diego, CA, 92108, (619) 260-8484, 11 am-10 pm

RA Sushi, 474 BRdway, San Diego, CA, 92108, (619) 321-0021, 11:30 am-11 pm

Rock Bottom, 401 ìGî St, San Diego, CA, 92101, (619) 231-7000, 11:30 am-12 am

Round Table Pizza, 1221 Garnet Ave, San Diego, CA, 92109, (858) 273-0600, 11:30 am-9 pm

Round Table Pizza, 16761 Bernardo Center Dr, San Diego, CA, 92128, (858) 487-4994, 11:30 am-9 pm

Round Table Pizza, 3250 Governor Dr, San Diego, CA, 92122, (858) 457-2334, 11:30 am-9 pm

Round Table Pizza, 10415 Tierrasanta Blvd, San Diego, CA, 92124, (858) 277-3111, 11:30 am-9 pm

Round Table Pizza, 13293 Black Mountain Rd, San Diego, CA, 92129, (858) 484-6800, 11:30 am-9 pm

Sizzler, 3755 Murphy Canyon Rd, Ste S, San Diego, CA, 92123, (858) 278-6988, 11 am-10 pm

Sizzler, 4445 Imperial Ave, San Diego, CA, 92113, (619) 263-5731, 11 am-10 pm

Sizzler, 2855 Midway Dr, San Diego, CA, 92110, (619) 224-3347, 11 am-10 pm

Todai, 2828 Camino Del Rio S, San Diego, CA, 92108, (619) 299-8996, 11:30 am-9 pm

Tony Roma's, 4110 Mission Blvd, San Diego, CA, 92109, (858) 272-7427, 11 am-10 pm

Uno Chicago Grill, 4465 Mission Blvd, Pacific Beach, San Diego, CA, 92109, (858) 483-4143, 11 am-12:30 am

Uno Chicago Grill, 7007 Friars Rd, Ste 356, Fashion Valley, San Diego, CA, 92108, (619) 298-1866, 11 am-12:30 am

Yard House, 1023 4th Ave, San Diego, CA, 92101, (619) 233-9273, 11 am-midnight

San Dimas

Sizzler, 101 N Village Court, San Dimas, CA, 91733, (909) 592-4585, 11 am-10 pm

San Gabriel

Sizzler, 5405 Rosemead Blvd, San Gabriel, CA, 91776, (626) 285-8958, 11 am-10 pm

San Luis Obispo

Hometown Buffet, 485 Madonna Rd, San Luis Obispo, CA, 93405, (805) 541-5594, 11 am-8:30 pm

Round Table Pizza, 1055 Olive St, San Luis Obispo, CA, 93401, (805) 541-5551, 11:30 am-9 pm

San Marcos

Bakers Square, 1650 Descanso Ave, San Marcos, CA, 92069, (760) 744-9637, 7 am-11 pm

Hometown Buffet, 288 Rancheros Dr, San Marcos, CA, 92069, (760) 471-9944, 11 am-8:30 pm

Tony Roma's, 1020 W San Marcos Blvd, San Marcos, CA, 92078, (760) 736-4343, 11 am-10 pm

San Pedro

Carrows, 28200 S Western Ave, San Pedro, CA, 90732, (310) 831-5903, 6 am-11 pm

San Ysidro

Coco's Bakery, 825 W San Ysidro Blvd, San Ysidro, CA, 92173, (619) 428-4981, 6:30 am-10 pm

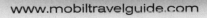

Santa Ana

Black Angus Steakhouse, 1350 N Tustin, Santa Ana, CA, 92701, (714) 558-3057, 11 am-10 pm

Claim Jumper, 2250 E 17th St, Santa Ana, CA, (714) 836-6658, 11 am-10 pm

Hometown Buffet, 2321 S Bristol, Santa Ana, CA, 92704, (714) 885-8187, 11 am-8:30 pm

Hometown Buffet, 1008 E 17Th St, Santa Ana, CA, 92701, (714) 541-3020, 11 am-8:30 pm

Marie Callender's, 1821 N Grand Ave, Santa Ana, CA, 92701, (714) 836-1513, 11 am-10 pm

Round Table Pizza, 212 E 17th St, Santa Ana, CA, 92701, (714) 542-6111, 11:30 am-9 pm

Round Table Pizza, 2860 S Bristol St, C-2, Santa Ana, CA, 92704, (714) 751-1600, 11:30 am-9 pm

Sizzler, 800 W 17th St, Santa Ana, CA, 92706, (714) 796-9243, 11 am-10 pm

Santa Barbara

Carrows, 210 W Carrillo St, Santa Barbara, CA, 93101, (805) 966-1227, 6 am-11 pm

Elephant Bar, 521 Firestone Rd, Santa Barbara, CA, (805) 964-0779, 11 amñ10 pm

Santa Clarita

Chili's, 25970 The Old Rd N, Santa Clarita, CA, 91381, (661) 260-3620, 11 am-10 pm

Hometown Buffet, 23154 Valencia Blvd, Santa Clarita, CA, 91355, (661) 253-2225, 11 am-8:30 pm

Romano's Macaroni Grill, 25720 The Old Rd N, Santa Clarita, CA, 91381, (661) 284-1850, 11 am-10 pm

Santa Fe Springs

Sizzler, 13225 Telegraph Rd, Santa Fe Springs, CA, 90670, (562) 944-0724, 11 am-10 pm

Santa Maria

Bakers Square, 1841 S BRdway, Santa Maria, CA, 93454, (805) 925-6661, 7 am-11 pm

Carrows, 1635 S BRdway, Santa Maria, CA, 93454, (805) 922-8538, 6 am-11 pm

Hometown Buffet, 1431 S Bradley Rd, Santa Maria, CA, 93454, (805) 352-0111, 11 am-8:30 pm

Marie Callender's, 229 Town Center West, Santa Maria, CA, 93458, (805) 928-1252, 11 am-10 pm

Round Table Pizza, 2508 S BRdway, Santa Maria, CA, 93454, (805) 614-4466, 11:30 am-9 pm

Santa Monica

Benihana, 1447 Fourth St, Santa Monica, CA, 90401, (310) 260-1423, 11:30 am-10 pm

Bubba Gump Shrimp, 301 Santa Monica Pier, Building 9, Santa Monica, CA, 90401, (310) 393-0458, 11 am-10 pm

Carrows, 3040 Ocean Park Blvd, Santa Monica, CA, 90405, (310) 450-1321, 6 am-11 pm

Coco's Bakery, 3440 Ocean Park Blvd, Santa Monica, CA, 90405, (310) 450-6257, 6:30 am-10 pm

Hooters, 321 Santa Monica Blvd, Santa Monica, CA, 90401, (310) 458-7555, 11 am-midnight

P.F. Changs, 326 Wilshire Blvd, Santa Monica, CA, 90401, (310) 395-1912, 11 am-10 pm

Sizzler, 2025 Wilshire Blvd, Santa Monica, CA, 90403, (310) 453-3250, 11 am-10 pm

Santa Paula

Big Boy, 55 Hallock Dr, Santa Paula, CA, 93060, (805) 421-1016, 6:30 am-10 pm

Carrows, 327 S Palm, Santa Paula, CA, 93060, (805) 525-0966, 6 am-11 pm

Round Table Pizza, 598 W Main St, Santa Paula, CA, 93060, (805) 933-1351, 11:30 am-9 pm

Santee

Chili's, 9804 Mission Gorge Rd, Santee, CA, 92071, (619) 258-5811, 11 am-10 pm

Hometown Buffet, Santee Town Center, 265 Town Center Pkwy, Santee, CA, 92071, (619) 562-1555, 11 am-8:30 pm

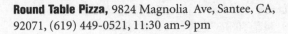

Round Table Pizza, 9824 Magnolia Ave, Santee, CA, 92071, (619) 449-0521, 11:30 am-9 pm

Seal Beach

Marie Callender's, 12489 Seal Beach Blvd, Seal Beach, CA, 90740, (562) 596-2797, 11 am-10 pm

Romano's Macaroni Grill, 12380 Seal Beach Blvd, Seal Beach, CA, 90740, (562) 598-5979, 11 am-10 pm

Sherman Oaks

Cheesecake Factory, 15301 Ventura Blvd P-1, Sherman Oaks, CA, 91403, (818) 906-0700, 11 am-11 pm

Fuddruckers, 15301 Ventura Blvd, Sherman Oaks, CA, 91423, 11 am-9 pm

Marie Callender's, 14743 Ventura Blvd, Sherman Oaks, CA, 91403, (818) 788-3983, 11 am-10 pm

P.F. Changs, 15301 Ventura Blvd, Sherman Oaks Galleria, Sherman Oaks, CA, 91403, (818) 784-1694, 11 am-10 pm

Romano's Macaroni Grill, 15301 W Ventura Blvd #103, Sherman Oaks, CA, 91403, (818) 981-3885, 11 am-10 pm

Simi Valley

Chili's, 25 W Cochran, Simi Valley, CA, 93065, (805) 527-0377, 11 am-10 pm

Coco's Bakery, 698 Los Angeles Ave, Simi Valley, CA, 93065, (805) 526-9122, 6:30 am-10 pm

Elephant Bar, 1825 Madera Rd, Simi Valley, CA, (805) 584-9119, 11 amñ10 pm

Hometown Buffet, 1855 Cochran St, Simi Valley, CA, 93065, (805) 583-3382, 11 am-8:30 pm

Marie Callender's, 20 W Cochran St, Simi Valley, CA, 93065, (805) 582-0552, 11 am-10 pm

Romano's Macaroni Grill, 2920 Tapo Canyon Rd, Simi Valley, CA, 93063, (805) 306-1303, 11 am-10 pm

Round Table Pizza, 1855 Cochran St, Ste 101, Simi Valley, CA, 93065, (805) 522-3488, 11:30 am-9 pm

Solana Beach

Round Table Pizza, 126 S Solana Hills Dr, Solana Beach, CA, 92075, (858) 755-6662, 11:30 am-9 pm

Soledad

Round Table Pizza, 2135 H De La Rosa Sr St, Soledad, CA, 93960, (831) 678-8700, 11:30 am-9 pm

South Pasadena

Carrows, 815 Fremont Ave, South Pasadena, CA, 91030, (626) 799-0561, 6 am-11 pm

Round Table Pizza, 1127 Fair Oaks Ave, South Pasadena, CA, 91030, (626) 441-4269, 11:30 am-9 pm

South Santa Ana

Carrows, 3355 S Bristol Ave, S. Santa Ana, CA, 92704, (714) 557-6733, 6 am-11 pm

Spring Valley

Godfather's Pizza, 685 Sweetwater Rd, Spring Valley, CA, 91977, (619) 462-6580

Round Table Pizza, 9676 Campo Rd, Spring Valley, CA, 91977, (619) 589-2424, 11:30 am-9 pm

Stanton

Sizzler, 12775 Beach Blvd, Stanton, CA, 90680, (714) 894-8894, 11 am-10 pm

Stevenson Ranch

Coco's Bakery, 24930 Pico Canyon Rd, Stevenson Ranch, CA, 91381, (661) 254-2776, 6:30 am-10 pm

Studio City

Todai, 11239 Ventura Blvd, #218, Studio City, CA, 91604, (818) 762-8311, 11:30 am-9 pm

Sun City

Coco's Bakery, 27990 Bradley, Sun City, CA, 92586, (951) 672-8003, 6:30 am-10 pm

Sunland

Sizzler, 10401 Sunland Blvd, Sunland, CA, 91040, (818) 951-2816, 11 am-10 pm

Coco's Bakery, 10521 Sunland Blvd, No 7, Sunland, CA, 91040, (818) 353-5677, 6:30 am-10 pm

Tarzana

Carrows, 18355 Ventura Blvd, Tarzana, CA, 91356, (818) 343-0782, 6 am-11 pm

Round Table Pizza, 18365 Ventura Blvd, Tarzana, CA, 91356, (818) 344-5054, 11:30 am-9 pm

Temecula

Black Angus Steakhouse, 27735 Ynez Rd, Temecula, CA, 92591, (951) 699-8000, 11 am-10 pm

Chili's, 27645 Ynez Rd, Temecula, CA, 92591, (951) 694-0099, 11 am-10 pm

Claim Jumper, 29540 Rancho California Rd, Temecula, CA, (951) 694-6887, 11 am-10 pm

Godfather's Pizza, 26479 Ynez Rd, Ste C, Temecula, CA, 92591, (951) 296-9477

Hometown Buffet, 40390 Margarita Rd, Temecula, CA, 92590, (951) 694-1116, 11 am-8:30 pm

Hooters, 27345 Jefferson Ave, Temecula, CA, 92593, (951) 506-0093, 11 am-midnight

Marie Callender's, 29363 Rancho California Rd, Temecula, CA, 92591, (951) 699-9339, 11 am-10 pm

Romano's Macaroni Grill, 41221A Margarita Rd, Temecula, CA, 92591, (951) 296-0700, 11 am-10 pm

Round Table Pizza, 27644 Ynez Rd, Temecula, CA, 92591, (951) 694-4488, 11:30 am-9 pm

Sizzler, 27701 Jefferson Ave, Temecula, CA, 92390, (909) 676-3630, 11 am-10 pm

Tony Roma's, 27464 Jefferson Ave, Temecula, CA, 92590, (951) 676-7662, 11 am-10 pm

Temple City

Hometown Buffet, 5535 N Rosemead Blvd, Temple City, CA, 91780, (626) 285-6229, 11 am-8:30 pm

Thousand Oaks

Black Angus Steakhouse, 139 W Thousand Oaks Blvd, Thousand Oaks, CA, 91360, (805) 497-0757, 11 am-10 pm

Cheesecake Factory, 442 W Hillcrest Dr, Thousand Oaks, CA, 91360, (805) 371-9705, 11 am-11 pm

Chili's, 100 S Westlake Blvd, Thousand Oaks, CA, 91362, (805) 370-1072, 11 am-10 pm

Claim Jumper, 2150 Thousand Oaks Blvd, Thousand Oaks, CA, (805) 494-9656, 11 am-10 pm

Fuddruckers, 401 N Moorpark Rd, Thousand Oaks, CA, 91360, 11 am-9 pm

Melting Pot, 3685 E Thousand Oaks Blvd, Thousand Oaks, CA, 91362, (805) 370-8802, 5 pm-10:30 pm

P.F. Changs, 2250 Thousand Oaks Blvd, Thousand Oaks, CA, 91362, (805) 277-5915, 11 am-10 pm

Piatti Locali, 101 S Westlake Blvd, Thousand Oaks, CA, 91362, (805) 371-5600, 11:30 am-10 pm

Romano's Macaroni Grill, 4000 E Thousand Oaks Blvd, Thousand Oaks, CA, 91362, (805) 370-1133, 11 am-10 pm

Round Table Pizza, 2000-B Avenida De Los Arboles, Thousand Oaks, CA, 91362, (805) 492-2403, 11:30 am-9 pm

Toluca Lake

Marie Callender's, 10050 Riverside Dr, Toluca Lake, CA, 91602, (818) 985-6862, 11 am-10 pm

Torrance

Bakers Square, 819 W Carson, Torrance, CA, 90502, (310) 533-8124, 7 am-11 pm

Benihana, 21327 Hawthorne Blvd, Torrance, CA, 90503, (310) 316-7777, 11:30 am-10 pm

Big Boy, 24021 Hawthorne Blvd, Torrance, CA, 90505, (310) 375-1800, 6:30 am-10 pm

Black Angus Steakhouse, 3405 Carson St, Torrance, CA, 90503, (310) 370-1523, 11 am-10 pm

Chili's, 21835 Hawthorne Blvd, Torrance, CA, 90503, (310) 792-9012, 11 am-10 pm

Claim Jumper, 24301 Crenshaw Blvd, Torrance, CA, (310) 517-1874, 11 am-10 pm

Coco's Bakery, 3615 Pacific Coast Hwy, Torrance, CA, 90505, (310) 373-6316, 6:30 am-10 pm

Coco's Bakery, 18120 Hawthorne Blvd, Torrance, CA, 90504, (310) 371-4086, 6:30 am-10 pm

Coco's Bakery, 21815 Hawthorne Blvd, Torrance, CA, 90503, (310) 542-2686, 6:30 am-10 pm

Elephant Bar, 21227 Hawthorne Blvd, Torrance, CA, (310) 543-5595, 11 amñ10 pm

Hometown Buffet, 3520 Carson St, Torrance, CA, 90503, (310) 921-6546, 11 am-8:30 pm

Marie Callender's, 21211 Hawthorne Blvd, Torrance, CA, 90503, (310) 540-9696, 11 am-10 pm

Marie Callender's, 23365 Hawthorne Blvd, Torrance, CA, 90505, (310) 378-4209, 11 am-10 pm

P.F. Changs, 3525 Carson St, Torrance, CA, 90503, (310) 793-0590, 11 am-10 pm

RA Sushi, 3525 Carson St, Ste 161, Torrance, CA, 90503

Romano's Macaroni Grill, 25352 Crenshaw Blvd, Torrance, CA, 90505, (310) 534-1001, 11 am-10 pm

Round Table Pizza, 4330 Redondo Beach Blvd, Torrance, CA, 90504, (310) 371-8009, 11:30 am-9 pm

Sizzler, 17544 Hawthorne Blvd, Torrance, CA, 90504, (310) 371-0775, 11 am-10 pm

Sizzler, 2880 Sepulveda Blvd, Torrance, CA, 90505, (310) 539-1617, 11 am-10 pm

Tulare

Round Table Pizza, 150 E Cross Ave, Tulare, CA, 93274, (559) 686-2222, 11:30 am-9 pm

Tustin

Black Angus Steakhouse, 3030 El Camino Real, Tustin, CA, 92782, (714) 573-4888, 11 am-10 pm

Coco's Bakery, 14971 Holt Ave, Tustin, CA, 92780, (714) 730-1540, 6:30 am-10 pm

Round Table Pizza, 13771 Newport Ave, #17, Tustin, CA, 92780, (714) 838-2242, 11:30 am-9 pm

Sizzler, 14042 Newport Ave, Tustin, CA, 92680, (714) 832-6892, 11 am-10 pm

Universal City

Tony Roma's, 1000 Universal Studios Blvd, Universal City, CA, 91608, (818) 763-7674, 11 am-10 pm

Upland

Carrows, 425 N Mountain Ave, Upland, CA, 91786, (909) 946-2315, 6 am-11 pm

Coco's Bakery, 60 W Foothill Blvd, Upland, CA, 91786, (909) 985-9604, 6:30 am-10 pm

Coco's Bakery, 150 E Seventh St, Upland, CA, 91786, (909) 946-2324, 6:30 am-10 pm

Round Table Pizza, 830 E Foothill Blvd, #5, Upland, CA, 91786, (909) 946-0741, 11:30 am-9 pm

Sizzler, 275 E Foothill Blvd, Upland, CA, 91786, (909) 982-3019, 11 am-10 pm

Valencia

Black Angus Steakhouse, 27007 McBean Pkwy, Valencia, CA, 91355, (661) 288-2000, 11 am-10 pm

Claim Jumper, 25740 The Old Rd, Valencia, CA, (661) 254-2628, 11 am-10 pm

Elephant Bar, 27063 McBean Pwy, Valencia, CA, (661) 799-8640, 11 amñ10 pm

Marie Callender's, 27630 The Old Rd, Valencia, CA, 91355, (661) 259-4675, 11 am-10 pm

Van Nuys

Coco's Bakery, 13733 Roscoe Blvd, Van Nuys, CA, 91402, (818) 786-3966, 6:30 am-10 pm

Hometown Buffet, 7868 Van Nuys Blvd, Van Nuys, CA, 91402, (818) 787-6007, 11 am-8:30 pm

Round Table Pizza, 17200 Saticoy St, Van Nuys, CA, 91406, (818) 609-7607, 11:30 am-9 pm

Sizzler, 7131 Van Nuys Blvd, Van Nuys, CA, 91405, (818) 781-4014, 11 am-10 pm

Sizzler, 16955 Sherman Way, Van Nuys, CA, 91406, (818) 345-5445, 11 am-10 pm

Ventura

Black Angus Steakhouse, 4718 Telephone Rd, Ventura, CA, 93003, (805) 644-7323, 11 am-10 pm

Carrows, 2401 Harbor Blvd, Ventura, CA, 93001, (805) 642-3780, 6 am-11 pm

Carrows, 4095 E Telegraph Rd, Ventura, CA, 93003, (805) 644-8539, 6 am-11 pm

Marie Callender's, 1295 S Victoria Ave, Ventura, CA, 93003, (805) 644-0147, 11 am-10 pm

Romano's Macaroni Grill, 4880 Telephone Rd, Ventura, CA, 93003, (805) 477-9925, 11 am-10 pm

Round Table Pizza, 4255-8 E Main St, Ventura, CA, 93003, (805) 654-0777, 11:30 am-9 pm

Sizzler, 4017 E Main St, Ventura, CA, 90003, (805) 656-2748, 11 am-10 pm

Victorville

Chili's, 11910 Amargosa Rd, Victorville, CA, 92392, (760) 244-1786, 11 am-10 pm

Coco's Bakery, 15570 Park, Victorville, CA, 92392, (760) 241-6686, 6:30 am-10 pm

Hometown Buffet, Costco Shopping Center, 14689-C Valley Center Dr, Victorville, CA, 92392, (760) 241-3311, 11 am-8:30 pm

Marie Callender's, 12180 Maiposa Rd, Victorville, CA, 92392, (760) 241-6973, 11 am-10 pm

Visalia

Bakers Square, 3301 S Mooney Blvd, Visalia, CA, 93277, (559) 625-9900, 7 am-11 pm

Carrows, 900 S Mooney Blvd, Visalia, CA, 93277, (559) 732-0934, 6 am-11 pm

Chili's, 4015 S Mooney Blvd, Visalia, CA, 93277, (559) 749-0213, 11 am-10 pm

Hometown Buffet, 1804 S Mooney Blvd, Visalia, CA, 93277, (559) 733-3660, 11 am-8:30 pm

Marie Callender's, 350 S Mooney Blvd, Visalia, CA, 93291, (559) 738-1442, 11 am-10 pm

Round Table Pizza, 1691 E Noble Ave, Visalia, CA, 93292, (559) 625-8753, 11:30 am-9 pm

Sizzler, 2121 W Caldwell, Visalia, CA, 93277, (559) 625-1290, 11 am-10 pm

Vista

Chili's, 255 Vista Village Dr, Vista, CA, 92083, (760) 639-1958, 11 am-10 pm

Coco's Bakery, 605 W Vista Way, Vista, CA, 92083, (760) 758-9340, 6:30 am-10 pm

Round Table Pizza, 923 E Vista Way, Vista, CA, 92084, (760) 941-1700, 11:30 am-9 pm

Walnut

Carrows, 21130 E Golden Springs, Walnut, CA, 91789, (909) 598-5359, 6 am-11 pm

West Covina

Black Angus Steakhouse, 455 N Azusa Ave, West Covina, CA, 91791, (626) 331-5381, 11 am-10 pm

Carrows, 101 S Azusa Ave, West Covina, CA, 91791, (626) 919-1618, 6 am-11 pm

Chevy's, 100 S California Ave, West Covina, CA, 91790, (626) 851-9400, 11 am-10 pm

Chili's, 2929 E Eastland Center Dr, West Covina, CA, 91791, (626) 915-8809, 11 am-10 pm

Elephant Bar, 200 S Vincent Ave W, West Covina, CA, (626) 918-3400, 11 amñ10 pm

Hooters, 3041 E Garvey Ave, West Covina, CA, 91791, (626) 974-4668, 11 am-midnight

Marie Callender's, 3117 E Garvey Ave N, West Covina, CA, 91791, (626) 339-5491, 11 am-10 pm

Romano's Macaroni Grill, 1230 Lakes Dr #107, West Covina, CA, 91790, (626) 917-9295, 11 am-10 pm

Round Table Pizza, 478 Plz Dr, West Covina, CA, 91790, (626) 960-3997, 11:30 am-9 pm

Sizzler, 1100 W Covina Pkwy, West Covina, CA, 91790, (626) 338-0610, 11 am-10 pm

West Hills

Chili's, 6775 Fallbrook Ave, West Hills, CA, 91307, (818) 704-9537, 11 am-10 pm

West Los Angeles

Marie Callender's, 11324 National Blvd, West Los Angeles, CA, 90064, (310) 478-0347, 11 am-10 pm

Westchester

Hometown Buffet, 8629 S Sepulveda Blvd, Westchester, CA, 90045, (310) 216-9208, 11 am-8:30 pm

Westlake

Marie Callender's, 3635 E Thousand Oaks Blvd, Westlake, CA, 91362, (805) 497-7437, 11 am-10 pm

Westminster

Marie Callender's, 16390 Beach Blvd, Westminster, CA, 92683, (714) 847-6600, 11 am-10 pm

Round Table Pizza, 16450 Beach Blvd, Westminster, CA, 92683, (714) 847-5517, 11:30 am-9 pm

Todai, 2008A Westminster Mall, Westminster, CA, 92683, (714) 891-0081, 11:30 am-9 pm

Whittier

Black Angus Steakhouse, 15500 Whittier Blvd, Whittier, CA, 90602, (562) 947-2200, 11 am-10 pm

Chili's, 13580 Whittier Blvd, Whittier, CA, 90605, 11 am-10 pm

Marie Callender's, 12402 E Washington Blvd, Whittier, CA, 90602, (562) 693-2724, 11 am-10 pm

Marie Callender's, 9829 La Serna Dr, Whittier, CA, 90605, (562) 945-3471, 11 am-10 pm

Woodland

Round Table Pizza, 421 Pioneer Ave, Ste F, Woodland, CA, 95776, (530) 666-3701, 11:30 am-9 pm

Round Table Pizza, 638 Cottonwood St, Woodland, CA, 95695, (530) 666-4477, 11:30 am-9 pm

Sizzler, 201 W Court St, Woodland, CA, 95695, (530) 666-1112, 11 am-10 pm

Woodland Hills

Black Angus Steakhouse, 21720 Victory Blvd, Woodland Hills, CA, 91367, (818) 703-6160, 11 am-10 pm

Cheesecake Factory, 6324 Canoga Ave, Woodland Hills, CA, 91367, (818) 883-9900, 11 am-11 pm

Coco's Bakery, 21844 Victory Blvd, Woodland Hills, CA, 91367, (818) 887-7848, 6:30 am-10 pm

Maggiano's, 6100 N Topanga Canyon Rd, #1330, Woodland Hills, CA, 91367, (818) 887-3777, 11 am-10 pm

P.F. Changs, 21821 Oxnard St, Woodland Hills, CA, 91367, (818) 340-0491, 11 am-10 pm

Todai, 20401 Ventura Blvd, Woodland Hills, CA, 91364, (818) 883-8082, 11:30 am-9 pm

Yorba Linda

Chili's, 18380 Yorba Linda Blvd, Yorba Linda, CA, 92886, (714) 524-8162, 11 am-10 pm

Round Table Pizza, 18518 Yorba Linda Blvd, Yorba Linda, CA, 92886, (714) 970-9295, 11:30 am-9 pm

Yucaipa

Sizzler, 33002 Yucaipa Blvd, Yucaipa, CA, 92399, (909) 797-2944, 11 am-10 pm

Yucca Valley

Carrows, 57044 29 Palms Hwy, Yucca Valley, CA, 92284, (760) 228-1232, 6 am-11 pm

Sizzler, 57084 Twentynine Palms Hwy, Yucca Valley, CA, 92284, (760) 365-0708, 11 am-10 pm

Notes

Notes

Notes

Notes

Notes

Notes

Notes

Notes

Notes